More Women Travel

Adventures and advice from more than 60 countries

There are more than one hundred Rough Guide titles covering
destinations from Amsterdam to Zimbabwe

Forthcoming titles include
Bangkok • Barbados • Central America
Israel • Japan • Jordan • Syria

Rough Guide Reference Series
Classical Music • European Football • The Internet • Jazz
Opera • Reggae • Rock Music • World Music

Rough Guide Phrasebooks
Czech • French • German • Greek • Hindu & Urdu • Hungarian
Indonesian • Italian • Japanese • Mandarin Chinese • Mexican Spanish
Polish • Portuguese • Russian • Spanish • Thai • Turkish • Vietnamese

Rough Guides on the Internet
http://www.roughguides.com

Published in 1995 by Rough Guides Ltd, 1 Mercer St, London WC2H 9QJ.
Reprinted in March 1996 and March 1998.

Distributed by the Penguin Group:

Penguin Books Ltd, 27 Wrights Lane, London W8 5TZ
Penguin Books USA Inc., 375 Hudson Street, New York 10014, USA
Penguin Books Australia Ltd, 487 Maroondah Highway, PO Box 257,
    Ringwood, Victoria 3134, Australia
Penguin Books Canada Ltd, 10 Alcorn Avenue, Toronto, Ontario, Canada M4V
    1E4
Penguin Books (NZ) Ltd, 182–190 Wairau Road, Auckland 10, New Zealand

Typeset in Bembo and Gill Sans to an original design by Henry Iles.
Printed in the UK by The Bath Press, Bath.

704pp

A catalogue record for this book is available from the British Library.
ISBN 1-85828-098-2

More Women Travel

Adventures and advice from more than 60 countries

Editors

Natania Jansz and Miranda Davies

THE ROUGH GUIDES

ACKNOWLEDGMENTS

This book belongs to its contributors. We could never have pieced it together without the help, advice, patience and unfailing goodwill (in the face of the usual catalogue of editorial adversity) of the 86 travellers and writers included here. Crucial as they were, however, they form the tip of the iceberg. We'd also like to thank the many women who have written in over the years with accounts and information, especially Peggy Gregory, Chris Johnson, Zuleika Kingdon, Jessica Carlisle, Naomi Roberts, Liz Maudsley, Ilse Zambonini, Jane Bryce, Anna McMahon, Dawn Ellis and Jacqueline Webster. Also Lucinda Montefiore, Laura Longrigg, Alisa Joyce and Jane Parkin for past but enduring editorial input, and Pat Holland for many discussions on travel and tourism.

For practical help in sleuthing out information and generously sharing knowledge, bibliographies and address books, thanks to: Sarah Anderson for her limitless knowledge of travel narratives; Sarah Austin who allowed us to browse endlessly in the excellent London *Travel Bookshop*; Janet Brown for bibliographies that arrived serendipitously from Massachusetts; Pilar Vazquez, Cath Forrest, Giovanna Iannaco, Lucinda Montefiori for commenting on manuscripts; Alison Murdoch, Josie Barnard, Mike Gerrard, Lucy Kimbell for providing contacts; Huw Molseed at *Booktrust*, Jeanne Muchnick in New York, and Janet Hayton, Mark Salter, Mia Ehm, Victoria Tubau, Oriol Nello, Charlie Hebbert and Annie Exton for background information.

Thanks too to fellow "Amazonians", in particular Dea Birkett, Sara Wheeler and Sarah Anderson, for a rich fare of travellers' talk, moral support, literary uplift and the odd pint.

From the Rough Guides office our thanks to Sam Cook for keeping us on course and supplying the lick and polish; Susanne Hillen, Henry Iles and Judy Pang for smooth production and inspired design; Michael Hill for the illustrated maps and Jerry Williams for their origination; Simona Sideri for proofreading; Richard Trillo, Jules Brown, Dan Richardson and Rob Humphreys for updates on the travel scene and Jean Marie Kelly for transatlantic guidance.

For back-up help in wading through the early stages of envelope-opening and page-sorting thanks to Ruth, Ella Reed and Nat. Also, for general support, thanks to Harriet Gaze, Peggy Jansz, Clifford Jansz and Sabrina Rees.

Last but far from least we'd like to thank Bridget Davies and Litza Jansz for steadfast support in a range of guises . . . and Mark Ellingham for his typically generous help, encouragement and direction at various stages in this project.

Grateful acknowledgment is made to Little, Brown and Company (UK) Ltd for permission to reprint excerpts from *Travels in a Thin Country* by Sara Wheeler.

THE EDITORS

Natania Jansz was the co-author of the first ever *Rough Guide*, on Greece. A Clinical Psycholgist, writer and editor, she currently divides her time between the NHS and media projects. She has worked with a feminist film collective, published fiction for children, and acted as consultant for a Channel Four TV series about women's travels, *Maiden Voyages*. Her own travels have taken her to Asia, North Africa, and most parts of Europe.

Miranda Davies is a writer, editor and translator with a background in women's studies, development and human rights. She has edited several books, including the two influential anthologies *Third World – Second Sex 1* and *2* (Zed Books, 1983, 1987); *Women Travel*, co-edited with Natania Jansz (Rough Guides, 1990), and *Women and Violence: Realities and Responses Worldwide* (Zed Books, 1994). Her travels have taken her to North and South America, Morocco and much of Europe. She lives with her daughters, Ella and Lucia, in London.

WOMEN TRAVEL: THE NEXT EDITION

We plan to produce a new edition of *Women Travel* in a couple of years' time, and would welcome any information of use in keeping the chapters as up-to-date as possible – as well as new, personal accounts of travel (including to those countries we have not been able to cover this time around). Should you wish to contribute or have information on contact listings, books or travel notes that you feel should be included please write to:

Natania Jansz and Miranda Davies
Women Travel, Rough Guides, 1 Mercer Street, London WC2H 9QJ, UK.

or

Women Travel, Rough Guides, 375 Hudson Street, 3rd Floor,
New York NY10014, USA

CONTENTS

Introduction

L ooking back to the mid–1980s, when we started work on our first anthology of women's travel experiences, it is hard to imagine how little there was in the world of travel and guidebook writing that women could identify with. We were part of a generation with unprecedented opportunities to travel, equal consumers in one of the world's fastest growing industries, busy asserting that our personal experiences (of home, work, relationships) had a wider importance. Yet in the way travel was presented our experiences were routinely sidelined. Guidebooks would enthuse about the interior wonders of a mosque without bothering to let half their readers know that they wouldn't be allowed in to see them; brochures would feature glossy views of an old quarter of town without commenting on the harassment a woman traveller might face in attempting to negotiate the labyrinthine streets alone. The early boom in travel literature had a distinctly male slant, and, as isolated voices, those women travel writers who were published could be dismissed as extraordinary "other" women, more resolute, eccentric or intrepid than the rest of us.

We knew that there was a rich seam of knowledge and experience that women shared with each other when they crossed paths abroad – in the private ways that women have always found to pass on the information that matters – telling of how we would be perceived and treated, the pleasures and pitfalls we might face. It was time to bring this to a wider audience. Our formula was simple. We advertised for travellers returning from abroad to write to us about their experiences, not in the authoritative and detached style of travel journalism, but woman to woman. Clearly we had touched a chord. Articles, advice and contacts listings arrived in sackfulls, and we published them as a book entitled, enthusiatically, *Half the Earth: Women's Experiences of Travel Worldwide*.

Two editions later and more women are travelling. More women are also writing, talking and presenting programmes about their journeys, keeping their feminine and/or feminist perspective very much in the foreground. Guidebook authors have begun to pay lip service to the fact that at least half their readers are women (the *Rough Guides*, our travelling companions over the decade, go much further), while the ever-accommodating tourist industry has at last acknowledged that we are equal consumers with men, planning our own journeys and paying our own hotel bills.

We like to feel that *Half the Earth*, and its subsequent edition *Women Travel*, have been part of the engine of change, and it's with pride that we note the number of contributors who have moved on to publish further travel narratives, become travel journalists, guidebook writers and foreign news correspondents. Our task, too, has over the years shifted in subtle ways. In *More Women Travel* we celebrate the range of women's contemporary experiences of travel. The tone and style of this new collection of personal accounts varies from the inspiring if simple testimony – "I'm a woman and I went there alone" – to an evocative sampling of places, encounters and scenes. That this book is primarily about relationships with people – guests meeting hosts – we make no apologies; there are other places to look if you want to see the sights. Some of the practical information and advice we include has filtered into guidebooks, but you won't find it elsewhere collected under one cover. This is a book of experiences, information and insights, something to dip into as a companion on the road. There are gaps, of course – we were led by the pieces we received – but as far as possible we've tried to keep the span wide, just as the focus is personal.

More Women Travel – and for a variety of reasons and to a variety of places. Of the women whose narratives follow, many have launched themselves abroad as a means of escaping the rut, relishing the chance to free themselves from the usual reference points, find new stimulation and a new perspective about the world in which we live.

Solo travel remains for many of us one of the more accessible means of testing our independence; handling the logistics and bureaucracy of a foreign country and carving out a new if temporary life. Job opportunities also feature as a motive, especially in the newly opened Eastern Europe, where the demand for English-speakers, in teaching jobs and the new media runs high. The most poignant reason for travel, however, came from Madeleine Cary who turned to the backpacking routes of Thailand following the death of her son, in the hope of regaining some lost sense of identity. An openness and compassion filters through in her writing, as does the theme of being changed by the influence of a new culture – perhaps the one common thread that unites most of the accounts in this book.

Whatever our reasons for setting off, shared concerns emerge about the relationship we have with the risks (fear of attack, illness, accident) and threats involved in coping with situations we may not fully understand, let alone feel in control of. Wendy Teasdill thinks nothing of traipsing off alone across the plateaux of Tibet, forging fast-flowing rivers in her attempt to reach Mount Kailash. Warnings from nomads that she will surely die are dispensed with stoically, even after being "dragged along the boulder-strewn floor by ice-cold water, convinced I'd drawn my last breath". Janey Mitchell fights off rape in Colombia. Ceri Sheppard finds herself sharing a bar table with a gun-toting drunk in Bay Island, Honduras: "And if you move I'll blow your fucking brains out" being just one of his propositions. Deborah Bosley gets a similar welcome on the New York subway. Helen Buhaenko scrambles out of a mace-filled bar in Kiev in the middle of an altercation between mafia gangs.

Yet behind these headline incidents there's the more insidious sense of intimidation that we feel when we can no longer fall back on any reliable knowledge of what might be offensive or dangerous. This is especially strong when travelling in more strictly segregated societies, such as orthodox Muslim areas, or within any traditional community where men's control over women's lives is more severe. Where men crowd the public spaces and mediate all dealings with foreigners, it is easier to feel exposed and vulnerable as a lone traveller. There are many parts of the world where the act of leaving home and family ties to travel places us more squarely in the world of men, and often as uneasy trespassers.

The line between being an "honorary man" and a more available sex object (symbol of the immoral West) is a hard one to negotiate. Pat Chell who spent two years teaching in Morocco provides some insights into the impressions we can create:

> If a woman is alone or only with women, what kind of woman can she be? No father would put his daughter at risk by letting her travel unless she was already "worthless". Her nearest equivalent in Moroccan society is the prostitute. She sits in cafés, drinks alcohol, smokes cigarettes or hashish, and will even comb her hair in public. She often dresses "indecently" – not even a prostitute would do this. She will also often be prepared to have sex if you can charm her into it. These are the kinds of attitudes I heard so frequently.

We discover, too, that in packing to travel, that most everyday question "What shall I wear?" takes on a new and profound meaning. There are many destinations where powerful stereotypes exist about Western women and where there are strict cultural codes to contend with. In these situations, we have to decide how to present ourselves as women, how far we are willing to go to merge in, and how far we can tolerate standing apart from the crowd. The effects of these choices run deep, influencing the most intimate relationship we have, that with our own bodies. In Iran, the first act of unsolicited kindness that Wendy Dison receives from a stranger is when a student, and fellow bus passenger across the border, gives her one of the scarves he is bringing home for his mother and sisters, to cover her head. In a Bangladeshi village, Katy Gardner finds that the rules are strict and that she becomes moulded by her new environment in unexpected ways:

> There are certain bits of you which must never be shown, especially your legs, and ideally your head should always be covered. You must talk quietly, not call out or run; you must be shameful and obedient to your menfolk ... When strange men came into the family compound, like the other women I too jumped up and ran inside, feeling genuinely ashamed. If I went out without an umbrella to keep my face hidden, I felt naked. It was alarming to say the least. If just fourteen months can have effects like that on such a product of Western feminism as I had considered myself to be, what would happen after two years or more?

In Brazil, Cherry Austin undergoes an equally intense – but reverse – transformation. Arriving in Copacabana she finds herself intimidated by (and disapproving of) the eroticism on display. However, as she allows the rhythms and ideas of new culture to seep in, and learns what "every Brazilian learns from birth: that my body is beautiful and should be shown off", she loses the negative feelings she has about her appearance and learns how to handle unsolicited attention without feeling threatened:

> By the time I got back to Copocabana I had the tan, the shorts and the walk. I could get into deep conversation with strange men, exchange phone numbers and saunter away with a smile. I could see newly arrived visitors staring at me with the same bemused distaste that they showed towards other half-clad women on the avenue.

There's a similar sense of loosening up and enjoying the party in Katy Noakes's beachwise view of Jamaica, while Nancy Stender enjoying her first visit to the Michigan Womyn's Music Festival tells us (and we believe it) that "You haven't lived until you've seen a group of naked women Country and Western line dancing". Between these extremes Lucy Kimbell treads the streets of Warsaw in her Doc Marten boots wondering at women dressed in microskirts and stilettos, waiting at bustops in the snow. Feminine glamour she learns has become even more imperative amid the new consumerism sweeping post-Communist Eastern/Central Europe.

Elsewhere, women write about how they are perceived and how their treatment compares with that of the women of the country. Often there's an uneasy guilt about identifying with men – who in many cultures are much more likely to approach and entertain passing strangers – and a regret at the barriers that exist in forging closer relationships with women. Indeed, there are times when asserting femininity can be a struggle, as Melanie McGrath showed in her routine banter with a market woman in Burkina Faso:

> "Why didn't I wear earrings", the woman wanted to know, "Why didn't I plait my hair, why was it so short, do I have fleas?". She said that I looked "comme un homme, quoi" and wiped tears from her eyes with the back of her hand.

Being an honorary man might have some advantages, but it can be unsettling to feel excluded as a bad influence or unfit companion for sisters or daughters, as Caroline Bullough discovered when invitations from Egyptian female students were politely withdrawn. It can also be hard to find yourself treated as an object of pity, with great concern expressed about your childless or unmarried state; the freedoms we proudly assert to delay or not have children become thrown into question among cultures where this is considered an essential rite of passage for women.

So much for the problems. An equally strong thread in the featured accounts is the way in which many of our contributors found ways to cross the cultural divide and gain acceptance. Lesley Reader who wrote to us from her new home thousands of feet up the Himalayas in a Bhutanese village, describes the warmth and solidarity she encountered from the women whose lives she shared:

> My friends here in Buli are women of all ages. Just as I am a woman alone, the majority of them are either widows, women with husbands absent in the army, or single women. They arrived in my house the evening after I reached Buli, bearing many bottles of local brew and we all got drunk. We have been together ever since.

The difficulty in adjusting to communal living where individual needs are submerged under those of the extended family is a recurring theme. Daphne Toupouzis, who lived for a while in a family compound in Senegal, writes:

> The women with whom I was closest seemed unable to understand my professed need to be alone once in a while or my occasional spells of gloom and loneliness. I was gently scolded for my self-indulgent attitude and forced to confront why privacy and independence as I understood them were so important to me.

Frances Hunt in Calcutta found that while she was expected to keep men at a distance (holding someone's waist while on the back of a bike was the only physical contact she could allow herself) a surprising closeness was normal between women:

> Asha finds it difficult to accept that I cannot share a bed with her. . . She says she finds it impossible to sleep alone and when her two sisters, niece and mother come round for the evening, they all sleep together on Asha's big bed. As the months go by and I feel relaxed enough to sleep with friends in the afternoons, I begin to realize how intimate it feels.

In most of the accounts that follow, there's a sense of finding some middle ground, of being accepted while remaining an outsider. The travellers are all too aware of the problems of stepping in and out of people's lives, and the cultural and economic differences that can intrude. Nonetheless, the residual effects of colonialism and inequalities between North and South get played out in everyday relationships. Valerie Walkerdine in Mexico comments that:

> Attitudes to gringos and gringas are about the hate and envy felt by an oppressed and exploited people. White women, especially with fair hair, are about the most hated, envied and desired of all. Any glance at the television screen makes it immediately obvious that white skin equals wealth and class in the Mexican popular imagination.

In China, Kerry McKibbin falls into the trap of romanticizing rural hospitality. Invited to share a meal with a peasant woman she finds herself disturbed when confronted with a bill.

I was angry at her and yet, as I pressed on, I realized I was most sickened with myself. In her wisdom (she) had managed to expose the holes in my dubious Western, political correctness. I had thought of myself as a traveller, not a tourist, determined to seek out the real, contemporary China. But she knew that I had wanted to see inside a real, Chinese, peasant farmer's house, to gawp at how she survived with no running water, to store details of her uneven, earthen floor. If this had been given freely within the framework of simple, unassuming peasant hospitality, I could have ignored my guilty motives.

Travel is supposed to broaden the mind, but we know that it can just as easily reinforce prejudices. A casual racism often pervades they way we look at other cultures, seeking confirmation through a host of petty inconveniences. If not careful, the insidious belief that we in the West know better and do things properly can creep in almost unnoticed. In India Frances Hunt learned to question the attitudes she adopted as a harassed tourist:

When I first arrived I used to shout "Go away!" at porters who approached me at the station; it's a lot more polite (and effective) to learn how to say "I don't need you" in the local language, in which case the porter – who's only doing his job, after all – can try and find business elsewhere. When I asked my friend Asha how to say "Leave me alone!" to people begging, she quietly told me that in Bengal they prefer to say "mab koro": "forgive me".

The most salutory reminder of the racism we export, however, came from Adrienne Su, an American of Chinese descent writing of her first visit to China:

(The privileges accorded tourists) feel more like the privation of the human rights of the Chinese than the extension of hospitality to their visitors...When I came across other white Westerners on the road their attitude towards me was high-flown and condescending until I spoke English. It wasn't entirely their fault; the environment had deluded them into seeing the Chinese as less than people.

The fact that travel is a privilege was reflected, too, in the predominantly white and middle-class background of most of our contributors. In the accounts that we've included from Black or Asian travellers, racism often supercedes sexism as an urgent concern. Maureen Mckarkiel found that her white Catalan friends were outraged by the gross discrimination she faced but had no notion of the everyday humiliations of being singled out and stared at as a lone Black tourist on the streets of Barcelona. Sylvia Okopu, in Warsaw, found herself caught in an ambivalent role, insulted by street racists as a "Black Devil", and pursued by admiring Polish men as "dusky exotica". On a more positive note, Denise Roach, a British traveller of Jamaican origin, discovered that her mother's prediction that Ghanaians are "just like us: Jamaican at heart" rang true on her trip to Accra. Initially sceptical about personal quests to discover "roots" in Africa she found herself reviewing her sense of her own history – and also discovered that beach gigolos have an entirely different concept of what it means to "unite the diaspora".

More Women Travel is a book that follows many routes abroad: journeys which throw up many more issues than can be summarized here. The act of writing about them – of retracing steps and re-evoking scenes   is, in many ways, another journey in itself. We like to view this book as a celebration of all these aspects of women's contemporary travels and, by the same token, a celebration of contemporary women travellers themselves. As Wendy Teasdill writes of her encounters in Lhasa:

> Each day we would meet one or two others who, by some wild chance or determined cunning, had slipped into the traditionally forbidden city. For some reason, most of these were women . . . resilient individuals with a lot of character and a streak or two of crazy wisdom – I love them all.

HOW THIS BOOK WORKS

More Women Travel is primarily a collection of individual narratives. In an attempt to provide some context to the travels described, though, we've included a brief introductory sketch of the politics, culture and trends of tourism for each of the countries covered, as well as general information that might not be included in the account(s) themselves. We also detail information about women's organizations and campaigns, as background for the contacts given at the end of each section.

Also included at the end of each section are brief recommendations of further reading. These book listings are highly selective, focusing on books that provide either a broader perspective of women's travels, or the lives that women lead, within the countries covered. The non-fiction books that we most recommend are starred; fiction works are not, for otherwise the stars would become a constellation.

Australia

A ustralia is massive, and very thinly populated: in size it dwarfs Western Europe and rivals the USA, yet its population is barely seventeen million. Moreover, despite the youthful vitality of the towns and cities – most of them founded little more than 150 years ago – this is an ancient

land. The Outback, which covers much of western and central Australia, is the most eroded, denuded and driest of continents, one whose attraction lies in bizarre wildlife, striking geological forms, and backcountry dirt roads.

For most travellers, the Outback is the core Australian experience, and perhaps best explored in a group. It can be a temperamental, unforgiving environment, and the vast distances make it an expensive undertaking. If your time and budget is limited, you may want to consider joining one of the numerous tours, which are geared to a variety of tastes and expectations. A few offer genuine contact with Aboriginal life in the Northern Territories; Australia's indigenous inhabitants predate the white colonizers in this continent by some 40,000 years and the last decade has seen their culture resurgent, alongside a strident campaign for land rights.

Australia's cities and coastline are an altogether different proposition. Most of the population live within 20km of the ocean, along an arc that stretches from Queensland to Adelaide, and visitors from the US and Europe will find the cultural *mélange* of cities like Melbourne, Sydney, Adelaide and Brisbane easy and familiar. The populations are far more cosmopolitan than most visitors expect, with immigration from Asia having done much to dilute Australia's Eurocentrism over the past forty or so years. If you are a British, Irish, Dutch or Canadian passport holder, and under 26, you can also acquire a Working Holiday Visa, and subsidize travels with temporary jobs.

Working in or travelling around Australia brings an almost inevitable confrontation with the continent's legendary sexism. The myths of male culture and bonding remain all too prevalent, especially in the interior, and you need to be prepared for a barrage of sexual remarks, shouted from cars, or from groups of workers who, you might imagine, have never seen a woman before. Walk tall and confident and, if you're travelling alone, avoid rural pubs, be wary of small town motels, and don't even think about hitch-hiking. Look to Australian women as your role models: they have a well-earned reputation for being robust and practical.

Australia has a strong **women's movement**, active on government, local and community levels – even conservative Queensland has a female senator. Equal opportunity and anti-discrimination laws introduced by the 1970s Labour government laid the foundations for an impressive network of women's refuges, rape crisis centres and health centres throughout the country, though changes in state and federal policies have meant a hard fight to maintain these services. All the major cities have resource centres and information lines, and there's a lively culture, too, of women's bookshops, magazines and galleries. International Women's Day (March 8) provides an excuse for a month-long series of events, culminating in enthusiastically attended street marches.

In Your Own Backyard

Margo Daly, an Australian living in London, was 27 when she was offered a job researching the *Rough Guide to Australia*. She returned to explore her country with a notebook and the requisite eye of an outsider. Her initial research took her to South Australia and Victoria, where she travelled in the middle of a rainy winter, mainly by bike. She is currently working on her first novel set in England and Australia.

After two years living in England it was odd that I chose to write and research a guidebook to Australia. For as long as I can remember I had dreamt of escaping my home country, fuelled by all the books I'd ever read. I was the first of my siblings to go abroad, having schemed to leave since I was sixteen when my best friend and I had gone as far as a guided tour of a cruise ship berthed at Sydney's Circular Quay. Our Year 12 leaving magazine judged us most likely to embark on a *Women's Weekly World Discovery Tour*. Instead, two weeks after my high school exams, I flew alone to England, my father's birthplace, for a very unglamourous year as an au pair and a bar attendant, with a few forays into France. At the same time my older brother had taken a year off from university to travel around Australia, writing to me in London as the Australian Pioneer Explorer – or APE for short. In his letters he chided me for going overseas without seeing Australia first, and it sunk in that he might be right.

The problem was that I had had a rather appalling glimpse of the "real" Australia as a child, which had made me dread the country's interior. I was eleven when Dad dragged us from the leafy, hilly northern suburbs of Sydney to northwest New South Wales. Wee Waa was suffocatingly inland, 500km from the sea, and the terrain around the small town was monotonously flat. The hotel where our father took us to live was one of only a few double-storey buildings in town; while he was its publican, we lived upstairs. On the Namoi River, Wee Waa is at the centre of Australia's highest yielding cotton-growing district. Sharing the climate and crop of the USA's Deep South, in the mid-1970s it also echoed some of the same racial attitudes.

I saw life here for the first time and it was brutal. The locals called my father's pub the "black hotel": the town's Aboriginal population drank in its public bar. There was an unspoken apartheid system in operation, which even extended to my best friend, an Aboriginal girl, who was not allowed to sleep over, despite my tears. At the height of the cotton-chipping season, at the hottest point of the summer, when most men were working and had money to throw about, the bar and the beer garden seethed. On hot Saturday nights, Country and Western music floated up to my bedroom and I'd fall asleep listening to the plaintive tones of *Satin Sheets to Lie on, Satin Sheets to Cry on*, to be woken up by the shouts and broken glass of a brawl. The "bull wagons" routinely pulled up outside the hotel on these nights and the police would literally pile the black population into the back. Or so it seemed to me, hanging out on the balcony, allowed a privileged view of Main Street.

> *My mother cooked knee-deep in brown water in the kitchen, while customers sat at the bar on high stools.*

Nature too, entered into my view of the "real" Australia. Wee Waa got its levy bank eventually, not long after we'd left, but in between the Namoi swelled its banks twice. My mother cooked knee-deep in brown water in the kitchen, while customers still sat at the bar on high stools, the salvageable contents of the cellar piled high before them. The Aborigines from Tulladunna, the Aboriginal reserve on the fringes of town, were put up at the two-storey Central School, and townies made cruel jokes afterwards about it needing to be disinfected. Afterwards, fine silt covered everything, and a smell like damp clothes left to rot pervaded.

When we left four years later I hated rural Australia, seeing no romance in the outback: boring stretches of backward nothing. Give me the sea and the city, I thought; give me culture, an outlook. And yet I remember as a young child in Sydney being amazed when I learnt that people came to the city for holidays, and being driven across Sydney

Harbour Bridge and the glittering harbour thinking, sullenly: why would anyone want to come here, it's so boring. I had still to learn that in order to really know and love a place, you need comparisons. Returning to Australia to begin work on the guide, I realized it was more complicated: that a place changes, becomes something else, each time you go away and come back to it. Now I was returning to Australia, not Sydney. I was thinking of my home as a continent, not a city or a state.

Just as my preconceptions about my country began to collapse on being tested, so did my ideas about myself. I had chosen to cycle on my first trip out to Australia, alone, and the decision for me was a big one. I was allowing myself to believe in my abilities, to say, "I can do that". I had always hated sport at school because it was competitive; I was a clumsy child, always tripping over my own feet. But being clumsy (and pale) doesn't prevent an enjoyment of physical activity and I loved swimming and walking. What I saw as a very Australian mania for sports and sun-worship had always been a mystery to me and sometimes made me feel like an outsider in my own country.

What I saw as a very Australian mania for sports and sun-worship had always been a mystery to me.

I had learnt to cycle quite late, at eleven, when my experience was restricted to the flat roads of Wee Waa. My first adult taste of cycling was a few months before leaving England for South Australia. Renting a mountain bike, I spent a weekend pedalling along the Ridgeway between Oxford and Marlborough. Covered in mud, rain pouring down, I sometimes wept as I tackled another hill, my friends furiously speeding off in the distance. But I had learnt that the sense of achievement at the end far outweighed the tears which, after all, were only temporary.

It was not that I had planned to cycle in Australia – the thought never crossed my mind until I was confronted by the realities of South Australia's negligible transport system. I'd taken the bus to the Barossa Valley, one of Australia's most famous wine-producing regions, but once there, how was I to get around? South Australia is a car state, made easy by lax registration laws so everybody, it seems, can charge around in a battered old bomb. Consequently, the transport system is abominable, with buses to the main centres but no public service to any spots off the main route. I couldn't afford a car and petrol, let alone the nightmare, cost and responsibility of a breakdown, but clearly needed my own transport to properly research the book. After renting a bike to cycle around the Barossa, I knew I had the answer: a pleasurable and inexpensive means of transport – idiot-proof too – that allows you to be part of the landscape, rather than viewing it at full speed through a glass screen.

In Adelaide, a city surrounded by vineyards, I based myself with some kind friends of friends who became my mates too. To them, with their full-time jobs, it must have seemed as if I was forever flitting off for mini-wine tours. Away I'd cycle to the Franklin Street bus station, load my bicycle, and arrive back a few days later with some more choice bottles for us to enjoy. My first expedition was to Victor Harbour, a seaside town on the Fleurieu Peninsula just south of Adelaide. With little to discover there, I cycled east along the coast to Goolwa, a river town on the Murray Mouth, and ventured into a surf life-saving club en route. Surfers, those almost mythical Australian characters, still intimidated me – a teenage hangover of a suburbanite attempting to brave the wilds of beach culture. I faced my fear, using the cover of the travel guide to speak to one for the first time, extracting all sorts of information about local surfing and finding this "waxhead" was in fact a human too.

Cycling demands carbohydrates and after the 40km return ride I craved a huge bowl of pasta. Italian restaurants are few and far between outside Adelaide, and in Victor Harbour I happily found one, its walls encouragingly lined with photographs of Italian cyclists. I stuffed myself with spaghetti, perfect fuel for the next morning's cycling. It was a liberation to be eating as much as I wanted, like I had as a teenager, with an enormous and unselfconscious appetite. Instead of living in my mind, I discovered that I had a body.

They insisted I must be scared, by which they meant rape and deserted country roads: cars and men.

My body was a machine, use of which was exhilarating. Like a car it needed water and fuel; when it was cold and started suddenly it would crank up, causing a painful left knee.

The Fleurieu Peninsula, besides its impressive coastlines on both its Gulf St Vincent and Southern Ocean coasts, has the undulating vineyards of the Southern Vales inland. With about forty wineries in a small concentration, mostly in bush settings, the area around its centre, McLaren Vale is perfect for cycling. Perfect anytime but winter, perhaps; Adelaide and its surrounding areas have a Mediterranean climate, just right for grape cultivation, of dry summers and rainy winters. I didn't know this until I'd done my research; ill-prepared with no waterproof gear whatsoever.

My second expedition (this time with a fetching, bargain-basement, clear plastic, wet weather suit) was to the Clare Valley, another wine region which has more in common with a down-to-earth farming community than the boutiquey feel of McLaren Vale and the Barossa. It is as much sheep as wine country, and my first night was spent at Bungaree, a grand old sheep station. Waiting for a night-time lift to the property, I sat drinking tea in a milk bar. The women behind the counter were curious about this night-time manifestation with a bicycle and amazed that I was brave enough to cycle around by myself. They insisted I must be scared, by which I knew they meant rape and deserted country roads: cars and men. But except for once or twice, I was never frightened and I knew why. It was as if I was on a mission. I had such a sense of purpose, and I was so busy getting on with it that there wasn't room for fear. I was determined not to fail, and besides, I never felt alone. My bike was company.

I found these wine areas refreshingly sophisticated yet with friendly, rural attitudes. But the Riverland – the long, irrigated strip on either side of the Murray River from Blanchetown to the Victorian border – came as a shock, resembling that atmosphere I'd experienced as a child in northwest NSW. The towns here all have the same raw edge, with little charm or sophistication, and an undercurrent of violence most apparent on drunken Friday nights. I found the area menacing, and several things happened there to make me hate it.

I'd planned to stay at the backpackers' hostel in Berri. Figuring that in the middle of winter there wouldn't be much competition for rooms, I left it until late afternoon to call, just to check if it was open. I didn't bet on the number of people fruit-picking at that time of year – the man who answered the phone said they were full up. I begged him to squeeze me in somewhere, as I had to come and look at the place for the travel guide anyway. Also, it was now early evening and there was nowhere else in Berri where I could afford to stay. Seemingly unimpressed, he insisted that there was no room. When I returned the next day to look at the hostel, after telling him of my panicked 24km cycle in the dark along a busy highway to the next town and a cheap place to stay, he sheepishly confessed that they weren't quite full, but he had turned me away on account of my Australian accent. Hostels are for travellers, and if you're travelling within your own country, you have to make the distinction between traveller and itinerant worker (read untrustworthy drifter) clear. Unfortunately it is often Australians who misbehave at hostels.

As travel goes, what seem like the worst of days can provide some of the best moments. I'd made an appointment to interview Ian Abdullah, an Aboriginal painter who lives in Barmera, a Riverland town known for its annual Country and Western music festival. I had first seen his paintings in Sydney at the Museum of Contemporary Art. Bright and childlike, the painting of the flood-lit rodeo at night struck at childhood memories. It was already getting late as I hurried to make the 14km from Berri to Barmera for the night. Riding along the highway towards a turning with a few cars waiting to pull out, I was disconcerted by the crude comments shouted at me from one vehicle; although it's a disturbing fact of life that men in cars in Australia heap verbal abuse at female pedestrians, I'd never experienced it on my bike. But at least he didn't knock me off, like the bloke who then turned left, without looking.

> *My shabby, unheated room seemed as spitefully far from the ladies as was possible.*

Picking myself up, all I could think about was my bike, my new bike. I shook my fist at the man and screamed that it was my right of way, in too much of a hurry to check if I was hurt or to take down his licence number. My bike was OK, so I headed on, feeling angry but strangely pleased that I hadn't burst into tears.

As in all of Australia, the Riverland's pubs double up as hotels, an often misleading term stemming from a legal requirement that drinking places provide at least a few rooms where customers can sleep off the night's excesses. Struggling on to Barmera, I arrived to a scene of typical Friday night drunkenness, men spilling out onto the streets from the very heavy hotel where I'd planned to stay. As I pushed my way into the public bar, I got the usual quota of stares and sexist comments. In public life, Australia has one of the best records for sexual equality in the world. However, an equivalent change in attitudes has not necessarily followed. Around the time that women achieved equal pay, public bars of hotels – which until then had traditionally refused to serve women – were stormed by women's groups. Now, you can get a drink anywhere, but the way in which these places are set up with two bars continues to reflect the old bias: you'll still see signs for the "Ladies Lounge", and it's nearly always a long way from the public bar to the women's toilets. My shabby, unheated room seemed as spitefully far from the ladies as was possible. Sitting on the worn orange towelling bedspread under a dim dangling light bulb, I examined my left leg and the painful yellow, purple and green bruise spreading across my shin, and did finally burst into tears.

The drinkers were still going strong when I wearily got on my bike to make my appointment. Beyond the hotel were fields and pitch darkness and I cycled as fast as I could in sheer terror through the unlit streets. I knew Ian Abdullah's house by the red, black and yellow Aboriginal flag outside. In 1970s' Wee Waa such a thing would have been unheard of, especially in – what I later learnt – was a mainly all-white street. Things in Australia were beginning to change; white

Australians were fascinated by Abdullah's paintings with their rural black perspective. Mostly evocations of his childhood and early adulthood, they show South Australia's Noongahs growing up along the banks of the Murray. For many they provide a realization that tribal existence was only one aspect of traditional Aboriginal life; just as my best friend in Wee Waa would look confused when I asked her about carved emu eggs and didgeridoos, Ian Abdullah began by trying to paint tribal images which didn't feel right and belonged not to him but to the Aboriginal people of the Northern Territory. The Murray River, teeming with water-life, supported a large Aboriginal population, and the area along the Murray still has a large black community. Abdullah is not tribal, but he had never moved far from his roots, working on the land, in the tradition of the unsung Aboriginal rural worker.

After the Riverland, I was glad to get out of South Australia and head for Victoria. I caught the interstate bus to Melbourne and my old friend Jackie, who lived in a turn-of-the-century run down terrace house right near the Victoria Markets, just to the north of the city centre. The Market, operating every day except Mondays and Wednesdays, is a lively showcase for all the varied cultures that thrive in Melbourne. Every vegetable and fruit imaginable is sold by all varieties of people hawking them in loud, raucous voices; and the food halls burst with delicacies, among them hybrid creations like brie wrapped in eucalyptus leaves.

When I cycled to Jackie's doorstep it was 6am but she'd already got up and lit a fire in her room to welcome me. It was a notoriously cold house and the all-women household used to take long hot baths to warm themselves in the midst of Melbourne's bitter winter. It was also the house where Helen Garner, one of Australia's most famous writers, had once lived, immortalized in her classic novel *Monkey Grip*, a tale of obsessive love and heroin addiction, played out in the shared communal households of the 1970s. Still gloriously ramshackle in best Melbourne inner-city grunge style, the house of women continued to be unconventional: artists, a dancer, a women's refuge worker. They all cycled, too, and were envious when I'd get out my gear and go off on a jaunt, away from the bars and the bands and the late nights of the city. Everybody, it seems, cycles in Melbourne, a mostly flat city with a transport system predominately of trams providing a quieter, less polluted and more predictable cycling environment. Cycling within the state is made easier with a bicycle-friendly and extensive train system. The high population density in Victoria, the second smallest state, means the system has stayed intact so it's very easy to get to out of the way places.

My grandfather had come from Victoria, and there was some mixed-up story about him being orphaned in a fire. He and his brother got shipped off to an orphanage while his four sisters were sent to a convent and became nuns, to torment my mother during her childhood. Mum said I still had some second cousins in Victoria, but could never quite remember whether they were in Ararat, Ballarat or Bendigo, all within the gold-rush area, north of Melbourne. I kept a lookout but it was not until Shepparton, in the fruit-growing centre of the Goulburn Valley northeast of Melbourne, that I spied a Doyle's bus. With about an hour to kill, I looked up them up in the phone book, expecting mild disinterest. Instead, a very excited Ken Doyle insisted I come straight round to the bus depot, where I found a short, very friendly man who looked just like my mother. He took me back to meet his mother, who sorted out the complexities of the blood ties for us: our grandfathers had to be brothers. A big dinner was arranged for me out on his sister's farm where I met Ken's wife Joyce, of Aboriginal descent, who taught Aboriginal studies at the local technical college, and their three blonde, brown-eyed children. I was touched by the kindness of distant relatives, so far removed yet familiar. I saw a photograph of my grandfather's brother, dressed in his WWII uniform. We'd lost our only photograph of Grandad, who'd died when I was five, and this seemed the closest I'd ever get to his dimly remembered image.

Throughout my journey, strangers became friends and friendships were strengthened. On my last night in Melbourne, I cycled with Jackie at midnight across the city to seaside St Kilda to see the last set of a local band, and drink some long, cool beers. It was exhilarating, the impulsiveness of our ride and having the tramless, near-deserted streets to ourselves. For once I took my friend's lead, launching myself across traffic lights and abandoning all rules of the road. Although I was leaving the next day, I felt as if I'd finally come home.

Six Months in the Outback

Nerys Lloyd-Pierce is a freelance journalist, originally from North Wales. After some time in Asia she travelled widely around Australia, starting with six months working on a remote cattle station in the west of the country.

Having spent four months travelling around Asia, a trip to Australia seemed a logical progression. My reasons for visiting that country were ambiguous. On a mercenary note, I knew I would be flat broke by then and had a good chance of earning money. The prospect of warm, sunny weather was also appealing after a succession of chilly English winters.

I arrived with the usual preconceptions about heat, flies and Bondi Beach, but was soon to learn that Australia had considerably more to offer. My first preconception was shattered as I flew into Perth. It was green! Greener in fact than the subdued winter face of the England I had left behind.

I saw a newspaper ad for a camp cook on a remote cattle station. Only later did I learn that I was the only applicant.

On the flight from Bangkok I had my first encounter with Australian hospitality. The young guy I started chatting to on the plane was shocked when I remarked that I had nowhere to stay, no connections and very little money, and offered me a place on his sitting-room floor, for as long as I liked. This gave me an invaluable base from which to look for the work I now desperately needed.

Finding casual work in Australia shouldn't be a problem, and the pay is good. The government is trying to clamp down on people working illegally, however, and it helps to have a working holiday visa. Those I met working without a permit hadn't had any problems, but the penalty if you are caught is instant deportation. Having enough money to tide you over does ease the pressure; I arrived at my first job with only thirty cents left in my purse.

Despite dire financial straits I really didn't want to do a mundane job like waitressing or working behind a bar. Having travelled halfway across the world I wanted to do something which was as much an experience as a job. The chance came when I saw a newspaper advertisement for a stock camp cook on a remote cattle station. I was accepted for the job with an alacrity which surprised me. Only later did I learn that the job had been advertised for three months and I was the only applicant! To the horror of my Perth friends – urban Australians rarely seem to venture into the bush – I set off, leaving them convinced that I would loathe every minute.

The bus journey from Perth to the cattle station brought home to me the vastness of Australia: close on 2000km of open space and travel for hours without seeing a solitary sign of human habitation. The station itself was 260km from any town and over 60km from the nearest neighbour.

The homestead formed a small cluster of houses in a vast bowl skirted by rugged magenta hills. A deep slow-moving river curled in crescent shape around these homes, creating an effective natural fire break. Families had their own houses while the unmarried stockmen lived in bedsits. I was lucky enough to have a house to myself, which gave me both space and privacy, essential elements in what could very easily become a claustrophobic environment.

Everyone used to meet up for coffee and a chat at morning "smoko" when I, being the "cookie", had to produce vast quantities of cake or biscuit. Food was of great importance to people leading such active outdoor lives. There was no television and evening entertainment revolved around barbecues, fishing, playing cards and scrabble. I was always amazed how the same group of people managed to laugh and joke together in spite of seeing each other every day. On the other hand, living in such close proximity you can't afford to fall out with anyone as there's no way you could manage to avoid them.

For anyone coming from a tiny country like England, the isolation of the outback is hard to imagine. The four-hour drive between station and town naturally made conventional shopping quite impractical; fresh produce was flown in on the mail plane every fortnight. If you ran out of anything in the meantime, too bad.

Every four months a road train brought in supplies of non-perishable goods, absolutely essential in the wet season when it was often impossible for the mail plane to land. During this period the dirt road connecting properties with the outside world would become altogether impassable, sometimes for weeks at a time. Communications were by means of a two-way radio with a shrill continuous call sign to clear the airwaves in the event of an emergency. In such a case the flying doctor plane would land on the nearest airstrip, but the patient still had to be transported from the scene of the accident to the waiting plane. Radio also plays an important role in children's education. The school of the air is part of their daily routine, the teacher no more than a disembodied voice. To qualify for a government governess a community must have seven or more children of school age.

> *We worked for three weeks mustering cattle in the bush, and a week at the homestead.*

The cattle station covered one-and-a-half million acres, a distance that I found hard to assimilate. Stand on a high point and literally all that the eye can see is one property. On arrival I naively commented that fifty horses seemed a lot in one paddock, only to be told that the paddock stretched over 12,000 acres.

My job out in the bush was to cook meals for fifteen stockmen, or ringers as they're known, on an open fire. We worked on the basis of three weeks mustering cattle in the bush, when we slept on "swags" (bedrolls) under the stars, and a week at the homestead. Every day we loaded up the gear on to the creaking chuck wagon and moved to a new camp, each of which had a name: Corner Billabong, Eel Creek, Old Man Lagoon.

This itinerant lifestyle led me to discover the hidden corners of a region that might simply appear barren and hostile to the casual observer: an arid outcrop of rocks hiding a tumbling waterfall, a pool framed by the luxuriant growth of pandanus palms, the sudden blooming of hibiscus on a dry plain or the strangely contorted branches of a boab tree clawing the sky.

At first I was afraid of getting hopelessly lost between camps – after all there was no one I could stop to ask for directions – until Phil, the manager, put my mind at rest with the wry observation, "No worries. If you've got the tucker they'll always come and look for you."

Despite the obvious novelty of being in a new place and seeing a different way of life, being a stock camp cook was far from easy. At times I felt very isolated from anything familiar and comforting. Physically the job was often hard work and as the cook is always the first up and last to finish, the hours were long. On occasions, struggling to lift billies of boiling water from the fire, sweat dripping down my face and clothes smeared in grime, I wondered why the hell I was doing it.

It's not easy to conquer the vagaries of cooking on an open fire.

To his amazement I socked him. Cooks are notoriously bad-tempered and I can see why.

In order to bake a cake or loaf of bread I had to build up the fire, only to wait for it to die down to a heap of glowing coals. The temperature of these coals was all important; too hot and the cake would burn, too cool and it would simply never cook. I can't remember how many times I found myself frantically piling on more coals in an effort to cook a loaf, while the middle remained stubbornly soggy.

Having put so much effort into cooking you become strangely possessive about the results! On one occasion I had been labouring over melting moments (biscuits which literally melt in the mouth), a task I wished I had never started, when John, the youngest of the ringers, strolled up remarking, "These look good, cookie" and grabbed a handful. Seeing him munching so indifferently after my labours was too much and to his amazement I socked him across the back with an axe handle. Cooks are notoriously bad-tempered and I can see why.

Eight of the fifteen stockmen were Aboriginals. Relationships between the two communities on the station were amicable but distant. I found the Aboriginal men good-humoured, easygoing company. The oldest among them couldn't have been more than fifty, though the deeply etched lines on his face suggested a much older person. He would tell me stories of how he first came into contact with white Australians – how, at the age of fifteen when he saw his first car, he got on his horse and chased it off his land. Despite their superficial friendship, a certain segregation clearly existed between the two communities. The Aboriginals always built a separate campfire in the evenings. This was done by tacit agreement and both groups seemed to accept the arrangement. During the twelve months I lived there I never met a white Australian who mixed socially with an Aboriginal and was shocked to find racial intolerance common, even among the educated elite.

Male attitudes perhaps resemble those in Britain twenty or thirty years ago.

Generally speaking, women in the bush tend to adopt the conventional female roles, and male attitudes perhaps resemble those in Britain twenty or thirty years ago. It is considered unladylike for a woman to swear and, by the same token, it really isn't on to swear in front of a "lady". On one occasion at camp I burnt my foot quite badly on the hot coals; all alone, angry and frustrated, I let loose the tirade of swearing I had so carefully been suppressing!

The three women on the station stayed at the homestead while the men and I went out into the bush. I was worried this might create friction, or that they might simply resent me for being an outsider intruding on their close-knit community, but nothing could have been further from the truth. I was welcomed and accepted from the beginning.

The women's role was different, though no less important than that of the men. They were responsible for the smooth running of the station during the men's absence; they organized the vegetable garden and the orchard and kept chickens. They also provided a balance in a male-dominated environment. The station manager's wife was a nursing sister and fortunate enough to be able to pursue her career as organizer of community health in outlying areas. She told me that without the job she could easily have found the lack of intellectual stimulation hard to handle.

Even though I was alone in the bush with fifteen men, I never at any point encountered sexual harassment. Both women and men went out of their way to make sure I settled in and felt happy and at home. Working on the station was an incredible experience, probably the last vestige of frontier spirit left in Australia. Several things will remain imprinted on my mind forever: the cloud of dust on the horizon heralding the return of stockmen and cattle; riding all day across that immense parched land; the sheer delight of coming across a cool shady water hole.

It was not without regret that I decided after six months that the time was right to move on. I wanted to see more of Australia and now had the finances to do so. As a leaving present the Aboriginal men gave me three boab nuts, carved with the traditional pictures of emu, goanna and kangaroo. Returning to the city was like emerging into another world, only this time it was urban life that felt alien.

TRAVEL NOTES

Languages English is the official language, but you'll also find Italian, Greek, Serbo-Croat, Turkish, Arabic, Chinese and numerous Aboriginal languages.

Transport A good system of trains, buses and planes connects major cities. Public transport is expensive, but prices are competitive and it's a good idea to look around. Fuel is relatively inexpensive – by British standards, at least – so it's worth buying your own vehicle if you have the time and money. Hitching alone is not advisable under any circumstances.

Accommodation Suburban motels tend to be much cheaper than those in central locations. Sydney, especially, has lots of hostels geared up to travellers. Australians are very hospitable so don't be afraid to use any contacts you may have. Noticeboards at women's bookshops (see below) and universities often have information on women-only accommodation and shared transport.

Special Problems Working visas are becoming increasingly hard to get, especially for visitors older than 26. Applications should be made well before you leave home and you will need evidence of sufficient funds to cover your trip.

Guides *The Rough Guide to Australia* (Penguin) includes excellent women's listings.

CONTACTS

It would be impossible to include here all Australian **feminist groups**. The following list focuses on some of the major cities – for more details like it from there. Feminist magazines include *Refractory Girl* and *Hecate*.

Canberra: *Women's Centre*, 3 Lobelia St, O'Connor 2601 (☎47-8070); *Women's Shop-front Information Service*, Ground Floor, CML Building, Darwin Place, Canberra 2600 (☎46-7266).

Adelaide: *Women's Information Switchboard*, 122 Kintore Ave, corner North Terrace (daily 9.30am–9.30pm; ☎223-1244).

Brisbane: *Women's Infolink*, 2nd Floor, Pavilion Building, corner of Albert and Queen streets (☎229-1264 or 1584). For women's radio in the city tune into *Megahers* on 102FM (Tues 5pm).

Darwin: *Women's Information Service*, PO Box 2043, Darwin 5794 (☎81-2668).

Melbourne: *Women's Information and Referral Service* (Mon–Fri 9am–9pm; ☎654-6844; toll-free 008/136-570).

Perth: *Women's Information and Resource Centre*, 103 Fitzgerald Rd, North Perth 6006 (☎328-5717).

South Hobart: *Women's Information Service*, 4 Milles St, South Hobart 7000 (☎23-6547).

Sydney: *Women's Liberation House*, 62 Regent St, Chippendale 2008 (☎699-5281).

SELECTED WOMEN'S BOOKSHOPS

Adelaide: *Murphy Sisters Bookshop*, 240 The Parade, Noward 5067 (☎332-7508).

Brisbane: *Women's Book, Gift and Music Centre*, Gladstone Rd and Dorchester St, Highgate Hill 4101 (☎332-7508).

Sydney: *The Feminist Bookshop*, 315 Balmain Rd, Lilyfield 2040 (☎810-2666).

Victoria: *Shrew*, 37 Gertrude St, Fitzroy 3065 (☎419-5595).

BOOKS

📖 **Robyn Davidson**, *Tracks* (1980; UK, Vintage, 1992/US, Pantheon, 1983). Powerfully compelling account of a journey across the Australian desert with four camels and a dog. Davidson manages to break out of the heroic mould to write with compassion and honesty of the people she meets in the outback and the doubts, dangers and loneliness she faces on her way. A classic of its kind.

Jan Morris, *Sydney* (UK, Penguin, 1993/US, Random House, 1992). Insightful and informative account of Australia's favourite city.

Daisy Bates, *The Passing of the Aborigines: A Lifetime Spent among the Natives of Australia* (1939; UK, Panther o/p/US, Putnam o/p). Fascinating combination of anthropological study and autobiography by one of the first travellers to take up the Aboriginal cause.

Julia Blackburn, *Daisy Bates in the Desert* (UK, Secker & Warburg, 1994/US, Random House). Beautifully written biography interweaving fiction with fact to conjure up the life of one of Ireland's most eccentric travellers (see above).

Pearlie McNeill, *One of the Family* (UK, The Women's Press, 1989). Vivid account of the author's often unhappy life growing up in Sydney during the 1940s and 1950s.

Susan Mitchell, *Tall Poppies* (UK, Penguin, 1983). These profiles of ten successful Australian women, from all backgrounds and nationalities, make an inspiring and well-balanced read. A phenomenal best-seller in Australia.

Dale Spender (ed), *The Penguin Anthology of Australian Women's Writing* (UK, Penguin, 1988). The best Australian women's writing from Elizabeth Macarthur to Germaine Greer.

Babette Smith, *A Cargo of Women* (US & Aus, NSW University Press, 1988). Painstaking account of the lives of one ship's "cargo of women" transported to Sydney: eye-opening and sad.

Sally Morgan, *My Place* (UK, Virago, 1991). Powerful and widely acclaimed account of a young Aboriginal woman's search for her racial identity.

Glenyse Ward, *Wandering Girl* (UK, Virago, 1988/US, Fawcett, 1992). The author, an Aboriginal from Western Australia, tells her own story of growing up in a white world.

Ruby Langford, *Don't Take Your Love to Town* (Aus, Penguin). Autobiography of a black woman's courage and humour in the face of tragedy and poverty.

FICTION

Jessica Anderson, *Tirra Lirra by the River* (UK, Penguin, o/p/US, Penguin, 1991). Richly evocative novel following an old woman's recollection of her troubled life as she returns from Britain to her childhood home in Brisbane.

Rosa Capiello, *O Lucky Country* (Aus, University Queensland Press). Powerful novel of the migrant's experience from a young woman's viewpoint, translated from Italian.

Helen Garner, *Postcards from Surfers* (UK, Bloomsbury Press, 1989/US, Penguin, 1986). Recommended short stories by one of Australia's finest women writers. Her novel *Monkey Grip* (UK & US, Penguin, o/p), is a gripping 1970s story of obsession, love and heroin addiction in inner-city Melbourne.

Kate Grenville, *Lillian's Story* (UK, Picador, 1994/US, Penguin, 1987). Funny, tragic tale, loosely based on the life of Bea Miles, the eccentric Sydney bag lady.

Dorothy Hewett, *Bobbin Up* (UK, Virago, 1985/US, Penguin, 1987). The only novel by one of the country's leading women playwrights, first published in 1959, this is an entertaining portrait of working-class life in Australia in the 1950s. Also look out for her autobiography, *Wild Card* (UK, Virago, 1990).

Gillian Mears, *The Mint Lawn* (Aus, Allen & Unwin). Award-winning first novel by a young writer, set in a perfectly captured northern New South Wales country town.

Bruce Pascoe et al (eds), *The Babe Is Wise* (UK, Virago, 1989). Excellent collection of contemporary short stories by Australian women writers.

Also look out for novels by Miles Franklin and Christina Stead.

Thanks to Christine Bond, Karen Hooper, Tessa Matykiewicz and Jenny Moore for their individual contributions to these Travel Notes.

Bangladesh

Burdened by massive foreign debt, a rural community devastated by floods and cyclones, and one of the highest population densities in the world, Bangladesh has few resources to spare for tourism. Dacca, the sprawling, overcrowded, capital, boasts a cluster of international-class hotels but in the country areas, where villages are connected by the occasional riverboat and paths lie submerged for much of the year under monsoon rains, travel is difficult and facilities non-existent. Most foreign visitors arrive as part of aid and development projects, swelling the ex-patriate communities in the capital's richer suburbs. It's rare to find women travelling independently further afield.

Bangladesh is a predominantly Muslim country, although not, like Iran, an Islamic state. Women are expected to conform to fairly rigid codes of dress and behaviour, a pressure that increases as the fundamentalist movement gains ground. Segregation is fairly strict and Bangladeshi women, when

they do venture out on the city streets, are often hidden beneath the traditional *burqua* (a type of veil) or escorted by a male relative. The extent to which these customs are adhered to, however, varies with class: among the educated elite there's far less pressure to veil in public. Wandering independently through crowds of men, however, can be unnerving and, even if you dress with extreme modesty and keep your eyes averted, you're bound to attract some disapproving comments and stares. That said, however, the attention rarely becomes personally threatening. Men often express genuine surprise and concern at the fact that you are alone and "unprotected", and some might even be sent as intermediary from an unseen woman to offer help and hospitality.

In rural areas, the sheer depth of poverty can come as a shock, even for those hardened by extensive travel on the subcontinent. With the main thrust of charity relief coming from individual sponsorship, people tend to look on foreigners as potential patrons and are quite open about requesting money. How you deal with this is up to your own personal politics, although it is important to be sensitive to the burdens even minimal hospitality imposes and reciprocate in kind. Other than this you should not underestimate the pressure of being an object of continual and endless curiosity. Often groups of onlookers will appear as if from nowhere to scrutinize and comment on your every act. In a society where there's frequently no choice but to live communally and where security depends on close family and community ties it can be very hard to explain a Western pre-occupation with solitude.

Women have remained very much second-class citizens within Bangladeshi society, their status dependent on their relations with men within a complex extended family hierarchy. In recent years development programmes have increasingly attempted to emphasize women's roles as care-givers and providers in ensuring the survival of rural communities. Since 1993 however, debates around the staus of women have been obscured, and the women's movement divided, by the uproar following the writings and pronouncements of Taslima Nasreen, a 32-year-old doctor-turned-writer. Her book, *Shame*, and, more importantly, her widely (mis)quoted criticism of Sharia law, was greeted with storms of protest and death threats from an obscure radical Islamicist group. Pressure mounted following further indictments of fundamentalism by Nasreen in the Western press, and in June 1994 the Bangladeshi government, who had already banned her book, issued a warrant for her arrest. For the next two months she disappeared into hiding while writers, intellectuals and human rights activists in Bangladesh, India and the West campaigned on her behalf. Several progressive organizations within the country came under attack and demands were made by the religious right-wing to expel foreign aid missions and development workers on the basis that they were encouraging blasphemy. At the beginning of August 1994, with government connivance, she was spirited out of the country to asylum in Sweden.

As with the "Rushdie Affair" there has been considerable equivocation among her fellow progressives in Bangladesh. Feminists who had laboured – themselves under death threats – to reconcile a wider freedom for women with Islamic precepts and customs applauded her principles but were perturbed by her frequently blunt and confrontational style. Her tendency to dismiss the work of other Bangladeshi women activists led to a deeper dismay, as did the Western media's stereotyping of Bangladesh as a country riddled with religious fanatics. Whether the left can regain its lost ground, and create conditions that might enable Nasreen to return, remains uncertain.

Home at the River's Edge

Katy Gardner first came to Bangladesh as an anthropology student and spent a year-and-a-half staying with a family in a small village in the north. Her book, *Songs at the River's Edge*, published in the UK by Virago, tells of her gradual immersion into the segregated world of Muslim family life.

A s the plane began its slow descent, a flat expanse of endless paddy fields and long winding rivers spread out beneath us. Closer down, scattered village compounds came into view: men driving bulls through mud, fishing nets spread across waterways, people working in their yards. At last we had arrived in Bangladesh.

It was the beginning for me of a sixteen-month stay. As a student of anthropology my task was relatively simple – to find myself a village and live in it, as much a part of the community as possible, to let the village people teach me about their lives. I had travelled fairly widely in India and Pakistan before, as well as in other parts of the Muslim world, and had always felt strongly drawn to the Indian sub-continent. I had also always found the role of a tourist, unable to speak the local languages, inherently frustrating. This time would be different. I would learn Bengali and actually get close to people where previously I had felt apart.

I made my base in Dacca, a sprawling and chaotic city which by any standards is hard to love, and tried to connect its modern streets and shopping arcades, its pristine parliament building and ghetto of luxury mansions owned largely by aid donors, to what I felt must surely be the "real" Bangladesh – a country which is mainly rural, with a depressingly large percentage of its population below the poverty line.

Like many foreigners I stayed in the district of Gulshan with a friend in a huge house owned by an American donor agency. There was a 24-hour guard service, a full staff, and more rooms than could ever be used. Dacca, like most South Asian cities, is a place of contrasts. Close to this area, although well hidden from sight, were the horrific *bustees* of Dacca – vast areas of huddled huts made from polythene sheeting and jute matting, and down the road, the smog and crowds of the central city.

I was to visit Dacca many times in the months to come, taking breaks from my periods in the village, and although I enjoyed those spells of getting away from it all, I found it disturbingly easy to lead a life there quite separate from Bangladeshi people. Sadly, many of the ex-patriates have little to do with Bangladeshis socially, and rarely leave Dacca. Perhaps because of this lack of contact, and because the middle classes usually speak good English, many never get round to learning Bengali properly, I was shocked, but perhaps not really surprised, by how quickly and easily some of the Westerners took to the master-servant relationships they were involved in. In some ways the Raj, albeit in the form of international aid, still continues.

Although you see foreigners driving around the city in their smart jeeps, they tend to stick to the relative havens of the middle-class suburbs. The streets of Dacca are crammed with people, but they are almost exclusively men. In the warren-like alleys and roads of the old city women, if seen at all, are hurrying past, wrapped up in their *burquas*, with faces averted. This does not mean that the atmosphere is hostile, but wandering about solo you do feel conspicuous, an easy target, and I always took the warnings not to walk alone around the city at night seriously.

A middle-class Bangladeshi said I would never survive the rigours of life without electricity.

So, after about a month of leading a lifestyle far more luxurious than I had at home, a development worker whom I had met on a trip up north to Sylhet introduced me to a family in his wife's village, and we decided that I should move in. Back in Dacca, a middle-class Bangladeshi said that I would never survive the rigours of life without electricity, or eating rice with my hands. White ex-patriates talked in terms of rabies injections and medicines, and I bought myself a mosquito net and a hurricane lamp.

I eventually moved into my new home one night in September, travelling by boat from the nearest road with a small group of villagers returning from a trip to Sylhet. From June to October much of the country is under water, and even under normal, non-flooded conditions (the recent floods which have been so disastrous are not part of this seasonal pattern), many places can only be reached by the painted wooden boats of the villages. In November, the clouds and heat clear, and with the cooler, dry weather, fields and paths miraculously emerge from a morass of mud. When the rains start in the spring these are inundated, and the landscape becomes watery once more.

That evening we passed straggling villages, waterlogged fields, and groups of children on the paths calling out "Inreji! Inreji!" (English) when they saw me. Very few white people venture outside the urban areas and those that do are always assumed to be English. They are viewed with a mixture of amazement and extreme curiosity. At the politest end of the continuum this leads to the eternal question: "What is your country?", at the other end huge crowds gather to gape and comment on your every move ("What is she doing? . . . Look, she's alone . . . She doesn't speak our language, she's white . . . Look, she's opening her bag . . . " etc, etc). Although I never enjoyed it, I gradually became used to the excitement my appearance inevitably generated.

Six hours later, and about five miles from the potholed road (the boat being not exactly speedy), long after the sun had set and the Bangladeshi sky turned violet, I arrived. Immediately I was surrounded by clusters of children and the many faces of my new adoptive family. I had of course already met them a month earlier, but I still had no idea who was who, especially as many of the children and younger women had felt unable to come out in front of me and the distantly related town man who had been my escort.

Now, everyone was present: Amma, my new mother, who took my hand and pronounced immediately that I should be just like a daughter to her; Abba, my dad, who shuffled in to receive my *salaam* and then with a chuckle went back to his *hookah*; and numerous young women – the sisters who were to become my closest friends. I understood hardly anything that was being said to me but it didn't really matter. In a process which was to be repeated many, many times in the following weeks by every family in the village, I was inspected and commented upon. "Look, she's so tall", they said, "Look, she doesn't wear a sari . . . Why don't you wear oil in your hair? . . . *Yallah*, she's not a proper *Londoni*, she isn't fat enough . . . Look at her great earrings . . . " and so on.

> *Compared with the other women, I was a complete oaf and indeed, hardly female.*

I didn't really mind these appraisals; they were a quick way of striking up friendships and of proving that I was no threat and quite prepared to make a fool of myself. More or less everything I did caused outbursts of laughter (whether I'd intended it to or not) and nothing more so than my pathetic attempts to speak the Sylheti dialect. Not surprisingly nobody understood why I should possibly want to live with them and learn. "How can you learn here?" they asked, "Where are your schoolbooks?"

Eventually most people accepted that for some extraordinary reason, I spent hours writing and asking exceedingly stupid questions and wanted to live in their village. "But why come here?" I was often asked, "Your country is a land of peace and richness. Why are you here when we all want to be there?"

Everyone agreed that I had to start at the basics if I wanted to live as they did. "Katy", one of my sisters, Khaola, announced as she eyed me making a mess with my supper of rice that first week, "you're just like a baby, but don't worry, after a year with us we'll make you into a proper Bengali." She was right, I had a long way to go.

Everything I did at first was watched, criticized, laughed at, and corrected. I had to learn how to tie a sari, bathe in the family pond, how to wash out my clothes properly on the stone steps, how to eat my rice, spit, use water in the latrine and much, much more. Compared with the other women, I was a complete oaf and indeed, hardly female. I was clumsy at cutting bamboo or vegetables on the great blades the women squat over, unable to light the fire, and hopelessly inelegant in a sari, which kept riding over my heels. Worse than that, I kept forgetting to cover my head.

As I let the village people mould me, however, I began to learn much about being a Muslim woman in rural Bangladesh. To be approved of, you must be as feminine and submissive as possible. You must dress in a certain way; your hair must be tied back and smoothed with oil, otherwise you will be seen as "mad" and manly; your sari must be tied properly and your blouse fit correctly.

When strange men came into the family compound, I jumped up with the other women and ran, feeling genuinely ashamed.

There are certain bits of you which must never be shown, especially your legs and ideally your head should always be covered. You must talk quietly, not call out or run; you must be shameful and obedient to your menfolk. An old adage, which village women often quote, is that: "A woman's heaven is at her husband's feet".

I certainly failed on most counts of modesty, especially as I never succeeded in changing into a new sari after bathing without revealing myself, or in keeping it continually over my head. But slowly, as I stayed longer in the village, I noticed that a transformation had happened in my values as well as my appearance. Not only had I begun to sit, dress and talk like the village women, but to my amazement I began to express the same sorts of ideas. "It is the will of Allah", I heard myself telling people, and when strange men came into the family compound, like the other women I too jumped up and ran inside, feeling genuinely ashamed. If I went out without an umbrella to keep my face hidden, I felt naked.

It was alarming, to say the least. If just fourteen months can have effects like that on such a product of Western feminism as I had considered myself to be, what would happen after two years or more? And what did it imply about the security of my beliefs if they could be so easily swayed by a new environment?

Of course this doesn't happen to all Western women who visit Bangladesh. My need to be open to the culture and customs of my hosts left me peculiarly vulnerable. Bangladesh is a very difficult country to get to the heart of, and many visitors leave feeling unsympathetic. This is perhaps because although extremely friendly, Bangladeshis tend to be on their guard with foreigners. The country has had a short, violent and politically unstable history, and foreigners, who originally came to Bengal to rule, now usually come as dispensers of aid or advice. "What project do you work for?", is almost as ubiquitous a question as "What is your country?", and many foreigners inadvertently end up as the patron of a Bangladeshi. I was continually asked for money by people in the village. Poor women would come into my room and ask for saris or *taka* – they felt that since I was rich, which I must have been since I was white, it was my duty to give. I nearly always refused, knowing that I could not manage the stream of requests and people's expectations of me had I taken those initial steps. However frequent this became I never managed to get accustomed to the requests and demands made of me, or my hollow excuses that I wasn't *really* rich. When I left, I gave away all my clothing, bedding, etc and even my bras, which various women had been eyeing all year. One of the last things that one old destitute woman said to me was: "Now you have your own poor, we are your responsibility now."

Just as relationships with foreigners can be coveted, leading as they might to patronage and help, they can also be regarded with horror, due to our dirty ways, loose women and alcohol consumption. This ambivalence is especially strong towards young white Western women. We are respected because we are probably involved in aid, and certainly rich, yet viewed with unease because of our independence.

Many of the villagers asked me to stay: "You can become a Muslim, we'll arrange a husband for you."

One of the most common reactions I had when meeting people from outside the village was a horrified: "But are you alone? Aren't you married?" So that after sixteen months I too began to see myself as some kind of freak.

Although people may be surprised, even affronted, to see a woman alone, I always felt that Bangladesh was a relatively safe place to travel in. Wherever I went, people were anxious to help me (whether I needed it or not) and get talking. I travelled by trains, local buses, planes and ferries, and always ended these journeys with new friends. Speaking the language helps of course, as does dressing appropriately – I always wore *shalwa camise* (baggy trousers and long tops), and an *orna* (scarf worn over the chest), or in the village, a sari.

My sex was far more of a blessing than a curse, which I have some-times felt it to be in other countries. Whilst most rural women would never talk to foreign men, wherever I went I was welcomed into women's quarters. Our Western inhibitions do not exist in these places and friendship is easily and unquestionably offered. "Why should we be afraid of you, sister?" I was told so many times, "Aren't we all women?"

Sixteen months after landing in Dacca, I began to prepare for leaving the village. Many of the villagers asked me to stay: "You can become a Muslim, we'll arrange a husband for you." I wasn't so sure about the conversion or the husband, but leaving was certainly extremely difficult.

The day I went, many people came to our homestead. A tinsel garland was put around my head, and Amma fed me the special sweetmeats she had made. A crowd of people then led me down to the river where a boat was waiting to take me back to the road across the flooded fields, this time for good. As was expected of us, we all cried. The boat punted me away while I looked back at the figures, dwindling against the green fields behind. I knew that my return to Britain would not mean that I would stop being their daughter and that we would write regularly. Now, after a few months in London I am already planning my return.

Bangladesh is a powerful and very beautiful place, with golden winters, lush greenness and kingfishers darting over great rivers of water lilies. My image of the country had been largely of a poverty stricken land, precariously surviving an endless cycle of famine, and bloody coups – swollen-bellied children with begging bowls staring out at me from the TV news or Sunday supplements. That poverty and suffering are very real, yet throughout my time in Bangladesh I was constantly reminded that the ways in which it is portrayed by the Western media conceal behind a cloak of sensationalism that the majority of Bangladeshis are extraordinarily resilient. They do as they have always done – they carry on.

TRAVEL NOTES

Languages Bengali. English is widely spoken.

Transport Flights between towns are incredibly inexpensive. There's a limited rail network and a few buses, but these tend to be old, decrepit and massively overcrowded. Boats, paddle launches and steamers are the usual forms of transport in the south. Bangladeshi women tend not to travel without a male escort and can easily be overprotective towards a lone woman. It's often possible to arrange lifts with foreign workers, many of whom have jeeps.

Accommodation Outside Dacca there are very few hotels (or any sort of tourist facilities). You may find rooms in guest houses but there's

nothing like the range in India or Pakistan. Bangladeshis can be very hospitable – the responsibility is yours to pay for as much as you can. As a guest you should always offer some sort of gift.

Special Problems As in any Muslim country, you should dress extremely modestly with loose clothes covering arms and legs. Non-Muslims are not allowed into mosques or shrines. Only a few hotels in Dacca sell alcohol and it would certainly be frowned upon for a woman to drink alone.

Guides *Bangladesh – A Travel Survival Kit* (Lonely Planet) is the best-known but can be inaccurate in places. *Bangladesh – A Traveller's*

Guide (Roger Lascelles) gives a useful overview.

CONTACTS

Bangladesh Rural Advancement Committee (BRAC), 66 Mohakhali Commercial Area, Dacca 12. A private, non-profit making organization of Bangladeshis engaged in development work. BRAC initiated the Jamalpur Women's Programme in the late 1970s, which focuses on skills training, health education and literacy. It has also set up many women's work co-operatives and publishes a regular newsletter.

Bangladesh Mohila Samity, 104-a New Bailey Rd, Dacca. A group geared towards campaigning for equal status and providing educational and employment opportunities, especially for rural women. It has branches all over the country and runs two educational institutions and a number of cottage industries.

BOOKS

Katy Gardner, *Songs at the River's Edge* (UK & US, Virago, 1991, o/p). The full account of Gardner's eighteen-month stay in the village above. Incisive, personal and deeply evocative, this edges you gently across the cultural divide.

Taslima Nasreen, *Lajja/Shame* (India, Penguin, 1994). The book at the eye of the storm in Bangladesh. *Lajja*, referring to Salman Rushdie's book of the same name, depicts a fictional Bangladeshi Hindu family who suffer atrocities at the hands of Muslim extremists following the destruction of the Ayodhya mosque in India. An immediate best-seller in Bangladesh and West Bengal, the book was banned by the Bangladeshi government on the grounds that its "inflammatory tone had increased misunderstanding between Muslim and other communities". Conservative Muslim leaders charged her with conspiring against Islam and death threats soon followed, leading her to seek asylum in Sweden.

Bhutan

Wedged between Tibet and northern India and for centuries virtually untouched by Western influences, Bhutan has come to represent the last of the truly remote Himalayan kingdoms. It remains, however, a notoriously difficult country to get into. Anxious to avoid the cultural havoc wreaked by open tourism in nearby Nepal, the monarchistic government of King Jigme Singye Wangchuck issues only two thousand or so tourist visas a year and limits these to accredited – incredibly expensive – luxury tours, well beyond the reach of most travellers. Travel is restricted to permitted areas, hefty levies are charged for each day spent in the country and trekking costs extra. The only way round this is to arrive as a volunteer or on invitation from someone already working in the country – foreign volunteers are allowed a quota of two visitors a year.

The landscape and culture of Bhutan varies greatly: the north and central high Himalayan areas are predominantly Buddhist, and the Buddhist clergy still hold considerable sway; the foothills of the south, on the other hand, are still home to a large Hindu minority, mainly of Nepalese origin. Recent years have seen an upsurge of state nationalism with increasing discrimination against the Nepalese Bhutanese; literally tens of thousands have been forced into exile across the Indian border and on to refugee camps in Nepal. Tourists, however, are carefully screened from these troubles. Few Bhutanese can afford to be drawn into political discussion and it would be hard to pick up signs of any unrest on a usual tour-bus itinerary. The abiding impression for most visitors is of an overtly gentle and tolerant culture.

Development has been slow to gain pace in the steep mountain valleys that cut through the interior. There are a few urban centres connected by road and supplied with electricity and the trappings of modern commercial life (including a handful of luxury hotels) but the populations remain small – Thimphu, the capital, is home to only 25,000 people. In these towns, among the small professional elite you might find English spoken, chosen as the language of instruction in preference to the obscure national language of Dzongkha.

Far away from the roads, in the villages where the majority of people still live, there has been little change in the centuries-old lifestyle of Himalayan subsistence farming. Travel is by foot, whole families work relentlessly hard to grow what food they need and news from the outside comes slowly, if at all. Foreign visitors to these parts are so rare as to inspire intense fascination, even fear. Although, as a local phenomenon, you will have to deal with being continually scrutinized and commented on, it's unheard of for Western visitors to be harassed or threatened in any way. Dangers are mainly physical – altitude sickness, exhaustion, a lack of medical help and poor diet, landslides, monsoon-swollen rivers – you'll also be warned by the Bhutanese against wild animals, black magic and ghosts.

Attempts are being made to introduce formal education to the villages (as part of a modernization programme) but many still rely on monastic teaching. **Women** are valued as the mainstay of the extended family and in many areas property is inherited through the female line. Other than this, customs and attitudes towards women (education, travel, marriage, divorce, adultery, single parenthood) can vary greatly, even between villages only a day's walk apart.

A White Ghost in the Himalayas

Lesley Reader, an educational psychologist, traveller and writer from England, first came to Bhutan in 1986 to take up a post as a volunteer teacher in the remote mountain villages of Ura and Buli. She was the only Westerner to have lived and worked amongst the villagers of this region. While still in Bhutan, she wrote and sent us the account below. We have also included her later experiences of of returning to Bhutan to work once again in a country that has long since become a second home.

"Well, there are jobs in Zimbabwe, Nepal, Kenya or Bhutan. What do you think?" The voice on the telephone paused. I looked out of the window on to the depressed and depressing Sunderland landscape and tried hard to conjure up the distant and exotic worlds itemized by the woman from the London Headquarters of Voluntary Service Overseas (VSO). It was impossible.

"I'd like to go to Bhutan," I said.

"What do you know about it? Where is it?" she asked. Not unreasonable questions in view of its size, inaccessibility to most people and absence from the world media.

"It's to the right of Nepal and I know enough," I claimed boldly.

I had applied to VSO in a state of boredom with my job, disillusionment with house-owning, disgust at the rat race and horror of the increasing materialism of life in England. It seemed to me that I could run away from it all or I could stay and try to improve matters by involving myself in politics at some level. I decided to run.

Four months after the phone call I was actually among the mountains of Bhutan. And two-and-a-half years later, as I write, I am still here. I realize now that I didn't know enough when I arrived, don't know enough now and, indeed, even if I stayed forever, would never know enough about this foreign land and its people where I feel so much at home.

It seems that there are two distinct Bhutans for me. One is the remote Himalayan Kingdom, last remaining Shangri-La, mystical, almost magical place described in guidebooks and glossy travelogues, with scenery beyond words, peace beyond imagining and people of such friendliness, generosity of spirit and contentment that they are special indeed. Remarkable as it seems, this is a true picture.

But it exists alongside the other Bhutan. The Bhutan of sheer slog and drudgery for its people, where ill health, illiteracy, ignorance, and a terrifyingly low life expectancy prevail; where people lead short lives made painful, both physically and emotionally, by hardship. I sat in my friend's house in the village the other evening and her mother looked at me carefully, and said "we go to the fields every day and we become old women very quickly. You teach in school all day and you will become old very slowly". She is right. Yet slowly things are changing.

They closed their eyes, covered their ears with their hands and shook with fear at my approach.

Increased contact with other nations, both by foreigners being allowed into the country and with Bhutanese people being sent abroad to study, has increased the awareness of the potential for improving the situation. But this is only among some. Much of the country is isolated and unvisited either by tourists or aid workers. I met a group of women on the path a few days ago. They closed their eyes at the sight of me, covered their ears with their hands and shook with fear at my approach. They had never seen a Westerner before and thought I was a white ghost. It will be a long time before any of the advantages of development touch their lives. But it will also be a long time before they have to cope with its disadvantages.

In the more urban centres crime has increased, consumerism raised its ugly head and dissatisfaction at the disparity between rich and poor affected the normal equilibrium of the Buddhist temperament. The balancing act being attempted by the royal government between improving the lives of the people while avoiding the worst pitfalls of "civilization" makes a tightrope walk across Niagara Falls look like a gentle stroll.

The majority of the Bhutanese are subsistence farmers. In harsh terms that means if you don't farm well you don't fill your stomach. It means working sixteen-hour days of hard physical toil when the work has to be done: dragging yourself weary from your bed well before dawn to get to the fields so as to make use of every second of daylight. The people of Buli did this for more than three weeks at a stretch during rice planting. In my enthusiam to take an equal part I managed a day-and-a-half with them one weekend and lurched back to the classroom on Monday morning, certain I would never walk upright again. For me it was a new experience, for them the stakes are higher.

In addition to the inexorable demands of the land they must expend considerable ingenuity to find a source of cash as money has become increasingly necessary, perhaps to take a relative to hospital. Sometimes the family or a neighbour helps out, sometimes they can sell butter, cheese or eggs. It isn't easy. They must live with the knowledge that they, their crops and their livestock are at the mercy of unseasonal weather, wild animals or disease. Most cannot read or write although the majority now send at least some children to school in the hope that they will eventually get a job away from the land and so have a steady income. One son, or maybe more if the family is large and the land is sufficient to support them, may be sent to a monastery to become a monk.

The main source of information is oral; the weekly government newspaper is incomprehensible to many villagers and any printed matter must be taken to a sympathetic teacher or Lama for understanding. There may or may not be someone in the village with a radio (and the necessary batteries) to listen to the daily broadcasts of news, information or music from the capital which is often many days' journey away. People do not travel much; there is no reason and it is expensive and time-consuming.

Into this land I arrived from my comfortable terraced house in Newcastle-upon-Tyne.

Into this land I arrived from my comfortable terraced house in Newcastle-upon-Tyne; central heating, automatic washing machine, freezer, a garden that was a wilderness as I knew nothing about growing anything, a car and deep feelings of wanting something different. As I passed my first few days in late winter at over ten and a half thousand feet in Ura, the tiny village in the Himalayas that was to be my home for the next two years, it dawned on me that I had certainly found it.

I was alone and relished what lay ahead, whatever that may turn out to be. I decided to learn the language, find out what life in this beautiful but harsh environment was about and participate in as much as I could. Of course, in some matters there was no choice: I had to adopt local ways; my water was in the stream with everyone else's, I had a pile of wood and an earthen cooking stove to get my food cooked and my pit latrine was out the back. The wind scythed through the myriad tiny cracks in the house walls as it funnelled up the valley every afternoon and the closest electricity was a long way over the horizon. For many weeks I considered it quite a feat just to feed myself, wash my clothes and keep warm. It was to be a long time before I even bothered about washing myself!

In other respects I did have a choice. I could have just spoken English and restricted my social contacts to the staff at school and the few other people in the valley who would understand me. I need not have adopted the national costume. I could have declined to drink the local distillation. I could have stayed in my school quarters and not moved out to live in the temple. I could have refused blessings from the local Lamas. I could have stayed home and not sallied forth with the archery team for a weekend in a neighbouring valley. I could have, but I didn't. And the fact that I had the pleasure of so many remarkable experiences was due to my Bhutanese neighbours.

I was the first Westerner to live in Ura. As such I was the subject of considerable curiosity. For my first two weeks there were twenty faces peering in at my windows each morning watching me eat breakfast. Their disappointment was palpable as they realized I opened my mouth, put food in, chewed and swallowed just like they did. The favourite occupation of some of the smaller children was to stand next to my washing line and watch my multicoloured knickers, bra, jeans and other exotic clothes flap in the wind.

"You're the Ura teacher. I'd heard tell there was a teacher there who could speak our language."

My entertainment value was considerable and every activity was scrutinized. As their confidence grew I was questioned as to why I took all my clothes off to wash, why I used paper after I'd been to the toilet, why I walked up the mountain at the weekend when I had no work to do there. And to their, and my, delight, after much struggle they could do this in their own language.

At first no one understood why I wanted to learn, then they despaired of me ever managing it, then every person I encountered took it upon themselves to teach me until I thought my brain would explode. Finally after two years they would proudly inform any visitor to the valley, "You know our foreign teacher? She speaks our language."

Once, when visiting a school a day's walk to the north of the village I met an old man walking towards me down the mountain path. We began the usual greetings. He stopped after a short while, "I know who you are," he said, "you're the Ura teacher. I'd heard tell there was a teacher there who could speak our language," he nodded, "it's true, you can." With encouragement like this it was hardly surprising I succeeded. It is the greatest achievement of my life.

In all their curiosity and interest there seemed to be no malice; they enquired, noted the differences and let me carry on, however bizarre they obviously found me. One question that came up again and again related to my family. As an only child (that was considered peculiar and sad enough in itself), they wanted to know how I could leave my elderly parents to travel for so many days across the sea to live amongst strangers. I tried, oh I tried, to convey curiosity, the reality of city life, itchy feet, philanthropy and whatever else my confused motives contained.

But I know that although they might be able to imagine themselves, if they tried very hard, in some of the strange situations I described – living with electricity, driving a car, buying everything from a shop, having a tap in the house – they could never imagine journeying so far from one's family and staying away for so long out of choice. Such a thing was strange indeed.

In Bhutan, the family are your mainstay in times of crisis; they and neighbours will rally round if food runs out, if someone falls sick, if someone dies or if more help is needed in the fields. They are the buffer in misfortune, easing your burdens physically and psychologically. In my case, contact with my family was limited to letters. In Buli the postman came every ten days or so, he can rarely have had anyone waiting with such anticipation for him to amble along the path.

The other means by which people achieve control over their fate lies in religion. In the northern part of Bhutan this is Tibetan Buddhism. Seeing its influence on the everyday lives of people, I sought to find out more about this gentle religion. Unfortunately I wasn't fluent enough to grasp the deeper philosophy but I began to attend ceremonies, leave offerings, receive blessings, and later

Coming back late from my friend's house I am warned about ghosts and bears. Fortunately, I have never met either.

I was given a Bhutanese name. I don't know what much of it means but I do know that it is about living in the present, and that's fine by me.

And where do women fit into all of this? Well, it depends. In the south of the country the majority of the population orginate from Nepal and have retained their language, culture and Hindu religion. Of this I know nothing. My life is among the Buddhists in the north. I have been told on many occasions by people far better travelled than I, that compared to the rest of Asia "it's not too bad".

I am not knowledgeable enough to argue.

The women I met were strong, vibrant, outspoken, bawdy and the mainstay of the community. On marriage a man moves to his wife's house and becomes part of her family.

Consequently the birth of a daughter is greatly celebrated as she will later bring much needed manpower to the house. In their everyday lives the women are not constrained as long as the work is attended to. They travel if they need to, they decide on their own work and they drink alcohol if they wish. It's the same for me; I am free to travel where and when I wish. Bhutanese custom dictates that one must offer all possible hospitality to visitors and travellers, and arriving anywhere at any time of the day or night one is immediately looked after. Any man approaching me to ask who I am and where I am going merely wishes to know who I am and where I am going. Coming back late from my friend's house I am warned only about ghosts and bears. Fortunately, I have never met either.

Women speak out at village meetings and, on social occasions, more than hold their own in the verbal sparring that inevitably takes place between the sexes. Yet in their everyday life it would be impossible to have a simple friendship with a member of the opposite sex. These expectations applied to me also; my friends in the village were all women. If any man were seen walking or talking with me it would be instantly assumed we were having an affair. And if he was married the wrath of his wife would traditionally descend upon me, as the "other woman", rather than upon the errant husband.

My friends here in Buli are women of all ages. Just as I am a woman alone, the majority of them are either widows, women with husbands absent in the army or single women. They arrived in my house the evening after I reached Buli bearing many bottles of local booze and we all got drunk. We have been together ever since. They bring me rice, vegetables, local alcohol, they teach me to plant, harvest and thresh rice, and cook me dinners of rice and chillies when they see that I'm struggling.

They try to understand why I don't want a husband and children, they worry about the fact that I will have no one to carry me to my cremation when I die and they answer my innumerable questions about their life, Universe and everything. I take their photographs, cook them egg and chips, read and write letters, cut their hair, help them out with cash and tell them about my life and country.

In their attempts to try and understand more about this strange, but entertaining phenomenon in their midst they ply me with questions; why the double-decker buses in the picture of London had no driver on top, where were our rice fields, where did we keep our yaks, how did we cook and keep our saucepans clean? They wanted to know about my parents' house and were astonished to see a picture of a block of flats. They sat mesmerized as I explained how my parents use a lift to get to the thirteenth floor and couldn't understand why I didn't know every single person in my village (London). I fear they have ended up with strange ideas of England. In some ways it doesn't matter, and in other ways it does.

I am rarely completely alone. As far as people here are concerned, to be on one's own is to be lonely and true friends make sure that I am never in that unfortunate state. Sometimes this can feel a burden. I once became sick. As is my habit I took to my bed to sleep. Every five minutes somebody arrived to wake me up and talk to me, they came in relays of two or three for three days. I was demented, I craved sleep, healing sleep. If I had possessed enough strength, the expression "bugger off and leave me alone" might have been verbalized. As it was I lay and suffered.

Inevitably I recovered and questioned my tormentors, although obviously torment was the last thing on their minds. They had come to protect me from the spirits. For spirits are particularly aware of vulnerable souls: those of the sick and anyone who sleeps during the day. They had come to look after me and I in turn have gone to visit sick people for this reason.

So I live all day in a crowd, I live with the constant knowledge that something strange and unexpected may be about to happen; my friends arrive to take me to a wedding, to the temple to get a blessing from an important Lama or from some sticks that have come by magical means from Tibet. I'm aware, however, that I can still only appreciate from the outside what it means to have been born here, to grow up and to expect to die in this tiny valley. To say there is never a dull moment is absolutely true. No it certainly isn't Shangri-La. It's better.

Big Mother Beckons

After a short spell back in England, studying, working and catching up on the social and cultural life she'd left behind, **Lesley Reader** again took an overseas voluntary job – this time in a refugee camp in Thailand. She worked there for two years before she found herself drawn again to the Himalayas.

I may have thought I'd finished with Bhutan, but Bhutan had certainly not finished with me. One night, while I was living in Thailand, my Big Mother came to visit me. Big Mother, "Ama Jigpallah", is the title for your oldest maternal aunt in Kengkha, the language I had struggled with in Buli. My Ama Jigpallah is the aunt of my best friend in the village. In that strange state between sleep and wakefulness, more vivid than reality, more substantial than dreaming, she appeared and spoke: "Kuzuzangpo, Lopen" – Hello, Teacher. She smiled and vanished. I feared she had died, and sent letters to her village, enquiring. She appeared again and again, always at the same time; she always said the same words. And then, out of the blue, came news of another job in Bhutan, a job I knew was for me. Once I'd made up my mind I didn't see Ama Jigpallah again until I saw her in the flesh in Buli. Neither she nor anybody else in the village was surprised to hear of my visitations in Thailand. I know that Westerners will see Ama Jigpallah as proof that I'd gone bush, been taking strange substances or finally cracked up. It can't be helped.

I returned to Bhutan two years after leaving. There was no overwhelming excitement, no tears, no drama. I stood in the clear mountain air and breathed deeply, gazed into the brilliant blue high altitude sky, and I was home.

The new job and life were very different from the old. Instead of living in one village and teaching in the local school, I was committed to visiting the eighteen schools in Shemgang District, or the Keng district as it is called.

The area is one of the most remote in Bhutan. Roads are very few, the villages are widely spaced and the countryside is wild and difficult. Rivers thunder through steep-sided gorges several thousand feet deep, with sides covered in thick inhospitable forest. People have settled wherever a water supply and enough flattish land are available for cultivation. Most of the villages are many days' walk from the road and Government services are widely dispersed. Schools, health units, malaria eradication officers, agricultural workers and animal husbandry officers cover wide areas and ease of access to these facilities varies greatly; some children live within half an hour of school (although this may involve a difficult river crossing on the way), others may walk for well over an hour in each direction while others again board at school from the age of six as the only way to receive education.

Within these villages electricity is a dream (a dream that is coming true as Save the Children provide small solar panels to run school lighting schemes), water supplies are sometimes clean, sometimes worrying, knowledge of latrines is rudimentary, there are no shops and life varies from hard through very hard to almost impossibly hard, depending on your village and the time of year.

Everything that a family needs they must produce themselves, or they must have the cash, time and energy to trek to the road (two, three or four days walk away) to buy it and carry it home. Every box of matches, every bar of soap, every bottle of kerosene for lighting has to be carried on the back of a man or woman or horse over countryside that is sheer up or sheer down. I never learned the word for flat in Kengkha: it's never used. To make that journey you must also carry your food for the trip, your pots to cook your food on the way and enough clothes to keep you warm while you sleep in the forest at night.

As well as family needs every pencil, book, piece of paper and blackboard for the school, every aspirin and needle for the health unit, every improved seed or grain of chemical fertilizer, all of these necessities of development must be carried along these well-trodden but often very difficult paths. One day I met a group of men carrying new "improved" blackboards to the schools, donated by an aid agency that had better remain nameless. Produced after much thought and consultation, the blackboards were three feet wide. Many of the footpaths in the area are much less than this. These men had to walk sideways like crabs for hours and hours on end, their loads strapped to their backs as they struggled up hill and down dale.

My job was to visit the eighteen schools scattered around this area as often as possible and support, help and advise the teachers and heads. I was based in Shemgang, the district head-quarters, but most of my time was spent trekking from village to village.

I would pack my rucksack, get a lift down to the place where the footpath left the road, hire a porter from the first village for the trek to

I discovered that I could cope with leeches on any part of my anatomy without having the screaming abdabs.

the next, and off I would set. At each village I would stop and change porters. Sometimes I would stay overnight in a village if the schools were too widely spaced; sometimes I would reach the next school within the day. Sometimes the day's walking was long, ten-and-a-half hours of solid slog; sometimes the day was short, six hours of solid slog.

At each school I would stay for two or three or four days, do my work and move on. There were various routes around the district and I always varied my route to explore new paths, visit new villages, meet new people. Six or seven weeks after leaving the road I would arrive back, hitch a ride to Shemgang, settle down for a week or two to recover, write my report, read my mail and do the washing before setting off again.

I became a nomad and learned that I could sleep equally well on the floors of classrooms, kitchens, forests, huts or supposedly haunted temples. I discovered that I could cope with leeches on any (and I mean any) part of my anatomy without having the screaming abdabs, was not much distressed by fleas, bedbugs or scabies and could sleep equally well with the headmaster's children or village grandmothers snoring beside me. I have the cast iron stomach of the truly lucky, but still cringe to recall the maggots I found in one plate of meat. I wish I had discovered them before digesting more than half of it.

I learned from my porters which water sources to trust and which not, which ferns to pick for curry and which plants never to touch, the almost dried leaves of which tree I could roll up and smoke if I so wished. For the porters, sometimes men, sometimes women, sometimes young, sometimes old, were my companions for hour after hour. Unfailingly cheerful, they chatted if I had breath to do so, sang and

BHUTAN

chewed betel nut while carting my rucksack up sheer slopes, knew how
to cross raging rivers in the monsoon, cut new paths through the forest
if a landslide had taken the original one away and were a fine source of
gossip and fun.

In a region where Westerners are very rare, I was initially regarded
with some concern: would I be able to climb the hills, drink the local
booze, sleep next to Grandma? One endless source of delight was the
look on people's faces when they realized I could speak Kengkha.

There was often initial uncertainty as to what I was. Dressed in trousers,
T-shirt and walking boots, I reached one village. The old couple plough-
ing in the field stopped, looked at me, frowned and quizzed the porter: "Is
it a man or a woman?" When I replied and pointed out that I did have
boobs, at first I thought they were going to die from the shock and then
thought their uncontrollable laughter might finish them off.

As well as bringing news and gossip from Shemgang and the villages
along the way, I spent endless hours describing my own country and
family and I usually managed to pack a different set of photos on each
trip for people to look at. For people were as keen to know about me as
I was to learn about them. In one house there was a belief that Western
women did not drink alcohol. I soon put them straight on that.

Depending on where the school was in relation to the village and where
I was sleeping, so my social life in each
school was determined. If I was staying
with a headmaster who maintained a
distance between himself and the local
people, then I tended to mingle with
the school staff and their families; but if
I slept in the classrooms or the head
was of a different disposition then things were very different.

*The comments were
uninhibited: "Isn't she
fat?" "Her flesh is
white." "She has hairs
on her legs."*

In one village I think I was probably visited by every woman who
lived there in the course of my stay. There was a constant stream of
visitors from dawn to dusk; they often woke me in the mornings and
left after I had crawled into my sleeping bag and nodded off at night. If
they missed me in my off duty hours they would often arrive at the
classroom windows for a chat.

One old lady, unaware of the conventions of schools, wandered into
the class as I was teaching, a bottle of the local distilled alcohol in one
hand and a mug in the other. "Have a drink," she demanded.

I said I would drink later.

She thought I was making excuses and wanted to know what was
wrong with her drink.

I tried to explain I was teaching.

38

"So?"

I said I couldn't drink while I was teaching.

"Why not? Here's the bottle, here's the mug."

My Kengkha was not up to the task. I gave in. The mug was very big. I taught the rest of the morning sitting down.

My novelty value was considerable. Washing in the local stream often attracted a crowd, particularly on my early visits. At first I thought that little old ladies standing beside me were waiting to get to the water, but they soon put me right: "Oh no, we've just come to watch you." As I struggled to wash all parts while keeping most covered the comments were uninhibited: "Isn't she fat?" "Her flesh is white." "She has hairs on her legs." One day I got up at four in the morning to wash in solitude.

Although in some ways my life was difficult, I was lucky in that every village I visited gave me something to look forward to; the prospect of someone or something that got me up the final five hundred feet, helped me forget my aching legs, my rumbling stomach and the discomforts I would find. In some villages it was a special family, friends; in others it was a wonderful stream for washing, a glorious view, a peach tree in season, a headmaster who always had fresh vegetables, a group of teachers to laugh with.

Yet whatever my hardships, they were nothing compared with those of the people I came to know and admire more and more as I learned about their lives.

I learned that Buli is a fortunate place: the people have paddy fields and enough rice, vegetables and forest food to keep them going for the year. Such is not the case throughout Keng. I visited villages where soil, rainfall and terrain make rice a luxury, where maize or millet are the staple crop. These are lower grade grains than rice, harder to digest, providing less goodness. In one village slash-and-burn agriculture is the method of production, difficult back-breaking

Ama Jigpallah looked stricken. "You have just come back, and now we will never see you again. You will die."

work. Forest experts may condemn this, but with no land flat enough for a permanent field it is difficult to see what else people could do.

I learned that sickness is a constant danger. I stayed in a tiny village in the middle of nowhere. One of the women in the house started taking her clothes off. "Please check my baby." She was pregnant, five or six months. I protested my ignorance. Her shoulders slumped; her last child had been stillborn and she was worried about this one. I suggested she go to the nearest hospital. It was the middle of the monsoon, the paths were diabolical, the rain, mud and leeches almost intolerable. It had just taken two of the worst days' walking I had ever done to reach the village. She pointed up at the mountains over which I had come, the almost sheer paths across them and shook her head. "It's too late. I can't walk." No health workers ever visited; she and her baby were in the hands of fate. I heard later that both were fine. This time.

I learned about festivals and pilgrimages, about a Lama reported to be able to bring water forth from dry stones and about poisoners, black magic and superstition. On my first trip back to Buli I explained my job and the route I would take around the district. Ama Jigpallah began to cry. She shook her head. "You must not go to Picor." This is a particular part of the district. "The people there will poison you, they are poisoners."

"I have to go. It's my work."

Ama Jigpallah looked stricken. "You have just come back, and now we will never see you again. You will die."

Her younger sister scurried into a back room and staggered out, pulling a sack of rice. "Do not eat in their houses. Take this rice: you must cook it and eat it yourself."

I gestured to the sack and my already bulging rucksack. Even they could see the point. I suggested I was going to eat in school: the Head was not from those parts. The sack was divided, divided and divided again. They packed and repacked my rucksack, squeezed in as much rice as they could and finally I promised to be careful where I ate, under no circumstances to touch a boiled egg (especially dangerous) and to send a message by some means, any means, to let them know when I was safely out of Picor. After several safe returns from the dreaded Picor and my admission that I ate anything I was given by anybody they decided that, as a Westerner, I was obviously immune in some way. Gradually I learned more about these poisoners and their awful characteristic – although they do not choose to hurt people, they sometimes harm people years after they have eaten in their house, and very often the trait runs in families. They appear to be looked on with a certain amount of fear, but without blame.

In contrast, black magicians, reputed to be rife in certain other villages, are generally feared and detested for using their learned arts to cause illness and death. The local prison held those convicted of black magic, while other prisoners had taken the law into their own hands and attempted to murder an old lady believed to practise such evil arts.

It seemed that every day I learned more, and gradually my perceptions of what I was seeing altered. On my first trip around the district the scenery filled my mind. During the monsoon I became aware of which bridges were likely to be washed away and which paths were prone to rock falls; I learned where I was likely to encounter a snake, where most leeches lurked and simply have to close my eyes to see again the tiger footprints in one part of the forest. I learned which paths had the cruellest inclines or no drinking water, and where and when my favourite wild fruits would be ripe. And while I enjoyed the friendship and good nature of the people, so too I saw the unrelenting hardship and the darker, sadder side of their lives. This was a privilege.

For some months now I've been back in England. To explain my comings and goings both to myself and to my Bhutanese friends, to explain why I feel no sense of culture shock in moving from one place to the other, I suggest that my soul is half Western and half Bhutanese and needs both places to thrive.

This time when I left I promised to return. I'll make sure Ama Jigpallah doesn't have to come and get me.

TRAVEL NOTES

Languages There's a great deal of regional variation in languages and dialects – all of which are hard to pick up. Dzongkha, the national language, taught in schools, Is native to the west of Bhutan. English remains the language of instruction, but with formal education being so limited very few people outside of the towns will speak it

Transport Bhutan has an airport at Paro and a national airline, *Druk Air*, which offers extremely expensive flights to Bangkok, Dacca, Calcutta, Kathmandhu and Delhi. The only other way in is via West Bengal or Assam (though for this you'll need an Inner Line permit, which are difficult to get). Travelling around is a slow and difficult task. Even tour-buses come up against landslides and blockages on the main roads. Local buses are inexpensive but often packed. Many villages, a long trek from the road, are impossible to reach without the help of porters. You should never underestimate the ardours of a relentless climb along difficult paths and at high altitude.

Accommodation Thimphu and Phuntsholing boast a few luxury hotels but otherwise accommodation is very basic – just a scattering of lodges and some rest houses for Bhutanese officials moving round the country.

Special Problems Unless you are travelling with an extremely expensive tour-group, visas are difficult to come by. You have to apply directly to the Director of Tourism, in Thimphu, three months in advance. Once you've gained entry, the main difficulties are coping with the climate

(very cold in the higher valleys) and the physical demands of trekking. The dress code for locals is fairly strictly adhered to, especially in the main urban centres where government policies are more easily enforced. As yet, the code (for women a long, tightly belted blanket-like garment) does not extend to foreigners.

BOOKS

Françoise Pommaret-Imaeda and Yoshiro Imaeda, *Bhutan: a Kingdom of the Eastern Himalayas* (UK, Serindia, 1984, o/p/US, Shambhala, 1989). A superbly illustrated, informative book by two eminent Tibetologists who have lived in Bhutan for many years.

Katie Hickman, *Dreams of the Peaceful Dragon: Journey into Bhutan* (UK, Coronet, 1989) and **Tom Owen Edmunds**, *Bhutan Land of the Thunder Dragon* (UK, Penguin, 1989). Katie Hickman and Tom Owen Edmunds travelled together through Bhutan. Her version of their epic journey is complemented by his collection of photos.

Peter Collister, *Bhutan and the British* (UK, Serindia, 1987, o/p). A detailed analysis of the obscure historical relationship between the two countries.

If you are coming to Bhutan from India it's worth checking out **Reliance Publishing House** and **Pragati Publications**, both in Delhi, for more recent English-language titles on Bhutan.

Bolivia

The second poorest country in South America (after Guyana), Bolivia is still relatively undiscovered by travellers, many of whom were put off by the political instability and drug scandals that blotted the country's reputation in the 1980s. In reality, despite its position at the heart of the world cocaine trade (cocaine is said to account for sixty percent of the nation's foreign exchange revenue), Bolivia suffers nothing like the level of drug-related violence of, say, Colombia, and the political situation has stabilized considerably in recent years.

This is a fascinating country and though getting around isn't always straightforward – schedules can be disrupted by anything from floods to bureaucracy – public transport and accommodation are inexpensive and plentiful. The landscape, encompassing rainforest, desolate plateaux (most notably,

the great luminous windswept expanse of the Altiplano), the Andean Cordillera and Lake Titicaca – at 3810m, the highest navigable water in the world – is often magnificent. And the people (two-thirds of them Indios) are steeped in tradition, captured in their distinctive dress and the haunting strains of their music.

For women travellers, the overwhelming presence of indigenous people makes Bolivia fairly unstressful from the point of view of harassment, though, as in all South American countries, you're unlikely to escape some of the day-to-day irritations of machismo. Outside the rural areas, in towns like the capital La Paz, Sucre or the more Westernized Cochabamba, passing comments from men are the norm, fuelled by the familiar cocktail of girlie images that permeate television and adorn every newstand. But the attention, however maddening, seldom feels seriously threatening.

Although concerned with issues like sexist media, especially in relation to male violence and sexuality, the **women's movement** in Bolivia is predominantly linked to the problem of widespread hunger and the need for economic and political change. An increasing number of *campesinos* (farmers) own at least a small plot of land, but most are still desperately poor, leading to an inevitable drift toward the cities where women, in particular, try to eke out a living as street vendors. Two of the most notable women's organizations are the widespread Women's Peasant Federation and the *Amas de Casa de la Ciudad*, a group of poor women who run a health clinic and various education programmes in the slums of La Paz. Both believe in the value of excluding men from specific discussions and decisions in order for women to gain the confidence to stand up for their rights. In addition, since the mid-1980s women have won themselves a strong platform in the COB (Bolivian Workers' Federation), where women delegates have long insisted on the need for more representation on its committees and participation in general.

An Inside View

Susanna Rance has been living and working in Bolivia since 1980. Former editor of the bi-monthly news analysis *Bolivia Bulletin*, her special interest is in grass-roots and development journalism, especially relating to popular women's organizations. She was also an active participant in the 1994 Population Conference in Cairo.

When I first arrived in Bolivia, I came with the idea of settling here permanently. Not just because La Paz was my husband's birthplace: on previous travels through Mexico and Central America en route to Venezuela, where I lived for two years, I had already got the "bug". I had fallen in love with Latin American culture, music, language, politics, a certain flavour of life which I found – and still find – warming and exhilarating.

On returning to London from Venezuela in 1977, I joined the Latin American Women's Group and became involved in discussion and solidarity work with women from a variety of backgrounds and countries. That experience confirmed my desire to live permanently in South America, and at the same time to change the course of my work – then teaching English as a foreign language – to something linked with the international struggle for social change.

As a gringa, I expected to feel out of place, even rejected. None of my fears were confirmed.

I flew into La Paz airport, reeling from the 4000m altitude, in May 1980. Winter, the cold dry season, was beginning, but La Paz was spectacular with its crystal clear air, blue skies and bright Andean sun. The beauty of the descent from the high plateau into the basin of the city has never lost its impact for me. The narrow back road winds down steep hillsides covered with a pastel-coloured hotchpotch of improvised dwellings, a sharp contrast to the avenues and high-rise buildings of the city centre.

As a gringa, arriving in the midst of a fairly traditional Aymara household, I expected to feel out of place, even rejected. None of my fears were confirmed. My husband's extended family welcomed me warmly and did all they could to make me feel at home.

Each of the small rooms around the cobbled courtyard housed several people, yet there were always invitations for us to visit, sit and share a meal or borrow what we needed. Twenty of us used one cold tap in the yard, the only source of water, which frequently dried up. Washing and cooking, both done squatting at ground level, were social activities, a time for the women of the household to chat, complain and catch up on family news. My husband was thought odd for joining in with these tasks, and our attempts to involve our nephews in household chores were firmly rejected.

Although our lifestyle was clearly different from that of the rest of the family, I found an atmosphere of tolerance, generated largely by my mother-in-law, a generous and open woman who was always loving and supportive to me, up until her death. "La Mama" was the hub of the household, a true matriarch.

Only three of her nine children had survived. In my terms, the others died of poverty; in hers, from a variety of supernatural causes: the evil eye, a sudden shock which sends the soul fleeing from the body, a strange illness called larphata which has all the symptoms of malnutrition.

My parents-in-law lived for most of the year in the subtropical Yungas valley, growing coffee, citrus fruits, bananas and coca on land which they had cleared from virgin forest. Our

After the coup, I felt panicked, ignorant, impotent to do anything about the repression we witnessed daily.

honeymoon was a month spent with them up in the woods, harvesting coffee, talking in the evenings by candlelight, preparing lunch at dawn on a wood fire before we set off to work.

La Mama worked energetically on the land, dressed in trousers and boots, wielding a machete. On her weekly trips to the nearest town, she would run the two-hour stretch down rocky paths, stopping at intervals to take off one of her work garments and replace it with a petticoat, a long vest, a layered skirt, Cinderella-style shoes and finally her bowler hat.

Despite the family's usual openness towards me, there was one period when I felt isolated. In our second year my husband, a folk musician, went abroad for months on tour. I was "sent to Coventry" by his younger brother's family for carrying on my life as usual, going out at night and staying over with friends: unseemly behaviour for a woman, which I could only get away with in their eyes if my husband was around to give his permission.

Nevertheless, I know that even now a lot of allowances are made for me because I am a gringa. One of my sisters-in-law, a Quechua from rural Potosi, often feels as much at sea as I do in the midst of Aymara customs and rituals. Yet as a Bolivian, she is expected to merge totally with the dictates of local and family tradition. Only I, as a foreigner, receive praise for any efforts to integrate, and understanding when I opt out!

Two months after I arrived in La Paz there was a military coup. I still knew very little about the country, and it wasn't until some time later that I realized this wasn't just another of the frequent changes of government for which Bolivia is notorious.

Being stopped in the street by military patrols after curfew, hearing sinister shots late into the night, seeing tanks blocking the university gates and the media censored – these were just symptoms of the more hidden violence imposed by the cocaine generals. Their two-year rule, ended by the virtual collapse of the Armed Forces, left a trail of exile, massacre and corruption, which remains a brutal reminder of the fragility of the Bolivian democratic system.

After the coup I felt panicked, ignorant, impotent to do anything about the repression we witnessed daily. I looked for ways of finding out more about what was going on. A couple of months later, I was offered the chance to join a small group of people in the clandestine task of collecting and processing information about the abuses committed under the military regime, to send to solidarity and human rights organizations abroad.

Through this work, I started to learn not just about the current situation but also about Bolivia's history and culture. Gradually the information project began to take up most of my time and I was able to leave my English teaching job and change my line of work, just as I had wanted to do before leaving England.

Meanwhile, I had also become politically involved, in the Women's Front of a party active in the resistance to the dictatorship. Our group, made up mainly of middle-class professionals, represented the first attempt to bring women's issues into the forefront of Bolivian left-wing party politics.

We fought against being relegated to tea-making and sticking up posters while the men met to make the "serious" decisions. We were criticized for doing popular education with women's groups in the shanty towns, instead of pushing the party line and rallying female masses to the demos. We were accused of dividing the struggle at a time when the urgency of the situation required unquestioning discipline. Eventually, the Women's Front was dissolved, but a women's education and information centre grew out of that first initiative.

My first three years in Bolivia were a time of almost total immersion in the life, culture and work around me. Most of my friends and work-mates were Bolivian and I had little time to miss my own country or people. Then two things happened to change my experience of Bolivia: I got hepatitis and lost a pregnancy; and we moved out of the family house to have our first child.

It wasn't until I was pregnant that I realized I was malnourished. Although my weight had fallen to a little over six stone, I had never given a thought to my diet. When the doctor asked me exactly what I ate each day, I said it was the same as the rest of the family, but I had to admit it wasn't very nutritious: dry bread and herb tea for breakfast, rice or noodle soup with potatoes or boiled bananas for lunch and the same again for tea and supper. No milk, butter or jam. Very little meat, cheese or eggs.

Cooking together at home, we all ate from the same pot, just adding a cup of water to the soup if there was a visitor. The main difference between me and the rest of the fami-

> *I suddenly realized that I couldn't go on subjecting myself to that diet, to that poverty.*

ly was that they were used to eating large quantities of carbohydrates to compensate for the lack of protein. Often, rice, potatoes and bananas would make up most of the meal, with a tiny sliver of meat and some spicy chilli sauce to give it all flavour. I couldn't take that much bulk, so I just ate less and lost weight.

Soon after this discovery I got hepatitis and had a miscarriage as a result. The next time a plate of watery rice soup was put in front of me I burst into tears, and I've never been able to eat it since. I suddenly realized that I couldn't go on subjecting myself to that diet, to that poverty. For the first time since arriving in Bolivia I felt horribly foreign and apart. I started to sort out what things I could and couldn't accept in the way of life around me. Some months later, when I had recovered and was pregnant again, we moved out into our own house, on a market street not far down the road.

The birth of my daughter was a wonderful experience. Apart from the joys of motherhood, encountered for the first time at 31, I discovered first-hand how children are welcomed and loved in Bolivian society, how they are accepted as part of everyday life, not segregated into a subculture of mums and toddlers as in my own country. Relatives and neighbours would ask for a turn with the baby. Market sellers would hold out their arms to give her a cuddle. As a mother, I had a new-found bond with the women around me, even if they shrieked with horror to see Nina being carried down the street in a baby sling, unswaddled and hatless.

I went back to my job a couple of months after Nina was born, working partly from home and sitting breast-feeding her in office meetings with the full support of my colleagues. However, I found it impossible to continue my political activity. Carrying my daughter on long, bumpy bus rides to smoky meetings, coming out late and waiting for transport in the cold, arriving home exhausted, with a broken night ahead of me – it was too much. Aside from the incomprehension of the male party militants, the women my age had all started their families ten years before me and weren't into babies any more.

Another isolation point. My life became a shuttle between home and work, and I started to miss the company of other foreign women who were late-starting mothers like myself, or could understand what I was going through. When I did start to find such allies, I was faced with a hard fact of having chosen to live so far from my own culture: the departure of a succession of friends who left Bolivia when their period of work or study ended.

One year, I withdrew and refused to make new contacts, knowing they would just leave again. But gradually I came to terms with the fact that despite the yearly exodus, these friends greatly enrich my life while they are here. Contact with many of them has continued and some, smitten with the Bolivia bug, return periodically to visit.

When Nina was two-and-a-half, our son Amaru was born. I carried on working full-time, thanks to the support of helpers, friends and neighbours. My husband took on the main parenting role during the months he was in La Paz, but continued to tour with his group for several months each year. Like working mothers everywhere, I felt the inevitable strain of combining parenting with a demanding job, and there was little time for relaxation or social activities.

A stay of several months in England convinced me that, despite some nostalgia, I far preferred living in Bolivia.

Meanwhile, the work of our small team had grown and developed into a documentation and information centre. With the demise of the military regime and the return to democracy in 1982, we were able to open an office, print and mail our news bulletins in Spanish and English and offer our services to students, researchers and journalists in Bolivia and abroad.

My own work was taking a clearer line as I alternated writing and editing on general topics with following up my specific interest: popular women's organizations. I started writing for publications in Bolivia and abroad on grass-roots organizations grouping women from the country-side, factories, mines and shanty towns, writing about their experiences and activities on the basis of direct testimonies.

The end of my eighth year in Bolivia marked a watershed in my personal and professional life. A stay of several months in England had convinced me that, despite some nostalgia, I far preferred living in Bolivia, which offered me many more opportunities to develop as a person, worker and mother than Tory Britain. I returned feeling confident in this choice, ready to start a new phase in my life. It was this new confidence which enabled me to make some unsettling changes: I left my job of eight years and my marriage, also of eight years, in the space of three months.

Belonging to the information centre had been a kind of umbilical cord for me almost since my arrival in Bolivia. It was there that I had become accepted as part of a team, made friends, learned about Bolivia and developed a new career. Finally, I was ready to branch out on my own.

As well as writing articles on development issues, I began to research a report for the National Population Council on the hot debate around (voluntary) family planning versus (imposed) birth control. This work has opened up new channels: the opportunity for training in population and development planning and the prospect of running a programme on legislation and women's rights.

Soon after I changed jobs, my husband and I reached the point of recognizing that our lives had become distanced and we had come to relate more as "co-parents" than as a couple. I started to experience the problems of being a single woman in Bolivian society, where stable couples are the accepted norm and machismo sets out the rules for most relationships.

But through it all, after nine years in Bolivia, I've finally found my own identity here as a gringa, person, mother and worker. I now have close Bolivian women friends with ideas and experiences in common. And I know that this is where I want to stay, where I want my children to grow up, the country I want to keep enjoying, discovering and writing about.

T R A V E L   N O T E S

Languages Spanish, Quechua, Aymara and other minor Indian languages.

Transport *Flotas*, or long-distance buses, run from the main bus terminal in La Paz to most other towns in the country. Trains are slow, but the journeys often picturesque. Air travel is very cheap.

Accommodation Although prices are rising, by European standards Bolivia still has plenty of inexpensive, basic hotels. Only La Paz tends to get booked up, so try to arrive early.

Women's Holidays In the UK, *Ms. Guided Tours*, 16B Vicars Terrace, Leeds LS8 5AP, offer women-only tours to Bolivia and Peru. Their aim is to offer adventurous travel while introducing and informing Western women about women's lives in the so-called Third World.

Special Problems Avoid going to a doctor, dentist, clinic or hospital unless you absolutely must. The Bolivian medical profession has an unhealthy reliance on the prescription of (unnecessary) drugs. Take sanitary protection with you as tampons are incredibly expensive.

Everything revolves around the dollar in Bolivia, so don't bring British currency. If you manage to change sterling it will be at a very low rate.

Guides The excellent *South American Handbook* (UK, Trade and Travel/US, Passport Press) includes roughly sixty pages on Bolivia. *Bolivia* (Lonely Planet), aimed more at the budget traveller, has plenty of reliable information.

CONTACTS

Centro de Promoción de la Mujer Gregoria Apaza, Edificio Muritto, 3rd Floor Office no 2, Calle Murillo, La Paz (☎327932). Postal address: Casilla 21170, La Paz, Bolivia. Women's centre carrying out research and popular education sessions with poor urban women.

Centro de Información y Desarrollo de la Mujer (CIDEM), Avda Villazon 1950, Of. 3a, 3rd floor (opposite University). Postal address: Casilla 3961, La Paz, Bolivia. Women's information and development centre – activities include the provision of health and legal advice, participatory research and the build-up of an audiovisual archive on the lives of Bolivian women.

Centro de Estudios y Trabajo de La Mujer (CETM), Calle España 624, Cochabamba, Bolivia. Information and research centre, again concerned with working with women's organizations in poor urban areas. Publishes a weekly bulletin, *Nosotras.*

BOOKS

☆ **Domitila Barrios de Chungara**, *Let Me Speak* (UK, Stage 1, 1978/US, Monthly Review Press, 1979). First-hand account of the life of one of the founder members of the Housewives Committees of Siglo XX, one of Bolivia's largest mining complexes, now closed down. A slightly more recent pamphlet by Domitila is included in **Miranda Davies (ed)**, *Third World – Second Sex I* (UK, Zed Books, 1983/US, Humanities Press). See also the general bibliography on p. 692.

Gaby Kuppers (ed), *Compañeras* (UK, Latin America Bureau, 1994). Subtitled *Voices from the Latin American Women's Movement,* this collection includes a short interview on the rise of Bolivian feminism with a member of the CETM (see *Contacts*).

☆ **Alicia Partnoy (ed)**, *You Can't Drown the Fire: Latin American Women Writing in Exile* (UK, Virago, 1989/US, Cleis Press, 1988). Moving anthology bringing together essays, stories, poetry, letters and lyrics by women in exile.

Susan George, *A Fate Worse than Debt* (UK, Penguin, 1987/US, Grove, 1989). Clear account of Latin America's biggest collective problem – debt – including some information on Bolivia.

Thanks to Ruth Ingram of *Ms. Guided Tours* for background information.

Botswana

Botswana tends to get cited as an example of post-Independence success in Africa. From being one of the poorest nations on the continent, the country has risen in less than three decades to a position of relative wealth, with a history of peaceful, multi-party democracy, unparalleled among the South African frontline states. Much of its wealth, based on the surprise discovery of vast diamond deposits only a year after the British left, has been successfully channelled into development programmes, particularly in the highly populated farming communities and urban centres in the eastern corridor around the capital Gaborone. Beyond this, cut off by the vast roadless wildernesses, a more traditional way of life persists. Tourism has also developed apace, with an industry based mainly around the spectacular wildlife reserves, notably the 15,000km of waterways, lakes and islands of the Okavango Delta, the Ghobe and Moremi reserves to the north, and the vast scrublands of the Kalahari Desert, crossed by herds of springbok and wildebeest.

Botswana is, however, an expensive destination. The government, in its concern to lessen the impact of tourism but benefit from its revenue, has a policy of promoting luxury tours and squeezing out ordinary backpackers. Daily charges are levied for each day in the reserves and there's often little option but to stay in the upmarket accommodation provided. However, if you do manage to escape official tours – possible if you're determined – travel can be affordable and very rewarding. What's more, this is one of the easier African countries for women travelling alone. Harassment, either sexual or racial, is uncommon and the crime rate very low.

Botswana's leaders, though pragmatic in their trading relations with South Africa, have long been staunch allies of the ANC, speaking out against apartheid and offering asylum to political refugees. Now that black majority rule has at last spread across the border, new vistas are opening for trade and foreign policy in the region (while defence against incursions from the South African Defence Force can be relaxed). Optimism is high, especially among the young, but this is tinged with apprehension at the volatile social and political situation brewing on the country's doorstep.

Nearly half of all households in Botswana are headed by **women**, due to the migration of men to urban centres and across the border to South Africa in search of work. The majority labour on small plots of land for a subsistence living, often supplementing their income by brewing beer. In recent years, as access to education and employment has improved, women have been gaining a higher profile in the commercial, professional and political life of the country.

A Personal Safari

Adinah Thomas is a writer and dramatist based in London. She went to Botswana at the invitation of two friends, but spent most of her two-month stay exploring alone.

During my visit, I went off alone into the hinterland using a variety of forms of transport. There is basically only one tarmac road in Botswana, running from Gaborone, the capital in the south, to Kasane in the north. Apart from a few good side-shoots, most roads are little more than dirt tracks, some quite reasonable but most impassable in anything other than a four-wheel drive vehicle. A single railway runs from Gaborone to Bulawayo in Zimbabwe. I never travelled by train, but the service is said to be reliable provided you can find someone to explain the timetable.

Despite primitive road conditions, I found travelling through the endless variations of desert fairly easy. I began by catching a bus from Francistown to Nata, a village on the edge of the Makgadigkaki Pans. The bus went on to Kasane where I waited for three hours with six white people and about thirty Batswana, all wanting to go on across the desert to Maun. Eventually I camped in a field belonging to the *Sua Pans Lodge*, a clean and friendly establishment owned by the most supportive man I had met in Africa, and his efficient wife. That night I had a minor hassle with an extremely drunk and callow youth who wanted to share my tent. I was rescued by "Mr Supportive", who got rid of him with a mixture of firmness and tact. "What sort of opinion do you want this lady to take back to her country about our people?" he exclaimed. The youth vanished.

That was the one and only hassle I had while travelling well over a thousand kilometres alone. The local men were polite, helpful, sometimes amused, sometimes a little reserved and always delighted by my pathetic attempts to string together my few words of Setswana.

I eventually got a lift to Maun with two South African farmers in a massive lorry that averaged 20km per hour. They were kind enough, but every time the engine boiled over, which was often, and we were left sitting in the middle of nowhere, waiting for it to cool down, they would moan about how dreadful it was that they were no longer allowed to shoot everything in sight.

The Nata–Maun road is renowned for its bad surface: 300km through desert that varies from scrubby savannah to vast and lifeless saline pans, empty of water in November, through the palm tree belt and sandy wastes followed by more scrub and trees, and more sand. It is not soft golden sand like you find in the Sahara, but a much grittier substance, tufted with dry grasses and thorn bushes and the ever-present acacias. When it rains, parts of the road get washed away. I was lucky and actually made the trip four times without either drowning or dying of heat.

Travelling on a truck, ostrich-spotting, sharing canned drinks at every bottle store, is an exhilarating way to get about.

In Maun I borrowed floor space from Barbara, an Australian teaching at the secondary school. Maun itself is set on thick, pale sand, with a shopping mall, *Riley's Hotel*, and a collection of rather upmarket Safari centres. I walked out of town several times, partly to explore and partly to find a swimming pool. On most occasions I got lifts at least part of the way, though I did once walk eighteen kilometres in blazing sun, with a towel draped around my head.

Local buses exist, but they are on the erratic side and tend to break down; either all the tyres blow, or the springs give way under the weight of what seems like hundreds of Batswana and their bundles. I frequently found myself with a lapful of parcels, a sleeping baby in one arm and my own luggage in the other. Very local public transport, connecting small villages, can comprise anything from converted lorries to open trucks, and vary accordingly in discomfort. But travelling on the back of a truck, ostrich-spotting, sharing canned drinks at every bottle store on the way and trying to understand what the hell people are talking about is an exhilarating way of getting about.

The Batswana usually charge hitch-hikers. The most I ever paid was 10 pula from Nata to Maun, and I paid far less for shorter and less bumpy rides. Sometimes I paid nothing at all. Whites don't normally charge, but do get uptight about their insurance policies and tend to make you promise not to sue them if they almost kill you by accident. Lorry drivers doing the north–south run will sometimes pick up passengers, but many are forbidden to do so by their contracts. Wherever you are, though, you will eventually get a lift, even if you have to wait a day or two in the more remote areas. Some people will ask for beer (drinking is pretty heavy in Botswana) or food, or even money – if you are white it is assumed you are rich, and by most Botswana standards you are – but it's unlikely that you will ever feel threatened in any way.

Tourism in Botswana concentrates on safaris, aimed pretty exclusively at the very wealthy. It is possible, I was told, to be set down by chartered plane in the middle of the Kalahari amid carpeted tents, with a chance to drink French champagne between taking the occasional blast at leopard from the back of a Landrover. I preferred to spend three unimaginably wonderful days being poled through the watery mazes of the Okavango Delta by a quietly polite and generous-hearted Bushman whose name I never did learn how to pronounce.

It is not only foolish but positively dangerous to roam the ever-changing Delta without the help of an expert, and *Kubu Camp*, who more or less organized every aspect of my trip, came up with a guide for me. I was collected from the school gates in a battered jeep, and driven through the bush for three-and-a-half hours to the pick-up point where the *mokoro*, a dug-out canoe, was waiting. My tent, tins of food, lotions, potions and water bottle were carefully loaded and I was arranged, with equal care, in the prow, so that I wouldn't upset the balance.

We pushed off into the whispering silence and beauty of the Delta. The poler knew exactly where he was going. Punting soundlessly though great beds of pink, white and lilac water lilies, swishing through reeds and rushes, nosing through rhododendrons, we paused only to gaze at the brilliant birds glittering overhead. At one point, I swam in warm water soft as silk, watching dark red weeds wrap themselves round my legs and getting tangled in lily roots. It was a new, clean, pristine world with its own laws and legends. The Bushman poler knew these laws. Alone, I would have been lost within minutes in those winding secret channels.

I was punted to a small island where I found I was to share a campsite with three Dutch tourists. There was just time to brew a cup of tea and set up my tent and set off across the bay for a game walk, before the sun did its vanishing act for the day. The Bushman moved softly, perfectly at ease; he belonged to the Delta, his knowledge was awesome and profound. We tracked – he tracked – a herd of buffalo, massive yet gentle until they saw us and vanished. We saw reedbuck, warthogs, assorted boks and beasts, and more species of bird than I could count. We met two giraffe, who loped off with easy elegance, and saw ostriches racing furiously through the grass. There was nothing but the wind, the tart, warm smell of animals and grasses, the clacking of palm leaves, the silky swish of water. The world suddenly made sense.

The next day we set off in the *mokoro* again to do a bit of hippo-spotting. We were lucky to come across a family of hippos, hugely enjoying a late splash, their vast jaws agape, almost grinning at us as they heaved and floundered, snickering to each other. On land, like elephants, they move almost soundlessly. It seems incredible that all these prehistoric creatures have such grace and gentleness. They won't attack unless they feel threatened, *The poler led me cautiously through tall grass to stare at what I thought was a tree until it moved.* although probably any one of these massive beasts could kill a man. They prefer to back off, to merge into the background, or in the case of hippos, to submerge, only their bright eyes alert and visible above the water. A couple of birds dive-bombed the mother hippo, who snapped back lazily as if knowing she would never catch it, and the cabaret continued until slow, warm rain sent the animals underwater and me back to the camp.

The final day meant another game walk, just after dawn. That night, I heard a lion roaring in the distance, and the poler found its spoor. We tracked it for a while, then lost it in churned-up mud. The poler, while so familiar with all the local animals, kept his respect and excitement for the wildlife intact. We went back to the beasts and the boks, endlessly graceful, their huge eyes dark and inscrutable.

I left with great reluctance the day after. The poler stopped about halfway along the journey, and led me cautiously through tall grass to stare at what I thought was a tree until it moved forward and I found myself so close to a giraffe that I could see its eyelashes. We stared at each other, the Bushman grinning from ear to ear with pride and satisfaction, before the giraffe became a tree again. We continued pushing through the lilies, pausing to swim and fill our water bottles from the clear river or simply to stop and watch the birds.

There was no sign of the jeep when we arrived at the pick-up point, so the poler and I sat in companionable silence, smoking, dozing, dreaming, until dusk. Out of nowhere a tall, thin man appeared, driving a safari truck with all the trimmings, and offered us a lift. We had gone about 2km when we met our jeep pulling three new *mokoros*. We swapped vehicles and drove at breakneck speed, first to the poler's hut then back to Maun, bouncing over potholes, grinding to a halt in sandpits, narrowly avoiding being pounded to death by startled kudu, and driving into one of the most magnificent electric storms I have ever seen.

TRAVEL NOTES

Languages English and Setswana.

Transport Hitching is widely accepted, as there are few buses away from the main roads, but you're expected to pay. Entering the country from Zimbabwe, it's best to take the train.

Accommodation Hotels are few and expensive, catering to luxury tour groups. There are hostels, mostly run by the different voluntary services, but most places have somewhere you can camp, though clearly at your own risk.

Guides The Rough Guide to Zimbabwe and Botswana (Penguin), very much geared to independent travellers, has a hundred or so pages on Botswana.

CONTACTS

Women's Affairs Unit, Ministry of Home Affairs, Private Bag 002, Gaborone. Run almost single-handedly by Joyce Anderson, largely concerned with supporting women's agricultural co-operatives. It also produces publications and helps organize workshops to spread information on women's legal rights.

BOOKS

Bessie Head, *A Question of Power* (UK, Heinemann Educational, 1974/US, Heinemann). Bessie Head lived in Botswana as an exile from South Africa until her death in 1988. This, the best of her novels, set in the village where she lived, is a beautifully written exploration of a woman's sanity. Other novels/short story collections include *Maru* (UK, Heinemann, 1987/US, Heinemann, 1988); *The Collector of Treasures* (UK & US, Heinemann, 1992) and *Serowe, Village of the Rain Wind* (UK & US, Heinemann, 1981).

Brazil

Arriving in Brazil from any neighbouring country, let alone from the USA or Europe, can be something of a culture shock. The reverberations are felt in the linguistic shift from Spanish to Portuguese, the sudden vast distances and extraordinary blend of people and landscapes, and not least the realization that the country holds some of the worst pockets of urban poverty in the world. Vast *favelas* (slum dwellings) spread out from all the main cities and as the coffee economy sinks further into debt, the numbers of homeless and destitute are rising. Upwards of half a million homeless children sleep rough on the *favela* streets, many of them organized into street gangs, hustling or drug-pushing for a living.

The death toll for these children, often at the hands of private killers hired to "clean up" parts of the city, is a scandal few politicians know how to address. For travellers personal safety has to be taken seriously: robbery, notably on deserted beaches, in Rio de Janeiro, and in the larger towns of the poverty-stricken northeast, is a very real threat.

In general, Brazilians are an open, easy-going people with a relaxed attitude to sex, encapsulated in the often outrageous eroticism of their annual *Carnaval*. At the same time, this is a strongly *machista* society. Whether it feels threatening clearly depends on the situation, but a woman alone, especially a foreigner, will inevitably attract a lot of physical attention from men. Hitching is most definitely out and it is inadvisable to walk in any city street on your own at night.

The diversity of Brazil's landscape, which ranges from the threatened tropical rainforest of the Amazon Basin, to partially arid Highlands, down to the heavily industrialized coastal strip, is matched by its varied peoples. After the centuries of decimation which began with colonization, only a fraction of Brazil's indigenous population remains. The rest is mainly descended from the Portuguese colonists, the African slaves they brought with them, and the millions of European families who more recently flocked to the country for work. Today whites or near-whites hold most of the nation's wealth, while black and mixed-race people constitute the bulk of the population pouring into the cities in search of employment. Along with high inflation, the problem of internal migration is one of the key symptoms of Brazil's ongoing economic crisis.

Brazilian women have a reputation for being feisty and upfront, giving as good as they get in an overwhelmingly male-dominated society. The fact that so many women have to cope with the pressures of single parenthood, struggling to make ends meet with poorly paid, insecure jobs, no doubt reinforces this stereotype. On average men take little responsibility for family life and relationships are rarely assumed to be monogamous. There has, however, been a strong tradition of women's political activism – many of the feminists who fled the country under the repressive years of dictatorship have since returned, lending impetus and eloquence to Brazil's growing **women's movement**. Contemporary groups range from autonomous feminist organizations campaigning on reproductive health, sexist education, racism, male violence and women's legal rights, to more hierarchical organizations directly linked to political parties. The country also has a national feminist paper, *Mulherio*, while groups dedicated to working with low-income women, such as the Carlos Chagas Foundation in São Paulo, produce excellent cartoon pamphlets to get their messages across.

The Luckiest Woman in Rio

In 1990 **Cherry Austin** took a break in her career as an advertising executive to spend some months travelling in the northeast of Brazil. She funded her trip by working as a hotel receptionist and tour guide. Since then she has returned at least once a year to compile and update the Brazil chapter for the *South American Handbook* and raise funds for the Passage House, a Recife-based project which helps homeless girls.

B ack in Rio, I was smiling. The corners of my stiff upper lip started curving when I stepped off the walkway into the airport, with its tropical mouldy-concrete smell. The taxi driver's nonstop conversation and three-lane Grand Prix performance made me laugh, as did the Coca-Cola balloon floating next to Christ, up above a gleaming bay. The sunshine did the rest. By the time I'd settled myself down with a cold beer, the smile was downright smug. One of the world's most stunning beaches in front of me, one of its most exciting cities all around; it was February; I was hot; I was happy.

The first time I went to Rio I hated it. I stayed three weeks, determined not to let any damn city get the better of me, and for three weeks I was miserable. Then I caught a bus to explore the rest of South America. I never left Brazil: just under a year later I was sashaying down Copacabana beach, making every second count before I had to force myself to board a plane for London. Brazil had got the better of me. It taught me a lot, changed some of my ideas, most of all, it changed my attitude to myself.

People tend to ask the same two questions about Brazil: "Weren't you worried about the violence?" and "Did you get a lot of trouble from the men?". When I first arrived, my mind was ringing with warnings. I was scared, mistrustful, and everything bewildered me.

Copacabana is erotic. Brazilian flesh comes in an infinity of shades of brown, and it's paraded – toned, tanned and glistening – not only on the sand, but around the streets, on the buses, in the shops. Surrounded by all this sexiness I felt threatened. I certainly couldn't compete, but worse than that, I didn't understand. My bikini was bigger than some of those girls' street clothes, and they were wiggling muscles I didn't even know existed – but they were so beautiful, they surely didn't need to be quite as obvious as that . There could only be one explanation. I remembered the voice of a friend who'd been here: "They're all prostitutes." "All of them?" "Yes, all. Some of the men, too". Her tour guide had confirmed it. Clinging on to my bag for fear of thieves, I tried not to stare. But people were staring at me. I felt like the unwelcome guest at someone else's party.

It didn't get any better. The streets sprouted market stalls on every spare inch; I fumbled about in a maze of lurid colour, confused by sounds, smells and sights that were totally unfamiliar to me. I stepped over whole families living in doorways and old women with leprosy. Permanently on the defensive, I marched through a forest of bronze bodies, and everywhere I went people stared. Back in my room each evening, I laboriously calculated the day's dollar rate against the cruzeiros I'd spent to see how much I'd been ripped off. Then I battled with my Portuguese handbook for an hour or so, trying to make sense of the day's abortive conversations. Not much wiser, I would put on some makeup and go out for dinner, steeling myself against the dangers of Rio at night, against beggars, robbers, and the approaches of incomprehensible men.

The calculations were a waste of time. Give or take a dollar, my sums always tallied. No one cheated me. I found it hard to believe: clumsy and uncomprehending, I was such an obvious target. I had to face the shameful fact that I was expecting to be short-changed, because in their position I thought I might have tried it. The traders on the streets of Rio were not only poorer than me; they were more honest.

The realization dawned that maybe I wasn't the centre of attention after all.

Someone did try to rob me, one hot Sunday afternoon. He was scruffy, shoeless, dishevelled and dirty, and carrying a big stick. He was too slow – I saw him coming. It was easy to hop on the bus with my bag under my arm, as I have done so many times at home in London, and then I wondered why I'd been letting fear restrict my movements. Years of roaming freely around my own risky city had already given me a fine street sense – and a philosophical attitude towards the occasional minor loss. There was no reason to assume Brazilian handbag thieves were any cleverer than our own sharp operators: ours don't even do you the favour of warning you by their alarmingly poverty-stricken appearance. Better still, nobody was planting bombs in the Rio metro. On balance, Rio was probably safer than London. Having rediscovered my common sense, I relaxed.

My Portuguese was improving, too. With my new-found confidence I started to stroll the length of Rio's black-and-white mosaic pavements at a slower pace, absorbing the sunshine, the music and the view. I took time out to enjoy the permanent party atmosphere around me. The realization dawned that maybe I wasn't the centre of attention after all. Everybody stared, certainly, but then everybody was staring at everyone. It was just what people did. Meanwhile, I still had to work out how to handle the constant onslaught of people wanting my money.

The critically poor were everywhere, most of them trying very hard to make or beg an honest living. Like other visitors to developing countries, I found it difficult to strike a balance between giving and ignoring, buying and rejecting. Whatever I did, I felt inadequate. And the kids broke my heart. Energetic gangs of good-looking youngsters hung out on the streets day and night, harassing passers-by with cynical humour. All the guide books told me to avoid them – but when you're eating a meal big enough for three, how can you refuse a homeless urchin asking for food?

The first time I offered, the child said something I couldn't understand. He looked at the plate, then at me, with open contempt, and moved on. Watching what the Brazilians did, I learned to use a toothpick to transfer the food, without touching it, into clean paper napkins, which the child can wrap up and take away. It's also quite normal to ask for the remainder of your meal to be packed in a foil container that you can give to someone hungry. However famished that boy may have been, he was not prepared to trough in my plate.

I tried a quote from the previous evening's soap: "I need to be alone!", delivered as dramatically as possible.

It was becoming obvious that, by Brazilian standards, my manners were appalling. With enough Portuguese by now to manage everyday transactions, I observed and copied all the small conventions that keep any society running smoothly. As soon as I learned to take time over greetings and thanks, life became simpler. People smiled and waved, "Come back soon!" The incessant cat-calls that had been bothering me now translated themselves into such comments as "Hey, Blondie!" – not very creative, but neither very threatening.

I had one big problem left to solve: a painless way to get rid of unwanted admirers. The action around me gave no clues. It seemed unlikely that the entire city was populated by hookers, but I could certainly understand why my friend had thought it was. The local girls were consistently seductive, polite, and charming to all comers, but trying to imitate them proved a big mistake for me. I couldn't work out what to do: merely showing lack of interest was not enough – the would-be suitor simply doubled his efforts. Guidebook advice about pretending to be married, or with someone, was useless. The average Brazilian man is convinced that he's the greatest lover in the universe, and will carry on giving you the opportunity to try him out for as long as you let him talk. I have never been seriously harrassed in Brazil, and know of no other woman who has been (groping, Italian-style, is almost unheard of), but I was getting into some very complicated situations, simply because I couldn't find any tactful means of persuading someone so persistent to go away. One day, I tried a quote from the previous evening's soap opera: "I need to be alone!", delivered as dramatically as possible. "Ah!", came the response, verbatim, "Sometimes it's good to be alone." Pushing my luck, I repeated the next line, which went something like: "Yes, there are many things I must consider. In solitude." I could hardly believe it when my new friend told me where to find him if I got tired of thinking, and left.

By the miraculous intervention of television drama, I'd hit on one of the few reasons allowable, in a sociable Latin society, for rejecting company. It wasn't ideal: it meant finishing conversations as soon as they'd started, when I wanted the practice. But it saved me from having to get up and leave places before I was ready, from shouting matches in the middle of the night, and from the near-fatal insult of telling a macho male you don't actually fancy him. I must have gained one hell of a reputation as a deep thinker around Rio de Janeiro.

> *"Imagine you've got a piece of chalk in your bum – now draw a figure of eight with it."*

The girls in the tiny shorts obviously weren't all claiming to be in permanent need of solitude, and I was no closer to understanding what it was they were doing. Women in Rio had no interest in me, other than commercial, and there was little more to be learned from stilted conversations with hotel staff, so to try and find out more about this intriguing culture I headed up to the northeast in search of the perfect beach and a small, friendly town with few foreigners.

I found it, and that's where I stayed. Maceió, the shambolic capital of Alagoas (an impoverished state the size of Wales), is one of hundreds of towns, villages and cities along that coastline, a seemingly endless chain of glorious beaches. My journey took me from crowded Salvador to São Luis, on the marshy fringes of the Amazon: two old slaving ports, each retaining its colonial architecture and an intense mystical culture carried over from West Africa. I tried peculiar fish and strange Amazonian fruits in Belem; drove through toffee-scented sugar plantations; drank cocktails by a lush river in the dozy town of Mossoró, visited dusty hamlets in the colourless Sertão, a desert covered with thorn bushes.

My new-found skills in Portuguese were largely useless when faced with varying regional accents, but people were generous with their time and patience. My answer to "Why are you travelling alone?" was simply that no one had been able to come with me. The idea that I had been so eager to visit their country that I'd actually left my family and friends behind appealed to most people. I rarely was alone.

Everyday life in Brazil is set to music. It seems most people can play an instrument, and know the lyrics to hundreds of songs. Children learn to dance as soon as they can stand; ordinary couples will get up and perform a dazzling lambada between the tables at a café; teenagers samba-reggae outside the record shops. In the northeast especially, everything seems to happen to a syncopated beat; Brazilians even walk with a swing. The smallest gathering around a roadside bar could turn into a party, with old ladies teaching me to samba ("Imagine you've got a piece of chalk in your bum – now try and draw a figure of eight with it"), and the kids who sell oranges to the bus passengers practising their English – usually one obscene word, picked up from television – to universal hilarity. I was invited to impromptu parties on starlit beaches, where guitars and drums would magically appear as if they had been somehow hidden in the palm trees, to dinner with extended families of twenty or more, and to birthday celebrations at two-room houses in *favelas*, where the one chicken that was cooked meant the entire household would do without meat for the rest of the week.

I could see why Lídia and thousands like her would marry almost any man, no matter how unpleasant.

I was never allowed to contribute more than the other guests did: maybe a couple of rounds of beer; often nothing at all. When I took some chocolates to a dinner party, as I might at home, the hostess was embarrassed. Such kindness to a virtual stranger astonished me: the humiliating reply to "Well, wouldn't you do the same if we were alone in your country?" was so painfully clear that nobody forced me to answer. Unable to return all this hospitality, I tried to be good company: at the least, my stiff-backed attempts to dance were a guaranteed source of amusement.

Many of the people I met lacked the money for basics such as dental care or changes of clothes (brothers and cousins shared their wardrobes, with one spare outfit between them). Competition was fierce for jobs that would barely pay the rent, and sometimes children had to work to supplement the family income. Their education was in any case limited by the inadequacies of the state school system, so families could easily become trapped in a cycle of deprivation.

The thing that brought the reality of hardship home to me was not the overcrowding in the poorest houses, or the malfunctioning drains flooding dirt roads where children played, nor the treatable illnesses suffered by people who could not afford to buy medicine. Perhaps all this was too far from my own experience. It was a comment by my colleague at the Maceió hotel where I found a job, that helped put this poverty into perspective. An educated girl of immaculate appearance, she was describing the life of a cousin who had managed to "escape" to Germany, where she worked in a factory. It sounded pretty grim to me. "She always has food in the fridge," enthused Lídia, "and she's got dresses she hardly ever wears!" Lídia had plenty going for her, including a decent job. She had five changes of clothes. If she was ill, she had to ask our boss to pay the doctor – and the boss decided whether treatment was necessary.

I could see why Lídia and thousands like her would marry almost any man, no matter how unpleasant, or would be willing to work in any demeaning capacity to break out of Brazil's oppressive economy. What I couldn't hope to explain to her was the sheer drudgery I imagined her cousin enduring, the greyness of a winter in Hamburg, or the apathy we Europeans call civilized behaviour. The vitality and determination Lídia took for granted in her surroundings were an inspiration to me: people often had to do two full-time jobs to make ends meet, plus an adult education course to improve their prospects, yet never seemed too tired for laughter, gossip, or their deeply complicated emotional lives. Every day was lived with relish.

It doesn't take much imagination to see how intricate sagas of love, jealousy, friendship and treachery develop.

The estimated proportion of adult women to men is eight – some say as many as thirteen – to one. Despite equal opportunity laws, the culture generally gives economic preference to men. Parents try to buy their daughters a home as early as possible to help defend against financial risks, but this doesn't alter the figures: some form of sharing is inevitable. Rather a lot of Brazilian men have a tendency to fall passionately in love several times during their lives, resulting in several families. Some of the women they set up house with might also have children from a previous lover.

The scenario is further complicated because households often cannot afford to move – so all the families end up living in the same neighbourhood. As a result, many of the young people on one block may be closely related, with fathers, half-brothers and sisters, mothers and stepfathers all living in different households. It doesn't take much imagination to see how intricate sagas of love, jealousy, friendship and treachery develop in such a setting. I began to understand why Brazilian TV soaps are so famously outrageous: nothing the scriptwriters invented could hope to rival the extravagant passions dominating their viewers' own lives.

These people respect their emotions, and talk about them: listen to a group of men, drinking beer at a café, and they'll be discussing football, politics – and relationships. To someone from a culture where it's better to admit to a case of measles than to being unhappy, it was a revelation. Portuguese has words for feelings that don't even exist in English. Experimenting with this new vocabulary, I did become more aware of changes in my own state of mind – and more sensitive to others' feelings. It was incredibly liberating; and, unexpectedly, I found my difficulties with over-persistent admirers dissolving. I started to make friends.

There were, of course, still plenty of men whose conviction that I'd come to Brazil purely for sex was unshakeable. These studs, ready to oblige, could be very hard to get rid of: one leaped into a taxi with me, and had to be removed by two incredulous drivers; one invited me to dinner with his wife, forgetting to tell either of us he was planning a little orgy after the pudding; one, having been refused entry to my hotel room, sat outside on the kerb all night "in case I felt like it later". Then there was the guy who asked the man I was with if he could borrow me for a while, asserting with total authority that "gringas" are liberated – and therefore sleep with anyone who asks them! The mystery of my sudden irresistibility was solved, especially when I took a closer look at the pornographic magazines displayed on every news stand – most of the images are imported from the USA, and represent, to some fevered Brazilian imaginations, all "first world" women. It's a rough equivalent of the way some British men think about Swedish girls.

I got talking to two girls at a beachfront bar one evening. They had been laughing at the amount of attention I'd attracted during the day, so I asked them about it: it did seem ludicrous, asking two golden women whether I was cramping their style, and so it turned out to be. "Look", said one of them, "You're foreign; you're different from us, you're from the first world. You're . . . "

"Exotic", filled in her friend, trying not to laugh too much: "But in the end, our men have got nothing in common with you. You seem like a nice person, but you're a diversion; you're just passing through . . . "

"Everyone's entitled to a bit of fun", offered the friend again, before they both collapsed into giggles. None of us were completely sober. I suddenly had a vision of how my friends and I would react if confronted with a similar question by a Swedish tourist. Mortified, I made a lame excuse and a rapid exit.

I had assumed that the imbalance between the sexes, coupled with male economic power, would lead to vicious competition among the women. It was one of a thousand mistakes I made by applying English values to what I saw in Brazil. Yes, women were restrained and restricted in many ways but these were matters for legislation; step by step, the women of Brazil were winning confirmation of their rights. They were feisty, these girls – they weren't sitting around waiting for male permission to get on with their lives. They just did things differently from the way we do.

I met one of Brazil's lamentably few female bank managers. She was always glad to see me on the beach because, she said, people thought it was peculiar when she sunbathed alone. We weren't by any means the only two unaccompanied females on that stretch: getting a suntan is something of an imperative, so if your friends can't be there, you go on your own. What made this woman different was that she was married. While she was bronzing her skin, her husband was with his long-term mistress. At four-thirty, the bank manager's lover – a friend of mine – finished work, and joined her for a few hours before going home to his wife. The bank manager knew everything about her husband's extramarital activities; but if he had known about hers, he would have killed her – perhaps literally. Male pride is a serious matter in this land of epic emotions. My friend had many other lovers, but adored his wife to the degree where he would – and did – drop everything if he thought she was in trouble. It would have destroyed him to know that she, too, had a gentle friend who kept her company while her husband was out.

I could see that very few of them had perfect bodies. What they had was confidence.

At first, all this confounded me: I couldn't quite believe that so many people's lives were so complicated, but, in context, I found it all a good deal more acceptable than I might have done at home. Spending my evenings drinking beer under palm trees with people who gave their phone number to anyone they were interested in, I started to wonder which was the better way. Letters were arriving from friends in England: a woman who was secretly frightened her man was being unfaithful; a man in distress because he thought he loved two women; a girlfriend depressed because she never seemed to meet any available men. Perhaps the oh-so-controlled British were not really very different from my Brazilian friends: just significantly less honest. At least the people around me respected – and enjoyed – their own and each other's sexuality.

There's a phrase, heavily used in Brazilian cosmetics advertisements, which, translated as "it's your duty to be beautiful", I found offensive. My samba teacher put me right. The phrase is a Brazilian proverb: "Whatever is beautiful should be shown off!". While teaching me to dance with my body "opened out", she also had to teach me what every Brazilian learns from birth: that my body is beautiful. I was about 40lb too heavy when I flew to Rio. Within two months, I'd lost all the excess weight without trying. Brazilian food is delicious, and I ate plenty of it. I believe it happened because I'd started to lose the negative feelings I had about my appearance. This wasn't because of any special event, it was in the air. Taking a closer look at those gorgeous people with the slinky walk, those sequinned dancers in the carnival, I could see that very few of them had perfect bodies. What they had was confidence. You don't have to be skinny to be beautiful in Brazil. All you have to do is be proud of what you've got, and show it off with style.

By the time I got back to Copacabana I had the tan, the shorts and the walk. I could get into deep conversation with strange men, exchange phone numbers, and saunter away with a smile. I could see newly arrived visitors staring at me with the same bemused distaste that they showed toward the other half-clad women on the avenue. By now, I knew the answer to the question that was puzzling them. Some of the girls are hookers, some aren't. Some do it part-time. For going on a date with a holidaymaker, spending the night and sharing his breakfast, they can make the equivalent of a whole month's pay. Me, I had a brand-new positive outlook, a fresh attitude towards people, passion and politics, a better body, a sense of rhythm; a ticket to London and a passport to a country with a stable economy. I felt like the luckiest woman in Rio.

TRAVEL NOTES

Language Portuguese. Don't assume everyone speaks Spanish. It won't be appreciated.

Transport Inexpensive, fast and comfortable buses criss-cross the country almost any time of day or night. Internal air travel is highly developed. Hitching is difficult and potentially very dangerous. Don't do it.

Accommodation There are plenty of inexpensive hotels throughout Brazil.

Special Problems Avoid going alone to isolated beaches or walking around alone at night in any city. Robberies and assaults on residents and travellers alike are becoming increasingly frequent.

Guides *The Rough Guide to Brazil* (Penguin) is the most comprehensive option. *The South American Handbook* (UK, Trade and Travel/US, Passport Press) has an excellent chapter on the country, researched by Cherry Austin above.

CONTACTS

There are far too many women's organizations to list here; also, groups are forever moving and changing. Probably the best central organization to contact is *Centro Informação Mulher* (CIM), Rua Leoncio Gurgel, 11-Luz 01103, São Paulo (☎229 4818); or Postal 11.399, 05499 São Paulo, Brazil. CIM publishes regular lists of different women's organizations throughout the country.

BOOKS

Alma Guillermoprieto, *Samba* (UK, Bloomsbury, 1991/US, Vintage). An account of a year spent in a Rio *favela* by one of Mexico's leading journalists. A compelling read, revelling in the drama of everyday life in the run-up to *Carnaval*.

Catherine Caulfield, *In the Rainforest* (UK, Picador, 1986, o/p/US, Knopf, 1984). Sharp-eyed journalist travels around the Brazilian Amazon. Full of atmosphere though sketchy on context. One of the best of the recent rainforest offerings.

Caipora Women's Group, *Women in Brazil* (UK, Latin American Bureau, 1993). Moving collection of articles, poems and interviews showing life for women in Brazil's shanty towns and peasant villages.

Helena Morley, *The Diary of Helena Morley* (UK, Virago Press, 1981, o/p/US, Ecco Press, 1991). Classic tale of a teenage girl growing up in a small Brazilian town: first published privately by the author in 1942.

Elizabeth Jelin (ed), *Citizenship and Identity: Women and Social Change in Latin America* (UK, Zed Books, 1990). Edited by an Argentinian sociologist, this book examines women's increasing involvement in grass-roots social change, from the *favelas* of São Paulo to the Bolivian Highlands.

Gilberto Dimenstein, *Brazil: War on Children* (UK, Latin America Bureau, 1991/US, Monthly Review Press). Harrowing journey through the underworld of Brazil's ten milllion street children, based on first-hand reportage, interviews and statistics.

Miranda Davies (ed), *Women and Violence: Realities and Responses Worldwide* (UK & US, Zed Books, 1995). Includes an account of the role of the women's movement and in particular the impact of women's police stations in Brazil.

Britain

For many travellers, Britain begins (and quite possibly ends) with London. The capital, with its individuality, lively cultural mix and plethora of entertainment, largely lives up to its myths and reputation. At the same time, along with much of southern England, it can often seem unwelcoming – and for many visitors it is outrageously expensive. Without friends to stay with, the cost of accommodation can be crippling, while the city's transport charges are the highest in Europe. Expense, in fact, is a problem throughout Britain and if your funds are limited, you may have to be prepared to rely on youth hostels – often pretty grim places – or else camp in notoriously unreliable weather, spend a lot of time hitching and cook for yourself.

That said, Britain is still a great destination for sightseers. Almost every town offers up some historic monument, from medieval churches or elegant Regency parades to relics of the Industrial Revolution, while countless picturesque villages nostalgically hark back to a rural age. Also, surprisingly, given the scale and population of the island, there are still large stretches of countryside – particularly in Scotland, Wales and the north of England – where you can wander for miles without coming across a soul.

Economically, Britain is at a low ebb; fifteen years of uninterrupted Conservative Party rule have led to a dramatic widening of the gap between rich and poor. This chasm is mirrored by the marked differences in prosperity between north and south and the growing number of homeless people and beggars all over London – a shock for many who have not visited for a while. Parts of Wales, Scotland and the north have been especially hard hit by government spending cuts, and the poverty and unemployment in cities like Glasgow, Liverpool, Bradford and Newcastle are the worst Britain has seen since World War II. But don't be put off exploring these parts of the country. Northerners tend to be more open and friendly than people in the south, with less of the traditional English reserve; accommodation is less expensive, and much of the countryside is spectacular and wild.

Sexual harassment varies little between England, Wales and Scotland. Apart from the odd wolf-whistle, you're unlikely to be bothered by men in rural areas, except, perhaps, in pubs. Big cities, however, like anywhere else in the world, pose a problem at night when you may feel uneasy wandering around alone. Racism is an additional problem, rooted in Britain's history as a leading imperialist power. You're undoubtedly more prone to abuse if you're black, but even white Australians report patronizing, colonial attitudes, especially at work.

The double issue of racism and sexism is a strong focus of the **women's movement** in England, which has many more Asian and Afro-Caribbean communities than neighbouring Wales or Scotland. The movement as a whole, as in the US and most of Europe, has greatly diversified since its inception in the early 1970s. As well as racism, questions of equal opportunity, reproductive rights, education and violence have been joined by a growing commitment to environmental issues. There is also mounting concern about poverty and homelessness, of which some of the worst sufferers are single mothers. British feminism may have lost its unity as a national movement but all in all, in spite of economic recession and a government devoted to disingenuous "Back to Basics" values, its spirit and aims remain very much alive.

"I Am Not a Tourist; I Live Here"

A German national, **Ilse Zambonini** lives and works in north London. She has seen many sides of the city over the past twenty years.

The first time I came to Britain, I was eighteen and on my own; I travelled widely, through England, Scotland and Wales, by bus, train and hitchhiking. Protected as much as anything by my naiveté, nothing nasty happened to me and I retained a nagging love for this country. In 1976, I decided to return to London for a while, and I have lived here ever since.

I did not know anyone in London, but I had an idea of what kind of people I wanted to meet and where to look for them. I also managed to find a teaching job through the Central Bureau for Educational Visits and Exchanges. Luck – but also my determination to find a way of staying here. Many people who have moved to London from abroad have told me how difficult it is to meet "English people"; they end up in ghettoes of immigrants, give up and go home. I did not find this a problem; it helps if there is a context of shared interest, for instance feminism, politics, education . . . perhaps being a parent.

Within a year, I had moved into a communal house full of English and Scots. At first I couldn't understand a word the Scots were saying: I thought they were speaking a foreign language. Now, like everyone else in Britain, I can place people by their accents – and people can place me, too.

I have never lost my German accent – it just won't shape into clipped English noises – which puts me outside the class structure. I could be anybody and I enjoy that. The only time I get a little short-tempered is when someone talks to me as if I were a tourist, very slowly and just a little patronizingly. How many English people speak German, let alone accent-free?

However, I never experienced any hostility directed at my being German, except for one English lady in the Portobello Road who called me a "stupid German cow" because I was in the way of her smart car – and she would have found something else to blame me for if I hadn't had a foreign accent. No one has ever complained about my taking jobs away from the British. They are too busy blaming black people for it. And Nazi films on television, where English actors speak with terrible German accents, have thankfully gone out of fashion.

In 1977 I joined a band and found myself in the middle of the Rock Against Racism movement. I was living on Social Security, and upon my return from a tour abroad with the band, I discovered that I had been turned out of the country. I was only admitted back on the condition that I would never again be a burden to the British tax payer. Under the Treaty of Rome, EC nationals are entitled to work and live in any member country. They are entitled to unemployment benefit once they have worked for a certain number of months or years, but not to Social Security benefits. So, I became a resident working alien!

> **This was the first time I had come into contact with people who were culturally different from myself.**

My life changed. I started out as a youth worker and began to get to know intimately the young unemployed of Islington and Hackney: whites, blacks, Cypriots, Asians. This was the first time I had come into contact with people who were culturally different from myself and my friends in age, race and class. I felt that I was beginning to understand more about London. I had to think about poverty, racism, about being white and working with young black people, and about being a childless woman and working with young single mothers.

When I moved to London, I had been warned about the dangers from muggers, burglars, murderers, rapists, all waiting there for me. At first, I walked about warily. One evening, on my way home, a group of young men walked up to me. "Here it comes, my first encounter with male violence', I thought. They stopped, looked at me, and one of them said: "You look like a hippie." I giggled all the way home.

How exciting, how amusing everything was then: having a key to a boyfriend's flat in Hackney; cycling from Holloway to Mare Street and finding shortcuts through parks; living in a decrepit squat that had open fires in every room but no electricity; having breakfast in my own garden; going on women's day marches dressed in purples, pinks and lace-up boots, carrying the small children of women friends . . . even the weather was glorious.

Nowadays, I am aware that violent attacks happen all the time, in London as everywhere else. But I move around as though I had a right to, day or night. The area I live in, Archway, in the north of the city, is on the way to "gentrification", though being burgled remains a day-to-day possibility. Sometimes I resent living as if in a fortress, with locks on the windows, locks on every door; lock up after you've let the cat out and unlock when she comes back in (and don't forget to lock up again!). But in a country where the divide

> *There is a Third World feel to many parts of London.*

between rich and poor is becoming as extreme as in the so-called Third World, this is the price I pay for not being at the bottom of the pile.

In Munich, there are people I know who leave their doors unlocked during the day, some even at night. In London, crime is all around you, and it is just another thing to live with. The dirt, the feeling of neglect, the ugliness of some parts of London, where you find yourself either in a shantytown or in a postmodern theme park, can be extremely depressing. Most of the housing estates are disgusting – full of dogs and dogshit, with dangerous elevators, broken windows and no lighting. But then I go to Hampstead and daydream about living in one of those mansions on the hill, where you breathe London's cleanest air.

There is a Third World feel to many parts of London: people waiting in line outside post offices and benefit offices; beggars; plastic bags full of rubbish everywhere; tatty goods in the shops. In a city with thousands of homeless people, and as many brand new cars, the contrast between private wealth and public poverty has become almost intolerable over the last fifteen years, and now, with so many hospitals under threat of closure, healthcare is going to go the same way. During the last three elections, I swore to myself that if the Conservatives were elected again I'd go back home to Mother, where everything is nice, clean and egalitarian, and ecologically sound. But I never did.

There have also been changes for the better. When I first moved here London was a culinary desert with no decent cup of coffee to be found. The word "café" was synonymous not with coffee and cake but with greasy food, and wine with overpriced sugarwater. During my first few years all visitors from Germany had to bring enormous food parcels full of real bread, real coffee, real chocolate, etc. Maybe I felt insecure. Now every supermarket sells ground coffee, and I can buy *Lebkuchen* from my local garage. Everybody knows what tagliatelle is (though no one knows how to pronounce it), and cafés with shining espresso machines can be found in Stroud Green Road, Clapham and even Dalston. Thanks to those deplorable yuppies, off-licences now have affordable as well as drinkable wines, and I can swill champagne in wine bars instead of going to a pub – the only British institution I have never learned to love.

London is, of course, different from other big cities in Britain. No other city is so much like a whole country in itself, a whole continent; it is hard to think of leaving, once established. Life in London is anonymous, certainly, and many people are isolated. But isn't this also why they came to live here? If you want to know all your neighbours and all the gossip, you live in the villages. London is a city of privacy, but a place where you can also say hello to the greengrocer or the garage cashier. It is exciting, full of things no one needs, full of useless discoveries, cinemas you will never go to, bands you will never hear, restaurants you might one day eat in. The one really negative factor is provided by its size – visiting a friend in another part of town can be a day trip.

I also enjoy the feeling of living in a city I still don't quite know. After twelve years I still discover new walks by the river or along the canals, parks I have never walked in, or some old bridge or railway station. There are dozens of galleries and museums which I still haven't seen, and I can shop at any time of day or night. In Munich, I hated the deadness that descends on the city at the weekend. Life there stops by noon on Saturday, and if you don't do your shopping by then, you eat out or not at all. No sweat in London.

A Scottish Adventure

Sarah Dale works as a solicitor in the south of England. This was her first trip to Scotland, where she went to Glasgow to visit a friend she had met on her travels in Southeast Asia (see p.335 & 381), before going on to a wedding on the Isle of Skye.

I arrived in Glasgow and couldn't believe how cold it was. With a backpack full of shorts and T-shirts I was wholly unprepared for the weather. It rained constantly and the Glaswegians all had a pinched look about them. My Glaswegian friend Mark was meeting me. He describes himself as a Fundamental Practical Realist. His first words to me were "softy southern shite" because I was shivering.

That's what Glaswegian men are like. They call a spade a shit shovel and communicate through a series of head jerks. A Glaswegian man I had only just met was popping down to the shops. He jerked his head back in my direction by way of asking if I wanted anything and I replied "Yes, I'd like some tampons with applicators and a tapered end." I was of course conducting my own private experiment to test the "sensitive-new-age-guyness" of the typical Glaswegian male. He slightly arched one eyebrow and shuffled off down the street. When he got to the end of the road he turned back and shouted "WHAT SIZE?"

The best thing about Glasgow is its buildings. It vies with Edinburgh for the coveted City of Architecture award to be anounced at the end of the century. The tenements are huge, old-fashioned, mansion-like places, with high ceilings and big sash windows. If you need something you actually have to walk across the room to fetch it. I'm used to London accommodation where a gentle lean to one side can put you in easy reaching distance of all you need.

The worst thing about Glasgow, though, is that people sound so aggressive. I overheard a guy talking to his girlfriend and he sounded as if he was going to headbutt her! I was ready to shout messages of support from a safe distance. Then Mark told me they were merely passing the time of day and there was no problem at all.

I asked people I met in Glasgow what they thought about Skye, where I was heading next for the wedding of my best friend. Grown men, the sort with hairy hands, would stumble and falter and come out with words like "breathtaking". Even Mark confessed that his heart starts pounding whenever he goes there.

I had the best fun in years stripping the willow and being swung round by hairy men in kilts.

I was dying to set off and was lucky to scrounge a lift from a friend of the bride's brother. We drove through Loch Lomond and Glencoe where the Campbells massacred the MacDonalds. The only man-made things in sight were the road and the twelve-foot poles which are used to identify it when it is obliterated by snow. I was stupid with tiredness but the beauty of the landscape compelled me to sit up, wide-eyed and gazing.

The church my friend was getting married in was The Free Presbyterian Church of Scotland. The "Wee Frees" are so strict as to make the Quakers look like fun guys to go raving with. The minister simply would not hear of the bride taking "obey" from the marriage vows. Intellectual and spiritual arguments could not sway him, neither cunning nor guile. Nothing would convince this man to "make a mockery of the house of the Lord". All that was left to my friend was to go through with it and cross her fingers.

The service was a miserable affair. The Wee Frees stand up to pray and sit down to sing and don't go in for musical accompaniment. We sounded grim warbling out "The Lord is My Shepherd", particularly as the minister got the ball rolling an octave too high. The bride swept down the aisle to complete silence, which was spooky. The minister spent the next hour and a half telling us what a lot of rotten sinners we were. When he eventually let us out, we followed the couple in their white Rolls Royce across barren bumpy landscape – a combination that seemed entirely incongruous.

The reception took the form of a *ceilidh*. In Scotland *ceilidhs* are not just preserved as a cultural relic like Morris dancing; they are alive and absolutely kicking. I couldn't get over the fact that everyone knew the steps, and had the best fun in years stripping the willow and being swung round by hairy men in kilts.

I was staying in a Bed and Breakfast owned by the MacDonalds. My friends were staying up the road in the next B&B. Their people were also called MacDonald, as was the taxi driver who drove us to the wedding. And the minister. They all looked worryingly similar, too. I was beginning to think that everyone on the island had the same surname and I was almost right: Sleat, at the bottom of the island where I was staying, is home to the MacDonald clan.

I asked Mr MacDonald which was his favourite place in Skye. He looked puzzled and just said "Sleat". Left with an awkward silence I filled in with something about that being lucky as it was his home. It transpired he'd been to school in Portree, the main town, and apart from Sleat had never been anywhere else on the island. I was flabbergasted. But then it's so beautiful I suppose you might well be quite content to confine yourself to the land around your cottage.

Mr MacDonald's cottage and small acreage of land formed a croft which had been passed down through his family for generations. Crofting is a form of subsistence farming where the crofter cultivates his own small parcel and has rights to common grazing land. From this common ground the crofters dig peat and pack it into small brick-like shapes which they can burn and use as fuel. Wherever you go in Skye you'll come across little mounds of peat like mole hills, drying for the fires. The crofters were almost entirely burnt out (literally) in the Highland clearances of the eighteenth century, when the landlords kicked them off the land in an effort to make more money by raising sheep. Now the whole system is under the tight control of the Crofter's Commission.

> *I expected oak-panelled taverns with open fires. Instead I found spartan rooms with simply a bar and a pool table.*

Once all the wedding guests had gone I was left alone. I decided to move to the *Backpackers Guest House* in Kyleakin, one of a chain throughout Scotland set up as an alternative to youth hostels. Compared to hostels they make your stay more like a holiday and less like a school field trip; you can stay out late and don't have to do chores. Everyone was really friendly and there's always someone to go down to the pub with.

I was disappointed with the pubs in Skye. I expected oak-panelled taverns with open fires and old men in kilts. Instead I found spartan rooms with simply a bar and a pool table. Strictly speaking I suppose that's all you need. The licensing laws more than make up for the lack of decor. Last orders never seems to arrive. The feeling of timelessness is exaggerated because the sun hardly sets. I was in Skye for midsummer's night when the sun went down for only one and a half hours. As for pub lunches, everything comes with oats, possibly beacuase oats are the only crop that will grow in the island's appalling climate. I saw oatmeal haggis, oatmeal whisky, oatmeal cream and whisky and even oatmeal cream and raspberry.

> *Suddenly I wanted to buy twenty Aran jumpers, change my name to MacDonald and start life all over again.*

One of the most enjoyable parts of my trip was Ted Badger's bus tour of the island. Ted Badger is a big brusque Australian who has lived on Skye for five years. He drives to his favourite spots and narrates a string of Celtic myths and legends collated over the years mostly through word of mouth. It's definitely not your usual sightseeing trip. I especially liked Kilt Rock, a sheer drop of pleated rock into the Atlantic. The wind was strong enough to throw you off were it not for the sturdy metal railings at the top. Another favourite was the Quiraing which we walked up for a spectacular view of the mountains and a loch. These mountains are responsible for a number of fatalities every year. Difficult climbs and a violent wind cause people to lose their footing and perhaps a few just throw themselves off into the sheer beauty of it all. Here the wind was so fierce that a mountain waterfall was actually being blown upwards into the sky. The sun beamed through a capricious cloud cover that caused shadows to skittle across the velvet mountains. Suddenly I wanted to buy twenty Aran jumpers, change my name to MacDonald and start life all over again in Skye.

Another way to see Skye is to rent a car which is easy to do. I drove around with two Aussies and a New Zealander who I met in the hostel. Each time we stopped the New Zealander, our driver, would disappear into the bushes, returning later with glazed eyes and an urge for ever greater speed. I eventually realized he had been sneaking off to smoke dope and felt he had to hide this from me. The others didn't seem to mind and my English reserve wouldn't allow me to yell at him to slow down; we hurtled through Skye in no time, straight over the mountains and up to Neist Point, another sheer drop into the ocean. For a minute I thought we were heading straight over.

I stayed in Kyleakin for the rest of my time in Scotland. Skye is extraordinarily unspoilt – I can't do it justice by describing it – but if it could have anything resembling an inner-city black spot, Kyleakin is it.

The place is flat and dull, and made worse by the ugly box-girder bridge that's being built between the harbour and the Kyle of Lochalsh.

Being an island is part of Skye's appeal and the ferry journey makes it that bit more remote and enchanting. In building the bridge one of the most important otter populations in Europe is under threat and a native collection of Scots Pine trees is being destroyed. Jenny, a Skye girl of about seventeen, told me of the consternation the bridge was causing. The workers employed were brought here from Newcastle despite the unemployment problem in the Highlands and the toll has been set at more than twice the cost of the car ferry. Jenny, along with many other islanders, was emphatically against it, and I could only sympathize and wish her luck with her campaign.

> *I was advised to dab malt whisky behind my ears if I wanted to catch a MacDonald man.*

Skye is certainly the kind of place where you can get to know the locals. That is if you can stay sober for long enough. Once you've done the Cuillin Ridge there's not much else to do but sit in the pubs and get drunk.

Twice a week in the local pub a singer called Jerry Coogan sits at his electric organ and belts out all the old singalong favourites, with every Beatles number and Elton John song you've ever heard of. However sophisticated your musical taste, after two pints you'll be swinging your glass and joining in with everyone else. After one such evening I managed to get myself invited back to the private party of one of the local girls. I later realized how well I was integrating when I found myself on my hands and knees wiping up Morag MacDonald's vomit from her carpet.

Skye women are tough. They look it, they sound it and they are it. They are the descendants of the crofters' wives who spent their time gathering kelp from the rocky shore line in bare feet to save on shoe leather. They carried big bags of the stuff on their backs to be used for fertilizer. It is also said they would knit as they walked along so that all their limbs were usefully employed!

Nowadays most women leave the island for jobs on the mainland. Most Skye jobs are of the traditionally male-oriented variety. Consequently there is an excess of men over women. By some strange quirk of fate, though, once the men come down from tending sheep in the mountains all they want to do is drink. They are notoriously disinterested in courting. I was advised to dab malt whisky behind my ears if I wanted to catch a MacDonald man. In fact so unromantic are these guys that instead of marriage they used to have a procedure called "handfasting". This was marriage on a sale or return basis. The woman would tootle off to live with her man for exactly one year, after which period all he had to do if he didn't like her was send her back. Added to this was the possibility that the clan chieftain might claim his right to the first night with every bride.

Things were no better in the spirit world. At Loch Storr there is said to be a celtic water spirit called Calpees, who turns himself into a hunky handsome man with "yellow" hair and entices women from the highway down to the loch. Once his captives are off their guard he turns back into the monster he truly is and drowns them. In Uig, however, women get their own back. Uig is on the west of the island and has a fairy glen. The scenery in Skye is generally vast and enormous but when you enter the glen the scale is dramatically reduced creating a wonderland of tiny hills called Siathans with Rowan trees growing on them that protect the glen from evil spirits. The wind doesn't howl here as it does on the rest of the island; it is very still and very quiet.

In the fairy glen reside "The Wee Folk". They only go out at night and by day stay in their tiny houses drinking, carousing and dancing to fiddle music. They are between four and five feet tall and are sceptical about men. If they come across a big person they ask them to solve a riddle. Apparently women always answer correctly because they are more in touch with the environment and their emotions. As a reward they receive simple gifts like bowls of milk and pins. But men are doomed to answer wrongly, so the Wee Folk pull out their fiddles and make these errant males dance to fiddle music until they drop. Then they pick the men up, hurl them in the air and drop them in giant cow pats!

TRAVEL NOTES

Languages English and Welsh; plus many dialects and languages spoken by different ethnic groups.

Transport An efficient, if costly, network of buses and trains connects all main centres, buses being cheapest for long-distance travel. Services in remote areas, especially parts of Scotland and Wales, are often slow and irregular. Hitching alone carries the usual risks and is not advised.

Depending on the exact area, big cities can be unsafe at night; if you're going to be out late it's wise to work out in advance how you'll get home. Public transport tends to shut down around midnight and taxis can cost a lot. London at least has a special minicab service, *Ladycabs*, run by women for women, though it doesn't operate around the clock and its drivers aren't exclusively female (you'll be asked your

preference when you book). The service is based at 12 Archway Close, N19 (☎0171/272 3091) and 422 Kingsland Rd, E8 (☎0171/254 3501 or 3314).

Accommodation In general expensive, especially in London, which is renowned for having some of the most highly priced hotels in the world. Rooms advertised as Bed and Breakfast can be reasonable and very comfortable, but fill up quickly in the summer, as do the many youth hostels, which, if you don't mind the regulations, are some of the cheapest places to stay. Most tourist information offices carry a list of rooms available in the area. Camping is safer than in many countries and often feasible outside organized sites.

Women's Travel Companies *Treadlightly Outdoor Activities for Women*, c/o Sheena Law,

146 Oakland Rd, Hillsborough, Sheffield S6 4QQ (☎0114/232 6055) organize cimbing, abseiling, canoeing, hiking and biking with experienced female instructors in the Derbyshire Peak District.

Special Problems Getting into Britain can be a harrowing experience, especially if you're arriving from a Third World country. Admission is at the discretion of the immigration officer and even marriage to a British citizen won't guarantee you secure entry. Make sure you have all the relevant documents, including entry clearance from the British Embassy in your home country where applicable, and proof of sufficient funds to cover your stay. Black women have been particularly discriminated against by the UK Nationality Act. If in trouble, contact the **United Kingdom Immigrants Advisory Service** (☎0171/357 6917), which has offices at Heathrow and Gatwick airports; and/or the **Women's Immigration and Nationality Group**, c/o 115 Old St, London EC1V 9JR (☎0171/251 8706).

Guides The Rough Guide to England (Penguin) is pretty comprehensive, as are the volumes to *Wales* and *Scotland*. *Hitchhiker's Manual: Britain* (UK, Vacation Work) has invaluable route information. *The Woman's Travel Guide to London* (UK, Virago/US, RDR Press) gives practical information combined with fascinating accounts of women's contribution to the capital's history, art and culture.

WOMEN'S ACCOMMODATION

Necessarily only a selection.

ENGLAND

The Only Alternative Left, 39 St Aubyns, Hove, Sussex, BN3 2TH (☎01273/24739). Feminist-run Bed and Breakfast, also used for small residential conferences.

Reeves Private Hotel, 48 Shepherd's Bush Green, London W12 (☎0181/740 1158). London's only hotel, restaurant and bar run by women for women. Not cheap, but all nine rooms are comfortable with private bath.

Shiplate Farm, Shiplate Rd, Avon BS24 ONY (☎01934/14787). Bed and Breakfast in a converted eighteenth-century farmhouse.

Women-Only Guest House, 19 Crossroads, Haworth, W Yorks, BD22 9BG (☎01535/45711; eves and weekends). Women-run Bed and Breakfast in the heart of Brontë country.

SCOTLAND

Belrose Guest House, 53 Gilmore Place, Edinburgh EH3 9NT (☎0131/229 6219). Women-owned and operated Bed and Breakfast.

WALES

Lan Farm, Graigwen, Pontypridd, Mid Glamorgan, CF37 3NN (☎01443/403606). Traditional Welsh farmhouse run as a hostel by two gay women. Exclusively gay, for both sexes.

Oaklands Women's Holiday Centre, Glastonbury-on-Wye, nr Hereford, Powys (☎014974/275). Tends to be booked up in advance by groups and can be chaotic and not always very friendly, but worth trying out.

CONTACTS

For details of individual women's organizations contact **Feminist Library, Information and Resources**, 5 Westminster Bridge Rd, London SE1 (☎0171/928 7789 or 7781).

WOMEN'S BOOKSHOPS

Just a small selection, but any of those listed below should be able to offer information about local women's groups.

ENGLAND

London: *Silver Moon*, 68 Charing Cross Rd, WC2 (☎0171/836 7906). Excellent feminist bookshop; a good central source of information. *Gay's the Word*, 66 Marchmont St, WC1 (☎0171/278 7654). Stocks a wide range of gay books and periodicals and has a café.

The city also has a number of radical bookshops, among them **Compendium**, **Housman's** and the **Africa Book Centre**, with extensive women's sections.

Birmingham: *Key Books*, 136 Digbeth, Birmingham B5 6DR (☎0121/643 8081).

Bristol: *Greenleaf Bookshop Co-operative*, 82 Colston St, Bristol 1 (☎0117/921 1369). Also a wholefood café.

Cambridge: *Grapevine*, Unit 6 Dale's Brewery, Gwydir Street, Cambridge (☎01223/61808).

Leeds: *Corner Bookshop*, 162 Woodhouse Lane (opposite university), Leeds 2 (☎0113/454125).

Liverpool: *Progressive Books*, 12 Berry St, Liverpool L1 4JF (☎0151/709 1905).

Manchester: *Grassroots*, 1 Newton St, Manchester M1 1HW (☎0161/236 3112).

Newcastle: *The Bookhouse*, 13 Ridley Place, Newcastle-upon-Tyne NE1 8JQ (☎0191/261 6128).

Sheffield: *Independent Bookshop*, 69 Surrey St, Sheffield S1 2LH (☎0114/273 7722).

York: *York Community Books*, 73 Walmgate, York (☎01904/37355).

SCOTLAND

Edinburgh: *West and Wilde Bookshop*, 25a Dundas St, Edinburgh EH3 6QQ (☎0131/556 0079).

Glasgow: *Changes Bookshop*, 340 W Princes St, Glasgow G4 9HF.

Cardiff: *108 Bookshop*, 108 Salisbury Rd. You should also make contact with the **Women's Centre**, 2 Coburn St (☎01222/383024), for information about women-only/lesbian bars and discos.

BOOKS

Katherine Sturtevant, *Our Sisters' London: Feminist Walking Tours* (UK, Women's Press, 1994/US, Chicago Review Press, 1990). Fascinating tours taking in the historic dwellings of countless women from literary figures to saints and prostitutes.

Joanne Shattock, *The Oxford Guide to British Women Writers* (UK & US, Oxford University Press, 1994). Lists more than 400 women from novelists to poets, scientists and translators, including bibliographies and assessments of their works.

Jan Marsh and Trevor Lummis in association with the National Trust, *The Woman's Domain* (UK, Penguin, 1993). Study of seven British country houses, using letters, diary extracts and local archive material to reveal the lives and thoughts of the women who lived and worked there.

Beatrix Campbell, *Wigan Pier Revisited, Poverty and Politics in the 1980s* (UK, Virago, 1984). A devastating record of the extent of poverty and unemployment in the north of England, and a passionate plea for a feminist socialism that responds to real needs. Also by the same author, *The Iron Ladies: Why Women Vote Tory* (UK, Virago, 1987) provides some astute insights into the Margaret Thatcher phenomenon.

Angela Carter, *Nothing Sacred* (UK, Virago, 1982). Collection of essays and writings, many of them autobiographical, by one of Britain's most talented contemporary writers who sadly died in 1993.

Daphne du Maurier, *Vanishing Cornwall* (UK, Penguin, 1972/US, Doubleday, 1981, o/p). Good overall view of Cornwall from an author who lived most of her life there and plundered the scenery as a backdrop to her wonderfully stormy novels, among them *Rebecca* (UK, Arrow/US, Avon) and *My Cousin Rachel* (UK, Arrow/US, Bentley, o/p).

Beverley Bryan, Stella Dadzie and Suzanne Scafe, *Heart of the Race* (UK, Virago, 1985). Insights into growing up as a black woman in Britain.

Amrit Wilson, *Finding A Voice* (UK, Virago, 1978/ US, Virago, o/p). Experiences of Asian

women in Britain recorded in their own words – still highly relevant.

Rosalind K Marshall, *Virgins and Viragos – A History of Women in Scotland from 1080–1980* (UK, Collins, 1983, o/p/US, Academy of Chicago, 1983). Over-academic but interesting in its exploration of little-known ground.

Angela Mason and Emma Healey, *Stonewall 25* (UK & US, Virago, 1994). Anthology of individual stories and essays by some of Britain's leading gay activists.

FICTION

Rukhsana Ahmad and Rahila Gupta (eds), *Flaming Spirit* (UK, Virago, 1994). Anthology of stories by Asian women writers from across Britain. Explores a wide variety of themes from identity and religion to sexuality.

Pat Barker, *Union Street* (UK, Virago, 1982/US, Ballantine, 1984). Account of the lives and struggles of seven working-class women and their men in the north of England during the 1973 miners' strike. Also recommended is Barker's *The Man Who Wasn't There* (UK, Penguin, 1990/US, Ballantine, o/p), an optimistic novel about the bridging of age and class barriers.

Buchi Emecheta, *Adah's Story* (UK, Allison & Busby, 1983, o/p). Having left Nigeria to join her violent husband, Adah finds herself living alone in London with five children to look after. An account of an indomitable woman who fights against the odds to realize her ambition to be a writer. Look out also for Emecheta's other novels and children's books.

Esther Freud, *Peerless Flats* (UK, Penguin, 1994/US, Harcourt Brace, 1993). Lisa, a young drama student, follows her glamorous sister to London and plunges into a troubled, exciting and confusing first year in the capital. London characters and scenes are freshly evoked by one of Britain's best young novelists.

Maggie Gee, *Grace* (UK, Abacus, 1989/US, Grove-Atlantic, o/p). Based on the events surrounding the extremely suspicious death of Hilda Murrell, an anti-nuclear campaigner, this novel deals with the threats inherent in British life.

Sara Maitland, *Telling Tales* (UK, Journeyman Press, 1983, o/p). Collection of short stories, some set in the present, others featuring women from ancient and biblical history. Very readable. By the same author, *Three Times Table* (UK, Virago, 1991/US, Holt, 1994), interweaves the lives of three women, combining fantasy with everyday observations.

Jeanette Winterson, *Oranges Are Not the Only Fruit* (UK, Pandora, 1985/US, Atlantic, 1985). A quirky, funny and original book based on the author's own experiences of growing up in a Pentecostal community in Lancashire. Barred from expressing her lesbianism she breaks away, establishing her independence at university. First and by far the most enjoyable novel by this increasingly controversial writer.

Of the many **literary classics**, essential reading are Jane Austen's *Northhanger Abbey* and *Persuasion* for their witty renderings of Bath's spa society; Charlotte Brontë's *Wuthering Heights* for her passionate portrayal of the Yorkshire moors;

George Eliot's perceptive insights into small-town provincial life under the shadow of the industrial revolution in *Middlemarch*, and Elizabeth Gaskell's *North and South* for a feminine perspective on the iniquities of the nineteenth century. All are published by Penguin.

Among **contemporary writers**, Angela Carter, Nina Bawden, Beryl Bainbridge, Rose Tremain, Michele Roberts, Gillian Slovo, Lesley Glaister and Fay Weldon are all recommended. Finally, if you're into modern thrillers, try Ruth Rendell, PD James and Sarah Dunant.

Burkina Faso

Landlocked and desperately poor, with an almost feature-less landscape of dry, arid grassland, few roads to travel on and even fewer places to stay, Burkina Faso seems a strange choice of travel destination. Since gaining independence from the French in 1960, the country has been ruled by a succession of leaders, launched to power in a series of coups and counter-coups. Since the early 1980s, their innovative and stringent reforms have boosted education and pride in the national culture but have so far had little impact on the unremitting poverty that blights most people's lives. Aid and development agencies have moved in, in the wake of the recent Sahelian droughts to the north, while large swathes of the population head south across the border to Côte d'Ivoire looking for work.

Yet travellers, albeit in small numbers, continue to arrive, using the capital Ouagadougou – an unprepossessing sprawl rising out of red dust – as a springboard for trips further into

West Africa. For ten days every two years the capital plays host to the now famous *Festival Panafricain du Cinéma* (FESPACO), drawing huge international crowds and filling all available rooms. Despite this cultural focus there remains little by way of any developed tourist infrastructure. The government, lacking resources and the political will to create a five-star industry, has been keen to stress the human dimension of tourism and the importance of making contact with local people.

As a traveller it is hard not to be impressed by the relaxed, dignified and effortlessly friendly approach of the Burkinabe. Even at the many military checkpoints dotted around the country, visitors are treated with a low-key respect and surprisingly little of the usual macho posturing. Travelling alone you may well be stared at but seldom threatened or harassed. Attitudes towards sex are fairly relaxed and, with Western women prized for their novelty value and relative wealth, you are bound to be propositioned. It's fine, however, to say no. In terms of dress, people are generally tolerant about tourist fashions, although it's polite to cover your legs. Burkinabe **women**, prominent as market traders, wear long dresses or long pieces of cloth tied round the waist with a *pagne* (a wide band of printed cloth). Trousers are disapproved of on the grounds of being mannish and wearing them you will have to fend off a constant incredulity about your gender. Amusing for a while but ultimately unnerving.

Other than the sheer physical grind of travelling – cramming onto buses, jolting over potholes, battling with heat, flies, dust and fairly basic food and accommodation – the main problem any visitor to Burkina Faso faces is dealing with their relative wealth. It's assumed that Western travellers have limitless funds and, in local terms, they do. It's usual to be asked to pay more and important that you find ways to reciprocate any hospitality you receive. The exchange of gifts remains a revered social custom.

Welcome to the Land of Whole People

Melanie McGrath, a freelance writer, spent a month with documentary filmmaker Carlyn Saltman in Ouagadougou. Her book about the American Southwest, *Motel Nirvana*, is published by HarperCollins. See also her piece about Mali in this book.

About two months after my father died, in early 1991, a friend called. "I think you should go away for a few months. Is there anywhere you just can't picture yourself?" "Africa," I replied. There was a pause down the line. "Good. I know just the person you should meet."

For four weeks in February and March Carlyn and I rented a big stucco house under bougainvillea vines in the northern outskirts of Ouaga. Carlyn was away much of the day, so to pass the time I would sit out on the porch with the radio on tuned to the World Service. At lunchtimes I was often joined by Moise, who was studying for his *baccalaureat* under a mango tree at the edge of the compound. "Paris, c'est tous, tous riche, quoi?", Moise used to say, which was his unqualified thumbs up for France and everything French. He didn't know about the black ghettoes strung out along the railway tracks north of the Paris *périphérique*, or about the rows of Senegalese traders flogging trinkets on the Place Vendóme. Nor did he invite discussion of such things. To him, France was free and rich, Burkina impoverished and politically second-rate. It was as simple as that. One day he would work in France and send money back to his homeland, he said. He didn't know how, only that it was inevitable.

Moise did not feel it safe to discuss politics. About a week after we met, he brought with him a leaflet headed "Le Patrie ou la mort, nous vaincrons," Burkina's national slogan. Inside was printed a crude history of the country's political struggles and a puff for the ruling party. He asked me to keep it as a memento of a particular point in time, which, although not significant in itself, made up part of the greater narrative. He said that if the government fell, the leaflets would be burned and new ones printed; mine would always remain as evidence. Evidence of what? He did not say, but I understood that he felt the struggle to live made a tawdry puppet show of politics and patriotism. At the back of Moise's leaflet was a little note: "Bienvenue au terre des hommes integres, Burkina Faso." Welcome to the land of whole people. I noticed it when I was back home, unpacking. There was a smear of sand stuck over the word *terre*, which drew my eye.

During the dry season in Burkina, the White, Red and Black Volta Rivers dwindle to little more than salt scars cutting the savannah. The mosquitoes are worse in the rains but even when the water was sunk low in the nearby reservoir, or barage, thick curranty clusters of the creatures pestered women washing their clothes. When the water level fell, it left behind it deceiving mud banks whose depths were as pliant and dismal as quick sand. A tyre up-ended in the mud vanished the following day. Plastic water bottles filled with silt and sank like stones. The water itself, on the other hand, always seemed inviting enough; steel blue and shiny under a matte Harmattan sky.

> *There was no mention of hunger, because it is too commonplace to be of much interest.*

In the heat haze, it was easy to mistake the fishermen and their craft for fat-bellied water birds. Moise had told us it was forbidden to fish, but then, people have to eat. All the talk around Ouagadougou at that time was of drought and food shortages, because the January rains were not good, and there would be no more until July or later. There was no mention of hunger, you understand, because it is too commonplace to be of much interest. Outside the cities hunger is a way of life. The predictions they were making on the street were for famine.

People begin to suffer long before the pot-bellies and fly-blown eyes of television images; long before the hatching of what will later become "a story". The suffering starts as a series of delicate acts of neediness. A child picks up some mango peelings and stuffs them into his mouth without brushing off the dirt; a woman takes a peanut from the road, closes her hand over it and walks on. The famine flashpoint is not a point at all but the accretion of many such tiny degradations, each of which helps edge the country nearer to starvation. West Africans treasure what little they have that can be relied upon; the weight of tradition, sincerity, an understanding for the value of acceptance. Beneath the brilliant currents of colour and theatricality which bring tourists to West Africa there persists a grave and subtle stoicism as unchanging as a well-used pathway. On the far bank of the barrage, beyond the scarlet pirogue, there were always vultures blustering about, picking at things not visible.

Just south of the big house, past the barrage and into the Bois de Boulogne is a compact copse of whitewashed acacia trees leading in to the centre of Ouagadougou. This was our route into town in the mornings to pick up baguettes from the bakery near the *Hôtel Indépendance*. If the sky were not blush and hot with Sahara dust from sunrise to dark you might momentarily imagine yourself bumping along some unloved road in southern France. Early each morning, a woman would set up her trestle table at this corner, a youngish woman in a blue *pagne* printed with portraits of the Pope. We bought our carrots from her, always three brilliant orange carrots tied up with plastic twine. Each day the same wide seductive smile, no teeth, baby on her back balanced inside a *pagne* of purple striped calico, another in the shade under the trestle. "Française?" asked the woman once. "Yes." In Burkina, all points between or at either side of Africa and France are secret *départements* of the French motherland or remote geographical irrelevances. Why didn't I wear earrings, the woman wanted to know, why didn't I plait my hair, why was it so short, do I have fleas? She said that I looked "comme un homme, quoi" and wiped tears from

She said that I looked "comme un homme, quoi" and wiped tears from her eyes with the back of her hand.

her eyes with the back of her hand. Then she threw in a mango with the carrots to thank us for our custom and waved us away, same wide smile. If I were to stop by on the way back she'd plait my hair, she said, laughter big enough to split her spleen.

One morning, about three weeks after we arrived, Carlyn had the idea of visiting an aquaintance of hers in the bush. He was old and illiterate, and she was unsure whether or not he was still alive; there had been no news of him. We drove our mopeds into town in search of kola nuts good enough to present as gifts. There were few sellers, since it was out of season and the nuts, in any case, have to be brought up from – where? – the coast, I think. In Burkina a gift is a sign of the measure of respect accorded by the visitor to the visited. An ill-considered or mediocre gift is regarded as an affront to the dignity of the recipient. Better to bring nothing but company. Towards late afternoon we found what we wanted and turned our mopeds north, back towards the big house.

Moise and his friend Jean were sitting in the shade of the porch, waiting, although the door was open. Solemn African patience. To what purpose did we so wholeheartedly lose ours? Perhaps, after all, we never had it. Jean had come with a message from his mother to ask if we would like her to bring over some of her cassava. We shuffled about and made eyes, locked in inner diplomacy; cassava to us tastes like mashed potato and raw egg yolk left in the sun to putrefy. No sauce, no accompaniment can ressurect it. It lies beyond the culinary pale. Finally, Moise said; "So what did you both do today?" Burkinabe are, as a rule, informal but effortlessly courteous people. Even the aggressive style of market haggling has its own implicit protocol. Overstep the mark, and you will find yourself outside the system altogether, with no possibility of re-entering it, as though the market had folded in on itself and become a dream-world, excluding all spectators. It's one of the strangest paradoxes of Burkina, and of West Africa in general, that a culture so embalmed in its customs, so riddled with social rules, can be at the same time so much more relaxed and sensitive than our own.

Next day two 50cc mopeds headed out on the Kaya road early, rumbling the silence and kicking up ochre dust, Jean and Moise driving, we two content to be passengers clinging on behind; pragmatism before femininism – one of the first great rules of female travel. A few miles north of Ouaga the burnt red soil gives out to a sickly chalk white laterite, which is where the savannah truly begins. Grey brown baobab trees stretch to the horizon, and along the route here and there are thatched mud *zakse* strung about with granaries and knotted into compounds. Yellow *termetières* make a coral reef of the plain. For the most part the road is unpaved piste, rutted into escalier, but every few miles there is a metalled section still surviving from the last grand government infrastructure construction scheme. Wherever there is a proximal village women will have set up impromptu arrets on the tarmac with stalls selling oranges, ginger beer and peppery brochettes. A string of women passed us on the road, headed towards Saaba for the market, their heads hatted with eliptical paniers full of calabashes, dry dates and bread cakes; the country's nervous system, these women. Now and then we scattered dwarf goats grazing in the drainage ditches either side of the road. A taxi brousse passed, leaving a dust devil whirling behind it. Grit built up in our eyes and noses, clinging to the skin like red barnacles, and matting the hair into hempish ropes. Heat pinched the air into strange smoky flues. By ten we had turned to the east, towards Nakambe – the White Volta – across a track razed from the bush.

> *The old man stared as one does when retrieving some detail from the memory, then smiled a big moon smile.*

The old man was sitting under a carob tree about twenty yards from his compound. Two years on and his left eye was cataracted over. On his head he wore an embroidered skull cap fixed with a booby grip. Carlyn knew him at a distance from his *boubou*, the same tear in the shoulder revealing a ladder of sinews. Hearing the put-puts, the old man looked up, stared without looking as one does when retrieving some detail from the memory, then smiled a big moon smile. Under the shade of an awning he inspected our kola nuts, pulling off a lobe and pushing it carefully around his mouth as if it were a piece of hardened wind-dried meat. When his wife returned with a calabash of *dolo* we gave her a piece of scented soap.

The old man produced a faded polaroid of his family, set in rows. He asked Jean to tell us that his sons and nephews were absent, working the fruit plantations down in Abidjan. He shook his head. "Burkina is become a nation of women and old men", he said, "just women and old men". When we left, he said "You have made me happy so I will leave your footprints in my compound until the wind takes them away," He squeezed his wife's arm. "She won't need to sweep today, so she's happy too."

To save ourselves from the worst of the sun, we stopped off at Saaba. A light hot breeze carried with it the smell of ammonia and tannin, and the stench of goat. A woman with heavy tribal cicatrices beckoned Jean and Moise with her right hand palm down, hissing. Who were we? Not development workers? The general feeling about development agencies in Burkina is that they should give more and get out.

"She doesn't think you are telling the truth. That is very bad. We like openness here."

Saaba's menfolk were settled under a carob tree, eating brochettes made from giant snails and playing cards. A couple of girls pounded millet together in desultory fashion, but it was too hot that afternoon to do anything much but doze and idle. The noise of a generator rose up on the heat haze. Inside a nearby hut a local entrepreneur had set up his video to show kung fu movies to the village youth. Jean and Moise headed over to the hut leaving Carlyn and I to begin negotiations for a handful of mangoes. The stall-keeper was a fat woman with lean eyes, the kind you wouldn't trust if you made contact with them on a city street. "Where are your children?" "We haven't got any." She stared out from those silted eyes with a mixture of amazement and scepticism, then reached for my earlobe and pulled. "How old are you?" She peered at the earlobes, trying to guage whether or not they were pierced; was I a woman as I had claimed, or merely some strange sexless thing? "Twenty-seven." "Ah, trop agée, quoi?" She shook her head. A man with cicatrices came up behind her and exchanged greetings. She said something to him in More, the language of the Mossi people, which made him laugh. "She wants to know where are your children?" he said in broken French. "We don't have any." He said: "What have you done with them?" The woman pressed his arm and leaned in towards his face. "She doesn't think you are telling the truth. You are not telling the truth. That is very bad. We like openness here." The woman reached behind her and produced a calabash of *dolo*. "That'll loosen your tongues. *Nous sommes en Afrique, quoi*," said the man with a smile on his face.

TRAVEL NOTES

Languages There are some sixty different language groups within Burkina Faso. French is the official language although, outside the larger towns, few people speak this with any fluency. Over half the population speak More, mother tongue of the Mossi who live in the central plains around Ouagadougou.

Transport *Air Burkina* operates domestic flights between the main towns and there is a train link from Ouaga through Bobo-Dioulasso and on to Abidjan. The usual way to get around is by *taxis brousse* – bush taxis – which are cheap but incredibly cramped, or the slightly more expensive *Régie X9* buses. Mopeds and bicycles make up much of the traffic in the main towns.

Accommodation Ouaga and Bobo have a few international hotels but otherwise the options are fairly basic. Don't expect to find running water and electricity in the smaller towns, particularly in the north.

Special Problems You'll need a visa before entering Burkina. If there's no Burkinabe embassy in the country you're travelling through, try the French one. Gaining visas from Ouaga for travelling on can also be tricky (quite a few West African states lack representation) so be sure to plan ahead.

Guides *The Rough Guide to West Africa* (Penguin) packs in just about everything you need to know in its chapter on Burkina Faso.

BOOKS

 Charlotte Bruner (ed), *Unwinding Threads* (UK & US, Heinemann, 1994). Very little has been published in English. For a general overview, this anthology of African women's writing includes stories from West Africa. See also the general bibliography on p. 692.

Burkinabe **film** directors and producers are moving from FESPACO onto the European film circuit, sweeping up awards and audiences as they go. Best known in the West are Gaston Kaboré's *Wend Kuuni*, and Idrissa Ouédreago's *Yaaba*.

Cambodia

S ince the final withdrawal of UN Peacekeeping Forces in
1993, Cambodia has been striving to achieve stability after
more than two decades of violence, and to place behind it
the traumas of genocide. In the last 25 years this small country,
bounded by Thailand, Laos and Vietnam, has been blanket-
bombed by the United States, wracked by civil war, invaded by
Vietnam and, until comparatively recently, largely isolated by the
UN and the international community. Central to this tale of
conflict and neglect is the terrifying force of the Khmer Rouge.
In their determination to radically restructure Cambodian society
along rigid Maoist lines, during their period in power under Pol
Pot (1975–79), the KR tortured and killed up to two million
people – roughly a fifth of the country's population. Pol Pot's
regime was eventually
ousted by the Vietnamese,
which brought with it a
backlog of support for the
KR from China and
Thailand, both keen to
control the spread of
Vietnamese influence in
Indochina. With additional
indirect backing from
Britain (whose SAS troops
train the KR in mine-laying

techniques) and the US (who provide aid) the Khmer Rouge soon embarked on a full-scale guerrilla war that lasted throughout the 1980s. UN intervention finally led to an ending of the war, but with significant strongholds in the west of the country, the Khmer Rouge still constitute a major threat to the nation's peace.

Surprisingly, given the precarious political situation, Cambodia is experiencing something of a tourist boom. Backpackers are keen to fill in on a big gap in the Southeast Asia trail, while the great temples of Angkor pull in a constant stream of package tour groups, mainly from France. (Like most of Indochina, Cambodia was colonized by the French.) In Siam Reap (near Angkor) and the capital, Phnom Pehn, hotels, guest houses and restaurants are springing up as fast as people can build them. At the same time, however, travel is still largely restricted. Many problems are due to the lack of infrastructure after years of neglect: even the main national roads are little more than dirt tracks, full of potholes and in places almost impassable. Other difficulties are directly caused by continuing instability in the country, exacerbated by banditry and gang warfare. Trains are sometimes ambushed, while taxis out of the major towns can be attacked or stopped at army checkpoints where soldiers demand protection money. There is direct danger still from the Khmer Rouge, who kidnapped and killed three Western travellers in 1994, and the mines that still litter the countryside are yet another potential hazard.

Generally speaking, tourists are warmly welcomed by the Cambodians as proof that their country is on the road to recovery and as a buffer against the wholesale atrocities of the past. Ordinary people are often eager to talk of their country's devastation and share their hopes for the future. In tourist areas there's little danger of violence and despite the desperate level of poverty muggings are uncommon.

It is hard to gather information about the status of **women** in Cambodia. Though men have a higher presence on the streets, it's not uncommon to see women running businesses, or walking out alone or with friends. There is also evidence of a burgeoning protest movement around women's issues, linked partly to the promotion of Buddhist principles: for the first time on International Women's Day 1994 around a thousand nuns, monks and activists marched with banners through Phnom Penh's red light district to protest against sexual exploitation and violence against women.

A Nation Struggling to Survive

In the spring of 1994, **Alison Tarrant** flew to Cambodia with her friend Julie whom she had been visiting in Singapore. The two friends met while living in Italy and have travelled extensively together ever since. Restricted by a return ticket to Britain, they were only able to spend a short time in Cambodia, but are determined to return.

One of the first things we saw in Phnom Penh were huge blue banners strung over the main streets. The slogans on them, written in Khmer and English, were slightly bizarre: "Rice seeds lift up the earth, women lift up men", read one. "A father is worth a thousand friends, a mother is worth a thousand fathers" announced a second. The third was more succinct, telling us simply that "Women's rights are sacred". We had arrived on International Women's Day.

We nearly didn't go to Cambodia. Only the day before we left Singapore for Phnom Penh the television news spoke of renewed fighting in the northwest. The Ministry of Foreign Affairs in Singapore advised us, if we had to go at all, to stay in Phnom Penh. Even the main tourist areas in Cambodia have not been readily accessible to independent travellers for long. More than two decades of civil war, punctuated only by the four years of murderous Khmer Rouge rule, isolated the country and made it dangerous or even impossible to travel in.

We are one of the more recent novelties, along with working telephones and a relatively direct mail service.

Our travel in Cambodia was limited by time as well as practical restrictions. With little more than a week in the country we confined ourselves to two areas, Phnom Penh and Angkor. It would be difficult to imagine two more different towns, but Cambodia is a country of contradictions. It demands a response, touches emotions which usually lie dormant.

Phnom Penh airport epitomizes the struggle Cambodia is having to keep up with the sudden surge of foreign visitors since the UN-approved elections in May 1993. Arriving there is a traveller's nightmare. As three international flights landed more or less simultaneously the chaos in the tiny arrivals hall grew to ludicrous proportions. Obtaining a visa on entry was easy – our passports were taken from us as we were compressed into the immigration counter, and we simply paid the statutory US$20 to get them back. Baggage retrieval was another matter. Packs and suitcases were piled into an enormous heap which I scrambled about in for a while before locating my rucksack, by that time ripped open. Nothing had gone, but an aid worker we met at the airport told us that bags are frequently rifled.

That seemed uncharacteristic of Cambodia. In general it is a country where travellers are made extremely welcome. We are one of the more recent novelties, along with working telephones and a relatively direct mail service (though the price of stamps fluctuates from day to day). People stop and greet you in the street, arrange their children into neat photographic compositions, sell you newspapers, books, fruit. Everywhere we went we were trailed by men on motorbikes who will take you anywhere in the city for a few riels. It's a great way to travel once you're accustomed to the insane traffic – which should be included in guide books as one of the sights. On one occasion my driver decided to catch up with his friend by the simple method of driving *through* the car blocking his way.

All over the city naked, malnourished children – many of them orphans – play in the filth or beg for a living.

The chaotic airport and even worse traffic typify Phnom Penh. The city is hectic, hot, vibrant and bursting with life. Everywhere you go you see slices of people's day to day existence. Two policemen squat on the pavement playing a complex version of noughts and crosses. A few yards away a family is washing under one of the communal hosepipes which are the only bathrooms available to the hundreds of street dwellers. There is no privacy here, no tidy distinction between houses and shops or building sites or temples. It is a jumbled up testament to daily survival.

Survival is what life is about in Cambodia. Twenty years ago the Khmer people suffered some of the most devastating bombing in history as US B52s – illegally – poured seven billion dollars' worth of explosives and napalm over their neutral country. The indescribable atrocities of the Khmer Rouge regime which followed have been well-documented. Less well-known is the fact that after the Vietnamese invasion that "liberated" the country, the United Nations withheld development aid to Cambodia for years.

The result is that Cambodia is a nation of desperate poverty. Phnom Penh has none of the hallmarks of a capital city. Only the major roads are tarmacked, others are just dust. There is a huge population of homeless people. Every open space you come to seems to have people camping in it, lying on makeshift beds or crouching over fires. In some areas the stench of human excrement is difficult to bear. All over the city naked, malnourished children – many of them orphans – play in the filth or beg for a living. Others, more fortunate, can be seen carrying sacks of rubble on building sites or heavy pails of water.

There are scarcely any big sights. The beautiful Royal Palace is like a quaint, provincial version of the Grand Palace in Bangkok. The National Museum is infested by bats. And Cambodia must be one of the few countries on earth where an empty building lot is listed as a tourist attraction. (It marks the spot where the National Bank stood, before the Khmer Rouge, in their determination to create a peasant society, blew the building up and declared money redundant).

Standing there, looking at exhumed mass graves, my brain seemed to lose its capacity to take in the implications.

Within hours of arriving in Cambodia you are aware of the country's tragic past. Everywhere there are limbless people – victims of the landmines that are still being laid. Even today up to 600 people, from a population of some nine million, are maimed or killed by landmines every month. It is estimated that for each person who reaches a hospital for treatment, another dies on the way. Many times in Phnom Penh amputee beggars or starving children asked me if they could eat the food I'd left on my plate.

And, if you want, you can find even clearer reminders of the recent horrors. The first thing I saw when I walked into *The Happy Guest House* where we stayed was the huge sign above reception. It read: TAXI TO THE KILLING FIELDS US$4.

The Killing Fields is the ground where, during the worst excesses of the Khmer Rouge regime, thousands of people were executed and bludgeoned to death. It is a strange experience to go along as a tourist to see such places. Standing there, looking at exhumed mass graves still littered with bones and the memorial full of neatly labelled skulls, my brain seemed to lose its capacity to take in the implications. Even worse is Tuol Sleng prison, the headquarters of the Khmer Rouge "security" forces. Liberated by the Vietnamese in 1979, it has been left largely as it was found, with only the bodies removed. Photographs of Khmer Rouge victims, taken by their captors, paper the walls from ceiling to floor. Paintings explain the use of the torture equipment on display – rough and rudimentary and horrifying.

Like many people I met in Phnom Penh I questioned my motives for going to these places: justifiable interest in Cambodia's history, or macabre fascination? It seemed voyeuristic, almost obscene, to trot along with a camera and spend a day seeing the sights of genocide. Yet some Khmer people we met were happy to show us or tell us about their history. They want to tell the outside world of the ruin of Cambodia and the years of despair they hope may one day come to an end.

> *Every night I woke up to the sound of artillery. The local people are used to it, and after a few hours so were we.*

It was with mixed feelings that we joined the tourist trail again, setting off for Siem Reap, the town everybody uses as a base to visit the magnificent temples of Angkor. It is more of a village than a town, a place of sleepy dusty streets and some of the friendliest people I have ever met.

The temples of Angkor are beyond description. Lurking in the forest depths of this small, insignificant country, famous only for its terrible recent history, are some of the greatest architectural achievements of all time. These phenomenal monuments stand untouched as they have done for centuries. Giant smiling faces gaze placidly out over the jungle, oblivious to change and turmoil. Yet here, in what seems a haven of peace and stability after bustling Phnom Penh, we were closer than ever to Cambodia's dark side. The first vehicle we saw in the town was an armoured car, covered with troops. There are soldiers everywhere.

Up around Angkor we heard shelling every day. The government had launched a new offensive against the Khmer Rouge bases in the west. Every night I woke up to the sound of artillery. The local people take no notice, they are used to it, and after a few hours so were we. Until one night, when the Khmer Rouge turned the tables by attacking the town itself. We weren't in danger; their target was a timber factory on the outskirts of town. But it was an alarming episode and one which gave us a brief, tiny insight into the experience of people who live their lives in fear.

The strangest thing about the day after the attack on Siem Reap was that everything carried on as usual. People went to market or to school, the women in our guest house carried on the dressmaking they do as another source of income. We carried on visiting temples. It seemed almost surreal. But as the day wore on the atmosphere of tension in the town became almost tangible. At night our guest house owner asked us not to go out. Discos shut early and the whole town seemed to black out under a voluntarily imposed curfew. Everybody knew, or at least believed that the Khmer Rouge were a mere 7km away.

It is partly for this continuing unrest that the Khmer people love to see foreigners and treat them with respect and great hospitality. We are a symbol of their security. The simple fact of our being there is a clear indication that their country is no longer an all-out war zone. Indeed, the presence of elderly French package holidaymakers in Siem Reap reassured us, as well as the local people, of our safety.

The attitude to Westerners is a refreshing change from many parts of Southeast Asia. It is impossible to overstate the friendliness of the Khmer people. It is a delight to travel in a country where the population either does not want or has not yet learnt to rip tourists off. Sadly it's difficult to believe that the situation is likely to last long.

It is not just that; like it or not, travel or tourism – call it what you will – destroys. Here there is an extra dimension. Even in travel terms Cambodia is still very much a victim of its past. Quite apart from Phnom Penh's bizarre tourist attractions, it is collecting a unique brand of traveller. Along with Vietnam, it seems to have achieved a cult status as an in-place to be on the road. Recently a war zone and even now hovering only on the edge of stability, Cambodia is attracting war tourists.

Compared to the rest of Southeast Asia, the travelling "community" is noticeably male-dominated. *The Capitol Hotel and Restaurant,* where most backpackers end up, was rich in Vietnam wannabes, too young to have been caught by the draft and working hard at recreating the spirit of *Apocalypse Now.* Lots of prostitutes hang around at *The Capitol* (a lot of them live at the *Happy Guest House*

UN soldiers had advised them how to get out of a minefield. The simplest option was to pay a Khmer person to walk in front.

just next door) and some travellers have no qualms about availing themselves of their services. I met one Swiss man who used a child prostitute – an Englishman with him set her age at no more than ten.

The Nam scene is not disguised. One man we met was trying to set up a business selling Vietnam vets' Zippo lighters, abandoned when troops moved out and now, apparently, important fashion accessories. And one of the men most interested in buying one was an Irish character who had worked as a volunteer for UNTAC, the UN body responsible for administering the country's first free elections. Martin was always stoned (dope is legal and widely used in Cambodia and a dollar buys an astonishing amount. The *Happy Guest House* reeked of it) and had a stream of good-time tales. He told us how much more exciting Cambodia had been when the UN was still there in force and the country full of ex-pats. His wage, as a volunteer, was far more than it is really possible to spend in Cambodia. Most of it seemed to have been used to fund wild weekends living it up in Phmon Penh. His reasons for being in Cambodia were clear.

By far the most disturbing of Martin's stories was his account of how UN soldiers had advised them how to get safely out of a minefield. Poking the ground with a radio aerial before taking each step was one option. The other, favoured for its simplicity, was to pay a Khmer person to walk in front of you. We never found out if the story was true or a wind-up, but it said more than enough.

Given such attitudes, it is perhaps surprising that the Khmer people are so welcoming to foreigners. Women are accepted with the same openness as men. Cambodia is one of only two countries I have been to where I have felt that we are no more vulnerable and that harassment of Western women because they are women is non-existent (the other was China).

If anything, being women meant we were treated with greater respect. Our guides at Angkor took us to the Western Baray reservoir. When we wanted to swim they showed us a good place and then pointedly left us alone. Conditioned to be wary, we said no when the armed guard at Preah Khan temple invited us to go and "see beautiful women" with him – he turned out to be referring to a bas-relief of the goddess Lakshmi emerging from the Ocean of Milk.

Probably the most telling experience we had was when we strayed into a brothel in Phnom Penh by mistake, thinking it was a bar. Two men working there treated us with great courtesy, giving us seats and a fan and taking us to the fridge to indicate what we would like to drink. The women, mostly whiling away the time playing cards, smiled cheerfully at us. It was only after some minutes that it occurred to us where we were (the discreet screens around the tables were the giveaway).

I wouldn't choose to travel alone in Cambodia, though I met plenty of women doing so quite happily. My reservations come less from problems specific to women than from the general security situation. Apart from the threat of banditry and national unrest, Phnom Penh after dark is dangerous, effectively ruled by gangs; two travellers I spoke to had witnessed street shootings. As in every country, travellers can be attacked and robbed. And there are more basic difficulties like the lack of health care. Cambodia is not a country I would like to be ill and alone in.

I was glad to have companionship. Cambodia is the kind of place that you need to talk about. In less than ten years it was ripped from its peaceful, sheltered, neutral existence, torn apart and ruined, with the death of one-fifth of its people. Understanding why it happened and how the Khmer people can still smile, how they can welcome strangers as friends, has become important to me. Of all the countries in Asia that I have travelled in, this is where I most want to return.

TRAVEL NOTES

Language The official language is Khmer – horrendous to learn. English is not widely spoken, though gaining fast in popularity (Phnom Penh has a whole thoroughfare – English Street – lined with rudimentary language schools). French is useful.

Transport Given the security situation, it's not easy to get around (see *Special Problems*). Air is the easiest way to Siem Reap and other provinces, but be sure to book in advance. Siem Reap is also accessible by boat up the Mekong River and across Tonle Sap. However, the journey takes days and is often impossible due to the river level (or lack of it) – tickets available from *Hotel Capitol*.

Accommodation Budget accommodation is burgeoning in Cambodia. *Hotel Capitol* and the *Happy Guest House* are the best-known places in Phnom Penh. According to Alison Tarrant, the *Happy* is fine, *Capitol* a dive. Siem Reap is full of clean, cheerful little family-run guest houses. Otherwise there are plenty of more expensive hotels.

Special Problems Continuing unrest is a problem. Ask advice from locals wherever you can; the tourist bureau in Phnom Penh is a good source of information. Travellers are advised to register with their embassies or representative in the country. Cambodia currently has no diplomatic representation in Britain or the US.

Overland journeys should be undertaken with caution. A sign in the *Hotel Capitol* reads: "Going to Saigon by taxi? Think twice". Many roads are controlled by bandits, army troops demanding protection money or the KR, who kidnapped and are believed to have killed three Western travellers in April 1994. Pay protection money if asked and bear in mind that if your taxi driver won't go somewhere he'll have a good reason for refusing. Buses are out of bounds and tourists are advised definitely not to travel by train. Do not travel in the west, where the Khmer Rouge still have strongholds, unless you're with

someone who really knows what they're doing. Take care, too, around some of the outlying temples in Angkor.

Most of the Cambodian countryside is still mined, though many minefields are now marked. Do not stray from marked roads and paths or touch any war refuse you see lying around. **Caution:** sometimes signs indicating minefields in the paddyfields behind are placed on road verges – often the verges are also mined, so don't go up to the notice to photograph it!

Money can be a problem. Travellers' cheques are not cashable. Take US\$ in cash, acceptable everywhere. US\$ are more or less interchangeable with riel; for many items you can pay using both, but hotels, air tickets and so forth, have to be paid for in dollars.

Guides *Cambodia/Laos* (Germany, Nelles Verlag) is the most recent, with some good historical/cultural background but few practical details. Also look out for updates to *Cambodia* or *Cambodia, Laos and Vietnam* in the Lonely Planet series.

BOOKS

John Pilger, *Distant Voices* (UK, Vintage, 1994). Includes five essays on Cambodia and examines events since the Khmer Rouge regime.

William Shawcross, *Sideshow: Kissinger, Nixon and the Destruction of Cambodia* (UK, Hogarth Press, 1991/US, Touchstone Books, 1987). Impeccably researched documentation of the US bombing of Cambodia and its effects.

Dr Haing Ngor, *Surviving the Killing Fields* (UK, Macmillan, 1987, o/p/US, Chatto & Windus, 1988, o/p). Chilling first-hand account of life and trauma under the KR by the actor who played Dith Pran in the film of *The Killing Fields*.

Special **thanks** to Alison Tarrant who provided much of the background for the Introduction and Travel Notes.

Canada

C anada is a country of less outrageous extremes than
the US, more famous for its great outdoors than the
hype and excitement of city life. There are far fewer
people and, for many, mountains, forests, rivers and vast
empty plains are the principal attraction. You should have
little trouble travelling alone or with another woman
although, as in the States, most cities have areas it is best to
avoid. Regional differences are hardly surprising in a country
of this size, but Canada is also very much split along national

lines, going back to the days of direct French and British colonization. There has always been a degree of tension between British and French Canadians, particularly in Quebec Province – home of Canada's liveliest and most cosmopolitan city, Montreal – which continues to move uneasily toward independence.

Like much of the country, Quebec is home to several nations of native peoples who have long been engaged in largely non-violent efforts to reassert their independence through the registration of land claims. These groups – mainly Inuits in the north, Iroquois to the south, Ojibwa and Blackfoot to the west and various tribes on the Pacific coast – suffered greatly from the Europeanization that began early this century. This concerted campaign to deprive people of their land and traditions (at the opening of the twentieth century certain ceremonies were literally banned) quickly reduced them to the status of second-class citizens. In recent years the Assembly of First Nations has sponsored a number of land claims, most notably supporting calls for an Inuit home-land in the north, but progress is slow and poverty and deprivation still dominate life on the reservations.

Struggles within national minorities for identity, rights and property have all influenced the **women's movement** and determined its diverse, regional and very active nature. Native women's groups are on the increase, there are active trade union women's groups and women's causes are supported in national political parties. In addition, almost every major town has a women's bookshop, café, feminist theatre, art gallery and local health centre. Yet, away from the main urban centres of Vancouver, Toronto, Ottawa and Calgary, despite Canada's apparent tolerance for difference and radical causes, the national ideal seems firmly entrenched in the image of the white nuclear family, loaded up with lavish leisure accessories, enjoying the great outdoors.

A Friend, Her Daughter
and the Man with a Chainsaw

Madeleine Cary has travelled extensively in Canada where she once lived for several years. Here she focuses on a trip to the Queen Charlotte Islands, an archipelago of some 150 islets off the country's west coast. A writer and television producer, she is also a contributor to *Soul Providers*, a volume of writings by single parents, published in Britain by Virago. She has also written pieces on Thailand and Malaysia for this book.

We must have made an odd trio, Marion and I decked out in ill-fitting plastic sowesters and borrowed wellies; Beth, Marion's teenage daughter, dreadlocked and wearing farming overalls with one old Doc Martin boot. The other foot was covered in plaster following a fall from a friend's trampoline days earlier. Somehow she juggled two crutches as well as balancing a rucksack and didgeridoo.

We were on our way to the Queen Charlotte islands, Canada's ecological gem in the North Pacific. The "Charlottes" lie only twenty odd miles south of Alaska, hence our rushed and loaned assembly of weather-proof garb, even though it was early summer. Whilst boarding the *Queen of the North*, the luxury ferry which sails through the "Inside Passage" from Vancouver Island to the northern mainland port of Prince Rupert, we attracted hostile stares from the well-heeled, Goretex-clad tourists on Alaskan fishing expeditions. We had been told that the scenery en route would be stunning and as it was a bright, rain-free day, we settled into a sheltered spot on deck to enjoy the view.

It was this promise of breathtaking sights on the three-day journey up to the Queen Charlotte Islands that had finally determined our decision to make the trip. My friend Marion, who was putting me up for a short vacation in her Vancouver Island home, had told me of two contacts she had on the Charlottes who would be able to house us. One was a recent acquaintance who had just purchased land and an old lodge on the islands and had offered to feed and house anyone who was willing to help him with renovation work. The other was a contact from Marion's nursing days who was now living and working as a district nurse in the small island community. Tedium was setting in during the long, lazy days in anodyne Victoria city and I craved adventure.

The Queen Charlotte Islands seemed a fascinating destination. Everyone who heard of our plan to visit them enthused unequivocally. The islands were known as the Canadian Galapagos, a treasure-trove for anthropologists, ornithologists, zoologists and ecologists. I can hardly think of one "ism" that was not mentioned as people described the place. It was home to the Haida native people, reputedly the most advanced and respected tribe in North America; it was an exquisite example of northern primal rainforest ecology, teeming with rare species of plants, birds and aquatic creatures; and sadly, like everywhere else on the arboreous west coast, it was being threatened with deforestation by the logging industry.

Our expectations of the boat trip were more than fulfilled. The route meandered through an archipelago of hundreds of snow-peaked forested islands, with deep gorges leading through to the Rockies on the mainland side. The area is a good sighting ground for whales and we spent most of the trip on deck scouting the waters. The occasional gasps from passengers with hightech binoculars and cameras confirmed that the jets of water we could see in the distant waters were spurts from Orcas or Grey Whales. There were plenty of playful dolphins dancing alongside the boat and if this wasn't enough, there was always the wide basin of technicolour blue sky to contemplate, the glaciers and island waterfalls to observe and eagles or sealions to look out for.

Eventually, the deck attracted more passengers, including a couple of other backpackers, nature fanatics and quite a few indigenous people. One fellow traveller, Bill, a Haida man who was returning from a fishing job on Vancouver Island, told me that when he was not fishing, he was carving. The Haida artistic tradition was alive and well, and many Haida artists produced carvings, etchings and paintings for the tourist industry in British Columbia. Bill's home was in Masset on Graham Island, the northern, populated island in the Charlottes. He knew all about the lodge we were going to and its new owner; that is how small the community was. He was delighted that travellers were starting to visit the island in greater numbers as he felt it was time to alert the outside world to the impending destruction of the environment by the Canadian timber industry. It also meant a financial boost to the islanders as visitors came to seek original Haida artwork and took paid tours to the remains of ancient Haida villages or the ecologically unique sites on the lower island of Moresby.

Marion spent much of the trip being hounded by an eccentric Englishman who travelled the world looking for examples of "God's Own Country", while Beth enjoyed the company of a couple of German backpackers who were entertained by her mastery of the didgeridoo. It was not clear if the bellowing blast from the weird instrument went down well with the other passengers. Some would spin around and look out to sea as if a gigantic whale had just called to them.

We felt relaxed and in adventurous mood when the *Queen of the North* finally pulled into dock at Prince Rupert, the northernmost port on the

Canadian coast. Although we were not quite in the land of the midnight sun, the sight of the sun poised some way above the horizon at almost eleven o'clock at night and the strange light levels that suggested dawn rather than dusk played havoc with the body clock. We disembarked with an energy and excitement that seemed out of place in the sleepy port.

Our lodging house in the town, the *Pioneer Rooms*, was a quaint surprise; originally built to provide board for early settlers in the area, the tall wooden house, with its gaily painted facade and original features, was reminiscent of wild west gold rush days. We entered a cosy lounge where two other guests stared at the blaring television. One, a strange, androgynous character in what appeared to be a nun's headdress, a long dirndl skirt and a huge pair of gumboots, looked round at us and ignored our smiles. The other, a young man from Quebec, took one look at us and said: "Queen Charlottes, eh?" He had just returned from a six-week trip there. "I hope you have friends on the island", he said when we asked him his opinion. He had gone there to seek solitude, but had ended up with more isolation than he could handle.

I was moved by Marion and Beth, a single mum and rebel daughter who lay laughing in the night like schoolgirls.

Our concierge was a kindly woman, the first on our trip to enquire sympathetically about Beth's broken foot. She took us up to our room, a tiny spick-and-span attic which looked out on the street. Later, we lay in bed with our heads by the open window, listening to the people wandering home from the bars, looking at the clear northern starlit night, breathing in the unpolluted air. We made great travelling companions, we agreed. I was particularly moved by Marion and Beth, a single mum and rebel daughter who now lay laughing in the night like a couple of schoolgirls.

After the final lap of our journey the next day, a seven-hour crossing out to the Queen Charlottes, we were all relieved to see Marion's lodge-owning friend waiting for us at the dock, as arranged. He sauntered over coolly and then broke into that North American gregariousness that can be a little overwhelming for British tastes, back-slapping, hooting and "giving five". Marion and Beth sat with him in the front of the truck and I willingly jumped into the open back, seeking some solitude to savour the sights and atmosphere of the island. The road cut out within minutes to a long, quiet beachside stretch that took us some 40km north to the small community where the lodge was situated. To my left the Pacific lapped quietly against the driftwood-covered beaches; on the right dense forests occasionally opened up to ranching fields. I lost count of the number of deer I saw at the roadside and spotted my first bald-headed eagle.

The lodge was set back from the main road in isolation, hemmed in by several acres of privately owned bush. It was a ramshackle affair in a state of renovation. Inside, the original living quarters were still in place with a huge old woodburner and several doors leading off to the rooms. Each door was covered with sheet metal pierced with bullet holes; apparently the lodge had been a favourite resting hole for deerhunters in the past and evening beer parties would lead to competitive indoor shootouts. The owner had sold the place in a hurry, failing to clear it out of its original supplies. In its present state, with cupboards full of old towels and sheets, shelves of books, old furnishings and utensils lying around, all covered with layers of dust, the place had an eerie quality. The new owner claimed the place was in desperate need of a "woman's touch". By this, we soon learnt, he wanted us to scrub, clean, dust, make curtains and get the kitchen, a fascinating old relic with a griddle fryer and double-oven, up and running. Marion and I chose to put up with this stereotypical division of chores, believing it was a small price to pay in return for a sojourn on the island. She did make an immediate effort to contact her nursing friend, however, *After being incarcerated with a white Canadian patriarch, there was something uplifting in the all-female baseball game.* and we simply assumed our lodge arrangement was a minor hiatus. Beth was already disgruntled. She had asked for a lesson on the chainsaw only to be dismissed with a guffaw and a reference to it being "man's work". She put her Michelle Shocked tape on at full blast and set about making some wholemeal bread.

Over the next few days, while continually leaving phone messages for the elusive nurse, we juggled time between working at the lodge and being "treated" to days out. Our host refused to let us use his truck so we had to rely on him for any excursions. This dependency was not something we had bargained for, especially as our experience of what the islands had to offer was bound up with someone else's taste. We were taken to a dull logging town to drink in a redneck bar when we were hoping to visit a Haida community. We had an endless lesson in clam-digging in a torrential downpour when we would have preferred wandering through a canopied rainforest. After an early morning lecture on a freezing beach in the art of spotting rare gemstones amid the millions of pebbles, we voiced our need for some freedom. Things were not quite going as planned, we explained. As we had no access to transport we felt somewhat stymied in our desire to explore the islands at our own pace. What we did not say was that he seemed to be less concerned with our enjoyment during our stay than with the opportunity it afforded him to show off his knowledge and wield power. Our assertiveness and openness got us nowhere. The man claimed we were ungrateful timewasters, started cursing like a corporal and ordered us into the truck. We decided it would not be politic to ruffle his feathers further for the moment. In a simmering silence, he bolted to the nearest town, Queen Charlotte City, and with barely audible instructions of a later pick-up time, virtually ejected us from the truck and scooted off in a cloud of dust. He could not have done us a greater favour.

It so happened that there was a community festival on in Queen Charlotte City that day. Relishing our freedom at last, we entered into the spirit of the occasion, regarding the people and their activities with wide-eyed curiosity. I have never been a fan of baseball and yet on that day I found myself rooting at a game with unbridled rigour. It was an all-female game. After being incarcerated for a week with a white Canadian patriarch, there was something particularly uplifting in this sight. We sat in the appreciative crowd, where husbands, boyfriends and offspring were cheering the women on, supping root beer and chomping on hotdogs. Most of the players were Haida or mixed race – strikingly handsome people with blue-black hair and honey coloured skin. Behind us, female elders, large, authoritative women, sat in trucks and cars handing out picnic goodies to the children.

While we were harbouring paranoid fantasies about chainsaw massacres, he probably throught we were trying to poison him.

It was a warm, dry day. The island's mountain range peaked over the clouds in the distance. A band started up in the church hall at the back of the playing field, rehearsing the evening's jamboree. Down on the beach, on an old overturned boat, a small group of people were moving in Tai Chi harmony. From where I sat I could make out a couple of ponytails, a headband, a bald head, something rainbow coloured. They were obviously members of the growing community of new agers living on the island. Baseball was probably not their scene. A passing truckload of local rednecks honked at the Tai Chi group, calling out obscenities and guffawing as they hightailed it down the main street.

This tripartite lifestyle of native inhabitants, new age/ecology freaks and logging industry rednecks gave the island a social tension which was palpable beyond its idyllic physical beauty. The Haida community lived in relative comfort with generous government support (much resented by the loggers) which at least allowed them decent housing and material standards. There was little evidence here of the oppression that has forced native people into alcoholism and poverty elsewhere in Canada and it was refreshing to see a community that had retained its dignity. Yet there was also an ongoing battle between the native people and the Canadian government over the rights of the major logging companies to cut down trees on the island. Deforestation was affecting the ecological balance of this special environment and the native people were now fighting to preserve the land. On their side was the growing number of ecologists and people seeking alternative lifestyles who had come to the island in recent years. The logging families were striving to keep their industry going, fearing a threat of widespread unemployment if the timber trade were curtailed.

Back at the lodge things went from bad to worse. We knew we were no longer welcome, but were still waiting to hear from the nurse. The more surly and aggressive the man became, the more heated were our private diatribes against misogyny. He seemed to be permanently attached to his chainsaw and we found we rarely ventured out of the kitchen. I noticed the guns over the door. Marion commented on how there were no locks on our bedrooms. He refused to eat with us. It was getting seriously out of hand. While we were harbouring paranoid fantasies about chainsaw massacres, he probably throught we were trying to poison him. With no public transport on the island and hardly any vehicles to hitch rides from, we knew that once we left we would be facing a possible forty-kilometre walk.

It was sheer good timing that brought the nurse to our rescue just as we were ready to wander out onto the lone wilderness road. We heard a car pulling up outside the lodge and ran out to see a pleasant, sane-looking woman stepping out. We hugged her with such gratitude, as if she had saved us from the death sentence. Chainsawman came out to check on the commotion and we introduced him to our saviour. He looked her over disdainfully, chewing on his cheroot, grunted and turned on his heel. We did not need to explain our situation; she had read all the signs. Within minutes we were packed and out of there, hooting like escapees from Colditz.

The nurse lived in an old house on the north beach which faced the Pacific and had sand dunes in the back garden. She shared the place with another woman and several cats. Somehow she managed to find beds for us all and made us feel safe and free at last. We had only a few days left before our departure, but it was enough time to finally savour the beauty and individuality of the island and its community. We indulged in long, beachcombing walks with no lectures. We explored the magical spruce and cedar rainforests where delicate mosses hung from intricate branches, and ancient trees reached up to impossible heights. We visited workshops and met Haida carvers and artists. In the northern town of Masset, I met Bill, my companion from the boat, and enjoyed a pub darts' game with him. Many of the homes on the north beach were owned by the self-sufficient alternative community who lived off the land and made a living by contributing to the new-age shops and cafés which were starting to blossom in the area. Beth was delighted to finally rub shoulders with the hippie scene. Marion, just surfacing from her feelings of guilt and shame about misjudging her so-called lodge-owning friend, felt vindicated by the nurse's unconditional kindness and hospitality. We were both relieved that the antipathy at the lodge had not strained our friendship, as it so easily could have.

On our return journey on the *Queen of the North*, most of the passengers were Haida people who were going to Bella Bella, a mainly native fishing community on the British Columbian coast which was only accessible by boat. It was about to host a major "potlatch", a festival with banqueting and exchanging of gifts, for Pacific native tribes. When the boat pulled into Bella Bella, we heard chanting and drumming. On the dock a group of people had gathered in native costume of wide cloaks and eagle headdresses. Some of the young men came forward in a dance, hopping from foot to foot to the hypnotic chanting of the women. A line of elders waited to receive the guests. Finally the oldest passengers, many blind and infirm, were escorted off the ferry and greeted by their hosts. As the dock filled with people, we watched the joyful reunions; young people greeting past lovers or potential future mates with excitement; older people tearfully meeting old relatives and companions. Beth found it all overwhelming. I knew that she was thinking, as I was, of how much we have lost in letting the extended family break down. Marion put an arm around her.

Hitching through the Yukon

Kate Pullinger is a Canadian writer living in London. Here she describes hitch-hiking through the Yukon Territory, a massive area north of British Columbia.

The Yukon is basically the "Great Outdoors", and not much else. Exceptionally underpopulated, with less than 25,000 people in an area almost as large as France, it is a mountain–lake–forest–river-lover's dream come true. I think the best way to see it, at least in summer, is to hitch-hike. I have always found hitching in the Yukon relatively fast, easy and safe, mainly because towns are far apart and nobody is going to leave anyone standing on the side of the road in the middle of nowhere at -20°C, or, in summer, in all that dust.

Last summer I stood on the side of the road outside the Yukon's capital, Whitehorse. My thumb stuck out, I was heading for Dawson City 556km away. The first vehicle to stop was an old Ford truck, bed on back with two extremely large sled dogs hanging out over its sides. They barked at me ferociously. A woman jumped out and asked how far I was going. I told her, and she said she was only going 85km, but that was a good start. So I jumped in.

I knew about this kind of van: lush interior, shag carpets on the walls, a stereo. They call them fuck-trucks.

She was young, had long plaited hair, and was wearing men's shorts and a felt hat. Next to her sat a small, dark baby, who looked at me curiously. The woman didn't say anything so neither did I. After a few miles she reached above the windscreen and pulled a cigar from behind the sunshade. She smoked it as she drove, clenching it between her teeth when she changed gear. I looked out of the window over the hills and vast, peopleless landscape. After 85km she pulled off the road on to the dirt track that led to her house and I thanked her and jumped out. I slammed the truck door so it shut properly and she and the baby sped off. The sled dogs barked at me until I was far out of their sight.

I stood again at the side of the road. A small Toyota two-door stopped. I put my pack in the back seat and climbed in front. This driver was also a woman, she wore a skirt and her hair was wet. We began to chat and I learned that she was just driving home from a swimming lesson in Whitehorse – a trip of 340km, which she made every Friday. There aren't very many swimming pools in the Yukon. The conversation led to a familiar story: she came up to the Yukon ten years ago to visit a friend and stayed. She said she wouldn't leave for anything, and now her brother lives up here too. I began to think there must be something special about this place.

Where she dropped me it was very quiet. There were trees everywhere I looked. In fact, all I could see was trees. I had to wait here around twenty minutes before I heard what sounded like a truck. I saw the dust before I could see it, great clouds of dirt billowing up into the sky. Then I saw the truck and stood on my tiptoes and tried to make my thumb bigger. The driver saw me and started to slow down. It took him a long time to do so and he went past me. I could no longer see, there was so much dust, and I held my scarf over my mouth. When it settled I walked to the truck – a long way up – and negotiated the lift, another 85km.

After hoisting my pack up I climbed in. The driver started the engine and headed down the road. I smiled to myself, thinking I was in front of the dust now. The truck driver seemed to change gears a hundred times before we were up to the right speed. Steaming along, past the endless lakes and hills, he told me about his children going to school, having babies and working in Edmonton. I listened and then asked how long he'd been here. He said he came for a year thirty years ago. There is something about this place.

Dropped at another turnoff I ran into the bushes for protection from all that dust. When he and his cloud were out of sight, I climbed back to the road. A few more cars went by and then a van stopped. It was a newish van, brown, with a sunset painted on the exterior. I knew about this kind of van: lush interior, shag carpets on the walls, a stereo. They call them sin-bins, glam-vans, or more straightforwardly, fuck-trucks. Thinking of my vulnerability, I took a look at the driver. He was male, of course, and looked about forty-five. He was wearing a nylon shirt with bucking broncos on it. He had a skinny black moustache and shiny hair. He asked where I was going and said he was too, he didn't know these parts and would like some company. The voice inside me said he was okay. I got into the van.

I talked and laughed with all the other gamblers I had met. Feeling rather rich and drunk . . .

The driver was called Dan and came from Fort St John. He talked away about his family and I began to relax. He said he was a professional gambler which made me sit up: gambling is illegal in most of Canada. Dan told me all about the gambling circuit in British Columbia, the late-night games in Trail, Kelowna, Hope, the nights when he'd walked away with $4000 in his pocket. He told me about the cards, the passwords and the bribes to the Mounties. I was astounded; this was a whole new side to "Beautiful But Boring British Columbia". I asked him what he was doing up here. Then I remembered: Dawson City is the only place in Canada where gambling is legal. And Dawson City was where I was headed.

It was evening by the time we arrived and Dan dropped me off at the crossing to the campsite. Satiated with gambling stories, I sat down beside the river and waited for the little ferry to take me across. It was full of other hitch-hikers: Germans, Americans, Québecois. It was 8pm and the sky was as bright as mid-morning. I ate and then took the ferry back across to the town, strolling along the wild west wooden sidewalks, past the false-front saloons, hotels and shops and ending up in front of *Diamond Tooth Gerties*, the casino. I went in, thinking I wouldn't play, just have a look around. The place was full and everyone was drinking, smoking and gambling. There were dancing girls, and a vaudeville show and card-dealers with waistcoats and bow ties and armbands. I had a drink and wondered if this was what it had looked like in 1905. Standing beside the blackjack table I figured out how to play, and watched as people won and lost. I wasn't going to play, just watch.

Many bottles of Molson Canadian and five hours later, I came out, $10 up. It was 2am, broad daylight; if the sun ever went down, I missed it. Running to catch the ferry back to the campsite, I talked and laughed with all the other gamblers I had met. Feeling rather rich and drunk, I crawled into my tent. Someone had built a campfire and people were milling about doing campfire sorts of things but it didn't seem right, campfire and campsongs in broad daylight. I closed my eyes and thought that perhaps after a few nights of lucrative gambling I would hitch that brief 250km up into the Arctic Circle. There is definitely something about this place.

TRAVEL NOTES

Languages English and French; in Quebec, French is the main language.

Transport Getting to the main centres is straightforward. There are Greyhound buses to most towns, good trains and efficient, fairly inexpensive internal flights. Public transport services in outlying areas tend to be few and far between. Here hitching, safest through agencies, may be your only option, but is not advisable alone. For long distances, college noticeboards are an excellent source of information; they specify people wanting or offering lifts and you get a chance to meet the people you'll be travelling with beforehand.

Accommodation YWCAs are usually a good bet: you can get full details from the national office at 571 Jarvis St, Toronto, M4Y JJ1 (☎416/921 2117). Outside term time, universities are also recommended.

Women's hoidays *Wilderness of Women* (WOW), Box 548, Tosino BC, V0R 2Z0 (☎604/725 3230). Wilderness trips for women on Canada's west coast. Political and spiritual workshops, backpacking and custom trips. Non-profit-making group that operates a sliding scale.

Guides *The Rough Guide to Canada* (Penguin) covers just about every facet of the country and its cultures. See also *The Rough Guide to the Pacific Northwest* (Penguin) for chapters on western Canada and the Canadian Rockies. Recommended for the Yukon is *The Alaska-Yukon Handbook* (US, Moon Publications).

CONTACTS

A very good source for addresses and information about the Canadian women's movement is the annual *Everywoman's Almanac* (Canada, Women's Press), which is distributed in the UK and available in women's bookshops.

The National Action Committee on the Status of Women (NAC) is the political arm and largest national women's movement organization in Canada, comprising a coalition of just under 6000 groups with a combined membership of close to three million women. Their main office is at 344 Bloor St W, Suite 505, Toronto, M5S 3A7 (☎416/922 3246).

Also useful, the *Canadian Women's Mailing List* for up-to-date information of events, publications, services is published by *WEB*

Women's Information Exchange, 9280 Arvida Ave, Richmond BC (☎604/274 5335).

Another way of gathering information inside Canada is via the free networking magazines available in kiosks in every large city. These list everything from gay, lesbian and ethnic groups to psychodrama, alternative health and ecology groups and more.

WOMEN'S BOOKSHOPS AND RESOURCE CENTRES

Alberta: *Commonwoman Books*, 8210 104 St.

Montreal: *Androgyny* (gay and women's bookshop), 1217 Crescent. Should stock the *Montreal Yellow Pages* which lists resources for women.

Robson: *Women's Resource Centre*, 1144 Robson, near Thurlow.

Toronto: *Women's Bookstore*, 73 Harboard St.

Vancouver: *Vancouver Women's Bookstore*, Cambic St (☎604/684 052).

BOOKS

Susanna Moodie, *Roughing It in the Bush* (UK, Virago, 1986, o/p/Canada, Beacon Press, 1987). Reprint of a classic by a Canadian writer about pioneering in the Canadian wilderness.

Jan Morris, *O Canada: Travels in an Unknown Country* (UK, Robert Hale, 1992/US, HarperCollins). Ten essays about Canadian cities by one of Britain's best-known travel writers.

Peney Kome, *Women of Influence: Canadian Women and Politics* (US, Doubleday, 1985, o/p). Somewhat academic, but a useful overview of women's place in Canadian political life.

FICTION

Margaret Atwood, *Wilderness Tips* (UK, Virago, 1992/US, Bantam, 1993). This volume of short stories is the latest work of Canada's leading novelist and poet. See also *Bluebeard's Egg* (UK, Virago, 1988/US, Fawcett, 1987), *The Handmaid's Tale* (UK, Virago, 1987/US, Fawcett, 1986), *Cat's Eye* (UK, Virago, 1990/US, Bantam, 1989) and earlier novels.

Joan Barfoot, *Gaining Ground* (UK, The Women's Press, 1980). Novel about a woman who leaves her husband, children and suburban security to live as a hermit deep in the Canadian countryside.

Willa Cather, *Shadows on the Rock* (1937; UK, Virago, 1984/US, Random House, 1971). Classic novel about French settlers in Canada.

Margaret Laurence, *A Jest of God* (UK, Virago, 1987/US, University of Chicago Press, 1993). One of Canada's foremost writers, whose novels explore the loneliness and frustration of women living in the stifling fictional backwater of Manawaka. See also *The Stone Angel* and *The Diviners*.

Alice Munro, *Beggar Maid* (UK, Penguin, 1989/US, Penguin, 1984). Best-known book of this Canadian author, set in rural Ontario and in Toronto. See also *Lives of Girls and Women* (UK, Penguin, 1989/US, NAL-Dutton), *The Progress of Love* (UK, Flamingo, 1988/US, Penguin, 1987) and *Friend of My Youth* (UK & US, Vintage, 1991) – all excellent short-story collections.

Jane Rule, *The Desert of the Heart* (1964; UK, Pandora, 1986/US, Naiad Press, 1985) and *Memory Board* (UK, Pandora, 1987/US, Naiad Press). Just two of the books we recommend by one of the country's leading lesbian feminist writers.

Ann Tracy, *Winter Hunger* (UK, Virago, 1993). Haunting story set in Northern Manitoba where an aspiring anthropologist has brought his family to study native Canadian customs.

Chad

S ince 1990, when the triumphant expulsion of Libyan troops marked the end of 25 years of war, Francophone Chad has been experiencing a great period of renewal and optimism. Public services remain somewhat lacking but compared to just a few years ago, much of the country – especially the more populated south – has changed beyond all recognition; buildings are being repaired, roads are being improved, the capital, N'Djamena, is buzzing and travellers are beginning to reinstate Chad on their Central African itinerary. The economy, largely reliant on cotton production, also appears to be reviving, though in reality the country remains more or less totally dependent on foreign aid.

Apart from the far north, which is still closed to foreigners other than aid workers, it is possible to travel around fairly freely – just don't expect to get there quickly. Though large-scale road development is under way and the number of buses is increasing – especially on the main route between N'Djamena and Sarh – much travel is still by pick-up truck or lorry, usually on top of a pile of goods. N'Djamena has its share of pickpockets and areas to avoid, but by and large crime against visitors is rare. Outside the two main cities, hotels are few and far between, but most villages seem to have a mission station where, once people have got over the shock of seeing a lone woman traveller, you will probably receive a warm welcome. Also you will nearly always find yourself among travelling Chadienne women, more than willing to look after you and help find you a bed for the night. Travel in Chad may be unpredictable and hard-going at times, but the absence of tourist hustle, coupled with vast stretches of wild and beautiful scenery, make it definitely worth the trip.

Oxfam and UNICEF focus a proportion of aid on **women's** income-generating and health projects but, despite an official Department of Women's Affairs, there appears to be little specific concentration on women's needs from within the country. Circumstances vary considerably from north to south, but generally women have only limited property rights and bear the brunt of water- and wood-carrying on top of childcare and general domestic chores. Women in the capital seek to ease their economic burden by running *pari-matches*, whereby a group of them rent a bar for the day and send out invitations to all their friends (though anybody can come), hoping to make money from the drinks. These gatherings are a great opportunity to hear the latest African pop music and get down to some serious partying.

Days on the Road

A freelance photographer from the northeast of England, **Chris Johnson** spent a year in Africa, researching the lives of local women and taking photographs for an exhibition. In Chad shortly before the end of the war, she travelled much of the time by lorry, hitching lifts wherever she could. At the time the country had few paved roads and those that were paved were usually in such bad condition that people preferred to make their own tracks.

From the capital, N'Djamena, a narrow strip of pot-holed tarmac runs north; we follow alongside on the broad sandy track through the scrub. It's hot and I'm thirsty. I look longingly at the bottle of water beside me, but it's the second day of Ramadan and as neither of my companions have had anything to eat or drink since sunrise it seems unfair of me to add to their misery by indulging myself.

At 4pm we stop for them to pray. The road continues through sparse red gold grass and past the occasional dusty tree. Half an hour later we reach a village where we stop to rest. The driver sends off for cans of cold orange juice and hands one to me, brushing aside my protests and insisting I drink. It feels like the height of generosity and is typical of my experiences with Muslim men in Africa.

As a visitor, I am accorded the status of honorary man and sit with them to eat. A woman waits on us silently.

En route again. We've now lost all semblance of tar, and in places there isn't even much semblance of track, just tyre marks in the sand. At 6.30pm we stop again to pray. The ordeal is over for the day and at last they can drink. They tell me the first three days of Ramadan are the worst; after that one gets used to it. The evening is a pearly grey-pink; above is the thin crescent of the moon. All around is vast emptiness. We drive on again, often through thick sand. A man comes by on his camel, our headlights picking out the rich colours of the woven saddle cloth.

We reach Chaddra, our first port of call, at 10pm. The vehicle is unloaded and we stop for a meal. Inside the courtyard, lit by the flicker of oil lamps, a group of white-robed men sit round the large mat. As a visitor, I am accorded the status of honorary man and sit with them to eat. A woman waits on us silently.

Then it's another two hours' rough driving. Exhausted, I keep falling asleep, only to be jolted awake again. At midnight we stop by a cluster of houses. We roll out our mats and the local inhabitants come across the sands to chat and to bring us more mats. I am aware of the faint sound of someone playing a thumb piano, before falling asleep.

Sometime in the early morning the cold wakes me and I crawl into my sleeping bag.

Prayers are at dawn and we are off by six. Apart from the occasional tree, the only vegetation is a pale green plant, about three feet tall and with leathery leaves. Mostly there is just sand. An hour later we pass a small group of rectangular houses with flat roofs; then, coming over a rise, see the village of Mao spread out on the hillside ahead. The single-storey houses are built of the local pale-coloured earth which is found in bands by the *wadis* (dry watercourses). They are very Arab looking – rectangular in shape, with flat roofs and little turrets at each corner and halfway along the long walls – and are entered through tiny gateways in the street walls.

One of these houses is my home for the next few days. The thick walls and tiny slit windows keep it wonderfully cool, a welcome contrast to the modern houses of the city. Inside the courtyard someone has planted trees and flowers; an awning keeps off the fierce sun and a gentle wind rustles my papers as I try to write.

Mao is the capital of Karem province and an ancient trading centre. As you enter the village the words "Sultanate of Karem" can be seen written in black over the white archway. The weekly market still brings in people from a wide distance and even the daily market is large, though it has little fresh food: most things are dried to preserve them. Especially good are the dried dates.

Along one side of the village runs a *wadi*. Down in its valley piles of bricks lie baking in the sun and there is constant traffic to and from the wall. A line of women, swathed in long black robes, walk back up the hill to the village carrying heavy earthen water pots on their heads.

At 6.30pm the *muezzin* calls the faithful again to prayer. Looking out across the walls, there are only four colours: the pinky-beige of the sands, which is split by a gash of white – the same white as the houses; the dusty green of trees; and the pale, pale blue of the sky. Veiled women greet me and laugh at my taking photographs.

Northwest of Mao is Nokou. It's definitely remote: if you travel northwest for about 320 miles you might, if your navigation is good, hit Bihua in Niger; travel northeast about 400 miles and, if you are lucky, you come across Zouar in the Tibesti Mountains; otherwise the nearest habitation is about 800 miles away in Libya.

We set off from Mao as soon as the prayers have finished. The empty landscape sweeps up into hills, nothing very high or steep, but on a grand scale. It's windy and the surface sand blows off like spindrift. Occasionally there's a sparse covering of grass which from a distance lends the hills a yellow-green colour; but as soon as you get close it is clear there's far more sand than grass. From time to time we see a few goats or a woman on a donkey, but mainly it's just camels: some roaming free, others ridden by men dressed in long white robes.

The people I am travelling with are involved in a project helping to cultivate the *wadis*. The water table in the *wadis* is very close to the surface and *shadufs* (pivoted poles with buckets at the end) are used to lift water to irrigate. Traditionally some people have always cultivated in this area: it's one of the features that distinguish it from the eastern Sahel. But when the drought came and thousands of nomads lost their entire stock and ended up in camps, someone decided that the answer was increased cultivation.

Nomadic people have always had their own way of dealing with drought. A Fulani friend explained how, when drought hit and they lost their stock, some of the tribe would go into the villages and work for the settled people, just for long enough to raise money to restock. Then they'd be off again. Maybe many will use the new aid schemes in the same way. Some, though, say desertification has gone too far, that the land can no longer support so many people in that old lifestyle.

A cloud of dust, out of which emerges an old blue Toyota . . . three turbaned Arabs will take me to Mussokori – for a price.

It's my last day in Nokou. I get up very early and climb the nearby hill to watch the sun rise behind the small fortress that looks out over the desert. Slowly the village wakes up. Women climb the hill, pots on heads; a man walks off across the desert, the wind tugging at his white robes; a laughing girl comes by on a donkey.

As I walk down and wander along the sandy streets taking photos I am sad to be leaving, but there is little option. If I don't get today's transport there won't be another vehicle until Tuesday; and my visa expires on Wednesday. My original intention had been to go west from here rather than going back to N'Djamena, but being Ramadan there are no vehicles going that way.

We leave at about 9am. Somewhere in the middle of an area of beige and white sand dunes something goes wrong with the vehicle. But, as always, they manage to fix it; meanwhile I go round taking photos.

As enquiries at Mao reveal no transport going either west to Lake Chad or south to N'Djamena I decide to go out with the project for the day. If there are any vehicles going south we will see them and if not I'll go back to Mao for the night and try again in the morning. For a long time the only vehicles we see are the French army, and one very broken-down lorry. Then, in the distance, a cloud of dust, out of which emerges an old blue Toyota. We flag it down, and its occupants, three turbaned Arabs, agree to take me to Mussokori – for a price.

Ten minutes along the way we get a flat tyre. They change it and we continue, shuddering our way over the rough ground. My companions speak no French and I little Arabic so our conversation is limited. Almost an hour later the next tyre goes. Luckily we are close by a small settlement. The schoolteacher, a slip of a kid who has probably only had a couple of years' secondary schooling himself, comes to greet us and takes me back to one of the huts. I am brought water and Provita – a nutritional supplement in the form of small biscuits, the result of some aid programme.

The hours tick slowly by. Several times I think I hear the sound of a vehicle, but on investigation it is only the wind. It is very hot. Again I think I hear the sound of a vehicle. I

> *I sit on a rug, feeling tired. Not just physically tired, but tired of the endless waits, of the uncertainty, of travelling alone.*

go outside and strain my ears; then over the horizon appears a cloud of dust, followed by two very large and very new lorries, each towing a trailer wagon and carrying a handful of passengers. I flag down the first one; the driver is happy to give me a lift and in I climb. It transpires that the lorries are part of a six-truck UNDP convoy returning from delivering food to displaced persons in the war zone.

Such lorries are not fast but they are relatively comfortable and I am well pleased with the lift. The driver has been all over, driving lorries across the Sahara to Tripoli, Algeria, Agadez, Tunis. The only problem with the journey is lack of water – I have stupidly managed to leave my water bottle in the fridge at Mao and by the time we reach Mussokori in the early afternoon I am so thirsty I can hardly speak. In desperation I manage to down 1.5 litres of disgusting Camerounian fizz.

The convoy of UN lorries is staying the night and I should probably stay with them; but I am short of time and anxious to get back to N'Djamena. A pick-up was meant to be leaving "toute de suite" so I decide to take it. At 4pm it still hasn't left. I transfer to another pick-up, we leave, get stuck in the sand, push it out, get stuck again . . . "toute de suite" passes us, we push ours out again and pass them, with much glee.

At 6pm we stop in a village where we are all instructed to dismount while the driver simply wanders off. I try to find out what's going on and am told that he has gone to meet his wife and that we'll be leaving again in an hour. I bet. I sit down on a rug, feeling very tired. Not just physically tired, but tired of the endless waits, of the uncertainty, of travelling on my own. At 7.30pm our driver comes back and we pile in, only to find the *Sûreté* suddenly want to see my papers – I have only been sitting outside their office for the last hour-and-a-half! Still, at least they are quick and pleasant.

We set off, stop to pick up wood – everyone off, load the cargo of wood, everyone on again – then, on the outskirts of N'Djamena, a motorbike roars up, overtakes us and demands we stop. Apparently we have failed to stop at a checkpoint. Back we go, off we get, and watch them go through all our baggage. Arriving at N'Djamena market at about 9.30pm, I flag down a taxi to take me to the house and collapse.

TRAVEL NOTES

Languages Largely Arabic in the north and French in the south, plus about seventy local languages.

Transport The number of surfaced roads is rapidly increasing, as are buses, though these remain largely confined to the south. Elsewhere your only option is to ask around for a lift. Travel this way is slow and erratic, but generally safe.

Accommodation Hotels are in short supply outside the capital. Again, your best bet is to ask around on arrival in a particular place.

Guides *Central Africa – A Travel Survival Kit* (Lonely Planet) has a concise but handy section on Chad.

CONTACTS

We know of no women's groups currently operating. Oxfam and UNICEF could put you in touch with development projects including women.

BOOKS

Margery Perham, *West African Passage – A Journey through Nigeria, Chad and the Cameroon* (UK, Peter Owen, 1983). Journal account of Perham's six-month tour of West Africa in 1931. Although she was sent out there on business, the liveliest accounts are of her unconventional free-time adventures.

 Charlotte Bruner (ed), *Unwinding Threads* (UK & US, Heinemann, 1995). Copious anthology of African women's writing that provides a good overview: see also the general bibliography on p. 692.

Thanks to Chris Johnson for supplying much of the information for the Introduction and Travel Notes.

Chile

For sixteen years Chile was home to one of the most brutally repressive military regimes in Latin America. Despite the army's ability to hold onto certain key positions, the establishment of democracy that began with the final defeat of General Pinochet in 1989 – if still somewhat fragile – seems likely to remain. That said, however, it is hard to forget the widescale political repression that overshadows the nation's recent past, evident in the sense of insecurity and genuine fear of another military coup that still pervades many people's lives.

Hundreds of political exiles have returned and the country is becoming more and more popular with all kinds of visitors, from foreign business people to package tourists and independent travellers; overwhelming hospitality and a general lack of crime against tourists – as well as a relatively low-key breed of machismo –

make this one of the more relaxing Latin American countries to explore. Most of the population is concentrated in central Chile, in and around the capital, Santiago, and in the beautiful lake district, home of the Mapuche Indians. Santiago is an attractive, lively city, though its magnificent setting with the snow-capped Andes as a backdrop is too often obscured by smog, while the lakes are some of the most picturesque in the world. Elsewhere, in the northern desert (covering roughly a quarter of the country) and south toward the glacial region of Patagonia, transport is more erratic and accommodation can be hard to find. Travel in general tends to be expensive with prices at their highest in the south and everywhere during the high season of December to March.

Women have long been very active in the political and public life of Chile and for several years Santiago boasted a higher proportion of women in the professions and in further education than most Western capitals. At the forefront of the country's struggle for democracy, many were also counted among the murdered, tortured and disappeared of the Pinochet era. Today there are numerous women's organizations, one of the biggest being CODEM (Defence Committee for Women's Rights) which co-ordinates a large network of working-class women's organizations. Local groups in different parts of the country develop training schemes for women in areas such as health and technical skills; they campaign for women's legal rights, for adequate housing, and for the release of political prisoners; and organize soup kitchens, alternative schools, cultural events and protest activities, especially in the *barrios* or shanty towns. Santiago also houses the main office of Isis International, a long-established women's information and communication service, that collects and distributes resources from all over the world, as well as co-ordinating a women and health network for Latin America and the Caribbean.

Travels in a Thin Country

Sara Wheeler spent six months travelling 2600 miles through Chile alone. The following extracts are from her book, *Travels in a Thin Country* (for details see *Travel Notes* at the end of this chapter). We take up the tale as she hitches a lift down from the Altiplano, where she has just spent a week at 15,000 feet near the Bolivian border.

The lorry skidded to a halt a few yards ahead of me, causing a minor cyclone, and I climbed up into the grimy cab, met by two sweaty and smiling dark brown faces. I reckoned the journey back down to Arica would take about eight hours. It was to turn out rather differently.

The truck was loaded with 34 tons of timber on its way to the United States. Simon and Rodriguez sat a couple of feet apart in the front seats and I perched on the narrow wooden bed behind them. A large plastic model of the Virgin in prayer, her body wreathed in fluorescent roses, was swinging violently from the mirror. (This, the South American equivalent of the furry dice, was to become a familiar sight on my trip.) Most of the metal in the cab was exposed and dented, and wherever possible it had been decorated with circular stickers printed with pithy Bolivian aphorisms such as "Virginity kills: inoculate yourself". Every few minutes the two men dipped their stubby fingers into crumpled paper bags on the dashboard and took out lurid jellyish sweeties. I ate one of these later. It tasted of chemicals.

> *On the wall were pinned two posters, one of Samantha Fox and one of a dying Christ: a typical, Chilean juxtaposition.*

I had underestimated the capacity of 34 tons of wood to slow a vehicle down. In addition, the height of the cab magnified the bumps (there were many bumps) and I often clenched my eyes in pain as *soroche*, as South Americans know altitude sickness, flooded back. When the sun began to set behind the furthest arid foothills I made a headrest out of my sleeping bag, and then the pink and orange liquid Andean sky turned my torture chamber into a palace.

The truck got a puncture, and it took two hours to fix it. When we set off again I asked Simon when we would be arriving in Arica. "En uñ ratito", he said, a phrase I had already heard many times in Chile. It had the same connotations as *manana* in Spain (without the sense of urgency, as the old joke goes). It was the first of many journeys which took far longer than it would ever have been possible to imagine at the outset, and by the end of my six months in Chile I experienced a sense of achievement whenever I actually arrived anywhere.

At midnight a building materialized out of the blackness. It was surrounded by Bolivian trucks. We pulled over, got out, and Simon hustled me inside, where an Aymara family were watching a black-and-white television behind a straw screen. On the wall someone had pinned two posters, one of Samantha Fox and one of a dying Christ: a nice, and typical, Chilean juxtaposition. In the front portion of the building Simon and Rodriguez greeted about fifteen of their compatriots and we joined them at a long table.

He lay down, breathing heavily. I sat rigid in the passenger seat.

Thus it was that at 13,000 feet on a cold night in the sterile heart of the Andes I ate greasy *cazuela* with seventeen Bolivian truckers.

We set off again. It was cold, and inky black. At about three o'clock Simon announced that we were going to snatch a couple of hours sleep, and he parked the lorry on a verge. The hapless Rodriguez was despatched into the back of the truck with blankets, and I was motioned forward while Simon made up the bed behind the seats. He lay down, breathing heavily. I sat rigid in the passenger seat.

"Why don't you come back here?" he said alluringly. "It's much more comfortable." After two or three further attempts at persuasion he fell asleep. I tried to do the same in the passenger seat, but the man could have snored for Bolivia, so I put my thermal gloves on and watched the stars until the sky transformed itself from deep black to the pale pearly shades of an oyster, and sunlight leaked from the east.

A cockerel crowed, but it was a very old cockerel, and halfway through his wheezy crow collapsed into a rasping cough. A small dairy farm coalesced out of the gloom. A man was chasing cows around a pen. Simon woke up with a snort. He shouted at Rodriguez, spat on the floor of the cab, got out and stumbled around outside. We left in a hurry with a lot of farting, past the man who had been chasing cows, standing now in the sunlight concentrating on a mirror hanging on a gatepost and working at his chin with a cutthroat razor.

It came as no suprise when, a few miles down the road, the lorry broke down. I reckoned we were about twenty-five miles from Arica. Despite the fact that I had a hard slog ahead of me to any kind of settlement, with only a brief period of pleasant air temperature between extreme cold and extreme heat, I couldn't stand another stultifying day literally getting nowhere with the Bolivians. Simon was displaying pointed indifference towards me. He felt the rebuff of the previous night, and the breakdown meant that he couldn't be bothered to fuss around a gringa.

So I picked up the carpetbag and started down the deserted road, the pale light of morning hanging over the Lluta valley ahead of me. As I left, Simon belched loudly.

Later in the trip Sara Wheeler spent a month in the capital, Santiago.

As I came to know the urban sprawl I found a home at the *marisquerias* (seafood bars) of the central market, where I could linger anonymously at a gingham tablecloth after a bowl of shellfish and a glass of cloudy wine, looking out onto wet fish counters piled with gleaming corpses, exotically nameless in English, and heaps of prawn tails and bristly sea-urchins. Men in black caps slammed machetes onto outsize chopping boards, and others pushed trolleys between the aisles, white boots meeting white rubber aprons. Itinerant guitarists played Violeta Parra folksongs to diners, and the waitress called me the South American equivalent of "pet". A handful of suited executives came in and out, but the market was largely the territory of the old school, slicked-back hair, cardigans and string shopping bags. I even got used to spooning shellfish juice into my wine.

We saw men dressed as nuns acting out a ritual which involved simulated oral sex and shooting up.

My new friends and I often went to *Spandex*, my favourite nightclub in Santiago. It was open on Fridays only and located in a cavernous old theatre in the centre of town. It was a great place to go at one or two in the morning after doing something else, and, as in all good nightclubs, it was perfectly acceptable to have a nap on one of the many sofas if you felt tired. *Spandex* exemplified counterculture, and it was full of eccentrics; I couldn't help wondering where these people were during the day, as I seldom saw anyone like them on the streets.

Most of the nightclubs in the city were located in the *barrio alto*, lair of the rich, and were peopled with glamorous society types and wealthy poseurs. The nouveau riche syndrome in Santiago was repellent. It was particularly unpalatable when observed among the young: men and women of twenty whose aspirations were to own a Landrover and eat in *Pizza Hut*, their cellular phones at their side, worshipping at their dual shrines of conformism and ostentation. Anyway, *Spandex* was different. Small podia were provided for solo dancing performances by anyone who felt the urge, and the evening was punctuated by the occasional floor show. These latter seemed to be predicated on the concept of cramming as many taboos into one act as possible. We saw men dressed up as nuns acting out a ritual which involved simulated oral sex and shooting up (not simultaneously), and a bizarre dance by three people dressed up as rabbits stretching condoms between their teeth. I didn't care much for the acts, but I enjoyed *Spandex* very much, as its laid-back flavour and sense that you could do anything or nothing without being watched were unusual qualities for a nightclub.

I never made it to closing time, though; the latest I managed was five, when it was still pulsating with energy. One night we ran into some Frenchmen there whom I knew; they were botanists, and had been working in Chile for eight months. I had first met them in the north, and had seen them socially two or three times in the capital. They were leaving for Paris the next morning, and had booked a private bus to take them and their friends from home to the airport so the party could continue for as long as possible.

After *Spandex* we went to their flat and drank *pisco sours* for breakfast; the bus, inevitably, failed to turn up. Undaunted, the leading botanist strode out onto Apoquindo, one of the main streets of Santiago (it was rush hour by now), leapt onto a public bus and offered the driver approximately twenty pounds in cash to collect everyone from the flat and proceed to the airport. "Everyone off!" shouted the driver without a moment's hesitation, and the disgruntled and besuited passengers disembarked into the polluted morning air.

The buses of Santiago are a phantasmagoria. Over a thousand per hour travel in each direction along the city's main artery at peak time. It is difficult to understand what Pinochet's total deregulation meant for the city. A transport economist at the Catholic University told me that average vehicle ownership among bus-service operators is two, and that as there are several large fleets this means that many people own just one antediluvian vehicle which they loan to a hapless driver who works on commission. It isn't surprising that both congestion and pollution stand at record levels.

After several months in Patagonia and Tierra del Fuego the author insinuated herself on a military plane from Punta Arenas to Antarctica.

A contingent of air force personnel larked around with redundant blocks of polystyrene, shouting above the noise of the Hercules's North American engines. Every single person except me had brought protective earphones. The bastards could have told me, I thought.

We advanced over the gunmetal Strait, the sky streaked with salmon pink and petrol blue clouds. The Strait was so narrow that I began to appreciate Magellan's achievement in finding it. The sepulchral islets of the Beagle Channel melted into the clouds, and when the plane next descended through the white blanket the Southern Ocean was pierced with icebergs. Everything was shining. It was like entering another universe, a surreal one, beyond us. A block of polystyrene flew across the cabin and hit me on the shoulder.

We landed in a roar. When the door was opened a glacial blast swept into the Hercules, and as I set foot on Antarctica, my heart singing, a man dressed like a yeti approached me.

"Mrs Sara Wheeler? Welcome to Antarctica. I am Comandante Leopaldo, and you are my responsibility on this icy continent."

He looked as though this were an onerous task, so I tried to be friendly, to break the ice, as it were.

On the third day in Antarctica I climbed a glaciated hill with a saturnine Uruguayan vulcanologist. It was hard work, but at the top the ice desert appeared in all its glory, aspirin-white and refulgent in the late afternoon sunlight. The circumpolar sea was rippling like a wheatfield, and as their shadows lengthened the icebergs took on an incandescent quality; I stood there and watched a single snow petrel fly among them, gliding through its private symphony against a Hockney-blue sky. There was no sound at all except the occasional metallic tap-tap as the vulcanologist, a hundred yards away, scraped snow into a specimen tin. Nobody owned it; that was the thrilling thing. It was like seeing the earth for the very first time, and I felt less homeless there than I had ever felt anywhere. I did not want to take a photograph, and I could not: I knew that moment would always be with me, and I did not want to betray it with a picture.

It was like seeing the earth for the first time, and I felt less homeless there than I had ever felt anywhere.

I did leave Chile, eventually. A friend threw a party for me, and with true South American brio it was still raging when I had to leave for the airport at six in the morning. The plane to Rio was delayed for three hours, which meant that I would miss my next two connections. I felt exhausted, miserable, hungover and desperate, and I hadn't even left yet. The airport was brightly lit, even at that hour, and the grime and litter of the concourse stood out in sharp focus, as did the anxiety and fatigue of the passengers who eddied pathetically around the coffee bar, which was out of coffee.

I found a red plastic seat and sat on it, my feet resting on the carpet-bags. There was nothing I had ever wanted to do less than leave Chile. With my eyes closed, to still the sick misery of that moment, I called up the memory of a birthday lunch on the shore of a bright blue lake – a bottle of warm champagne, the crisp, still air, the saffron steppe and purple mists of Patagonia, the trail of ducks breaking the surface of the water, the ponderous curlicues of smoke rising from the rim of a volcano, the trill of the chucao and the sweet taste of the box-leafed barberry, the synchronous shadows of a flock of black-necked swans on an Andean mountain – and after a few minutes the calm elation of that day came to me again, and I knew I would make it come many times over the months and years which would be known as "after Chile", so I wasn't really leaving at all.

TRAVEL NOTES

Languages Spanish and some remaining indigenous languages.

Transport Buses are many and frequent. Travelling directly from north to south, or vice versa, internal flights are quick and comfortable, but you obviously miss out on much.

Accommodation A wide range of hotels and pensions at all prices can be found throughout the country. There are also quite a few youth hostels. Most towns have a tourist information office and it's easy just to ask someone in the street to direct you somewhere.

Special Problems Remember to buy Chilean-made products whenever possible. You are usually offered brand-name imported goods at highly inflated prices. Beware of taking part in any overt anti-government activity. A foreign passport doesn't necessarily make you immune to police brutality.

Guides *The South American Handbook* (UK, Trade and Travel/US, Passport Press) has a helpful, though somewhat limited chapter on Chile. Also recommended is *Chile and Easter Island – A Travel Survival Kit* (Lonely Planet).

CONTACTS

For up-to-date information, contact *Chile Democratico*, 15 Wilkin St, London NW3 3NL (☎0171/284 2400). Or write to *Isis International Women's Information and Communication Service*, Casilla 2067, Correo Central, Santiago, Chile (☎490 271). *Isis* has a huge network of contacts, especially in Latin America and the Caribbean, produces publications and houses an excellent resource centre to which visitors are welcome.

BOOKS

★ **Sara Wheeler**, *Travels in a Thin Country* (UK, Little Brown, 1994). A pacy, informed account of the author's six-month solo journey zig-zagging the entire length of Chile. Wheeler manages to pack in an extraordinary diversity of experiences, from camping in Patagonia to hitching a lift on a supply boat around Cape Horn, and relays it all with verve and intelligence. One of the bold new voices in British travel writing.

Marjorie Agosin, *Scraps of Life: The Chilean Arpilleras – Chilean Women and the Pinochet Dictatorship* (UK, Zed Books, 1987/US, Red Sea Press) *Arpilleras* are artisan women who make lacquered cloth wall hangings; this book is an examination, through their accounts and art, of their sufferings under the dictatorship. Many lost husbands to the military: they tell stories of jail, torture and bureaucracy. Moving, if a little short on analysis.

Joan Jara, *Victor, An Unfinished Song* (UK, Jonathan Cape, 1983). Moving account of her life with Victor Jara, the legendary Chilean folksinger who was murdered by the military in 1973.

Sheila Cassidy, *Audacity to Believe* (UK, Darton, Longman & Todd, 1992).Tells of the author's experiences in prison during some of the worst years of the Pinochet dictatorship when, as a British doctor, she was incarcerated and tortured for treating a wounded revolutionary.

★ **Alicia Partnoy (ed)**, *You Can't Drown the Fire: Latin American Women Writing in Exile* (UK, Virago, 1989/US, Cleis Press, 1988). Anthology of essays, stories, poetry, letters and songs by 35 Latin American women, including Veronica de Negri, Cecilia Vicuna, Marjorie Agosin and Isabel Morel Letelier from Chile.

Jo Fisher, *Out of the Shadows* (UK, Latin America Bureau, 1993). Fascinating account of the rise of the autonomous women's movement in Latin America: includes two chapters on Chile.

Elizabeth Jelin (ed), *Citizenship and Identity. Women and Social Change in Latin America* (UK, Zed Books, 1990). Examines women's roles in Latin American movements for social change, ranging from the Mothers of the Disappeared in Argentina to trade union organizations in Chile.

FICTION

Isabel Allende, *House of the Spirits* (UK, Black Swan, 1986/US, Bantam) and *Of Love and Shadows* (UK, Black Swan, 1988/US, Bantam). Two compulsive novels, the first interweaving family saga with political events in an unnamed Latin American country; the second dealing with a passionate love affair against a similar background of violent political turmoil. See also *Eva Luna* (UK, Penguin, 1990/US, Bantam, 1989).

Also look out for novels by José Donoso, Ariel Dorfman, Antonio Skarmeta and the poetry of Pablo Neruda and Gabriela Mistral.

China

Outwardly, China is booming. In the years since 1989, when the world watched in horror as Chinese tanks crushed the students' pro-democracy movement in Tiananmen Square, the pace of change has been frenetic. The shift toward a "socialist market" economy, central to the modernization policy set in motion in the early 1980s by Deng

Xiaoping, has led to a massive rise in annual economic growth. Stock markets have opened, tourism has become a profitable business and millions of new consumers are flocking to buy the electronic goods now flooding the shops. Yet China's "economic miracle" has brought with it a new set of problems. Soaring inflation (widely blamed on the investment craze) suggests the prospect of recession, while rising unemployment and the widening poverty gap fuels a simmering undercurrent of social discontent. Crime is also on the increase and many China-watchers have grave doubts whether the government can cope with the demands of its people, exacerbated by the uncertainty of what will happen after the death of Deng Xiaoping. The events of Tiananmen Square may be long gone, but the brutality of the government crackdown stands as a reminder of the lengths the leadership is prepared to go to in its determination to preserve the political status quo.

China is vast (the third largest country in the world) and immensely varied, both in the scale and breadth of its landscape and the legacies of its history, stretching back some five thousand years. The countryside, from the great northern plateaux bounded by Tibet down to the peaks and caves of Guilin in the southwest, is often breathtaking. And though few monuments survived the years of the Cultural Revolution, there is still a thrill to be had from the chance to penetrate deeper into the world's oldest civilization.

The official enthusiastic approach to tourism and subsequent opening up of all but the most remote border areas in recent years have made it easier to get around. On the other hand, travel in China is still rife with frustrations. Bureaucracy, involving anything from the hazards of negotiating two currencies (foreigners are encouraged to use special Foreign Exchange Certificates rather than *renminbi* or "people's money") to waiting in line for a bus ticket, can be a nightmare. It's standard practice to charge foreigners more than local people for virtually everything. Western visitors are never allowed to forget or ignore their status as *wai guoren* (literally "outside country persons") and you can expect to be constantly stared at, especially outside the major cities like Canton, Shanghai or the capital Beijing. As a woman, having elected to abandon family and "motherland" in order to travel across the world, you're even more of an oddity. Chinese women today are still expected to seek fulfilment and social sanction through marriage: not having a husband or children to cement you in the family structure makes you an incomprehensible entity to most Chinese. Although safety does not appear to be a particular problem and reports of foreign women experiencing sexual harrasment are rare, you may prefer to travel with a companion just to share the attention.

Many of the prominent student leaders during the democracy movement, and some of the most outspoken and brave sympathizers among journalists and intellectuals, were **women**. In heralding a new, and as yet unborn China, the movement gave voice to a group of female political activists on an equal status with men for the first time. For these women, concern for the future of their nation took precedence over feminist issues.

China has always been a patriarchy. The Communist era heralded enormous changes for women, while at the same time institutionalizing the problem of dual labour. According to Mao's two zeals, women were expected both to help build the socialist future and fulfil their traditional family role. Many women now have full access to education and employment; contraception is free, abortion legal, and divorce instigated by wives is common. But the traditional view that women are specially suited to certain jobs (childcare and housework) and incapable of others (anything too mentally and physically taxing), as well as the Confucian ideal of the three obediences to father, husband and son, are as strong as ever. The clearest and most frightening demonstration of women's subordinate status has been the increase in female infanticide, associated with the introduction of the one-child-per-family policy. Whether the fourth United Nations World Conference on Women, hosted in Beijing in

1995, is merely a public relations exercise on the part of the government or will bring about a genuine improvement in the status of Chinese women remains to be seen.

On the Trail of the Great Chinese Economic Revolution

After graduating from university **Kerry McKibbin** taught for over a year in Japan, where she became disillusioned with the sexual harassment encountered from both students and the boss of her language school. Eventually she escaped by boat to China where she spent three months on her own backpacking from Beijing down to Hong Kong. Originally from the Isle of Man, she currently works as a freelance television researcher in London.

On board the China Shipping Line ferry from Japan, I had no need of my guidebook's hints on "How to Meet the Chinese". My fellow passenger, Ken Ki Cho had volunteered herself as my guide and together we spent three surreal days speaking pidgin Japanese in the ship's sauna. Curiously darting glances across at each other's naked bodies, this unusually intimate situation provoked deep discussion of our recent histories, our relationships and future plans. Like the majority of passengers, Cho had just completed three years of privileged study in Japan. Her professors had shown her countless newspaper and magazine articles written by Japanese businessmen worried and amazed at the rapid expansion occurring in China. What did her family think of that, I asked. She wasn't sure. Her only contact with China had been an occasional letter from her mother and sisters. But they worked on the land and would know nothing of the changes occurring in Beijing or Shanghai. Now in the luxurious heat of the sauna she dreamed of a high-flying, well-paid career in electronic engineering.

On the third day there was sudden commotion. Mah Jong boards were abandoned and card games gathered up as passengers piled on layers of thermal underwear. I stood shivering on the deck with wet hair. The afternoon was overcast. It was sleeting heavily. This was my first solo backpacking journey outside the security of Japan and for the first time, it struck me that everyone else was going home: Cho was meeting her student friends in Beijing, other passengers were giddily returning with gifts for their relatives. I was nothing more than a lone speck on some exotic map. As I stared down at the armed guards marching along the Tianjin harbour wall a knot twisted in my stomach.

In the chaos outside the ferry terminal a hoard of khaki-coated men pressed in on Cho and myself and bundled us onto the nearest bus where I sat squashed up against a frozen window while the driver – a Castro look-alike in an ex-army greatcoat complete with shoulder stripes – revved the engine to screaming point before lurching forward onto the main highway, a string of plastic grapes swinging wildly across his windscreen. Unwilling to halt at signals, he blasted his way through traffic lights, passengers haring after us, prostrating themselves across the doors and clambering in while we were still in motion. Oil constantly leaked from the gear box and mixed with spit and tea leaves on the floor. On he raced, Beijing Opera music flooding out of the front speakers. A mother sitting next to me leant over, slid my window open slightly and stood her little boy on my knee so that he could pee through the crack.

The woman dragged us from our seats, out of the doors and dumped our bags down into the slush.

As we neared Beijing, a fight broke out between the tight-faced woman ticket-collector and a male passenger. Cho anxiously revealed that the initial fare had inexplicably gone up and that those who refused to pay would be thrown off. After several frenzied attempts at extracting the supplement from us, the woman dragged us from our seats, out of the doors and dumped our bags down into the slush. And so it was that I first entered China, bouncing along the black, shiny streets in a smart sidecar, grinning up at my new friend Cho who was strapped behind the solid woman driver. "My business!" shouted back our driver proudly. "International taxi service!"

Was it a year spent walking clinical Japanese streets that made the out-skirts of Beijing so shocking? The road ahead was pitch black, cars and lorries flashing their headlights to warn us of their presence. Fruit sellers displayed their wares by candlelight; I was surprised when we overtook a horse-drawn cart. This was more an Elizabethan landscape than a capital city. In the lights of the headlamp I picked out four chickens dangling upside down each side of a bicycle's handlebars. The owner had tied them on by the feet and cycled along, legs held at right angles, out of pecking range. Street lights began to appear and I could make out low, crumbling houses with felt roofs held down with bricks. Outside, cabbages were slung over coal cellars. We raced past one narrow *huton* (alley) after another. Each was incredibly narrow and muddy. I wondered down which *huton* Cho would sleep that night.

At the hotel Cho found me, the owner claimed she only had double rooms. The building felt suspiciously empty. I was surprised to find a caretaker on each landing. The first was reclined, feet up on her desk;

the second was knitting with a bright yellow ball of wool; the caretaker on my floor was almost asleep. Scowling, she led me to my room and dumped a flask of boiled water on the table. Two cups sat still filled with the dregs of jasmine tea and the bed was unmade. A locked door in the en suite bathroom adjoined the next room where a woman and man were arguing. I lifted the toilet gingerly – all was mercifully clean. The woman's voice grew more high pitched and frantic; from the car park came the sound of a windscreen shattering. Shouts, a scuffle, the sound of running footsteps. Beijing felt out of control.

I did not want to leave that hotel the next morning. Dire though it was, I dreaded setting forth into the street; but I had to find my bearings. Men loitered on the street corner but said nothing as I walked by. Outside a noodle shop, children played a game with fistfuls of straw. Garbage cans with their lids up lined the street, overflowing with rotting vegetables. At the end of the street, a mountain of cabbages stood twelve feet high. I

A man flung himself at the ticket booth. Two uniformed women stood on a ledge, beating him back.

turned down a narrow alley where a group of workmen were squatting by the gutter, slurping noodles from metal basins. A woman took my arm and led me away, indicating that it would be dangerous to continue. Suddenly we were on a wide boulevard with high-rise buildings, cars, trees in tubs. It could have been anywhere in Europe.

These were the streets Cho insisted we stick to when I met her later. I noticed that the white leather shoes she had carefully cleaned before we stepped off the boat were now scuffed and muddy. "Look at that posh hotel!" she would exclaim. "That wasn't there three years ago . . . Over there on the right – that's an American clothes shop, isn't it?" We ate at Kentucky Fried Chicken, drank coffee on the top floors of glass-fronted hotels and shopped at the Friendship Store. Cho was ecstatic to be back in Beijing.

She insisted we arrive at Tiananmen Square by taxi. The square was very large and very empty. I looked in vain for evidence of the atrocities I had read so much about but it was as though nothing had ever happened. A few families bought ice cream from stalls and hawkers tried to sell wind-up paper birds which flew for a few seconds before clattering down on the paving slabs. In the subway beneath the square, a football match might have just finished. Hundreds of locals were packed together, some squeezed behind stalls. A man at the plimsoll stall held a bewildered old woman by the throat, shouting into her face. Cho dragged me to the train station where the same frantic atmosphere awaited me. I had been warned about queues at stations but had never imagined that each would be six bodies deep. As the customers pushed against each other, one would suddenly pop out of line and fight to regain their place. At the front, a man flung himself at the grille which protected the ticket booth. Two uniformed women stood on a ledge level with the counter, beating him back.

I was determined to travel to Guiyang in the south of the country and bought a ticket from a black marketeer. Guiyang had its problems (six million beneath the Chinese poverty line), but according to my guidebook it was typical of the current economic development in China. I wanted to see what this great and unexpected twentieth-century miracle looked like there. Cho couldn't understand why I should trade Beijing's luxury for Guiyang, but she waved me off from my hotel as I took a rickshaw to the station the next day.

Like every transaction in China, negotiating the bicycle rickshaw for the short journey to the station involved lengthy negotiation. The driver had started with complicated Chinese hand signals to signify numbers, but we soon reverted to bargaining on paper. As fifty yen became twenty-five, shoemakers, cooks, a butcher and an ironmonger stood watching from the sidelines. Each gave his opinion on whether the price was fair or not. Eventually the driver strapped my rucksack between the bicycle and his two-wheeled cart and moved off into the sea of traffic.

A cook pedalled hard next to us, a steaming canister sloshing about behind him; a bus screamed across our path. I shut the canvas side flaps of the roof canopy, praying for a safe arrival. The driver snorted, coughed and spat onto the street, first to the left, then to the right. I remembered the signs in English I had pointed out to Cho: "Do not spit!" According to her, the Chinese translation was slightly different: "Aim your spit carefully!" The driver snorted again, this time using his hand to blow his nose with great precision, spraying mucus first over my left foot and then over my right. On the way he'd met a collaborator. They had cycled level with each other, plotting. On reaching the station, the collaborator thrust his head through the canvas side flap. "Fifty yen" he hissed, flicking a knife blade in front of my face.

Guiyang city centre assaulted my senses the moment I stepped out of the hotel. Red brick dust blew in my face. I had to walk the main street with half-closed eyes, my scarf pulled right up to protect my mouth. Every building was gutted; every road surface mercilessly torn up. A man picked his way across a crumbling wall, silhouetted against two gleaming, new towerblocks. My ears nearly exploded with the constant pounding and drilling. I passed a team of men who were breaking bricks by hand. Others were tottering in plimsolls over heaps of jagged rubble, shoulders breaking under heavy yokes.

Rain had begun, transforming the brick dust into a light brown, swimming mud. A line of hard-faced women stood freezing at a makeshift bus stop, hands in their trouser pockets, stiletto heels perching them high above the slime. Buses and jeeps spliced their way around exposed, metal sewer covers, leaving the women angry in their spattered patent. Everywhere, crazed development was out of all proportion and control. A butcher sold sheep's innards from his bicycle; the bright red stomach hung over the crossbar like a deflated rubber ball, passing shoppers fingering it despondently. Disorientated inhabitants emerged from breeze-block shacks with hungry eyes; they neither knew nor cared that Cartier had hit Shanghai. They stared as I photographed the plastic tables with their gaudy, fringed umbrellas which stood next to the noodle stands – a touch of the Bahamas on the edges of Hell.

Inhabitants emerged from the breeze-block with hungry eyes; they neither knew nor cared that Cartier had hit Shanghai.

Back at the dank and freezing hotel lobby in Guiyang, the receptionist was chatty as usual. We were the same age which, in China (as I would later discover to my disadvantage), spelt instant camaraderie. She was preparing for a wedding reception that afternoon but found time to devour my British postcards. "Who sent you to China?" she constantly asked me. It was beyond her comprehension that I could have earned enough money alone. "No matter how hard I work, my money is worth nothing outside this country" she sighed. "China's face is changing but it's still the same people who travel and fill the beds in this hotel." I recalled the moment at the airport where I had surprised a group of Mao-suited, communist die-hards swilling copious amounts of imported whisky in the splendour of the first-class waiting room. "And I don't even want to emigrate," she continued "only go outside – only to look." Her words stuck with me. I was sure this natural desire to get away and put one's life in perspective was inherent in the collective frustration, the fighting and the tension I had witnessed on the Beijing streets. There the people aren't just accepting flimsy promises of material change. They want to experience the results now.

The wedding party trooped past singing at the tops of their voices. Heartened, the receptionist translated the song as a wish for the birth of a baby boy. Their song still echoed in my ears days later as I tramped along the backs of the fields below a certain Yunnan mountain. Women were bent over their vegetable patches and hadn't noticed this

Western traveller closing in on them from behind. Looking down, I had been balancing along the grass strips which separated some disused patches when suddenly – shockingly – I had spied a baby's skull sticking up out of the soil. Another lay close by, barely covered by a thin layer of earth; a few more holes were dotted around. I watched the women intently, but if any really had murdered their baby daughters, they didn't flinch – just carried on, heads bent, tilling the soil.

> *Alone on the mountain side, we stopped. "Ka-ree", he began. "Perhaps we can become special friends."*

Buying breakfast on my first day in this isolated Yunnan village I had met the local entrepreneur, James, as he called himself. Emerging from behind a screen, he had drifted over to take my order. He was wearing a smart jacket with a fur-lined collar, which gave him a luxurious air I had seen in few Chinese people. Discovering we were both born in 1969, we chatted as Chinese equals and he invited me to join him and his friends on a hike.

Our party consisted of James (sporting a bright red cravat and trilby), his friend from the rubber factory (where a power failure had resulted in an impromptu holiday) and an old man who insisted on buying bread and bananas before our ascent.

The vegetation was semi-tropical. Big palms and ferns lined our path. No one wanted to carry the bag of bananas so we stopped regularly to eat, admiring the village lake below us. Half way up the mountain, I went to pee behind a line of fir trees, finding when I came out that our chaperones had disappeared. The climb up to the top would be too much for the old man, James explained. As we continued climbing right up into the snow James began to annoy me; he insisted on taking my hand to help me over icy patches on the slopes. Completely alone on the mountain side, we eventually stopped. "Ka-ree", he began. "Perhaps we can become special friends." Warning bells were clanging. And what exactly did he mean by that? "We can write to each other" he explained. "Then one day, we can get married like my friend. He met a Dutch girl here. Now he has his own car and apartment in Amsterdam and", he added, "his wife is still a modern career woman."

He was offended at my amused refusal. "Don't you like me?" he asked incredulously. I mumbled a guilt-ridden criticism of oppressive regimes restricting free travel. "Agh! But you misunderstand my heart!" he retorted, angrily. "Can't you see? The gods have sent you! We were both born in the same week of the same month of the same year – the year of the Rooster. You are my chicken and I your cock!"

Yet another free enterprise venture was operating outside Yangshou village. Having spurned the tourist pilgrimage to Moon Hill, I had rented a bike which soon revealed itself to have a flat back tyre. Not to be put off, I ground heavily onwards out of the town, marvelling at the mysteriously formed hills rising sporadically like salt pillars from the surrounding flat plain, determined to seek out the real Yangshou. A mile later it came to me. A wiry, upright woman with bright eyes and an open smile neatly propped her bicycle against the hedge and proceeded to pump up my back tyre with great vigour. "Do not worry!" she called over her shoulder. "I only want to practise my English." After giving the tyre a last professional squeeze, she whisked a pocketbook out of her bicycle basket and handed it to me for examination.

Two young girls snuffled their way in from school, unsurprised to see a foreigner shelling peanuts in their living room.

It was crammed with foreigners' accounts of this woman, who introduced herself as Lee, a local farmer. The accounts praised her desire to improve her English, thanked her for her generosity in inviting strangers into her own home. Would I care to come to supper too? All she asked was that I buy a few traditional print postcards of the surrounding area. It was the least I could do. I congratulated myself on my good luck as I whizzed behind her back along the main road, the white-painted tree trunks which lined the ditches blurring as we passed.

Swiftly hoisting the bikes over the threshold, Lee slammed the huge barn door behind us, leaving only a square of light to come in through an open back door. She steered me towards a reclining, wicker chair piled high with knitting and offered me a cup of jasmine tea. Somewhere, a pendulum clock ticked. Did I like pork? she inquired. Was it too dark in here? Suddenly a naked bulb dangling from the ceiling was snapped on, illuminating a side of bacon hanging from the same wire. She took a cleaver, hacked off a slice and exited through the back door, leaving the bacon swinging. Huge, yellow, bulbous vegetables dangled from the exposed rafters. A large black-and-white photograph of a stern old woman dominated the white-washed back wall. Every few seconds a fizz and a hiss emitted from a collection of sealed pots beneath a table. Lee lifted one of the lids to reveal slowly pickling vegetables.

Two young girls snuffled their way in from school, unsurprised to see a foreigner shelling peanuts in their living room. Lee shrieked instructions from the outside kitchen and the reluctant pair took over the shelling.

Directly outside was a red, iron pump with a sandstone drainage area. A line of brightly coloured hand towels hung drying on a bamboo pole tacked to the wall. Next to this was a cotton holder with pockets containing four upright toothbrushes. Lee was merrily chopping vegetables on top of a smooth, stone slab. Behind her, a tarpaulin roof protected three squat brick ovens on top of which woks sat comfortably sizzling. My camera burned in my pocket.

At the low table, Lee urged more pork on me and taught me to push the rice quickly into my mouth by putting the bowl rim inside my bottom lip. As I brought the dish up, a bracelet bought in Yunnan glinted in the light. Would I buy one from her? At last an opportunity to show my gratitude (though I was embarrassed that her hospitality should be reduced to money). She pocketed another 10 yen and produced the pocketbook which I dutifully filled with praise: "By opening up her home, this woman is doing more for international understanding than the whole government put together. Keep up the good work." Immediately I had finished, she snapped it shut. Silence. The children perching on their upturned stools stared intently. The clock ticked. "One person; one meal – 20 yen", Lee stated in a business-like voice.

In her wisdom, Lee had managed to expose the holes in my dubious Western, political correctness.

The children giggled mockingly as I set off on my heavy bicycle. Silly, gullible foreigner jolting over pot holes in the pitch black, blinded by truck headlights, only the white-painted trees preventing me from falling into the steep ditches along the side of the road. How dare she mock my gratitude with her fake hospitality! I was angry at her and yet, as I pressed on, I realized I was most sickened at myself. In her wisdom, Lee had managed to expose the holes in my dubious Western, political correctness. I had thought of myself as a traveller, not a tourist, determined to seek out the real, contemporary China, to be a living part of history in the making. But she knew that at the bottom line, I had wanted to see inside a real, Chinese, peasant farmer's house, to gawp at how she survived with no running water, to store details of her uneven, earthen floor. If what I had wanted had been given freely within the framework of simple, unassuming peasant hospitality, I could have ignored my guilty motives. How did her neighbours regard her? I wondered. Did they admire her for making more money in one afternoon than they could imagine in a week?

The moon loomed behind the mysterious hills with all the beauty of Lee's picture postcards, but I didn't stop to savour the scene. Could no one see past my white, Western features in this country? I recounted those I had met on my travels. Almost every person I had been in contact with had been obsessed with the get-rich-quick syndrome and when they had spoken to me, it was to ask advice on how this might best be done. Had Cho, too, only been using me as a rice ticket, showing me glitzy Beijing hotels so that, with me, she could gain entry; showing me around the city just so she could exchange her People's Money for my foreigners' currency? I had hoped that our lengthy discussions meant more than that. I pedalled harder, breathing heavily to extract the doubt which stuck in the back of my throat.

One year later, I dropped into The Chinese Shopping Emporium off London's Kilburn High Road. The owner, Mrs Woo obligingly agreed to translate a letter I had received that day from Ken Ki Cho. Fetching her glasses, she leant over the counter. "She says you were the first British person she'd ever met," she began. "That you shared many thoughts together and that always you are in her mind. What's this?" she squinted. "Something about a sister?" Then she looked across at me, smiling admiringly. As a Chinese, she pays you the greatest complement of all. She says " I want to call you sister."

An Eastern Westerner in China

Adrienne Su, an American of Chinese descent, completed a year's study at Fudan University in Shanghai in June 1988. Her experiences of being mistaken for a citizen of the PRC (People's Republic of China) forced her to reconsider the privileges foreign travellers routinely depend on.

Not until a customs official at my port of entry into China berated me for speaking halting Chinese did I realize that my Chinese ancestry would exert a powerful influence on all my experiences in this country. My dealings with the Chinese differed from everything I had read in guidebooks. I had never questioned my being an American, but no one in China could tell I was one.

By government policy, a foreigner's dissatisfaction carries more weight than that of a Chinese citizen. If a road accident involves a foreigner, rescue forces arrive efficiently; if only PRC citizens are involved, the ambulance takes its time, if it comes at all. There are not enough ambulances around to accommodate everyone's needs and as a result the Chinese pay for the comfort of foreign guests.

In ticket offices, citizens may have to stand in line for a full day or more, therefore having to take turns with friends and relatives. Foreigners, on the other hand, are free to walk straight to the front. Soft sleepers on trains are available only to an elite few but any foreigner is free to buy a ticket. Large tourist hotels admit Chinese visitors only when accompanied by foreigners and once inside the staff treat the guests of their own nation with contempt while all but kneeling to their foreign companions. Unfortunately this policy is conducted on such a wide scale – the whole country – that it feels more like the privation of the human rights of the Chinese than the extension of hospitality to their visitors.

I detested this policy on arrival, but after a few months became accustomed to it and even grew to expect it. It's not only the expectation of special treatment that changes one's character; the daily observation of the Chinese in a lower position leaves a deep mental image. I was on the verge of thinking myself worth more than the Chinese when I reconsidered my experiences of being mistaken for a local resident. It had been mortifying to be ignored, shouted at, put last in line, and even pushed in favour of white tourists, while fellow Americans enjoyed an attentive service and paid no heed to my abuse. Just as I was appalled by the Chinese acceptance of a secondary status, I was ashamed of American travellers for riding on their privileges after all their talk about human rights and racial equality.

I was ashamed of American travellers for riding on their privileges after all their talk about human rights.

Repeated inhospitable receptions transformed my feelings of sympathy and kinship with the people of my ancestry. Until I made local friends, I found it hard to stay courteous and detached. Acquaintances from Japan, Taiwan, Hong Kong and Korea reported similar difficulties of feeling guilty for using privileges and angry at being denied them. (The black visitors I met faced even more extreme reactions; even in Shanghai, they had to contend with people staring, pointing and drawing away, all of which massively increased the pressures of travelling.) When I came across other white Westerners on the road, their attitude towards me was high-flown and condescending until I spoke English. It wasn't entirely their fault; the environment had deluded them into seeing the Chinese as less than people.

I also, however, found that there was an advantage to blending in, in that I could observe the street scenes without becoming one. Subtle differences in manner made me stand out, even when I dressed inconspicuously, but I could conceal myself in heavy traffic and large crowds, both of which China has in plentiful supply. Most people took me for a citizen of another region in China, or a tourist from another Asian country, and dismissed me as less strange than a Westerner, leaving me at peace to watch and not be watched.

In spite of the inconveniences I faced, I always felt reasonably safe. A solo woman is unlikely to encounter violence. Crowded buses make all women (and men) easy prey to wandering hands, and theft is on the increase in touristic cities like Canton and Guilin. But physical harm to a foreigner invites grave punishment and rarely occurs. It is easy, however, to drop precautions considered routine in the West simply because state media controls keep domestic crime inconspicuous.

Seldom does a Chinese man open a door for a woman, and on trains I have struggled alone to push my bag into a high luggage rack while Chinese men smoked and stared. Their attitude I attribute to the Cultural Revolution (1966–76) and not to Chinese culture itself. In comparison to most Asian cultures, the PRC has made great strides in restoring equal treatment of the sexes. Men and women all receive jobs upon finishing school, with comparable (although scant) salaries. The blue proletarian garb of Mao's China does away with feminine beauty and visually transforms the man and woman into nearly identical units. While many people still wear the old uniform, the streets of Canton and Shanghai boast short skirts, high heels and casual Western-style sportswear for both sexes.

A woman by herself evokes concern among the Chinese, who see convenience in numbers, if only to fight bureaucracy.

Too often, visitors dismiss the Chinese as an homogenous mass of people without considering the many different groups and classes that make up their society. To someone unfamiliar with Chinese ways, general similarities such as black hair, black eyes, plain clothing, and a slighter build than the average Westerner will make people of totally different characteristics seem identical. Until you have developed a sensitivity to cultural differences within China you will blame all Chinese for the offences of a few unhappy encounters. One obstacle is that many who consider themselves well-bred and educated feel it is improper to approach strangers unintroduced, which immediately limits the type of spontaneous contacts you'll make.

An advantage of travelling alone in China is that you do have more opportunities to meet people. The sight of a woman on the road by herself evokes concern among the Chinese, who see convenience in numbers, if only to fight the bureaucracy. Outside large cities, I was invited into homes, given food and escorted around town. One rule to keep in mind is that the Chinese almost always try to pick up the bill even if they haven't the money. Be sure to emphatically resist this and make a genuine effort to pay your share or both; not only is it rude to accept, but most PRC citizens live on minimal salaries that would make one foreign dinner guest a burdensome expense. By tradition a Chinese family gives the best of everything to a guest, even at great personal cost.

The extended absence of foreigners has very much increased their mystique, giving rise to rumours about our strange cuisine, etiquette, religions, courtship and rituals. Because no one trusts the government-printed newspapers, reports of the world outside are in high demand. People will treat you as an object in some places, but although you look unusual to them their fascination is more for the world you represent than for your personal peculiarity.

Every Shanghaiese there on the eve of the revolution remembers the British sign on the gate of a park: "No Chinese and dogs."

The Chinese conception of the *wai guoren* (foreigner) has been shaped by a dramatic history. Every Shanghaiese who was there on the eve of the revolution remembers the British sign on the gate of a Shanghai park: "No Chinese and dogs allowed." The European "spheres of influence" and the establishment of the Shanghai International Settlement humbled the Chinese, while foreigners enjoyed immunity from local law. Japanese atrocities in the 1930s left indelible memories.

Today, shortages and an enormous population require the pooling of the best resources in order to house, transport and feed foreign guests comfortably, and, considering past injuries, the Chinese are noble hosts. Most live in overcrowded quarters, whole families to a room, without indoor plumbing, and for everyone south of the Yangzi River, without indoor heating. Winter brings a harsh chill to Shanghai, Hangzhou and other southern cities. The discomforts of visitors, such as inefficient service, limited hot water, and difficulties in transport, are minimal compared to the limitations on the local quality of life. The tendency among foreigners, however, is to blame the Chinese for these inconveniences.

And it's easy to feel angry at China; every bus is early or late, many clerks are hostile, crowds push and clamour, and boarding trains, planes and coaches demands a physical struggle. People stare openly at foreigners, sometimes gathering in small crowds to observe while rash youths follow you around, trying to practise English and get a foreign address. You can quickly become overwhelmed by a language you do not properly comprehend and by customs, hemispheres removed from your own.

But beyond all this, there's no denying the grandeur of China's natural scenery, its position on the world scale and the influence it exerts over the rest of Asia. China requires patience, flexibility and humour. The unpredictability of wandering the Middle Kingdom has its rewards, and for women going it alone, it's bound to feel safer than home.

TRAVEL NOTES

Languages Standard Chinese (*putong hua* – "common speech" or Mandarin) is based on Beijing Chinese and understood everywhere to a degree. In addition there are major dialects such as Cantonese and Fujianese, plus distinct minority languages. English and Japanese are the main second languages taught in schools, but English is still spoken mainly in the bigger cities and by younger people. It is essential to learn some Chinese words and phrases and recognize the basic place names in characters.

Transport Visas are easy to obtain, though applications are complicated by having seven different types – be sure to contact travel agents or your nearest Chinese embassy in good time. Trains and buses are fairly efficient but incredibly cramped (unless you opt for first-class). Also beware of being overcharged. Hitching is officially frowned upon although it is possible to get lifts from long-distance lorry drivers. The main risk you'll face is arrest and a fine from the Chinese patrols – your driver, however, could lose his licence, face crippling fines and continuing suspicion by the authorities. It's important to pay as much as you can for your lift. Most towns have bicycle rental shops willing to rent out to foreigners, though it's worth buying your own if you aim to cycle for much more than a week.

Accommodation Tourists are designated specific hotels, generally the more expensive; it can be possible, however, to get a bed in their dormitories or cheaper rooms. Men and women are often clumped together but you can insist on a women only-room.

Special Problems None that affect women specifically. In general terms you should be sensitive to the political climate and discreet in your dealings with people you meet. The black market for FECs (Foreign Exchange Certificates), especially in the south, is still a going concern. You can exchange your money for *renminbi* at lucrative rates – but be aware that the authorities are clamping down on this. Chinese can get jailed or shot if caught, while tourists are deported first-class at their own expense. The use of false student cards is also now being cracked down upon.

Health problems include colds, nose and throat infections caused by the dry atmosphere and industrial pollution. Pharmacies, however, are well-stocked and local pills potent.

Guides *China – A Travel Survival Kit* (Lonely Planet) is an almost encyclopedic, 800-page guide, carried by just about every Australian in China, though some readers feel that its tone encourages appalling behaviour on the part of travellers determined to cut costs.

CONTACTS

All China Women's Federation, 50 Deng Shi Hou, Beijing or Box 399, Beijing. Branches in most cities, but you will probably need a special introduction by someone at the university or other body of authority in order to meet any representatives. Set up in 1949 under the umbrella of the Communist Party, the federation is often criticized as a Party vehicle, especially as regards the one-child-per-family policies. On the positive side it does provide crucial legal advice and help for women as well as acting as a pressure group to monitor and increase political representation.

Society for Anglo-Chinese Understanding (SACU), 109 Promenade, Cheltenham, Glos GL50 1NW, UK. A good source of information; offers short language courses. Publishes a quarterly magazine, *China Now*.

BOOKS

★ **Mary Morris**, *Wall to Wall: A Woman's Travels from Beijing to Berlin* (UK, Flamingo, 1993/US, Doubleday, 1991). Starting in Beijing, Morris tells of her journey through China, Mongolia, Russia and Ukraine to the Berlin Wall. Personal, highly readable account of travelling through countries teetering on the brink of change.

Christa Paula, *The Road to Miran* (UK, HarperCollins, 1994). Accompanied by a taxi-driver, described as a "Chinese James Dean" Paula's quest for the ancient kingdom of Shanshan uncovers a little-known China of nuclear testing sites, forced labour camps and rising political discontent.

Jung Chang, *Wild Swans* (UK, Flamingo, 1993/US, Doubleday, 1992). Best-selling memoir, chronicling three generations of the author's maternal family during a time of enormous political change and personal upheaval.

Anchee Min, *Red Azalea: Life and Love in China* (UK, Gollancz, 1994/US, Pantheon). Another (much briefer) memoir of a girl's upbringing during the Cultural Revolution, this time dwelling on the day to day joys and anguishes of her awakening sexuality under a pernicious, puritanical and vindictive regime.

★ **Agnes Smedley**, *China Correspondent* (1943; UK, Pandora Press, 1984). Compelling account of women's role in the Revolutionary period by one of the US's most unjustly unsung, great feminists. Her autobiography, *Daughter of the Earth* (UK, Virago, 1977, o/p/US, Feminist Press, 1987) is an inspiring and engaging read.

Jan MacKinnon and Steve MacKinnon (eds), *Agnes Smedley, Portraits of Chinese Women in Revolution* (UK, Virago, 1988, o/p/US, University of California Press). Eighteen of Smedley's pieces on Chinese women written between 1928 and 1941, based on interviews and observations.

Elizabeth Croll, *Chinese Women Since Mao* (UK, Zed Books, 1983/US, M E Sharpe, 1984). Informed analysis of the effect of Revolutionary policies on the lives of women.

Elizabeth Croll, Delia Davin and Penny Kane, *China's One Child per Family Policy* (UK, Macmillan, 1985/US, St Martin's Press). Important for understanding the pressures women face in choosing to have children.

Emily Honig, *Sisters and Strangers: Women in the Shanghai Cotton Mills 1919–1949* (US, Stanford University Press, 1986). A model of good, readable labour history – though academic. Interesting and with masses of evidence, examining family life, workplace tensions, strikes, and the Revolutionary period.

FICTION

Wang Anyi, *Baotown* (UK, Penguin, 1990, o/p/US, Norton Press, 1989, o/p). Moving account of village life written in the style of a folktale.

Maxine Hong Kingston, *The Woman Warrior* (UK, Picador, 1981/US, Vintage, 1989). A beautifully crafted book unravelling the Chinese cultural traditions and myths that helped form Kingston's identity as a first-generation Chinese American.

Zhang Jie, *Leaden Wings* (UK, Virago, 1987). One of China's most popular and controversial writers; her absorbing account of life in an industrial town was both praised and condemned as a powerful contemporary satire. Published in the US as *Heavy Wings* (Grove-Atlantic, 1989, o/p). Also translated are her short stories, *As Long as Nothing Happens, Nothing Will* (UK, Virago, 1988/US, Grove-Atlantic, 1991, o/p).

Yu Luojin, *A Chinese Winter's Tale* (Hong Kong & US, Renditions, 1990). Intensely personal chronicle of life during the Cultural Revolution.

Su Tong, *Raise the Red Lantern* (UK, Touchstone, 1994/US, Morrow, 1993). Tale of women's wasted lives in pre-Revolutionary China as four concubines desperately compete for the attentions of their husband, a worthless landlord. This is the novel on which Zhang Yimou loosely based his superb film of the same name.

Mo Yan, *Red Sorghum* (UK, Minerva, 1994/US, Penguin, 1994). Atmospheric family saga of endless warring in twentieth-century China with a vivid feel for the physical world.

Special **thanks** to Zuleika Kingdon for background notes to the Introduction.

Colombia

South America's oldest democracy, Colombia has a lamentable human rights record. Thousands of people are gunned down or disappeared every year, among them scores of street children targeted as "vermin" by notorious death squads, often supported by the police. Robberies and muggings are common and, as centre of Latin America's illicit drug traffic, whole areas of the country have been taken over by the cocaine trade. Yet not all foreigners are put off by Colombia's violent, gun-toting reputation. Not only is this an overwhelmingly scenic country, with its four Andean ranges, fertile valleys, wide eastern plains and steamy Caribbean coastline, but it has a unique vitality, evident in the seductive popular dance culture that permeates all walks of life.

The Caribbean coast, especially the lovely old colonial port of Cartagena, is becoming an increasingly

popular focus for inexpensive package tours, but elsewhere (perhaps not surprisingly) foreign travellers are comparatively rare. As a woman, it's not easy travelling in a strong *machista* culture and without a male companion you are almost bound to experience sexual harassment, mainly in the form of passing comments and invitations to "learn how to salsa". As always, how this affects you is largely a matter of confidence, patience and humour. Probably more than anywhere else in Latin America you will need quick wits and a good knowledge of Spanish to get by. On the other hand, those who brave it almost invariably find that the country gets under their skin. Away from major industrial cities like Medellín, Cali and the capital, Bogotá, lie a staggering variety of landscapes from deep green mountains and sweltering rainforest to the vast cattle lands dotted with palms that lead east to the border with Brazil. Transport is straightforward, accommodation is inexpensive and plentiful and, however daunting it may feel at first (especially in macho preserves such as bars), provided you heed warnings of no-go areas, conceal any conspicuous signs of wealth and keep a vigilant eye on your belongings, travelling will feel safer as you get to know people, most of whom are only too willing to be helpful to strangers.

Feminism in Colombia has made much progress since the first groups started up in the mid-1970s. However, reaching women of all backgrounds is a major problem in a country where social and economic divisions are so rigid. One of the most successful groups is *Cine Mujer*, a women's filmmaking collective that is attempting to gain access to the all-important mass media of cinema and television. Even the poorest families in Colombia tend to have TV, and cinema is a popular form of entertainment. *Cine Mujer* have made several short films about the position of women in Colombian society, which have been shown in cinemas throughout the country. As long as they don't openly attack the Church or the hallowed concept of the family, the group can use this access to a mass audience to challenge many popular myths. As they take advantage of the increasing use of video, there are hopes of spreading their message even further.

Taking the Rough with the Smooth

Janey Mitchell spent a year teaching English at a state university in the Andean market town of Tunja, three hours from the capital, Bogotá. She used her holidays to travel around the country, mostly on buses and occasionally hitching.

I was nervous about going to Colombia, a feeling confirmed by the discovery, on arrival at Bogotá airport, that half the contents of my rucksack had evidently flown in a different direction. However, any doubts I had disappeared in the first weeks and today I look back with amusement at my own and others' exaggerated preconceptions of the country.

I cannot deny that Colombia has multiple and currently insoluble problems and it certainly isn't the safest country for a woman to travel alone. I am writing from the point of view of someone who spoke reasonably fluent Spanish on arrival and picked up a great deal more as the year progressed. This is a huge advantage, but you still cannot help drawing attention to yourself. Clad in poncho, local hat concealing any trace of blondness, and dark glasses, I was no less conspicuous than otherwise. It's in your walk, your height, your demeanour. You can't escape it.

> Besides two Moonie missionaries, I was the only so-called alien in the place where I was teaching.

Conspicuousness brings *piropos*, catcalls, comments – even when you have just crawled out of the house with a hangover at seven in the morning. Whistles and "pssts" from men, as if calling a dog to heel, are blood-boiling, but they are human and once you show yourself to be human too, the situation becomes far less strained.

Acute visibility as a foreign woman can even be an advantage. Besides two Moonie missionaries, I was the only so-called alien in the place where I was teaching and naturally provoked considerable curiosity. Blue eyes, white skin and unjustly magic words like Cambridge open all the doors; I was spoilt with constant companionship, invitations into people's homes, VIP treatment, and paid not one peso of rent. I can't help feeling guilty at the undeserved esteem that British nationality seems to inspire and would like to think that the high regard and interest are mutual. However, I fear that Latins in Britain are, in general, poorly received.

During my first month in Tunja the words "es la gringa" followed me everywhere. "Gringa" is the female version of the term for all Western foreigners, although it essentially refers to North Americans, and, as local people regard the States as a rich, powerful, and much envied Big Brother, the word is often used derogatively.

The one conversation when I attempted to clarify the difference between the British and North Americans provoked genuine interest, besides revealing people's far from infallible knowledge of world geography. Many believed England to be a little island off the US coast. By the time a month was up, the words "es la inglesa" echoed in my wake.

Colombian women generally have a raw deal unless they hail from affluent families, have perhaps been educated abroad or, for whatever reason, have come to challenge traditional expectations. Machismo rules and men with means may have any number of girlfriends. In this respect women simply cannot achieve an equal footing with men, even in the most open of relationships. In indigenous areas a woman who two-times or is merely seen in public *I probably would have been branded a complete slut had I been local.* with different men is invariably classified as a whore. While women are a domestic necessity or pastime, a pregnant woman, even unmarried, is conceded a level of courtesy. Travelling alone, when I felt most at risk, I sometimes used a small padded rucksack over my stomach and inside a coat as a talisman.

The university environment brought me into contact with a huge range of people. Women were inquisitive and warm, but simultaneously suspicious and envious of my liberty, ability to travel (concomitant with money) and my novelty. I rarely went out with unaccompanied women as most had families and husbands and, for Colombian women, socializing is inseparable from contact with the opposite sex. Dance is a vital element of social life. Salsa, merengue and cumbia are barely conceivable in a single sex environment. Merengue in particular is a fast dance requiring man and woman to swing from side to side with their bodies as close as possible. It wasn't easy to accept that such sudden physical proximity could be less significant than buying someone a drink.

I found myself in a unique position in Tunja. Being foreign, I was far less obliged to conform to the unwritten local code of conduct. The vast majority of Colombians are Catholics and in a community rife with gossip and assumed unblemished personal virtue, hypocrisy has the upper hand. Though I hardly escaped criticism for mixing with as many men as I did, I probably would have been branded a complete slut had I been local.

I actually lived with two men for most of the teaching year and was constantly cornered by women demanding to know whether I was sleeping with them both or, if just one, which. It was unthinkable that I could be cohabiting with two men without having a relationship with either one. I was incredibly lucky to meet this pair who were like brother-bodyguards to me and unusually lacking in machismo. They even cooked and washed up!

Through these two I was initiated not only into the art of dance, but that of drinking *aguardiente*, a sugar-cane based quasi-toxic liquor flavoured with aniseed. It is customarily drunk in liqueur-sized glasses, but don't be misled by the size of the glass. "Fondo blanco", meaning "down in one", becomes a dreaded phrase, as to refuse is impolite and can cause offence. Although women are excused for lacking stamina, it may take a lot of determination and some strategically placed flowerpots to avoid inebriation. Beware of men using intoxication tactics to try and weaken your will.

As far as travelling in Colombia is concerned, no advice is complete and I can only offer guidelines. A woman alone will inevitably be harassed, but common sense and care go a long way. Thieves and pickpockets riddle bus stations in particular so stick to the obvious precaution of not displaying watch, jewellery or camera in public. Local women have a huge advantage in the Andes in that they wear countless layers of clothing in which to conceal a purse. Most carry notes in their bras. I wore a money belt and had dollars sewn into the hem of a T-shirt until washing it became a problem and I transferred them to the waistband of a pair of trousers. I once stupidly left the $240 T-shirt in a hotel room (in San Agustin) in a pile of clothes. It disappeared and I still seethe with fury to think of somebody going through every inch of clothing to find my money. Using hotel safes is generally safe, but if there was any doubt about the security of money in deposits, I would split my cash, and wear half in my clothes.

Colombian women rarely travel alone and it is hard for men to envisage a culture that allows women such independence.

Even more than anywhere else I would advise women against hitching in Colombia. I did so rarely, only in daylight and in areas where tourists were few and far between. This may seem to contradict a warning not to wander too far off the beaten track – lone travellers have been known simply to disappear without trace, especially around guerrilla strongholds and the remote foothills used to cultivate coca and marijuana.

But, where foreigners are rare, local people tend to be less wise to means of ripping you off and more likely to take a genuine interest in the whys and wherefores of a woman travelling alone. Here I found that white lies about my Colombian husband did not go amiss. It's wise to explain the reasons for your solitude, whether it means inventing a partner or honestly trying to outline your position. Just remember that Colombian women rarely travel alone and it is difficult for men to envisage a culture that allows women such independence. Hitching, in particular, also may require a degree of physical and mental stamina as you crouch, squashed between pumpkins and yams, ears deafened by the sound of squealing piglets.

On one occasion, I leapt over the back of a high-sided lorry to find myself landing on a heap of oranges from the valley, in which a bunch of distinctly pickled pickers lay sprawling or half buried. My instinctive recoil was met with a helping hand which then hesitantly offered a petrol can. It turned out to contain their local *trago*, a distilled sugar-cane hooch. They probably thought they

Attempted rape radically altered my attitude to travelling alone.

were hallucinating as I appeared. However, a spattering of English was successfully dragged out from somewhere in my honour and I even managed to add to it. I soon discovered that making moves to pay the driver is appreciated, but money seldom changes hands.

There were times in Colombia when I knew I was at risk, but after my first few trouble-free months I had become ridiculously blasé about the whole thing. My sense of invulnerability subsequently took a beating.

I advise women not to arm themselves with any kind of weapon as men are likely to act more aggressively under threat. I had taken general self-defence classes at the university before setting off alone during the holidays and when I did find myself under attack my automatic reaction was to aim for the organs most likely to debilitate. I was lucky in that in both cases the attacker was unarmed and my aggression won. The scrotal sac is woman's one concession against male physical strength. I remember little of the actual struggle: yelling, uncontrollable shaking afterwards, curiosity on seeing human hair between my knuckles and a recollection of the jelly-like texture of the eyeball as my fingers lunged.

Attempted rape radically altered my attitude to travelling alone. I was astounded by my own physical strength and mental determination to fight off attack. Full accounts of what happened would entail lengthy explanation; it is sufficient to say that, in each case, I had wrongly trusted my intuition and demonstrated a degree of friendliness. Travelling unaccompanied and without contacts in an unfamiliar city, it isn't easy to reject all approaches from men and I cannot stress enough that these violent incidents came about through a slackening of caution.

Mine was a conscious choice to travel alone and my fluent Spanish made it easy to make friends. Had I been travelling in company and with a person of less fluency, I would not have become as integrated into the communities I visited or have felt as close to their culture. I was often with people so trustworthy that I became blind to the proportion of the population who regard a Western woman travelling alone as a piece of flesh to be bought or taken by force.

Following these incidents, however, I took a great deal more care, making an effort to team up with fellow travellers and, where possible, share rooms with women. As it is, those experiences have given me a deep spiritual resilience. I know that I'd travel alone again under similar circumstances. The good times – visiting Colombia's lesser-known Caribbean islands, dozing in steaming volcanic pools, exploring prehistoric sites on horseback – far outweigh the bad.

A Lot of Dire Warnings

Susan Bassnett is Professor of Comparative Literature and Director of the Centre for British Cultural Studies at the University of Warwick. An author and poet, she has also translated works by a number of Latin American women, including Margo Glantz, Alejandra Pizarnik and Silvana Ocampo. She has four children and visited Colombia with one of her daughters, at that time eight years old.

Although I had worked on Latin American literature for some years and taught courses in Britain on Latin American culture, I hadn't visited a Latin American country until I was invited to go and do some teaching at the Universidad de los Andes, Bogotá, Colombia.

I was given a lot of dire warnings before setting out, many by people who had already visited the country. I was told about the high level of street violence, of areas which are effectively civil-war zones and the dangers of walking anywhere alone. When they learned that I was also proposing to take along my eight-year-old daughter, the warnings increased and I was told horror stories about kidnappings, child prostitution rings and ransom demands. I left Britain in a state of some anxiety. My experiences of the country revealed a lot about the way in which Europeans and North Americans perceive Latin America.

Viewed from afar, the South American continent seems like the final bastion of civilization: the place to which embezzlers and train robbers flee, the place that harbours undiscovered war criminals and to which people go to lose themselves and change their identities. Seen from the

North American fastness, it is source of a steadily creeping communist menace, it is "down below" with all its associations of hellishness and incivility added to the European's image of distance and solitude. And however much we may dismiss these images of another continent, they do exist and consequently colour our own perceptions. Despite all that I had read, despite the many friends from Latin America that I had made over the years, traces of these negative images remained.

Once I landed in Colombia, after a brief stopover in Caracas, everything changed. The visit remains one of the high points of an extensive travelling life and I can't wait to go back. It is an extraordinarily beautiful country, with a huge range of completely different landscapes, from the high Andes to the glorious Caribbean coast around Cartagena, the great fertile plateau and the Amazonian jungle. It is the

I was careful not to wear jewellery, not even earrings, or anything that might seem ostentatious.

only country in South America to have a Pacific and a Caribbean coastline, and stands in a unique geographical position, which no doubt is why the conquistadors, the English pirates and later North American profiteers, drug smugglers and the Mafia have always seen it as a prime target for exploitation.

The history of Colombia is a history of violence and there is no denying that it is a country where you have to take certain precautions. When I arrived, the regular traffic police had been replaced by military units, and on every street corner in Bogotá there seemed to be a nervous teenage soldier clutching a sten gun.

It is also a country that makes you face up to what it means to be – in the terms of those millions living in appalling shanty towns – a wealthy foreigner. We may not perceive ourselves as rich; but the boy who held up a British Embassy official at knifepoint the week I arrived and stole his coat, his watch, his wallet and his glasses clearly saw the possession of those things as a sign of wealth. Most people carry limited amounts of money; if you are held up at knifepoint or gunpoint, it is best to hand over a small sum straight away and the thief will then simply take it and vanish.

Colombia, of course, has abject poverty, and stealing from the rich is a way of surviving. I lost count of the number of times Colombian friends told me about their fears in North American cities such as New York, where their doors were fitted out with more padlocks than a Colombian would ever dream of and where you cannot be assured of safe delivery from a mugger if you simply hand over two dollars or an old watch. This difference illustrates two concepts of social crime that cannot fairly be compared.

I lived in Candelaría, the old part of Bogotá, an area reputedly unsafe. I did not walk on the streets at night, but I did walk the fifteen minutes or so to the place where I was working, and never felt remotely uneasy. My daughter and I used to go shopping, visit some of the magnificent churches in Bogotá and wander around quite happily. I used public transport and the ramshackle Bogotá taxis quite normally. However, I was careful not to wear any jewellery, not even earrings, or anything that might seem in any way ostentatious. Occasionally a shop assistant would remind me not to let my daughter carry a package, in case any-one snatched it from her as we passed, but otherwise we behaved as though we were in any big city. Bogotá is an extraordinary city, with some beautiful colonial architecture and one of the finest museums in Latin America, the Museum of Gold. Best to walk quickly past the men who hang around outside the museum, with handkerchiefs full of emeralds for quick sale to tourists: a refusal to buy might easily turn into something unpleasant.

Travelling across the country is easiest by air or, if that proves too expensive, by bus. The buses may not look it, but they tend to be very efficient and quite safe. Nevertheless, I never mastered the rationale behind catching an inter-city bus outside a station: you go to the out-skirts of the city and then leap out into the road at a passing bus – and it stops! When uncertain, it is always best to go to the central bus station and start the journey from there.

I did not have enough time to travel down to the Amazonian jungle, which I would dearly love to do one day. Crucial to any visitor's itinerary is a trip to Cartagena, the magnificent coastal town that, in the sixteenth century, was considered the jewel of the Caribbean. Northern Colombia, with its hot coastal flatlands, has been made famous by the author Gabriel García Márquez who was born and raised there and who contrasts the fertile plains with their brilliant sunlight with the colder, wetter climate of the high Andes. Bogotá is one of the highest capital cities in the world and although close to the equator is rarely hot. In fact the climate of Bogotá is not unlike that of an English summer, and can be very wet indeed.

A highlight of our visit was a trip to one of the oldest colonial towns in Colombia, Villa de Leyva, about four hours' bus ride from Bogotá. This amazing old town, constructed around the biggest stone-paved plaza I have ever seen or could ever imagine, stands at the edge of the desert, and the hot, dry winds blowing across the barren landscape have produced a geological miracle.

Close to the town are the skeletons of thousands of prehistoric animals, and all the stonework is full of fossils. Eighteenth-century colonial architects with baroque sensibilities played with the raw materials available, and so there are fountains built out of giant ammonites, courtyards paved with the vertebrae of dinosaurs, ornamental stonework in which the patterns are made out of fossilized bones of all sizes. You can wander around and pick up fossils everywhere, or buy rarer examples for very little from local children who roam around the plaza in groups, looking for likely sales.

I learned a lot from having a child with me. Responses to children were magnificent everywhere.

The combination of whitewashed houses built around little courtyards that are full of red and purple blossom (apparently all the year round) with the grotesque richness of bones and fossils everywhere was truly memorable. My other, strictly personal, memory to cherish from Villa de Leyva is the sight of my daughter running wildly down a hill in her pyjamas in pursuit of a contemptuous llama who had obviously seen too many enthusiastic small girls before.

I learned a great deal, too, from having a child with me. Responses to children were magnificent everywhere, and something of the wonder of a completely new continent can be lost when adults (and intellectual adults at that) exchange experiences. My daughter kept a home-made diary of the trip, collecting postcards and bus tickets and anything else of interest; and she wrote about the things that most impressed her. I felt that only with a child as a companion would I have sat in a colonial building now converted into a restaurant and stared in amazement at the mummified alligators and boa constrictors hanging from the oak beams above our heads. And having a child with me made me acutely aware of the cruelty of social inequality, where boys younger than mine are out at work or begging in gangs in the streets. One disconcerting fact that my daughter drew to my attention was the absence of girl children either as beggars or as child labour. Though no accurate figures exist, the implication of this absence suggests that the route through life for destitute girls, even at a very young age, is the brothel.

As in many Latin American countries, the position of women is profoundly ambiguous. On the one hand, the cult of machismo relegates women to low status as sex objects in the eyes of most men; and yet there are also many powerful women in political and business life who exercise a great deal of authority.

As a centre for Latin American publishing, Colombia is also very much a focal point for the region's culture and there are a growing number of women writers whose work is well-known and widely read. Working in a university context, there was not much evidence as yet that women's studies have begun to gain much ground, but there are women keen to promote them. Montserrat Ordonez, the feminist writer and critic who has spent some time teaching in the United States, was enormously helpful in introducing me to some of the problems of a Latin American feminist movement – the absence of models except those offered by European or North American women, the need to work specifically with the history and culture of women from Colombia, the problems of class and education that are so extreme in such a hierarchical society.

Colombia is a fascinating country to visit, with a rich history and an extraordinary variety of landscapes. It is volatile politically, and the battles between the government and the drug barons mean that violence is never far away and some parts of the country are more dangerous than others. Many of my friends have lost relatives in recent years, randomly murdered by unknown assailants, but there is certainly not the sense of fear you can find in some British inner-city areas, and provided travellers exercise a certain amount of caution in terms of dress codes, ostentatious displays of wealth or venturing into known trouble zones, there should be no difficulties.

I came away with feelings of affection and enthusiasm for the country and the people. My partner goes out to work with actors in Bogotá and Medellín every summer. One of these years I'll hopefully go back too.

TRAVEL NOTES

Languages Spanish.

Transport Buses are inexpensive and frequent, and all long-distance routes are covered by coaches – comfortable but a bit more expensive. (See *Special Problems*, below, for more on buses.) There are few passenger trains. Never travel in a taxi without a meter as you'll be overcharged.

Accommodation The poor exchange rate on the peso makes Colombia one of the most expensive South American countries. However, hotels outside the main cities can be very cheap. Camping isn't advised.

Special Problems Thieves and pickpockets are rife – hang on to your luggage at all times, watch your pockets and don't wear a flashy watch or jewellery. Expect harassment from all kinds of men, including the police and the military. Colombia is perhaps the worst country in South America for machismo. Bus stations can be particularly unnerving places. The drug scene is very heavy. Buses are periodically searched by the police and it's common for drug pushers to set people up.

Never carry packages for other people without checking the contents. Sentences for possession can be very long.

Guides *The South American Handbook* (UK, Trade and Travel/US, Passport Press) includes a sizeable chunk on Colombia. *Colombia – A Travel Survival Kit* (Lonely Planet) is more in-depth.

CONTACTS

Casa de la Mujer, Carrera 18, No 59–60, Bogotá (☎2496317). Women's centre run by a long-standing collective.

Cine Mujer, Avda 25c 49-24, Aptdo 202, Bogotá (☎2426184). Women's film collective.

BOOKS

Susan Bassnett, *Knives and Angels: Women Writers in Latin America* (UK & US, Zed Books, 1990). Collection of literary criticism on Latin America's leading women writers.

Jenny Pearce, *Inside the Labyrinth* (UK, Latin America Bureau, 1990/US, Monthly Review Press). Thorough examination of Colombian society, including the role of unions, political parties, guerrillas and civic movements, by one of Britain's leading writers on Latin America.

 Alicia Partnoy (ed), *You Can't Drown the Fire: Latin American Women Writing in Exile* (UK, Virago, 1989/US, Cleis Press, 1988). Moving collection of essays, stories, poetry, letters and song, including several contributions from Colombia.

Alonso Solazar, *Born to Die in Medellín* (UK, Latin America Bureau, 1992/US, Monthly Review Press). Through interviews with teenage contract-killers, their families, priests and self-defence vigilantes, the author provides a riveting insight into urban violence in Colombia's second city.

FICTION

Lyll Becerra de Jenkins, *The Honourable Prison* (UK, Virago, 1989/US, Penguin). On Virago's teenage list, this extraordinary tale of political intrigue is based on the author's own life in Colombia.

Charlotte Méndez, *Condor and Humming-bird* (UK, The Women's Press, 1987/US, Wild Trees Press, 1986). Passionate novel around North American woman's visit to Bogotá with her Colombian husband.

Gabriel García Márquez, *One Hundred Years of Solitude* (UK, Picador, 1978/US, Avon, 1986). Arguably his best novel. It's worth reading any books by Colombia's most famous contemporary writer, who brilliantly captures the magic, beauty and madness of his country.

Costa Rica

One of the main attractions of the tiny country of Costa Rica is its reputation as a peaceful oasis of democracy amid the political turmoil of Central America. Compared to most of the continent it is also a less intimidating destination for women travellers. Machismo prevails: relationships between the sexes are dominated by traditional values and foreign women, in particular, are considered fair game; men will hiss and make passing comments, especially in the streets of the capital, San José, but such attention seldom becomes threatening. Independent travel is made easy by an inexpensive, efficient bus network that serves most areas and, although prices are creeping ever upwards, there's still a reasonable choice of low-budget

accommodation. Camping is popular, especially in the country's numerous national parks, though not recommended alone.

With no army, a relatively high standard of living and its own national health service, Costa Rica is undoubtedly the most socially and economically advanced nation in the region. This, plus beautiful beaches and a rich abundance of wildlife and tropical vegetation – much of it preserved in well-kept nature reserves and national parks – has been more than enough to earn it the tag "tourist's paradise", especially in the United States. In return, Costa Rica is heavily dependent on the US, the influence of which is everywhere, especially in San José. There's a darker, disturbing side to all this, too: the sight of male tourists, blatantly hovering in and around San José's more lurid nightspots, attracted by the flourishing sex industry or, in a growing number of cases, the more long-term prospect of finding a wife. Though by no means as established as the prostitution scene in Thailand or the Philippines, the similar trend in Costa Rica appears set to stay.

As in bordering Panama, there is little evidence of an indigenous population. Apart from a tiny minority of Indians and a few Black communities, concentrated on the Caribbean coast, most people are of Spanish descent. Costa Ricans, known as Ticos (said to stem from the colonial saying "we are all *hermaniticos*" – little brothers) are generally proud of their European origins. Although officially protected, the five thousand or so remaining indigenous people have suffered a particularly raw deal, repeatedly tricked by large companies into selling off their land so that most live in dire poverty, either unemployed or forced to take very low-paid work in order to survive.

The weight of poverty is also carried by a large proportion of Costa Rican **women**. Fifty-two percent of families are headed by single women, burdened with all the responsibility of earning a wage and looking after children, old people and itinerant men. As a result, in poor neighbourhoods, they tend to be the first to get involved in any kind of community action. Although the women's movement in Costa Rica is largely middle-class, a number of grassroots campaigns do exist, especially around issues such as childcare, violence, sexuality and women's health.

McDonalds and Coffee to Go

Nicky Solloway first travelled to Costa Rica in 1992 where she worked as a freelance journalist and English teacher for nine months. She returned a year later and is currently a journalist with a development organization working with the indigenous communities of Talamanca.

I was initially enticed to Costa Rica by accounts of an army-free enclave of social welfare, free speech, and some of the most diverse ecology on the planet. As it was my first solo voyage, I was also reassured by reports of its relative safety for women travelling alone.

The bus journey from the airport was a blur of flashing neon signs, burger bars and traffic jams: I felt as if I'd landed in some seedy back yard of the United States. It was nightfall and I wandered up busy Second Avenue to look for a taxi. Rickety old cars with broken headlamps trundled past mounds of rotting rubbish. Smoking street stands selling barbecued meat huddled below the glare of the towering glass *Holiday Inn* and the sound of salsa and cumbia spilled out of dark bars.

The taxi driver had never heard of the Peace Centre where I planned to spend my first night and we jolted around the black streets while I desperately thumbed my phrasebook. Eventually he took the phone number and called for directions before carefully delivering me to the front door. It was then that I began to believe that this might really be a safe destination.

At the Peace Centre I was welcomed into a packed room and spent my first evening watching a slide show and discussing Cuban politics with a predominantly North American audience. Costa Rica is known as a safe haven for political refugees who flock from the more oppressive regimes of Latin America to set up campaign headquarters in San José. Aside from the political exiles, there is an expanding population of North American *pensionados*, attracted by the country's pacifist and progressive ideals, as well as, it has to be said, a number of tax perks and privileges. Others arrive in search of a Tica wife. The local English-language newspaper is littered with appeals from ageing male Americans in search of "beautiful Tica ladies" while a few of the capital's shabbier bars resemble Bangkok pick-up joints as scantily dressed teenage girls openly bargain with potential clients in the street outside.

After a couple of nights in the Peace Centre's hostel, I moved into a flat in downtown San José with an American woman before eventually sharing with a young Tica in the shrubby suburb of Sabanilla. To my disappointment – shared by many of the European travellers I met – the fast-food-baseball-cap culture is everywhere, especially in San José where drive-in *McDonald's* signs dominate the skyline and *Pizza Hut* adverts hijack the radio airwaves. It was always a relief to escape into the uniquely Costa Rican Central Market, tempted by the whiff of freshly ground coffee and new leather. Inside the narrow, buzzing building neatly layered stalls were piled with kettles and pans, sacks of multi-coloured beans and rails of saddles and shiny machetes. Further on, little soda cafés selling *platineau* (plantain), fried fish and beans were wedged between vegetable and meat stalls. Exotic herbal remedy stands stuffed with seaweeds, herbs and dried leaves displayed cures for everything from cancer to impotence.

It was also good to escape sometimes from San José. As a journalist I hoped to find some type of relevant experience and through my first land-lady I was introduced to an educational radio statio broadcasting to rural farmers, or *campesinos*. Having arrived with barely a smattering of Spanish, it took a few weeks before I could communicate on even a basic level, but the radio producers went out of their way to help me and I was invited on several bumpy trips to the tiny radio studios dotted around the country.

Costa Rica's 51,100 square-kilometre territory offers a huge diversity of ecological zones. The dripping cloud forests in Monteverde descend into the baked, brown plains of Guanacaste while a five-hour journey acrosss country leads you to the rhythmic, steamy Caribbean jungles. Temperatures vary dramatically according to altitude. A bus trip from the cool capital can drop you in a humid and sun-soaked province only half an hour away.

Mario, our guide, finally showed up, complete with rippling muscles, a string of medallions and a portable car disco.

One of the places I fell in love with on my first visit was Santa Rosa National Park, a remote stretch of dry tropical forest close to the Nicaraguan border. Crammed with passengers, the bus to the frontier groaned its way up the hill leading north out of the city. Eventually the engine picked up and we rumbled through the purple and orange valleys, past roadside peanut and avocado sellers and men on horseback, elegantly trotting along in huge cowboy hats and highly polished boots. The scenery turned browner and crispier as we neared the frontier with Nicaragua; huge plains of scorched grass spread into infinity and white, hump-backed cows panted beneath shady yew trees.

The bus dropped us at the entrance of the park where we paid a small fee before setting off along the rocky road toward the beach, some three hours' walk away. A family in an ancient VW van offered us a lift to the first campsite, a couple of kilometres into the park. Then, except for the wildlife, we were on our own. Iguanas rustled in the parched undergrowth and we glimpsed white-faced monkeys swinging across spindly branches. The track led through mountain, forest and dry plain until we finally arrived to watch the red sun disssolve into puce behind the silvery sea. Easter campers had strung pieces of canvas and plastic sheeting between the palm trees to make a rough campsite. With mosquitoes screaming in our ears, we quickly assembled the tent. Our torch flickered and failed and thrown into the treacly blackness we could do nothing but attempt to sleep. A patter of small feet followed a family of raccoons scuttling about the campfire. I woke with a start the next day to find an iguana a couple of inches from my face, breakfasting on the tent. I scrambled to the ocean for a bathe. Pelicans dived for early morning fish and massive waves yawned overhead before sighing into a rush of cool water to knock me off my feet.

We weren't long in the bubbling water before Mario decided to chance his luck and suggest a massage.

Another early trip I'll always remember was to Arenal, said to be one of the most active volcanoes in the world. It last erupted in 1968, swallowing a whole village in red-hot lava and caustic fumes. My friend, a German woman, and I were the only tourists in the town of La Fortuna, from where we decided to take an organized night tour of the volcano some 20km away. We waited by the gas station as instructed by the tour operator. Mario, our guide, finally showed up, complete with rippling muscles, a string of medallions and a portable car disco. We squeezed into the front seat beside him and sped off in the direction of Arenal. As the paved road gave way to more and more pot holes Mario slammed the jeep into four-wheel drive and we bounced across the volcanic craters to the beat of Merengue music before crunching to a halt at the foot of the steaming hill. Suddenly, as if on cue, there sounded a deep, gravelly roar and a spurt of orange lava burst into the black sky. We stood and marvelled for a few minutes as the volcano hissed and spluttered a fiery, red rain before racing off on the next part of our tour: the hot springs. We stripped to our T-shirts and had immersed ourselves in the bubbling, steamy stream when we spotted Mario, stark naked, striding toward us. He had decided to join us and dived in. We weren't long in the bubbling water before Mario decided to chance his luck and suggest a massage. Though the force of the water was strong, we managed to pull ourselves away from him, but we each felt glad that we hadn't set out on the excursion alone.

As in most macho societies, foreign women are prized in Costa Rica for their assumed availability. Men will constantly remark on your appearance and believe they are paying you a compliment as they "Pssss" and mutter at you in the street. Although it's annoying to be treated like a dog being called to heel, I never really felt threatened. However, since returning to the country with my Costa Rican fiancé, I've been especially irritated by the assumption that if a woman has a serious relationship, she can't meet alone with other men. In fact it is not generally accepted that women and men can merely be friends. When my partner and I were staying with his family, my future mother-in-law almost forbade me to meet a mutual male friend while my fiancé

Many families are headed by single mothers – in Costa Rica male infidelity is an accepted fact of life.

was away. I brushed off her disapproving glares, but when the friend came to the house she insisted on sitting in the same room while we talked, acting as a kind of chaperone. Another time I went to a café for a drink after class with a male colleague from the language school. That night two separate "witnesses" from the café telephoned my friend's wife and told her we were having an affair!

While these type of traditional values still predominate, with literacy rates at 93 percent, a fairly equitable land distribution and a large middle-class population, women generally have a fairly strong and decisive place in society. In fact they make up roughly half the workforce and are rapidly increasing their strength as doctors, lawyers and government officials. All my English teaching classes were dominated by women, most of whom were balancing day-time jobs and study with house-work. Many families are headed by single mothers – in Costa Rica male infidelity is an accepted fact of life – and the country has an active women's movement which has initiated a number of grassroots campaigns, including one of the country's few organic farming projects and a feminist radio station.

Women's health is also a priority among women's groups. Costa Rica's national health service ranks among the top twenty in the world. The larger boulevards are cluttered with homeopathy clinics, mammography x-ray suites, and osteopaths competing for the attention of North Americans who flock to San José in search of cut-price medical care. In addition, an overt contraception campaign which placed condom packets on supermarket check-outs has cut the average number of children per family from seven to three. However, the consequences of an unwanted pregnancy in this strongly Catholic country were brought home to me when my twenty-year-old flatmate fell pregnant. Her boyfriend had left some weeks before and despite the ostentatious liberalism of many Costa Rican women, I was shocked to see that even her best friends didn't come near her during her ordeal. Abortion is illegal and she was lucky to find a doctor willing to help. The first attempt failed and she had to go for a second, at even greater cost. Though she was clearly suffering intensely, I felt powerless to help since she begged me not to call the hospital as both she and the doctor risked a sentence in jail. Somehow she coped and the friends reappeared.

Despite the country's peaceful image, during this first stay in Costa Rica I was constantly warned to be on my guard against robbers, a fear which sadly preoccupied many people to the point of obsession. Most houses, save for the roughest shack, look more like homemade prisons. Iron bars criss-cross every window and fierce guard dogs patrol gardens encircled by barbed wire. Gun-wielding security guards are deployed at every public building, from the museum to the supermarket. I could never get used to the man with the pistol who would hover round the lobby of the British Institute, as if poised to shoot anyone who might enter through the wrong door.

My most common mishap was getting lost. Streets aren't named and house numbers usually obscured. The local address system is to describe a destination in blocks from a "well-known" landmark. Short of carrying a compass, I was forced to ask passers-by, which didn't always work. Costa Ricans have a curious habit of sending you off in completely the wrong direction rather than admit they don't know. I was once directed to an organization in a suburb of San José: "From the old fig tree in San Pedro walk 150 metres south and 300 east," said the secretary on the telephone. Simple, had the fig tree not been chopped down six months earlier!

TRAVEL NOTES

Languages Spanish is the main language, but quite a few people speak English in tourist areas. It's best not to depend on it however. Don't be surprised to hear a kind of Jamaican-style patois (along with reggae music) in and around Puerto Limón on the Caribbean coast.

Transport Buses are modern, inexpensive, punctual and serve most areas. It's best to book a day or two in advance for long trips and arrive an hour before departure to be sure of a seat. From San José taxis are worth taking to the suburbs or late at night.

Accommodation San José tends to be expensive, but outside the capital there are quite a few inexpensive, basic hotels. More expensive, and more luxurious are the national park lodges, often worth the money simply for their magnificent settings. Camping is commonplace in the national parks, too, but obviously carries an element of risk.

Special Problems Pickpocketing is on the increase in large towns, especially San José.

Guides *The South American Handbook* (UK, Trade and Travel/US, Passport Press), updated yearly, has some thirty pages on Costa Rica, including listings for hotels of every kind. Christopher Baker's exhaustive *Costa Rica*

Handbook (US, Moon Publications) has a good section on conservation and wildlife.

CONTACTS

CEFEMINA (Feminist Centre of Information and Action), Aptdo 5355, San José 100, Costa Rica. Longstanding women's organization dedicated to self-help with a strong emphasis on health. A useful source of contacts throughout the country.

BOOKS

Paula Palmer, *What Happen: A Folk History of Costa Rica's Talamanca Coast* (Costa Rica, Ecodesarollos, 1977). Sensitive account of the peoples of Costa Rica's Caribbean coast, written by a former Peace Corps volunteer.

Richard Biesanz, *The Costa Ricans* (UK, Prentice Hall, 1982, o/p/US, Waveland Press, 1988). Good overall political history.

FICTION

Anacristina Rossi, *La Loca de Gandoca* (Costa Rica, EDUCA, 1993). Novel about a conservationist's attempts to prevent the construction of a hotel complex. Written in Spanish, but not too difficult to read.

Cuba

With the collapse of the Soviet markets and the continuing stranglehold of a US trade embargo, Cuba is in dire need of hard currency. Blackouts and shortages of basic commodities are common, industries and transport are grinding to a halt, and most people, from the professional elite of Havana to rural workers, routinely face days without food. The desperation that many Cubans feel about the siege atmosphere in which they live was brought to national attention by the extensive media coverage of the mass exodus of boats and rafts in 1994. With the new treaty on refugees ratified by Cuba and the US (and the dumping of boat people back in the American base at Guantanamo), this eventually slowed to a trickle. But tensions within the country continue to simmer.

In an attempt to import much needed dollars, Fidel Castro's government has been busy stepping up mass tourism. Luxury resorts now dot the tropical coastline, offering exclusive sun-sea-and-sand holidays for a new, privileged class of dollar-wielding Westerners – though North Americans still have problems getting visas – while hard currency hotels, shops, restaurants and even taxis

have sprung up in the capital and main towns. Politically motivated tours are still organized, but the impetus to demonstrate the achievements of the Revolution is fast giving way to the demands of the more mainstream holiday industry.

For the average Cuban, denied access to the facilities freely available to foreigners, resentments are beginning to surface. Cuba has long had a reputation as a safe haven for travellers and for many years street violence was almost unheard of. Tourist muggings are now on the increase and although the numbers are negligible compared with other South American or Caribbean countries, it's a fast growing trend. Travelling independently, you're bound to experience some degree of hassle from illegal money changers. Sexual violence, however, is rare. Cuban men can seem as steeped in machismo as their Latin American counterparts, but the propositions and comments you face seldom seem aggressive. If you feel at all uncertain take stock of the cursory way that Cuban women deal with unsolicited approaches.

Traditions of hospitality run deep in Cuban society and people tend to be friendly, helpful and interested in making contacts with foreign visitors. Much of this is sincere, but you do need to be sensitive to the practical needs of your hosts – anything from providing the food and drink for the party you've just been invited to, to offering help with visa applications or sending parcels after your return. In the same way an apparently casual holiday romance can have much higher stakes for the Cuban involved, possibly as a first contact for self-exile in the West. It helps to be as straightforward as possible and find out what the expectations are. That said, the genuine warmth and openness and the desire people have simply to explain what is going on in their country, can at times be humbling.

For **women** the revolution brought real and lasting change in terms of legal rights, and access to education, health care and unemployment – much of this co-ordinated through the powerful Federation of Cuban Women. Successive generations now take these advances for granted. For younger Cuban women, however, new and potent frustrations have emerged. The task of looking after home and family – still the domain of women, despite attempts to legislate for the equal division of housework – has become a heavier burden in a climate of shortage. More importantly, younger women are refusing to place on hold their economic and creative potential. Many want out, and by whatever means possible.

Freedom to Travel

Lulu Norman is a freelance translator and writer living in London. She has travelled extensively, starting in 1983 when, at the age of eighteen, she journeyed alone for three months on her own specially planned itinerary across the former Soviet Union. This was her first visit to Cuba.

I wanted to go to the Caribbean, but not to those tourist enclaves where, in my imagination and a thousand colour brochures, local life was a brief tableau to be glimpsed on the way to the beach or the luxury hotel. The prospect of Cuba was intriguing: the Soviet system of Communism mingles strangely with the capitalist legacy of the 1950s under the Batista dictatorship, when Cuba became the playground of the American rich. The mythologies of Cuba are legion, comprising a heady mixture of heroism, romance and idealism against the odds. Invaded and occupied again and again throughout its history, by the Spanish, the Americans and the British, it claimed self-rule only in revolution, and still Castro presides, thirty-four years on, having seen out eight US presidents.

I wanted to go before the unique social and political fabric changed dramatically or disappeared completely, and I wanted to travel independently. I had travelled alone across the former Soviet Union for three months back in 1983 and knew something of what to expect in terms of the bureaucracy and the practical difficulties of travelling solo in a Communist country, where organized group travel is the norm and you are regarded as being very strange or even suspect as a lone traveller, let alone a woman. In Cuba I travelled both alone and with my (male) partner.

As an independent traveller in a country not yet geared for them, the problems you face mirror those of the inhabitants, although to a much lesser extent: I spent a great deal of time trying to find food and waiting for petrol, neither of which is easy to come by. An organized group tour is designed to smooth out these difficulties, making the experience of the country not only less intense but less representative. I was encouraged to plan ahead, but in practice this was not necessary. I preferred to take the chance and allow the unexpected to happen rather than decide where I would be and stick to it; it was always possible to find a place to stay when I arrived, although it was the tourist season. In the last few years, public

It should not be surprising or offensive to travellers that relations with foreigners tend to be governed by economics.

transport has become extremely haphazard and difficult even for Cubans and renting a car is expensive. I only had enough time (and money) to explore one half of the country, the northern half as far as Santa Clara.

It should not be surprising or offensive to travellers that relations with foreigners tend to be governed by economics; once you have accepted the fact that everything is coloured by this disparity, it will not prevent genuine friendships from developing. Castro has fostered an educated class that questions his leadership and is critical of his rule and its daily privations. Political discussions are eagerly entered into – people need to tell of their suffering, inform you about how they live, how they feel, and they are curious to compare attitudes and learn your story. In Havana I had the luck to meet a young couple called Rosa and Guillermo. We went for a drink in one of the few tourist bars where Cubans accompanying tourists are tolerated; most hotels will demand to see their identity cards and find some excuse to reject them. By the end of my trip we were firm friends.

Cubans are proud and begging is practically unknown, but what is often a small service to perform is a great one to receive: seeing friends too shy to ask, I would sometimes offer to accompany them to the tourist shops, the only shops with anything to sell. This charade usually entails a money exchange (although pesos are practically useless to a foreigner), a long wait while they shop and then hand over the goods for you to pay for in dollars; it is also peculiarly painful to watch the avid frenzy brought on by such brief opportunity. Rosa and Guillermo bought mainly clothes for their two boys, taking care to buy them far too big so they would last longer. It is a measure of the government's desperation that a law has now been passed permitting Cubans to possess US dollars.

Life takes place on the street – the idea of public space versus private space has little meaning. In cities there is a familiar stench of diesel fumes and leaking drains in unlit narrow streets where bicycles veer, kids run amok, men sit round a table on the corner intent on a game of dominoes, the women talk and couples dance and kiss. Music is everywhere and all at once: on the streets, through the windows, a band starts up in almost every bar and restaurant. The radio blares and schoolchildren sing along with their teacher on the street: "*Guantanamera*".

There is little theft and homelessness does not seem to exist. Mugging is of course more common in cities, and has increased in proportion to the economic decline, but is no worse in Havana, say, than in many other capitals and much less frequent than most other countries nearby. You should take care of your belongings, however, since the temptation is understandably great; your clothes are more likely to disappear than your camera.

Foreigners come for cut-price sun, sea, and sand, but also for sex.

If you do suffer unwanted attentions, most probably from black marketeers wanting to change money or sell cheap cigars, a firm "no" will usually do the trick. It is unwise to reveal which hotel you are staying at, simply because your "friend" will turn up outside or in the lobby to wait for you. When alone, I never suffered any form of harassment, sexual or otherwise and never felt afraid or threatened. As a foreigner and a woman you will be stared at, though usually with curiosity and respect.

Cuban women stand tall and proud and look you in the eye. Often scantily clad, no strangers to lycra, they seem uncommonly at ease with their sexuality and claim their equality with men. I asked Rosa about chauvinism and sexual equality: what does she do if Guillermo steps out of line? She laughed and mimed kneeing him where it hurts. Since the Revolution, much progress has been made in terms of women's rights, despite Latin machismo. Men are legally bound to do half the housework and the penalty for rape is death. Women make up forty percent of Cuba's workforce and have succeeded in gaining equality in the professions, although the proportion of women in managerial positions is still fairly small.

Foreigners come for cut-price sun, sea, and sand, but also for sex. Prostitution is increasing rapidly, at a rate estimated at as much as two hundred percent in two years. My partner was propositioned many times in word or gesture by women who probably weren't professional prostitutes but, like the urban "entrepreneurs" of the black market, stood to gain something – anything – from an association with a Westerner. The possible spread of AIDS is thus giving cause for alarm, although the rate of infection is still extremely low.

Marriage in Cuba is very popular, not least because each married couple is entitled to the rare privilege of two nights in a hotel and a free crate of beer, but homosexuality is still severely discriminated against; any public display can lead to prison. The "where's your husband?" line of questioning, often put to women travelling alone in other countries, was seldom pursued. I felt safe enough to take the odd hitch-hiker when driving alone, and once picked up an old boy, all skin and bones, who did ask. I said I had no children and wasn't married myself, what about him? He had never had a family, he said, because he ate too much.

I had not arranged a rented car (or anything beyond the obligatory five nights in a hotel) in advance. There were no cars to be had, I was told at *Havanautos*, not a chance. The only hope lay in phoning every car rental agency in Havana each morning in case someone hadn't turned up, which soon became tedious as my hopes of seeing any of the country diminished daily. Walking listlessly round Havana, I stopped in a tourist centre to make one of these calls. Inside, a woman with a broad smile stopped me and asked if she could help; I told her the problem. "There may be something I can do", she said, and reached for the phone. In an improbable twist, which I came to recognize as characteristic of Cuban life, it transpired that the boss of

> *He clasped my hand. Why could I visit their house and they not visit mine? Why did I have so much and they so little?*

Havanautos was her lover; they had been living together since college days. She told me to return armed with a couple of bottles of rum (*Havana Club* is best) and ask for Rolando. Make sure you get him alone, she said, and tell him Natividad sent you. Two hours later I was driving out of the city in a rented Nissan.

Cubans love travelling, but fuel shortages now mean there is a dearth of public transport. Some Cubans have cars but cannot afford to run them. The Carretera Nacional, the highway stretching from one end of Cuba to the other, has a massive eight lanes but these days traffic is scarce, not to say nonexistent, and the queues for fuel long. Taking hitch-hikers is a great way to meet people; you become as involved in their journeys as they are in yours, each stage has and becomes its own story, and the car often turns into a little party on wheels.

Despite great hardship, Cubans are among the warmest, most friendly people I have ever encountered, characterized by generosity, gentleness, much hilarity and a dry wit. As rations run out towards the end of the month, life gets harder, brightened by the prospect of the new month's supplies. Almost everyone I met asked me home for a meal, to their New Year fiesta, or offered me a part of whatever they had. I was quite relieved to have my first argument; it is more than a little discomforting to know one has more rights in Cuba than a Cuban and somewhat incredible never to see any sign of resentment because of it.

Stopping on the road to take a photograph, I was beckoned over by a gentle, handsome man standing on the porch of a house, his family milling around. I was offered a ride on their horse and was then introduced to the large, extended family, among whom were his son and brother, a typically unruly, drunken uncle figure. He clasped my hand and would not let go, staring unsteadily into my eyes for balance. Why could I visit their house and they not visit mine? Why did I have so much and they so little? The son prised me free, apologizing for him, but angrily continued the discussion himself. Of course they were right, I said, I come from a rich country and Cuba is in economic crisis. But it was not so much a question of economic disparities as of liberties; the problem was also the prohibition of travel; I had the freedom to go wherever I liked, and was permitted to acquire enough money to do it if I was able. Castro talks proudly of the Cuban democracy, but there can be no democracy without such basic rights as the freedom to travel.

Raúl corresponded tirelessly in the hope that someone might be coaxed into an offer of marriage or an invitation to visit.

Cuba offers a great chance to explore and discover; since most visitors to Cuba still travel in organized groups, meeting other travellers is rare except in the main towns and hotels. The beauty of the Cuban countryside is unrivalled: to the west of Havana is the fertile land of the Pinar del Río region, with its endless fields of swaying sugarcane, small country lanes lined with red earth and lopsided, fading signs exhorting workers to greater productivity; the roads still ring with the resonances of a decades-long struggle. Tiny huts stand festooned with small bright flowers and the day's washing; families sit out in the shade.

Towards Trinidad on the southwest coast I crossed the Escambray mountains with their multitudes of pine trees and small agricultural co-operatives growing the deep green leaves of tobacco. *Rancheros* were rounding up cattle cowboy-style in the fields and I happened on a fantastically rough Sunday afternoon rodeo. Small abandoned railways and transport depots abound, pink stucco columns hold up the fading grandeur of colonial style houses in one-horse towns.

Looking for black market meat for my supper, a friend took me to visit some small farms and houses in the country. Everywhere we went we stopped for a chat and were offered some rum. It was an old-style country idyll that seemed not to have changed in centuries: a soft light played on the tall, gawky palm trees, coconuts were cut down for me to drink from. Beans lay drying in the sun, women were weaving mats across their porch from reeds and wild flowers, and men driving oxen before the plough with what looked like just a piece of string.

According to the unwritten law that states that what is forbidden becomes the object of greatest desire, Cubans can be obsessed with all things Western and particularly American. In Santa Clara, a lively university town in the centre of the country, we were approached at the hotel by the resident nurse, Raúl. His sister was a dancer, touring Europe – he was writing to her, urging her to leave the troupe and stay in Italy so that he could join her. He showed us photos of an extraordinarily beautiful woman and then pointed out a brawny Canadian often draped round her. This man was her boyfriend and had promised to marry her. He had stayed half a year in their house and suddenly disappeared without trace. Raúl had reams of letters from Westerners he had met through the hotel, he had corresponded tirelessly in the hope that someone might be coaxed into an offer of marriage or an invitation to visit, paying the fare for him to join them (which he assured us he would then work hard to pay back). If anyone ever agreed, he sighed, he would probably die of excitement. He had tapes of American rock music, his walls were plastered with posters of supermodels. There was a big concert that night, a famous Cuban band playing under the huge statue of Che Guevara, but he wouldn't come with me, he said, because Cuban music was pathetic. In fact he was now lost to Cuba, or Cuba was lost on him; he had rejected his entire culture because of the freedoms he has lost, the privations he endures, and could get excited only by Western culture and ideas. He was embarrassed by his family in the country, with their humble provincial ways, and lived in a no man's land, neither within Cuba nor without, waiting, restless and bored, for the day his fantasy would come true.

TRAVEL NOTES

Languages Spanish. Few Cubans speak any English.

Transport Train services, though extensive, tend to be slow and inefficient Buses and taxis have been hit hard by fuel shortages and existing services are erratic and crowded. Travel agencies lay on their own transport.

Accommodation Independent travellers are advised to book in advance through the official *Cubatur* office, Calle 23, No 156, Velado, Havana (☎32-452), as the cheaper hotels fill up quickly,

especially in the provinces. Staying with families is forbidden.

Special Problems Most visitors only need a tourist card available from travel agencies or the Cuban Embassy in London. The exception is for US citizens who are not usually permitted by their government to visit Cuba – unless on business – and always need a visa. A useful source of information in the US is *Marazul Tours*, 250 West 57th St, Suite 1311, New York City, 10107 New York (☎212/582 9570).

You may well be hassled by money-changers, especially outside the main hotels; it's best to steer clear.

Guides Simon Calder and Emily Hatchwell, *Cuba* (UK, Travellers Survival Kit). An excellent book; the first comprehensive guide to Cuba to be published.

CONTACTS

Federation of Cuban Women, Calle 11, no 214, Havana, Cuba. Central organization for making contact with women's groups throughout the country.

Cuba Solidarity Campaign, 129 Seven Sisters Rd, London N7 7QG, UK (☎0171/263 6452). Useful source of information on current events in Cuba – strongly against any form of US blockade.

BOOKS

Jean Stubbs, *Cuba, the Test of Time* (UK, Latin American Bureau, 1989). Iluminating, well-researched look at contemporary Cuban life.

Margaret Randall, *Women in Cuba: Twenty Years Later* (US, Smyrna, 1981). Good, if slightly dated, socialist-feminist analysis of women's gains in Cuba in the first two decades of the Revolution. Offers a positive view of advances in legal, political and workplace rights and positions, and in particular gains made by women against machismo in family life.

Inger Holt-Seeland, *Women of Cuba* (US, Lawrence Hill, o/p). Interviews with six women, from farm worker to university teacher.

Elizabeth Stone (ed), *Women and the Cuban Revolution* (UK & US, Pathfinder Press, 1981). Collection of speeches and documents, including the thoughts of Fidel Castro.

Pedro Perez Sarduy and Jean Stubbs (eds), *AfroCuba – An Anthology of Cuban Writing on Race, Politics and Culture* (US, Center for Caribbean Studies, 1993). Looks at the Black experience in Cuba through the eyes of the island's writers, scholars and artists.

Jacobo Timerman, *Cuba – A Journey* (UK, Picador, 1994/US, McKay, 1992). Gloomy assessment of the country's progress by a socialist who once shared the dreams of the Revolution.

FICTION

Cristina Garcia, *Dreaming in Cuban* (UK, Flamingo, 1992/US, Ballantine, 1993). Set in New York and Havana, this haunting first novel centres on the lives of four strong-willed Cuban women from the same family.

Achy Obejas, *We Came All the Way from Cuba So You Could Dress Like This?* (US, Cleis Press, 1994). Witty and erotic lesbian novel by one of a growing number of Chicana writers.

The Czech Republic

No sooner had the 1989 Velvet Revolution brought an end to over forty years of Soviet-imposed isolation, than Western tourists began flooding into Prague. The beauty of the Czech capital – which has preserved a wealth of art and architecture despite more than six centuries of wars and occupations – was enticement enough. With the added attractions of a rapidly developing tourist infrastructure, low living costs, a Westernized and cosmopolitan outlook and all the appeal of witnessing history in the making, tourist interest boomed. The city now ranks as one of the five most visited destinations in Europe, especially popular with young Americans as a cheaper,

and far trendier, alternative to Paris. Many stay on to soak up a 1990s version of bohemian life (Prague, after all, gave birth to the concept) and to cash in on the expanding job market for English-speakers and media-workers. Few, however, venture outside the capital and for most Westerners the towns and villages of Bohemia and Moravia remain as obscure as they were in the Soviet era.

The Czech Republic – formed when the two halves of Czechoslovakia split in 1993 following a surprise election victory for the Slovak nationalists – has proved better equipped than most of its East European neighbours to cope with the transition to democracy and the enterprise culture (certainly more so than the conservative, Catholic Slovak Republic). Much of this owes to the former strength of the economy and the international standing of Václav Havel, the country's dissident playwright and reluctant president. However, like in so many other former Eastern Bloc countries, the sweeping aside of Communism left fertile ground for a host of other social ills. Street crime is rocketing, the mafia is creaming off a large slice of the new tourist wealth, racketeering and corruption are endemic, and pollution in the cities a major health hazard – Prague being among the most afflicted. Those who have not found their niche are facing a degree of hardship and insecurity inconceivable in the Communist era.

Czechs have a reputation as a liberal, outward-looking people, and Prague is the obvious candidate for the political and cultural centre of the new *Mitteleuropa*. Resentments are, however, beginning to surface at the foreign take-over of the capital. The joint-venture clubs, bars, restaurants and hotels springing up in the historic centre are well beyond the means of ordinary city-dwellers and the constant demand for rooms is pushing up rents. Prices are routinely doubled or tripled for tourists and tourist muggings are on the increase. As elsewhere in the Eastern Bloc, racism, particularly towards the the large Romany population, is rampant, and Black and Asian tourists are facing increasing harassment from local skinheads. It's a sad fact that few Czechs consider racism a cause for concern.

For most **women** there are few problems in travelling around alone. Prague has its no-go areas (old-style pubs, particularly, are all-male preserves) but the city is no more intimidating than most Western capitals. Sexual harassment is rarely an issue – if anything, Czech men tend to take on a protective and chivalrous stance towards women – although it's wise to follow your instincts about who to trust. The ever-present and largely unchallenged pornography can be disquieting, especially as few are prepared to acknowledge any offense or unease about this. Feminism, meanwhile, has long been discredited as part of the old Communist rhetoric and women attempting to speak out against widespread sexual discrimination face considerable antagonism.

Stalking the Revolutions

Stacy Gilbert travelled extensively in Eastern Europe in 1987 while completing a degree in Soviet and East European Studies. She returned two years later with a Thomas J Watson fellowship to study vampire fact and folklore but found herself in the midst of the revolutions of 1989 instead. She currently lives in New York where she is enrolled in a Masters Degree at Columbia University.

I have always felt inexplicably drawn to this country. Perhaps I came to Prague looking for a home among these people with whom I share more than just the typically round Slavic face and high cheekbones. Having been cradled in the melting pot of America, I am partially of Czech and Slovak descent. My great-grandmother was born in Czechoslovakia but emigrated to the United States in search of a better life for her children. In a well-intentioned attempt to make a home in the new country, she insisted her children speak only English, but in doing so, they lost their connection with their history and heritage.

I first visited Prague in 1987, while I was a student in Vienna. Even seen through the chilly mist of the fading days of autumn, the city was breathtaking: the regal architecture along the banks of the Vltava; the wavy, red tiled roofs of Malá Strana; the rough cobblestone roads and narrow, winding streets of the Old Town, and a skyline of spires. I couldn't believe such beauty, such elegance, such grace could exist behind the Iron Curtain. I fell in love with Prague and with Czechoslovakia – its rich history and culture – but, admittedly, not immediately with its people.

In those days of constant police surveillance contact with foreigners was considered highly suspect and a simple query about directions to Charles Bridge would be met with a dismissive wave of the hand. But I could not reject the Czechs as easily as they seemed to reject me. I blamed their icy attitude on the frosty weather and chilly political climate.

Two years later, almost exactly to the day I first visited the country, I was again in Prague, but this time in the midst of the Velvet Revolution. I had hitched a ride from Berlin with Pavel, a Polish emigré on his way to Prague for an Esperanto conference. We stood together watching the wild celebrations in Wenceslas Square that followed the announcement that Czechoslovakia's Communist government had resigned. Cars filled with jubilant students brandishing the Czech tri-color sped past the statue of King Wenceslas while champagne corks popped and people hugged each other, cheered, cried and sang in triumph. As night fell and the temperature plummeted we began to search for a way out of the crowd, desperate for refuge from the biting wind and snow. Alena, an old friend of Pavel's, lived only two blocks from Wenceslas Square in a building still pock-marked by bullets from the street-fighting that took place twenty years earlier during the 1968 Soviet-led invasion of Czechoslovakia.

Two weeks ago she would not have allowed me into her apartment for fear that it would endanger her job.

Already carrying low in her final month of pregnancy, she had been watching the commotion on the square from the furthest corner of her living room window when Pavel showed up with me in tow. She herded us in quickly, poured out some shots of *Becherovka*, and begged us for details of what was happening. She was as flushed with excitement about the unfolding events as we were from the sudden transition from the freezing wind to the cosiness of her flat.

As we warmed up, the conversation turned serious. I asked her what she thought the future would hold for her and her job as instructor of Marxism-Leninism at a technical school in Prague. Yes, she had thought of that. It was all uncertain now, she said as she absently stroked her huge belly. For her country, this new, unpredictable future was certainly preferable to the predestined one they knew too well: the Five Year Plans and May Day parades, censorship and lies. She looked me squarely in the eye and admitted that two weeks ago, she would not have allowed me, an American, into her apartment for fear that it would endanger her job. Raising her cup of tea, she proposed a toast. We laughed and cheered as teacup clinked with Becherovka glasses: "To the Revolution!"

I have lived in Prague since those amazing days of November 1989 and have seen the fundamental changes in this country's politics, economy,

The key to getting past their cautious shell is to make the first move.

and indeed, in Czech society as a whole. But I concede that the Czech character continues to elude me. It is far easier to stereotype their neighbours: the efficient Germans, the adventurous Poles, the passionate Slovaks, the brave Hungarians, the cultured Austrians. Czechs are enigmatic, private, cautious and fatalistic. They are, in a word, bohemian. Their national hero is the shrewd, self-protective but lovable Good Soldier Švejk who fights (and wins) wars of attrition, never aggression. At first, Czechs can seem distant and cold, but if you do manage to break through the cynical exterior, you discover a tender Slavic soul.

Unfortunately, the Czechs I encounter daily at almost every ticket counter, shop queue, metro or tram still seem to be the same indifferent, rude, sometimes downright nasty people who brushed me off when the country was still a police state. Its hard to imagine that these might be the same people who invite me to dinner, stuff me with dumplings and homemade cakes and toast my health and future.

The key to getting past their cautious shell is to make the first move. I can think of many times when a chance encounter – checking an address, for example, has led to a spontaneous invitation to join family or friends at a weekend cottage or to go mushroom-picking in the mountains. Though impulsive, these invitations have always been sincere and have led to lasting friendships. I still get phone calls, holiday cards and dinner invitations from people I exchanged addresses with during the demonstrations on Wenceslas Square in 1989.

But it is sometimes difficult to find Czechs to talk to. Before the Revolution, it seemed they were all too busy shopping and standing in lines. Now, they are too busy working, shopping and standing in lines. And, from early Friday afternoon, the city empties onto the roads for the weekly exodus from the urban Stalinist housing estates to weekend cottages in the country. Never pass up an invitation to someone's cottage – it is here you will find Czechs at their bohemian best, hiking, mushroom-picking, gardening and, of course, drinking.

Very few women in their mid-twenties or older have time to sit and chat over a coffee. Usually they have to rush home to take care of their families. Even well-educated Czechs tend to get married and have children relatively early and I know that at least some of my Czech friends find it odd and maybe even a little uncomfortable that I am still single. I can almost see new aquaintances stepping back to assess my "abnormality"; surely any normal woman would have a husband and family by the withered age of 26!

My marital status has become the subject of a weekly ritual at a near-by vegetable market. An amiable old woman from whom I buy fresh flowers always checks my hand for a wedding ring before dramatically shaking her head and inquiring when I will get married. "I'm too young", I tease. She chuckles and admonishes me affectionately with the warning "Like Christmas cake!" – short for the proverb, "A woman, like Christmas cake, is no good after 25."

Reactions to me as a foreigner have begun to change since I first arrived. Standing in Wenceslas Square the night the hardline government resigned, I was speaking into a tape recorder describing the whirlwind of ecstatic chaos around me when someone tapped me urgently on the shoulder. I turned around and an old man with bright eyes asked me where I was from. When I told him America, he whipped out a harmonica from his coat pocket and launched into a robust rendition of *Yankee Doodle Dandy!* In Western Europe, I became accustomed to being accused of all my country's inequalities and ineptitudes, but for the Czechs, I was "ta Američanka" – "the American" and treated with a reverence I found strange. For them it seemed, I was a bitter-sweet reminder of all they had lost in the last forty years as well as a symbol of the higher ideals and better life they wanted for their children.

> *It has its own acronyms: YAPPIEs (Young Americans in Prague) or POPs (Poets/Painters/ Parasites of Prague).*

The opening of the country has brought with it a flood of Westerners, mostly young Americans: financial consultants, entrepreneurs, English teachers, writers, or simply those with enough money to hang out for a couple of months. So many, in fact, that the phenomenon has its own acronyms: YAPPIEs (Young Americans in Prague) or POPs (Poets/Painters/Parasites of Prague). Few bother to learn more than a few words of the language, or venture outside the poetry-reading, club-hopping exclusive Western clique they've established almost to the complete exclusion of the less financially carefree Czechs.

With the influx of foreigners in the capital, I am just one of the crowd: one more body on the metro, one less job for the Czechs. In smaller towns and villages though, conversations still halt abruptly when they hear me speak "Ameri-Czech". Older people smile broadly and proudly tell me of their uncles or cousins who have emigrated to Chicago, to Florida, to America.

This is a country undergoing fundamental political, economic and social change. The opening of what may well be one of the strongest economies of the former Soviet bloc has brought a flood of "imports" from the West: *McDonalds* and Madonna, investment bankers and young 90s-style beatniks, crime and unemployment, pornography and prostitution; all apparently part and parcel of "democracy" and the new enterprise culture. Many are critical of what they describe as a wild free-for-all, made up entirely of rights but with few acknowledged responsibilities. Unfortunately, a plague of hard-to-cure social ills has found fertile breeding ground in this fledgling state.

I've started to hear stories of violent attacks on women, no longer simply the prey of pickpockets and rip-off artists.

In a crowded, late afternoon metro, four young Czech skinheads began harassing two Asian men. One boy started to swing from the overhead bars, bringing his knees up closer and closer to one man's face. Distressed that other passengers either watched with indifference or blatantly ignored the boys' increasing aggression, an American friend and I decided we had to intervene. Stunned and confused by finding two strangers suddenly shouting at them in English, they scampered off at the next station. Looking round at the equally surprised and embarrassed expressions of the passengers it was hard to feel we'd achieved anything. Racism thrives on complacency.

Numerous times my Czech friends have warned me to beware of the African moneychangers, the Arab drug dealers, the Russian mafia, the Polish gun smugglers, the German skinheads, and the Gypsies who, according to Czechs, are the most loathsome of all. However, I've found that in the few cases where I've been ripped off, it has been by Czechs: the taxi drivers who charge foreigners exorbitant fees for round-about rides, the waiters who covertly add extra items to the bill, and the cashiers who regularly short-change customers.

I live and work in the city centre and generally feel a liberating sense of safety, even alone and at night, that I have never felt in an American city. In fact, more than once I've been stopped by a police car during my early morning run around the perimeter of a nearby park. Not noticing my personal stereo, running shoes and less-than-reckless pace, they ask if I'm OK, is anyone chasing me? But lately I've started to hear stories of violent attacks on women, no longer simply the prey of pickpockets and rip-off artists. I've taken my name off my doorbell buzzer and mailbox and like other women, have taken to carrying an illegal canister of mace in my bag, just in case.

Inevitably, foreign friends who come to visit me in Prague remind me of things I've become frighteningly used to, among them the pollution. Certainly, few modern cities escape the acrid fumes of car exhausts, but Prague has these and worse. The charming eighteenth-century buildings are generally still heated by an eighteenth-century method: brown coal, the effects of which, in turn, give Prague its year-round romantic haze. The winters can be crippling when the city's furnaces are going full blast. Last February during an especially bad week, I went out just to do some shopping and run some errands.

> *When I described a female friend as a feminist to Alena, she grimaced as though I had presented her with a dead rat.*

After only a few minutes outside, my eyes began to water and my nose stung. Within an hour I was forced back to my apartment by a brain-splitting headache that even the extra-strength aspirin I was gulping down could barely touch. On arrival, I dashed to the toilet and threw up, relief for my nausea but the headache became excruciating. I lay on my bed and cried myself into a fitful sleep listing the number of women I knew who have had miscarriages and even mildly deformed children. Is this the price I too will pay for living here?

Foreign friends are also shocked by the pornography that litters the streets of this otherwise majestic city: foreign and Czech skin-zines alongside knitting monthlies and children's comics, girlie posters in public transport, cheesy calendars and obscene matchboxes in reputable businesses and respectable hotels. Public display of these pictures is not thought of as being offensive to women. Indeed, few Czech women seem to notice, let alone complain about them. When a Czech friend accompanied her teenage daughter to a police station to report an attempted rape, they were confronted with bare-breasted models on posters covering the walls and desk of the officer-in-charge. The mother's complaints about the inappropriate pictures were simply dismissed as the foolish ravings of a feminist.

There is no other so-called Western "import" as contentious or ambiguous as the word "feminist." When I once described a well-educated, bold and opinionated female friend as a feminist to Alena, she grimaced as though I had just presented her with a dead rat. Alena, also well-educated, bold and opinionated, then proceeded to argue that our mutual friend was in fact an admirable person: intelligent, respectable, hard-working, and she had a boyfriend. I couldn't under-stand how we could have an argument when we both agreed on all these points. But it wasn't the characteristics we were arguing about, but simply the word "feminist".

Here, "feminism" is derided as just another "ism", like Marxism, Communism or Socialism; a banner under which you had to march, a cause you had to support. Having been forced into Women's Unions and International Socialist Women's Leagues for so long, Czech women welcome the freedom not to be associated with "feminism" anymore. Eva, a young colleague, rolled her eyes when describing "International Women's Day," a "holiday" heavy-handedly encouraged by the Soviet Union. Men would give their female colleagues flowers then leave work early to go to the pub. This ritual was repeated at home with the husband bringing flowers, eating dinner, then joining his friends for a night of heavy drinking.

Men are still expected to be subtly chivalrous in their dealings with women, giving up a seat on the metro or taking care of the restaurant bill. In fact, men tend to get deferred to in all matters concerning money. Similarly, women tend not to venture off on their own but go out in mixed couples or groups. This is not because they fear for their safety but because, in a subtle way, it is still considered impolite for a man to send a woman off on her own. Czech men are also extremely possessive and don't like to let "their" women out of their sight. In some areas, such as the local pubs, there's a palpable feeling that women are unwelcome. The last remaining bastions of "real men", the pubs are dingy places, dense with tobacco smoke, spilt beer on the tables and the obligatory porno posters covering the walls.

I have never experienced problems travelling alone in the Czech Republic or Slovakia, regardless of the mode of transportation. In fact, I've found the most rewarding way to travel is by hitch-hiking, especially between villages where the bus connections are too slow for my wanderlust. I was once picked up by a well-tailored gentleman in a sleek red sports car while trying to flag down a ride in the rain about a half an hour outside of Prague. His English was impeccable and his knowledge of Czech history seemed to be as personal as it was comprehensive. He effectively evaded my questions about his profession, what he was doing in Prague and where he learned to speak such beautiful English. Upon our arrival in Prague, he chauffeured me to my destination and finally introduced himself as the Prince of Bohemia.

When people ask me why I have stayed in the Czech Republic so long – in light of the increasing crime and cost of living, less than liberal attitude toward women, environmental dangers ad nauseam, etc – I give a farrago of reasons: the history, the beauty of a Prague Spring, an apartment with a functioning phone, research to be done, vocabulary to learn, things are changing, and I've been here so long, I can't imagine leaving. To put it quite plainly, I'm a Czechophile.

But the single, most significant experience that has kept me here so long resulted from some old black-and-white photos that my mother found in my grandmother's attic and sent to me after I settled down in Prague. On the back was a spidery scrawl in a language she assumed was Czech or Slovak. Armed with these aged photos and a yellowing letter with two names and addresses, I set off for the valley region south of the Tatra mountains in the easternmost part of former Czechoslovakia. I didn't expect to meet any long-lost relatives; surely they had all died, moved or emigrated. The best I could hope for was a house that was still standing or graves with the name "Matsko" somewhere in the vicinity.

My destination was a small village a few kilometres away from the nearest train station. I walked along the country roads to the church, the geographical, historical and spiritual center of any Czech or Slovak village where I paused to check again the names and addresses. No sooner had I unfolded the paper than two elderly women dressed in ebony brocade dresses, their heads covered by shiny, black kerchieves, approached to offer assistance. I explained that I wanted to see the house in which my great-great-grandmother had lived and handed them the letter. They peered intently at the yellowing piece of paper then asked the two questions that I would become very familiar with: "Američanka?" ("American?") and "Samá?" ("Alone?")

Each woman linked a large, solid arm around mine and waddled down the main road, calling gleefully: "American!" "Alone!"

Each woman linked a large, solid arm around mine and waddled down the unpaved main road with me, calling out gleefully to the other villagers: "American!" "Alone!" People peered at us from kitchen windows; children on bikes rode in front, craning their heads around to look at me; a handful of old men walked their bikes behind us and numerous others joined in what amassed to be a parade following us down the dusty road.

As if on cue, the entourage came to a halt in front of a white house and the muscular old arms that had securely held my own fell away. I unhitched the gate and walked up the short path to the door. I rang the doorbell and nervously bowed my head looking again at the piece of paper. A stout, stern-looking woman, elderly but of indeterminate age, answered the door and I explained in Czech, "I'm sorry to bother you. I have these addresses. I think my family lived here." She took the paper and read it, once, twice. She looked up at me slowly, her eyes glistening as she asked me the only question she needed for confirmation, "From

America?" I nodded and she threw her arms around me in an engulfing hug to the applause and cheering of the crowd that stood at the gate. I was home.

TRAVEL NOTES

Language Czech, a Slavic language that's famously difficult to learn. Though German is the standard second language of the older generation, and Russian was obligatory until 1989, learning English has almost become a national pastime for everyone from the president to the little old lady sitting next to you on the metro.

Transport Czech transport is reliable, extensive and remarkably inexpensive. Even train tickets to Western Europe and especially to the former socialist countries are cheaper to buy in the Czech Republic than in the West. Tram and metro tickets in Prague are also good value. Avoid using taxis unless you really want to be "taken for a ride".

Accommodation In an attempt to ease the room-finding frenzy that begins in May and continues until late October, new hotels and hostels, pensions and private rooms and a plethora of private accommodation agencies have sprung up in Prague. Foreigners are charged a higher rate than Czechs because of the "favourable exchange rate for foreign currency". Even with this legally dubious but widespread, two-tiered system, accommodation is still generally less expensive in the Czech Republic than in the West.

Guides The Rough Guide to the Czech and Slovak Republics and The Rough Guide to Prague (Penguin) are informative, entertaining and packed with up-to-date accounts of the political scene, artistic movements, literature and current social problems. A guidebook that can be read like a novel, *Sadakat Kadri's Prague* (UK, Cadogan Books), offers an in-depth and often odd history of Prague and its sights. A lively book even for those who think they know the city.

CONTACTS

Gender Studies Centre, Legerova 39, 12000 Prague 2 (Tues–Thurs noon–6pm; ☎02/24 91 1667 or 5041). Houses Prague's largest selection of books, journals, magazines, academic abstracts and general information for and about women. The centre also has a regular programme of reading groups, seminars (in Czech and English), and English-language courses. A good place to

begin making contacts. A similar centre may open soon in the Czech Republic's second largest city, Brno. For more information, contact: Charlie Buchanan, Filosofická fakulta, Masaryková universita, Arne Novaka 1, 600 00 Brno.
Mercury Club, Kolínská 11, Prague 2.
Lambda L-Club is a social gathering for lesbians, both Czech and foreign, held here – for now – every other Wednesday at 6pm. The place and time are subject to change, but the club's owner will be happy to give you the latest information. *Lambda* also has an evening telephone help-line (☎02/57 73 88) for men and women, occasionally staffed by English speakers.

To find out about women's groups in **Slovakia**, contact Jana Čziková, c/o *ASPECT*, Stáromestská 6, 815 69 Bratislava (☎07/37221).
Aspekt Magazine is a recently founded scholarly feminist journal – in Slovak – highlighting a different theme each issue. Contact Jana Juraňová, Bilíkova 3, 841 01 Bratislava, Slovakia.

BOOKS

Eva Hoffman, *Exit Into History* (UK, Minerva, 1994/US, Penguin). Eva Hoffman, a Polish-born writer, returns to Eastern Europe to bear witness to the changes wrought by the fall of Communism. A literary *tour de force* – erudite, lucid and knowing.

Lesley Chamberlain, *In the Communist Mirror: Journeys in Eastern Europe* (UK, Faber & Faber, 1990/US, Faber, o/p). Chamberlain describes herself as "a discontented Westerner dazzled by austerity" – just part of the honesty she brings to bear in relating her travels in the former Eastern Bloc. Her chapter on Czechoslovakia, set in the mid-1980s, evokes the sense of the absurd that made life just bearable under the Communist regime.

Martha Gelhorn, *A Stricken Field* (1940; UK, Virago, 1986, o/p/US, Penguin). Martha Gelhorn provides a fascinating, if sometimes sentimalized, account of a country on the verge of occupation, based on her experiences of arriving as an American journalist in Prague just as the Nazis marched into Sudetenland.

Misha Glenny, *The Rebirth of History* (UK, Penguin, 1993/US, Penguin, 1991). A thorough account of the elements that fueled the Eastern

European revolutions in 1989 by the BBC's highly acclaimed Central and Eastern European correspondent.

Timothy Garton Ash, *We the People: The Revolutions of 1989* (UK, Granta Books, 1990). Ash's personal and amusing anecdotes of the revolutions in Poland, Hungary, East Germany and Czechoslovakia are as entertaining as they are enlightening.

Václav Havel, *Living in Truth* (UK, Faber & Faber, 1989/US, Faber, 1986); *Letters to Olga* (UK, Faber & Faber, 1990/US, Holt, 1989); *Disturbing the Peace* (UK, Faber & Faber, 1990/US, Vintage, 1991); *Open Letters* (UK, Faber & Faber, 1991/US, Vintage, 1992). Includes essays and the prison letters Havel wrote to his wife, Olga, often under great duress (and heavy censorship). A revealing, frequently moving collection of one man's thoughts, experiences and hopes.

Miranda Davies (ed), *Women and Violence: Realities and Responses Worldwide* (UK & US, Zed Books, 1995). Includes a contribution on women and violence in post-Communist Czechoslovakia by Jirina Siklova and Jana Hradilkova, founder and co-ordinator of the gender studies centre (see *Contacts*).

FICTION

Eva Kantůxrkov, *My Companions in the Bleak House* (UK, Quartet, 1989, o/p/US, Penguin, 1991, o/p). Set in the detention cell in a women's prison outside Prague, this novel provides a tale of survival in the face of human stupidity.

Zina Rohan, *The Book of Wishes and Complaints* (UK, Flamingo, 1992/US, Hutchinson). The story of a young country girl who moves to Prague during the months of the 1968 Prague Spring.

Lidmilla Sovakova, *The Drowning of a Goldfish* (US, Permanent Press, 1990). Sharply observed story of how the Communist takeover changed one woman's life.

Zdena Tomin, *Stalin's Shoes* (UK, Dent, 1987, o/p). First novel by Czech dissident, now living in Britain, which draws from the events leading up to Prague 1958 and the subsequent collapse.

David and Peter Turnley, *Moments of Revolution in Eastern Europe* (US, Stewart Tabori & Chang Inc, 1990, o/p). Twin brothers David and Peter Turnley's 1990 Pulitzer Prize-winning book of photos of the 1989 revolutions in Eastern Europe.

Denmark

Perched on the fringes of mainland Europe, Denmark, the smallest and southernmost of the Scandinavian countries, comprises the jagged peninsula of Jutland and four hundred islands, the largest of which, Zealand, is dominated by the capital, Copenhagen. Although more in line with the rest of Europe in terms of its cost of living and drinking laws, Denmark shares the same kind of affluent lifestyle and enlightened welfare policies of its northern neighbours. You'll find a marked tolerance for so-called alternative interests, from street theatre and summer rock festivals to experiments in education and communal living. Attitudes to sex and sexuality are also more relaxed than in southern Europe – gay marriages were legally sanctioned in 1989.

Most visitors head straight for Copenhagen with its lively cosmopolitan feel, quite different from the more insular, slightly old-world atmosphere of the provinces beyond. The capital has everything, from interesting museums and galleries, and plenty of green space, to bars, cafés and clubs galore. Elsewhere Denmark's largely green, flat landscape is peaceful and undramatic with pretty villages and some fine sandy beaches, especially on Funen and other smaller islands. Being flat, this is an ideal country for cycling and virtually half the Danish adult population (around five million) owns a bike – partly due to a huge tax on cars. For the less energetic, most places are connected by an excellent network of trains, buses and ferries. Finding a place to stay is similarly straightforward, though hotels can be expensive. As in most of Europe, youth hostels and campsites – both usually excellent – are the most economical option.

Despite a generally more progressive approach to sexual relations, for most Danish **women** nuclear family units and traditional sex roles are the enduring prototype. Communes and collectives in both agrarian and urban settings have proliferated since the 1960s but they're still viewed as a largely middle-class alternative. On the other hand, within fields of adult education, women's studies have made an impact across both class and regional boundaries. Courses on aspects of women's lives are now part of most high-school curricula and in the late 1970s a Women's School, the *Kvindehojskolen*, was esablished in the south of Jutland.

Under an Alternative Flag

Leo Sykes was drawn to Denmark by the work of an experimental theatre group, Odin Teatret, whose performances she first saw at the age of eighteen – an experience she describes as the closest she has ever come to physical addiction. She visited the country for over eight years before finally settling in the small town of Holstebro in northwest Jutland to study and work with the group.

All my preconceptions about Denmark turned out to be true. It is cold, expensive, flat, small, and the Danes do eat pickled herrings and are mostly tall and blonde. But they also hold wild parties and sunbathe nude in public parks, have continental-style cafés and beautiful beaches. I have joined the crowd and sunbathed topless in the middle of Arhus (one of the largest and most attractive towns in Denmark) and was not harassed once. Afterwards I went to the local supermarket, and on leaving saw a man cycle past, completely naked.

Apparently it is now illegal to go about totally nude in town centres, as it's considered hazardous to traffic, but the mentality is still the same. Recently my mother came to visit and, reminding me of my prudish British roots, asked me if she could keep her knickers on in the sauna, a practice unseen in uninhibited Denmark.

After I first settled here, whenever I returned to Britain, my friends used to ask me how my Swedish was coming along, or how I was enjoying Norway. Denmark was apparently too small and anonymous for anyone to remember. Until, that is, the country did two very noticeable things. First it won the European soccer cup, at which point people began asking me if I was proud to live in Denmark; and secondly, it said "no" to Maastricht. Suddenly this small and anonymous land had become a fiery rebel, putting sparks back into the monolith of Europe. Or at least, that is

> *I have never felt unsafe; I always have the freedom of going out alone, no matter where and no matter when.*

how the Danes like to see it; such independent thinking barely conceals a disturbing xenophobia. Most of the immigrant communities in Denmark are refugees, and while the majority are obliged to learn Danish, those from former Yugoslavia are not allowed to make friends with their Danish helpers, let alone take a job or get an education. I don't know how this compares with the treatment of refugees in other countries, but I do know that the Danes are strangely torn between their liberal, socially minded ideals and their national identity as a small country isolated in the north of Europe, and would like to retain both the smallness and the isolation.

Denmark is not an exciting or socially stunning country, nor is it (except for Copenhagen) crammed with beautiful architecture, breathtaking church spires or internationally famous galleries and museums, but it does have many pretty towns and small but interesting galleries. One of the high points of my year is to be able to sit in the sunshine at midnight. It only happens for a very short period, but it is quite a special experience to be lying in bed at midnight with the sun still coming through the window. Life is pleasant, easy and convenient but it can also seem a bit too bland. Living out in the provinces, the main things I miss are people, crowds, excitement, the anonymity of vast cities and the choice of things to do. Foreign guests have asked me "But where are all the people?" Well, there really aren't that many. On the positive side this means you can get everything done fast and efficiently. And I have never felt unsafe; I always have the freedom of going out alone, no matter where and no matter when.

Danish banks, an emblem of the safe and unparanoid lifestyle, are totally open-plan, with customers and employees wandering freely around the different desks. The only thing that stands between you and the cash till is a bowl of free sweets. I was recently in a building society in London when an attempted robbery took place. Metal shutters crashed down along the counters, isolating the money from the robber and the rest of us. We stood there, staring at each other, until the automatic alarm sounded and he ran out. There are no metal shutters in Denmark, and there are also very few robbers. Of course crime is on the increase as it is everywhere, but we often leave our house open when we're out and so far nothing has been stolen.

When I first began watching the news on Danish TV I thought there must be a huge feminist meeting or political debate.

Equally, this is the country in which to have children, the idea being that they're the responsibility of society and not just the individual parent. As soon as kids can pedal, they cycle themselves to school. Trains, ferries, shops and banks have play areas, and there is even a train escort service for young children. Parents can share a six-month "maternity" leave, and babies can go to crèches from the age of three months. All fathers, even if they were only there on the night of conception, are obliged to pay child-care until the child is eighteen. Marriage doesn't come into it.

Denmark is also a state of social services. The unemployed have their social advisers, children have free hot-lines to child psychologists, old people receive home visits. Public buildings are big and clean. This is partly made possible by taxation at fifty percent, which helps create the effect of an apparently classless society. Of course there are rich and there are poor, but walking down the street you can't immediately place people by their clothes and Danish accents give clues as to geographic origins, not class status.

Another contributing factor is the highly egalitarian state education system, supported by a wide choice of free or very inexpensive schools. Academic achievement is not the sole, or even the main, aim of the Danish school system. As much focus is put on the development of children as people as it is on their exam results. In many ways this is the ideal plan, based on the kind of philosophy I have always believed in, but again I have to acknowledge that I miss the variety and energy of a more diverse society. Even the Danish queen, who is very popular, seems like a "normal person", waving out of her bedroom window to the crowd and the television cameras on her birthday, in her dressing gown and with unbrushed hair.

Denmark is sexually very liberated and highly promiscuous: it's all there for the asking. One of the best forms of entertainment in the long winter evenings is to ask a Danish friend about their sexual exploits and adventures. These hilarious and extraordinary tales keep me rapt for hours and are infinitely more amusing than anything to be found on Danish TV. And this is not just frivolous indulgence on the part of a few individuals. Danish legislation reflects the different aspects of sexual liberation. Gay couples can get married, with a church blessing, and I was recently invited to my first ever lesbian engagement party. The other side of this coin is the free availability of pornography. There is no top-shelf, behind-the-counter mentality here: titles such as *Anal Sex* are offered on the same shelf as liquorice ribbons and chocolate mice.

When I first began watching the news on Danish TV I thought there must be a huge feminist meeting or political debate going on. But this debate went on and on. Lots of women were voicing their opinions. Every day, many of these unapologetically self-assured women would be being interviewed. Slowly, as I got more used to the Danish news and began to get some grasp of the Danish language, I came to realize that these women were Danish politicians (so many of them!). What is more, the majority of news-readers are women as well. Danish women aren't particularly feminist, but they are without doubt the most emancipated women I have ever seen; I say this as my Danish boyfriend sits sewing me a dress in the other room.

Mostly due to watching English and American films, which are subtitled rather than dubbed on Danish TV, all Danes speak impeccable English. This is wonderful for the tourist or visiting business person, but can be a problem for someone who comes to live here. I have had to refuse point blank to speak English, not only to my colleagues at work but also to strangers, just in order to have some chance of learning the language.

Denmark is interesting in terms of its national identity. On any festive occasion, be it a birthday or the greeting of a relative or friend at an airport, out comes the Danish flag. You can buy packets of them in a variety of sizes, sold in supermarkets next to the cake candles and streamers. I was very taken aback by the first Danish birthday party I attended as the room was awash with these red and white flags: it looked horrifyingly nationalistic. But for the Danes the flag is a sign of festivity, not nationalism. Last week we held a birthday party for a ten-year-old. When I asked her if she would like to keep the "Danish flags" from her birthday cake she answered that they weren't Danish flags, but party flags, even though she conceded that they looked identical.

Another kind of party is very particular to Denmark. Known as the "family party", this is a gathering of probably little seen family members at which coffee, schnapps and homemade cakes are the centre pieces. But what is fascinating is the singing: traditionally, each guest arrives with a gift of a specially written song about the host, who in return has prepared a special song of thanks. Although each person is supposed to write their own lyrics, those lacking inspiration can turn to professional song-writers – mostly old women – who for a fee will compose a song.

Danish parties are not for the faint-hearted. They usually last until sunrise and consist of getting totally drunk. This applies to all ages from eighteen upwards. Schnapps and Gammel Dansk, a brown liquor that tastes like cough medicine, are what get the parties swinging while the evening is rounded off with beers, believed to help people sober up and avoid hangovers the next day.

The more "alternative" side of Denmark is encapsulated in Christiania, a small area of Copenhagen that became self-governing in the early 1970s and has been a focus of national controversy ever since. Featuring self-built houses, a large and active concert hall, some bars, openly available drugs and a vegetarian restaurant Christiania remains occupied by a largely self-sufficient community of around one thousand. No one pays electricity bills and the streets are of dirt, but at last this is somewhere where not everything is concerned with cleanliness, punctuality, decency and convenience. Even this enclave of lawlessness is not threatening, however, and it's a relief to finally hear loud music, see grubby-looking kids and dogs wandering around and be able to buy cheap and cheerful food. Christiania is scruffy, open, loud, and as close to being in London as I have ever felt in Denmark. It may have lost a lot of its original ideology, but it's still a lively place, and by standing in direct opposition to the more puritanical values of provincial Denmark, undoubtedly retains its own historical and emblematic importance.

TRAVEL NOTES

Languages Danish – similar to Norwegian and Swedish – with English and German widely spoken.

Transport An excellent system of trains, buses and ferries connects most of the country. Special routes make it safe and pleasant to cycle everywhere.

Accommodation A good option is to stay in private rooms, similar to British Bed and Breakfasts and listed in local tourist offices, which can also recommend the less expensive hotels. Youth hostels and campsites are plentiful and seldom full.

Special Problems Non-meat eaters will have a tough time finding places to eat out, as vegetarianism is a very foreign concept in Denmark. Buying food for yourself can be surprisingly expensive: potatoes, for example, though normally quite affordable, can be exorbitant if you buy the wrong kind or at the wrong time of year (the first potatoes of the season, which come from the island of Samso and are regarded as a great delicacy, can cost the equivalent of £100 for a kilo!).

Guides *The Rough Guide to Scandinavia* (Penguin) contains a good section on Denmark. The highly readable and witty gay and lesbian guide to Europe, *Are You Two . . . Together?* (UK, Virago/US, Random House), by Lindsy Van

Gelder and Pamela Robin Brandt, has an enthusiastic chapter on Copenhagen.

WOMEN'S ACCOMMODATION

Kvindelejren Femo, c/o Femogruppen Kvindehuset, Gothersgade 37, 1123 Copenhagen (☎33/91 15 57). A women-only camp on the Danish island of Femo, held annually during the *Femogruppen* (women's group) International Week. Children welcome.

CONTACTS

Dannerhuset, Gyldenlovesgade 37, Copenhagen (☎33/14 16 76). The city's chief women's centre, which includes a café and bookshop. Also good for information about women's activities in the rest of the country.
Kvindehuset, Gothersgade 37, Copenhagen (☎33/14 28 04). Smaller version of the above.

BOOKS

Inga Dahlsgard, *Women in Denmark, Yesterday and Today* (Denmark, Nordic Books – available from the Danish Cultural Institute, 3 Doune Terrace, Edinburgh, EH3 6DY). Refreshing look at Danish history from the point of view of its women.
Mary Wollstonecraft, *A Short Residence in Sweden, Norway and Denmark* (UK & US, Penguin, 1987). Searching account of Wollstonecraft's three-month solo journey through southern Scandinavia in 1795.

FICTION

Dea Trier March, *Winter's Child* (UK, Serpent's Tail, 1986/US, Bison Books). Wonderfully lucid sketch of modern Denmark as seen through the eyes of several women in the maternity ward of a Copenhagen hospital.
Peter Hoeg, *Miss Smilla's Feeling for Snow* (UK, Flamingo, 1994). The central character of this beautifully crafted tale is a tenacious Greenlander named Smilla Jaspersen who sets out to investigate the cause of a small boy's death. Published in the US as *Smilla's Sense of Snow* (Dell, 1994).

Egypt

E gypt's tourism industry is in an uncertain state. In the summer of 1992 the industry ground momentarily to a halt as news reverberated that Islamic radicals had begun targetting foreign tourists in bombing and shooting campaigns as a means of undermining the economy. The Valley of the Kings, one of the oldest and most popular tourist destinations in the world, suddenly emptied, leaving the pyramids standing in an isolation unknown to the site for centuries. Staunch reassurances from the government, backed by blanket policing, have done much to allay fears – within a year over a quarter of a million tourists arrived from Britain alone – while the security coup of the contro-

versial 1994 Cairo Conference on Population boosted confidence still further (protection of delegates was used as justification for mass detentions and a long list of civil rights abuses). At the time of writing only the Middle Nile region around Assyut has been declared out of bounds for visitors. It's advisable, nonetheless, to get an update from the foreign consulate before planning your trip.

Security apart, Egypt has never been an easy country for women travelling alone. The clamour and hustle of Cairo; the sheer numbers of touts, "guides" and street-traders who congregate on the main tourist areas, not to mention the fairly constant level of sexual harassment, can leave you feeling confused and intimidated. It can also take a while to come to terms with being a symbol of affluence (to some people, the only viable source of income) in a country where unemployment is high and poverty intense.

Western women are assumed to have a far more casual approach to sex and morality than their Egyptian counterparts. The fact that so many choose to leave the confines of family and wander alone in areas dominated by men (even share rooms with men they are not married to) is used to fuel the myth of the available Westerner. Travelling alone you are likely to come up against a stream of comments and propositions, and, though this rarely reaches threatening levels, it can be a strain. It helps to dress as inconspicuously as possible, covering arms, shoulders and legs, and to follow the more conservative behaviour of Westernized Egyptian women. If you come to Egypt to work, however, these problems are less intense. Egyptians are renowned for their open-handed hospitality and the care and protection they offer to anyone accepted as guest. It's worth remembering that no Egyptian woman would put up with the harassment and propositions routinely meted out to tourists. If you find yourself on the receiving end of blatant sexual harassment remonstrate loudly and turn to a woman for help; the chances are that she will wade in, pouring scorn on your abuser for his shameful act. The Sinai Peninsula, the homeland of the Bedouin, is noticeably more relaxed than elsewhere and about the only place where you might feel comfortable sunbathing on public beaches. Many women spend days on camel tours in the desert with Bedouin guides without any concerns whatsoever about safety.

Women in Egypt are returning, sometimes voluntarily, but also under considerable social pressure, to traditional roles. While in rural areas they continue to labour for long hours under arduous conditions to maintain a subsistence living, the all too familiar scapegoating of women who attempt to retain their positions in the workplace during a climate of recession and high unemployment is particularly strong. The **women's movement**, as such, exists only underground – the assassination of the liberal writer Farag Fouda, accused of daring to mock the Islamic societies as "unenlightened groups of darkness", imposes an unofficial but frightening censorship of the progressive left, and the development of an autonomous movement seems an ever more distant prospect. Despite this, women have continued to speak out in defence of their civil rights and to attempt to find new, and Egyptian, ways of reconciling secular egalitarian ideals with the precepts of Islam. Among the small number of women who have distinguished themselves through feminist writing, Nawal el Saadawi (see *Books*, p.207) was the most influential throughout the 1980s.

An Instinctive Kind of Caring

Kate Baillie, a freelance writer, lived in Cairo for two-and-a-half months teaching English and learning Arabic. While her piece is set in the early years of Mubarak's rule, just after the assassination of Sadat, the sense of emerging conflict that she describes and the attitudes she encounters, have an enduring relevance.

E gypt is the West's pet Arabic country, "moderate" being the favourite adjective. It's important to know that this reflects little of the internal situation, but is simply Egypt's pro-Western economic and diplomatic policy. In reality, Egyptians are imprisoned for criticizing the government; censorship of the arts and media is commonplace; political parties are suppressed, and Cairo and the provincial capitals are infested with armed police and soldiers. In the Cairo press and television centre, levelled rifles greet employees from a sandbag emplacement inside the foyer. The oppression is not quite as bad now as it was under President Sadat, but while a few political prisoners are released and the odd paper is allowed to publish again, American enterprise continues to prise apart Egyptian culture, values and economy.

A new polarization has appeared above the basic division of peasant and bourgeois, villager and Cairean. Those in the pay of the multinationals form their own super class. Speaking only English, adopting Sindy-Doll and grey-suited dress, their living standards leap while their lives become subservient to work patterns evolved for a very alien climate and culture. Speed, greed, glamour and competitiveness are the requisite values. Meanwhile, the majority, who don't or can't choose that rat race, remain in their desert robes and poverty, upholding values and a vision of society derived from a history much older than the West now knows.

The re-emerging strength of Islamic fundamentalism has to be appreciated in this context. An apparently fanatical religious social movement is hard for many to comprehend. What has to be grasped is that Islamic fundamentalism is both political and religious and there is no distinction because of the nature of Islam. The Muslim faith is a set of rules for a state, not just for individuals and it is in this that it differs so much from Christianity. Inevitably, the religious text, the Koran, is open to all manner of conflicting interpretations.

There is a communion between women that our Western conception of sisterhood could never emulate.

It can be argued – contrary to actual practice in Egypt – that the Koran stipulates the right of women to choose their husbands and to leave them. The financial rights it lays down for women were not achieved by European women until the nineteenth and twentieth centuries. Its banking policy would make you open an account tomorrow. Its precepts on virginity and menstruation would make you run a mile. During the Prophet's lifetime, some women complained that only men were being addressed. From then on, the two words for male believers and female believers appear. There is nothing in the Koran about female circumcision.

Leaving behind the fifth and sixth centuries, the struggle for emancipation was started by Egyptian women at the end of the last century. In 1962, under Nasser, they obtained the vote, access to free education at all levels, and a woman minister for social affairs was appointed. In the last twenty years, women have entered the professions, factories, the civil service and business, though they are not allowed to be judges. In the public sector, equal pay is legally enforceable. Women now comprise almost fifty percent of the workforce though nearly half of those are peasant women working in the fields with their men as they have done for centuries. Abortion remains illegal and clitoridectomy, proving virginity on the wedding night and the punishment of adultery are still practised.

Sadat created an official Women's Movement with his Madison Avenue-bedecked wife Jihan as president. Although they managed to push through certain reforms, such as allowing women the right to

EGYPT

instigate divorce, the movement had little popular support. It was seen as little more than a tea party circle of her friends enjoying the freedoms of power and riches. The real Women's Movement, though inevitably made up of educated urban women, is pan-Arab and takes its position from Arab history and experience, not American or European feminist texts.

In the villages and among the urban poor, where feminism is unheard of, there is a communion between women who share work in and outside the home, in ways that our Western conception of sisterhood could never emulate. In Cairo, I experienced from women this almost instinctive kind of care and protectiveness. On several occasions women who were strangers to me and spoke no English rescued me from situations in which I was unwittingly at risk. Wandering, heat-dazed and lost, in a slum behind the Citadel, a woman took my arm, smiled at me and led me out of the maze, shooing away the men and little boys who approached us. A few days later I tried sleeping in Al Azhar mosque, unaware that this is forbidden to women, let alone infidels. A soldier appeared with the intention of arresting me, but I was saved by a woman who sat me behind her and talked at length to what were by now five soldiers and seven other men grouped around. Presumably she explained my ignorance: the only words I could catch from the men were "Police" and "Koran". But she succeeded, the men left and the woman smiled at me and patted the ground to show I could stay.

> *I avoided any words the dictionary gave for "atheist", which carries the same connotations as saying you eat babies.*

Aside from the pyramids, the mosques are the sights to see in Cairo, both from the "gaping at beautiful buildings" point of view and to experience the use Muslims make of their places of worship. A note on dress – you always have to take your shoes off and in the more tourist-frequented mosques you may have to pay to get them back. Though not usually enforced, I'd advise wearing a scarf, out of courtesy if nothing else. As for shorts, short skirts, punk hair styles and bra-lessness with clinging clothes, forget it, whether in mosques or in the street.

Mosques can also be the best places to meet Egyptian women – especially where a women's area is curtained off. Not long after the incident in Al Azhar, I was very comforted to be separated from the men. But I still wasn't sure about the sleeping rules, so I gestured an enquiry to a woman, in her fifties I supposed, veiled and gowned to the floor in black. She immediately bounced up to me, talking nineteen to the dozen and then went off to fetch two friends who spoke some English. With their fifty odd words and my fifteen of Arabic, gestures, pictures and a dictionary, and joined by two more women, we passed several hours together in enthusiastic discussion. They asked me the two standard questions that had opened every conversation I had had in Cairo with men or women: "What's your religion?" and "Are you married?" the latter, once answered negatively, would be replaced by "Where's your friend?".

The first question had involved me in metaphysical arguments I had long forgotten, and I learned to avoid any words the dictionary gave for "atheist", which carries the same moral connotations as saying you eat babies. I don't know what these women understood about my religion or lack of it, but they burst into delighted laughter at the fact of my having not one "friend" but lots. They removed my scarf, combed my hair, called me *halwe* (sweet, pretty) and invited me to eat with them later.

Egyptians are renowned for their kindness, humour and generosity. It was these qualities that I appreciated in the Egyptian men I became friends with. I was treated with great respect and my views were listened to without having to force a space to speak. But when it came to anything to do with sex, they were pathological. One group of colleagues assumed, on zero evidence, that I was having an affair with one of them. They persuaded his wife that I was, expected their turn to be next, and were baffled by my astounded refusals. Their image of Western women and their idea of American companies are similar illusions: free sex and fast money. What I found again and again after similar and worse experiences, was a childlike shame, profuse apologies and misconception of my attitude when I taxed them with their behaviour. These men were all liberals or socialists and well-educated.

However, don't let this put you off getting into conversation with Egyptian men. Though I don't know the statistics for rape and assault, I'd stake a lot on Cairo being a safer place than London for a woman on her own. But even if you encounter no unmanageable difficulties, Cairo is an exhausting experience. Oxford Street during the sales has nothing on every street in the centre of the city all day and most of the night. Crossing roads is like trying to fly a kite at Heathrow. The fumes, heat and dust, the noise of car horns and shouting, and the spilling, squashing buses are a nightmare. And manoeuvering through this you have to contend with constant pestering, mostly verbal, from the passing male masses. There are times when you feel very exposed and wish you were robed and veiled.

A Student in Alexandria

Caroline Bullough has travelled extensively around the Middle East. After completing a degree in Arabic and Persian, she moved to the University of Alexandria to spend a year studying Arabic.

The arrival of thirty British students of Arabic (half of them female) caused quite a stir on Alexandria University's dusty concrete campus. I was lodged, along with three other women, in a newly built hut, already falling down, in a far corner of the campus and it was soon surrounded by a gaggle of curious onlookers. For the first few weeks we were showered with invitations and accosted by students eager to practise their English.

Most of these were men. The female students were initially shy and perhaps a little wary. Those who did approach us were obviously considered "forward" and therefore disapproved of. It was also clear that many parents disliked the idea of us associating with their daughters – friendships were suddenly broken off or invitations withdrawn without warning. The very fact that we were four girls living in a flat of our own without parents or guardians was enough to guarantee their disapproval. As foreign women it was frustratingly difficult to maintain platonic friendships with Egyptian men as at some stage it was always made clear that more was expected.

Foreign women are well-known as "easy game". Every Egyptian man claims to have at least one friend who can testify to the willingness of a foreign woman he once met. In a society in which pre-marital sex is officially taboo and a complex set of rules govern even informal relations between the sexes, the freedom enjoyed by most Western women is easily misinterpreted. I was asked constantly what my relationship was with the male students on the course. That they should be my close friends and no more seemed beyond comprehension. Those Egyptians who had begged for invitations to our parties, with the expectation of witnessing orgiastic mass coupling, were disappointed.

We could do little to dispel the myths which abound about foreign women (amply reinforced by imported American films and television programmes). However hard I tried to adopt an appropriately decorous way of life, I could not escape the fact that I was foreign and all that it implied. I was evicted from my first flat for having my fellow students (some male) to tea!

To live each day facing a barrage of comments, whispered or shouted, humorous or insulting, can be a strain. I became increasingly adept at avoiding particularly difficult situations, such as passing groups of young boys, who learnt at an early stage to imitate their elders' attitude to foreign women, or crowded pavement cafés. I learnt to ignore, and sometimes not even hear, the comments and asides. I learnt to stride purposefully through the milling crowds, defying passers-by to challenge me. The hassle was often at its worst when we were in groups of girls or pairs, but seldom did I actually feel under any physical danger. I was followed on several occasions both in Cairo and Alexandria but this never happened when I was alone and because I had got to know the area, it was less frightening than it might have been.

Leaving a crowded bus I was prodded from behind and shouted at by a woman concealed by a thin black veil and cape.

I often went out alone and found a café where I was able to sit undisturbed, my back to the road. I longed to be able to wander at will but it was only when I was with someone else that I felt confident enough to look around me. Alone, it was easier to walk head bowed, ears closed rather than risk attracting anyone's attention. This was the stance adopted by many Egyptian women who are themselves the object of unwanted attention.

Nowhere are wandering hands or, for that matter, wandering bodies, quite such a problem as on crowded buses and trams. Morning tram rides to the university were a constant nightmare of sweaty bodies, grinding hips and whispered comments. However, if you find yourself seriously cornered you should make a fuss, and other passengers will invariably help you out.

Egyptian students seemed to pay far more attention to appearance than their British counterparts. Most were dressed in smart Western clothes. Growing support for Muslim fundamentalism with its restrictions on dress was, however, clear. During my last months at the university, there was a student election in which a large number of known members of the Muslim Brotherhood were elected. During the week of the election the walls of the university were plastered with banners exhorting all female students to dress in the prescribed Muslim manners. Bizarre fashion shows were organized on the university campus to demonstrate suitable garb.

Few women in Egypt have returned to full Islamic dress but a woman covered from head to foot in a black, Iranian-style *chador* is an unnerving sight. The voluminous garments and thick veils rob her of human shape or form. Her feet are carefully concealed under the floor length folds of her skirt and her hands are covered by thick black gloves. Once, leaving a crowded bus (all public transport in Egypt is crowded), I was prodded from behind and shouted at by a woman concealed by a thin black veil and cape. Her strident tone of voice and colourful language astonished me and seemed at odds with her devout appearance. The force of her impatient curses was undoubtedly increased by her anonymity.

Alexandria is more Mediterranean than Arab with its elegant colonial buildings and pavement cafés. The Alexandrians are proud of their city and "Welcome in Alexandria" or "Welcome in Egypt" is on everyone's lips. At night the city is bright and vibrant, the streets teeming. Because of terrible overcrowding at home and particularly in hot weather, most Egyptians spend a large part of their lives on the streets. Coffee houses are exclusively male preserves but respectable restaurants and cake shops are full of women and families tucking into large platters of *ful medames* (a stewed bean dish) and small cakes oozing with honey.

The city is famous for its beaches which attract visitors from throughout the Middle East. In fact they are over-crowded during the summer and rather windswept in winter. Most Egyptian women remain fully clothed on the beach and even in the sea. Hassle is inevitable – Alexandria has its share of rather overweight "beach bums"– but not unbearable. Swimsuits are, even now, sufficiently rare to arouse interest in all who pass. There's a private beach in the grounds of the Montazeh Palace on the outskirts of Alexandria where we were able to swim and sunbathe almost undisturbed but bikinis are rarely seen even there.

Standards of medical care in urban Egypt are generally high, at least if you are rich or a foreigner. However, although many Egyptian doctors have been trained abroad, there seems to be considerable ignorance of specifically female ailments. Suffering badly from thrush, I visited a doctor associated with the university with whom I had been registered on arrival. Most drugs are available over the counter in any pharmacy so, had I known, I could probably have treated myself. Instead I was subjected to a rather ham-fisted internal examination and a long series of questions. It was clear that the doctor assumed that I must be suffering from a sexually transmitted disease and seemed only partially convinced by my protestations. To be fair, though, the medication I was prescribed, made in Egypt under licence, was extremely effective.

Working with the Bedouin

Emma Loveridge first visited Sinai as part of her postgraduate studies of early Christian Art. In 1991, still in her mid-twenties, she set up a travel company, *Wind, Sand and Stars*, that aimed to combine a tour of the historical sights of the desert with an understanding of the Bedouin way of life. She now also works with the Bedouin in the Western and Eastern deserts of Egypt.

Hundreds of small camp fires were already burning as I picked my way through the trucks and camel trains of those arriving, like myself, at the annual festival of the Bedouin at their ancestral shrine in the desert. I watched as the sun shifted behind the mountains throwing the great valley into shadow. Laughter burst out from the family groups gathering around the fires. Women cooked, men gossiped, toddlers raced across the sand from one fire to the next and teenagers, much as they do anywhere in the world, painstakingly dressed themselves for the public occasion. The light from the fires caught the bright colours of the girls' dresses, glinting beneath their black, creaseless cloaks worn partly for modesty, partly for warmth against the chill night air. The young men carefully smoothed out their spotless white robes and arranged their long flowing headdresses. Flirting had already begun from a distance. Later they would dance into the night, a long line of men and a long line of women, clapping, singing, giggling, and some tentatively agreeing to marry before the official arrangements could be made between families in the daylight. I was greeted by the Sheikh and some of his relatives with whom I work;

"Emma, Emma *Maksoufa* (the shy), Welcome."

"Are you strong", they asked.

"May God give you strength", I replied.

"Your company brings light to our gathering."

"From you light has come upon me also", I answered.

Then they laughed and teased me because I could never talk enough, eat enough or drink enough to satisfy them. But it was a strangely sympathetic tease. English reserve is as much a Bedouin trait.

The Sheikh beckoned me to join his group and I sat cross-legged on colourful hand-woven mats while great trays arrived laden with goat's meat, a rare treat for the tribe, and home–made unleavened bread. There was something of an annual English picnic about the event: family members assembling, some welcomed, others tolerated; small groups laughing or bickering, discussing politics; over-excited toddlers shouting and crying. I felt oddly at home.

Yet there was one startling difference. I was the only female adult in a circle of men. A little girl lay stretched out, her head in her father's lap, overcome by excitement and exhaustion, but, otherwise, only the men of the family and their male guests had gathered around the food.

One of the advantages, however, in being a woman is that I could enter both circles, male and female. Halfway through the evening I rose, excused myself and went to greet the wives, sisters, mothers and daughters. Three kisses on the right cheek, three on the left and three on the right again. Veils were put aside in this all-female corner. The fire was quickly rekindled and the tea began to flow. "In which valley will your next group sleep?" they asked. "How many camels will you take?". The women longed to have the same knowledge as their menfolk.

Eventually I said my farewells and wandered back to the circle of men. A bit of laughter, a bit of gossip and I knew it was time to go. The evening was still young, I was pressed to stay, but I had an instinct that the Sheikh had some politics to clear which he couldn't do with a guest on his hands. I also felt the unease of my Egyptian business partner who had driven me to the feast. He is Christian and, though more relaxed in the company of unrelated women than his Egyptian Muslim contemporaries, he was not entirely comfortable. His upbringing, which discouraged him from sititng with a woman socially, was gnawing at him. Business was no problem, but this occasion was purely social. For the good of the future it was time to leave.

For some years now I have worked in the interior of Sinai, taking small groups of foreigners to the ancient sites and helping them to learn about the Bedouin way of life. There are advantages and disadvantages to being a woman working independently among a desert tribe – my greatest joy is the contact I am allowed to have with the families of the men I work with.

My mountain guide has four young daughters aged three to ten years old. His wife is exactly my age and I spend much time in her home. Culturally the women are less free and boy children highly prized, but not always. Hussein's four girls come running to greet him when he returns from a four-day mountain trek. He loves them totally, has no regrets that they are girls and has hopes that his eldest will go to university as she is the brightest at the local school. Individuals within any culture can bring surprises.

Only the men of the tribe work as guides in the mountains although, as a woman, I can bring their wives and mothers into much closer contact with my travellers than would otherwise be permissable. The women are always keen to gain some first-hand experience of the quirks and demands of the foreigners that they have heard so much about and often say that this knowledge helps them to be more tolerant of the men's work. The work of the women, however, is to tend the gardens and herd the flocks of sheep and goats. The mountains are filled with walled gardens and lakes, both fed from the rains and melted winter snows. The ancient Byzantine stone cisterns still used by the Bedouin supply water throughout the dry summer to the fruit orchards and olive groves. The women and children lead the goats to higher pastures where you can hear the sound of their reed pipes echoing across the valleys. We wave in passing, but it is when I come back down to the village that I have most contact.

She was knocked down by a car and lay in the rubble behind the new tourist resort while passers–by thought she was asleep.

After some days in the mountains I go to visit Hussein's family. We usually sit together in the back room of their house for tea and fresh almonds. On this particular occasion, however, Hussein's wife Hamda looks unwilling to move from the kitchen area. I am invited in with the women.

Hamda looks tired and she explains she lost her unborn child. There were complications and her husband took her to the hospital in Suez, a six-hour journey away. She is now recovered and laughs when I express sorrow. "Look", she says, "I have four beautiful girls, it is enough". Tea is served before the sugary herb liquid goes next door for the men and then I hear the family news.

The five-year-old, with some delight, shows me the scars down her face. A few weeks previously she was knocked down by a car on the new road outside the village. She lay in the rubble behind the new tourist resort while passers–by thought she was asleep. It was three hours before her father found her unconscious. She too, however, has recovered and is as cheeky as ever.

The old women complain of the sewage leak from the hotel now up the valley. The sewage is running down past the houses and breeds mosquitoes. Complaints at all levels seem to go unheard, but there is good news too. Their cousin is home from the army and has returned to tend the fruit gardens left him by his father in the nearby valley. He is a close friend as well as a relative and has been much missed. I am invited next time I come to go with the family for the autumn grapes and tea under the shade of the almond trees in his garden.

Despite illness and the growing problems of commercial activity the family are hopeful of the future. To me they seem happy. I have seen more love matches and affection in the lives of the Sinai Bedouin than in any other country in the Near and Middle East. The men and women I know are affectionate parents with happy children despite the nawing hunger that can come when the rain does not fall, the bushes are barren and the goats' milk dries up. Security of close family ties, as well as the sheer strength of body of these desert people sees them through winter snows and summer droughts, as well as balmy months of plenty. The desert can be kind as well as cruel.

Tourism has, of course, had its effect on the Bedouin and their families, not all of it negative. Inspiring a love of their land is as rewarding to the Bedouin as the cash foreigners bring with them. Sadly as the Egyptian controlled air-conditioned buses arrive on the desert road and the Bedouin are separated from the visitors by glass, cash is more readily available than inspiration. Not that

> *Bedouin courts impose vast fines on any man found guilty of harassing a girl, and his family usually have to pay.*

cash is to be scorned; it brings food and medicine, but when it comes with an interest and willingness to learn, it brings also something more enduring but intangible. What comes from your heart, the Bedouin women say, is greater than what comes from the hand only.

The Egyptians are, on the whole, open and honest towards foreigners. The main tourist traps can be places of hassle and harassment, but then so can the commercial centres of London and New York. I have not travelled much alone in mainland Egypt as I rarely have business there and am usually rushing through en route to the desert, but I have always found Egyptians helpful and courteous on a short-term basis, so long as you are sensitive to their customs.

Sinai is a separate world, totally exempt from all the religious tensions south along the Nile. The Bedouin have a rare respect for individuals. The only place in Sinai where I have cause to worry about harassment is from a few of the Egyptians now living on the coast. They see so many bikini-clad Israelis and Europeans looking for a man to turn their head, that they assume this is true of all tourists. It is no excuse and their behaviour infuriates me, but I can also see their confusion.

The Bedouin are different. I take teenage girls and women of all ages into the remote desert and mountains with the Bedouin and I never have a problem. Their own women travel with goats and sheep far from home for four, five or more days looking for pasture. This freedom can exist only because the trust women have in men and the respect men have for women is upheld. The Bedouin courts of justice impose vast fines on any man found guilty of harassing a girl, and his family usually have to pay.

Despite being a woman in a male-dominated land I enjoy working with the Bedouin enormously. I have to say that a little domestic ineptitude, a serious failing in my English life, has done me no harm in the Bedouin world. It is a very practical display of the different way of life that I have come from. Without words of explanation the Bedouin women intuitively know that my aspirations differ from theirs beyond all measure. The women gently tease me and send instructions with the men to take particular care of me and my travellers in the desert. To what extent they envy my freedom I shall probably never know, but, as an outsider, I feel accepted.

TRAVEL NOTES

Languages Arabic. English is spoken in the tourist areas but it's useful at least to be able to read Arabic numerals.

Transport Buses and trains are inexpensive, but very crowded. Egyptian women avoid sitting next to strange men, which is how prostitutes solicit customers. All women, Egyptian and foreign, are subjected to gropes and pinches in the crush. You should make a fuss and enlist the help of women nearby. Efforts have been made to assign single-sex sleeper compartments on trains (and complaints are honoured in case of mistakes). Although second-class cars are not segregated and women have been hassled on overnight journeys, most Egyptian women travel second-class during daylight. Taxis are readily available in the cities and main towns.

Accommodation There are hotels at all prices. In the high season (Oct–March) the expensive places tend to be fully booked, but finding a cheap room is rarely a problem.

Travel Companies *Wind, Sand and Stars*, 2 Arkwright Rd, London, NW3 6AD, UK (☎0171/433 3684). Emma Loveridge (see above) often takes groups of women into the Sinai Desert.

Special Problems Harassment – particularly if you're on your own. Though many tourists do wander about in shorts and sleeveless T-shirts, this is considered both offensive and provocative. It's best to keep arms, legs and shoulders covered.

Other Information Along the Mediterranean coastline there are both private and public beaches. On public beaches there are few foreign tourists and almost all Egyptian women swim in their clothes. Private beaches do not cost much and you'll feel far less self-conscious as you'll be amongst other women (both tourists and Egyptians) who will be wearing swimming gear. It's a good idea to carry coins with you for *baksheesh*, the small tips that ease your way in many situations.

Guides *The Rough Guide to Egypt* (Penguin) combines practical information with informed and highly readable accounts of the country's entangled history and politics.

CONTACTS

Arab Women's Solidarity Association, 25 Murad St, Giza, Egypt (☎Cairo 723976). Strongly supported by Nawal El Saadawi, AWSA is an international, non-governmental organization aimed at "promoting and developing the social, cultural and educational status of Arab women".

BOOKS

Katherine Frank, *Lucie Duff Gordon: A Passage to Egypt* (UK, Hamish Hamilton, 1994). Sympathetic, detailed biography of the eminent nineteenth-century traveller whose classic *Letters from Egypt* (1865; UK & US, Virago, 1983), written in illness from the author's house in the Luxor temple complex, remains one of the best travelogues ever written about the country.

Nawal El Saadawi, *The Hidden Face of Eve* (UK & US, Zed Books, 1980). Covering a wide range of topics – sexual aggression, genital mutilation, prostitution, marriage, divorce and sexual relationships – Saadawi provides a personal and often disturbing account of what it's like to grow up as a woman in the Islamic world of the Middle East. Also recommended are *Women of the Arab World* (UK & US, Zed Books, 1989), in which she introduces a group of essays by the Arab Women's Solidarity Association and her novels: *Woman at Point Zero* (UK & US, Zed Books, 1983), a powerful and moving story of a young Egyptian woman condemned to death for killing a pimp, and *God Dies by the Nile* (UK & US, Zed Books, 1985), the story of the tyranny and corruption of a small town mayor in Egypt and the illiterate peasant woman who kills him. Her latest novel is *The Innocence of the Devil* (UK, Lime Tree, 1994/US, University of California Press).

Gay Robins, *Women in Ancient Egypt* (UK, British Museum Press, 1993/US, Harvard University Press). Absorbing study of the lives of Egyptian women between 3000 and 332 BC. Essential reading for sightseers.

Alifa Rifaat, *Distant View of a Minaret* (UK, Heinemann Educational, 1987/US, Quartet, 1993). Rifaat is a well-known Egyptian writer in her fifties. Here she expresses her revolt against male domination and suggests solutions within the orthodox Koranic framework.

Nayra Atiya, *Khul-Khaal: Five Egyptian Women Tell Their Stories* (UK, Virago, 1988/US, Syracuse University Press, 1982). A fascinating collection of oral histories, recorded over three years, which reveal the lives and aspirations of working-class women in contemporary Egypt.

Huda Sha'rawi, *Harem Years: The Memoirs of an Egyptian Feminist* (UK, Virago, 1986/US, Feminist Press, 1987). A unique document from the last generation of upper-class Egyptian women who spent their childhood and married life in the segregated world of the harem.

FICTION

Olivia Manning, *The Danger Tree* (US, Atheneum, 1977) and *The Battle Lost and Won* (1979). The two final books in Manning's *The Balkan Trilogy*, set in World War II Egypt.

The Faroe
Islands

Made up of eighteen islands of volcanic rock, rising sheer out of the Atlantic half way between the Shetlands and Iceland, the Faroes may seem an unusual choice as a holiday destination. A few tourists, mainly Danish or Norwegian birdwatchers and hikers, arrive each year at the islands' tiny airstrip or off the ferry boats at Tórshavn, the capital, only town and main harbour of the group. Most visitors, however, are deterred by the obscurity and ruggedness of the islands and the uncertain, changeable weather.

Although officially part of Denmark, the Faroes have enjoyed home rule for nearly fifty years with their own parliament, national language media and bank notes. Centuries of self-sufficiency, based on fishing and small-scale farming, have left their mark in a strong local identity

‸at persists despite the recent drift of younger Faroese leaving to work in Copenhagen. Approximately two thirds of the islands' tiny population (a mere 45,000 in total) live in villages interconnected by roads, bridges and tunnels with Tórshavn, not much larger than a village itself but the hub of the islands' commerce and cultural life. In recent years the economy has been undermined by a depletion in local fish stocks, and taxation and inflation have risen, yet the standard of living remains high, with houses equipped with all the modern comforts neccessary for lasting out the dark, chilly winter months. Positioned in Gulf Stream waters, the islands escape the freezing temperatures that you'd expect at such a high latitude, although the constant strong winds are a force to be continually reckoned with.

The few travellers tempted by the unusual terrain and teeming bird-life (including large puffin colonies) arrive almost exclusively in summer when the nights are short and the weather mild. Travelling around the islands is fairly straightforward, with good bus and ferry connections, but hotels tend to be few and far between. Costs are high – pitched at Scandinavian levels – and apart from a few homegrown entertainmnents and local festivals there's little to do in the evenings other than dry out your clothes and plan the next day's outing. Unlike their Scandinavian counterparts, the Faroese have a reputation for a gruff warmth and friendliness and are always willing to offer advice and help. Crime levels are very low and harassment towards visitors almost unheard of. However, socializing tends to be a private affair, carried out in each other's houses, and it can be hard to break into the circuit.

Wet Rocks in the Atlantic

Margaret Hubbard, a teacher living in Edinburgh, set off on a cycle-trip around the Faroe Islands with her American friend, Carol. They met in the early 1970s while teaching in a small Australian town and joined each other for regular expeditions throughout that decade.

On a clear July morning Carol and I wheeled our bicycles onto the *St Clair* at Aberdeen harbour for the first leg of our journey to the Faroe Islands. It had been twelve years since we had last set out together, cycling around the Western Isles of Scotland, and we were both a little apprehensive about the trip. Twelve years is a long time. I had since been divorced and had travelled far and wide on my own in the school holidays, and Carol had been bringing up a daughter while continuing teaching at home in America. Would we be able to rekindle the old camaraderie we had shared on the road? We neither of us worried too much about our destination. The Faroes, we imagined, would be like the Western Isles – perhaps a little starker.

Twelve hours later, in the middle of a howling gale, the *St Clair* edged into Lerwick harbour in the Shetlands where our connecting boat, the *Smyril*, was waiting to heave anchor. Ahead of us lay a sixteen-hour journey across some of the worst seas in the world to Tórshavn, the Faroe Islands' capital. We had hardly left the harbour when we were both struck down by sea-sickness. I remember lying on the floor of the lowest deck of the ferry, wallowing in nausea and self-pity, wondering if my holiday insurance covered being airlifted off the ship.

The Faroese are a hardy seafaring race. Not for them the slower more roundabout route along the currents or moving in accordance with the

Customs officials stared when they saw two pale, shaken, middle-aged women disembarking with their old bikes.

wind. Draw a straight line from Lerwick via Dunrossness, the channel that wrecked the *Braer* oil tanker, to Tórshavn, and you have the route of the *Smyril*. Faroese children by the dozen played happily as the boat rolled through what appeared from my horizontal position to be 180°.

We arrived at seven in the morning. The sky was overcast, the wind was strong and it was raining. Even the customs and passport officials stared when they saw two pale, and rather shaken, middle-aged women disembarking with their old bikes. It seemed we were not the usual visitors to the islands.

Our first task was to find some breakfast and recover from the passage. There was nowhere open. In the end we had to resort to an expensive hotel (Scandinavian prices with high freight charges on top) where the puffin on the menu, a local delicacy, did little to settle our already queasy stomachs.

Not the most prepossessing beginning. And yet, over the weeks that followed, these crazy islands bore into my soul to the extent that almost a year later, not a day goes by when I don't think of them.

What first captivated me about Tórshavn was its colours. In contrast with the grey of the weather the houses are painted bright yellow and green. Many have traditional turf roofs, kept short by the sheep grazing on top. And the stillness! The town is so calm, it seems that neither traffic nor human sounds can penetrate the quiet.

The town is effectively run by the Plymouth Brethren, who until recently banned the sale of alcohol. Now it is available in supermarkets, but there are no pubs. In the evenings you see large groups of teenagers and fishermen, some of Inuit origin, settling down for a long night's drinking on the streets and in the parks. Graffiti, vandalism and drunkeness, the well-documented results of alienation and boredom, have left their mark on the streets of Tórshavn. Pubs, I felt, would have been much less harmful.

Finding somewhere to stay proved no easy matter. Youth hostels and hotels are few and far between and there are none of the usual other options: no bed and breakfasts or boarding houses. In Tórshavn we ended up in a Sports Hall, which doubled as a hostel in summer, run by a local school teacher who was supplementing his income with a summer job.

Our initial plan had been to set out from Tórshavn and cycle round the islands, but this proved impossible. First there was the weather to contend with. The Faroese kept telling us that it was a freak summer. So be it. We were buffeted by force 8 gales, driving rain and an unseasonal wind blowing straight off the Arctic. (We had been led to believe the weather would be like Scotland in April. Not so: it was more like a very bad January.) Then there were the tunnels. These we also knew about, but no one had told us that they were unlit. Our bicycle lamps made little impression on the blackness that suddenly enveloped us as we entered, and slowing down to a snail's pace, left us in real danger of carbon monoxide poisoning. Added to this the lack of accommodation meant that it was quite possible to end up stranded in some uninhabitable spot, in the driving wind and rain with nothing but a long dark tunnel behind us.

Our solution was to base ourselves in the Sports Hall and cover the islands on a series of day-trips. Each day we listened to the English-language weather forecast at 8am and, if the weather promised to be fine, we would cycle. If not, we bussed. It's interesting how one's perceptions change when travelling. The definition of "fine" weather was anything less than a force 7 gale, no likelihood of sleet and the temperature reaching 5°C – conditions which would probably have kept me inside back home.

Curiously, we never considered giving up the trip. Neither of us were in it for an easy package-style holiday; we had come to see the Faroes, to cycle and spend time quietly together in the evenings, catching up on each other's lives. And we both had enough experience of the rough side of travel to know we could manage. Almost immediately we fell into our old patterns, knowing intuitively when to offer a word of encouragement, when to stop for a coffee-break, cycle ahead or drop behind, and the risks we'd both be prepared to take.

I felt overwhelmed by the violence and the power of the elements. One severe gust could blow me away completely.

The islands are effectively the peaks of a submerged mountain range that rise sheer out of the water with barely a beach on their extensive coastline. The roads seem to go either up or down, with only a few stretches on the flat. From the top of these windswept rocks the only view for miles around is of the Atlantic, churning in the distance or hurling itself against the cliffs below. More than anywhere else I have been, I felt overwhelmed by the violence and the power of the elements. One severe gust could blow me away completely. Cycling downhill, pushing hard against the oncoming wind, became routine. A waterfall blowing upwards as it fell, so that the water made a U-shaped arch, came as no surprise. The birds, the wind, the water, triggered musings about the crucible of nature. An island popping up from the bed of the sea would have hardly seemed strange. I was emptied of words and could only look on silently.

Travelling every day in this landscape we grew stronger, developing muscles we didn't know we had and relishing our food and sleep. We also grew attached to our bikes, tending to their every noise and complaint, drying them off and ensuring they were carefully stowed for the night. Initially, I admit, our thoughts turned to warmer, drier climes but as we grew used to the harsher aspects of life these other places receded.

The transport system in the Faroes is excellent and when we chose to hitch (sometimes with the bikes!) we were always successful. People were extremely friendly, as if they felt a need to bond against the elements. We were asked, of course, what had brought us to their remote corner of the world and sometimes a note of defensiveness crept in when people suspected we might be Greenpeace members and anti-whaling. The Faroese still hunt whale as food, an activity they consider integral to their livelihood as well as their culture. They defend it as vehemently as the Spanish do bullfighting.

Tórshavn is the only town in the Faroes. All the other habitations are villages, invariably grouped round a whitewashed Lutheran church built on the cliff top nearest the sea, so that it is both the first and the last sight for the fishermen. The village houses are brightly painted, the land is green and, when the greyness clears, the sky and the sea are blue. The prettiness of the picture belies the toughness of the people and the harshness of the life.

It is so far north that it never really grows dark in summer. At midnight people play tennis without electric lighting. At 2am I could read outside. I tried to imagine the long dark winter months with their eighteen hours of night but failed; it seemed just too gloomy a proposition.

I remember standing on a cliff in Vidoy looking due north over three miles of water that are impassable for much of the year, to the neighbouring island of Fugloy. Its 1,500ft cliffs reared out of the sea defying the vastness of the ocean pounding the rocks below. There were no trees in sight, yet a huddle of houses clung on to the wet rockface. How do they live? I wondered. What could you do except just try to survive in such an isolated place? Gjogv is a village of one hundred people jammed hard between a mountain and a cliff top. The only way in or out is by road over the mountain or by boat, both impossible for long stretches of the winter. How do its inhabitants perceive the world?

One afternoon we cycled against movement-defying winds to the black sands south of the island Sandoy. A cliff-top football match was in full swing. The goal nets had long blown away, but the children were as absorbed in their game as they are anywhere. Watching it I became curious about the strange arc the boys took to follow the ball upfield until it suddenly clicked that they were taking into consideration the wind blowing the ball off course. That geometry had to be calculated also when kicking the ball any distance, and of course it had to be re-computed every time the wind changed direction! I chuckled at the prospect of the World Cup in the Faroes.

The isolation of the islands has led to a very rich local culture. In the Nordic House in Tórshavn Faroese films are shown, weekly. The majority of the audience are locals; the films are not marketed to the tourists. Nor are the ring dance evenings. The photographic exhibitions too are rich in colour and wildlife (not surprising considering the quality of the light in this unpolluted place), while the museums in Tórshavn are among the best I have seen anywhere. Wandering around the town is a delight: the varied and intriguing life of the port unending.

The Faroese are a proud, dignified people who manage to establish a quality of life that eludes many people living in much easier circumstances. Until recently the fishing industry brought in extensive wealth and, despite the recent recession, there is very little evidence of poverty. Old people live with modern conveniences and in houses bought by their children. None of the greed of the new rich is evident in Faroe – you don't see old folk living in hovels while their families drive BMWs. Labour is divided in traditional ways between men and women but I was struck by the mutual respect that went with this. Faroese women are strong. The constant threat of disaster at sea means that they might suddenly be left to cope single-handed. (There is one deserted and ruined village on the Faroes where all the men drowned in a single accident, and where the women were forced to disperse and carve out new lives for themselves.) Also, despite the strictly masculine work that so many men are involved in – the fishing fleets and merchant shipping – they seemed unafraid to show their gentle sides. Perhaps, with so many real dangers surrounding them, there's no need for macho posturing.

The Faroes captivated me. I was cold much of the time. Sometimes I was very frightened of the weather but I knew I had found somewhere very special indeed. Few tourists come to Faroe, even fewer stay. We gave it respect.

Next year we're going to Alaska.

T R A V E L   N O T E S

Languages Faroese, a Nordic language. Danish and a basic English are also widely spoken.
Transport There are good links bewteen all the islands by ferry, tunnel or bridge. The bus network is wide and efficient if a little expensive. You can rent bikes or cars in summer.
Accommodation Limited, although a few hotels and some youth hostels are dotted about the islands. You can often arrange private accommodation in more remote villages.
Special Problems The weather. Pack foul weather gear and get into training for walking against the wind. Stock up with duty free alcohol,

as you're unlikely to be able to buy any once you arrive and whiskey is a valued gift.
Guides *Iceland, Greenland and the Faroe Islands – A Traveller's Survival Kit* (Lonely Planet) includes a hundred pages on the Faroes.

BOOKS

Schei and Moberb, *The Faroe Islands* (UK & US, John Murray, 1981). Highly readable account of the history and culture of the islands.
Kenneth Williamson, *The Atlantic Islands*. Enthusiastic account of island life by a British soldier who, billeted on the islands during World War II, met and married a Faroese woman.

Finland

Despite the obvious attractions of a wilderness of lakes and forests, a stunningly modern capital city, and easy access by ferry to St Petersburg, Finland tends to be overlooked as just a little too remote, obscure and expensive for most ordinary travellers. For those who can afford it, however, the tranquility and architectural fascination of the towns and cities, and the natural beauty of the countryside – trees petering out into the stark, haunting terrain of Lapland as you move north – hold an enduring appeal.

Finland is an easy country to visit alone or with other women. Expenses apart (and the cost of living can be cripplingly high), your biggest problem will be coping with the isolation as you travel. People offer help if needed but for the most part leave you to yourself and, in the more remote countryside, you

might well get a frosty and suspicious reception from older Finns. It is much easier to break down barriers of reserve in Helsinki, a cosmopolitan and progressive city with a strong alternative culture, although the government restrictions on alcohol can dampen even the liveliest night out. (It's worth remembering that many Finns use the boat and rail crossing to St Petersburg for their drinking sprees and on late night trips the atmosphere can get pretty obnoxious.)

In political and economic terms, these are critical years for Finland. The end of the Cold War and the collapse of the Soviet markets have deepened an already well-established recession, while wiping out the value of the country's hard-won neutrality. Standards of living have been falling since the mid-1980s, with unemployment endemic in the north, and many of the country's more progressive welfare policies threatened by a political swing to the right. Increasingly Finland is pinning its hopes on gaining entry to the European Community but, as Europe continues in a state of flux, success is by no means guaranteed. Meanwile apprehension grows at the volatile situation brewing across the border in Russia.

Finland was the second country in the world (after New Zealand) in which women achieved suffrage and the current parliament has a record 38.5 percent women representatives (one of whom, the current health minister, Eeva Kuuskoski, was the first minister to give birth while in office). Progressive equal opportunities legislation, backed up by good childcare facilities and maternity leave, has ensured that women retain a high profile in all aspects of public life. Younger women, especially, seem aware of, and confident in, their rights to equality. Sexual harassment and violence towards women are relatively rare (interestingly, in the case of prostitution it is the punters not the women who face prosecution under the law).

The contemporary **women's movement** is now fairly small and centred in Helsinki. Women who were active in the early 1970s tend to have moved into more mainstream politics or joined various peace and environmental campaigns. There are a few autonomous lesbian organizations which also operate in the capital (attitudes tend to become more conservative as you move further away from Helsinki), the largest of which is a group called *Akanat*.

A Halcyon Summer

Penny Windsor has worked as a teacher, youth worker, freelance writer and performance poet. She spent a month travelling with her partner around the south of Finland.

A ll journeys are, of course, personal journeys, but my journey to Finland last summer was a peculiarly emotional one. I was three months pregnant and, at the age of 41, with an eighteen-year-old daughter, felt deeply uncertain about my future. My travelling companion had studied Finnish literature and history for many years and had shared his dreams with me of visiting the country. At the end of June, when we had earned enough money to pay the price of the air fare to Helsinki – measured out in potatoes picked in the fields of Pembrokeshire – we began our trip.

Without doubt it was the right country to visit at the time. We had weathered the many curious questions of friends and acquaintances – "Why Finland?", "Where is Finland?", "Won't it be cold?" – insisting Finland was indeed a European country of considerable interest and beauty and the summers were often warmer than our own.

In bald terms Finland is one of the Scandinavian countries, bordering Norway to the far north and with a long frontier with Russia in the east. It has a population of about five million people, many of whom live in the major cities of Helsinki, Tampere, Turku, Lahti and Oulu. Swedish is the official second language, and although a small proportion of the people speak Swedish as a first language, the overwhelming majority speak Finnish, a strange and unique tongue with affinities only to Hungarian (and making no distinction between "she" and "he" – the pronoun for both sexes being *hän*). English is widely spoken but my companion's efforts to speak Finnish at every opportunity were greeted with surprise and delight.

Other than these facts . . . Well, Finland is an independent, democratic republic, the first European country to give women the vote (in 1906). It has an excellent human rights record, and a long history of fighting for national independence from Sweden and from its giant neighbour Russia. (Finnish history makes fascinating reading, a spellbinding account of a David surviving the onslaught of a Goliath.)

We arrived in Helsinki at midnight and put up our small mountaineering tent in Hesperia Park, in the middle of the city, next door to Finlandia House, the international conference centre. It was our first experience of the Finns' "laissez-faire" attitude to all except those who flagrantly break the law. At no time during our three weeks stay were we told not to do anything. Rules were kept to a minimum and the country seemed to run on the assumption that people would behave well if left to go quietly about their business.

For the rest of our time in Helsinki we camped between fir trees on the island of Seurasaari, a few miles from the city centre. The island is an open-air museum full of historic buildings from all over Finland – a fact we didn't realize until we saw the place in daylight. The red squirrels and even the hares that live there seemed unafraid of people.

Helsinki can be too much like the perfect, suburban dream, full of rosy, stable, nuclear families.

From this secluded camping place we explored the city – the National Museum where grand scenes from the Finnish national folk epic, the Kalevala, were displayed; the monument to the famous and much-loved musician Sibelius, a vast organ of silver pipes; the island fortress of Soumenlinna, built originally by the Swedes to fight off the Russians; the markets on the harbour fronts; the *Academic Bookshop* in the main shopping street, which has the largest selection of titles in Europe.

Sometimes I explored the city with my companion, at other times alone. I was never hassled in any way, whether I was wandering about the city centre after dark, whiling away a sunny afternoon reading in the park, or sitting drinking coffee in the green-draped, elegant waiting room in Helsinki station. There were a few drunks, predominantly men, at Helsinki station and various inland stations, but I never felt under any sort of threat from them. Alcohol is expensive and only light lager is easily available -- other drinks are sold at state-run stores, called Alkos, which have mysterious opening hours. Drinking trips are often made to Sweden and across the border to St Petersburg where alcohol is cheaper and more readily available.

Helsinki is a pleasant, restful uncity-city – an orderly place where things work well, people appear prosperous and healthy. Sometimes, perhaps, it can be too much like the perfect, suburban dream, full of rosy, stable, nuclear families. It rocks along gently with its well-dressed people, nicely displayed museums, beautiful parks and buildings and lovely harbour views. If it lacks altogether that dynamic, volatile, wicked quality of many other capital cities, I can only say it was the perfect place for me last summer, a place where nothing I saw was ugly or violent or dirty, where I could wander freely by myself, thinking and writing.

Leaving Helsinki we travelled north to Hameenlinna, birthplace of Sibelius, then east through the cities of Lahti and Imatra to the province of Karelia, near the Russian border and in a wide loop back to Hameenlinna by way of the industrial cities of Varkhaus and Tampere. We travelled by a mixture of train, bus and hitch-hiking.

By our standards all prices were high in Finland, particularly for food. As for travel, the train is marginally cheaper than the bus. As with all public places, trains are comfortable and clean and the waiting rooms provide toys which don't appear to get either vandalized or stolen. The toilets have baby-changing rooms and potties, in some cases in the men's as well as the women's sections. This last seemed to me a litmus test of equality – I was truly impressed.

Hitch-hiking is difficult. We had a number of short lifts but had to wait long hours for them, even on the main road between towns. We came to the conclusion that this was in tune with the national Finnish character – they are, after all, a nation renowned for their reserve and insularity, wanting, it seems, not much to do with an outside world which knows and cares little about them. They treasure the quality of *sisu* – youthfulness, independence of thought, "guts", embodied in the characters of the life-giving, daring Lemminkëinen and the dour, brave Kullervo, the adventurers in the *Kalevala*.

As far as national characteristics can be true, yes, the Finns did seem to be reserved people but, once approached, proved almost overwhelmingly courteous and helpful. I hold warm memories of the family who gave us supper and breakfast and asked us to camp in their garden outside Lahti, when we stopped to ask the way; the man on the bicycle in Hameenlinna who went off to photocopy a street map of the town for us; the guard who scrupulously looked after our interests on our strange circular journey across the country when we had taken the wrong train.

We sometimes breakfasted on mustard and onion sandwiches and windfall apples.

We did not use official campsites, preferring to put up our tent in the forest and by the side of lakes. However, the campsites we saw were, like everything else, well-organized and clean.

Our biggest problem was money – basic items of food, even in large supermarkets, often cost double the price charged in Britain. We sometimes breakfasted on mustard and onion sandwiches and windfall apples. On the other hand, nobody bothered us in the remote forests where we camped, unless you count the restless midnight mole in the glade above the Aulanko Lake and the early morning woodpecker. Bathing naked in the great quiet lakes of Aulanko Forest and Karelia we were similarly undisturbed. And the sunsets on the lake marshes as we watched the short summer turn to autumn at the end of August were brief, dramatic and perfect.

In those weeks I spent in Finland, I grew accustomed to the gentleness of the country, the mild intimacy of the wilderness forests and the sudden openness of the lakes. It was restful to be in a country which did not seem to deal in unnecessary rules, but where the streets were free of litter, where factories and houses were hidden by trees, and lakes and rivers were clear and full of plants and bird life.

For me, it was definitely the right country to visit that particular summer, but also the right country for any woman traveller who just wants to sit or wander, reflect and daydream, without comment or interference.

T R A V E L   N O T E S

Languages Finnish. Swedish is the official second language although many people also speak English.

Transport There are plenty of highly efficient and speedy options – both trains and planes are comparatively inexpensive (in Finnish terms). The overnight ferries or trains to Sweden or St Petersburg, which tend to be used as cheap boozers and can develop an aggressively sexist atmosphere, should be avoided. Hitching is perfectly acceptable and (as much as it can ever be) quite safe, although you'll have to wait a while for lifts.

Accommodation Again the various options are expensive. Many women camp on their own. (See under *Contacts* for details of a Women's Summer Camp.)

Other Information It's fairly common to find *Naistentanssit* dances organized specifically for women on their way home from the office, usually after 4pm or so. Women rather than men take their pick of partners. Some mainstream discos also arrange evenings for women (*Sekahaku*), where men and women choose partners freely.

Guides *The Rough Guide to Scandinavia* (Penguin) has a useful and concise section on Finland.

CONTACTS

The Women's Movement Union (Naisasialitto Unioni), Bulevardi 11a, Helsinki (Mon–Fri 10am–1pm & 2–5pm; closed mid-June to July; ☎90.64.3158). The oldest and largest of the women's organizations, established in 1892. It's worth dropping by to get information about the range of groups currently operating. The *Unioni* also owns *Ida Salin's Summer Home* which houses the Open Women's University. As well as various consciousness-raising courses, a Women's Summer Camp is held in the grounds once a year. There are plans to open a "book café" and reading room.

The Organization for Sexual Equality (SETA), PO Box 55, 00531, Helsinki (☎76.96.42 or 76.96.32). Has information about current lesbian groups and provisions.

Akanat, PL 55, 00551 Helsinki (☎76.96.4). A lesbian collective that publishes a campaigning and listings magazine, *Torajvva*.

BOOKS

Rosa Liksom, *One Night Stands* (UK, Serpent's Tail, 1993). First appearance in English of Liskom's razor sharp short stories – dark, minimalist tales of the post-punk generation.

Christer Kilman, *The Downfall of Gerdt Bladh* (UK & US, Peter Owen, 1989). Novel about a businessman unable to come to terms with his wife's infidelity; gives a flavour of Helsinki life.

France

By far the most visited country in northern Europe, France attracts more or less every kind of tourist and traveller. Yet despite the obvious appeal of its food, landscape and city life, it can be a hard place to get to know. An image of exclusive chic permeates the centre of Paris, the much glamourized Côte d'Azur and the Alpine ski resorts, and the country as a whole has a reputation for cliquishness. Without educational, business or social connections you may find it hard to slot in, no matter how good your French might be. Regional affiliations are very strong and local communities tend to be tightly knit. If you do manage to break down the barriers, however, the rich culture of France, the appreciation of the qualities of life and zest for politics may well have you hooked.

Travelling around is generally straightforward, although you may come up against fairly low-key sexual harassment. This ranges from running commentaries from men who overtly size you up as you walk past to the more persistent attentions of a specific type of creep whom the French refer to as *les dragueurs*. Attempting to cash r on the myth of the romantic French lover, these are men of all ages, who hang around the main tourist areas of any city or resort to literally "trawl" for women. Having managed to catch your eye, he will smile, greet and very probably follow you, uttering banal compliments or launching into the usual banter about "love at first sight". The best policy is to try ignoring him completely – if you're going to lose your temper, make sure there are plenty of people around.

A further difficulty is where sexism merges with racism. French people, and particularly Parisians, will warn you against "les Arabes". If you come from an Arab or North African state, or look as if you do, you may have to contend with some pretty blatant discrimination, finding that hotels are suddenly fully booked, etc. The same applies if you're Black (whatever your nationality), and you might find obstacles in gaining entry.

First-time visitors may be angered by the constant barrage of exploitative images in advertising. French **women**, however, appear largely unperturbed; when during her reign as the first minister for women's rights, Yvette Roudy tried to introduce a law banning sexist advertising she found herself shouted down by women and men alike. Similarly a law against sexual harassment, passed in 1993, seems to have had little impact on attitudes and behaviour between the sexes. As American feminist Susan Faludi remarked when in Paris to promote her book *Backlash*, a special edition needed to be written for the French market. Excellent maternity benefits and state-run crèches allow seventy percent of mothers to go out to work, yet these services threaten to be undermined as the conservative government, faced with economic crisis, proposes the introduction of financial incentives to encourage women back into the home. With women representing only six percent of parliament, whether such proposals are allowed to gain ground remains to be seen.

Living in Paris

In her early twenties, **Maria Pavlopoulos** was assigned a work experience period (*stage*) in the office of a large European organization in Paris. For five months she worked as a trainee in the Press Office, handling general enquiries about matters relating to the organization and dealing with the Press. She then went on to work as a trainee for a PR company for a further four months. Although she spoke fluent French, she had no previous work experience of this kind.

I set out for Paris full of preconceptions and ideas I had fostered since seeing *An American in Paris* starring Leslie Caron. These had been reinforced by two brief visits while still a student. Both the film and the visits contributed to give me a naive and somewhat fairy tale view of one of the most beautiful cities in the world. I anticipated encounters with artists and poets, long afternoons in steamy cafés absorbing the atmosphere and refining my meagre knowledge of the art of sophistication, which seemed to me to have been invented by Parisians. My experience proved to be different. I certainly encountered many of the things I expected, but I soon came to realize that while Paris has much to offer, there is a harsh and often impersonal side to Parisian life.

An eternal optimist, I arrived in the city to stay with friends just over a week before I was due to start work. I was convinced that I would find a spacious, furnished flat within my strictly limited means, at the drop of a beret. I scanned the newspapers for several days and visited numerous studios (no two-bedroom palace for me, I soon realized) which were in general just large enough to squeeze in a bed.

Every flat in Paris is described in terms of *mètres carrés* (square metres) and most of those which are rented by students or *stagiaires* like myself measure a generous fifteen. (This has its advantages, in that you can just about turn the TV on with your toe without actually having to shift out of bed.) These palatial spaces are meant to combine a bedroom, a kitchen and, if you are lucky, a semblance of a bathroom. I intended to be lucky which made my task all the more difficult.

The basis for most of these studios are the infamous *chambres de bonne*, roughly translated as the maids' rooms, invariably located on the top floor of the majestic six- or seven-storey nineteenth-century buildings. Trudging up hundreds of steep stairs, it dawned on me why so many Parisian women maintain their sylph-like figures into old age.

I scoured the less salubrious areas of Paris trying to come to terms with what now seemed a herculean task. Furnished apartments just didn't exist. Tenants are supposed to provide for themselves, no doubt from the furniture dumps that littered the streets. I had begun to resign myself to the prospect of living in the *banlieue* (suburbs) and kissing goodbye to any social life for the next five months (it was that or a ferry back to England) and then suddenly I stumbled on a studio right in the centre of town. The only drawback was the rent: it was time to put my translation talents into practice.

I moved in the next day and, needless to say, the first night was a catastrophe. Within two hours of my arrival the tap had exploded. "SOS Plombiers" were called and arrived stoned at 3am to stand and giggle at how badly I had been ripped off and charge me about £70 ("Yes, but it's Sunday night, *Mademoiselle*") to disconnect the tap. When I finally got to bed, I was woken up to the sensation of a large insect crawling slowly across my face. I lay there paralysed with horror as I felt it move nearer to my mouth. It was my first introduction to my new tenants, the cockroaches. A chat with a neighbour (during which a giant roach crawled across the kitchen table) soon revealed that they were regular visitors, as in fact they are to most pre-war Parisian buildings. I was to spend some of my most creative moments devising traps for them on those lonely first nights . . . I was also to spend many hours removing the sparse furniture for the regular ritual of the *désinsectation* which got rid of them for about two days, after which they reamassed in what seemed stronger force, bigger, dirtier and ever wiser to my traps.

I sensed a ravine between myself and the other women working there. I was an alien dress fiend.

Having achieved the flat my next gargantuan task was to attempt to open a bank account. I had approached a number of banks armed with a large cheque which was supposed to see me through my five months in Paris. This, I assumed, would be enough to please any banker. *Mais non!* First, I was required to produce proof of my identity. No problem, I thought, and cheerfully whipped out my passport. This, it appeared, was insufficient. They needed my birth certificate. Clearly, I was one of those rare foreigners who do not travel with their birth certificates concealed in the heel of their shoe for such tricky moments. Once I had obtained this with considerable difficulty, I presumed I was in the clear. This was when I was asked for a recent electricity bill to prove the validity of my residence. I pointed out that this was rather difficult given that I had been resident there for under a week. Finally a letter from my landlord sufficed. With that, I felt I was supposedly a valid *Parisienne* (for nine months at least) with a studio, a few friends and a cheque book. It was now time for work.

My first day at the office was not a success. After a 45-minute commute, I was greeted by a security guard, standing in an empty room, who informed me that my employer had relocated at the end of the previous week to a destination five minutes away from where I was living. This minor fact had obviously been of too little significance to mention to me the week before, when finalizing arrangements. When I did manage to make my entrance at the correct place, I immediately sensed a ravine between myself and the other women working there. I was an alien dress fiend. First, my fingernails were not painted scarlet, nor did I have dyed and perfectly coiffed hair, nor was I sporting the regulation short skirt, high heels and dark fitted jacket with gold buttons and, worst of all, I didn't wear make-up. After all, I was being judged purely on appearance. This, combined with other incidents, led me to conclude that Parisians have some of the most sexist attitudes of any citizens in Europe.

Women are given opportunities to hold positions of responsibility and to find high-powered jobs, but once they are installed, they are expected to conform to certain standards of dress and behaviour which are dictated by men. They are faced with constant pressure from the media, their employers and indeed their partners, to strive for eternal youth and physical perfection. If there were a youth elixir available, it would probably sell best in Paris. If, however, you are foreign and do not conform, it is simply attributed to your nationality: "Ah, la petite Anglaise!" soon became a catchphrase. Nevertheless, I was soon to realize that my non-conformity would be no drawback in terms of my work-related social life. Most of my male colleagues felt obliged to make a perfunctory very public dinner invitation to justify their masculinity. In view of the reaction to my polite but negative response, I gathered most other female trainees had consented. Without wishing to shatter any illusions, the unanimous opinion of the foreign women I knew in France, is that French men's reputation as the world's best seducers and lovers is a myth. Presumably there are exceptions, but in general their sliminess, persistence and inability to take a hint definitely bestows upon them a unique title, and it is not the above. Many French men are also very short (remember Napoleon and Toulouse-Lautrec), which unfortunately makes them just the right height to ogle your chest but also perfectly sized to have their eyes elbowed by mistake. Thus, I survived my first experience of the French art of sharking in the knowledge that I was not that desperate for a free meal.

Desperation did, however, soon set in, although I never took up the dinner offers. Paris must be one of the world's most expensive cities to live in. Unfortunately when doing a *stage* it is the norm to receive no wages; employers regard the sharing of knowledge and the gathering of experience as an honour bestowed only upon those who strive for places or whose parents know the right people. As a result, places for stages are generally highly competitive and unpaid. I had already realized that in order to survive I would have to find an alternative source of income, and had quickly started doing some translation and research work which I could carry out at home and on weekends.

During my free time I tended to associate with a core group of fellow foreigners living in Paris. We all met in our common search for part-time employment at the American Church, which has the best reputation for providing this type of information. It begins with the scuffle for a good viewing position before the notices are put up; after a few minutes of treading on other people, things tend to warm up and everyone chats. It is a meeting of kindred spirits, all of whom are equally broke, sharing similar experiences and committing the same *faux pas*. A group of us started to meet and would devise various money-making schemes, none of which ever materialized. Once we realized this, we began looking for low-budget entertainment instead.

> *I would expose my white body amid rows of oiled brown flesh, in the hope that the sun would turn my skin a more Parisian shade.*

While exploring the infinite possibilities of ways of spending time, I stumbled across a curious custom: the Parisian art of dog-owning. Never have I come across people who love dogs more. They have dog shops, dog beauticians, dog wear, special dog toilets and they even take their dogs into restaurants with them. However, the dog-worship cult culminates in the legendary machine, the poopa-scoopa. This fluorescent green beast is either a three-wheel van or a motorbike with a big fat hoover-tube on the end which slurps up dog mess off the streets. Rumour has it that the city council preferred the expense of installing and operating these machines, as opposed to fining dog-owners, for fear of alienating a substantial section of the electorate. I became intimately familiar with these horrendous machines since I used to pass the Poopa Man, as I called him, every day on my way to work. One morning he sped after me on his motorbike. Standing there in his green plastic, disinfected boiler suit, astride his machine with the hoover tube still on full suction power, he asked me out for a drink. Faced with the combination of suit, scoopa and the inevitable charisma, I was at a loss for words. Eventually, as politely as possible, I declined and made a run for the office.

As I got to know Paris better, one of my favourite haunts became the *Piscine Déligny*. Moored on the Left Bank, just near the Assemblée Nationale, this pool offered sanctuary from the bustle of the city. As it was not far from my workplace, I often nipped across at lunch, aided by the guard who would let me slip in free. The swimming pool was in the middle of a large barge, with decks and mattresses all around the edge for sunbathing. I would periodically expose my white body amid rows of oiled brown flesh, in the hope that the sun would turn my skin a more Parisian shade. From the deck I could see the obelisk of the Concorde, the dome of the Grand Palais and, on a clear day, the Sacré Coeur. For me, this was Paris at its most magnificent.

In the eternal pursuit of cheap pastimes, I spent hours wandering along the *quais* looking at books, art and hand-drawn maps. The stall-holders were often older native Parisians, full of fascinating stories of Parisian life, tracing changes they had witnessed in this vibrant city. I visited museums where I could get in as a student, my favourite being the *Musée Rodin*, and gaze at the masterpieces. Often, I would simply end up in the café at St Sulpice, alone or with friends, making a coffee last for several hours and watching the passers-by.

Another of our haunts was Les Halles, full of cheap clothes stores, fast-food joints, tourists and buskers. Hours and even days were spent wandering round watching the buskers sing, dance and skateboard for a living. Occasionally we would venture into *Café Costes*. Designed by the much-hyped Philippe Starck, this notorious minimalist café is a posers' paradise, especially if the

> We often just watched TV, cringing at the sexist adverts: semi-naked women advertising coffee, cars, soft drinks.

fashion crowd are in town. Scores of perfectly coiffed and groomed men and women sit watching each other and sipping coffee as designer ribbons of smoke waft up from their ashtrays. It's also a good place to observe the art of *la bise*, when acquaintances brush or skim (never actually kissing – this is lethal as it could smudge make-up) the cheek of the person they are greeting with their own cheek, two or three times. As a general rule, the less you know or like someone, the greater the number of mock kisses. The highlight of this particular establishment, however, is the men's urinals.

On the rare evenings when we did go out to eat we would invariably end up at our favourite restaurant, in rue Jacob: small, and one of the most camp in Paris, with fake leopardskin tablecloths, fake leopardskin lampshades and waiters wearing fake leopardskin aprons. From our first visit we loved it. We celebrated our birthdays there and any visitor offering to take us out was put through the rue Jacob ritual. Otherwise we would spend lively evenings at home and all sit on the floor eating chunks of baguette with paté or the ever cheap *Vache qui Rit* cheese. We often just watched TV, cringing in horror at the sexist adverts: semi-naked women advertising coffee, semi-naked women advertising cars, semi-naked women advertising soft drinks. Everything seems to come down to breathy lip-licking and nudity. I wondered whether to be featured in an advert in France you had to take a special course in the art of lip-licking . . . I wouldn't be surprised.

On the few occasions we trespassed to Parisian bourgeoisie (commonly referred to as BCBG, the *bon chic, bon genre*) social gatherings, we found there was an immense snobbery directed towards us. As foreigners, we elicited the kind of condescension which only Parisians can generate; we did not dress *correctement*, nor did we share their Parisian

> *My unease peaked when the police informed me that my effects had been found on a corpse in Calais.*

humour. Not being able to appreciate the latter's finer points and transgressing all social etiquette, we exposed ourselves to the full force of Parisian superiority. For most of us, it was this that made our stays finite, since these were precisely the sort of people we would have as colleagues. After an initial few months we all had opportunities for living in Paris indefinitely and yet without exception, the ten of us all chose to return home.

By the time I was attending such events, I had built up a circle of friends and knew my way around. I felt comfortable and things were going quite smoothly, until the day I was mugged. It was a strange scene for a mugging: Saturday morning in a busy crowded street just by the market in the rue de Buci, five minutes from my home. I was walking down ready to arm myself with a weekend's worth of baguettes and cheese when a large man punched me twice, full on in the stomach. As I bent over searing with pain, he grabbed my wallet and ran in the opposite direction. Several other shoppers had seen the event and stopped to stare in that typical Parisian "Bof, je m'en fous" (I don't give a damn) fashion.

I gathered myself up, still in considerable pain and tried to decide whether to pursue him or go to the police. He had already disappeared into the crowd so I took the latter option after first calling the emergency bank number (it is frequently possible to cash a cheque without ID). It took an hour before I was interviewed at the 6e arrondissement police station and completed the necessary paperwork, which caused much mirth as I was a foreigner, and was given a *déclaration de vol*.

That was that. I lived in considerable unease for the next two weeks in the knowledge that my assailant had my address and most of my personal details. My kindly bank manager refused to change my account number, on the basis that the thief would not "have the nerve to cash any cheques as he would have to go to the branch". Given that he had

had the nerve to mug me in broad daylight, it struck me as more than possible that he would try. Such basic logic was not well-received and I subsequently closed my account. Primed by my previous experience and equipped with the remainder of my cheque I was able to open an account at another bank relatively simply. My unease, however, peaked when I was contacted by the police who informed me that my effects had been found on a corpse in Calais. "At least it wasn't you" they joked . . .

Shortly after this incident I found myself facing the option of returning home or staying in Paris permanently. I did not find it a difficult decision. Weighing up the advantages of staying and those of leaving, I realized that although much of the beauty and romance of the city still remained, it had lost its fascination for me. Paris was also a city of snobbery and prejudice, full of disturbing, exploitative images of women. I did not want the negative aspects to smother the positive. I wanted to keep a part of the fantasy intact and that meant moving on.

My last night was spent on a tour of all my favourite places. Dinner at rue Jacob, dancing until dawn at various night clubs where I was greeted like a long lost sister, and finally the most beautiful scene, watching day break in the middle of Place de la Concorde, free from traffic and entirely empty apart from myself and two friends. It was an exquisite moment and one which I look back on with nostalgia.

Cycling on the French Riviera

Carla King, a freelance writer from California, lived in Nice for six months while researching a bicycling guide to the French Riviera. She has also travelled in Germany, Britain, the Irish Republic, Portugal, the Netherlands and cycled through West Africa, from Senegal to Côte d'Ivoire.

I stood on the edge of the cliff and surveyed the terrain I'd covered that April morning. The Mediterranean sparkled blue only 15km away as the crow flies, but I'd cycled 40km along smooth, curving, black-paved, lonely roads to get from sea-level to my 1000 metre-high perch. Behind me, in the distance, were the snow-capped Alps. The guys who passed me on their racing bikes had told me they often go there on weekends, after the snow has melted. Unlike these kilometre-counting, colour-clad fanatics, I was happy to stop in the field of grass and wild flowers atop this protruding, round-faced cliff the Niçoises call a *baou*, and call it a day.

I was loving this time I was spending in Nice and the towns and countryside around it, much more than I had on my previous trips to

France. Soon I realized that being on a bicycle was the key to my current experience. Besides my own sense of personal accomplishment and well-being, the French, being cycling fanatics, almost always treated me with respect and kindness – despite my less-than-perfect grasp of the language.

I was biking in the *arrière pays*, or "back-country", which is situated behind the Riviera, in front of the Alps, and southeast of Provence-proper. In the tiny villages perched in the hills though, it was Provence. After the first climb of the morning I'd stop at a little café to rest, eat something, and contemplate the Alps to the north, the Mediterranean to the south. It was just me and my mountain bike, the trusty five-year old Rock Hopper I'd modified with suspension and touring racks for previous, more ambitious tours. The children ran their hands over it, pointing out my California license sticker, and asked me questions about America while I sat under the perpetual sunshine of the Côte d'Azur . The waitress worried over me. "You should eat more than that *chèrie!*" she said, slipping me an extra portion. "Think of the energy you will use." I could almost hear the Italian mamma in the accents of many of these village women, insisting, "Mangez! Mangez!"

It had taken all morning to get to my perch on the cliff and from now on it was downhill. I felt pretty proud of myself. After my last tour, a three-week stint in Switzerland three years before, I hadn't done much bike touring. In California I had been considered a mountain-biking dilettante by my more athletic friends. But now I was doing three or four day-trips a week from Nice, of forty to a hundred kilometres each, navigating by contour maps to find the forgotten roads and tracks, preferably leading to a castle ruin or an old fort.

"Aren't you scared riding around by yourself in the woods?" a French woman asked me. It could be lonely on the trails and the fire roads, but I was never frightened. Occasionally, teenage boys on motorcycles would race past, barely glancing at me, and the few others I met were usually busy collecting mushrooms or herbs. They would give me chanterelles and puffballs and fill my packs with leaves and berries to make a *tisane,* good for strength.

It was the solitude I liked about biking. I listened to my body work, I had time to think, time to enjoy the abundant natural beauty, and time to contemplate the history of this area. Each mountain has its tiny *village perché* with fountain, church and a cobblestoned square. Here time seems to have stopped; women in black scarves tread slowly along in groups, carrying bags of produce from the marketplace; old men play *pétanque*, a form of *boules*, on a flat dirt court. Others sit at the nearby café and drink beer or *pastis*, the perpetual column of smoke from their Gitanes curling up past their hat brims.

To reach some of the more remote villages I had to take a train into the hills. The controllers were bored and never minded that my French was bad or that sometimes the train wasn't authorized to carry a bike. A lot of them were cyclists themselves and were anxious to give advice on the best roads, the best areas, the best bakeries and crèperies (cyclists eat a lot). After two or three hours of pedalling through the mountains I'd descend to the platform, the only passenger at some deserted station, and start my journey back to Nice.

The hills were a relief from the city, which I loved but sometimes found tedious. At Nice train station men would freely offer their opinion on my physical appearance: "I don't like women with muscles", one might say, looking me up and down disapprovingly. Another would point out my legs to someone else and grin: "Look at those legs . . . *très musculées*." The men in Nice are not shy.

Interestingly enough, I was hassled less when I wore skin-tight biking gear – ten times sexier than the baggy shorts and T-shirts I wore riding around town. I attribute this difference in attitude to image. When I was dressed in professional biking gear, men saw me as an athlete first, a woman second.

In Nice I had a room in a villa converted into apartments, rented out to students and long-term tourists by Madame and Monsieur Dupuy. This couple immediately became like family; Madame Dupuy helped to correct my French and Monsieur Dupuy, always the clown, taught me all the words that weren't in the dictionary. After telling them about my day I'd run down to the beach to take a quick swim before going out in the evening.

Nice has many good clubs and bars, including for foreigners, three Irish Pubs, a Dutch pub, and a big American-style place called *Chez Wayne's* in the old section that attracts a young rowdy crowd. A cosier place is *Jonathan's*, a basement club where Jonathan, an ex-patriate American hippie, sings and plays his guitar – mostly American and British folk songs – and lets French bands try their hand at Bruce Springsteen and The Beatles. The club feels like a corner-bar, which made me comfortable there alone.

The old section also has markets and a good selection of cafés and small shops selling quiches, snacks, and sandwiches. *Bar René-Socca*, popular with everyone from students to business people, is cheapest for lunch when everyone relaxes for a while with their *socca* or pizza, washed down with a beer or glass of the local rosé, always served ice-cold. But here, like everywhere else, I found it too easy to meet French men, and too difficult to meet French women. For one thing, women seem to prefer jogging or aerobics classes to cycling. And their culture is still traditional enough to keep them occupied with most of the housework even though many work outside the home. They just don't have time to sit around in cafés unless they schedule it into their day. I had one French friend I'd worked with in Lyon several years before; another brief friendship with a woman I'd met who worked at a tourist office; and I met two women, a mother and daughter, by trading English-for-French lessons. But we were always working our meeting times around their husbands' or boyfriends' schedules.

During a slow month my landlord, Monsieur Dupuy, and I often went to the railway station in the mornings to meet the trains from Paris and Rome to recruit tenants for his other apartments, but many people were too suspicious to take us up on it. Monsieur Dupuy would lean on the open door of his Renault, smoking, squinting under his cap, while I tried to convince people that we weren't working a scam to rob them, but truly had a nice, reasonably priced apartment to offer as the tourist season was slow.

My bedroom with shared bathroom cost 2400F per month, and though I thought this was a bit steep, the other foreigners I met were envious of my deal. The Dupuys' place was behind locked gates in a quiet residential neighbourhood on a hillside only a five-minute walk from the beach. The back garden was shaded by orange and peach trees, and we ate at the tables by the flower beds. I made friends with a couple from Vancouver who stayed there for a few weeks, and it was always fun to play *pétanque* with everyone in the evenings before dinner.

> *"Don't ignore them. Before they speak to you, look back at them like they're the lowest life-form on the planet."*

Though I lived in one of the safer areas of town, someone mangled the cable lock on my bike, and if they'd had bigger snippers they'd have owned it. In town, even small towns in the hills, I locked my bike with two locks. A friend at school locked his with three. Petty theft is an everyday occurrence and violent crime is not uncommon.

Theft, harassment, and violence is most apparent around Nice's primary tourist attraction, the Promenade des Anglais – a wide sidewalk built next to the 3m-high sea-wall that stretches the several kilometres between the airport and Nice's shipping port. The promenade, overlooking the town's stony beaches, is where everyone walks, jogs, exercises their poodles, or just hangs out. I wanted to rest on one of the promenade's blue chairs that the city has so thoughtfully provided, or on its benches or on the wide edge of the cement sea wall. I wanted to stare out to sea, to write, to read . . . but the men who hang out there are relentless. My first day in Nice, I had only taken a few steps on the promenade when I was approached by a man. "Are you Swedish?" he asked in English. I shook my head and kept walking. "Danish?" he continued. "English, American, German, Italian, Spanish?" he persisted. "Why won't you talk to me?" he pouted. Finally I replied in French, "I want to be alone." He stopped with a scowl and I continued on my way. One minute later: "Hello. You are American, I can tell." Another persistent fellow.

Every foreign woman I met had the same experience, no matter what nationality or mode of dress. French women seem to have the best defence system against excessive harassment. I was advised by a local: "When they look at you, don't ignore them. Before they speak to you, look back at them like they're the lowest life-form on the planet." It's cold but it works. Being polite has no effect.

I would not walk on the promenade late at night, though it is well-lit. At that time the guys who hang out there are often high or drunk. During my stay I saw three knife fights, one of which was over a girl who'd walked by – they were fighting over who got to say hello to her first.

This seemed to be more of a problem in Nice than in the other towns in the Côte d'Azur. I visited all the coastal cities between Cannes and Menton, and occasionally crossed the Italian border to bike in the hills behind Ventimiglia – an entirely different world.

All in all, my bicycle seemed the perfect method of transportation. I could throw it on a train going to Antibes, and ride to the Picasso Museum. Or to Menton to see the Cocteau Museum. Everywhere I went people were nice to me because of it. "*Courage!*" they would shout as I puffed up a hill. I never lacked a subject of conversation. I learned all the French words for bicycle parts and tools. I passed cars sitting in city traffic jams. I could take long trips or short trips or just give up and take the next train home.

In the end I was sorry to leave. Even after six months I had not seen all the perched villages, I hadn't seen all the museums and forts, nor had I begun to look at the caves and important archeological sites. I hadn't gone to Corsica as I had intended. (An eight-hour ferry ride away, it's reputed to be a hiker's and mountain biker's paradise.) Next time I will stay with the Dupuys again. I'll go to the *Alliance Française* and study for a language certificate. I'll ride my bike to all the caves. I'll see the perfumeries I missed in Grasse and go to the culinary arts museum in Biot. Maybe I'll take sailing lessons or rent a kayak, go horseback riding, learn to hang-glide or para-sail. Or I'll start a women's bicycling club.

Back at home now, I find myself flipping through the brochures and guidebooks as eagerly as if I'd never seen the place.

A Pilgrim on the Chemin de St Jacques

In 1991 **Claudia Campisi** walked the Chemin de St Jacques, following a route from the borders of Germany through France and northern Spain to Santiago de Compostela in Galicia. We've included her account in this chapter, as the heart of her journey lay along the French footpaths and in the cloisters of the French convents. Half German/half Italian, she now lives in east London, doing drama, dance and music with people with learning difficulties.

It was during the Gulf War in the winter of 1990–91, while men fought about oil – the guarantee of power – wasting human lives and destroying nature. Back then we were demonstrating in London and Berlin, smog-choked and unemployed, without hope, without vision of a future worth living for, with no delight in the present either. I suddenly thought of that map hanging in my flat in Berlin and decided "I am going to walk". If this was the end of the world, this was the last thing I would do in my life: go back to Germany, walk to Santiago, camp and live outdoors, as free as I could be, far away from the Moloch. It didn't matter that I had never done anything like this before, that this was *terra incognita* for me. I did it because I wanted to. Simple.

Santiago de Compostela – a thousand years of pilgrimage. I wasn't interested in it as the grave of St James. Though a Catholic, I am not into relics, shrines and saints. But I was attracted by the idea of following a path that has been trodden by millions of feet, with works of art and anecdotes left along the way.

Having said my official goodbyes to friends and relatives in Berlin, Munich and Milan, thus following the pilgrim's ritual, I set off on April 7th from Tubingen, a Swabian town as old as the Middle Ages and as young as the thousands of students buzzing about. The modern equipment I had gathered together set me apart from the old-fashioned pilgrims of long ago, who travelled light in cape and sandals, carrying only a shoulderbag, a flask and a stick. Still, my battered leather hat, shortage of money and searching spirit united me with them.

My idea was to avoid using fuel-burning vehicles and staying in organized tourist accommodation, camping sites included. I would surrender myself to Providence. A friend wanted to join me, but I said no, this is one of those things you have to do on your own.

My trek started like an ordinary Sunday afternoon stroll through the woods with friends, except that they returned home and I carried on.

"I bet you're back in a week", said one. I knew he'd lose: this was the first of 109 days.

10th Day. Apricot-coloured sky. End of a day in T-shirt in the vine-covered hills of the "*Kaiserstuhl*". I sit outside my tent, waiting for tea water to boil, with two maps spread out, one for France and one for Spain. Tomorrow I'll cross the Rhine into France.

I can't. It's impossible; it's too big for me. Walking to Freiburg was a game: now I am going to start the real thing. My adventure with the stag calling his wives by twilight, the drunken fishermen in front of my tent during the night by the lake in the forest, and the top tent piece I lost in the morning and found with the help of a farmer's son in the evening, 25 kilometres back – that seems like Kindergarten!

11th Day. I lie in a horse stable and imagine being trapped, raped and murdered. I could vanish, just like that. I tremble with fear and rage. If only I was a man! That I look like a man protects me. That I am a woman makes people less suspicious; and yet, I feel vulnerable. But it's just in my head. Maybe I am too much influenced by the French customs guards who warned me about the dangers a woman on her own has to be aware of. The two grooms who invited me to dinner and wine are just impressed by my project and my knowledge of French, that's all.

14th Day. In the middle of my first night in the Vosges, I woke up and listened to the crispy sound of snowflakes settling down upon the tent roof. Several times I had to crawl out and shovel off the white mass to prevent my tent from collapsing. This morning I panicked. I couldn't see the trail; I wasn't prepared for an expedition to the North Pole! Still wondering whether to return to the valley, I saw a woman coming out of nowhere. "Would you mind if I came with you?" she asked with an Alsacian lilt. Would I mind! I was intrigued. (Up on the Petit Ballon we parted, and today we still write postcards to each other.)

Now it's the second snow-morning. I am sitting in a mountain café, opened especially for me by its stunned owner. While I sip my comforting hot chocolate, I am joined by two wet Dutchmen wanting to climb the Grand Ballon – in this weather! "Just to say that we've done it", they say.

15th Day. I am the only person in the world. I melt into the wavy valleys. I become one with the mountains unfolding before me. Adieu les Vosges!

20th Day. I have a day of rest. Yesterday, as I came walking into Dannemarie, some children of this small village in the north of the Jura followed me and persuaded me to put up my tent on the land of their friends, Didi and Lilli, who owned a dairy farm. One of them fetched the rest of the gang to come and say hello. They wouldn't leave until I had promised to stay a day and play with them.

Today, between games, I had lunch with Didi and Lilli and then a dinner party with the kids and some parents who looked rather embarrassed. We sat outside by candlelight, singing silly songs and rolling around. Maybe they have doubts whether I am a grown-up woman or a kid. I am not so sure myself!

22nd Day. Before I can follow the Swiss-French border, I have to climb down Les Echelles de la Mort (Death's Ladder). Metal bars covered with ice. I feel my rucksack pulling heavily backwards. Yesterday I felt great, dancing along the road accompanied by *mes amis les enfants* until the next village. Now I feel like a wimp.

Having arrived at the banks of the River Doubs, a man offers me a lift in his car. I explain. He frowns: "But that's a penance!" "No, it's a gift."

25th Day. It's all fog now. I've climbed Mont d'Or and shovel snow from the plaque which tells me all about the splendid view. An hour later I am still running around with no clue about where I am or where I am supposed to go. Suddenly I can make out something black bouncing about. My heart jumps. A jogger! I stop him: he looks annoyed, stirs his arm into the milky soup to give directions and then hops off before I can even nod. Eventually I get back to the trail which leads me to Mouthe. After I get settled in the barn of a rather suspicious farmer, I walk to the nearby *gite d'étape*. I want a glass of wine to cheer me up. The woman at the door eyes me up and down – a scruffy, bedraggled unwashed traveller – and says, "Sorry, but I think you'd better go to the pub at the other end of the village". This is not a *gite*, but a plush, posh club and I don't want it anyway – boo!

27th Day. At the *Maison du Montagnon* I gladly accept the offer of a hot shower, the first since Freiburg, and a hot chocolate in exchange for the promise of a postcard from Santiago.

29th Day. I leave my route at the Col de la Faucille to descend into the valley of Lac Leman, looking forward to resting with a friend's relatives. In the night I am sick and get the runs: it must have been from the stream where I drank earlier. This will teach me not to forget to take enough drinking water. I'm just lucky that now I'm well looked after.

I will stay for three days, just watching the fog fingers reaching over and down the ridge, slowly stretching out along the rocks, down, down into the valley, wrapping us up with giant hands . . .

36th Day. I am trapped in the suburbs of Lyon, with nowhere to camp. The pensioner couple I'm asking for advice don't hesitate. "I'll take her back", she says to her husband. Before I understand what is happening, I sit in the hut on the allotment where Mme and M. Calendre spend their days. The woman talks fast while she rushes from table to cupboard to sofa to me, opening fridge, drawers, tins, baskets, bags. "Please help yourself to whatever you like." She'll have to lock the garden door: Tomorrow morning her husband will come to let me out. I stay up late, not used to having a real house all to myself, and above all a radio! This is humankind at its kindest. Providence is still on my side!

37th Day. I walk into the Lioness, the "true capital of *La Belle France*", I've been told. I'm looking forward to meeting Martine, a woman I met in a hamlet while asking for water a few days ago. She works for IGN, the French map publisher. Through her, I can have all the maps I'll need to get to Spain, discounted. She has also arranged accommodation for me in Lyon. I start to believe in miracles . . .

40th Day. "It's time to unwrap Christmas presents" somebody in the Monts Lyonnais says, commenting on the weather. It's May 16th.

47th Day. Since my detour to "La Chaise Dieu" (God's Chair) where I indulged in the silence, space and sacred curiosities of a dimly lit abbey not yet invaded by swarms of tourists, at last it's become summer. Heat makes me retreat into the shade for a siesta. I can't stop being amazed and excited at the richness of the Massif Central, its breathtaking views and spicy scents.

Today I'm full of suspense, approaching Le Puy, end of the individual part of my walk and beginning of the official pilgrim route. It's just after Pentecost: tourists people the church of Polignac, forever clicking their cameras.

In the afternoon I stand at the porch of a convent of Poor Clares in Le Puy, waiting for the grumpy nun in brown-white robes and veil to tell me whether I can stay with them for a few days. She comes back smiling. Although the guest house is still closed, they will put me up and feed me. "You've got to eat a lot!" she commands with a shaking index finger and a frown.

50th Day. I go to Sunday Mass in the cosy convent chapel and then join the nuns for a chat in the parlour. They bombard me with questions: How many kilometres do you walk each day? Are you not scared? What do your parents say? Are they not scared? Why do you do this? Have you heard of the woman who walked to Santiago with a donkey? How much does your rucksack weigh? When do you think you'll arrive? Etc, etc. The abbess refuses to take any money: "You'll need it".

I part from the nuns with a heavy heart. In spite of the floods of tourists and the rows about the inappropriateness of the travel business and consumerism in holy places, I had a wonderful time in Le Puy. I felt like part of the family, going out with the cathedral attendants, sitting with the beggars, my pilgrim cousins, on the cathedral steps, and having dinner with the family next to the convent. I would have liked to stay on, but I am a pilgrim and the journey has just begun.

Wrong. In order to become a "real" pilgrim, I need to go through the ancient ritual of the benediction of pilgrims. In the cathedral I get hold of a priest who has some minutes to spare, and indeed it takes but a few moments for him to reel off his prayers.

Much later, out of town, something unexpected happens. Clutching the scallop, Santiago's symbol passed on to me by a former pilgrim yesterday at my "last supper", I sit and cry with passion. I feel so alone.

55th Day. What a strange landscape, Aubrac: hill-less, tree-less and endless. Hairy cattle with impressive horns on bleak muddy grass. No sounds. Complete stillness. God? . . .

56th Day. It's the fourth thunderstormy day in a row. I descend into the valley of the Lot. Following the river's snaky, calm and dreamy movements, I come to Espalion.

I am attracted by the tradition of pilgrims finding shelter with church people. The priest I ask takes me to Cistercian nuns who live rather isolated in the thick forest up in the hills. I don't mind sitting in a car as my feet hurt – something that's becoming a problem. It's off the route, anyway.

Unlike my Poor Clares, the nuns here are invisible. In church, we visitors, already seated in a far corner, are further separated from the nuns by a grille. From my only neighbour I hear that the two priest–monks who say Mass enter through a special tunnel. The nuns' heavenly singing is such a contrast to my earthy life, I can hardly believe that this is reality.

59th Day. Conques, which is supposed to be a highlight of the Chemin de St Jacques, is a flop for me. I am suffocated by tons of schoolkids rolling out of coaches into the Basilique and out of the super-expensive cafés into the narrow cobblestone lanes. I'm off to have my first encounter with a free-living viper! But she brushes along without paying any attention to me, and once more I'm disappointed.

60th Day. For a few hours I have company: two Swiss women who do the pilgrimage in chunks in their vacations. They sleep in cheap hotels and *gites*. I feel sorry for them because they can't be "real pilgrims" and they feel sorry for me because I have to carry such a big rucksack.

63rd Day. This is my second detour, this time to Rocamadour, a village built into vertical rocks. I visit *La Vierge Noire*, but actually she's just one of many Black Virgins of this region. I sense the strong energy this place emanates. In the chapel I kneel before the altar with my palms on the stone floor, eyes closed. If people are staring at me, I don't care. I'm a pilgrim. A fool. So what.

67th Day. I'm sure that the two women who run the little café in Cahors where I sit writing postcards and sipping my Grand Crème are dykes. We grin at each other. Yeah, must be!

It's incredibly hot. I need more rests, and wherever I can I have a cold footbath.

72nd Day. Tonight I'll sleep in the bed of a farmer's son who's gone to do his military service. I'm now in the Gascogne, land of the Musketeers.

So far, I've met quite a few nice Sisters of different congregations. I'm really torn. As much as their churchiness, I do love the warmth and attention they give me.

75th Day. My first complete "nuns' day", with all their offices. Not with them, though, as they are enclosed Carmelites, but alongside, staying in a hut in the guest house garden. The abbess calls me for an "audience". She wants to know whether I have a vocation. Huh? With insight, she exclaims: "Must be the Benedictines for you!"

"Why?"

"Because they are musical!" She's heard me playing the penny whistle.

I don't tell her that I'm reading the account of an ex-Poor Clare, a rather gruesome story.

81st Day. Orthez. I've sent off my tent; I don't need it any more. Spain and its free *refugios* for pilgrims are close. Somehow I'm depressed. I want to stay: it's nice here. Poor Clares again. And Maite from the Pyrenees who's absolutely gorgeous. But I fear she'd fall out of her shoes if I made any advances.

91st Day. Back in Orthez. The sun is rising. I'm going to hitch-hike to St Jean Pied de Port, near the Spanish border.

Been there before, a week ago. Walked. Stayed with Maite and her family Sunday night. Drove back to Orthez with her on Monday morning. Couldn't do it. I'm exhausted. Fed up. Scared by the next chapter: Spain. Is this my "Border Syndrome"? Also, my Spanish is virtually nil.

But now I've got to go. Marie, the very rich nuclear power station engineer, now a Poor Clare postulant, took care of me and brought me to Lourdes for a retreat in silence. After three days in this first-class hotel, mesmerized by her continuous rambling and Lourdes's multitudes of very international visitors thirsting for holy water miracles, I feel like a bird in a gilded cage. My benefactor understands and buys me a ticket back to Orthez.

Oh God, Orthez! I had told Marie about the chilling book I was reading, wondering aloud "which convent it could be?" It's in Orthez, she says matter-of-factly.

The abbess later tells me it's all lies, but what else could she say? It doesn't matter, as I'm leaving anyway.

92nd Day. Roncesvalles. At last I made it to Spain. Tonight I won't sleep. How could I, with about twenty other people in the same room, snoring, giggling, shuffling and making the beds creak. Suddenly I am engulfed by pilgrims, mostly Spanish men, cyclists and walkers. The only other woman so far is E from Reims. She started in St Jean and is out for a flirt (definitely straight). 787km to Santiago. Where's my tent?

94th day. I had been looking forward to seeing Pamplona, with Hemingway's tales in my mind. It's July and time to run with the bulls. My curiosity is quenched by the sharp smell of urine mixed with vomit. The city has turned into a big, filthy loo. We leave Pamplona as quickly as we can.

107th Day. Sahagun. I can't stand this anymore. Ten days ago it was nice in Viana, the last town in the province of Navarra. I met some Irish people I could talk to without problems, even gossip about the Spaniards racing along in ill-fitting trainers and treating their numerous blisters with hot needles, dramatic red spray and sewing thread. In Viana I even had fun. There was a fiesta and loud music on the plaza, to which I danced with wild Spanish kids.

The dreaded Meseta, flat as a table, in the year's hottest season. No shade; the land dry as bones. The reddish dust creeps in everywhere. This is a desert, not without a particular fascination, but I'm unable to take it in. I hate all these snoring men around me. I hate the man who attacked E while she was walking on her own. I hate the Spanish inhabitants, who are disinterested, of course. How many pilgrims do they see passing through their villages every day, month, year? I hate myself for not being able to keep my own walking rhythm. I hate my feet, which are on strike.

I sit on the floor of the chapel, feeling shattered. "Do what God wants you to do", nuns usually say. To hell. What do *I* want?

I want to arrive, that's all. The abbess here in the Benedictine convent advises differently: "There's a train. In Santiago you can stay in our sister convent. They are nice."

It's the end of my walk. I'll take the train. I'm not a martyr. Tomorrow I'll go to Leon, the day after to Santiago.

And that's what I did. I arrived on July 24th, one day before the festival, the *Dia de Santiago*. I was so tired and worn out that the nuns had to force me to go out to the fireworks. At first I did nothing but eat, sleep and tend my feet which had given up because they couldn't stand in worn-out walking boots any longer. When I woke up, there was a lovely woman taking care of me. I stayed on until the first of September, indulging in romance and pretending to have a vocation: the Carmelite abbess had been almost right.

In the following year I went to Santiago three times. The last time, I finally walked off my "leftovers". I learned a lot about the region of Galicia: its nationalism, hostility to strangers and feminists (identified with Lesbians) and its darkest Catholicism; but also rough coasts and gentle *rias bajas*, very pagan, a bit Celtic. It needs time to understand Spain and to get to love it – much more time than it does with France, I find.

This summer, Santiago saw its first Lesbian and Gay Pride Parade. I went for my last visit. I still had to go to Finistère. To finish everything to do with the *Camino*.

To End.

TRAVEL NOTES

Languages French. Basque and Breton, as well as regional dialects, are still spoken but losing way. Perhaps more important today are immigrant/migrant languages – Maghrebi Arabic, Portuguese, etc. English is spoken reasonably widely but you'll find it frustrating to depend on.

Transport The French rail network, SNCF, is the best in Europe – efficient and extensive; bus services play a relatively minor role. Cycling is big and you can rent bikes from most train stations and in all towns of any size. Few French women would even consider hitching. If you must, make use of *Allostop*, an organization for drivers and hitchers to register for shared journeys.

Accommodation Plentiful, though if your money is tight you'll need to depend on the numerous youth hostels and campsites. In rural areas you can stay in *gites* which are friendly little Bed & Breakfast-type hotels. On the Riviera, ask for the brochure *Hills and Alpes*

d'Azur (available in English) from the tourist office, which lists accommodation, festivals, and activities for many of the hill towns. There are also a few women's holiday camps (see *Women's Accommodation*).

Guides *The Rough Guide to France* (Penguin) gives a refreshing alternative perspective while also covering all the traditional tourist interests. For exploring the capital, *The Woman's Travel Guide to Paris* (UK, Virago/US, RDR press) includes interesting information on women's contribution to the city's history, art and culture, as well as useful listings.

WOMEN'S ACCOMMODATION

The following is just a selection: write first for a prospectus to: Barriare, *Les Essades* (holiday camp), 16210 Chalais (☎045.98.62.37).

R.V.D. Plasse (holiday camp), Les Grezes, St Aubin des Nabirat, 24250 Domme (☎053.28.50.28).

Chez Jacqueline Boudillet (guesthouse), Langerau à cere la Ronde, 37460 Montresor (☎16.47.94.34.63).

Saouis (guesthouse with camping), Cravenceres, 32110 Nogaro (☎0033.62.08.56.06).

CONTACTS

The following contacts are reasonably established and should be able to provide full and up-to-date contacts for other French cities.

Paris: *Maison des Femmes*, 8 cité Prost, 11e (☎93.48.24.91) is the capital's best-known feminist centre. They publish a fortnightly bulletin, *Paris Féministe*, run a cinema club and radio station, *Les Nanas Radioteuses* (101.6Mhz; Weds 6pm–midnight), and provide a meeting place for most Paris groups including *MIEL*, a lesbian organization that runs the centre's café – *L'Hydromel*.

Marseille: *Maison des Femmes*, 95 rue Benoit Malon, 5 (people around Tues & Thurs 6–10.30 pm). A meeting place for all groups.

WOMEN'S BOOKSHOPS

Paris: The following feminist bookshops stock the French feminist calendar/guide and *Lesbia*, a monthly lesbian listings and events magazine.

Librairie des Femmes, 74 rue de Seine, 6 (☎43.29.50.75).

Librairie Pluriel, 58 rue de la Roquette (☎47.00.13.06).

Marguerite Durand Library, 21 Place du Pantheon, 75005 (☎43.78.88.30).

Marseille: *La Librairie des Femmes*, rue Pavillion. Feminist bookshop.

Nice: *Le Papier Maché*, 3 rue Benoit Bunico. Co-op bookshop, restaurant and arts centre – a friendly leftist haven and meeting place for feminist, ecology and radical groups.

LESBIAN/FEMINIST BARS

Paris: *La Champmesle*, 4 rue Chabanais (6pm–2am; ☎42.96.85.20). Popular bar; the front is mixed, the back is women-only.

Katmandou, 21 rue de Vieux Colombier (11pm–dawn; ☎45.48.12.96). The best-known and most upmarket of the lesbian nightclubs, with Afro-Latino and international atmosphere.

Marseille: *La Boulangerie Gay*, 48 rue de Bruys. Contact point for *La Douce Amère*, a lesbian campaigning group.

BOOKS

Mary Ellen Jordan Haight, *Walks in Gertrude Stein's Paris* (UK & US, Gibbs Smith, 1988; US o/p). Five literary walks through bohemia, with some good quotes and anecdotes.

☒ **Shari Benstock**, *Women of the Left Bank: Paris 1900–1940* (UK, Virago, 1987/US, University of Texas Press, 1986). Full of information about women's contribution to the ex-pat literary scene and the founding of literary modernism.

Morrill Cody and Hugh Ford, *The Women of Montparnasse* (UK & US, Cornwall Books, 1984; US o/p). Collective biography of English and American women on the Left Bank between the World Wars.

Marilyn Yalom, *Blood Sisters – The French Revolution in Women's Memory* (UK, Pandora Press, 1995/US, Basic Books, 1993). Fascinating collection of memoirs chronicling women's experiences of the French Revolution, from the servant who attended Marie-Antoinette in her last days to Mme Roland, Mme Genlis and other writers of the time.

☒ **Simone de Beauvoir**, *The Second Sex* (1949; UK, Picador, 1988/US, Vintage, 1989). Groundbreaking feminist work by one of the founders of French feminism and existentialism.

Deirdre Bair's *Simone de Beauvoir: A Biography* (UK, Vintage, 1991/US, Touchstone Books) provides an illuminating revaluation of her life.

Anaïs Nin, *Journals 1917–1974* (1966; UK, Peter Owen/US, Harvest Books, both published in 7 vols 1967–91). In Paris during the 1930s, Anaïs Nin rubbed shoulders with the likes of Henry Miller, Antonin Artaud and Otto Rank. She manages to capture the energy of those times with subtle, often beautiful prose.

Janet Flanner, *An American in Paris* (UK, Hamish Hamilton, 1940/US, Simon & Schuster). Collection of articles written when Flanner was Parisian correspondent for the *New Yorker*. Includes illuminating profiles of many of the leading artistic and literary figures of the time.

Elaine Marks, *New French Feminism* (UK, Harvester, 1981/US, Schocken). A part of the continuing debate that divides French feminists – de Beauvoir described Marks' book as "totally distorted".

Claire Duchen, *Feminism in France* (UK, RKP, 1986/US, Routledge, Chapman and Hall). Chronicles the evolution of the women's movement in France from its emergence in 1968 to the present. Highly recommended.

Francine du Plessix Gray, *Rage and Fire – A Life of Louise Colet* (UK, Hamish Hamilton, 1994/US, Simon & Schuster). Fascinating biography of the nineteenth-century feminist writer and central model for Flaubert's *Madame Bovary*.

Simone Berteaut, *Piaf* (UK, Penguin, 1973/US, Harper, 1972, o/p). Gripping biography by the singer's half-sister.

FICTION

Djuna Barnes, *Nightwood* (UK, Faber & Faber, 1950/US, New Directions, 1946). Brilliant novel set in Paris by one of the city's flamboyant literary characters.

Simone de Beauvoir, *The Woman Destroyed* (1967; UK, Flamingo, 1984/US, Pantheon, 1987). Just one of the challenging novels by France's most famous feminist writers providing an intense, beautifully written view of male/female relationships.

Colette, *Chéri* (UK, Penguin, 1990/US, Ballantine, 1986); *Gigi* (UK, Penguin, 1990/US, Signet, 1973, o/p); *The Pure and the Impure* (UK, Penguin, 1990/US, Farrar, Straus & Giroux, 1975, o/p), and many more. Semi-autobiographical novels by notoriously bohemian model, actress, journalist and writer who was the first French woman to be given a state funeral.

Shusha Guppy, *A Girl in Paris* (UK, Minerva, 1992/US, Heinemann). Arriving in Paris from Iran at age 17 to study French at the Sorbonne, Shusha Guppy gradually eases in to life on the left bank.

Eveline Mahyère, *I Will Not Serve* (1958; UK, Virago, 1988, o/p). Powerful lesbian fiction set in Paris in the 1950s.

Anaïs Nin, *The Four-chambered Heart* (UK, Virago, 1992/US, Swallow, 1959). Chronicle of a passionate love affair set on a canalboat on the Seine. Nin, renowned for her bold and sensuous fiction, also wrote *Henry and June* (UK, Penguin, 1992/US, Harcourt Brace, 1990) and several volumes of erotic short stories.

Jean Rhys, *Quartet* (UK, Penguin, 1992/US, Carroll & Graf, 1990). Poignant story of a single woman manipulated by all those around her; set in the damp streets and smoke-filled cafes of Paris between the wars.

Françoise Sagan, *Bonjour Tristesse* (1954; UK, Penguin, 1971/US, NAL-Dutton, 1983, o/p). Novel of a girl's awakening sexuality set in the blazing heat of the south of France. Caused quite a stir when first published.

Marguerite Yourcenar, *Coup de Grace* (1957; UK, Harvill, 1992/US, Noonday, 1981). The first woman to be elected to the *Académie Française*, Marguerite Yourcenar's novels show an incredible breadth of scholarship and experience.

Look out, too, for Katharine Mansfield's short stories and cartoons by Claire Brétècher and Catherine Rihoit.

Ghana

For many years travellers steered clear of Ghana, deterred by its reputation as one of the most economically distressed countries in West Africa. The enormous wealth and prestige it had amassed before retrieving independence from the British in 1957 had all but collapsed, leaving the country floundering in political conflict, corruption and famine. Under its recent "era of recovery", however, much has changed. Poverty has eased, food is again filling the market places and independent travellers, drawn by the low costs, the vast, empty stretches of palm-fringed beaches and the rich and vibrant lifestyle of the Asante homeland, are returning in force. Facilities remain pretty basic, relying on a crumbling colonial infrastructure of government rest houses and hotels, but, with a good road network and plenty of buses, there are few problems in getting around.

For women arriving across the border from the hyped and commercialized tourist destination of Côte d'Ivoire, Ghana can come as a welcome respite. Ghanaians show a warmth and hospitality toward visitors unrivalled in the region, and this, coupled with a familiarity and tolerance towards European culture and a widespread knowledge of English, make it a relatively easy and safe country to travel around alone.

As an *Obruni* (literally "whitey", but used regardless of colour for any obvious Westerner) you are bound to attract attention. Taxi-drivers and traders will tout for custom but most of the men who approach you on the streets or in bars have a genuine interest in getting to know you and helping out. The most casual encounters can end with invitations to stay at someone's home, visit relatives in nearby villages or get down to some serious celebrating at a local high-life concert. As ever, you should follow your own instincts about who to trust. The role of host is taken seriously, and while men are happy to let you know that they'd like to sleep with you, this is rarely pushed to the point of being threatening or offensive.

Like in many parts of Africa, women cover their legs, wearing long dresses or printed cloth tied at the waist. Donning shorts and undertaking mannish activities – riding a bicycle, for example – are frowned on, although no one will publicly criticize you for this. The atmosphere is generally relaxed and even in the north, where Islam prevails, the culture is far more tolerant than in, say, Mali or Senegal.

Women in Ghanaian society maintain a high profile, particularly in their established role as market traders; the vast Kumasi market, for instance, is exclusively governed by women, each section having its own Queen Mother who sets prices and allocates stalls. Polygamy, usually involving a wife and several "girlfriends" is common, but for many women the reality is much like single motherhood, where the burdens of childcare and providing for the family fall squarely on their shoulders. Even within the semi-matriarchal Asante region, where inheritance passes from a man to his sister's son, the secondary status of women holds firm.

"So Why Am I European?"

Denise Roach, a Black British woman of Jamaican origin, travelled to Ghana after a challenging two-year spell as an English teacher in Dakar, Senegal. Before this trip to West Africa she had done relatively little independent travelling. She currently lives in London and works in the book trade.

One thing I give West Africa: the people of its many nations are amazing salespeople and will encourage you, by persuasion or just through the example of their genial approach to life, that visiting their country will be the best decision you will ever make. Thanks to a group of Ghanaian students at Dakar University I decided a trip to Accra and beyond might just live up to the hype. Having spent two years in Senegal I had grown weary of the glitz and squalor of Francophone Africa and blasé about the bureaucratic stiffness the French do so well. I was itching to move on. I wondered if my newly learnt survival skills would translate to a former British colony. Were, indeed, all African men the same? I felt I couldn't merely rely on mum's assurances that I'd be OK because Ghanaians were "like us": Jamaicans at heart.

Arriving in Accra in the sticky heat of a Sunday afternoon with no hotel or hostel reservations was, perhaps, a mistake on my part. The arrival at the airport of Mr Ogbarmey-Tetteh, the father of a friend of a friend, cushioned what could have been a serious setback and demonstrated once again that in Africa the most tenuous links can turn out to be the most dependable. I had planned to head for the YMCA – full, of course – but ended up being led to GNAT (Ghana National Association of Teachers), an all-male hall of residence. GNAT, as its name would suggest, was not exactly five-star comfort, but it matched the basic criteria I'd set for choosing a room; that is it had a working toilet with a flush, a shower, and a lock on the door. Unfortunately my room was next to the said toilet with flush (teachers, I found, get up early and perform their ablutions with unreasonable vigour), but I was grateful to offload my rucksack, shower and collect my thoughts. Mr O-T seemed happy to take care of me and I welcomed the gifts of toilet rolls, mosquito spray and bottled water as well as the massive meal he treated me to later that night.

If you have the right contacts or are willing to "dash" a little something in the right direction, it's possible to find rooms not listed in any guidebook. Mr O-T's contacts and influence allowed me access not just to GNAT but to the Commission for Scientific Research guest house and finally the Ghana Institute for Management and Public

Administration. I don't really know what Mr O-T did in the day (a lawyer, but with amazing amounts of free time on his hands) as he seemed to devote most of his time to shuffling me from one guest house to another, in search of "the right place". I was just happy to be clean.

Accra itself is an urban sprawl, shabby and decayed, its old colonial mansions and system of open sewers standing in contrast to the slick modernity of Dakar's commercial district. Some Ivoirians I met considered the absence of skyscrapers and cinema complexes a serious failing, which told me more about Ivoirians than it did about Ghana. But what Accra lacked in flash it made up for in fume-filled ambience and sheer noise. Traffic queues are endless. Much of the city's serious hustling is concentrated around the massive roundabouts or "circles" that provide convenient dropping-off points for taxis and *tro-tros* (passenger vans) and which mark out the capital's commercial and industrial areas. Street traders and hawkers work the crowd, taking advantage of any gap in the general whirl: a traffic jam, an argument, to offload their goods – anything from musical bibles to clothes pegs – while stalls are set up on every corner with cheap food to "chop"(eat). I got the impression that Accra was a city trying hard to be a capital and not quite making it.

Coming from Senegal I was immediately struck by the sense of warmth and how undaunting it all seemed. Don't get me wrong – hanging around in lorry parks surrounded by spitting women and diesel fumes, or waiting for a *tro-tro* to be sufficiently packed to make it absolutely unsafe, were not "warm" moments. But asking for directions and being led all the way to where I wanted to go, really put a glow in my heart. After Dakar, admittedly, I was a tad easier to please.

Unfortunately the sheer craziness and urgency of the city's routine makes it difficult to sit back and people-watch. For this you need the beach. Tucked away behind the International Trade Fair site, Labadi Beach is where Ghanaians come to strut their stuff, as noisily as possible, of course. Having come across all manner of chat-up lines in Dakar, I felt unbothered by the cries of "Hey, so, lady, where you from?" and pleas to "take me to England" that came thick and fast as soon as I stepped on the beach. The cheeky calls to "unite the diaspora", did impress me however – I'd never heard the phrase used in that context before.

Any agenda I had was sketchy to say the least. My main priorities were to establish where I was going and get the currency to pay my way. FOREX (foreign exchange) bureaux offering competitive rates were dotted around Accra, and while I tried to change small amounts of CFA at a time, I still ended up coming away with what looked like the whole of the Bank of Ghana in used notes. The cedi looks and feels like

Monopoly money and I dispensed with great wads of it as if I were buying Park Lane.

Though I had by no means exhausted Accra, it was time to move and this meant entrusting myself to the rigours of Ghana's public transport system. I resigned myself to being squashed into a *tro-tro* and flung about over innumerable potholes on the road to the Gold Coast. It could have been worse – most seats had some form of cushioning and, for once, I was grateful for my own sturdy rear end that proved a much more reliable shock absorber than the mechanical ones on offer. Fortunately, also, I had had the fore-

> *Something about the way the TV pastors said "fornication" every other word sent shivers down my spine.*

sight to pack only sports bras, for minimal bounce. There's an etiquette to *tro-tro* travel that keeps what is essentially a dangerous and volatile grouping of people both patient and resigned. Journeys start with a communal prayer and continue under the shared belief that while the Lord is in his Heaven he will keep the rustiest of rust-buckets safe and in business. For less than 30p in most cases, who was I to question comfort and road-worthiness? Having the prayers of my fellow passengers thrown in for free, seemed a bit of a bargain.

Christianity would follow me through Ghana, pervading the Ghanaian daily scene as Islam does in the Middle East, with a prolifera-tion of churches in all forms, shapes and sizes. It disturbed me only because it came from something familiar. There was something about the way the TV pastors said "fornication" every other word, and the way the choirs seemed to look out of the TV right at me, that sent shivers down my spine. But despite this I managed to find comfort in the irony of it all and, walking from one ramshackle shop to another, I couldn't help grinning at the idea that someone, somewhere, was enjoy-ing the joke. The local "chop bar" where I chopped *fufu* (yam mash) and light soup had, thanks to faith and perseverance, been transformed into the "Salvation Belongs to God Chop Bar". Hairdressers were advertised as the "Thy Will Be Done Salon" and the "Blessed Resurrection Beauty Parlour". And as for public transport, there were signs proclaiming "Thy Kingdom Come". Hardly reassuring.

Ghana has worked hard to maintain the country's heritage and display the history of its contacts with European slavers and colonialists and of the traditional kingdoms. I was impressed by the desire of all Ghanaians I met to preserve and respect the traditional culture, so easily threatened in large urban centres by contact with Europeans and Americans. The sight of men draped in rich *kente* cloths and wearing elaborate sandals, all paunch and pose, was inspiring. It was on the Gold Coast, however, that the real significance of my journey became apparent. I had always maintained a healthy, even robust, cynicism towards personal quests for

> *In Ghana my Britishness was a burden. I wanted to lose it and take back all the times I'd claimed it.*

meaning and self, and had poured scorn on African Americans and others from the diaspora who claimed to be looking for roots but ended up chasing an image. A visit to the castles at Cape Coast and El Mina changed all that. Things started to fit. Other visitors and their comments ceased to matter as I became aware of my place in the whole frightening picture. At castles resembling warehouses, complete with dungeons and chapels (and, in the case of El Mina, built before the discovery of that "New World" which would provide eager buyers for their supplies) the scale and sequence of disastrous events became clear.

"Cape Coast is the answer", I was told after chatting to Charles, a tourist officer working in Kumasi.

"What's the question?"

"Why am I European?"

Both Ghanaians and Jamaicans have suffered exploitation and betrayal at the hands of the British, and I'm the product of that. In Ghana my Britishness was a burden. I wanted to lose it and take back all the times I'd claimed it. Yet at the same time I knew that I wanted to go home eventually, and that "home" was a small corner of north London that I love to hate. I wasn't expecting to feel such a part of history, and it pushed me to make discoveries that I'll draw on for a long time.

Ghana's respect for its traditions does not prevent the country tackling modern issues and crises. At a grand *durbar*, a traditional festival, the local chiefs and dignitaries assembled not just to mark the start of the fishing months but to be criticized by the highest chief present, for their poor standards of hygiene and education and their apathy in the face of the challenge of tourism. All were taking part. I watched women with elaborate gold-decorated beehives standing next to a family-planning stall – history meeting the present and future. Messages about sexual responsibility provided a poignant backdrop for a retrospective on Ghana's links with Europe, and images of marauding, raping slavers were never far from my mind. "Liverpool Street" and "Trafalgar Square", once home to women and their mulatto children, were literally a stone's throw away.

For the next stage of my journey – to Kumasi – I took the train. I had looked forward to the comfort and the chance to collect my thoughts and sort out an itinerary. Sleep was out of the question. The non-reclining plastic-covered seats were obviously designed with taller insomniacs in mind. And of course I chose the carriage with the one-woman Pentecostal choir, who kept me awake with her tuneful, if unnecessary, rendition of *Trust and Obey* that lasted the entire trip. So I sat upright and pondered the coastal sands and their towns given life by the slave trade, the green of the south, home to the grasscutter and bush meat stew (rodent! I ate rodent!) and headed for Kumasi, with fumes and traffic to remind me that life is smog.

By the time I arrived my feet, back and head hurt, which didn't bode too well for a place of unrelenting noise. A kind taxi-driver asked me where I wanted to go; and since I didn't really know he offered to take me to Dichemso, a lively corner of town full of Ivoirians and Nigerians. Home was *The Fabulous Hotel*, a drab building that made brave but futile attempts to live up to its ambitious name. The rooms were as clean as the cleaner/receptionist/barman could keep them although the general absence of windows gave the place a prison-like feel. Foolishly, I chose a single room and was conse-

I was probably just another confused Black woman, a fool to drag herself around in the most unladylike fashion.

quently forced to encounter the worst communal bathroom horrors of my journey. But I liked the *Fabulous* for its people and its faults. My new friends would drag me into their homes to look at their photo albums and offer me protection and advice. It all proved much more helpful and inspiring than I would have imagined when I first set eyes on the pornographic frescoes on the lobby walls or the curious signs in the toilet: "don't squat on the w.c.", "don't spit on the walls" – I mean, why would you want to?

Kumasi seems to be built around the central market, a massive crater filled to capacity with corrugated iron shacks selling everything you could possibly want, new or used. Like jumping into a pool of piranhas, I didn't think I'd make it out alive. But there was little to fear and, establishing a harmless flirtatious conversation with a *kente*-seller and his family, trying my best to sound like an old hand at this bargaining business, I managed to find my way back to my landmark, the Malta Guinness stand, bargains and confidence intact.

If there was danger, I perceived none, and certainly felt no antagonism between Ghanaians and the few tourists I encountered. Tourists were the target of the odd bit of extra attention, more demands for a little "dash" or a parting gift. But where I prepared myself for the worst I was rewarded with politeness and openness, even when my desire to explore led me down alleys and through police barracks or to outlying villages to see traditional weavers and craftsmen at work. One man remarked that he felt it would be a shame and a waste if he were to refrain from helping me and then die without being some service to someone in some way. Melodramatic perhaps, but it made my day. For once it seemed guide-book generalizations about the warmth of the people were right.

I thought of the friends I made – like Smiler the ex-decathlete police-man who offered to help me out if ever I got into "trouble", and Charles at the tourist office who gave me dress tips for visiting the palace and let me hitch a ride with him to the magical Lake Bosuntwe – and wondered what they made of me? I was probably just another confused Black woman, a fool to herself to drag herself around in the most unladylike fashion. I certainly felt like that at times. I only ever aimed to scratch the surface of this many-faceted country and I came away with much more than I had bargained for. My own preconceptions and priorities had surely changed. I missed Dakar's crêpes and ice cream, but I discovered Malta Guinness, my past and much more besides.

A "Foreign Expert"

Naomi Roberts, a clinical psychologist living in Bristol, spent eight months living and working as a volunteer in a Ghanaian village.

Only a few parts of West Africa have opened up to tourists – little strips of beach backed by new hotels – and even here the slightly adventurous traveller has only to walk past the barbed wire inland for a few hundred yards to discover a very different continent. If you want to you can stick to a life on the fringes – or you can try, with some difficulty, to penetrate the less glamorous and more struggling daily life.

I lived for eight months in a village in the coastal forested region, about 120 miles from Accra. I had been brought out by a British volunteer agency to assist in setting up primary healthcare programmes. I stayed only eight months because I became uncomfortable in my role as "foreign expert". The undue respect I received seemed to be based on little more than my being English and therefore seemed demeaning to the people who gave it. My job had been worked out between the British agency and a Ghanaian central government department and no one local had been properly consulted. No effort had been made to see if a Ghanaian could have done my job.

However, putting these deep objections aside, my time in Ghana was full of interest. I lived with people who were unused to tourists and entirely generous and accepting. They welcomed me into their homes so uncritically that even in such a short time I felt I had gained a new family. The job, although not working out, gave me an entry into a shared way of life that will forever make our boxed Western existence seem thin.

My stay began with a few weeks training, after which I was taken out to the district where I was to work. A truck had been laid on and loaded up with a bed, a table and two chairs, a few buckets and saucepans, a kerosene stove and lamp and a water filter, as well as my suitcases from England. The journey, although only 25 miles, took about six hours. The truck came at dusk and we drove out into the bush as night fell, over roads which were almost continuous pot holes with vast puddles shining in the moonlight. The towering forest trees and the thick, jungly growth beneath them lined both sides of the road. Occasionally we passed through small villages, crowded and tumble-down, their only signs of life a scattering of roadside stalls, lit by small points of light from oil-lamps. There were dogs tearing along the road-side in the light from our headlamps and strange birds which crouched on the road waiting to streak off, striped plumage flashing, into the forest darkness.

We arrived in the village at about one in the morning and drove off the road up to a large, low house with its door locked and wooden shutters closed. After pounding on the shutters around the back, the door was pulled back with a great scrape. There was a young woman, a man and a small child, smiling but shy, holding back except to help with carrying my belongings. I didn't know yet just how extraordinary it must have seemed to them, so much stuff arriving with just one person.

I had come to live in a compound house of the chief of the village. It was five miles away from the small district capital where I was to work but no one had been able to find a room for me there. One of my future Ghanaian colleagues, Tony, had found me the room. He lived in the house, too, and that first night he helped me place my things in my room, hiding them as far from view as he could and warning me to keep my shutters closed at all times. He was a city dweller and convinced that all my belongings would be stolen by these ignorant villagers. When I later stopped following his advice, nothing was ever taken from my room.

Next morning the household was awake well before 6am, banging, chopping, sweeping, talking. As soon as I emerged from my room there were many, many introductions, as half the village had come to see the new arrival. Everyone shook hands and, as I had learned a very few phrases in the local language – "How are you?", "I am well – how about you?" – there was a great deal of laughter.

The Chief was referred to as Nana (the name for all chiefs) and was about 65 years old, very tall and erect. He looked benign and wise. I felt that he was pleased and proud that I had come to his house, although very shy and embarrassed too. Through an interpreter he welcomed me and told me that the women would do everything for me that I needed doing – cooking, washing, sweeping. I could go to work and then relax in the evenings with him. It was clear that I could become an honorary man in this household. The other men in the house were Nana's younger brother, called Teacher, because that was what he was, and another lodger – an unattached man whose wife, I later learned, had left him and who was visited by his little daughter who lived elsewhere in the village.

There were many more women. The Chief had four wives, although only two lived in the compound. His senior wife lived in the next village, looking after her ageing mother. The next lived in the compound and so did the youngest wife, who was in her early twenties. Teacher's wife, Beatrice, who was herself also a teacher, became my closest friend. There were three single women relatives and about ten children. Round the back of the compound lived several teenage boys and young men. They did not have much to do with the rest of us.

Over the next few days I began to learn about the first basic, practical problems of everyday life: how to light a kerosene stove and lamp, how to wash myself in a bucket of water, how to get to the wash house at night carrying my bucket, lamp, soap and towel, how to wash my clothes and how to cook. But whatever I did, someone immediately came to help, took over, carried my bucket or washed my clothes for me. I had very mixed feelings about this. I did not want the people I lived with to think that I took them for granted and thought of them as servants, and I really wanted to learn how to do things for myself. Nevertheless I was so slow and clumsy at these tasks, making all sorts of mistakes and having accidents like scalding my hands all over with boiling water when I tried to sterilize my water filter. The young children were much more efficient at so many things: at stripping the skin off plantains and at washing clothes and even sweeping the floor.

I shopped in the local market and bought the same ingredients as the Ghanaians that I lived with: mainly vegetables and dried and smoked fish. But I used to cook them the way I would at home – omelettes when I could get eggs, and stews with large lumps of vegetables and fish, ten times as much fish as any Ghanaian would get to eat. The results were looked on with horror and only a few brave people wanted to try some of my mixtures. Nana was sure that my food would make me ill and urged me again and again to let his wives look after me.

Proper Ghanaian food took hours to prepare. At about 3pm every day the women started to prepare the vegetables for the evening meal: mainly plantains and cassava. After boiling in big pans on wood fires, the vegetables were smashed and mixed together in a large wooden bowl, the children taking turns to pound with a long heavy pole. A steady thud of regular pounding was a late-afternoon sound wherever you went in Ghana. The sticky mixture produced was called *fufu*, and had a texture like uncooked bread dough. This would be eaten in bits torn off by hand and dipped into a very peppery soup made of ground vegetables and fish.

I attempted nearly everything at least once, including great land snails, though I did baulk at roasted bat.

The women and children ate together while the largest portions would be taken to the men, who ate alone. I used to prepare my English-style meals over my own kerosene stove and take them over to eat, sitting with the women. We would try bits and pieces from each others' plates. I attempted nearly everything at least once, including great land snails, though I did baulk at roasted bat. The fruit, however, was wonderful – oranges, avocados, paw-paws, pineapples, mangoes and bananas so good that I haven't been able to enjoy the hard, bright yellow ones in English shops since.

On weekdays I went to work in the "office", sometimes biking there, sometimes catching the passenger lorry or *tro-tro*. Some days of the week all the family went to their farm, which was a good hour's walk out into the forest. They came home at the end of the day laden with plantain, yam, fruit and firewood. On one of my first days off I went with them. At the end of a hot and exhausting walk all I could do was sit on the ground and watch them work: which, at that time of the year (November), involved cutting down the plantain and cassava crops. Women and children worked together and carried the great loads on their heads. Men also went to the farm to work and, on our farm, were involved in tapping palm wine and distilling it in a little dark shed in the forest. But men never carried anything back home. It seems that once a man is old enough to have a wife it is considered improper for him to be seen carrying anything on his head. I had offered to carry a basket of oranges but was defeated by the head carrying; the basket slithered every way on my head and my neck started to ache after a very short while. A little seven-year-old girl took the basket from me, put it on her head and jauntily walked ahead all the way home.

When we were not working, we relaxed together; mainly just sitting and chatting. I loved to be outdoors day and night. My room, despite my attempts to decorate it with a batik tablecloth and postcards and photos of my family stuck to my wall, seemed dark and enclosed. In the evenings we would sit in the courtyard of the compound, an outdoor "drawing room", brilliantly lit on nights with a full moon. Luckily there were few mosquitoes where I lived. Nana would be visited by a stream of people coming up from the village, often consulting him on business or about disputes that he would be asked to settle. They would talk in a little group on one side of the courtyard and drink the palm wine brought home from the farm. The women and the children and I would sit in another group. I could only understand little bits of the language and to learn more I would write down words and phrases in an exercise book. Although my language skills improved, I remained dependent on those people who were able to speak English to me.

Beatrice and I soon became friends. At first she must have felt a dutiful concern for me and took responsibility for showing me how to do things and for seeing that I was not lonely, for saying goodnight to me and for enquiring how I felt each morning. If I went for a walk, she would find out and send her nine-year-old son, Kofi, to accompany me.

In the evenings Beatrice and I would talk together, sometimes about her life, sometimes about mine. She asked me questions: what did it feel like to be cold, how did we carry our babies, were there tall mountains in England, which were the biggest towns, what did we export, what did we import? Some of these facts, the sort that must have been in the geography textbooks of her school-days, really interested her. After a while we talked more intimately. I told her about my frustrations at work and if I was feeling homesick and she gradually and very discreetly began to tell me about Teacher and his other wife, an older woman who lived with her aged mother in the village. I had begun to notice that Teacher was often away at supper time and later on in the evening. On those evenings Beatrice was much more ready to come and talk to me.

I questioned the luxury we have as Westerners to pop in and out of other people's lives.

Her reaction to the whole affair was mixed in just the same way as any wife's might be, although she said in a rather defiant sort of way "I don't mind as I don't want to bear any more children". She had five already. As Teacher left the house in the evening, Beatrice would call out "ochina" ("till tomorrow"), embarrassing him by her openness. If I called out "ochina", too, Beatrice and I would laugh together, aware of causing discomfort. When Teacher did spend an evening at home, though, Beatrice was very keen to be with him, leaving me to read my airmail *Guardian Weekly*.

I had other companions, though I could talk less easily to them. Kofi would come into my room to see me in the evenings. He would draw pictures with my coloured crayons and especially liked me to set him rows of sums to do. Nana had a sister who told me that she was adopting me as a daughter. She used to come and sit in my room, smiling at me and holding my hand. She was an old lady whose children had all left the village and who lived with just one grandchild, a little boy of about six. He would be sent up to see me with presents – some mangoes or some beans that she had cooked.

Being in my mid-forties, I did not naturally become part of the village courting and coupling activity that took place in the main street after dark. Many of Nana's friends told me that they wanted to marry me and there were lots of jokes with Nana telling them that they would have to apply to him as he was my father now. I did have a more serious suitor, who used to come and talk to me in the evenings and made it very clear that he wanted me to come with him to his room. I did once, but I didn't want to again and he put no pressure on me.

Generally I think women travellers are relatively safe with men in Ghana. I felt no danger from harassment wandering about in the village or in towns day or night. Obviously one should be careful about physical relationships, as aware of the problems of AIDS as you would be in Britain or America.

Over the months that I lived in the village the family became more and more aware of my frustrations at work and my homesickness. In the spring my plans to return began to shape and there was genuine sadness – plus, I felt, a bewilderment that I was such a free agent, that I alone decided whether I came or went. Didn't my boss in Accra have to give me permission to go home?

On my last evening we had a party. Earlier in the week I had brought five live chickens and lots of vegetables and that day the women prepared a vast quantity of chicken stew. Even so, Nana had invited so many important men from the village that my friends in the compound stood at the edge of the crush and never got any party food. There was dancing and I tried to get Kofi to dance with me. Like many boys at an age just before growing into manly confidence he hated to show off. He looked on and seemed lost in sadness. That night he just came and slept in my room. After I had left next morning with goodbyes all round the village and was driven off towards Accra, I questioned the luxury we have as Westerners to pop in and out of other people's lives.

If you do manage to stay for a while in a village, there are basic courtesies to observe. Take presents; it is unlikely that anyone will let you pay any rent. Once in a village you must, first and foremost, pay a call on the Chief. He may be able to find you somewhere to stay or will introduce you to the "Queen Mother", the head of women's affairs in every village. If my experience is anything to go by you will be treated with great kindness and generosity as well as being a source of excitement and curiosity. Both sides can give a lot to the other, so much more than when a tourist sticks to a hotel by the beach, getting impatient because of the time it takes to bring the beer.

TRAVEL NOTES

Languages English is widely spoken, especially in the towns. Twi, the language of the Asante region, is also used in the south, whilst in the north there are many different languages – Dagbani, Mampruli and Wala, to name but three.

Transport State-run buses operate between the major towns. In the towns there are small buses (*moto-way*) and mini-buses (*tro-tro*) but these, like the wooden trucks (*mammy-wagons*), are massively overcrowded.

Accommodation There are a few hotels in Accra and in all the state capitals, otherwise you are dependent on fairly basic, but quite safe, guest houses. It's very likely that you'll be invited to stay at someone's house – be conscientious about the expense this imposes on your hosts by taking gifts and paying for food and entertainment.

Special Problems Take any health provisions (contraceptives, tampons, etc) you may need – little is available.

Guides *The Rough Guide to West Africa* (Penguin) has a good section on Ghana.

CONTACTS

Federation of Ghanaian Women, PO Box 6236, Accra.

BOOKS

Maya Angelou, *All God's Children Need Travelling Shoes* (UK, Virago, 1987/US, Vintage, 1991). The story of Angelou's emigration to newly independent Ghana and her growing sense of disillusionment.

Wendy Belcher, *Honey from the Lion: An African Journey* (US, Dutton, 1988). Descriptive account of a young woman's time in Ghana working for a Christian organization.

Mary Gaunt, *Alone in West Africa* (UK, T Werner Laurie Ltd, 1912). Widowed, middle-aged and strapped for cash, the Australian writer Mary Gaunt set sail for the Gold Coast. Her fearless travels, that sent her swaying in her hammock with her sixteen African bearers deep into the Asante heartland, enthralled her Edwardian public. Sadly the book has not been reprinted, but **Dea Birkett's** *Spinsters Abroad: Victorian Lady Explorers* (UK, Gollancz, 1991/US, Blackwell, 1989) provides some illuminating anecdotes of her trip, and helps place her amongst her contemporaries.

FICTION

Ama Ata Aidou, *Our Sister Killjoy* (UK, Longman, 1988/US, NOK Publications, 1979). Noted Ghanaian playwright explores the thoughts and experiences of a Ghanaian girl on a voyage of self-discovery in Europe.

Ayi Kwei Armah, *The Beautiful Ones are Not Yet Born* (1968; UK, Heinemann Educational, 1988/US, Heinemann, 1986, o/p). An insightful tale of the politics, greed and corruption of post-independence Ghana, seen through the eyes of a railway clerk.

Asiedu Yirenkyi, *Kivuli and other Plays* (UK & US, Heinemann, 1980; UK o/p). One of Ghana's best-known playwrights. *Kivuli* is about the break-up of a family strained by inter-generational conflict.

Greece

E ach year, millions of independent travellers flock to Greece, attracted by the easy-going Mediterranean culture, the myriad islands and legendary ancient sites. It's a country that gets into people's blood, and many return year after year, exploring a different circuit of islands, perhaps, or — increasingly popular — walking in the mountainous countryside of Epirus, in the north.

Foreign women also have a strong work presence in Greece, most often as English-teachers in the hundreds of language schools. If you want to spend a year in the country, and to learn Greek, this is by far the most promising possibility.

Travelling about the country is pretty straight-forward, with good transport (by bus and ferry) and a pleasingly low-key network of campsites, rooms and hotels. Harassment from a particular breed of Greek men (known as *kamakia*, or literally harpooners) who congregate around the main resorts to pick on "easy" tourists can dampen experiences, though it's more on the nuisance level than anything threatening. Even in Athens you rarely feel unsafe. A bigger problem perhaps is the low public presence of women. Off the tourist track, in the villages, you'll find the local *kafenion* (café) is often the only place to get a drink – and that it's completely male territory. As a foreign woman your presence will be politely tolerated, but, travelling alone, you won't always feel comfortable. The major concern for most travellers, though, lies in escaping fellow tourists. Greece has seen some of the Mediterranean's most rapid development over the last decade and a tiny hamlet one year might well become a mass of hotel blocks the next.

In political terms, Greece has been rocked by a series of government scandals over the last few years – corruption and phone-tapping being high on the list – in the midst of a worsening economic crisis. On top of this, nationalist feelings were outraged when the Yugoslav Republic of Macedonia declared itself independent in 1991 and began calling itself Macedonia – a name that Greeks considered to be the sole preserve of the northern province of their own country. Unlikely though it might seem that a tiny and impoverished new republic would take on a fully armed member of NATO, Greek politicians considered the purloining of the name to be tantamount to a threat of annexation. Pressure was successfully placed on the government to impose a trade embargo (though many felt only invasion could solve it). At the time of writing the drama has cooled somewhat, and the focus of attention returned to the ineptitude and disarray of both the socialist government and its main conservative rival.

As for **women's issues**, over the past decade, the Women's Union of Greece, closely identified with the socialist party, PASOK, has helped to push through legislative reforms on family law – dowry is now prohibited, civil marriage recognized, and equal status and shared property rights stipulated. The reforms may have had limited impact in the rural areas, but they at least provide a legal reference point. Another positive, if small-scale, achievement has been the setting up of Women's Co-operatives in rural communities; these provide loans for women to run guest houses, and an opportunity for visitors to experience local village life.

An Island Idyll

Janet Zoro has long held a passion for Greece. Sparked off by an initial visit in the late 1960s, she now makes a habit of returning twice a year, travelling alone to wherever she can get the cheapest last-minute flight.

I fell in love with Greece on my first trip, twenty years ago. I was a student then, surprisingly politically naive at a time when others were sitting down in Grosvenor Square. The Colonels were in power and I should not have gone, but I did and discovered an almost instant affinity for the place. The affair continued intermittently but it was in 1986, when I made my first solo trip, that the flame rekindled. Now I go in spring and autumn, usually for two weeks, but for longer if I can get a suitable flight.

What is it about Greece? The country is so full of clichés: the perfect blue harbour, the white-cubed houses climbing the harbour slopes, the sunsets and moonrises, smell of oregano and grilling fish, cool, shaded waterside bars, white beaches and brilliant glass-green water; but the clichés work every time. Whenever I arrive and cross the burning tarmac of the island runway, fight through the tin customs shed and head off to yet another idyllic fishing village, my heart beats faster and my spirits lift; I feel as if I am coming home. Familiarity breeds a warm and ever deepening affection.

I am not attracted by the archeology. I go to Greece to swim and walk and paint and recharge my batteries. I do not want discos or bars or water-skis or umbrella-covered beaches. I want my own vision of Greece: a perfect place to travel alone; no one bothers me if I do not wish to be bothered.

I can sit for hours in solitude over a drink, writing postcards, watching the harbour lights, listening to other tourists talk, or I can strike up conversation with the waiter or a fellow diner. The odd occasions for evasive action inevitably arise – the elderly gentleman from the tailors-cum-shipping agency who presses dinner invitations; the bored boy soldier who ignores my protestations that I am old enough to be his mother; the sailor on the little inter-island steamer who cannot understand that I should choose to be alone – but I would never call it harassment. I find I can accept lifts, drinks or compliments from Greek men and when I smilingly say "no" they shrug and smile and buy me a drink anyway. I never feel worried or lonely.

The Greeks generally welcome foreigners and, though an obvious curiosity as a lone traveller, I feel easily accepted. I have picked up enough words to gather the gist of basic questions and in signs and single words explain that my husband is in England, I am travelling alone, I like to paint and walk, and I have no children. Sitting in the shade of some village square, the old men express amazement while the women offer congratulations. Greek women are slaves to their boy children who, as far as I can see, are allowed to do anything they like as soon as they are mobile enough to elude the maternal embrace.

I wish I knew more Greek. I want to talk to them, the women who run shops from dawn until late, let rooms upstairs, hang out hand-washed sheets each day and still have time to water and weed their miraculous polychrome jam-packed gardens; the women who call to me from balconies as I sit and paint in some un-tourist-frequented hill village, who speak no English at all, but smile and admire my picture and give me apples; the old women who let white cool shuttered rooms with makeshift plumbing and give me coffee and figs for breakfast.

In the Dodecanese, some people speak Italian (compulsory in schools during the Italian occupation), and anywhere in Greece you'll often find men who have picked up a bit of English on their travels as merchant seamen. Others have Australian connections. In Ithaca a very old woman hailed me as I wandered into a village: "G'day, are you looking for the beach?". It turned out she had left Australia when she was twelve, but reckoned she'd kept a bit of the accent! In Limnos I was sitting in a tiny bar-cum-shop, slaking my thirst with cold beer, when a woman came in to fetch one of the men for Sunday lunch. Glimpsing me on my perch behind a sack of onions, she immediately burst into delighted conversation; home from Australia, she was going to lunch with her cousin and invited me to join them for tea. The cousin was about to make her first trip out to visit a son she hadn't seen for twenty years and, over sweet Greek coffee and even sweeter honey pastries, my help was enlisted to try and teach her a few words of English. I struggled home hours later, laden down with bags of grapes and peaches.

She can laugh and joke with foreigners, but spend half an hour alone with a village boy and there would be hell to pay.

Now that tourism is big money and English taught in all schools, the family pattern is changing. There is a new kind of young Greek woman. Increasingly in small villages I find the local restaurant tends to be run by the daughter, aged perhaps nineteen or twenty. She speaks good English and/or German, takes the orders, does a lot of the cooking and will talk to the customers about anything: life, politics, tourists, Greece.

She is the pet of her regulars, the English, German and Australian captains of sailing holiday yachts who bring their passengers to eat there throughout the summer. They hug her; she hugs them. They joke and laugh throughout dinner. If she has a husband, he probably builds apartments over the winter, helps in the restaurant during the tourist season or catches fish for her to cook. He may add up the bills. There may be a baby who toddles round the café, harnessed on a long string, tying tables, chairs and tourists into knots. And all the while, in the background, are the parents who, with little grasp of English, cook, carry and watch.

Here, in her tourist empire, the daughter is in charge. At the same time, her education is limited and she has little chance of breaking away. Nor can she escape Greek mores. She can laugh and joke with foreigners, but spend half an hour alone with a village boy whom she has known since birth and there would be hell to pay. No doubt this too will change. Ten years ago these bright, tough girls were with their mothers at the kitchen sink. Learning languages has given them a kind of freedom which in itself has become an economic necessity.

The actual physical business of getting around in Greece is part of the pleasure. Best of all are the boats. They are a sort of game. First, you go to one of the shipping offices that cluster round the harbour. Often these deal with only one line, so you ask for some island and they shake their heads: "Ah no, not there. Try the office next door!" Then there is the timetable; no office will ever admit to its fallibility, though I soon found out that a bit of a gale might well delay a boat for as much as one or two days. However, if you have asked around you will have found a man in the grocery shop who knows. He is in actual telephonic communication with the next island and knows that the ferry is running six hours late. Thus the man who sells you the ticket will say 3am, absolutely definitely; the man in the shop will say 9.30am. It makes a difference.

Although it takes a while to get the hang of ferries, the effort is rewarded by the sheer joy of racing through that dark blue sea beneath a cloudless sky, watching for the shadowy shapes of islands in the distance and sometimes, if you are very lucky, seeing a school of dolphins racing and jumping alongside in the creamy wake. Boats are good for sunbathing. They can also be useful for exchanging travellers' information: you'll nearly always meet island-hoppers with news of elsewhere, or someone to team up with in the search for the perfect place to stay.

I love to walk in Greece. There is something about the dry, blue, herb-scented heat that invigorates me. I walk miles in totally unsuitable shoes, armed with my paints and my swimsuit and a beer in case I don't reach a village. And I take lifts if someone stops, as they generally do. Usually, even if I am not thumbing, passing vehicles – anything from German tourists in Mercedes to those rickety three-wheeled trucks full of potatoes – will stop and offer a ride. Again, I've never encountered any problems. Because there are relatively few vehicles in country areas it is the natural thing to do, as it used to be in rural parts of England. I even take lifts at night.

A German girl who stayed one winter said she would never do it again, as there was really no place for her in society.

I think what I love about being in Greece is that it is closer than anywhere I know to how I feel life should be. I should be able to sit on a balcony overlooking the sea for my early morning coffee and late night brandy; I should be able to go out for a whole day leaving my door unlocked and knowing that nothing unpleasant will happen. The sky should always be blue and the sea transparent.

Greece for its people, though, is not heaven. The Greeks work very hard, particularly the women. Where there are a lot of tourists, the country's character is being sadly eroded by English-style pubs, bars and big hotels. But it is extraordinary how slow this erosion is and I am somehow confident that the Greeks will weather the onslaught of mass tourism: they are intrinsically so much themselves.

I have considered living there, naturally, but I really think Greece is a hard place for a foreign woman to settle in. There are, of course, some women who have stayed on and had a wonderful time, picking up work and drinking with the men in the bars. I met a German girl who stayed just one winter and said she would never do it again, as once the tourists had gone there was really no place for her in society. She could neither drink with the men, nor sit and crochet and talk babies with the women. And the few women I have encountered who have married Greeks don't seem very content, having little choice but to fit into their husbands' lifestyle, the extended family, the cooking, sewing, gardening, washing and having-babies way of life that Greek women lead. As far as I am concerned my spring and autumn visits are perfect.

Teaching in Thessaloniki

Jackie le Poidevin travelled by bus from London to Thessaloniki, Greece's second city, to take up a job teaching English at a private English-language school. At the time of her visit in 1993, feelings were running high about the Macedonian question (see p.260). She currently lives and works in the British Channel Islands.

The bus journey through Serbia to northern Greece couldn't have been safer. The roads were deserted and we sped along, making up for the time we had lost during the lengthy detour through Hungary, avoiding the savaged carcasses of Croatia and Bosnia. At the border of Yuogoslav Macedonia (known to Greeks as *Ta Skópia* after its capital), our rickety old Balkan bus was brought to a halt. Much to the outrage of Alexander's "true" Hellenic heirs, which included our excitable Greek driver, the border guards demanded to see our visas. Few of us had any inkling that we needed one and it was no easy matter to scratch together enough hard currency to pay our way through. Finally our bus was waved on and we crossed the tiny republic into Greek Macedonia. At Thessaloniki, my home for the next six months, I resisted the offer of a bed for a night from an obese and obdurate Greek man and headed off in search of my hotel room.

I had come to teach English in one of the thousands of private schools known as *frontisteria* that supplement the abysmal state system. The hotel, where my school chose to lodge me until they could secure me a flat, was on an excavation site for a new underground car park. This was admittedly sorely needed in a city where cars double park bumper to bumper in the narrowest of streets, blocking access to the pavements which are in any case pot-holed and planted with telegraph poles, frustrating anyone attempting to use a pushchair.

This is a family-oriented society and with few state provisions to turn to for support, close family bonds are a necessity. The kids I taught were, for instance, shocked by suggestions of not caring for one's elderly parents at home and talked with an impressive respect about their own grandparents. I never did manage to explain to them what an "old people's home" was, which I found wonderful but also a bit depressing. Part of me was beginning to believe that this traditional family set-up was the only sane and effective system. Couples marry young, mum goes out to work, forced by the high cost of living to continue earning, and a relatively youthful granny looks after the children.

In the holidays families escape the city and head for the coast or a mountain village where at least one set of grandparents generally still lives. When the grandparents become enfeebled they move in with their children, who inherit the country house as a holiday home. No fifteen-year-old child to whom I spoke could suggest any disadvantage in this arrangement. Perhaps they were too young to understand the tensions; perhaps there simply were no tensions and the three generations could live together in reasonable harmony.

I remained sceptical, however, about the family idyll. Maybe it was the persistent rumours of widespread wife-beating; maybe it was the *kafenia*, the men-only ouzo bars that were already busy with backgammon-players before breakfast; or the fact that a guy masturbating openly next to a friend of mine in the cinema was regarded as a hazard only to be expected by her Greek companion; or the news that the majority of divorces here are initiated by women, claiming that their husbands are good-for-nothings. Or maybe I found it oppressive to be continually told that a girl over twenty-five is past it in the marriage stakes. "We'll find you a nice Greek man, don't worry", the secretaries would say to us hapless English teachers, still spinsters in our mid-twenties. I tried explaining that I already had a boyfriend, whom I had no intention of marrying because I didn't need the reassurance, but this was easily discounted.

One woman had become a secretary after working for six months as an architect without ever getting the pay due to her.

The belief that twenty-five is a magic number, the threshold of old age, is fairly widely held in Greece. Until then, it seems, parents pamper you rotten, do anything and everything for you; but after that it's your turn. You start wearing gaudy flounced blouses, get fat, as every Greek woman under twenty-five will assert, and devote yourself entirely to your children. Many fathers find work in Germany and on their return use their savings to build a house for their offspring. Until the roof is added no taxes need be paid, which accounts for the building site appearance of major Greek cities.

Those who can't fall back on family support are left struggling to survive the high inflation on a very low first wage. We were amazed at how the secretaries, earning less than the teaching staff, could afford to patronize the smart nightclubs when we certainly couldn't fork out the three or four pounds demanded for a single vodka. The truth was, they couldn't either. Their parents were still giving them "pocket money". Their mothers would drop round at the weekend, bringing a hamper full of cooked meals. That is how the young people get by, not thanks to any reasonable pay structure. One woman had become a secretary after working for six months as an architect without ever getting the pay due to her.

My own perspective may seem somewhat distorted from having come into contact only with children whose parents were ambitious or concerned enough to pay out for extra lessons. But with a total of four thousand *frontisteria* in Greece, this is by no means an elite minority.

It is the norm to distrust any form of state interference, legal or otherwise. That is why, with a police force perceived as corrupt, the Greeks park illegally and never bother to pay the fine. That is why, when the government recently increased the tax on tobacco, it was rewarded by a dramatic loss in revenue. The locals simply bought their cigarettes from the East Europeans who smuggle in sports bags packed with black-market Marlboros over the Bulgarian border.

In a bar in Edessa, a town renowned through the ages for its waterfalls, and more recently for being close to the Yugoslav border, I got into a conversation about taxes and politics. A man about my own age, Nikos, warmed to the theme.

"If you pay your taxes", he pronounced, "they call you *malaka*, you know?" I did. It's a Greek word that would apply rather well to the aforementioned sleazeball in the cinema. "The government take the money for themselves. Look around you. Look at the schools, look at the hospitals. What have they done for us?" I couldn't help wondering out loud how the government was supposed to provide services if no one was prepared to supply the money? But Nikos insisted that the then Prime Minister Mitsotakis was corrupt and, moreover, war-mongering. He believed that only a change of government could prevent Greece from becoming embroiled in the Balkan conflict. Nikos had relatives in Skopje, as well as in Athens, and didn't much care what Skopje called itself. How could such a tiny country pose any threat? My letters at this time were arriving home postmarked with the slogan "Macedonia is in Greece". I told Nikos about this and about the Greek (not Macedonian) soldier in Corfu who, on hearing that I lived in Thessaloniki, had yelled out, "Macedonia is in Greece". Nikos resented the assumption.

"They keep telling me: 'You must be Greek first'. Why must I? We are laughed at here, because our accent is not proper and our grammar is not good. They call us stupid, but Big Alexander was Macedonian. Lots of people were Macedonian . . .". His voice trailed off, as if gradually losing its drift.

We had been drinking *tsipero*, an aniseed home brew superior to ouzo. I suggested it was getting to him, despite the sour, salty *mezes* that we were nibbling to stay sober – anchovies, strong white cheese, olives and vinegary salad. But no, this was impossible. "The *tsipero* is totally pure", he insisted, "You can pour it on your wounds."

The other men in the bar were philosophical. Yes, there could be a war. They didn't want to, but yes, they would fight, and on different sides too. But for now, it was time to drink, and enjoy themselves.

Issues of identity in Macedonia are complicated further by the Greeks' attitude towards the Turks. In the main they despise their former conquerors, and liken themselves to their easy-going Latin brothers. But in truth, the crazy drivers and shambolic street scenes of nearby Istanbul bear closer resemblance to life in Greece than do the wide boulevards of Milan or the air-conditioned buses and palm-fringed parks of Malaga.

The ancient ruins in Thessaloniki, surrounded by dirt-coloured post-earthquake flats, are filled with dust and rubble, crawling with stray dogs and cats and littered with crisp-packets. The topic of pollution produced little reaction among the children. They were merely relieved not to be in Athens, which is *really* bad. The thing is, the Greeks don't walk. They take the car or a taxi. The only walking that anyone contemplates is the daily parade along the *paralia*, which means "beach", but refers to the promenade pressed between four lanes of blaring traffic and the stinking, sewage-contaminated sea. However, the sunset over the twin peaks of Olympus across the bay is still spectacular and the view down to the bay from nearby Mount Hortiat is breathtaking.

After a search for the right bus station, I set off with two female colleagues into the largely unspoilt countryside. Away from the city the retsina and *melitzanasalata* (aubergine dip) are cheap, the private pensions are welcoming and the smallest attempt to speak Greek brings warm reactions. Our room in Kastraki, under the pinnacles of the rock-perched Meteora monasteries, had a cylindrical stove that our host lit with a shovelful of burning coals from the kitchen grill. Our room in the mountain town of Ioannina was on the tiny island in the lake, looking over the reed-grown shallows where wooden fishing dinghies were moored. The snow-covered villages of Mount Pilion, where the centaurs lived and where mules laden with olive branches still pick their way down the cobbled paths; the isolated village of Metsovo atop the sheer Katara Pass; the dramatic peninsulas of Halkidiki and the depths of the Vikos gorge, all became favourite weekend haunts. Mountainous areas were inaccessible by bus for parts of the winter, and it was too early in the year to go climbing on Olympus, but we could hike along roads with no tour-bus in sight and enjoy the mild "halcyon days" of January, granted by Zeus

> *The ideal husband was someone who wouldn't hit them when they made a mistake.*

to his beloved kingfisher as a brief respite from the cold in which to lay her eggs.

Greek friends warned me against the dangers of the mountains, convinced that they were the refuge of cut-throat Albanian refugees. The crime rate seemed negligible to me, but the Greeks insisted that the new immigrants were either murderers or thieves who would cut your throat because they couldn't find anything better to do, or else steal work from the locals. Despite this, I felt safe in Thessaloniki and, unlike in Italy or the Middle East, I scarcely ever got hassled or followed, even when walking alone along narrow old streets at four in the morning.

Back at school I questioned my class about sexual equality. Most of them reckoned that women in Greece were equal, but not as equal (fortunately, they claimed) as women in America, who were "too free". Some boys chivalrously announced; "I may let my wife work." The ideal wife was a good cook with blonde hair and blue eyes. The ideal husband, the girls confided, giggling, was someone who wouldn't get angry and hit them when they made a mistake.

One school director, lodging a new male teacher with two female ones, felt obliged to first ask permission from the neighbours. Whether he also asked permission from the teachers concerned, however, is doubtful. The neighbours were in fact relieved, having previously assumed that two girls living together without husbands could only be running a brothel. The employer of another teacher, Natalie, stipulated in writing that on completion of her contract she must not engage in any bar work, which would damage the school's reputation. Intrigued, she enquired more closely, to be told: "All bar girls are prostitutes." English teachers, meanwhile, were all "drunks and layabouts", for which claim there is, admittedly, rather more truth.

If you come to Greece to teach, you'll often have accommodation arranged for you. Don't expect too much. There was no telephone or fridge in my flat. There was a single hot plate for cooking, which I supplemented with a wobbly camping gas burner, suspiciously widely available in the shops. The shower leaked and had no tub beneath it. My employer indicated the flat's generous proportions, but this only made it look all the emptier. The sole furniture – a sofa, a chair and an unsteady table – had been taken without asking from the flat of two other teachers, who duly handed in their notice. Yes, it was the boss's old furniture, for the loan of which they were eternally grateful; yes, the school had arranged the flat for them. But they paid the full rent and expected to be allowed to treat it as their home without invasions of privacy.

They were mistaken. Greek employers expect to own you. Because they act as go-betweens and interpreters with the landlord and lend you some saucepans and a plastic tablecloth they feel they have a right to come and go as they please. They own your time – all of it. By Greek standards they believe that your wage is generous, and flatten you with piles of marking. "You're only here to work for us", they argue, unaware that your one motive in tolerating the poor working conditions is the opportunity to see something of the country. It is sad that they fail to understand why they only get inexperienced teachers and why, as soon as teachers gain that experience they move elsewhere.

Some secretaries are equally tyrannical. I glance at an English-teaching newspaper left on my boss's desk. "Please don't touch anything on Mrs Sonia's desk", Poppy, the secretary, orders. She has made too few copies of something I need urgently. But the smart red cloth is hung over the photocopier like a royal pall. "I can't copy anything now", Poppy claims. "I have to ask Mrs Sonia". Only Mrs Sonia isn't here. Another time, I need a single blank piece of paper to use as a mark-sheet. "I'll phone Mrs Sonia," says Poppy.

Sonia was, in fact, superficially pleasant to me, in pointed contrast to her treatment of my colleagues. She called me "my dear", drawing out the vowels as she inhaled cigarette smoke through an autocratic holder. I knew she was storing up her friendliness to blackmail me. Sure enough, the bubble burst in my final week. One-way flights from Greece are expensive, and the cheapest I could find left at five in the morning, presenting major problems in returning the key of my flat. The contents would have to be checked, the cutlery counted, the precious furniture inspected. Some teachers had been known, said Sonia, in the few hours between such an inspection and their early flight the following morning, to empty their flat and sell off the entire contents, curtains and all.

Immediately after inspection I was supposed to hand over my key and be turfed out with my baggage for the remaining twelve hours before my flight.

"Stay with one of these friends of yours. Every weekend you go away with them, you have so much free time, you have so many friends", Sonia countered, reminding me of my earlier reassurances to her pretended concern that, yes, I was settling down and making friends. "Stay in the hotel – we paid it for you for two weeks. We've been so good to you. I am so good to all my teachers. You take advantage of me. Why are you English all so dishonest?" This from the woman who was trying to cheat me out of my National Insurance stamps.

"But I've paid my rent for that night", I argued. I had, in fact, paid her a fortnight's rent too much, which she refused to hand back, leaving the message, "Tell the girl she won't get a penny."

TRAVEL NOTES

Languages Greek. It's worth at least learning the alphabet to work out bus destinations and timetables. English (if only tourist essentials) is widely understood, as many Greeks have worked abroad, tourism is a major industry, and there's a proliferation of English-language schools.

Transport An efficient, reasonably inexpensive bus service connects main towns and major resorts. Hitching – relatively safe – is accepted, if slow, in the isolated regions where buses do a daily round trip, if at all. Be careful of mopeds, rented out on most islands. Maintenance is a joke and accidents common on the dirt tracks. Island ferries get crowded so arrive early and leave time to get back for your flight – bad weather, strikes and out-of-date timetables make them unreliable.

Accommodation Plenty of cheap hotels, rooms in private houses and reasonably good campsites. Camping wild is illegal but often tolerated (police attitudes vary). On islands you'll be offered rooms as you get off the ferry – usually a good option for a first night.

Women's Holidays The Greek Council for Equality, in collaboration with the Greek National Tourist Organization and Greek Productivity Centre, has organized holidays with Women's Agro-tourist Co-operatives. Contacts include: **Ambelakia**, near Larissa, central Greece (☎0495/93296); **Arahova**, near Delphi (☎0267/31519); **Hios**, c/o The Prefecture of Hios (☎0271/25901); **Lesvos**: Petra, Mitilini (☎0253/41238), and **Maronia**, near Komotini, Thrace (☎0533/41258).

In the UK, *Trek Out*, 54 Edrich House, Binfield Rd, London SW4 6SS (☎0171/627 5561) organizes moderately priced women's holidays that incorporate walking, painting, Tai Chi and yoga in an unspoilt part of the island of Crete.

Special Problems *Kafenia* (cafés) are traditionally male territory and can be uncomfortable places for women on their own.

Guides *The Rough Guide to Greece* (Penguin). A practical and honest guide, good on background, and which doesn't romanticize those islands that are spoilt.

CONTACTS

Comprehensive listings for all **feminist groups** and centres in Greece appear in the women's *Imerologio* (diary) published in Athens by *Eyrotyp* (Kolonou 12-24), and meetings are often advertised in the English-language magazine, *The Athenian* (monthly from news stands). Those groups listed below are the more accessible

contacts, particularly if you don't have good command of Greek.

Athens: *Women's Bookstore*, Massalias 20 at Skoufa. Feminist bookstore, useful starting point for all contacts.

Selana Bookstore, Sina 38. Athens' other key feminist bookstore.

Genovefa "Our Ouzeri", 17 Novembriou 71 (☎653-2613). Women's café-bar.

Woman's House, Romanou Melodou 4 (entrance on a side street of Odos Dafnomili), Likavitos (☎281-4823). The city's main feminist meeting point.

Xen, Amerikis 11. The Greek YWCA offers language courses for women and maintains a library and archive on feminism and women's issues.

Ioannina: *Steki Gynaekon*, M Kakara 25. Women's bookstore.

Thessaloniki: *Spiti Gynaekon*, Yermanou 22. Women's bookstore.

BOOKS

★ **Sara Wheeler**, *An Island Apart* (UK, Abacus, 1993). In her first published travel book, Sara Wheeler recounts a five-month journey across Evia, Greece's second largest island. Her sure touch with Greek history and culture, and frank and open approach to the people she meets - Orthodox nuns, goatherds, Albanian-speaking villagers, intellectuals - bring her travels buzzing to life.

Sheelagh Kanelli, *Earth and Water: A Marriage in Kalamata* (Greece, Efstathiatis). An inspiring account of that rare thing - a foreign (in this case, British) woman integrating successfully into provincial society. Her short, lucid novel, *Nets* (UK, The Women's Press, 1983), reconstructs the events leading up to a disaster in a small Greek coastal village.

Feminist journals include *Dini* (Zoodohou Pigis 95–97, Athens), *Hypatia* (Piliou 1, Athens), and *Katina* (Vass Irakliou 19, Thessaloniki).

FICTION

Katerina Anghelaki-Rooke, *Beings and Things on Their Own* (US, BOA Editions, 1986). Powerful erotic poetry, full of sexual metaphor and sensuality.

Eugenia Fakinou, *The Seventh Garment* (UK & US, Serpent's Tail, 1991). Novel which relays Greek history from the war of independence to the Colonels' junta through the life stories of three generations of women.

Ursule Molinaro, *The New Moon with the Old Moon in Her Arms* (UK, The Women's Press,

1990/US, McPherson & Co, 1993). Witty and passionate novel, set in Ancient Athens, about a young poet who interprets the waning of the Moon Goddess, Circe, as an omen that women's position in society must be strengthened.

Dido Sotiriou, *Farewell Anatolia* (Greece, Kedros). A modern Greek novel, reprinted more than fifty times since its appearance in the 1960s. It's an epic chronicle of the traumatic end of Greek life in Asia Minor following the Balkan Wars of 1912 to 1922.

Aliki Zei, *Achilles' Fiancée* (Greece, Kedros). A recent best-seller, exploring identities and values amid a maze of twentieth-century timeshifts.

Hispaniola

The Caribbean island of Hispaniola is shared by two very different countries: Haiti, a former French colony, takes up the western third, while the Spanish-speaking Dominican Republic covers the rest. Regular flights connect the respective capitals of Port-au-Prince and Santo Domingo, but apart from the breathtaking scenery of the interior mountains and a coastline of wide, sandy beaches, they hold little in common.

Haiti, the world's first black republic, is poised on the brink of great change. Following the much publicized US military intervention of September 1994, the untold levels of political violence and repression suffered by the people of this desperately poor country have – for the present, at least – eased. Father Jean Bernard Aristide who, four years previously, had been forced into exile by a military coup only days after being voted into power, has

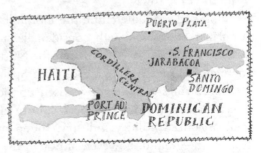

now been restored to his presidential seat. The task for this unassuming priest, revered for his work among the poor, is awesome. Not only does he face the challenge of meeting the expectations of a people, many of whom regard him as their messiah, but he also has to juggle with the almost impossible problem of satisfying the demands of the Americans, who expect a return with strategic interest on their multi-million development package, without altogether compromising his socialist policies.

In the current atmosphere of uncertainty, travellers – even more than usual – are rare. In its few relatively stable years, the country attracted visitors to its mix of music and voodoo culture at Carnival, and a couple of resorts were maintained as isolated ports of call on cruise itineraires, but Haiti has never really established itself as a tourist destination. Those visitors who know the place are devoted to it, though most have strong reasons for being there – most often, in the case of North Americans, through volunteer aid work. The country's sporadic violence aside, however – and this is a big aside – Haiti's approach to foreigners has always been relatively relaxed. Sexual harassment is not a major issue and while beggars, street traders and gangs of children are bound to crowd round, this rarely becomes threatening. Obviously it's important not to flaunt your comparative wealth, as thefts are fairly common in the capital and people routinely tell you to keep your doors locked at night. How safety and attitudes to travellers will be affected by the prolonged occupation of US soldiers and other foreign "experts" – due to remain in the country until 1996 – it's again too early to say.

Things are very different in the Dominican Republic, which has been marketing itself with considerable success over the last few years as a holiday haven – mainly for North Americans, although there are package holidays, too, from Spain and to a small extent Britain. Strings of hotels have risen up along the coastline, their guests protected from the local culture amid the trappings of a well-organized holiday industry. Independent travellers are still few on the ground, however, although the excellent beaches have become established in a small way on the surfing and windsurfing circuit, and, again, Carnival is a growing attraction. The country's stability, relative prosperity, and its inexpensive, efficient public transport certainly lends itself to independent travel. It is not, however, the easiest destination to handle, especially in Santo

Domingo, where machismo is upfront and it can be hard to escape the continual comments, propositions and hassle from men on the street. For the most part you need to tough it out, keep a sense of humour, and stay at arm's length until you feel sure you can know who to trust. Some knowledge of Spanish undoubtedly helps, while, inland, away from the resorts and cities the atmosphere eases considerably. People are far more likely to approach you with a genuine interest and hospitality.

Both Haiti and the Dominican Republic have a great many grass-roots organizations, working largely on popular education projects with the urban and rural poor. In Haiti, most of these are affiliated to the church, the only place where people could get together to share their feelings under political repression. The Dominican Republic has a long history of **women's organization**, much of it co-ordinated by the Research Centre for Feminine Action (CIPAF) which produces excellent popular education pamphlets on issues such as women workers' rights, rape and domestic violence. Women's groups only really got going in Haiti after the departure, in 1986, of the hated dictator "Baby Doc", when women discovered themselves gaining more confidence in separate meetings. According to Claudette Werleigh, a leading Haitian educationalist (strongly tipped for a high position in Aristide's cabinet), "the men are very aggressive and sometimes throw stones at them or the places they meet . . . the men think that the women are getting together just to criticize them." But despite resistance, such meetings have formed the basis for a growing movement to campaign for women's issues within the framework of fighting for a better society.

Travels with a Voodoo Soundtrack

Anna McDermott, in her early forties, lives in London with her young son. She works as a freelance press officer/journalist and is currently completing a course in television and film production. This was her first trip to Hispaniola.

The plane touched down in Port-au-Prince during a curfew, prior to the start of a general strike next day. Zombie-like young men lurked in the foyer. The glazed look in their eyes was more likely the result of crack/cocaine addiction, the advanced stages of leprosy or AIDS than any posthumous recreation. A peeling painting of *Oloffsons Hotel*, made famous by Graham Greene in his book, *The Comedians*, hung untouched since the Duvalier days.

The question I had been asked so many times since leaving London echoed in my head. Why was I, a lone European woman, travelling to Haiti? Non-Haitian visitors were usually missionaries from North America or prostitutes from the neighbouring Dominican Republic. I wanted to find out more about post-Duvalier Haiti, now known as the AIDS capital of the world, as well as the poorest country in the Western hemisphere. My reasons were simply the self-indulgent preoccupations of a single traveller, unencumbered by responsibility.

Discovering I was pregnant the night before I left for Port-au-Prince meant this was to be my last such untrammelled travelling. The flight was booked and the holiday planned, which was more than could be said for the pregnancy. I knew immediately I would go ahead with both. My flight from London's Heathrow was via New York and Miami and I spent the two hours' check-in time explaining to Pan Am security staff that I was not carrying a bomb. My Irish passport containing an Egyptian stamp from a visit years before had marked me out as prime terrorist material. Too preoccupied to be angry or embarrassed, I noted the empty seats near mine on board the plane.

Waiting for a connecting flight at JFK in the early hours of the morning, I felt the temperature plummet. Jet-lagged and frozen, I put on all the clothes I could fit and finding nowhere else, fell asleep on the floor. I awoke to find a security guard kicking me, mistaking me for the homeless bag lady I now resembled. American immigration officers were both suspicious and amused that I should want to visit Haiti, known only for the hundreds of boat people desperate to leave. At Miami, dazzling sunlight confused my weary brain and overdressed body. The flight to Port-au-Prince set off late then returned to base, much to the consternation of my neighbouring travelling companions. I felt protected on either side, as one woman prayed to a Christian saviour and the other to a voodoo god. Unfortunately they were not praying for my backpack which lost its way in transit.

My first night in Port-au-Prince there was a full moon and I was disturbed by a dream with a voodoo soundtrack. The next day I realized the drums were in honour of the full moon and not some hormone-induced fantasy. As there is no call for low-budget accommodation, I had accepted a lift from a big bluff American businessman called Jim from the airport to his hotel, *El Rancho*. With a swimming pool and marble floors it was clearly not in my price range for a long stay. At breakfast I savoured the view over the mountains near Pétionville, as I waited for Bob, Jim's driver, to take me to collect my mislaid baggage. Bob expertly navigated the route, more pot hole than road, reassuring me that he had acted as a driver for the last National Geographic expedition to Haiti. My backpack (with every bottle top removed, resulting in a glutinous mass of shampoo and moisturizer mixed with vitamin pills) successfully reclaimed, Bob took me to the children's clothing factory Jim had come to inspect.

The Haitians' pay and conditions guaranteed Darryl the type of lifestyle he could never have afforded elsewhere.

As we drove through the factory entrance, hopeful prospective employees tried to stop us to ask for work. One woman's eye gazed so intently, imploring and offering herself at the same time. Darryl, the factory owner, explained the tax breaks and other financial advantages of manufacturing in Haiti. From his air-conditioned office overlooking the shop floor he described how, if production was low, he locked the workers into the factory until they achieved a satisfactory output. He had a hard face and limped. I was glad not to be his enemy.

Predictably, the Haitians' pay and conditions guaranteed Darryl the type of lifestyle he could never have afforded elsewhere. That evening he invited me and some of his colleagues to dinner at his home in the mountains. More marble floors, but this time the swimming pool was shaded by palm trees and reflected fake Doric columns in the moonlight. Inside was the closest I ever hope to get to apartheid as black uniformed servants waited at the table which displayed an array of T-bone steaks and European wines beyond the imagination of most Haitians. My taste for alcohol had evaporated in my first few days of pregnancy, but my companions had no such inhibitions. I declined my host's later invitation to a club that sounded more like a brothel and Bob drove me back to *El Rancho*, where I slept on a settee in Jim's room, politely rejecting his fairly half-hearted, drunken amorous advances when he returned in the early hours. A few days later I moved from the hotel to Kyona Beach. I needed a change of company.

The trip to Kyona Beach by taxi was uncomfortably overpriced. To make his point, the driver switched off the rattling and ineffective air-conditioning when I disputed the cost. Somewhat circuitously we arrived at an "idyllic Caribbean paradise" as the manager, Elvis Jean, described it. During the week I was his only beach hut resident with an occasional passing donkey for company. He reminisced sadly about the Club Med days when the beaches were fully exploited by foreigners and rich Haitians. In spite of my basic accommodation, and bearing in mind that my personal financial straits could not compare with that of most Haitians, I was running out of money fast and could not travel or live as cheaply as pre-pregnancy. As my hormones played thriller videos in full colour in my dreams every night, I felt in need of more comfort and protection.

That weekend at the beach some American women invited me to eat with them. They were working at a boys' orphanage in Port-au-Prince. They weren't of the pious "Jesus saves" type of missionary – all prayers and promises of an afterlife with nothing for the present. It was clear that they worked hard and cared for the boys. I liked them even more when they told me the orphanage took paying guests and we arranged they would pick me up at *Oloffsons Hotel* the next weekend. I hitched a lift back to Port-au-Prince with some French Canadians working on a development project. The "dead houses" in the cemeteries we drove past looked more inviting than the shantytowns for the living. Women and children washed in streams by the roadside. Approaching town, more *tap-taps* (open-backed trucks), with their God-fearing slogans, jostled for space to avoid the pot holes on the rough untarmacked roads.

Arriving at *Oloffsons*, the staff made it seem like a homecoming. It was assumed I must know Andy Kershaw, the British writer and broadcaster, who had just left. Since the days of Graham Greene the hotel has acted as a sanctuary and research base for journalists and writers from all over the world. More by accident of hard times than design, I suspect, the white wooden colonial-style edifice remains much the same.

I was appropriately allocated a room in what had once been the maternity wing when the hotel was used as a hospital. I was not reassured to learn that the trench in the middle of my floor had been for draining blood. But that night, it was the sound from the streets and a loud radio next door that kept me awake after the silence of the beach, rather than any past or future ghosts of childbirth. After a late breakfast of hot currant bread and Creole omelette on the balcony overlooking the gardens and the tree-shaded swimming pool, I set off to walk into town.

A young man approached me and before I could argue, convinced me I should pay him to act as my guide. His logic was undeniable: he could make my life easier and I would give him a little money so that he could eat. We walked past the *Palais National*, painted bright white and standing apart and alien in its surroundings. Now heavily guarded, the palace was once home to the Duvaliers. In theory Baby Doc had disbanded the Tontons Macoutes, his father's private security police, but their presence was palpable.

Graffiti written in French defaced many walls around the city, but the expected coup had not happened. Even the general strike had passed

Measles would not register when dealing with babies dying of AIDS, leprous adults and day-to-day hunger and homelessness.

unremarked. Memories of the 1988 Tontons Macoutes massacre – when thirteen members of Father Aristide's congregation were killed at St John Bosco church – hung in the air. In the words of Andy Kershaw: "Foreign correspondents fear Haiti more than any other hot spots because the forces of terror don't play by the rules."

We passed on to the *Marché de Fer*, the Iron Market with its misplaced Moorish design, destined for elsewhere – it had been shipped mistakenly to Haiti instead of India. Inside, rude wooden carvings with fantasy-length penises were proffered by grinning craftsmen. A woman offered me voodoo potions to deal with any number of eventualities. I refrained, unwisely with hindsight, from having a hex put on my baby's father. A glass jar held the head of a blond doll with only one eye. As the only fair-haired person in sight I hurried on and did not ask for an explanation of this symbolism. A display of over-bright naive paintings clamoured for attention, but no one tried to hard sell me anything. Tourist trade is too distant a memory for most, who merely sit and wait in the cool, domed market. On the way up to the hotel entrance I thanked my guide as he held out a leprous stump to be paid.

That night, the women I had met at the beach arrived to join in the hotel's show of dancing and fake voodoo performance. Afterwards, as I was climbing into the back of their pick-up truck, a pre-maternal twinge prompted me to ask the driver, Michael, if there might be German measles at the orphanage. He laughed and reckoned I would be all right. We drove past the palace and and saw bands playing *compas* music to the crowds outside. It looked like a semi-successful public relations exercise. The revellers were not entirely relaxed.

I saw the reason for Michael's amusement when we reached the orphanage. An illness as mild as measles would not register when dealing with babies dying of AIDS, leprous adults and day-to-day hunger and homelessness. I was told the priest in charge of the orphanage rescued homeless boys from the slum known as Cité Soleil – his priority was those without shoes since he thought they were least likely to survive, an image that contrasted sharply with the young men in the latest trainers, dancing to New York rap from ghettoblasters on the balcony before going to evening prayers. Once in the orphanage they had no need to worry about going barefoot, until they left. Donations from North America ensured the boys' welfare and they flourished.

I was welcomed with flowers and slept soundly, undisturbed by the cacophony of roosters and dogs. The room next to mine was occupied by a young American woman working in one of the clinics. As an unreligious and very lapsed Catholic, I was moved and impressed by her serenity and dedication. Haiti is a punishing place to try and survive. On leaving, I tried hard not to cry when the boys sang a farewell in Creole and hugged me en masse.

On the short flight from Port-au-Prince to Santo Domingo on the other side of Hispaniola, I sat with a diplomat from the American embassy. Not the most sought-after post at the time and even less so, latterly. She was looking forward to her break in the wealthier Dominican Republic, but I felt very sad to be going. With a sense of foreboding I recalled Bob's tales of Haitian workers on Dominican sugar plantations being treated like slaves and some even killed.

There is an hour's time difference between Haiti and the Dominican Republic and a century in development. Flying over the devastated forests of Haiti into the green lush Hispanic Dominican Republic, I had not expected such a dramatic change. Nor was I prepared for the shock of such a cultural and linguistic schism on the same island. The customs officer leered and tried to flirt as he slowly went through my personal belongings. My immediate sense of unease did not dissipate during my stay. It had seemed logical to visit the Dominican Republic while on the island, but now I was not so sure. The capital, Santo Domingo, is a modern concrete city with the added disadvantage of water and electricity rationing and the worst machismo I have ever encountered. With so many armed soldiers on the street I decided to only change money through official channels, after which I booked into a cheap and nasty hotel room, not much larger than a cupboard and with no ventilation. Maybe it was a cupboard.

Men on mopeds kerb-crawled, dangerously rotating their heads to ogle me.

As soon as I left the hotel to walk to the restored Spanish-style Zona Colonial, I was stopped in my tracks by catcalls from passing men. Men on mopeds kerb-crawled, dangerously rotating their heads to ogle me. Having checked that I was fully dressed I could not find anything about my appearance to merit such attention. Somewhat pink and sweaty, I was flat-footedly plodding along, fairly tired and rather grubby. In contrast Dominican women were gorgeous, sashaying sexily in cleavage-revealing blouses and shorts, wearing high-heeled shoes. They oozed seduction in direct inverse proportion to my total lack of libido. They smiled while I frowned bad-temperedly when accosted. It took me a while to realize that it was perhaps because I was alone that the men felt they could take such liberties. There were other non-Hispanic-looking women tourists around, but they stayed in particular areas, travelling in tour groups.

Some armed soldiers were so affronted by my lack of compliance that they ordered me out of the Catedral Santa Maria La Menor. After refusing to acquiesce when they harassed me I was followed into the cathedral where I had gone to see Christopher Colombus's tomb. The soldiers told me in Spanish that I was improperly dressed. This was clearly not the case but I left anyway. I try not to argue with men with guns.

Adjusting to the raw chauvinism of these Latin men after the more gentle and dignified Franco-African mix in Haiti was sapping my energy and I decided to leave town as soon as possible and head for Jarabacoa, a health resort in the mountains. The cupboard manager booked me a taxi, which turned out to be relative's pick-up truck, to take me to the bus station.

The bus stopped before it reached the town at an aptly named *Hotel Montana*, a 1930s-style low-rise sprawl with masses of rooms, mostly empty. The few other guests were all in couples and I soon realized this was a honeymoon hotel. It was certainly romantic, looking out over my balcony at what the guidebook described as the "coniferous and cloud forests" of the Cordillera Central. The rain which started that evening was comforting after the heat and dust of previous weeks. My view of the mountain range disappeared in the torrential downpour and I retired to bed, reading Margaret Atwood's *The Handmaid's Tale*, a present from a friend unaware of my condition. This surreal story centring on women's fertility fitted my new hormone-driven existence. Days passed in the quiet room surrounded by long empty corridors and I felt no desire to venture into the town ten miles away. I mostly ate alone in the hotel restaurant, speaking only Spanish. One evening I noticed a couple of large mice (or small rats?) scuttling across the floor and understood why I was usually the sole human dinner guest.

Feverish dreamlike sequences filled my waking and sleeping hours. When I had finished reading all the books I had with me, I took a cold shower and finally set off for Jarabacoa. This turned out to be a town of a zillion motorbikes and after a quick *bocadilla* and *refrescos* I headed back gratefully to my hideaway in the mountains. Still, it was time for a change, so I joined up with a passing American to hitch a lift to La

Vega, from where I intended to catch a bus north to the beach near Puerto Plata. Apart from the odd breakdown and the manic war film played on board at full blast, the journey of several hours passed uneventfully.

The beach at Carboreta was teeming with surfboarders and rich Europeans posing. Not my idea of a holiday, but then I guess they would not covet my bumpy bus rides on the local *guaguas* or the paper thin walls between me and the guest in the next room. (My accommodation was now downgraded from cupboard to cardboard box, but it was so cheap I was not about to haggle.) For me the essence of travelling is the unpredictability of the journey, getting lost and finding the unexpected. On my last day in the Dominican Republic I sensed something of that; maybe it was just a sense of relief at leaving, but I was moved by the smartly dressed band playing *merengue* music at 6am in the dark and empty square in preparation for Duarte's Fiesta later that day.

At the airport I met a lively young German called Stephen, who was crippled with polio or perhaps thalidomide. We instantly clicked, so I wasn't surprised that he was heading for Haiti. In retrospect, I wonder if meeting Stephen quelled my subconscious fears about my baby being handicapped. Before leaving Britain I had been given the polio vaccine, unaware that I was pregnant or of the harm it might do to the foetus. When Stephen left the plane at Port-au-Prince, a large Haitian took his place. I felt at ease as he chatted about his hopes to return home and set up a general store opposite the Iron Market. Exile is a common theme in Haiti.

At Miami airport I celebrated my escape from the Dominican Republic with ice cream and chocolate. Bad weather, delays and near misses dogged my journey back to London. Travelling would never be quite the same again.

TRAVEL NOTES

Languages All Haitians speak Creole, derived from French and African dialects. The fifteen percent or so who have had schooling also speak French and often some English. Spanish is the official language of the Dominican Republic.

Transport Collective taxis, known as *publiques*, and *tap-taps* run between all Haiti's main towns, usually leaving whenever they are full. The Dominican Republic has an inexpensive, efficient bus network and you can usually find mini-buses or pickups, known as *guaguas*, in rural areas.

Accommodation In Haiti low-cost rooms, often including one or two meals, can be arranged through various religious missions. Port-au-Prince also has a few major hotels, but lodging in the countryside is best arranged in advance. The Dominican Republic has a good range of modest guest house accommodation, as well as a number of smart five-star hotels.

Guides *The South American Handbook* (UK, Trade and Travel/US, Passport Press) has a small but useful section on Hispaniola.

CONTACTS

Haiti: There are a number of missions and human rights groups. Recommended contacts are the *Holy Ghost Fathers* in Port-au-Prince or *Mission Wallace* outside Pétionville.

The Dominican Republic: A significant feminist force since the late 1970s, the *Research Centre for Feminine Action* (CIPAF), Benigno Filomeno Rojas 307, Santo Domingo, campaigns on issues such as work, rape, domestic violence, prostitution and health.

BOOKS

Amy Wilentz, *The Rainy Season: Haiti Since Duvalier* (UK, Vintage 1994/US, Simon & Schuster, 1990). Account of Haiti in the years immediately after the departure of Duvalier in 1986. Wilentz also paints a vivid portrait of Aristide, then a rebel priest.

Claudette Werleigh, *Working for Change in Haiti* (US, CIIR, 1989). This short booklet, published by the Catholic Institute for International Relations, describes the work of Haiti's popular education movement.

Ian Thomson, *"Bonjour Blanc" – A Journey through Haiti* (UK, Penguin, 1993, o/p). Fascinating account of travelling to the far corners of the country.

James Ferguson, *Papa Doc, Baby Doc: Haiti and the Duvaliers* (UK, Basil Blackwell, 1987). Lively and accurate account of the rise and fall of the country's notorious dictatorship.

James Ferguson, *Dominican Republic: Beyond the Lighthouse* (UK, Latin America Bureau, 1992/US, Monthly Review Press). This excellent introduction to the country exposes the inequality and corruption that lubricates its economy, as well as exploring the complex and tragic relations between Dominicans and Haitians.

FICTION

Julia Alvarez, *In the Time of the Butterflies* (US, Algonquin Books, 1994). Powerful novel based on the story of the three Mirabal sisters who were martyred thirty years ago for their opposition to the dictator Rafael Trujillo.

Honduras

Widespread illiteracy, high unemployment and a heavily dependent economy underline the poverty of Honduras, only recently surpassed by Nicaragua as one of Central America's poorest nations. Political power, sustained by a series of dubious military regimes, rests largely in the hands of landowners and foreign investors, in particular the US-owned United Fruit Company whose monopoly of the country's banana plantations led to its designation as the original "banana republic". On top of its economic interests, North America has long focused on Honduras for its strategic importance regarding US operations in the region. For instance, in the 1980s, it provided a convenient base for the infamous Contras, key

figures in the destabilization of Nicaragua's left-wing Sandinista government. It's too early to know whether the latest president, Carlos Roberto Reina of the Liberal Party, will be anything more than a puppet figure controlled by the military, though his position as former president of the Inter-American Court of Human Rights gives some grounds for optimism.

Most travellers pass through Honduras as quickly as possible on the way to Guatemala or Nicaragua. There may not be a tourist infrastructure, but the country does benefit from cheap transport and accommodation and there are certainly enough attractions to warrant it a place on any Central American itinerary. The magnificent Maya ruins of Copán are deserted most days and the capital, Tegucigalpa, while bearing all the hallmarks of urban deprivation, has lively street entertainers and several radical cafés/bookstores. There are also dramatic mountains to explore, as well as the curious Islas de la Bahía (Bay Islands) described by Ceri Sheppard below. The overwhelming US influence – further evident in food, music, clothes and media – has led to some antagonism toward fair-skinned gringos; as in Mexico, people tend to be more open and friendly if you say you're from Europe. Machismo is the norm and women travelling alone can expect comments and approaches from men, but these are rarely aggressive. As usual in Latin America, the more Spanish you know the more likely you are to feel at ease.

The 1980s were a period of widespread human rights abuses with torture, "disappearances" and extra-judicial executions at the hands of the military, sanctioned by the government. While the number of atrocities has fallen significantly in recent years, the military continues to act in most cases with impunity and abuses still occur against human rights activists, trade unionists and others perceived to be a threat to the ruling elite. Honduran **women** – themselves severely discriminated against – are often the guiding forces behind campaigns to recover "disappeared" relatives and to force the government to be accountable. They also have a long history of organizing for their rights (the first recorded group was founded in 1923) and have initiated a number of grassroots projects aimed at improving the status and health of women in the poorest sections of society.

"Boy, Teacher, You Must Be Real Poor!"

Ceri Sheppard and her friend Emma spent six months teaching English on one of the Bay Islands off the coast of Honduras. Having spent a large part of her adult life travelling and living abroad, in Asia and California as well as Latin America, she currently works as a freelance human rights researcher in London.

The Bay Islands (or Islas de Bahia) lie off the coast of Honduras in the Caribbean Sea. Thanks to good fishing and close links to North America and the Cayman Islands, they are relatively prosperous – certainly compared to the mainland. They are also curiously untypical of Latin America. Once the home of native Americans, followed by Dutch and British pirates, the islands are now inhabited by a staggering mix of ethnic groups ranging from people of African descent to the pale, red-haired descendants of pirates and prospectors. The population is largely bi-lingual in Spanish and English, the latter being the language of power and wealth.

When Emma and I arrived to carry out our six-month teaching contract we only had a vague idea of the social complexities of the curious world we were stepping into. In truth, nothing could have prepared us for life in this anachronistic and vibrant society. While all our assumptions were challenged within days of arriving, we also had to tackle the cherished assumptions that the islanders had about us. For starters, we continuously had to explain that we had not been sent by the Queen, Margaret Thatcher or the head of the British Navy. Secondly, there was the problem of our wealth, or lack of it, depending on perspective. To the poorer members of the population, we were of course, inordinately rich. But in the scheme of the island as a whole, we were merely one of the middle classes. True, we had the luxury of being able to get on a plane and fly to the UK at a moment's notice, but several island families, rich from exporting lobster, were in a position to send numerous children to school and college in the USA, to buy and sell land worth many thousands of pounds, and to holiday in Florida and California. While the richer parents never visited our school house (a wobbly wooden building on rotting concrete stilts, almost constantly engulfed in the smell of diesel and the crashing noise of boat engines), their children would occasionally stare at our crumbling walls, half missing windows and gaping floor, and say pityingly, "Boy, teacher, you must be real poor!". And while we had enough money to survive, there were times when we skipped meals, stretching our last few lempira while we waited for outstanding fees from the wealthier families and local businesses. Echoing the heartwarming kindness I have experienced before, desperately poor families would insist on our accepting gifts of fish, mangoes and coconut bread.

During the months that we lived on the island, we began to develop senses, or at least sensitivities, which we had never before imagined. Living in such a tiny place without any of the buffers of urban life, the sea and the weather took on a far greater importance than we had ever experienced. At first, when we were still green, children used to take great delight in frightening us with solemn predictions of massive hurricanes and certain death. While hurricanes were certainly not unheard of on the island, it was far more common to catch the outer storms of one passing over the Caribbean than the full weight of the real thing. In fact, such storms were routine in September and October, when the normally tranquil sea would take on another life, surging toward the houses tottering on their flimsy stilts, and tossing boats on its gigantic waves. The air would become thick with the largest raindrops I've ever seen, and within minutes, the concrete streets would be ankle-deep in water. Despite the rain and wind, the temperature only very rarely dropped to the point where we had to put on sweaters. In such storms, the ingenuity of the island design would come into its own. While enclosed paths quickly became waterlogged, most were simply strips of planks nailed together, like a maze of mini piers. Although they became slippery and we would have to take care not to miss our footing, they immediately drained down into the canals which crisscrossed the island.

We learnt very quickly that notions of privacy were non-existent.

The island itself was far too small for cars, or indeed anything resembling a road. Because the weather and the behaviour of the sea directly affected all aspects of life, we, like all the other islanders, became amateur weather-watchers, and learnt to predict squalls from the feel of the air, the look of the sea and the behaviour of animals (mostly cats and dogs). We even learnt to watch the numerous cockroaches with whom we shared our house. We were convinced that they became more active just before earthquakes – we experienced a few of these but they were only small, creating a sensation similar to the jolt of boats bumping against the house as they moored. We also managed to control our landlovers' fear of the sea, and by the end of our stay, we were hopping on and off wobbling *dories* (small wooden canoe-type boats), even in flip-flops! Not that we ever lost respect for the sea, nor for the creatures in it. Everybody on the island knew people who had been killed in boat accidents, and although the local sea creatures were relatively benign, there were still various species of shark and sharp-toothed fish to which we gave deferential space when snorkelling.

We learnt very quickly that notions of privacy were non-existent. With an island population of over three thousand in an area of just a quarter of a square mile, this was as much down to practicalities as anything else. Our house was typical in that every part of each room was clearly visible from outside. This even included the rooms facing the sea, which were overlooked by the fishermen who slept on boats tied to a nearby dock. The weather was another contributing factor.

> *We were incensed to discover that one particular "friend" had made a bet that he would get to sleep with at least one of us.*

Owing to the heat, houses are always open, and people spend all day (except siesta) on the streets, chatting, eating, and watching the world go by. In a very positive way, I became less obsessed with building a barrier around my own personal space, and began to value enormously the benefits of community life. The joy of sitting on the balcony in an old wooden swingchair, rocking away the stress of the day to the nearby beat of reggae or salsa, and exchanging *prensa* (gossip) with passers by; that was a hard feeling to beat. On the downside, however, neither Emma nor myself were ever able to accept the fact that everybody's lives became public property, and that nothing was allowed to pass unnoticed – especially the behaviour of the English teachers, which was scrutinized, discussed and judged according to a set of very strict moral codes.

The general lack of concern for privacy led to endless "courtesy" visits to our house by a long line of men. They would spend hours talking at us about the biggest fish they had ever caught, or the best football goal they had ever scored, or the most money they had ever made. During the first weeks, anxious not to offend cultural norms, we put up with it, imagining that we were under an obligation to act the dutiful hostesses. Our eyes would glaze over as we stared into the distance, across the bright blue sea, and imagined ourselves on one of the deserted, palm-dotted islands that surrounded the busy and noisy piece of land where we lived. It didn't take us too long to realize that such tolerance wasn't doing us any favours, and that far from fitting in with the local culture, our behaviour was seen by the moralists as improper, and by the others as naive and soft.

As time went on and we became more familiar with local culture, we became a lot more assertive in our attempts to maintain a degree of autonomy over how we lived and who we spent time with. But we still found that we were meeting far more men than women. Being European clearly made us exotic and challenging, for we were constantly approached by men, though it was virtually impossible to make genuine male friends. In one instance, we were incensed to discover that one particular "friend" had made a bet that he would get to sleep with at least one of us. Another man in his early twenties told me that he found the idea of having female friends quite strange. Men and women, it seems, view each other in terms of sex, economic support, or in the case of families, in terms of blood relations. Friendship is something much more rare. But while we would feel annoyed and insulted by continual male advances, and particularly by the rippling "tsss tsss tsss" of men on the streets trying to catch our attentions, many island women expected and welcomed such behaviour. In the absence of other contact between the sexes, this is how early courtship is carried out. It still made us feel uneasy.

Upon her partner's return she retreated into her house, only surfacing now and again with bruises and black eyes.

Our friendships with women were slow to develop, partly because of our strangeness as foreigners belonging to another class. However, the bonds we eventually made ran deep and were a great source of strength. Many of these women's partners were absent, either working on the fishing boats or on the Cayman Islands, and we'd spend raucous evenings chatting, telling jokes, drinking beer, dancing and eating *baleadas* (tortilla bread, refried beans and cheese). Lack of local employment made this a normal state of affairs, so that women were generally a stronger and far more consistent presence on the island than men. During our stay, the Mayor was a woman (nicknamed Thatcher by the islanders owing to her curt manner and autocratic style), and the Women's Club (a collection of the most wealthy and powerful women on the island) was a true force to be reckoned with. Others, left on their own for months on end, developed businesses, reared children (with the help of extended families) and made their own decisions. But when the men returned, it was all change; their pockets lined for the first time in months, many would go on benders, spending weeks in drunken stupors, terrorizing their wives and sleeping around. One good friend was a loud, confident and funny woman when we first met her, but upon her partner's return she retreated into her house, only surfacing every now and again with bruises and black eyes – despite her assurances that she gave as good as she got, she only lost her timidity when her partner returned to work overseas and she was free to be her own woman for another eleven months.

One group of notorious women did not need to compromise their routine. These were the few, but very open lesbians. While the island people tended to be blatantly homophobic in principle, gossiping maliciously about these women's lifestyles, they appeared to be tolerant in practice, living and working together with no obvious problems. No doubt it helped to know that they were nearly all of the same flesh and blood anyway.

Violence and early death are very much a part of island existence; men are regularly lost at sea, children die from common ailments, and guns are two a penny. Frighteningly, promiscuity combined with a minimal level of education and low expectations from life, offers fertile ground for the spread of AIDS which is already making its mark as a killer with the capacity to decimate the community. A local doctor, commenting on this possibility, laughed at our earnest approach to the problem, saying that since early death is such a common occurrence anyway – whether it be from malaria, malnutrition, gunshot wounds or pirates at sea – people are more complacent about the risks, preferring to live fast and die young.

"And if you move, I'll blow your fucking brains out".

Their situation between South and North America make the Bay Islands a useful link in the international cocaine trafficking network. In addition to organized trade, bags of cocaine sometimes get washed up on the shores, to be sold or given away on the islands. The mixture of drugs, guns and alcohol is a fearsome cocktail, likely to affect the community more and more as drug use spreads among the population. Nevertheless, I only felt truly in danger twice during our stay. On the first occasion, Emma and I had been sitting in a bar with a friend when a pillar of the local community descended on our table, extremely drunk and brandishing a gun. Straight out of a bad cowboy movie, he waved his weapon around in the direction of our heads and demanded that we drink with him. I'm sure that we were picked at random, being nearest to the door, and the first table he tripped over on entering the room. In any case, this was obviously no time for heroics and we accepted. Once the drinks were downed he repeated his demand, adding in slurred but easily audible words: "And if you move, I'll blow your fucking brains out". When he eventually got up to go to the toilet, we scarpered, diving behind a fence in time to see him emerge from the bar and stagger off down the street, gun held aloft as he swayed from side to side. Familiar with these habitual forays, people all along the street ducked behind anything they could find. He turned out to be one of the wealthier islanders, and so his behaviour was consequently left uncurbed.

The second time I felt in immediate danger was far more chilling since the threat was specifically aimed towards me as a woman, and probably a Western woman at that. I often used to walk around the island at night, never feeling in the slightest bit vulnerable. While domestic violence is common and disagreements easily develop into shoot outs, incidents like muggings or stranger rape seemed non-existent. On this particular occasion, I'd heard a group of young men behind me in the dark, but thought little of it – indeed, the freedom to walk alone at night was something I relished. I was only a few metres from home when a hand suddenly grabbed my shoulder and spun me around. The young man, who'd broken away from his mates to catch up with me, started talking angrily in Spanish; fuelled by drink and drugs, his hate needed no translation. Telling myself to keep calm I tried not to show any fear and in Spanish said that if he didn't let me go, I would shout out. With a sneer and a tightening of his grip, he told me that he had a gun in his pocket and would use it if I made so much as a sound. For what seemed an eternity we engaged in a battle of wills, he ranting on threateningly while I stared defiantly back. Eventually, the rest of the group caught up and gathered round to view the spectacle. I told one of them to make his friend let go of me, after which there was a dreadful silence during which I hardly dared imagine what might happen if they all decided to join in. I wouldn't have stood a chance. Thankfully, the pendulum swung my way, and my attacker allowed himself to be pacified by his mates, one of whom insistently offered to walk me home. I retorted that he'd make better use of his time criticizing his friend's behaviour and obvious lack of respect for women – a pathetic show of bravado maybe, but it made me feel better. Walking back to the house, I kept my hands stuffed in my pockets so no one could see them shaking.

In such a small community, it was easy to find out where my assailant worked. It turned out that he was employed by one of the rich "English" families as a nightwatchman and could easily have been carrying a gun. I told his employer what had happened, whereupon he shouted at the young man for twenty minutes in the presence of myself and around fifty other people in the street. I have mixed feelings about this form of public humiliation. I knew that had I been a "Spaniard" from the mainland, nobody would have taken any notice of my story. Or if my attacker had been one of the powerful "English" island men (themselves quite capable of insistent harassment in the bars and disco), it would probably have been laughed off as a bit of harmless fun. Despite these misgivings, I couldn't help feeling relieved. And although we passed on the streets many times, he never looked me in the face again.

A year later, Emma and I returned for a holiday. Although a few people greeted us as long lost friends, many said their hellos as if we'd only been there yesterday. The older folk simply nodded and reminded us of their prophesies; that all who taste the magically pure water of the island have no choice but to return. And the children, on seeing us in the street shouted, "Hello teachers", followed by: "When does class start? Am I late?" Time is a wily old devil at the best of times. On the Bay Islands, it plays its most disarming tricks.

TRAVEL NOTES

Languages English, followed by Spanish on the Bay Islands, plus Miskito and Garifuna on the mainland's Caribbean coast.

Transport Buses – cheap and very slow – cover most routes. Passenger boats ply the sea around the Bay Islands; otherwise it's possible to arrange lifts on fishing boats.

Accommodation Inexpensive and easy to find in main towns, where travellers are expected. Otherwise ask around for hostels.

Special Problems Don't be deceived by the evident US influence on Honduran culture. Modest dress is appreciated – and advisable for safety. On the coast and islands most women wear longish shorts and T-shirts. It's also best to be discreet regarding any interest or involvement in human rights issues.

Guides There are no guides specifically to Honduras. The best of those covering all of Central America is probably *Central America on a Shoestring* (Lonely Planet). *The Central America Handbook* (UK, Trade and Travel/US, Passport Press) though useful for mainland Honduras, contains several inaccuracies on the Bay Islands.

CONTACTS

Central America Human Rights Committee, 83 Margaret St, London WIN 7HB (☎0171/631 4200). Main campaign and education group in Britain. Good for further contacts in the region, including women's groups.

Comite Hondureño de Mujeres por La Paz (Honduran Women's Committee for Peace), "Visitación Padilla", Apdo Postal 1796, Tegucigalpa, Honduras (☎383704). Named after an early female peace campaigner, this group originally focused on ousting the US military from the country. It is now concerned with improving women's rights.

BOOKS

Elvia Alvarado, *Don't Be Afraid Gringo* (US, HarperCollins, 1989). Moving first-hand account of life as a Honduran woman in the countryside. *Woman of Maize* (US, Saoirse Press, 1993). The story of Margarita Murillo, a Honduran political activist, translated from interviews with Steve Sefton.

Tom Barry and Kert Norsworthy, *Honduras: A Country Guide* (UK & US, Inter-Hemispheric Education Resource Center, 1990; US o/p). Not a travel guide but a comprehensive analysis of Honduran history, politics and popular movements. In the UK the book is titled *Inside Honduras*.

Special **thanks** to Ceri Sheppard who provided much of the information for the Introduction and Travel Notes.

Hungary

W hile the Communist regimes of Eastern Europe were grappling with *perestroika*, Hungary was busy unravelling the iron curtain along its borders and recreating itself as a multi-party democracy. Not a shot was fired and, against the revolutionary fervour of 1989–90, the election in Hungary of a conservative nationalist government seemed almost an anti-climax. Four years on and the country has voted back the old reformer Communists, seen ironically as the best candidates for completing the transition to capitalism and safer hands for the massive influx of foreign investment currently flooding the country.

Prestige cars, ritzy nightclubs, bars and designer shops have proliferated on the streets of the capital Budapest and main cities, testifying to the spending power of the new entrepreneurial elite. The majority of Hungarians, however, have little chance of affording the imported luxuries on offer. Prices may have adjusted to Western levels but average wages certainly have not, and most incomes fall well below those of neighbouring West European countries. Behind the slick business centres and five-star facades of Budapest there hangs a pervasive sense of

alienation and dejection. The loss of state welfare provisions and pensions are leaving many old people destitute, while among the nihilistic youth sub-culture of the cities, suicide has been elevated to the ultimate cult act.

For tourists Hungary has long been a popular destination. Budapest, with its café culture and grand architecture on the banks of the Danube, plays host to thousands of foreign visitors each year, and the resorts around Lake Balaton do a burgeoning trade in inexpensive package holidays. The country has always kept one step ahead of its neighbours in providing a range of facilities for tourists, and travelling around independently or finding good-value accommodation is relatively straightforward, even for women travelling alone. Safety is a growing concern for city residents dealing afresh with the problems of pickpockets and other street crimes but, even in Budapest, you're unlikely to feel in more danger than in any Western capital. The same applies for sexual harassment. Prostitution is a major industry but punters know what they're looking for and even in the red-light areas there's relatively little hassle to contend with. Most Hungarian men still subscribe to notions of chivalry in their public dealings with women – bouquet-giving and flattery are the norm – and it's rare for women visitors to come up against sexual aggression. Rural Hungary is far more conservative than the capital and anything slightly outlandish – wild hair-colours or nose studs, say – are frowned upon. In these traditional backwaters the fact of being well out of your teens and without a husband or children is considered strange enough.

Hungarian **women** have long had the sole responsibility of looking after home and children foisted upon them, while often working at more than one job to make ends meet. Since the demise of Communism the pressure has increased to meet ever-higher standards of glamour, while access to higher education and better paid jobs is being eroded by more rampant forms of sexual discrimination. As in much of Eastern Europe, feminism has a bad name – for Hungarians the term reeks of stale Communist propaganda and images of man-hating, sexless women. Women's organizations do exist, and have spearheaded campaigns to set up women's refuges and publicize the problems of domestic violence, but these have a low profile in the mainstream political life of the country.

A Hack in Budapest

Lucy Hooker has been living in Budapest since 1991. She initially worked as an English teacher but has since moved into journalism and currently writes regular articles for the British newspaper *The Guardian*.

Hungary is a schizophrenic old place. One moment it is the heart of the Balkans full of deep-rooted conservativism and Christian values. The next moment it is "the Bangkok of Central Europe". There are streets lined with strip bars and *Playboy* is as common as the *Daily News*.

When you arrive, probably at one of the city's vast and dingy stations, you won't be confronted with the "hands on" approach of some countries further south. Hungarians pride themselves on their gentlemanliness – roughly translated as doors swept open in front of you and bills taken care of as you leave.

For Hungarian women, this gentlemanly behaviour means that they remain sole child-raiser, housekeeper, cook and hostess without the intervention of reconstructed man, who is still a strictly Western affair. And thanks to forty years of the glorious women-as-tractor-drivers policies under Communism it is quite normal for women to also hold down one or two jobs.

As a visitor the most noticeable consequence of this is the weary, run-down appearance of women over thirty. Youngsters on the other hand know how to celebrate their youth. Summer heralds the competition for the most revealing pair of shorts, a sight enough to raise the most liberal eyebrow. And while hems are up, cleavages are down. All this baring of flesh means you can make the most of the constant rays of summer sun which beam down from May until September. Numerous outdoor baths are dedicated to the bronzing of the human body. But that may not be your cup of tea.

A favourite haunt, that I'd return to with my mother on her visits to the city, is the indoor medicinal hot baths in the famous *Gellért Hotel*. Swathed in enormous white sheets, we'd stroll about like Roman empresses, enjoying the ornate Art Deco surroundings as much as the luxury of a big hot bath. Here, as my mother points out, almost anyone feels slim and youthful compared with the rest of the female clientele, most of them testimonies to the damaging effects of fifty years of Hungarian motherhood and a fatty diet.

You can add to the experience with a massage and pedicure. Enjoyment of the massage, however, can get clouded by knowing just a bit too much of the local lingo. Last time I found myself an involuntary party to the masseuses' discussion of the (whack) piece of pork (pummel) they had bought for Easter dinner (whack). By the end I felt I could sympathize with her joint under the tenderizing hammer.

After the baths we would while away the afternoon drinking strong coffee and sampling the pastries in a sumptuous Art Nouveau café. Happily there are plenty of these to choose from in Budapest. The grandest of all is probably the *New York Café* on the ring boulevard, where you sit at marble tables under a high arched ceiling. Happily again, gone are the days where it was purely a male preserve for playing chess, smoking and philosophizing. These days we can join in too.

For the first year of my stay I was stuck out in a suburb of Budapest in a large, clean flat which had lots of black leather furniture, chrome and glass tables, but no telephone. I felt a bit cut off. What is more, I knew my neighbours resented a young woman having such a spacious flat to herself. Most young couples in Hungary can't afford to rent their own place and are forced to move in with their parents for the first few years. It is virtually unheard of for a woman in her mid-twenties to have the space that I did. Although it was actually a nicer part of town, every time I put my name on the doorbell I would find it scratched off, and somebody broke into my post box. Unfortunately my Hungarian wasn't good enough to ease the tension and in the end I simply moved out.

On a short stay you are unlikely to trigger these sorts of resentments – even if you do, you won't understand what people are saying about you. Hungarian isn't the kind of language you just pick up accidentally. But it has one endearing quality for anyone who has battled in the past with "le" versus "la" or "der, die, das": one word – "ö" – means both he and she and there is no such thing as gender. The answer to the eternal debate over chairpeople, personholes and hu-manhandling, you might think. Unfortunately, however, it doesn't stop Hungarians assuming the world of politics, business and management is the sole preserve of men.

One word guaranteed to raise the hackles of Hungarians of both sexes is "feminism". "You're not a feminist", is the usual reassuring response, "You can't be, you're nice!" No amount of clever arguments and persuasion will shift your average Hungarian's view on the proper roles of the sexes. Recently though, a group of women activists have set up a long overdue hot-line for women and are trying to organize refuges for women who need to get away from their domestic situation.

After a year spent teaching English to a class of construction engineers at a technical college, a job I'd pre-arranged through an organization in England, I started to pick up a bit of journalism. Writing for a local English-language weekly was a good way to meet people and understand more of what was happening in the country. I caught the journalism bug and stayed on.

Being referred to as a "little miss" doesn't do a lot for your self-image as a hard-hitting hack . . .

Now I live in the centre of town, in the old Jewish district, which became the Jewish ghetto during World War II. Some of the buildings still bear the marks of those traumatic years and several stand empty because the city council has no money to renovate them. At the same time people go homeless and I often find old people on the street outside my flat begging or rummaging through the bins for left overs. The 45-year-old cosmetician next door comes in to borrow the phone every now and again in her skin tight leggings and bouffant hairstyle. She is probably after your boyfriend, the landlady reassures me.

Going to interviews, I found the most common ice-breaker from middle-aged men was: "I didn't know your paper had such pretty young reporters." Best ignored. Being referred to as a "little miss" doesn't do a lot for your self-image as a hard-hitting hack, but you get used to it. Once a local television crew asked me if it wasn't terribly emancipated of me to come and work in Hungary on my own. Patiently I tried to explain that actually it was quite ordinary. If it wasn't surprising for a man to do it why should it be for me?

Hungarians are not sure they want to change, but they are willing to learn. So while most Hungarians are stubbornly homophobic, Budapest has always offered a lot of fun for gays east of the crumbled iron curtain. My lesbian friends kiss and cuddle in public without earning too much attention.

And while Hungarians insist that women cook and men work, a few determined women are beginning to filter to the top in business and professional life. Those who do still face the concomitant prejudices. Said Zsuzsanna, who heads her own business services company: "One client told me that when he met me, he thought I had probably gone to Italy as a dancer or a whore and that was how I made the money. Men don't like the idea that women can be beautiful and have brains. They can't believe it."

Bearing in mind you are travelling though, it can sometimes be just as well to disguise your objections and try not to baulk if a young man commences his chat up speech by telling you how beautiful you are. It is quite usual for Hungarian males to be overeffusive along these lines.

There used to be only one perfume, called "The Red Square". Now you have a choice and can make a style statement.

Around the corner from where I lived last year in Budapest a fresh-faced 17-year-old sat at the super-market cashtill. No matter whether I was in tracksuit or mini-skirt, hair unwashed, straight out of bed in the morning or crawling in at 10pm he had a stock pile of compliments on how nice I looked that day. And he had no intention of taking it any further than that. Hungarian men tend to value their chivalrous image over putting unwelcome paws on a new foreign acquaintance.

Hungarians are more friendly than the British. They have a natural curiosity and are likely to want to talk to you. Anyone lucky enough to be invited to a Hungarian country festivity, be it a birthday, wedding or grape harvest, is firmly advised to drop all thoughts of dieting for that day and go the whole hog. This is the only way to avoid offending the persistently generous Hungarian country mother – not to mention having a taste of a real party.

One of the best times I have had in Hungary was a day's grape-picking in the countryside near Budapest. Being Western and a woman I managed to talk my way out of more than one glass of *palinka* – strong Hungarian plum brandy –before ten o'clock in the morning. But I couldn't get out of the five-course meal to celebrate our morning's harvest. They wanted to know why, at 23, I wasn't married yet and when I thought I was going to start having children. In the countryside girls are still often married off at seventeen to start their own families. I left feeling like I was being fattened for slaughter, but definitely like one of the family.

While Hungarian women, like Atlas, support the twin burdens of family and the economy, it doesn't stop them being mesmerized by the new-found glamour of western consumerism. Western clothes companies from fur shops to Marks and Spencers have moved in to tempt them, flanked by Lancome and Chanel.

"Suddenly you can be more female", my friend Kriszta explained. "Before, you had one type of shampoo or spray, everyone looked the same. There used to be only one perfume, called 'The Red Square'. It was so horrendous you couldn't use it. In the early Communist days, even wearing lipstick was frowned upon and labelled bourgeois. Now you have a choice and can make a style statement."

For Hungarians who have trudged through forty years of one-brand monopoly there is a revolution to be had in self-expression: if, that is, you have the purchasing power. Unfortunately too many are struggling to make ends meet to afford even the luxuries of disposable nappies and pre-prepared food, let alone fancy underwear and cosmetics.

Back in the old days, pre-1989, pornography was also banned, as a wicked vice of the West, and although prostitution thrived it was far more low key than it is now and easy for officials to ignore. These days pimps tend to be Mafia so officials still look the other way and Budapest has become a half-way house for girls from further east, from the former Soviet republics or Romania. They learn "Western ways" before going on to "careers" in Germany or Italy.

Fortunately the prostitution doesn't mean your freedom as a visitor is curtailed. Kerb-crawlers stick to what they came for and although there are one or two more seedy areas of town, Budapest is still relatively safe. Local transport is efficient and runs all night and taxis whizz past as often as you could wish. And if Budapest is secure the countryside is more so. At the risk of sounding naive I would say that in two-and-a-half years of walking about the streets in comfort at night and waiting at bus stops alone, I have seldom felt worried and I have never suffered any worse harassment on the street than the odd comment.

Nobody should be complacent of course. And, as anywhere, there are dodgy types about. You may well encounter them as you climb off the train among the crowd who want to offer you a room. If you aren't bedding in the local four-star, either opt for the harmless little old lady with a room to spare or, in summer, the university residences. During the holidays these get converted into enormous youth hostels. You may have to share the shower with ten other people and probably as many spiders, but you have the added advantage of meeting hundreds of fellow travellers and partying every night.

TRAVEL NOTES

Languages Hungarian – an incredibly difficult language to pick up. German is widely understood, but English is only spoken in the more heavily touristed parts of Budapest.

Transport Visas are necessary but are issued routinely on entering the country. Travel within the country is fairly straightforward by bus and train and you can go wherever you want. The "black train" (any train leaving Budapest for the northeast between 4pm and 7pm on a Friday) is best avoided. The carriages are crammed with migrant workers heading home for the weekend. Serious drinking is the norm and the atmosphere can get pretty oppressive for women on their own.

Accommodation Budapest covers the range of options, from luxury hotels to private rooms. You need to book ahead in peak season, however, when the city fills up. Around the country, *Turistahaza* dormitory hostels are useful and campsites plentiful, as well as the conventional hotel network.

Guides *The Rough Guide to Hungary* (Penguin). An excellent book – informative, insightful and a gripping read.

BOOKS

⭐ **Eva Hoffman**, *Exit into History* (UK, Minerva, 1994/US, Penguin, 1993). Eva Hoffman, a Polish-born writer, returns to Eastern Europe to bear witness to the changes wrought by the fall of Communism. Her travelogue, a literary *tour de force*, includes a chapter on Hungary.

Lesley Chamberlain, *In the Communist Mirror: Journeys in Eastern Europe* (UK & US, Faber & Faber, 1990, o/p). Chamberlain describes herself as "a discontented Westerner dazzled by austerity" – just part of the honesty she brings to bear in relating her travels in Eastern Europe shortly before the dismantling of Communism. Her chapter on Hungary, which she visited with her four-and-a-half year old daughter, is set in the mid-1980s.

Ivan and Nancy Volgyes, *The Liberated Female: Life, Work and Sex in Socialist Hungary* (UK & US, Westview Press, 1977, o/p). Looks at the position of women in Hungarian society from feudal times up to the 1970s.

Iceland

Perched on a volcanic rift just a few degrees south of the
Arctic Circle, Iceland epitomizes the wilderness of the far
North: remote, mysterious and rugged. Long popular
with geologists for its weirdly beautiful landscape of volcanic rock
formations, geysers, hot pools and glaciers, and with birdwatchers
for its vast nesting colonies, the country has gradually established
a more mainstream tourist industry. New hotels have sprung up
in the capital Reykjavik, and tour-buses ply the single road that
circles the coastline. Yet, for all the modern comforts of the island's
capital and the generally high – Scandinavian-style – standard of
living, this is no easy destination for independent travellers. Costs
are exorbitant, public trans-
port infrequent, shops and
supplies are often long
distances apart and the
weather notoriously changeable. In a country the size of
England but with a population of only 250,000 it can
be hard to grasp the scale of
the emptiness you encounter.

Icelanders themselves have a reputation for being self-reliant,
insular and notoriously hard to get to know. Though they're
ready to give help when needed it's up to the visitor to make the
first move – even then the likelihood is that you'll be spending

long evenings on your own. It is however, a very safe place for lone women travellers and, provided you like the hardy outdoor life, you'll find ample rewards in the scenery, which is unlike anything else in this part of the world.

The Icelandic **women's movement** has long had an impact at the heart of mainstream politics. *Kvennalistur*, the "Women's Alliance" was the world's first feminist party to win seats in a national parliament and is well-used to holding the balance of power at local as well as national level. In 1985 the movement demonstrated its full collective power by calling a one-day strike for equality in the workplace and parity of wages. With the unequivocal support of Iceland's woman president, Vigdis Finnbogadottir, thousands of women walked off their jobs, closing down schools, shops and government offices. The alliance together with the enlightened leadership of Finnbogadottir (now in her fourth term) continues to provide inspiration to feminist campaigners throughout the North.

Cod Row

Cathryn Evans spent ten months working in a fish factory in the northwest fjords before setting off alone on a tour of the country.

I'd spent a few weeks' holiday in and around Reykjavik in the summer and really wanted an extended stay. After searching unsuccessfully for a job and a work visa I decided to try and join the quota of overseas women employed in the fish factories on the coast. Unfortunately the jobs are set up by agents in England who insisted that I return to London for an interview.

They offered me an eight-month contract, with a free return flight thrown in if I lasted the course. Within a fortnight I was flying back to Iceland, heading for the village of Flateyri in the northwest fjords with ten other women. Some were travellers, from Australia, New Zealand and Europe, lured by the chance to fund their fare home in a short time, while others from the Southern hemisphere came out of curiosity, knowing only that they were guaranteed a white Christmas.

Before leaving, most of the people I met seemed to think of Iceland as a snow-covered wasteland populated by Eskimos fishing through holes in the ice and living in igloos. They certainly couldn't imagine a socially and technologically advanced nation with a very high standard of living.

The northwest coast is one of the best fishing grounds and, consequently, Flateyri one of the country's wealthiest and best-equipped villages. As with most of the settlements outside Reykjavik, the village only existed because of the fishing industry. The factory was run on a co-operative basis, its profits servicing the community of 425 with a swimming pool, sauna, shop, snack bar, library, surgery, school and guest house – outstanding amenities for a place of its size. We were given a large house next door to the factory – an instant introduction to the all pervasive smell of fish.

The day after our arrival we were plunged into work. Donning aprons, gumboots, baseball hats and layers of warm clothes we watched apprehensively as Salla, the quality controller, showed us how to shear the backbone away from the meat, pluck out live worms with a deft flick of the wrist and cut out some nauseating blemishes. It was best not to think too hard about what we were doing and switch to automatic. The hours were long and hard in cold, wet conditions and by the end of the first week we ached all over. Some of the women were already plotting their escape during the coffee breaks.

I was a little surprised by how clearly the labour was divided. Filleting and packing were termed "women's work" while the men unloaded crates, watched over the gutting machines and loaded trays into the freezer. It was a highly mechanized factory, but there was no getting round the sheer monotony of packing, alleviated only by the prospect of different fish to work on. Nevertheless it was a comforting routine and very much the focus of life in the village. At the end of the week there was always a rush to finish the week's catch and if there was a particularly big haul at the height of the season the whole village would turn out to help. There was a tremendous community spirit and, as part of the workforce, we gradually felt accepted within it.

At first, of course, we were viewed with what seemed like cold indifference. Foreign workers had been coming to the village for twenty years and we were just another batch. The village mentality, which thrived on gossip and newcomers, focused on us. But they were also shy people, and their reticence was taken by some of the foreign women as stand-offish. There was certainly no great reason for them to be especially welcoming. The younger women, in particular, saw us as coming to their country merely for the money and as potential rivals for the affections of the men. Obviously, there was a precedent to this as it was something of a status symbol to go out with a foreign girl, and the trawlermen with money to burn would often shower visitors with gifts, adding to the recipients' money-grabber image.

On an individual level, however, the people were very friendly and hospitable and it was a pleasure to share with them their great passion for their country and community. I became closest to a woman called Hjordis, the headmistress of a tiny school. She had represented Iceland at the United Nations and travelled a great deal but had settled on her own in a house at the far side of the fjord from Flateyri. She spent the summer charting the different migratory birds and was dedicated to nurturing a forest in the harsh climate and thin soil. Another good friend was Stina, an imposing figure who had the dubious task of counting the number of worms in the crates of fish and calculating how long it would take us to pluck them out. With a family of three to raise on her own, she supplemented her income by running the swimming pool and gathering expensive eider duck feathers from her farm in summer. She would patiently help me to grasp Icelandic, a language that has changed little from the time the great sagas were written.

The villagers always made sure that we joined in the celebrations of major festivals and would explain to us the different feasts and rituals, such as the pancake feast to mark the last glimpse of the sun before the dark winter days. Men, women and children each had their own festivals, dating back to the gods Odin and Thor. The feast of Thorrablot, for the single men of the village, was a memorable trial for the tastebuds. Traditional fare such as braised sheep head, rotten shark, rotten eggs and sour ram's testicles was served. The only thing I really acquired a taste for was *skyr*, a sour yoghurt-like liquid mixed with sugar. Most food is bought in from Denmark and is very basic. The tiny store often looked like it was operating food rationing, especially in winter when road, air or sea routes were closed and supplies couldn't get through.

Icelanders put this heavy drinking down to boredom and depression in the winter months.

Boredom seemed to be a big problem in Flateyri, especially among the younger people; they spent hours cruising round and round the village or burning rubber up and down the one main road. The women I worked with who were not great nature lovers and were used to big city life found it hard going as well. Dances with live bands were held every fortnight in summer but less frequently in winter.

Being the largest house in the village, our quarters became the party house at weekends and we would often get impromptu visits from people in neighbouring villages. Icelanders are by nature self-contained and undemonstrative and many relied too heavily on alcohol to let their hair down. Sadly, drink problems were common – even in such a small place, there was a regular "Alcoholics Anonymous" meeting. The sale of beer had, until very recently, been illegal, but as fourteen-year-olds would down a bottle of spirits at a time, this, like the high prices, seemed a futile measure. Icelanders put this heavy drinking down to boredom and depression in the winter months.

Every clear winter night there was a fantastic display of the Northern Lights, with whirling, flickering bursts of colour.

The whole country had an air of being untouched by commercialism, although it was clear that this was changing. Even Reykjavik, which was busy promoting itself to attract foreign investment, had none of the big city atmosphere, not even the usual neon lights. It was striking at Christmas that most adverts were for books. As a legacy of the long, dark winters, writing, poetry, music and chess are still very popular pursuits, with a high number of experts for such a tiny country. However, videos are set to supplant this and mail-order mania has taken grip in the villages. Keeping up-to-date with fashions has become increasingly important for both sexes and it's a matter of pride among the free-spending trawlermen to have the latest hi-fi and cars.

Although winter, with only three or four hours of daylight and snow-fall cutting off the village for many weeks, seemed a bleak prospect to most of the villagers and foreign workers, its novelty made it the most magical time for me. Every clear winter night there was a fantastic display of the Northern Lights, with whirling, flickering bursts of colour covering the sky. I enjoyed trekking on the mountain slopes on skis and whizzing across acres of snow on a snowmobile, stopping on a ledge and looking out on to the village below. Flateyri had many houses hugging the sides of the mountains so there was real danger of damage from an avalanche. Sometimes even a walk up the road was too risky. This was brought home dramatically one day, when with a great roar a cloud of snow and dirt subsided leaving a vast mound of snow just short of a row of houses. The risks of making a living by the sea were also made clear as three fishing boats in the region were lost within the space of one stormy week.

Gyllir was the name of our trawler. A crew of fifteen would go out on voyages of seven to ten days. It was fitted with the latest computerized instruments as well as the comforts of a sauna and videos. For all this the conditions at sea were arduous. When taken on a trip we had to stay below deck while the men struggled above with the nets in fierce winds. The catch was gutted on board, a very tiring process, and the six-hour shifts seemed an eternity. It was a great feeling, however, to sail back into harbour with a large haul which would be turned into neat packets of fillets during the next week. It's strange to think what a high level of job satisfaction there was working in the factory, singing along to the Icelandic pop songs on the radio and picking up pidgin Icelandic, even though this largely consisted of the different names of fish.

After my contract finished I found it hard to break away from the cosy routine of the community, and especially from the beautiful, peaceful environment. It was a total retreat from the hassles of city life, and as the summer approached I would spend long evenings walking at the edge of the fjord watching the boats turn into the harbour, seals and eider ducks on the beaches and the snow thawing to create cascading

The barren volcanic cratered areas were used to train the American astronauts.

waterfalls. The endless daylight made it hard to stay indoors and, much as I enjoyed the winter, I could see why the villagers were so cheered by the summer sunlight. One of the best moments was climbing up the steep mountainsides and crossing the still snow-covered plateau to watch the Midnight Sun.

However, I had spent ten months hardly leaving the confines of the village, so excitement slowly overtook my regret at leaving Flateyri, as I took off for Reykjavik to begin a tour of the rest of the country. I travelled mainly by bus and hitched to the less accessible spots. Taking advantage of the six weeks in the year when it is possible to travel across the interior, I joined a sturdy bus which was to cross the Spredgisandur route. The whole journey only took a day, but it was a battle to keep the bus moving through the glacial desert wasteland of sludge, sand, and ice-cold rivers. Crashing waterfalls, dark volcanic peaks and imposing glaciers contrasted with slabs of multicoloured rocks and steaming hot pools. Only a handful of drivers were qualified to take this route and we had to help out several stranded cars along the way.

Hitching can be quite difficult in Iceland. The most interesting places are often off the main road and there may only be a few cars passing. Trudging wearily along in enigmatic weather was quite demoralizing, but I never felt at risk and the lack of cars meant that if one did pass me, it would invariably stop. I spent many days exploring Lake Myvatn in the northeast, fortunately picking a time when the midges were taking a breather. This area has always been a magnet for bird watchers as it attracts a huge variety of migrating ducks in the summer. Great geological turbulence has produced many strange features – the barren volcanic cratered areas were used to train the American astronauts.

Close to this is a sulphurous plain with bright yellow crystals and bubbling pools of grey mud. The twisted statues of lava, called *Dimmuborgir* (dark castles), have still not been satisfactorily explained. There remains a suspicion that they might be sleeping trolls. It is usual for any giant boulder to be attributed to these mythical creatures, and often the course of roads has been altered to avoid disturbing them.

The geothermal activity in this area has some unusual spin-offs. In Hveragerdi the hot earth has been used as the basis of a greenhouse centre where exotic flowers and even bananas are grown. It also acts as an oven to bake delicious sourbread. In Svartsengi, the run-off from the heating plant has created a mineral-rich hot pool. It was a real luxury to bathe in the steam rising from bright turquoise water surrounded by craggy black lava. Throughout this time I stayed at youth hostels, which were always well-equipped and sited around the main routes. They ranged from farm outhouses to school halls and were friendly, relatively cheap places to spend the night. Camping was even better as the level of tourism means that there are few restrictions on where you can pitch a tent.

Iceland is not a place to spend time if you don't like the great out-doors and are expecting a bustling nightlife – outside Reykjavik there are few entertainments laid on. But the spectacular unspoilt landscape and relaxed lifestyle are reasons alone for taking a trip. It will hopefully be some time before the aggressive tourist and business drive now beginning to operate in the capital spreads to the rest of the country.

TRAVEL NOTES

Languages Icelandic and Danish: most people speak some English, too.

Transport No particular problems for women; hitching is probably as safe as it can ever be, but be prepared for long waits between lifts.

Accommodation Again, no particular problems for women. Many Icelandic women camp and hike alone (though see *Special Problems* below). There's a good network of youth hostels.

Special Problems Costs can be devastatingly high. Don't underestimate the dangers of hiking or driving into the interior; the terrain can be treacherous and your chances of being found if you have an accident are alarmingly slim.

Guides *Iceland, Greenland and the Faroe Islands – A Travel Survival Kit* (Lonely Planet) has a fairly comprehensive section on Iceland.

CONTACTS

Kvennaframbodid, Gamia Hotel Vik, Adalstraeti, 101 Reykjavik. Main office of the women's movement, used as a meeting place for various groups and for advice sessions on legal, social and health matters. They also publish a bi-monthly magazine, *Era*.

BOOKS

We've been unable to find any books in translation by Icelandic women. Any suggestions would be welcome.

India

India provokes intense reactions among travellers. However much you read, or are told, little prepares you for the richness of the various cultures, the variety of landscapes and the vast disparities of wealth among the people you meet – not to mention the sheer beauty of the place. In many ways it is misleading to talk about India as one country. With its six major religious groups, its differing stages of development, and proliferation of local cultures and languages, it is a collection of states easily as diverse as Europe. For a traveller on a short trip, one or two areas are more than enough to take in.

Countless women travel the country alone, and have done so from the days of the Raj through to the hippy era. The lingering hippy stereotype can be burdensome at times, connoting scruffiness, promiscuity and drug abuse, but it also has its positive side in an established trail and a legacy of inexpensive accommodation. Sexual harassment tends not to

be a great problem. This is not to say it doesn't occur; in strongly Muslim areas (concentrated in the north), wandering around on your own is considered a provocation in itself, inviting comments and jeers, and all women in India face the problem of being groped in crowded buses and trains. However, actual sexual violence, at least towards foreign visitors, is extremely rare, and any potentially dangerous situations can mostly be avoided by making a public outcry – passers-by or fellow travellers are bound to help you.

Much harder to contend with – in the cities, at least – is the frequent experience of being in a crowd and the volume of hustlers and beggars. Begging carries none of the social stigma that it does in Western societies and Indian people routinely give something. How you cope with the outrageous disparities of wealth is up to your own personal politics. But whatever you do, or don't do, you'll need to come to terms with your comparative affluence and outsider status – and the attention this inevitably attracts.

Although India's **feminist movement** has become established in recent years, it remains predominantly urban, the arena of highly educated, middle-class women. At the same time, however, many women's centres and action groups have been set up and with women's magazines such as *Manushi* and the feminist publishing company *Kali for Women*, the network is widening daily. Creative and diverse local actions include the formation of SEWA, a collective organization of lower-caste street workers in Ahmedabad as a means of protecting themselves from police harassment and the exploitation of money-lenders. One of the chief concerns of the women's movement is to involve more rural and urban-poor women in various broad-based campaigns – against dowry (the number of dowry deaths remains alarmingly high), discrimination in the workplace and disparities in pay and education.

A Troubled Guest

Rachel Armstrong travelled to Maharashtra as a final year medical student with the aim of spending three months as a trainee in a local hospital. She was invited to stay at the family home of the hospital's leading benefactor, a rich businessman, in the centre of Poona. Now medically qualified, she lives and works in London, combining her medical career with freelance work as a cartoonist, illustrator and photographer.

The glaring concrete failed to obliterate the waft of rank flesh and faeces that mingled with the hot air blasting into the airport lounge. A shadow floated across my burnt-out eyes. "Madam is to take the car to Mr Ahmed's residence!"

It was Randu, Mr Ahmed's chauffeur. He had a good eye for faces and had spotted me quickly from photos sent to the medical school. Poona was a long way from Bombay, he explained, and the journey was not safe for a woman on her own. Stupefied, I let him take hold of my meagre luggage.

Inside the yellow oven of his car I lost the will to make small talk. My mouth became mummified at each attempt to wet my lips. I was passed boiling hot water to drink which gave me little relief from dehydration. My eyes were scorched and sore. As blue returned to my visual palette I became aware of traffic on the busy Bombay highway. Ancient cars buzzed and tooted at each other. Bareheaded scooter riders weaved randomly in and out of the jamming cars, with little regard for safety. I shut my eyes.

Stirring from sleep, I found my gaze sheltered by rusted corrugated tin, fencing the highway. There appeared to be no pavement. We slowed down for a traffic light.

"Madam you must wind your window up, we are in the city!" Randu warned, but he was too late. The rising glass was darkened by a crowd of faces, hands rocked the car while voices clamoured for money. A woman with a cleft palate ground her tongue against the cavity as she pressed her child against the window. A one-eyed man with bandaged hands, barely able to to hold his staff, fixed me with dark hollows. A naked child salaamed with tears in his eyes prostrating himself on the bonnet of the car. I had stopped breathing, waiting for the ambush to crack the car open. The lights changed and the beggars fell away.

My vision became sharper. There were people on the sidewalk. Bombay was a city of bodies. Some shapes barely moved, mummified in the heat. Dark specks of flies crawled in and out of bloodless mouths. Decay was all around us and the nauseating airport smell crept into the car again. Randu informed me that we were close to the point where the entire city's sewage drained into the river.

"There are many people in Bombay", he exclaimed. "The river is important for washing and cooking." I shut my eyes again, unable to cope.

A dusting of salt crusted my flesh when I woke. The countryside was scorched with wheat and sticks that may once have been trees. The huts became smaller and darker. We were gradually gaining altitude. Red valleys broke through the precarious track which Randu protested was a road. I saw a grey wisp of train crawling far below me. I had no questions and my eyes closed. The sounds of Hindi, *sitar* and unmuffled exhausts plagued my daydreaming. I was dreadfully uncomfortable.

"How long now, Randu?"

"Just another two hours. Is madam comfortable?"

I nodded, rolling over to die.

Poona greeted us with a spiky wave of palms. Real shadows had formed, cooling the air. White clothed people stared into the car as we passed.

"Not long now, madam! The Ahmed household is in the centre of the city. Very beautiful, you are very fortunate to be their guest."

I had accepted the offer of residence with these strangers to appease the hospital management. The Ahmed family were benefactors, investing a great deal of capital in the establishment of the Medical Clinic. The empire of these successful building merchants extended to schools, housing development and recently, politics. The Ahmeds were very important people and had been insistent that a Western medical student would be more comfortable in their Westernized household than hospital accommodation.

I looked for the source of a voice blasting in stereo. A bearded man wailed a moving chant from a mosque. It was Ramadan; I was hearing the call to prayer. Randu was pleased at the thought of arriving in time to break the fast.

The tyres crunched against a gravel drive and a tall modern building garlanded in climbing plants rose from nowhere. Randu got out and passed my luggage to a grinning manservant. Spectators watched as I stretched my aching body. A chubby boy greeted me.

"I am Kafan. This is our house. You are most welcome! Excuse me, but they said you were a doctor. You look far too young to be a doctor."

I introduced myself, explaining that I was in my final year at medical school and thanked him for letting me stay.

"Don't mention it! Nothing is too much trouble".

The boy could not have been more than seventeen, but asserted himself with the authority of someone far older. We took the lift to the third floor. The doors slid open and two younger boys bounced up to take a look at me.

"Leave the poor girl alone! Rajif! Ali! That is no way to treat a guest, give her some room!" came the voice of Mrs Ahmed, mistress of the household. "My husband is upstairs with the men. They are talking politics", she announced, "Please, come in!"

An enormous woman beamed gold and pink in front of me. She pressed my baking hands in her limp palms. I curtseyed, feeling awkward at my apparent importance. I stooped to lift my hand luggage.

"No! leave it!" she snapped, clapping her hands, "We have someone to do that for you! Now, come! I will show you your room."

I padded behind her, escorted on both sides by the boys. A welcome chill kissed my face as I ducked under a fan and accepted the offer of a drink. The woman's soft hands patted together and this time, I watched as a skinny young girl raced towards us. Kafan spoke roughly to her, in Hindi. She disappeared with a curtsey. I did not ask after her. Four pairs of eyes scrutinized my face as a luxurious bedroom was granted as my own. I felt weak from dehydration. Rather than disappoint them, I sprang into life, praising everything I saw. They seemed pleased and hovered. I was expected to continue. I wanted to curl up on the bed, take my clothes off and cover myself in glacier water.

My jeans felt very dirty and my white T-shirt vulgar.

Mrs Ahmed swung the cupboard open to reveal saris and cotton trouser suits in technicolour. Of course, I would not know how to wear a sari but with pins and brooches I would soon look the part of an Indian princess. My jeans felt very dirty and my white T-shirt vulgar. I would be wearing traditional clothes and should change immediately so that we could break the fast together, before dinner. They finally left me to welcome solitude.

I felt extraordinarily ungrateful. These strangers had spared no expense to accommodate me. They had ensured my arrival in India was safe and that I was as comfortable as possible. I decided my disease was no more than homesickness. A soft knock brushed the door. Mrs Ahmed presented a child to me, holding a glass of melon juice on a silver tray. I thanked the child, with a disapproving look from the mistress, and was instructed to pull the bell rope in the corner of the room if I needed anything at all. I was to do absolutely nothing for myself. We would dine as soon as I was ready. Playing with a drip on the bottom of the glass I was instructed on Muslim custom. Men and women did not eat together; I would be with the boys and herself. The master of the household would see me later. I nodded with downcast gaze.

"There is no need to wear a veil but you should join us in prayers. We want you to share our customs."

She left with a hiss of silk.

Looking out across the courtyard from the bedroom window, Poona glowed like a sleepy volcano. Purple light streaked my skin showing the filth that had accumulated over the day with ultraviolet intensity. I needed to wash.

The grime swirled soapy down the shower plug and I felt clean and bright. The air remained hot, I needed something cool to wear. I chose a linen trouser suit from the vast wardrobe and left off my underwear. The bottoms were secured like pyjamas by a drawstring and the shirt hung loose, buttoning at the neck. The cut was unflattering and boyish. I had abandoned vanity and declined the effort of even a lick of make-up. I was ready to sleep. Dreamily, I looked out of the window. The sky had darkened, inky with beads of orange light bleeding upwards into its vastness. Insects chirruped in courtship, drowning the hum of traffic.

A sudden knock caused me to stand rigid to attention. The large face of the mistress fixed on me from the door.

"You are ready?"

I nodded.

"Here, you have got the shirt on backwards, the buttons go down the front like this!"

I was required to strip to readjust my attire. My drawstring was also incorrectly tied.

"That's better! Come!"

She swept forward, holding her sari at her shoulder and tossing her long plait to one side to balance the weight of the material.

"We will break the fast outside."

As she climbed the carpeted stairs to the roof I noticed she was breathing heavily. She was hugely overweight. Surplus chins gave an added breadth to her smile and her movement slowed to a regal glide. She turned, beckoning me impatiently.

The three chubby boys were tucking hungrily into bowls of fruit and cakes, using their fingers skilfully to roll up each morsel of food into little balls. They could talk and eat at the same time.

"Help yourself to whatever you want!" they all beamed.

I chose a good helping of fruit, buttered raisin bread and a large glass of sparkling water. I pulled up a soft chair next to the children and savoured each morsel. The faces of the boys and Mrs Ahmed were fixed intensely on me. I smiled and stretched out to relax.

"Please, have some more. You have hardly eaten a thing!"

"I'm very happy thank you. That was exactly what I needed."

"But you must have more! It's our hospitality! You have not touched the mango, the apples, plums, sweetcake or any of the pastries. Here, try these!"

A plate piled with food was handed to me and they arranged themselves around me to watch my appreciation. I really could not manage any more but I obliged my audience, almost to the point of pain, finishing off the contents of my plate nodding and smiling. They were happy with my performance.

Beyond the family stood manservants and small children. The Ahmeds appeared oblivious to the presence of these people. I wanted to ask about them but suspected it would not be etiquette to raise the subject.

Haunting music floated from the pipe of a musician who had been standing behind me. He swayed with each pulse of sound. A child stepped next to him slapping a hollow drum. The chant tempted my feet. I found myself rising to dance, shutting my eyes and swaying. India. I was so glad I had come to India.

"Please! No dancing! It is forbidden. We do not dance here! You are humiliating yourself in front of the servants! Come! We will have dinner now. The master is waiting downstairs."

More food. Much more food. Too much food. I was already very, very full.

Mrs Ahmed's putty hands pressed gently on my shoulders coaxing me to take a seat at a table hidden by silver dishes of multicolour delicacies. I was to at least try something of everything. As I explained that I had no appetite five pairs of eyes looked at me with gravity.

"Are you on a diet?"

"No, I'm just tired from the journey and have had more than plenty upstairs."

"You are far too thin, it is not attractive. You must eat more."

Rice dishes, vegetables in a greasy orange sauce and shreds of bubbling flesh were handed to me. I was vegetarian and madly wishing that there was some excuse which would spare me from the torture my insides endured. My fingers shifted food around my plate. Rolling rice into neat little balls with your fingers was not as easy as it appeared. I was not one of those poor mad Western girls who had problems with food, was I? I asked myself the same question.

I was desperate not to offend my hosts but incessant feeding was intolerable.

My hosts had been fasting all day and ate with further relish. I could not believe the volumes of food that were comfortably wolfed down. Their obesity reminded me that too much food made you fat. I would start a diet immediately. I never wanted to see food again.

"You look so unhappy! Do you find our hospitality offensive?"

A pair of skinny hands flashed past the kitchen door. I heard a gentle slap and squeak as the girl's hair was pulled in punishment for disturbing a guest of honour at table. I wandered what she ate for evening meal. The folly of my resistance made me feel ashamed. There were so many people in this country who would willingly change places with me. I braced my stomach to eat again, even managing a smile.

At last! I was permitted to go to my room. To de-bulk my belly was the only logical way to provide relief. I would make myself sick. Timidly my fingers crept on to my tongue. No result. My fingernails scratched at my tonsils and my stomach heaved. Braver from the promise of success, I pushed my fingers down my throat. Torrents of thick paste dropped over my fingers splashing in the pan, leaving beads of water on my face. I stood up and felt greatly relieved. I flushed the Western-style toilet, crept into bed and cried. I was terrified! I had never behaved in such a fashion! I needed help. I was desperate not to offend my hosts but incessant feeding was intolerable. I consoled my sobbing body with the prospect that things may change tomorrow. I would manage with a light breakfast and make my way to the hospital.

I had been excused on the grounds that it was important for someone in my "condition" to take good care of myself.

I slept deeply and woke to a burning sensation on my cheeks. Crystal light streaked my face through the blinds and strange birds were singing their triumph over night sounds in the morning air. The sun was warming the city outside so I washed and dried myself roughly to let my skin cool by evaporation. I rummaged in my bag for the map to the hospital.

My heart sank as I heard a soft pat against the door.

"Did you sleep well?"

I stretched a smile across my face to simulate pleasure, hoping the mistress would read my response as a greeting of appreciation and friendship. I desperately wanted to forget the previous evening.

"You look very pale and tired. I do not think it is a good idea for you to go to the hospital today."

"But I simply must go! Dr Wadir is expecting me!"

"I will telephone him. You look so weak. It is only sensible to stay here a little longer!"

"No! I insist that I go to the hospital today!" A feeling of panic began to shake my body. I gripped my muscles so that the mistress would not see my distress. Her eyes moved over my face.

"We shall discuss it after you have had a good breakfast."

The fried breakfast and chocolate cake was selected to excite my Western tastes. Sophisticated Indian food was obviously not suited to my constitution. The mistress would not join me as she was fasting; she would simply make sure that everything was as I desired.

The religious festival was in full swing. Mrs Ahmed had said prayers with the rest of the family at daybreak. I had been excused from the ritual on the grounds that it was important for someone in my "condition" to take good care of myself. I later discovered that she had been referring to my period. A servant had noticed the soiled cotton dressing discarded after I had arrived the previous night. Not wanting to risk blocking the toilet I had carefully wrapped the menstrual waste in toilet paper so that it would not offend my hosts. It would have required some curiosity and persistence to discover the unpleasant contents of the paper package. I wondered if the servant had found the partly digested food in the toilet bowl from last night too.

I shovelled the chocolate cake and fried food into my sore mouth, declaring revitalization and the need to go immediately to the hospital. I ignored the supicious glare which met me across the table.

"More? You seem hungry, at last!"

"Just a little, thank you!" I refused to give her cause for concern and won the release my belly ached for. I was permitted to go to the hospital.

Randu was worried that all I wanted to bring was my white coat and stethoscope. To stop him insisting that he should carry them for me I wore them to the car. I knew Mrs Ahmed would be watching from the window. I did not look up, feeling an overwhelming sense of freedom. As the car tyres bit on the gravel my stomach reminded me that oppression had embodied itself in the ritual of eating. Autonomy was the ability to choose what and when to eat. I wished car-sickness upon myself for liberation from the clutches of breakfast.

Poona was Scooterville; there were surprisingly few cars on the humming road. Randu was swearing in Hindi at bobbing riders and pinions as they weaved their way frantically in front of the sturdy bonnet. Grinning faces peered into the car windows to acknowledge the pallor of my skin. Everyone was going somewhere, urgently. Randu wound down the window and stopped with the rest of the traffic. Scooter riders jammed closer and closer. There was an immoveable obstruction on the highway. No one could move forwards, reverse or turn round. We packed tighter, inch by inch.

"What's the matter, Randu? Has there been an accident?" My medical curiosities were aroused. Randu did not hear. He was preoccupied. I watched his betel nut-stained teeth grind in his oyster pink mouth.

The crowd started to hum and motors revved louder, expectantly. I saw her stand, her flesh as white as my own. She looked at the impatient male drivers with disdain in her deep brown eyes. Her heavy eyelids fluttered and she lowered her pitchforked horns. The glorious beast faced us with her front feet splayed, ready to charge. The scooters whined a little more loudly, but did not move. Bored by the response to her challenge she tossed her head and neck folds, seeking better company with three chickens and some wiry goats. The flag had been lowered, the mini grand-prix raced up the highway to those pressing destinations. A sacred cow had stopped the traffic!

A sudden grunt confirmed that Randu had fallen asleep. I lifted the lock on the car, opened the door silently and fled.

The main highway was veiled in rich foliage. Lips of fluted pink flowers pouted from tall palm trees. Most of the houses were set well back from the road behind elaborately sprayed gardens. I could taste moisture in the morning air.

The Ruby Hall Clinic was a disappointing, 1960s' concrete lump. Randu turned into the dust track to the main entrance and halted at the barrier. An armed guard climbed leisurely out of his station, finishing a cup of tea and a bite of breakfast. I was discussed in Hindi. We passed to park in the courtyard by the main entrance. Now I could find Dr Wadir and my studies could begin. I grabbed the door handle to leap out.

"No! Madam is not to leave. It is not fitting to open the door in this public place. I must take five minutes sleep. The journey to the hospital has exhausted me. You will wait here in the car and we will go together to the hospital." He locked my door from the inside.

I was hot, frustrated and wanted to leave immediately. Instead of provoking a direct confrontation I pretended to settle. Randu's hairy neck shortened as he slid down in his seat and tilted his cap over his face. A sudden grunt confirmed my suspicion that Randu had genuinely fallen asleep. I lifted the lock on the car, opened and shut the door silently and fled.

At the main entrance I insisted that Dr Wadir was expecting me. I was not surprised to be spoken to in perfect English, but was astonished to win assistance to my cause.

"Of course doctor! His office is just down the corridor on the right. You are Dr Armstrong?" I had forgotten I was wearing my white coat. My sandals skidded on the cool tiled floor as I made my way a little too fast between staring people. I knocked boldly, looking over my shoulder for Randu. I did not see him and entered on command.

"Welcome to Poona, I trust you have had a pleasant journey!" My white skin and forwarded photographs made a formal introduction redundant. A strong hand took mine in greeting. I sat nervously on my chair glancing towards the door for the duration of our first conversation. At any second Randu would come to chaperone me.

"What is troubling you, Rachel?"

I confessed everything; my bewilderment at the oppressive hospitality of my hosts; the unwanted organization of my activities and now, the prospect of being "shadowed" around the hospital grounds. Dr Wadir looked concerned.

"This will not do. These people are trustees, not consultants. You are my responsibility. You must be free to learn everything you can whilst you are here. The difference in culture is very difficult to manage. Even within Poona people have very different ways. I for example, am a Parsee; our household is run very differently to a Muslim one."

He tugged at his chin and turned to look out of the window at the stream of people buzzing in and out of the emergency entrance.

A group of women were waiting on their haunches outside, some salaaming the ground and wailing loudly. There had been a death that morning; it was customary for the relatives to come and grieve publicly at the hospital.

Our pensive reflections were interrupted by a furious hammering on the door and a gruff voice shouting in Hindi. Randu! He stood at the open door, next to the armed guard with a menacing gaze. I leapt to my feet in horror. The chaperone was pointing at me and shouting accusingly. Dr Wadir remained silent. Was he going to turn me over? Then, a slow staccato of Hindi hissed from the consultant's mouth and the two men backed out of the room, bowing incessantly. When the door shut very gently indeed, the consultant looked composed.

"I told your driver that you were my responsibility now and that his was with the car. This has to be sorted out, sooner rather than later. You will spend the day here, with me and return to the Ahmed household tonight. I shall speak directly with them. Tomorrow will be different!"

Back to Bengal

Having lived in the middle of Asian communities in England and taught English to Asian women, **Frances Hunt** felt it was time to go to India. In 1991 she spent five months travelling around the subcontinent. A chance meeting opened up the possibility of a teaching job in Calcutta and, after temping in England for six months to earn her fare, she returned, this time to a job, a home and a network of close Bengali friends.

"Ladies? gents? you?" The policeman at the station had been questioning us about our stolen luggage for twenty minutes, had even taken our names and looked at our passports. My friend Liz was wearing make-up, but he still couldn't figure out her gender. Probably it was the short hair and trousers that confused him, or simply the fact that we were roaming freely around this vast country. We were used to the next question, "Married? Unmarried?" Whichever way we answered we were sure to be pitied, either for being spinsters, obliged to wander around aimlessly, or for having husbands too spineless to prevent us from doing so.

This was my first visit to India; Liz had been before. She was with me for three weeks and showed me the ropes, and then I was off on my own for four months. It helped to realize that from the start I was fighting two basic preconceptions: that, as a Western woman coming from a "free-sex country" I had no morals whatsoever and that as a Britisher I was "too formal", in other words cold and aloof. It was often hard to strike a balance between the two. We of course have many preconceptions ourselves, one of the main ones being that in such a densely populated country, we will never be left alone. It's a feature of our self-important imaginations that we assume we'll be dogged at every step by crowds of curious onlookers. In reality, Indian men and women have better things to do than hang around a dirty, ill-dressed and often rude foreigner, unless, of course, they need the contact to earn a living.

When I asked how to say "Leave me alone!" to beggars, she told me that they prefer to say "mab koro": forgive me.

When I first arrived in India I used to shout "Go away!" at porters who approached me at the station or outside New Market in Calcutta; it's a lot more polite (and effective) to learn how to say "I don't need you" in the local language, in which case the porter – who's only doing his job, after all – can try and find business elsewhere. When I asked my friend Asha how to say "Leave me alone!" to people begging, she quietly told me that in Bengal they prefer to say "mab koro": forgive me.

It's easy in India to get embroiled in conversations with men and we often need that human contact, especially when travelling alone. Yet, it's important to apply the same rules that we use at home. We also have a cultural card to play. If the conversation is really not wanted, one appropriate response can be "Forgive me, in my country ladies do not talk to men they do not know" – which is, after all, true.

An Indian friend had warned me of robbery on the trains with the triumphant air of someone performing a conjuring trick: "The train slows *down*, the hands go *in*, the train pulls *out* – your bag is gone!" Allusions were also made to *dacoits* (bandits) rampaging through the compartments. In England I had been led to believe that there would be Indians clinging precariously to the roof of the carriages (they don't) or hauling livestock on board as luggage (well, they never did in my experience). I think we get these images from films of India under the British; in reality, the system is efficient. There's a tourist quota for foreign travellers which means a guaranteed reservation, and, as in the West, if someone is in your seat you can show them your ticket and ask them politely to move (unless of course it's a sweet old lady sitting in the window seat, in which case it's not really done to boot her out). There's always the option of the ladies' compartment, although I invariably felt more conspicuous locked into this special coop and, with several children sharing the berths, the atmosphere can become incredibly noisy and chaotic.

> *If I didn't pay someone to sweep my room, make tea and wash my clothes it would be cheating them out of a job.*

Usually I opt for open, mixed compartments and I can't think of anywhere, Western Europe included, that I have felt so safe. You can ask other passengers to keep an eye on your things if you leave your seat for a while; fellow passengers have often commented on my lack of food for the journey and given me some of theirs – it is their duty to look after a stranger – and, although there is always some risk of theft, I have never felt under any personal threat. This is a country where people would definitely not look the other way if someone was being attacked.

Out in the corridors the train transforms itself into a mobile bazaar, with hawkers picking their way through the passengers, shouting lists of just about anything you could conceivably want on a journey: cold drinks, chocolates, cigarettes, newspapers, magazines, a quick shoe polish and, of course, the ubiquitous *chai*. An old blind man comes down the train led by a young girl. He sings, and the man next to me translates: "I am an old man and very poor. I know, as we all know, that wealth brings with it no happiness. So why not give your money to me?"

My first whistle-stop tour of India made such an impact on me that I returned within six months to take up a job teaching the under-fives in a suburb of Calcutta, living in a room above the school. In those first days I tried desperately to get a supply of bottled gas, to cook my own food, but my new family discouraged it. No one really thought I was up to the task. Instead the caretaker's wife cooked for me, and as the weather became more humid, I realized they were right, and am now grateful not to be anywhere near a source of heat. People in India defer to their elders. For a foreigner travelling independently this can be so hard to learn and yet, once you get used to it, it comes as a relief to accept advice.

I teach in the mornings and then, as my friends laughingly say, "go roaming here and there". They cannot understand why I would want to go into the teeming city centre on an almost daily basis. My first stop is invariably the buffet at Howrah station, a large, dark room where I sit at a corner table under a fan, plotting the rest of my day while the waiters hover with fresh pots of tea. The first-floor balcony looks out onto the Ganges and the immense Howrah Bridge of which the Calcuttans are so proud. Later I join the commuters on the ferry across to Babu Ghat, savouring the river breeze and the views of decaying colonial mansions and warehouses lining the banks, or the more domestic scenes of people bathing and washing clothes in the sacred water. Calcutta, I tell my English friends, is the Manchester of India, with theatre, music and dance continuously on offer. The famous writer and musician Tagore and filmmaker Satayjit Ray were both Bengalis, and Saraswati, the goddess of education, is a town favourite. The people here are highly politicized, with strike meetings and demonstrations under the Marxist banner on the grassy *maidan* (park) several times a week.

Everyone I know has servants, including me; I reckon that if I didn't pay someone to sweep my room, make tea and wash my clothes it would be cheating someone out of a job. I start off by telling the caretaker's wife we are equals and I will therefore call her by her first name, Nancy. But later the head of the school takes me to one side and chastises me. "You must call her *bowma* (son's wife), to show her proper respect as the head of this household." In fact, people rarely call each other by their proper names. Younger people in the family are called by their pet name; others are addressed in terms of their relationship to you, *didi, dada* (elder sister, elder brother) for someone about your own age and slightly older, *mashima* (mother's sister) for an auntie, *takma* (mother's mother) for a grandmother figure.

I have my own Bengali family. Asha, who also lives in the school, believes we were sisters in a previous life, and her daughter Khuku calls me auntie, or even "hello-auntie" because I call "hello!" so often. I have my own aunties living nearby, acting as my local guardians. Protima-auntie teaches me *sitar*. She has also tried to instil a love of music into her teenage daughter Tota, who is, however, more interested in meeting her boyfriend on the corner after dark and going for illicit motorbike rides. In my new role as elder sister I try to remonstrate with her, but more often I squeeze on behind them and we cruise the neighbourhood. Having *sitar* lessons is really an opportunity for social contact, a way to have a break from the school and the intensity of living there. One evening I go round. "Go in, go in", says my uncle, "Your auntie is waiting for you". I am shown by a servant into the drawing room. Auntie and Tota are lolling on a sofa watching an old black-and-white Bengali film on the television. The servant sits on the floor in the corner, also watching. I go and sit on the floor next to Protima-auntie; who smiles and strokes my hair. "This is a very old, sad movie", she tells me, and I can see from her crumpled sari end that she has used it several times to wipe her eyes. The cook brings us all a glass of Horlicks and some thin arrowroot biscuits on a plate. The ceiling fans whir. There is a strong smell of Flit (used in the evenings to kill mosquitoes); I still go home that evening with 43 bites on one ankle and 52 on the other.

> *I lie seething on my bed.*
> *Can't she understand?*
> *What is wrong with her?*
> *She, of course, is thinking*
> *the same about me.*

Asha tells me I must not be seen alone in a rickshaw with a man after dark, even if it is a friend's older brother escorting me home. As the months go by I begin to crave physical contact. Young women I meet shyly hold my finger, but the idea of Asha and I hugging is out of the question. On the other hand, she finds it difficult to accept that I cannot share a bed with her, and when a European I don't know too well comes to visit and I make a bed up in another room, Asha's idea of British coldness is reinforced. She says she finds it impossible to sleep alone and when her two sisters, niece and mother come round for the evening, they all sleep together on Asha's big bed. As the months go by and I feel relaxed enough to sleep with friends in the afternoons, I begin to realize how intimate it feels.

The head of the school tries to convince me that going to bed at 7.30pm and getting up at four in the morning is the healthiest regime, I listen politely and tell that in my country we cannot think of such a thing, and if I try and adapt too quickly it will make me sick. The idea of a quiet, unbroken night's sleep seems unknown to many of my friends and noise is the biggest cultural difference I have to try and get used to. I never do. At 5am *bowma* switches her radio on at full volume and is astounded when I, with several hours sleep ahead of me, fly down to the yard like a madwoman. "Turn it off! Turn it off!" I scream. I stamp back to my room and lie seething on my bed. Can't she understand? What is wrong with her? While she, of course, is thinking the same about me.

It's tiring being an ambassador for your country all the time. When my other auntie's son, Sanjoy, suggests a bicycle ride after dark and I realize there's only one bike, and that I will have to put my arm round him in order not to fall off the luggage rack, I jump at the chance. It hasn't been really cool since March, not even at night, but this evening the pre-monsoon rains have dampened down the dust and brought the temperature down a couple of degrees. We cycle for two hours, hardly speaking, my arm clutching his waist, my head sometimes leaning against his back. It's a miracle no one in the neighbourhood sees me and reports back, but this evening I don't care. This is the greatest intimacy I can imagine here.

I'm teaching one day when my friend Modhomita rushes in: "Frances, I have come to invite you to my wedding!" she exclaims, "It's next Monday!" I am rather startled, as I saw her a couple of weeks ago and she mentioned nothing then, but she is 29 and so I suppose time is of the essence. I ask her what the prospective groom is like, but as she's only met him a couple of times, and always with family members present, she can't exactly say.

On the afternoon of her wedding I arrive to find she's been up since dawn and hasn't eaten a thing. She's just spent four hours with the beautician and her face is wonderfully made up. Her voice has been reduced to a nervous croak and, against the tradition, her friends secretly slip her a drink of water and a snack. Throughout the day about two hundred guests mill around and eat the food that Modhomita's father has laid on. Around midnight, with half the ceremony completed, I search her out. She and her half-husband are seated side by side on a dais, receiving more guests and many more presents. They are waiting for the most auspicious hour for the completion of the wedding, about one thirty in the morning. "I'm absolutely starving", she confides in me as I sit next to her for a photo. She then asks me quietly, her voice shaking, "What is he like? Do you think he is a good man?" I go round to his side and have a few words – a few more than Modhomita herself has had. He seems nervous too, which I take as a good sign, and I reassure her as best I can.

Next day, at the leave-taking ceremony, Modhomita severs all ties with her former life and submits entirely to her husband's rule. She touches the feet of her much-loved aunties and uncles and everyone is distraught. "How are you enjoying our Bengali wedding?" I am asked many times by smiling relatives, "You must find it very interesting." I find it difficult to know what to say. At times like this I find it hard to stop myself from commenting that although in my country "sex is freely available" at least a woman doesn't feel obliged to sleep with a man she has never even had a conversation with.

At some point – and it's hard for a foreigner to discover when – you become accepted as part of the family. After that, people continually raise their eyes to the ceiling and cry "Why be so *formal*?" (If I ask for a second cup of tea, saying please, for example, or maybe say thank you for the first one.) When this point came with me I thought I had finally adjusted, and then things became more difficult. I think I'm beginning to understand and then I relax too much and offend. Asha doesn't talk to me for a week after

> *I was inspected and pitied – a pale, short-haired Britisher with no make-up, no jewellery, no husband and dirty feet.*

an argument where I end up telling her that if she's going to shout she can leave my room (apparently the most offensive thing I could have said and I'm lucky she ever came back); and where I shouldn't have disagreed with her in the first place, as I'm her younger sister (the age difference is maybe a couple of years). We only make up because, she says, she is prepared to make allowances for me being British. I also make the mistake of being too relaxed with the fathers of the children in my class. Being asked to visit is awkward sometimes – too often it is the husbands who invite me round to find out what an English woman is really like, while the wives spend a couple of extra hours in the kitchen preparing special food. It's tricky also when the husband walks you to the gate and tells you how restrictive arranged marriages are, what a lot of adjustments have to be made and, by the way, what beautiful hair you have.

It's not surprising that misunderstandings should occur across cultures, when there are so many differences between Indians themselves of caste, class, ethnic background. Two of my students live across the road. They are Marhoori, the business caste from Rajasthan, looked down on by Bengalis as *nouveau riche*. And they are rich indeed, with a mini-bus, a car (with driver), a motorbike, a Nepali houseboy, and a doorkeeper. The Rotary Club meets at their house and while the men discuss the minutes of last month's meeting, the women lounge on divans, waiting to criticize the food. I was invited, inspected and pitied – a pale, short-haired Britisher with no make-up, no jewellery, no husband and dirty feet. These are the monied elite of Indian society and, for most of the evening they ignore me.

But I am not poor. Sanjoy, coming with me to the pictures one day, was shocked when we were pursued by a woman begging. "They don't try so hard with us", he said. Her words translated as "Have pity on me. You are young, you have your mother and father. I have no one, no son or daughter to care for me." I go to New Market and buy lemon tarts or fudge brownies from the Jewish bakery; I browse in *Oxford Bookstore* or read my daily paper at *Flury's* while waiting for my order of Viennese coffee and fresh cream meringues. There is even a branch of *Benetton* here, and a man with eaten-away fingers asking for money in the street outside. No matter how much I think I have adjusted, I know I can always leave, and it is having options, rather than actual money, that makes all the difference.

After six months in Calcutta I began doing some work at Mother Teresa's. It had been so long since I was with other foreigners that it seemed strange to mix with them again: to go sightseeing or drinking in a group, flirting mildly, exchanging gossip – odd but interesting and good for me, a chance to relax into the shared experiences with no need to explain myself.

By June it is getting hot and the humidity becomes intense, about ninety-eight percent. I wake in a sweat every morning at 5.30am, tired and irritated. The evenings are blotted by pre monsoon showers. I switch off my fan and listen to the rain, to the caretaker's music, to a *puja* in the park, street-dogs fighting and the nightwatchmen blowing their whistles round the block. I lay dreaming of street cafés, of watching TV, relaxing in a hot bath and having a good night's sleep. When I start to listen to Western cassettes I know it must be time to leave; for six months music from home has sounded strange and out of place. I battled it out in my diary: "Oh, to be home. Oh, not to be home."

It is strange to think of being in London within a couple of days, working with a wealthy British family. The past six months condense into a series of flashbacks; of conversations on balconies, on verandah steps, in the dark; of moments of intimacy where secrets are told; of tensions that both sides have to adjust to. I wonder if, knowing I could leave at any moment, this country can ever be more than two-dimensional, a place to dabble, watch, be detached. On my last day everyone comes to see me off, *bowma* and her husband, Asha's family, my aunties, all crowd to the gate and straggle down the road behind me, waving and calling. I cry and cry; we're all too choked to speak. Sanjoy takes me to the station. The local bus lurches over Howrah Bridge and I let Sanjoy organize me onto the train.

It's difficult to return to English life. Everything seems strange, much stranger than India when I first arrived there. Lying on my English auntie's sofa with a cat on my lap, eating granary toast, and getting out of a hot shower and feeling cold (instead of the other way round); the pavements seem so wide and empty, and the supermarkets have such an excessive selection of goods that I panic. People ask me "But how did you cope with the poverty? Didn't you get sick? Isn't it very dirty?", and more than that they don't seem to want to know, or perhaps can't really grasp.

I am preparing to go back again, my plan being to return every two years. Hopefully, one day my friends will be able to visit me at home and understand more about my culture. In the meantime, I realize how much I've learnt from them; I value my family more and visit them a lot more often. I'm also not so complacent; it's very sobering to have close friends for whom life is a real struggle and it helps me to be more clear about decisions I have to take. And I've learnt not to be so independent, to listen to the experience of others and realize that I don't know it all.

Between Two Cultures

Smita Patel, a British Asian woman, took five months off from her job at a feminist publishing house to travel with her boyfriend to India and Southeast Asia. At that time it was still possible for travellers to visit the state of Kashmir, now considered a no-go area as a result of guerrilla attacks and tourist kidnappings by Kashmiri separatists.

This was not my first visit to India. Like most second generation Indians I had been taken to the subcontinent as a child and young teenager. But these journeys had always been considered as a duty or "family visit", not as a means of exploring the country or even mixing with the community at large. I had always been aware that as an Indian girl my role was to accept the guidance and protection of my relatives. Returning as an adult independent woman, I knew that I would face problems and dilemmas, and even more so travelling with a white boyfriend.

Our trip had been planned as part of wider travels to the East spanning five months. I was fairly confident about travelling independently (having done so alone and with friends to Europe and Africa) but the warnings of other Asian women surprised and disturbed me. India, I was told, would be different and travelling with a white partner I should expect much more harassment and abuse. My mind was full of doubts and pre-judgments but I drew comfort from the fact that India was a country which has witnessed hordes of travellers of almost every race and nationality, exploring every inch of its land.

I remember arriving at Delhi airport at 3am, feeling apprehensive, excited and with really no more idea of what to expect than any of the other travellers from the West. After waiting hours for our baggage we made our first tentative steps onto the independent travellers' trail. It was now 6am and though the sun had barely risen the whole area outside the airport was packed with people: families, beggars, police, rickshaw wallahs, fruit vendors, taxi men, and of course the famed hotel touts, urging bleary new arrivals to follow them to the "best room in town". Luckily we had got talking to an American woman on the plane who was being met by her brother who had been living in India for three years, and despite being heavily jet-lagged we managed to struggle out of the chaos and find them. As Ben had been living on a low budget for a year he steered us towards India's cheapest mode of transport, the local bus. It looked ancient and decrepit and I was convinced it would never make the distance into Delhi city.

Even though I had witnessed such scenes as a child, I was still bewildered at the extreme deprivation we came across.

In India you learn quickly how to shove your way to the front. We piled on to the bus with what seemed like hundreds of others although, as a woman, I was immediately offered a seat by one of our Indian fellow passengers. It took about an hour to reach the city along a road marked by small dwellings and shanty towns made out of cardboard, rubber, tin, in fact anything that the poor could get their hands on. Even though I had witnessed such scenes as a child and heard of India's poverty, I was still bewildered at the extreme deprivation we were to come across during our stay.

Our first week in Delhi was just as I had visualized it and childhood memories suddenly flooded back. We were staying in the Main Bazaar area of Delhi, near the railway station. This is an old marketplace, full of tiny shops and ablaze with colour. Strange and exotic smells hang in the air while fruit and vegetable sellers clamour over the prices for the day, and rickshaws and bikes swerve through the streets, avoiding the sacred cows that amble in their path. At that stage we were using other travellers' tips and living on a very tight budget. Like most backpackers we tended to be attracted to hotels and eating places where white travellers would meet or end up. To begin with I was unaware that my presence among mostly white men would be seen as strange and immoral behaviour by the Indian men who ran the hotels and eating places.

From the moment of our arrival both Max and I had taken care to dress and act according to Indian customs. At no time did we publicly show affection towards each other such as holding hands, kissing or even being physically close. In England I had been brought up to dress "respectfully" in the presence of family and community so this was not new to me. However, despite our attempts to merge in I soon discovered that being an Asian woman travelling among independent travellers I was perceived very differently by Indian men. People didn't always notice that I was with a white man, especially if Max and I were looking at different things, but as soon as we were together the stares intensified and men would start making comments and even touching me as they walked past. Understanding Hindi made me aware of all the insulting comments being made about me.

As a child growing up in an Indian family I had learnt intuitively when to be silent. In India I was silent again.

Sometimes this would lead to more direct harassment, with men changing seats so they could touch me, often in full view of Max as if wishing to provoke a reaction from him as well. On one occasion, six men got into the compartment and all took turns to offend me, including trying to sit on my lap. I also often heard men describing white women as loose and sexually available. It was clear that to them I was a "white product", a British-born woman doing what mostly white women do, flaunting my independence by travelling around with a white man.

We also experienced men approaching Max and talking about me as though I was invisible and had no mind of my own. I was made to feel like an appendage, passive and speaking only through him. Towards the end of our travels I had given up trying to explain my own point of view and simply let Max do all the talking. I felt caught between differing sets of values, having to play an uneasy shifting game of what was expected from an Indian woman. As a child growing up in an Indian family I had experienced a similar "balancing out" of values and had learnt intuitively when to be silent. In India I was silent again, superficially accepting men's behaviour towards me simply to get through a hassle-free day of travelling. But this passivity became much harder as time wore on. Things came to a head in Varanasi, where after only three days I had been subjected to so much abuse and harassment that I retreated to my hotel room and wept. I knew this was not an overreaction or paranoia as white travellers had noticed and commented on how differently I was being treated.

I was left with the feeling that perhaps the two different sides of me just did not fit into Indian life. My attempts to cover up my feminism and, by taking a passive role, to try and gain the approval of Indian men, soon gave way to overwhelming resentment. It was mortifying when I realized that I was dismissing part of my own culture in a way that can only be described as racist. Unfortunately, being so isolated from other Indian women – I experienced little or no contact with them – my experiences in India were very much male-dominated.

These extremely harassing times contrasted with some blissfully relaxed moments. After leaving India to spend a while trekking in the Himalayas we returned to spend our last three weeks in Kashmir and Ladakh. Kashmir is known as a tourist attraction and in the month of June many Indians themselves leave the hot plains to cool off in the Kashmir hills. We headed for Dal lake and found a house run by an old Kashmiri man who was obviously respected in the community. We were taken under his family's wing and I experienced no sexual harassment during the stay; due mainly, I am sure, to the fact that his many relatives acknowledged and therefore protected us.

Travelling around India I learnt what it felt like to be an outsider in a culture which I regard as part of my own. My experiences, however, were very personal and I really couldn't say how much they'd apply to other British Asian women travellers. Certainly, the prejudice we encountered as a mixed race couple is not confined to India alone. Returning to England left me in complete culture shock and finding my bearings in British society has again taken time.

T R A V E L   N O T E S

Languages Although Hindi is the official national language there are hundreds of other regional languages and dialects. A hangover from the days of the Raj, English is widely spoken and generally understood.

Transport Trains are the main form of transport. Most tourists use second-class reserved seats (second-class unreserved gets ludicrously crowded and is best avoided). Some trains also have compartments reserved exclusively for women. Buying and reserving your tickets may take time; sometimes there are separate queues for women – worth taking advantage of since they massively cut down time. If you've got money you can fly between major cities but you should be prepared to face frequent delays.

Accommodation A whole range of hotels from expensive luxury palace-style accommodation to bug-ridden cells. There is no shortage of inexpensive, clean and perfectly safe places to stay. A government tourist bungalow (middling price range) is usually a safe bet. With so much choice there's never any need to stay in a hotel where you feel uneasy.

Special Problems If you don't take care with your diet, various kinds of dysentery and infective hepatitis are hazards, though you might get away with just a dose of "Delhi belly". It makes sense not to drink unboiled water or to eat unpeeled fruit. Always get enough rest – many travellers set themselves exhausting, unrealistic itineraries that no Indian person would ever attempt.

Tales of theft and pickpocketing are, in general, vastly exaggerated. Crime levels in India are a lot lower than in Western countries. In the cities, however, you will find scores of hustlers fighting for your attention, and should you learn quickly how to stay calm and clear-headed. It's a good idea to carry small change to give to beggars, or a little food to share with children.

Women's Holidays Tiger Travel is a women's travel company that organizes specialist women-only tours to all parts of the subcontinent. Highly recommended for their expert knowledge of the main destinations and sensitive, unpretentious approach to travel. Besides their general tours, they offer adventure packages (mountain biking through Ladakh or white river rafting down the Indus) and offer tailor-made holidays for small groups of women. In the UK contact 6 Silver St, Buckfastleigh, Devon, England (☎/fax 01364 64370): in Delhi; J67 Kirti Nagar, New Delhi, 110015 (☎011 5419719; fax 91 11 5453434).

Guides The Rough Guide to India (Penguin), a new title in the series, draws together almost all the information you could conceivably need on a tour round the subcontinent. Lonely Planet publish regional guides to Ladakh and Zanskar and a trekking guide to the Indian Himalayas. For cultural detail the Murray's Handbook to India (UK, John Murray), though originally published half a century ago, remains in a class of its own.

CONTACTS

New Delhi: Institute of Social Studies (ISS), 5 Deen Dayal Upadhyaya Marg, New Delhi 2. Voluntary, non-profit research organization – concentrates on women's access to employment and role in development, also on strengthening women's organizations. The group publishes a newsletter.

Indian Council of Social Science Research (ICSSR), 11PA Hostel, Indraprastha Estate, Ring Rd, New Delhi, 110002. Runs a women's studies programme and carries out wide-ranging research. They also organize numerous workshops and symposia on feminist themes.

Manushi, c/202 Lajpat Nagar, New Delhi 110024. Publishes the monthly journal Manushi – an excellent source of information on news and analysis of women's situation and struggle in India. Written in English and Hindi. The journal can be obtained in the UK from Manushi c/o Colworth Rd, London E11; in the US from Manushi, c/o 5008 Erringer Place, Philadelphia, PA 19144.

Kali for Women (feminist publishers), N 84 Panchshila Park, New Delhi, 110017.

Bangalore: Streelekha (International feminist bookshop and information centre), 67, 2nd floor, Blumoan Complex, Mahatma Gandhi Rd, Bangalore 560 011, Karnataka. Stocks all manner of feminist literature, journals and posters, and provides space for women to meet.

Bombay: Feminist Resource Centre (FRD), 13 Carol Mansion, 35 Sitladevi Temple Rd, Mahim, Bombay 400016. Carries out action-oriented research from a feminist perspective on a range of issues: health, sexuality, violence against women, discrimination at work.

BOOKS

⭐ **Dervla Murphy**, Full Tilt (1965; UK, Flamingo, 1995/US, Overlook Press, 1987). A seminal piece of travel literature. After years of confinement looking after her parents in rural Ireland, Dervla Murphy cycles three thousand miles to India. Extraordinarily intrepid and inspiring in the warmth and openess she brings to life on the road. On a Shoe-string to Coorg: An Experience of Southern India (1976; UK, Century, 1985/US, Transatlantic Arts, 1977) charts her return trip to Asia with her five-year-old daughter Rachel. Dense forests, mountains, paddy fields and coffee plantations are viewed afresh through the eyes of a young child.

Elisabeth Bumiller, May You Be the Mother of a Hundred Sons: A Journey Among the Women of India (US, Fawcett, 1991). Perceptive travelogue focusing on women – from feminists and Indira Gandhi to Bombay actresses and impoverished village women.

Sarah Hobson, Family Web (UK, John Murray, 1978, o/p/US, Academy of Chicago Publications, 1993). While living in a village in rural Karnataka, Hobson recorded everyday conversations, often verbatim, touching on the status of women, sex, family-planning, kinship and local politics.

Sarah Lloyd, An Indian Attachment (UK, Eland, 1992/US, Hippocrene Books). Lloyd writes of the two years she spent in a remote Indian village with her Sikh lover. An accomplished account but one which leaves you wondering about the exploitative aspects of writing.

Imogen Lycett-Green, Grandmother's Footsteps (UK, Macmillan, 1994). The grandmother in question, Penelope Betjeman, visited India throughout her life, later leading tours in the Himalayas where she died in 1986. The author's account of retracing the steps of an unforgettable trip they made together is much enlivened by extracts from Betjeman's letters and diaries.

Gita Mehta, Karma Cola (UK, Fontana, 1979/US, Simon & Schuster, o/p). Now slightly dated, this is still a sharp and cynical look at the way Indian spirituality is marketed for Western devotees.

Philippa Pullar, The Shortest Journey (UK, Unwin, 1984, o/p/US, Trafalgar House, 1982, o/p). Unimpressed by a successful career in the West, Pullar seeks enlightenment on a trip to

India. She discovers, unsurprisingly, that the path to freedom lies within, but at least gleans an amusing travel book from the well-worn journey.

Heather Wood, *Third-Class Ticket* (UK, Penguin, 1984/US, Penguin, 1990). A rich landowner left some money to the villagers in a small Bengali village, in order that they might "see all of India". Heather Wood joined them for a part of their journey.

Emily Eden, *Up the Country: Letters from India* (1866; UK, Virago, 1983/US, Virago edition available). Having accompanied her brother to India when he took up the post of Governor General, Emily Eden amused herself, and an avid Victorian public with these witty finely tuned accounts of life on the road – in a regal cavalcade heading towards Shimla.

Madhu Kishwar and Ruth Vanita (eds), *In Search of Answers: Indian Women's Voices* (UK, Zed Books, 1984/US, Humanities Press, 1984). Collection of articles from *Manushi* which provides a comprehensive, powerful and lucid account of women in Indian society.

Jeniffer Sebstad, *Women and Self-Reliance in India: the SEWA story* (UK, Zed Books, 1985/US, Humanities Press, 1986). Account of the formation and achievements of SEWA (see the chapter introduction).

FICTION

Urvashi Butalia and Ritu Menon (eds), *In Other Words. New Writing by Indian Women* (US, Westview, 1994). Edited by the co-founders of *Kali for Women*, these lively stories paint a vivid picture of womens' lives in post-Independence India.

Anita Desai, *Clear Light of Day* (UK, Penguin, 1980); *Baumgartner's Bombay* (UK, Penguin, 1981/US, Knopf, 1989). The best-known titles from a widely acclaimed and prolific writer. Her books chart the changing position of women in a rapidly developing society.

Leena Dhingra, *Amritvela* (UK, The Women's Press, 1988). Stylish account of a middle-aged woman's return to her native India after a life in England.

Attia Housain, *Sunlight on a Broken Column* (UK, Virago, 1988, o/p/US, Penguin, 1989, o/p). Set against the backdrop of Indian Independence this centres on the life of an orphaned girl growing up in a fundamentalist Muslim community.

Ruth Prawer Jhabvala, *Heat and Dust* (UK, Futura, 1976/US, Simon & Schuster, 1987); *A Backward Place* (UK, Penguin, 1979), and others. Famous as a Booker prize-winner and long-time collaborator on Merchant/Ivory films, Jhabvala's writing charts the more irrational responses to Indian life.

Padma Perera, *Birthday, Deathday* (UK, The Women's Press, 1985). Short stories, most of which explore the contradictions for an Indian woman educated in the West on returning to her homeland.

Sharan-Jat Shar, *In My Own Name* (UK, The Women's Press, 1985/US, Salem House Publications, 1987). Autobiographical account of growing up in the Punjab, a life that includes forced marriage and emigration.

Indonesia

I ndonesia extends over a vast chain of more than ten thousand islands. Though remote and exotic by European or American standards, for millions of Australians and New Zealanders this island nation constitutes the nearest form of "abroad". Consequently, at least on better-known islands, Indonesians are well used to independent travellers and, alongside the thriving package-tour industry (with developments particularly along the beaches of Bali), there is plenty of inexpensive, basic accommodation.

Despite being rich in resources, Indonesia has a very low standard of living, exacerbated by a rapid growth in population. This is most evident on the island of Java which now holds over 160 million people – most of whom are crammed into its polluted, chaotic, and heavily policed capital, Jakarta. As the

nation's administrative centre, Java's influence, known as "System Jakarta", is widely resented and often disparaged as the successor to Dutch colonial rule.

In a nation of so many cultures, religions and languages, it is perhaps surprising that different groups manage to coexist and that the country as a whole has an image of stability. But the underside of this is the harsh, swift, and often brutal suppression of any opposition to General Suharto's regime, that has included the forced resettlement of islanders and the brutal military occupation of East Timor and West Irian.

The people of Indonesia are predominantly Muslim but tend to be tolerant towards the different habits of Westerners. It does help, however, to show respect for local customs and dress modestly with arms and legs covered. Except in the relatively undeveloped island of Sumatra (see p. 334) reputation as something of a troublespot for women travellers, and provided you are careful to respect local customs, you are unlikely to encounter sexual harassment on an aggressive scale. You will however attract a fair amount of attention (often just steadfast curiosity) which can feel oppressive at times. Indonesians neither share, nor sympathize with, the Western preoccupation with personal space, and privacy is something you have to learn quickly to do without. One of the more disturbing aspects of this trait are the peepholes you may find in the walls of your hotel room.

Indonesian **women** certainly seem more independent and visible than in many Islamic countries. The islands' interpretation of Islam does not demand that women are veiled, government schools are co-educational, and there is relatively little discrimination between the sexes with respect to subjects studied and the number of years spent studying. Whether this will endure is uncertain. Despite government curbs, Islamic fundamentalism has recently gained ground, attempting to reaffirm Malay culture in opposition to Western influence.

An Uneasy Choice of Companion

After a short spell working in Japan (see p.381), **Sarah Dale** visited Sumatra, one of Indonesia's largest islands, still relatively untouched by tourism. This was her first trip to Southeast Asia, where she travelled alone, only occasionally linking up with other travellers.

Oddly enough, it was the challenge of Sumatra's reputation as a "no go" zone for women travelling on their own that enticed me away from the more well-beaten Southeast Asian track. It was therefore a bit of an anti-climax when I arrived, only to encounter a bunch of other similarly challenged women, plotting their journeys south. Annoyed at being thwarted, I decided to head north instead to the remote island of Pulau Weh. I could either take the newly laid coastal road from Medan, the capital, or the old dirt track through the middle of the country, an area known as the Gunung Leuser National Park. With 800,000 hectares of virgin rainforest, this is one of the largest parks in the world, hosting such exotic animals as gibbons, orangutans, monkeys, elephants, tigers and the rare Sumatran rhinoceros. I plumped for the dirt track.

One of the girls that I met in Sumatra, Rachel, also fancied heading north. Knowing the region was little visited by travellers we decided to go together. Our departure point was Kutacane Bus Station. Bus stations, it has to be said, are the most stressful places to be in Sumatra if you are a Western woman. One step in and you get besieged by dozens of touts screaming manically for your business and then charging you triple the real fare. Most irritating, though, are the groups of men who frequent these places and whose sole purpose in life seems to be to pinch girls' bottoms. My strategy in these situations was to alight the bus with confidence, my day pack strapped across my front – thereby pre-empting any unwelcome boob-grabbing – and my larger pack on my back. One firm swing could fell up to three bottom-pinchers in one go!

Our bus was the usual ramshackle collection of metal, gaily adorned with brightly coloured bunting around the window tops. Buses are ideal for people watching. The women sit surrounded by children, the smallest tied to their bodies with sarongs. Wide grins betray what's left of their teeth and gums, stained scarlet by the tranquil chewing of betelnut. Meanwhile the men draw on strong sickly smelling clove cigarettes and fill the bus with smoke.

There are no timetables: buses simply leave once they are bursting at the seams. You know you're on your way when the driver switches on an ear-splitting cacophony which passes for music, guaranteed to jangle the nerves. The narrow, winding road was filled with potholes making for a bumpy ride. Around us everyone was vomiting, which surprised me as I thought local people would be used to such conditions. There was no fussing with sick bags or aiming for windows. Passengers just threw up on the floor – too bad if your backpack or your bare feet were in the way. I coped by looking stoically into the distance, not hard since the park's views of cloud-capped mountains, open fields and thick dense jungle were the most glorious I have ever seen.

The window seat had its drawbacks. While men happily let their children chuck up on my backpack, they would be especially careful not to drop their cigarette ash on the floor. So careful in fact that they would have to lean right across me in the manoeuvre to flick it out of the window, managing to brush against my breasts. A steel cap bra would have come in useful, but a firm stare usually did the trick.

Touching in public between members of the opposite sex in Sumatra, as in most Muslim countries, is absolutely taboo. Touching between the same sex however is rampant. It never ceased to surprise me that pairs of middle-aged men could stroll happily down the road arm in arm. It seemed to have no sexual connotation, simply revealing a healthy understanding of the need we all have at times to touch and to be touched.

Rachel merrily went about wearing skimpy shorts, sleeveless tops and no bra.

Covering up was *de rigueur*. The locals were offended by bare flesh and despite sweltering heat and my longing for a tan I always wore long trousers, socks and a long-sleeved top. Rachel on the other hand merrily went about wearing skimpy shorts, sleeveless tops and no bra. Every time our bus bounced over a pothole so did Rachel's boobs. When we hit a kangaroo jump her breasts and the men's eyes rose and fell in perfect synchronicity. I tried to mention something about respecting the local culture but her view was that since the men did not respect her she could not respect them back. Apart from the very poor, Sumatran women were always covered up. I found it was safer and less hassle to follow suit. There was a marked difference in the men's behaviour to the two of us; Rachel attracted all of the touching yet seemed totally unruffled. The further north we travelled, the more women concealed themselves until eventually we hardly saw them in public.

One of the joys of travel can be the other travellers you meet along the way, especially when travelling alone. It's made me more open about people, whom I've generally learned to accept for whoever they are. I must admit, though, that Rachel took some accepting. Sometimes a degree of circumspection about fellow travellers might be advisable. For instance, Rachel told me that she was psychic. This was all well and good when she stuck to predicting that I would one day be married with 2.2 kids – the best she could come up with on the husband front was a short balding doctor. But it was another story when her psychic powers led her to take instantaneous likings to complete strangers on buses, telling men what beautiful faces and wonderful auras they had.

In school, Indonesians learn that "Hello Mister" is the polite salutation for foreigners, be they male or female. Each day before we stepped out I had to psychologically prepare myself for the hello brigades that patrolled every corner. From fifty different directions we would be fired with a battery of "Hello Mister. What your name? Where you from? Where you go? I love you!" Rachel chattered away oblivious and I admired her resilience; the attention never wore her down. However, I didn't admire her habit of touching her breasts each time she referred to herself. This sort of thing was precisely what caught the men's eyes like magnets. Whenever we came to rest her bra would be off again. It was all too much for the local men. Places were panting.

Nothing provoked a reaction as nothing could be odder than the sight of our white skin, corn-coloured hair and big noses.

It was hours since our departure and we had travelled only thirty kilometres to Ketembe, the first village on route. We should have rested here overnight, but we had the bug for charting new territory and decided to soldier on a further forty kilometres to the next village, Blangkejeran.

We were penetrating deeper into the jungle. By this time our tiny winding potholed road had become an even tinier and more winding gravel path. We had to leave the big bus and climb aboard a *bemo*, a pickup truck with seats for about six people and a roof for storing baggage. The floor was lined with bags of grain and coconuts upon which perched some twenty Sumatrans, one of whom had two live chickens to sell at market. Once we were well into the jungle and away from officialdom the driver let me climb on to the roof. The panoramic views were spectacular as I clung on for dear life, drinking up the beauty with the wind rushing past my face. I was on top of the world.

Suddenly a torrential downpour started. Reluctantly I left the roof and found a coconut to perch on beside Rachel. We chattered away whilst the chickens pecked our bottoms and flapped in our faces. It quickly grew dark and with our legs dangling out of the back of the *bemo*, we stared into the deep blackness, counting fireflies.

The *bemo* had broken down several times already, so when it stopped yet again we didn't worry too much. Then the woman with the chickens did a spectacular mime of a downpour of rain causing a huge landslide down the mountainside and finally the penny dropped. We climbed out to inspect and found eleven *bemos* parked where we had halted. I walked to the front one, but it was too dark to see the landslide blocking the path. It became obvious that we were stuck in the jungle for the night. People lit bonfires to keep warm and staved off hunger pains with tomatoes meant for market. It got very chilly and we pulled on every single item of clothing from inside our backpacks. By this time the other twenty passengers and the two chickens had stretched themselves over our spaces in the *bemo* and there was no room left for us. Eventually one of the drivers gave in and said we could sleep upright in the front of his truck, where we spent an uneasy night, jostling each other for room.

We awoke to the sunrise and the windows of our truck surrounded by children, held in a trance. They had never seen white people before. We smiled, but their faces betrayed no reaction. The more this inscrutable sea of children stared the more we twitched and winked and pulled funny faces until it became faintly embarrassing. Nothing could provoke a reaction because nothing could be odder than the mere sight of our white skin, corn-coloured hair and big noses.

In daylight we could see that the landslide was 4m high and about 5m across. Before any of the *bemos* could continue the journey we had to wait for a bulldozer to come and move the landslide away. Amazingly one arrived and in pristine condition – this was clearly one event the Sumatrans were prepared for. The landslide took one and a half hours to shift, as the machine lumbered back and forth hurtling a mass of rubble and uprooted trees down the mountainside. Soon afterwards two German hikers coming from the opposite direction told us there were twelve more landslides stretching over the next three kilometres. Unless we were prepared to spend another night in the jungle we had to start walking.

Rolling up our trousers legs, we took off our trainers and socks and got stuck in. The ground was soft and wet; each footstep began with mud gurgling up between our toes and finished with a thigh-deep plunge. The road was in a terrible state. Huge chunks of it had literally been cut away by the landslides and great waterfalls gushed over the edges. But walking was the the best way to appreciate the park: with no engine noise we could listen to the sounds of the jungle and slowly luxuriate in the views.

When we eventually got through there was a trusty *bemo* waiting for us on the other side. It was full so we climbed on to the empty roof, where-upon all the male passengers got out and joined us. Maybe it was the adventure of the landslides that got them going, but these men were especially taunting. They had a way of laughing that jeered and allowed the paranoia to flood in. They pushed one another and dared each other to touch our arms, our faces, our hair. I was still wearing my long trousers and long-sleeved top and in the equatorial heat I was managing to brew up a healthy whiff. Something I hoped would act as a deterrent! The Muslim religion is pretty strict about sex and the Gunung Leuser National Park is very remote. Consequently foreign girls present an exciting opportunity to a populace whose only contact with the West is the occasional Hollywood movie. An illustration of this was told to me by a girl I later met who cycled through the park. She was pedalling through a particularly remote village when packs of people burst out of their houses and recognizing her haircut ran after her shouting "Demi Moore, Demi Moore!"

> The walls were littered with peep holes. As I set to stuffing them up, Rachel declared that she was going to sleep naked.

We finally arrived at Blangkejeran, having taken twenty-four hours to travel just forty kilometres. Consisting of one main street flanked by wooden buildings, the place reminded me of a dusty mid-American town straight out of some Western. While men sat outside their houses talking and smoking clove cigarettes, women were barely visible except in the market.

A crowd of enthusiastic villagers showed us to Blangkejeran's main guest house and it was great to have a place to rest and take a *mandi*, the Indonesian equivalent of a shower. Every bathroom has the usual crouch-down toilet and a large bath filled with cold water which you scoop up and throw over yourself. Bathing this way is wonderfully refreshing in the sweltering heat. However, the *mandi* in this guest house had a school of fish swimming in it. The landlord said I must not mind but should try not to throw any of the fish over me since they were destined for dinner that night! We went out to eat.

The walls of our room were littered with peep holes. As I set to stuffing them up with a roll of toilet paper and elastoplast, Rachel suddenly declared that she was going to sleep naked that night. It was so hot, she argued, and even if our neighbours did make new peep holes it would be too dark to see. "But it's broad daylight now," I snapped and threw a sarong over her. I was exasperated. She simply could not seem to appreciate that as we were travelling as a couple each of our actions bore consequences for the other. I pulled on my smelly trousers and tried to sleep.

We were kept awake by the incredibly loud TV and then woken up at 5.30am by the man in the next room chanting his morning prayers. The walls were very thin and there was no hope of sleep, but I felt soothed by the regularity of the prayers which were strangely reassuring. Then I noticed fresh peep holes on the side of the praying man, who ripped out a fart mid-prayer. Our suppressed giggles got Rachel and I on speaking terms again, until she started to make loud raspberry noises and did a horrible imitation of the praying. I expected the wrath of Allah to fall down on us and just waited, cringing in shame.

Takengon was a beautiful town at the end of the park. It had a huge lake and would have been a treat to explore, but I was keen to move on to Pulau Weh. We said our goodbyes and I took the next bus to Aceh, the capital of Northern Sumatra.

At last I was alone. I got the usual stares, but none of the earlier shouting or touching. While I was waiting for the bus to Aceh I became friends with a young Muslim girl who was dressed in the traditional long clothes and head dress. I really noticed a change in the men's behaviour when I was with her. I was no longer hassled and I could sense the respect they had for her as a Muslim woman, something I had previously underestimated. I don't know if this difference in behaviour was because I was out of the jungle where the people seemed so raw or because I was with her and I was covered up. I was just happy to feel at ease.

On reaching Pulau Weh I was glad to have met the challenge of the park and seen all its beautiful scenery. At the same time, it was a relief to be on my own again and I felt a lot safer and more in control of my own destiny. I like travelling with other people and have made some marvellous friends this way, but have learned also to be a little more careful about who I travel with. I have to admit, though, that even now – more than six months since I met Rachel – I still keep half an eye open for a short balding man with a medical degree.

A Plant Collector's Dream

After spending four weeks in the well-travelled islands of Java, Lombok and Bali, **Janet Bell** spent six months collecting medicinal plants on Seram, a small island in the Moluccas in the far east of Indonesia.

Joseph and Meli were transfixed by the teabag I had produced from my pack. It wasn't until we lit a fire and made a brew that they were fully satisfied that its contents were what I'd promised. What delight! Joseph's face lit up at the taste and he chuckled quietly.

The light was fading and the almost saturated mist had become quite chill. I still couldn't believe that we were only two degrees south of the equator and I was craving a woolly sweater. The drop in temperature associated with altitude seemed more pronounced than I was used to, but by now the only too familiar mountainous terrain had also modified my attitude to height, when I considered that we were already about the same height as Ben Nevis.

Indonesia's dramatic and varied scenery continued to amaze me. Seram was completely different from the fertile, highly-populated, volcanic islands of Java, Bali and Lombok, which had served as my introduction to this huge and diverse country.

While I cooked some food for our demanding stomachs, Joseph and Meli collected ferns and made a mattress under the overhang, our shelter for the night. Little did I realize at the time that it was for my benefit, not theirs. We ate our rice with some dried spiced fish from the coastal village we'd left that morning. Rice was something of a treat for all of us since, unlike most of Indonesia, sago was the staple diet in the Moluccas. However, its wallpaper-paste-like consistency scarcely lent it the characteristics of good hiking fodder, and neither did the flavour.

Joseph and Meli experimented with a teabag themselves while I dealt with my pack. Everything I produced was questioned – "Apa ini?" (what is it?), "Untuk apa?" (what's it for?); my torch, my knife, my first-aid kit, even my loo roll, for which I could provide no explanation. The things I considered essential seemed trivial, when all my companions' needs fitted into a small pouch. Still, they seemed grateful for the odd garment I offered for the night.

I snuggled down on my temporary bed and contemplated the sky above me. It was rare to have the opportunity to sleep under the stars without fear of a night-time downpour. The overhang would protect me sufficiently without blocking my view. I looked up the steep gorge, which was strongly illuminated by the moon, despite the night being somewhat overcast. I thought that if I were to awake during the night once the clouds had cleared, I would probably think it was morning. Already a long way beneath us, I heard the Wai Lala rushing down from the ridge we were heading over, its swirling blue waters ricocheting relentlessly against the sides of the gorge as it plummeted to the south coast.

The morning was chilly. Meli prepared himself for the climb by viciously rubbing *sila* leaves all over his legs and producing huge red welts similar to nettle stings, but far more painful. The locals used the leaves whenever they undertook a long trip to ease weariness in their limbs and to ward off cold at higher altitudes. It seemed more like shock treatment to me. Still, I made a note in my book to add to my ever-increasing list of plants used by the local people.

That was, after all, my reason for being on this rugged, paradisical island, 2500km from Jakarta. This particular trip was taking me inland over an 1800m pass, one of the lowest points in the dramatic ridge that separated the interior villages from the coast, a formidable barrier that still isolates them from the fingers of commercialism which have encroached upon the coastal villages. The ridge, I learned, is much more than a physical barrier, but has a significant role in the history and mythology related to the Seramese culture. It also represents the division between the northern and southern tribes on Seram, the Manusela and the Nuaulu.

Further to our west the ridge climaxed in the stark limestone outcrop of Gunung Binaia, the "mother mountain", the greatest spirit force in the eyes of the people and the foundation for the matriarchal lineage that characterizes the whole island. This association, coupled with the fact that Islam has no great hold on the island, has meant that the women have rather more of a respected position in society than might be expected. Even in the parts of Indonesia where Islam

Taller and broader than most of the men, let alone the women, white-skinned and Western, I didn't go unnoticed.

dominates, women have a better position than in the more fundamentalist areas of the Islamic world. This is the reflection of a culture that has evolved by picking up, adapting and modifying the various religious and cultural waves that have swept through its land over the centuries. As a fulcrum of the Indo-China trading axis, Indonesia has distilled diverse influences to create an identity of its own.

Our hike took us up steeply into the mysterious serenity of the moss forest. There was an uncharacteristic calm and quiet at this height, in sharp contrast to the riotous noises of the lowland rainforest. Misty epiphytes hung from moss-covered trees, beards of soft pastel-coloured lichen draped themselves between the branches, the scenery black and white in soft focus; all my senses were muffled by the mist. My feet sank silently into the spongy moss beneath us, giving life and a new spring to my stride. But this was a false paradise; from time to time my legs would crash straight through the luxurious covering, taking me thigh-deep into a limestone gully.

A rapid descent led us to Manusela, where we received an extraordinary welcome. Taller and broader than most of the men in the village, let alone the women, white-skinned and Western, I obviously didn't go unnoticed. Joseph and Meli had evidently found our little trip together as amusing and curious as I had, and I was frustrated that my Indonesian didn't stretch to interpreting their breakneck account of the hike.

We had attracted quite a gathering of small, smiling people. The women were surprisingly uninhibited in their approach; touching me, playing with my hair, and patting my bottom and thighs in sheer disbelief. "Kaki besar!" (big legs), the Bapak Raja's wife had exclaimed. But, for once it wasn't an insult, simply an observation.

The villagers in the interior were even smaller built than their coastal counterparts, which is partly accounted for by their more impoverished diet. The creation of a National Park whose boundaries had encroached into their hunting grounds had resulted in dependence on their gardens, a few domestic chickens (which never seemed to be eaten), and a few tiny fish and prawns from the rivers. Where hunting was still permitted, it was generally the man's job, but out of the hunting season they would tend the gardens with the women; these were often situated at least an hour's walk away from the village. It was also a common sight to see a man cradling an infant and looking after the small children.

Plants were such an integral part of their lives that they couldn't look on them objectively or in isolation, as I did.

We were invited to stay in the house of the Bapak Raja, the village leader, literally the "father king". In Manusela the Bapak Raja not only acted as the father figure and the law, but appeared in church on Sunday morning as the pastor, preaching from the pulpit, his head emerging from underneath the festoons of glittering streamers that I usually associated with Christmas. It was a rare sight in that simple wooden building with magnificent views up towards the heavy rounded form of Merkele Besar and its smaller and more elegant partner, the pyramidal Merkele Kecil. No organ here, just a choir of simple pipes and the rich sounds of what are reputedly the best voices in Indonesia.

Despite Seram's geographical isolation and inaccessibility, it didn't survive the invasion of the missionaries. Most of the villages were at least nominally Muslim or Christian. In the interior they were predominantly Christian, although it soon became obvious that the traditional animist beliefs remained very strong. I was told a story about the history of the island by a man who lived in a neighbouring village. Noah's Ark apparently came to rest on the top of Binaia's neighbour, Merkele Besar, the paternal mountain. The villagers in the interior believe that the whole of the human race diversified from Manusela; their Bible stories all seemed to incorporate this strange blend of Christianity and local mythology.

I had the good fortune to spend a few days in one of a very few villages to fully maintain its animist traditions. The villagers were proud of their culture and looked down on the rest of the island for having succumbed to other religions. They did not travel out of their territorial areas to any great extent and spoke a dialect which was difficult for even my Indonesian companions to understand. On our way to Houalu we stopped a night at another village on the coast where we came across a huge timbered monstrosity among the bamboo huts.

This, it transpired, was a missionary house, and its residents were focusing on the last bastion of traditional Seramese culture: Houalu. I couldn't help but smile inwardly when we learned that although the missionaries had been there for over three years and were constantly trying to gain approval from the animists to build their house in Houalu, so far no permission had been or seemed likely to be granted. So far there were no converts either.

The day always began in the same ways while I was staying in these villages. I would wake up to the sound of cocks crowing, babies crying and people coughing. At dawn the river was a hive of activity as the children filled the bamboo poles which served as elegant water carriers. The adults would make off for the gardens as soon as it was light to avoid the heat of the day. Sometimes I went with them, picking up endless plants along the way and enquiring about their uses. I soon learned that direct questions about the way they used plants for food, medicines or construction materials yielded precious little information, simply because they didn't understand the question. Plants were such an integral part of their lives that they couldn't look on them objectively or in isolation, as I did. Most of my records were derived from observation or pointing out a plant and questioning its use.

During my stay I collected over three hundred plants which served some useful purpose, but I had the feeling even then that I was only scraping the surface. Many of these had medicinal value, but others could be used in quite curious ways. For example, mashed young pineapple became a DIY perming kit and the serrated and corrugated leaves of one creeping plant acted as toothbrushes.

The use of medicinal plants is not limited to isolated parts of Indonesia though, for in Java there are small factories which have been set up to produce "Jamu", as traditional medicine is known there. This small but profitable industry is run almost entirely by women and is regaining popularity as the preferred form of treatment, even where Western drugs are readily available.

It was very hard to leave Seram and its peaceful way of life, and I wondered what the next few years would bring; how far the logging road will penetrate into the interior, whether the missionaries will achieve their goals in Houalu, how long it will be before Manusela sees its first shop and the dawn of consumerism, how long before Coke cans clutter the pristine pathways between the bamboo houses in Manusela. Jakarta brought me down to earth with a bump, the city of the great hypocrisy, attempting to unify and represent a country as diverse in culture and ideology as they come. "Do they hunt with bows and arrows in England?", one Bapak Raja had asked me on Seram. His country's capital would have presented him with as many surprises as a trip to London.

TRAVEL NOTES

Languages The national language is Bahasa Indonesian, relatively easy to learn at a basic level. There are over two hundred languages and dialects among ethnic groups. Younger people and those working in the tourist industry generally speak some English.

Transport Boats, buses and *bemos* (mini-buses) are plentiful and cheap; hitching is uncommon but possible and relatively safe.

Accommodation A wide range of places to stay, from luxury hotels to beach huts. Look out for *losmen* – basic rooms with probably just a bed and a table – which are cheap and usually clean.

Guides *Indonesia Handbook* (US, Moon Publications). A classic guide, banned for sale in Indonesia – though you can carry it in.

BOOKS

Shirley Deane, *Ambon, Island of Spices* (US, John Murray, 1979). Fascinating account of two years teaching English on an Indonesian island. Dramatic descriptions of the people, food and music, along with accounts of trips to various other islands.

Nina Epton, *Magic and Mystics of Java* (UK, Octagon Press, 1975/US, Institute for the Study of Human Knowledge, 1974). Interesting travelogue with anthropological slant.

Raden Adjeng Kartini, *Letters of a Javanese Princess* (UK, Heinemann, 1983/US, University Press of America, 1985). Letters of a nineteenth-century Indonesian feminist and national heroine.

Kumari Jayawardena, *Feminism and Nationalism in the Third World* (UK, Zed Books, 1986/US, Humanities Press, 1986). Includes a chapter on the rise of the Indonesian women's rights movement.

John Pilger, *Distant Voices* (UK, Vintage, 1994). Includes reportage from East Timor which Pilger entered secretly in 1993 and where a third of the population has died as a result of Indonesia's genocidal policies.

Minority Rights Group, *Women in Asia* (UK, MRG, 1982). Contains an interesting section on Indonesian women.

Iran

I ran, the showcase of Shi'ite Muslim fundamentalism and its
– supposedly – ancient puritanical values has become a
strangely schizophrenic country. In public, the theocratic
government of president Rafsanjani peddles the same anti-
Western, anti-modern rhetoric of the 1979 Islamic revolution,
imposing tight restrictions on a population already burdened with
the traumas of the Iran/Iraq war and struggling with soaring inflation,
unemployment and shortages. In private, Iranians are making their
own accommodation with a regime that is fast running out of moral
credibility. Western goods and
satellite televison have found
their way into urban middle-
class homes and, away from
the prying eyes of the revolutionary guards and hierarchy
of *mullahs*, a parallel culture
continues, drawing heavily on
modern Western as well as
Eastern influences.

In recent years a few
Western tour agencies have
been allowed to operate in
the country, offering expensive package deals. It is still notoriously
difficult to get hold of transit visas for independent travel – awarded
in line with diplomatic relations – and British and American

women may have to shop around far-flung Iranian embassies en route. Once in, almost all aspects of your journey will be dogged by stern bureaucracy and a minefield of cultural restrictions. Dress codes are severe; all parts of your body must be covered and hair hidden beneath a veil. Yet, no matter how hard you attempt to shroud yourself and merge in, you are bound to feel conspicuous and vulnerable. Public areas are almost exclusively crowded with men, and wandering around on city streets it's impossible to avoid attracting comments and stares. Most of the more blood-curdling anti-Western slogans are directed at governments not individuals, although a woman travelling alone (flaunting her independence by leaving the protection of her family) becomes an obvious target for harassment.

In contrast, however, you can encounter incredible warmth and consideration from strangers stepping in to offer help or from women welcoming you into their own segregated areas. Iranians have a strong tradition of hospitality and will go to great lengths to protect and entertain anyone they perceive to be their guest. Frequently strangers will invite you into their homes, seizing an opportunity to make international contacts and to share their hopes and concerns about the future of their country. You have to be careful, however, not to compromise your hosts – it's actually illegal for an Iranian man to spend time alone with a woman who is not a relative.

Despite these very real deterrents, women do still make the journey across Iran, drawn by the undeniable beauty of the country and the nostalgic romance of the overland route to India. Also, in purely practical terms, travel is fairly easy. There are good roads and bus networks and plentiful, though now rather dilapidated, budget hotels.

While the rise of fundamentalism and the re-introduction of Islamic law has affected the status of **women** throughout the Muslim world, Iran provides some of the more potent examples of women's repression under, and resistance to, this trend. Women had been at the forefront of the revolution that toppled the Shah in 1979. Within the first few days of Khomeini's regime 25,000 women took to the streets of Teheran to protest their rights against pronouncements that women should veil in public. Many were beaten and imprisoned. Since then wave after wave of legislation in accordance with Shi'ite interpretations of the Koran has been passed, effectively relegating the status of women to that of "absolute property" of the man at the head of the family.

With a woman's testimony legally defined as worth half that of a man's, the dangers of being denounced to a popular court (usually for crimes of sexual immorality) are severe; lengthy imprisonment, flogging and stoning remain common punishments, particularly for working-class women who have no recourse to bribery. Women have continued to oppose these laws, which are seen as threatening their security at the heart of the family and society. In addition to mass demonstrations and spontaneous acts of defiance (anything from going unveiled to assassination attempts on Ayatollahs), large numbers of women have supported oppositional parties such as the People's Mujahideen and have been vocal in protests against the Iran/Iraq war.

By the end of the 1980s over 20,000 women had been executed for "counter-revolutionary" or "anti-Islamic" activity. (Holland has been one of the few countries to accept Iranian women as political refugees on the grounds of the sexual discrimination they face.) While feminist groups in Iran have been forced under-ground, many still operate in exile.

A Lonely Journey

Deciding that a career in administration was not for her, **Wendy Dison** set off first around Europe and Africa and then on to Asia, crossing Iran alone on her way to the Himalayas. This trip was made before the death of Ayatollah Khomeini.

"Salaam, Salaam." The face of the Iranian immigration officer at the border creased with pleasure when I greeted him in Farsi. Over his desk hung a sign which read "No East. No West. Islamic Republic", and next to it a portrait of Khomeini glared at me.

As the official inspected my passport, looking from my face to the photo and back again, the smile was replaced by a frown. "Monsieur? Madame?" he asked. My short hair confused him and when he realized that I wasn't a man he made urgent gestures that I must cover my head.

I put on a woollen bobble hat which satisfied him, though the young men I talked to on the bus to Tabriz advised me kindly that to comply with Islamic law I must wear a scarf covering my hair and neck. They were students returning from Izmir university and had brought Turkish scarves, prettier than Iranian, for their mothers and sisters and they generously gave one to me. I must wear a knee-length coat too, they said, to hide the shape of my body.

I was taut with resentment while photos of my family were inspected and my journal read.

The February sun was warm and the discomfort of wearing a scarf and long jacket increased my resentment. As we travelled through the pale, stony landscape, the students talked to me of the repression and cruelty suffered in Iran since the Shah was overthrown in 1979 and Khomeini created his Islamic Republic. Never before had I felt such foreboding on entering a country.

Between the border and Tabriz, a distance of 300km, we were stopped six times. Sometimes the police wanted to check our passports, other times Revolutionary Guards, wearing military-style uniforms, stopped us. Their job was to enforce the strict Islamic code and they searched our bus for drugs, arms and alcohol, forbidden foreign music and indecent pictures. They emptied handbags, confiscated cassettes, and ripped pictures of women with bare arms – or worse – from magazines.

We were treated with contempt and I was taut with resentment while photos of my family were inspected and my journal read. Probably few of them could read English but after this I kept separate notes, buried deep in my rucksack, of anything likely to cause trouble. At one stop we were ordered off the bus and herded behind a wall under spotlights. The guards bullied us and an old woman was crying. I was taken with the women into a hut where we were body-searched by a female guard, all but invisible under a black enveloping *chador*.

It was dark when we arrived in Tabriz; night is a bad time to arrive in a city and the darkness made me more than unusually aware of the security I was leaving. A man I'd talked to on the bus also got off here. He told me he was visiting his sister and when he learnt that I had no plans he invited me to her house. "She will be happy if you stay with her", he said.

> *All I could see of the women around me were the triangles of eyes and nose visible under the chadors.*

In a modern suburb of the city his sister, Eshrat, lived with her two young children and sister-in-law, Parvin. The women were delighted to see their brother and they fussed happily round both of us. They displayed a talent not rare in the East; that of making me feel at once a special guest yet very much at home. We sat drinking tea around a tall wood stove on Persian rugs, their half-forgotten English slowly returning as we talked.

Parvin and Eshrat were married to brothers who had been imprisoned for "being intelligent and lacking sympathy with the government". With bitterness they talked of life before the Revolution, when the Shah's policies of Westernization and the new wealth from oil had brought a flood of nightclubs, dance halls, cinemas and bars to the cities.

Religion and politics have always been closely interwoven in Iran and with the overthrow of the Shah the religious leaders, angered by the growing materialism, banned these trappings of decadent Western culture. Only religious or classical Persian music was permitted, fashionable imported goods disappeared from the shops, and the menus in restaurants were restricted so much that people no longer ate out for pleasure. For those who weren't religious there was little joy in life.

Far more invidious was the position of women, who had been forced to return to their traditional role in society, denied freedom, further education and the opportunity to work. Parvin's medical training had been curtailed. Because female staff are needed in girls' schools, Eshrat was able to keep her job as a teacher, one of the few occupations still open to women.

Her uniform was a loose, dark tunic and a cowl that left only a circle of her face exposed. Most women wore the *chador*, a black sheet draped over the head and hanging shapelessly to the feet, worn over indoor clothes when outside the house. Those against the regime could keep within the law – though earn disapproval – by wearing a loose knee-length coat and headscarf pulled well forward to cover the hair. I hoped my jacket, which reached mid-thigh, was sufficiently modest, for I was warned that the Revolutionary Guards who patrolled the streets would stop any woman not considered decently dressed.

The Iranians I met hated the regime they were forced to live under and all talked of leaving Iran. They dreamed of living in Britain or the USA but passports were not being issued and the few people who left the country did so illegally. Demand for hard currency by those planning to leave has resulted in a thriving black market. Of course, because Khomeini's supporters would disapprove of a veil-less woman, I met only pro-Western Iranians and my impressions were necessarily one-sided.

Next day Parvin and I dressed in our street clothes and caught a bus to the bazaar in the city. I was shocked to find separate entrances on the bus for men and women and that inside we sat segregated by metal bars. All I could see of the women around me were the triangles of eyes and nose visible under the *chadors*. When they struggled on and off the bus with a baby and a shopping bag they had difficulty remaining covered and most of them habitually used their teeth to trap the *chador* tightly round their faces. I felt revulsion against a society that treated women like this.

Women took advantage of one area where they could show their individuality. Though they were always black, the fabric of *chadors* varied from plain nylon to finely embroidered silk – reflecting the taste and social standing of their owners. Other clues to identity were given by elegant high-heeled shoes peeping below a hem, the flash of gold rings on well-manicured fingers or a hennaed pattern painted on the back of a hand. Except for the odd turban and the popularity of beards, the men, in trousers and cotton jackets, looked like Europeans.

When I left Tabriz, Parvin guided me through the jungle of Persian script at the bus station and wouldn't let me pay for my ticket. We hugged goodbye, both sorry that I couldn't stay longer, but my visa barely gave me enough time to cross the country. We hoped we might meet again in England. As a result of the Iran/Iraq war doctors were in demand and Parvin was to be allowed to complete her training, possibly in London.

The journey to Teheran began with prayers led by the driver, who possibly had his erratic driving in mind. Frilled curtains hung at the windows and an elaborate arrangement of silk flowers obstructed the driver's view. This was a deluxe bus but there was no air-conditioning nor did the windows open. As the sun rose so did the temperature inside the bus, and I suffered in my jacket and scarf. On the back of the ticket was printed "Please observe regulations as to the Islamic covering", which seemed unfair under the circumstances.

The restaurant where we stopped for lunch was a large isolated building in the desert – functional and soulless. As in all Iranian restaurants we paid on entry, a procedure simplified by limiting the menu to one item, invariably *chello kebab*, a bland dish of rice and grilled meat. Meal stops were short and people ate rapidly, leaning over their plates. This time I only wanted tea and was directed to the kitchen where, in the dark and confusion, a man beckoned to me. He gave me tea but held my arm to prevent my leaving while another man thrust a hand up under my jacket.

For a long moment I wanted to throw my tea over them, but they laughed at my anger and I fled. I found a seat and sipped my tea, trying to look calm. A woman sat at my table and we exchanged smiles, allies in a man's world. Back on the bus I wanted to share a bag of pistachio nuts with my neighbour but her *chador* enveloped her so completely that I couldn't talk to her. My feeling of isolation was acute.

Apart from the incident in the kitchen I wasn't bothered by men. The stares I often attracted were curious rather than lecherous. Though I received much Muslim hospitality and people were kind and helpful, I didn't relax in Iran. People seemed afraid to show too much friendliness and usually remained distant and guarded. I was nervous too, not knowing the power of the various authorities. In Teheran when I was taken by police to the station for questioning, even though they were courteous I thought anything could happen and I was worried.

With a two-week visa I hadn't time for more than a superficial look at the cities I passed through, and I only saw the countryside through a bus window. Yet I was left with vivid impressions: mud villages that appeared to grow out of the earth, high snow-topped mountains forming a background to arid plains, goats foraging around the black felt tents of tribal nomads, ancient bazaars with lofty brick-vaulted roofs, tombs of medieval poets in rose-filled gardens and, in every village and corner of the city, the graceful turquoise domes of the mosques. I remember in particular the splendid Royal Mosque at Isfahan, decorated inside and out with intricate patterns of rich blue and gold mosaic tiles which completely cover the walls and domes.

Once we got in his car, his nervousness showed that he knew the risk he was taking.

The beauty of Isfahan was marred, however, by the giant paintings of Khomeini that hung in prominent sites. The heavy brows, hard staring eyes and thick lips appeared merciless. Because of the association with this cruel face I no longer enjoyed the singing of the *muezzin* calling the faithful to prayer. The chant now sounded menacing.

In Shiraaz I became friendly with a man staying at the same hotel as me and accepted his offer to drive me to see Persepolis, the sixth-century capital of Persia. Once we got in his car his nervousness showed that he knew the risk he was taking – Islamic law forbids an unchaperoned woman to be with a man who isn't a relative. "If we are stopped you must say I am your guide and that you are paying me", he said.

Away from the city he relaxed. We explored the ruins, stopped in a village that produces the best halva in Iran, and had lunch of kebabs and grape juice at a roadside café. It was good to be out in the sunshine even though I couldn't take off my jacket and scarf. My hotel room was the only place I could remove them; even crossing the landing to the bathroom was considered public.

Checking out of the hotel the next day I discovered that my passport, left at reception, was missing. The next 24 hours were a nightmare. The British Consul in Teheran said he couldn't replace the passport but would issue me with papers to enable me to fly back to England. I wept with frustration. The hotel owner suspected my friend. Wasn't he desperate enough to leave Iran? The idea appalled me that the thief could be someone I trusted.

The police were very concerned and treated me kindly. That night they came to the hotel to question the staff and evidently frightened the thief so much that he jettisoned my passport. I found it lying on the stairs next morning and cried with relief. The hotel owner put an arm of comfort round my shoulder but as soon as he realized his indiscretion he pulled away quickly. "What a bloody country" I thought, smiling at him through my tears. I caught the next bus to Zahedan on the Pakistan border.

TRAVEL NOTES

Languages Farsi, Turkish, Kurdish, Arabic. In the main towns and cities quite a number of people speak some English.

Transport Trains and buses are relatively inexpensive and well-run. In the former there are women's compartments, which provide a welcome feeling of comfort and security. The bus system however is more extensive and generally quite comfortable and efficient. In some cities the buses are segregated, with women seated at the front.

Accommodation Plenty of reasonably priced hotels remain in the medium-sized towns. For your own peace of mind it's best to carry your own padlock.

Special Problems The most obvious one is gaining entry to the country in a time of fluctuating diplomatic relations. The best bet is to apply for transit visas at the Iranian Embassy in Turkey or Damascus. It helps to wear a *chador* or veil in any photos you submit or attend interviews for visas with a male chaperone.

There's no option about dress: you need to cover yourself completely, preferably in sombre clothing. This must include a scarf that covers all your hair.

Security is stringent and Revolutionary Guards will stop and search coaches fairly frequently. You might also be body-searched when you cross the border into Iran.

Guides *Iran – A Travel Survival Kit* (Lonely Planet) is the first and only post-revolution guide. Comprehensive, practical and optimistic – the next most important item to a visa.

CONTACTS

Committee for Defence of Women's Rights in Iran, c/o London Women's Centre, Wesley House, 70 Great Queen St, London WC2B 5AX, UK. A broad-based solidarity group geared towards publicizing women's struggles in Iran and co-ordinating international campaigns to protest the conditions faced by women. They produce an occasional bulletin in English.

Iranian Community Centre (Women's Section), 465a Green Lanes, London N4, UK (☎0181/341 5005). Resource centre producing a women's newsletter in Farsi.

Women and Struggle in Iran. Quarterly publication produced by the Women's Commission of the *Iranian Students Association* in the USA. Copies available from ISA (WC-ISA), PO Box 5642, Chicago, Illinois 60680, USA.

BOOKS

Freya Stark, *The Valleys of the Assassins* (1934; UK, Arrow, 1991, o/p/US, JP Tarcher, 1983, o/p). Another world – and another classic piece of travel writing.

Christina Dodwell, *A Traveller on Horseback in Eastern Turkey and Iran* (US, Walker & Co, 1979). More intrepid adventures from the doyenne of fearless travel.

Tabari Azar et al (eds), *In the Shadow of Islam: The Women's Movement in Iran* (UK & US, Zed Books, 1982, o/p in US). Written by three Iranian women, this book covers the women's movement in Iran since the revolution, concentrating on the relation between Islam and the struggle for women's emancipation.

Guity Nashat, *Women in Revolution in Iran* (UK & US, Westview, 1983, o/p in US). Study focusing on the central paradox of women's participation in a revolution that deprived them of many rights. Analysis of the pre- and post-revolutionary periods as well as the revolution itself.

Farah Azari (ed), *Women of Iran* (UK & US, Ithaca Press, 1982, o/p). A collection of papers by socialist-feminist Iranian women which bring a fresh approach to the political debates surrounding the revolution.

Sousan Azadi and Angela Ferrante, *Out of Iran: One Woman's Escape from the Ayatollahs* (UK, Warner, 1993). Harrowing account of a refugee's flight from her country.

Shusha Guppy, *The Blindfold Horse* (UK, Minerva, 1992/US, Beacon Press, 1993). Memoirs of a childhood life amid the intellectual aristocracy in pre-Khomeini Iran.

Miranda Davies (ed), *Third World – Second Sex 2* (UK & US, Zed Books, 1987). Includes part of a study on crimes against women in Iran by Simin Ahmady.

FICTION

Manny Sharazi, *Javady Alley* (UK, The Women's Press, 1984). An outstanding novel set in Iran in 1953, and seen through the eyes of a seven-year-old girl whose childhood certainties are coming under threat.

Ireland

Cautiously, and with hopes reined in, the people of Northern Ireland are surveying the possiblities of peace. Since September 1 1994 the IRA guns have been silent; the loyalist paramilitaries followed suit a month later, and British army patrols are being gradually confined to barracks. Despite the fragile mandate of all the potential negotiators – and widely voiced fears of a backlash bringing renewed and much worse violence – a new impetus is noticeable in the six counties of the North. In Belfast an arts festival is already underway, property prices are beginning to edge upwards and hotel rooms are being booked out by visitors from the Republic, many of them spending their first night over the border.

Tourism is a major hope for a peace economy in the North. Some tourists have been returning for years to villages and coastal resorts where "the Troubles" (as the Occupation and twenty-five years of sectarian violence are labelled by the British press) barely impinge on day-to-day life – at least from the perspective of an outsider. Yet it will take a solid, sustained peace before mainstream tourists, especially from Britain, can be persuaded to view Northern Ireland as a holiday destination.

By contrast, visitors of all nationalities flock to the Republic of Ireland, enticed by the idea of a rural haven steeped in traditions of myth-making, music and literature. Famed for its relaxed approach to life and easy hospitality, Ireland has a reputation as a relatively safe and hassle-free destination for women, even for those exploring alone. Sexist attitudes certainly prevail, but are far more likely take the form of an old-fashioned male courtesy and genuine bewilderment as to why you should choose to be on your own, rather than any overt sexual harassment. The cost of living, which is at least 25 percent higher than in Britain, can be an initial shock; alleviated in part by the fact that this is perfect country for cycling and camping.

Women have played a significant part in Ireland's struggles for self-determination, though the movement for national liberation has not necessarily gone hand in hand with that for women's liberation. Votes for women were introduced into the Republic six years ahead of Northern Ireland and Britain, but women's rights were, and continue to be, severely restricted by a constitution that enshrines many Catholic values. In Northern Ireland, women are, in strictly legal and economic terms, better off, but their rights have always lagged behind those gained for women in Britain.

Northern Irish women played a prominent role in the civil rights movement of the 1960s, and in the 1970s a small but articulate feminist movement emerged, made up mostly of middle-class women. They attempted to operate across the sectarian divide, arguing that such issues as childcare provision, wife-battering, contraception and abortion (still an imprisonable offence throughout Ireland) should be brought in line with British law.

A division arose between those feminists who looked for emancipation through operating within the British government system, and those who saw it proceeding from British withdrawal. The divide still persists today, although notable campaigns – such as the setting up of the Belfast Well Woman's Centre and Rape Crisis Centre – have received widespread support.

Many similar developments have occurred in the Republic, with women campaigning throughout the 1970s for access to contraception (at the time banned even for married couples), equal pay for equal work, state benefits for unmarried mothers and legislation for divorce. Over twenty years later there has been a slight slackening in the laws against birth control but divorce remains outlawed by the constitution, as does abortion. An estimated 4000 women arrive in Britain each year seeking terminations, although since 1986, it has been illegal for Irish agencies even to offer counselling or contact addresses. A landmark Supreme Court ruling in 1992, allowing a pregnant fourteen-year-old girl who was raped by the father of a friend to travel to England for an abortion may herald some degree of reform. A note of optimism was sounded the previous year by the surprise election of Mary Robinson as president of the Republic. In a country whose political life is almost entirely dominated by men, the presence of a progressive female voice, unafraid to speak out on women's issues, has been welcome indeed.

Lesbians, on both sides of the border, have long had to struggle against entrenched prejudice. It took a ruling by the European Court of Human Rights in 1982 to bring Northern Ireland's homosexuality laws into line with Britain. In the Republic, anti-gay laws have recently been repealed although the atmosphere of intolerance remains.

Behind the Picture Postcards

Hilary Robinson has often visited the Republic of Ireland. In particular, she tries to go every summer to County Clare where she travels with fiddle to the annual music summer school at Miltown Malbay.

I t is all too easy to be utterly romantic about the Republic of Ireland. The beauty of the landscape, the numbers who still live on a small scale close to the land, and the generosity of spirit of so many of the people that you meet: all combine to encourage an idyllic view. Add to this an almost universal ignorance of Irish history on the part of the British (can you remember being taught any at school?), and the notion of a "Real Ireland" encouraged by the tourist trade, and you have the stuff of all romantic dreams – a place with an immutable essence where you can put aside the aspects of the twentieth century that you want to escape.

Now, I've spent some of my happiest times in recent years in Ireland, but I feel very strongly that the romanticized "Real Ireland" does not exist, not generally and especially not for women. There are elements, of course, on the visual level. It's very easy to clamber up some hillside in Kerry or Connemara and to sit, breathing in the clean air, and gaze out at the fields of luscious green, the Atlantic in the distance, perhaps a whitewashed cottage with a couple of children out in the yard, a small holding, a man driving his eight cows home for milking . . . This is when the fantasies start about giving everything up to come and live here on the land, where the children can grow up healthily.

However, each time I go, and as I get to know the country better, the mismatch between the picturesque image of the Tourist Board and the differing realities for the various people I meet seems to become more pronounced.

The parts of Ireland I know best are Dublin, Galway and County Clare, though I have made occasional trips into Connemara and Westport, to Kerry and Kilkenny. I've travelled there for various reasons, but mainly because of Irish music. I play the fiddle a little and try to get to Miltown Malbay in County Clare each summer for a music summer school. It's great fun and draws people from all over the world, as far as India and Australia, to play and listen. Although most of the traditional musicians who have made recordings are men, and some of the playing in some of the bars is competitively macho, a large number of women also play and attend the school. I found many of the older Irish people, in particular, to be delighted that a non-Irish person should show such an interest in their culture – quite a humbling experience as an Englishwoman.

One of my trips to Ireland was to research part of a thesis about contemporary women artists, when I went to speak to women (mainly in the Dublin area) about their work; another time I went cycling with a boyfriend around Clare, Galway and Connemara, with a tent strapped to the back of a bike.

I have several times had heated arguments with Irishmen who insist that Ireland is a matriarchal society. Their reasoning was based on the romantic ideal that women should be respected simply for being women, mixed with a dollop of mythology about motherhood and strong female figures; I felt it left out any appreciation of the day-to-day realities for their own mothers and sisters, and of the links between Catholicism and the State in Ireland. The recent divorce and abortion referendums (both won by the Church and conservatives) would be a case in point.

A discussion of sexual politics was almost like "talking dirty" to the man I was in conversation with.

The Irish population is nowhere near as dense as in Britain, but it is far more evenly spread across rural areas. Farms are handed down through families and have been important in the past in the support by families of prospective marriages. One of the arguments in the divorce referendum was that women would not only split families but farms, many of which survive only just above subsistence level. Ireland remains the only European country besides Malta to forbid divorce. Not surprisingly, a Dutch friend marrying an Irishman and going to live in Ireland deliberately chose to marry in Holland.

On a practical level, motherhood is held in higher esteem than it is in England: something I noticed in little things like the sympathetic attitude of shop assistants to women with children in tow. With regards to sex, it's not uncommon for Irishmen to assume that if you're not Irish you must be on the pill and therefore have no good reason to refuse their advances! On one occasion I realized that a discussion of sexual politics was almost like "talking dirty" to the man I was in conversation with.

In some ways attitudes are similar to those of the British in the 1970s, but for different reasons. The laws around contraception may not be as extreme as they used to be, but the moral climate of Ireland is still a far cry from the so-called permissive era we experienced in Britain. In theory you can buy condoms across the counter in chemist shops; in practice I found it to be a lot more difficult, since many chemists, even in the centre of Dublin, refuse to sell them "on moral grounds". Another difference is that in Britain in the 1970s, men expected sex in the name of "free love". In contrast, the Irishmen that I have met are far more likely to be romantic, to talk about falling in love, to want to take me across the country for the weekend to meet their parents, to demonstrate a level of romantic seriousness, despite the fact that I am only visiting – in short, to "court".

I have heard non-Irish women say that there's a vulnerability in this attitude that can be refreshing after the horribly repressed emotional life of British men. Personally, I've found the "back on top of a pedestal" position, although intended as flattering, deeply uncomfortable. Furthermore, for me to relax into it in a kind of "holiday romance" mode would only end up abusing the man concerned. I learned this the hard way, causing pain on all sides. Irish women would, of course, say something else again; one spoke to me very persuasively of what she called the deep conservatism of Irishmen's notions about women. On looking around a crowded bar in Doolin, County Clare, which every summer is filled with people chasing Irish music, and today seemed mainly to consist of Irish men and German women, she said she was waiting for the first case of herpes to be heard of in the village: then "all the men would soon go home".

There are two aspects of travelling as a woman in Ireland that I especially appreciate. The first, and most practical, is that this is the only European country that I have visited where I've felt happy about hitching alone. Obviously, I got offered lifts on my own more easily than when I was one of a couple, either with another woman or with a man; and I am not denying that things can go wrong. But I've never once had cause to feel threatened and, compared to many countries, hitching in Ireland is much more accepted as a way of getting about. Train fares are high, car insurance astronomical, and buses rare out in the country. Consequently you see all sorts of people at the sides of the road, from old men cadging lifts to teenagers trying to get into town.

A number of people said they'd stopped for me because they saw the fiddle case, and was I sure I wasn't Irish? Sometimes families would stop and once I got a lift all the way across the country from a soldier in the Irish army – we shared a similar dislike of the Tory government, so that was okay. I once got a lift from a single woman driver who told me she always offered lifts to women because she used to hitch herself, and had once or twice been in awkward situations. She never offered lifts to men.

The funniest time was a few miles outside Miltown, the day the summer school ended. It was tipping down, my friend and I were miles from anywhere, had been walking for an hour and were soaked to the skin. A car finally stopped; the man driving had seen the fiddle cases and took pity on us. He'd stopped for another woman (plus fiddle) earlier, and stopped again for another (plus guitar) a few miles further on.

The second thing I'm grateful for in Ireland took a bit of time to notice and that's the absence of pornography. No doubt it's around somewhere in some form, and no doubt it's missing for all the wrong reasons – repressive attitudes towards sexuality in general, rather than radical attitudes towards the representation of women. But it's just not there when you go to buy a newspaper; which is a holiday in itself.

TRAVEL NOTES

Language English and Gaelic.

Transport Buses and trains are very expensive. A good, inexpensive, way of exploring the countryside is to rent a bicycle. Hitching is relatively easy and safe, perhaps the greatest problem being lack of cars. Sunday traffic is usually the worst, when you find either cars packed with families or single men with time on their hands looking for some "fun".

Accommodation You can camp more or less anywhere in the countryside, as long as you ask permission of the landowner. Youth hostels get booked up in the summer so it's wise to book in advance. Bed and Breakfasts are usually relaxed and comfortable.

Special Problems Travelling in the North you may well be stopped by British Army or RUC patrols, and asked for your name, address, date of birth and immediate destination. Whatever your feelings or politics it's best to remain civil and to the point. It is now legal to sell contraception, although some pharmacists refuse to stock condoms. Ireland is notorious for its continuing abuse of gay rights. It's a good idea to get advice from a gay group about the local scene.

Guides *The Rough Guide to Ireland* (Penguin) is easily the most informative.

WOMEN'S ACCOMMODATION

Amazonia B&B, Coast Rd, Fountainstown, Cork (☎21/831 115) is a women-only bed & breakfast with campsite, beautiful views and various outdoor activities.

The Southern Ireland Wimmin's Holiday Centre, "Amcotts", Clonmore, Piltown, County Kilkenny, Eire (☎Waterford 43371), offers luxury accommodation in a tranquil rural setting, plus good food, a library, cycles for rent and a convivial, hospitable atmosphere.

CONTACTS

The yearly *Irish Women's Guidebook and Diary* provides a comprehensive list of addresses for individual women's/lesbian groups throughout Ireland. It is available from feminist bookshops in Britain and Ireland or direct from *Attic Press*, 44 E Sussex Street, Dublin 2.

In Ireland itself, the entertainments guide, *In Dublin*, and the gay magazine, *Out*, both have listings on women's groups. In the North be sure to pick up a copy of the *Irish Women's News*, Ireland's only women's magazine

WOMEN'S GROUPS AND BOOKSHOPS

Belfast: *Women's Centre*, 18 Donegall St, Belfast BT1 2GP (☎0232/243363), and *Just Books*, 7 Winetavern St, Smithfield (☎0232/225426), are good for contacts. You could also try *Lesbian Line* (Mon–Thurs 7.30–10pm; ☎0232/222023).

Dublin: *Dublin Resource Centre*, 6 Crowe St (☎01/771974), and *Women's Centre*, 53 Dame St, Dublin 2 (☎01/710088), will provide you with information about local groups and campaigns.

Women's Centre Shop, 27 Temple Lane (☎01/710088); *Books Uptairs*, Market Arcade, off S Gt Georges St (☎01/710064), and *Spellbound Books*, City Centre, 23–25 Moss St (☎01/712149), all have a good selection of feminist and lesbian literature and stock.

The Hirschfeld Centre, 10 Fownes St (☎01/910139), is a recommended gay/lesbian meeting place.

BOOKS

Dervla Murphy, *A Place Apart* (US, Devin-Adair, 1978). Conversations with people representing the full spectrum of political opinion in Ireland. Murphy's *Wheels within Wheels* (UK & US, Penguin, 1981) is a wonderfully sensitive account of growing up in a small Irish town, caring for her crippled mother. Extraordinary to think that before reaching her 30s this leading travel writer had ventured no further than the occasional bike trip.

Sally Belfrage, *The Crack* (UK, Deutsch, 1987). Readable, if romanticized, anecdotes and impressions by an American journalist who spent a year in Belfast. Published in the US as *Living with War: A Belfast Year* (Penguin, 1988).

E O Somerville and V M Ross, *Through Connemara in a Governess Cart* (1893; UK & US, Virago, 1990). Amusing account of a week-long drive in Ireland by venerable Irish cousins. Wittily written, with a shrewd ear for dialogue.

Fileen Fairweather (ed), *Only the Rivers Run Free: Northern Ireland, the Women's War* (UK, Pluto Press, 1984/US, Pluto Press, 1989). A selection of women describe the everyday realities of life in the North.

Eilean Ni Chuilleanain (ed), *Irish Women: Image and Achievement* (UK, Arlen House, 1985, o/p). Ten essays by specialist authors tracing the position of women in Irish society from ancient to modern times.

Nell McCafferty, *A Woman to Blame* (UK, Attic Press, 1985/US, Attic Press, 1989). Brilliant study of the "Kerry Babies Case" by one of Ireland's most acclaimed journalists. It examines the grip on Irish women by the Church, patriarchy and culture. Also look out for McCafferty's selection of articles and essays, *The Best of Nell* (UK, Attic Press, 1984/US, Attic Press, 1989)

★ **Liz Curtis**, *Ireland: The Propaganda War* (UK, Pluto Press, 1984/US, Pluto Press, 1985). An unanswerable indictment of the truth-bending of the British media.

FICTION

Emma Cooke, *Eve's Apple* (UK, Blackstaff, 1985/US, Dufour, 1985). Set against the 1983 Irish abortion referendum campaign, this novel describes a woman's isolation and desperation with middle-class provincialism and the hypocrisy of religious values.

Mary Lavin, *Mary O'Grady* (UK, Virago, 1986/US, Penguin, 1986). Best-known work by a prestigious Irish writer about a woman who leaves the country life to set up home in Dublin. Also worth reading is *The House in Clewe Street* (UK, Virago, 1987, o/p/US, Penguin, 1988), a family saga that uncovers the problems and pitfalls of an Irish Catholic upbringing.

Deirdre Madden, *Hidden Symptoms* (UK, Faber & Faber, 1988/US, Grove-Atlantic, 1987). A hauntingly evocative novel that centres on a woman's attempt to reconcile herself to the sectarian murder of her twin brother.

Frances Molloy, *No Mate for a Magpie* (UK, Virago, 1985/US, Persea Books, 1986). Tragicomic tale of a Catholic girlhood in Ireland.

Edna O'Brien, *Johnnie I Hardly Knew You* (UK, Weidenfeld & Nicolson, 1990/US, Avon, 1984, o/p); *The Country Girls* (UK, Penguin, 1970/US, Plume, 1987). Accomplished novels from a popular and prolific author. Both explore issues of emerging female sensuality within rural Ireland's repressive social climate.

Julia O'Faolain, *No Country for Young Men* (UK, Penguin, 1980, o/p/US, Carroll & Graf, 1986). Devastating story of human and political relations in contemporary Ireland.

Italy

Many Italians regard Italy as two distinct countries: the north and the south. The first, ending at Rome, enjoys an image of prosperity and innovation; the second, encompassing the notorious Mafia strongholds of Calabria and Sicily, is considered poor, corrupt, backward and, at least in the minds of most southerners, cruelly neglected. Compared to the thriving industrial centres in and around Turin or Milan, the south is indeed desperately poor. It's also more traditional and conservative and, in this respect, less easy for travellers.

As a people, the Italians are hospitable and talkative, and it takes little to be drawn into long conversations, however poor your grasp of the language. Train journeys provide the perfect setting and, perhaps unsurprisingly in the light of widespread street harassment, several women report these as among their most enjoyable experiences. Fellow passengers are keen to practise their English and everyone tends to pool their efforts to keep a conversation going. Travelling with a child, you'll be made even more welcome. All over

Italy children are doted on and fussed over, providing a wonderful passport for meeting people and gaining their respect. It's quite common in a restaurant for your child to be whisked off to the kitchen and showered with kisses and treats for a couple of hours while you enjoy your meal.

Travelling alone, or with a female companion, you'll be treated as a curiosity. But the attention you receive can vary from quite genuine concern about your isolation (and possible loneliness) to incredibly brazen and persistent harassment. The cat-calls, propositions and kerb-crawling tend to get worse as you head further south and in Sicily, especially, it takes a tough skin and plenty of determination to stick out a holiday on your own. As usual the hassles and misconceptions fade as you become known in a place and even the most frustrating moments can be tempered by singular acts of great warmth and generosity.

Italian society (with the weight of the Catholic Church behind it) is so strongly family-oriented that it's hard for the older generation, at least, to understand any female desire for independence. Mamma may appear to reign at home, but outside machismo is irritatingly prevalent. Italian men are stereotypically proud, vain, and not easily rejected, and in any situation like to at least be seen to have the upper hand.

Italian **women** have a lot to battle against, and today every city has at least one feminist organization; several have their own bookstores (also meeting places) and documentation centres. The roots of the movement lie in the generation referred to as the "Sixty-eighters", political activists who, during that period of political turmoil, gradually saw the need for women to organize separately from men. Many did and still do belong to the once huge Italian Communist Party (known since 1991 as the Democratic Left) with which *Noi Donne*, the country's first ever feminist magazine was originally linked. *Noi Donne* has survived, but in the current political climate, dominated by the right-wing Forza Italia party, women more than ever need to strengthen their voices if they don't want to see past achievements – such as the winning of divorce rights and legalization of abortion – undermined.

Living in Florence

Kerry Fisher first went to Italy as an au pair in 1985, while studying for a British university degree in European Studies. After graduating she spent three years teaching English in Spain and Corsica, before returning to Italy as a holiday company representative in Florence. She has lived in the city ever since where she works as a freelance researcher and writer for travel guides.

I taly. What a maddening, frustrating yet addictive country. After two and a half years in Florence, I am still not sure whether I love it for its variety and vitality or detest it for its prejudice, bureaucracy and contradictions. I have spent several years abroad and no country has ever aroused such strong emotions in me – hardly surprising when many Italians spend half their lives bemoaning the shortcomings of their country in one breath and extolling its beauty in the other.

When I was offered a job as a representative for a British tour operator, it seemed like a belated Christmas present. Although I knew that living and working abroad was very different from two weeks in a holiday atmosphere, sneaky little images of sunshine and ice cream crept into my head. My arrival soon dispelled any illusions. Florence is a serious city where tourists are tolerated for economic reasons rather than warmly welcomed. The city depends quite heavily on income from tourism, yet the average hotelier treats clients as though they have just insulted his mother.

On first contact, the Florentines seem abrupt and almost rude. My encounters with Italian bureaucracy reinforced this view. Everyday errands have become a major chore. Sending a parcel, paying a phone bill, going to the bank – you must first find your way around erratic opening hours, then locate someone who is not having a coffee break, or studiously ignoring the massive queues in favour of discussing where to go for lunch. I tremble in my shoes when I have to obtain any official document, such as my

> *By the time I've visited four or five shops, I know a lot about Italian politics, football, which grapes make good Chianti. . .*

foreigner's permit of stay. I know that such a simple request will result in queueing for several hours, filling in a whole rain forest's worth of forms, being sent from office to office then being asked to return ten days later because the office closes at 11.30am and I've run out of time.

The only way to move things along quickly in Italy is to be *raccomandato*, to have friends in high places. If you know the right people, anything is possible. Although the whole system goes against my every principle, the only alternative is frustration and disappointment. My advice to anyone staying in Italy for any length of time is to cultivate your contacts. It is not a country for the shy and retiring – you are expected to ask and return favours. This applies to all areas of life; getting a job, even if you are well-qualified, is difficult without inside help. A word in the right ear opens a myriad of doors: papers are stamped and handed over, apartments are found at the right price, parking permits are produced, speeding fines disappear.

The Florentines, as I've already intimated, are not a smiley breed, yet once you break through their outer reserve, they can be really charming and helpful. While tourists are often treated with ill-disguised disdain, resident foreigners arouse good-natured curiosity. I may be referred to as the *Inglesina*, rather than by name, but there is no malice intended. Originally, I felt very defensive about being foreign, adopting Italian mannerisms, dress, anything which

Italians seem to work on the law of averages – if they ask out ten women, one will eventually say yes.

would make me less conspicuously English. I desperately didn't want to be considered an ex-pat, indifferent to the host country's traditions and way of life. Now that I am proficient in the language, and I can express my individual attitudes and ideas quite eloquently, nationality has ceased to become an issue. I just feel European. If I catch myself thinking nostalgically about polite shop assistants and orderly queues, I remind myself of the delicious food, breathtaking architecture, and colourful personalities that brighten my daily life.

Florence's cultural wealth has exposed the city to international tourism. Nevertheless, it has retained a small town atmosphere. As a result, it is fairly easy for an outsider to gain a sense of belonging. There are no supermarkets in the centre of town, so even grocery shopping is a social event. By the time I've visited four or five shops, I know a lot about Italian politics, football, which grapes make good Chianti, and how to make good pumpkin soup. Having breakfast in a bar is one of my favourite activities; forefingers are stabbed and jabbed as cappuccino flows alongside lively discussions about corruption, taxes, and the latest bribery scandal. People are rarely too busy to have a coffee and a chat. In the cafés and bars that I frequent, I am automatically included in conversations – people assume that you want to talk, even when you would sometimes prefer to be left alone.

Florence is a relatively compact city and I enjoy the sense of security that familiarity with the people and places engenders in me. For myself and many other women, one of the most positive aspects is the lack of violent crime against women. In Britain, I would never walk home alone at ten o'clock at night, and would worry about travelling on public transport after 9pm. Here I am quite happy to go out and catch the late bus back without looking over my shoulder to see if I am being followed or if the local axe-wielding madman might be on board. Of course, I am not suggesting that there is no crime, but it is rare that you hear of a woman being attacked on her way home.

> The pressure is on women to be slim and beautiful. This does not extend to men.

This may have something to do with the Italians' attitude to alcohol. Unlike Britain in particular, social life is not based around drinking and people tend only to drink with meals, and never on an empty stomach. Drunkenness is frowned upon and masculinity does not depend on how many pints you can hold. In fact, there are very few places where you can just drink, and those that exist are expensive. It is far more common to see a group of young people going out for an ice cream on a Saturday night than queueing up at the bar for a fourth or fifth beer.

Day to day harassment is another matter. Italians seem to work on the law of averages – if they ask out ten women, one will eventually say yes. Their chat up lines are outrageous: I've had people tell me there was a bus strike and offer me a lift home, ask me directions to the Ponte Vecchio when I was standing on it – any excuse to get talking. However, most overtures are lighthearted and not very persistent. In fact, I often get the impression that men feel a social duty to flirt and comment on women. It is annoying when a man invites himself to join you in a bar or restaurant, or trots along beside you in the street; but these encounters are rarely threatening. I just find myself marvelling at their huge inflated egos! Once you dispense with the map and learn to walk with a determined step, the would-be latin lovers usually transfer their attentions to the next pale-skinned tourist.

Commenting on appearance is the great national sport. Looks are all-important and people are quickly divided into two categories, *bello* and *brutto*, beautiful and ugly. Attractive people have a definite advantage. Opinions are freely expressed, flattering or otherwise, by men and women. You don't need scales in Florence to know when you've put on weight, because there will always be some little charmer to point it out. Heaven help you if you are unlucky at the hairdressers. Clothes are of crucial importance to the snobby Florentines and the more ostentatious the designer label, the better. The streets are a confident blur of neatly tailored jackets and soft leather boots. The emphasis placed on appearance irritates me. Typically, the greatest pressure is on women to be slim and beautiful. This does not extend to men – even the most unattractive view themselves through their mother's adoring eyes and seem rather protected from moments of self doubt.

The relationship between men and women is a complex one. Lip service is paid to equality – there are women bus drivers and refuse collectors – but very few women hold top level management positions. Women remain entirely responsible for the household burden, and this situation is passed down from generation to generation. Sons are not expected to lift a finger around the house, but daughters must learn to run the household. If you don't get married, you stay at home regardless of age with parents expected to support their children financially until well into their twenties. Consequently, young people tend to be less independent; at 24, it may still be necessary to ask your parents' permission to go on holiday with your boyfriend. Although sex before marriage is very common, a pretence is usually maintained for the family. The average Italian male sneaks back home just before dawn to keep mum happy.

In terms of liberated attitudes, I would say that Italian women are at least a decade behind their British or American counterparts. There is definite social pressure to find a husband, preferably a rich one, and single women over thirty are an object of pity. Because of this, many women stay in unhappy marriages, turning a blind eye to an unfaithful husband as long as appearances are maintained. Being divorced is still a social stigma although it is becoming less so.

However, for every narrow-minded attitude, there are huge compensations. The warmer climate means that there is more life in the streets. I love walking around at midnight in the summer or watching the world go by from a café terrace. Social life is very much based on good food, and eating out with Italians is a pleasurable experience. They are basically generous people, with no quibbling over the bill – they are far more interested in the quality of the *porcini* mushrooms, or wild boar than the price. The strong community spirit appeals to me: open-air concerts are performed in the summer with free food and drink for the local neighbourhood; social events are planned without any commercial goals. One of my favourite evenings is the celebration of San Lorenzo in August when strains of Mozart float on the warm air, as lasagne and watermelon are handed out in the square.

In Florence the bank clerk shouts at me for not having a pen. But I can drink wonderful coffee outside in December. People look down their nose at me because I'm not wearing designer clothes. But I can walk home at midnight. I didn't get the job I applied for because it was given to the director's niece. But children are accepted anywhere. No, it's not perfect. But when the sun shines on the Ponte Vecchio and I'm heading for my favourite cellar bar for pasta with fresh basil and tomato sauce and a glass of Chianti, it'll do for now.

TRAVEL NOTES

Languages Italian, with strong regional dialects. If you can't speak Italian, French is useful. People working in tourist services usually speak some English.

Transport Trains and buses are reasonably inexpensive and efficient. Hitching is easy enough but risky and not advisable, especially in the south.

Accommodation *Pensioni* (and more expensive hotels) are plentiful throughout the country.

Special Problems Machismo rules and harassment can be a problem, especially in the south, which some women find quite unbearable. Railway stations everywhere are particularly hazardous. You should spend the least possible time in them, and never sleep in a station; you run the risk of theft and sexual assault. In general the most obvious strategy is to avoid eye contact. Whatever clothes you wear, you're still likely to be followed, pushed and touched and have your route blocked. Italians are quite amazingly adept at identifying foreigners.

Beware of the police, too. According to Diana Pritchard who has lived and travelled extensively in Italy: "Their conduct is an unpleasant combination of abuse of authority (even the Italian public are cautious of them) and an apparent lack of respect for foreign women. Some of my worst experiences have involved the *Carabinieri* – the armed police – ranging from the indiscreet fondle of my breast as I walked by, to a time when a group of *Carabinieri* demanded that I open the door of a tiny bedroom in which a female friend and I were staying. Although I eventually managed to get them out of the room, we were followed the next day until we left town."

Guides *The Rough Guide to Italy* (Penguin), plus separate guides to *Sicily, Venice* and *Tuscany and Umbria* in the same series are all recommended. *The Woman's Travel Guide to Rome* (UK, Virago/US, RDR Books) is a good read, as well as being packed with information.

CONTACTS

Often bookshops (*librerie*) and centres (*case*) are combined in the same building. A *biblioteca* is a library and suggests a more academic place.

SELECTED WOMEN'S CENTRES AND BOOKSHOPS

Roma: *Ufficio Progetti Donna*, Gabinetto de Sindacao, Via del Campidoglio 1 (☎67 10 38 98 or 99). This information service publishes a free booklet, *Roma la citta delle donne* divided into three sections covering services, women's organizations, and history and culture – available from main tourist offices.
Libreria delle Donne, Piazza Farnese 103. Rome's main feminist bookshop.
Alessandria: *Casa delle Donne*, Via Solero 24, 15100.
Ancona: *Biblioteca delle Donne*, Via Cialdini 26.
L'Aquila: *Biblioteca delle Donne*, c/o AIED, Corso Federico II 58.
Bologna: *Librellula*, Libreria delle Donne, Strada Maggiore 23/e.
Centro di Documentazione Ricerca e Iniziativa delle Donne, Via Galliera 4 (8am–2pm). Centre promoting research on women's issues: includes a small but growing feminist library.
Circolo Culturale, "28" Giugno, Piazza di Porta Saragozzae (☎43 33 92). Gay centre, bookshop and library that often holds lesbian meetings, social events, etc.
Civitavecchia: *Centro Donna "Terradilet"*, V G Abruzzeze, 00053.
Firenze: *Libreria delle Donne*, Via Fiesolana 2B; Casa delle Donne, Via Carraia 2.
Milano: *Libreria delle Donne*, Via Dogana 2. *Casa delle Donne*, Via Lanzone 32.
Centro per la Difesa dei Diritti delle Donne, Via Tadino 23.
La Nuova Idea, Via de Castiglia 3 (☎68 92 73). Gay bar. Thursday is lesbian only.
Modena: *Casa delle Donne*, Via Cesana 43.

Parma: *Biblioteca delle Donne*, Via XX Settembre 31.
Pisa: *Centro Documentazione Donne*, Via Puccini 15.
Reggio Emilia: *Casa della Donna*, Viale Isonzo 76.

BOOKS

Fiona Pitt-Kethley, *Journeys to the Underworld* (UK, Chatto & Windus, 1988/US, Chatto, 1990). English poet searches Italy for the sibylline sites, spending a good third of her time in Sicily – a healthy appetite for sexual adventure provides her with plenty of distractions.
Mary Taylor Simeti, *On Persephone's Island* (UK, Penguin, 1988, o/p/US, North Point Press, 1987). Sympathetic record of a typical year in Sicily by an American who married a Sicilian professor and has lived on the island since the early 1960s.
Lisa St Aubyn de Terán, *A Valley in Italy* (UK, Hamish Hamilton, 1994/US HarperCollins). Subtitled *Confessions of a House Addict*, this is the story of the novelist's obesession with restoring a villa deep in the Umbrian hills.
Judith Hellman, *Journeys among Women: Feminism in Five Italian Cities* (UK, Polity Press, 1987/US, OUP, 1987). Good, readable study of the womens' movements since 1968 in Turin, Milan, Reggio Emilia, Verona and Casserta. Slightly limited focus – mostly on the activities of the *Unione Donne Italiane* (UDI).
Lucia C Birnbaum, *"Liberazione Della Donna": Feminism in Italy* (US & UK, Wesleyan University Press, 1986). Good general survey – focuses on post war developments.

FICTION

Sibilla Alermo, *A Woman* (UK, Virago, 1979/US, University of California Press, 1980). A classic in Italy, first published in 1906, the semi-autobiographical story of a girl growing up, dominated by her love for her father, but determined to break away and forge her own life.
Natalia Ginzburg, *The Road into the City and Dry Heart* (1963; UK, Carcanet, 1989/US, Arcade, 1990) and others. The constraints of family life are a dominant theme in Ginzburg's writing, and her own upbringing is the source for this rigorous yet lyrical work. A radical politician who sits in the Senate in Rome, she is Italy's best-known woman writer, and most of her books are available in translation.
Dacia Maraini, *Woman at War* (UK, Lighthouse Books, 1984/US, Italica Press, 1989). By one of Italy's best-known contemporary writers, this book records, in diary form, a woman's growing self-awareness, beginning on holiday with her husband. It encompasses weird characters, political argument and a wealth of sensual detail. By the same author, *The Train* (UK, Camden Press, 1989), a brilliant satire on student life in the 1960s, follows a group of friends on their way to an international socialist gathering in Helsinki. Her latest work is *Isolina* (UK, Peter Owen, 1993), a historical novel based on the true story of a young working-class woman, murdered for her lively spirit in 1900.
Elsa Morante, *History* (UK, Penguin, 1985/US, Vintage, 1984, o/p). Capturing the experience of daily Roman life during World War II, this is probably the most vivid fictional picture of the conflict as seen from the city.
Sharon Wood (ed), *Italian Women Writing* (UK, Manchester University Press, 1994). Thirteen short stories – in Italian – written in the turbulent period since World War II.

Thanks to Diana Pritchard and Jane Harkess for useful insights, and Susan Bassnett, who obtained most of the addresses listed above.

Jamaica

L ush green mountains, idyllic beaches and a tropical climate attract foreign visitors to Jamaica year round. Tourism is integral to the national economy and strings of discos, expensive restaurants and watersports centres line the coast roads. However, this is not an easy destination for women travelling alone. Jamaican culture is unquestionably macho, fighting talk is big, reggae lyrics often misogynist, and the popular cult of Rastafarianism, however benevolent its philosophy may seem, is firmly based on woman's subordination to man. That said, however, if you hang on to your self-confidence and keep a sense of humour it's possible to have a great time.

A history of rebellion and political gun-slinging has given Jamaica a reputation among its Caribbean neighbours for being "ruff and facety" (feisty). Political tensions have calmed considerably since the 1993 election, but the continuing deep recession, chronic unemployment and high taxes still leave large sections of the population in a poverty trap. Street crime is common and the large numbers of usually well-heeled tourists are an obvious target.

Kingston has the worst reputation for muggings and people will warn you, with good reason, against wandering around the capital at night. Other warnings, just as freely given – against the "quashie dem" (low life) who hang out in the tourist resorts, against "dreadlocks" and "baldheads" (without dreadlocks) – needn't be taken so seriously.

While there is no general threat of sexual attack, it's hard to escape the assumption that a white woman travelling alone is rich and on the lookout for a holiday lover – someone to share a good time and hard currency with. You can expect all manner of comments and every type of pick-up line from the sweet and caressing to the blatantly upfront. If you do accept an offer, be aware that you'll be expected to stick with the same man in any one place; ugly scenes can and do arise from women attempting to pick up and drop partners. A delicate balance of exploitation goes on between locals and tourists in the main resorts and it doesn't take much to offend macho sensibilities. Once you've become known in a place you'll find the atmosphere noticeably relaxes.

None of this makes for easy contact with local **women**. Unlike the men, they may show no particular interest in striking up conversations, partly because they're too busy making ends meet, and partly because they see Western women, with all the allure of wealth, as dangerous competition. While men are traditionally seen as the breadwinners in Jamaican society, a large number of women – almost half the adult female population – are single mothers who shoulder supreme responsibility for children, both economically and in terms of household work. This contradiction, together with the assertion of women's importance in preserving African tradition by passing down customs through the family, is powerfully highlighted in the work of Jamaica's most radical women's group Sistren (see *Books* at the end of this chapter). In recent years, too, young Jamaican women have become a forceful presence in the country's traditionally male-dominated music scene. The extraordinarily aggressive sexuality of the female posses who have come to dominate the dance halls provides a refreshing, if complex, response to the the overtly misogynistic lyrics of ragga megastars. "Dancehall Queens", the most outrageous, sassiest dancers of all, are frequently as much in demand as the male DJs, while some women have taken up the mike in order to respond to the sexist taunts of their male contemporaries.

Ruff Spots and Rent-a-Dreads

Katy Noakes works in a black arts resource centre in Bristol. She went to Jamaica with a friend, Fiona Parker, in late 1993. This was their first trip to the island.

G oing to Jamaica was accidental. We'd planned to go to Cuba, but lacking the stamina to face the travel agent's queues, we grabbed the first bookable flight heading anywhere south of America. And so we came to be at Montego Bay's Donald Sangster airport, armed only with a five-year-old guidebook listing hotels which were way over our budget even then, and surrounded by a planeload of Bud-swigging red-faced American college boys. A group of women in national costume danced and sang in the sweltering heat, adverts for lord knows how many different types of rum plastered the airport walls; everybody everywhere seemed to have something to sell and were intent on selling it. The realization that we were in at the deep end slowly dawned, but like well-briefed independent travellers we set about looking confident, acting as if we knew what we were doing and trying to give off a "no messing or ripping us off" vibe. We should have known better.

Jamaica relies on tourism for nearly fifty percent of its income; the island attracts over a million visitors a year, its population is only 2.2 million and more people of Jamaican origin live outside the island than on it. It doesn't take a mathematician to work out that the islanders have an international outlook and a streetwise front isn't really going to fool anyone – most people have seen it all before.

Opting for the taxi driver with the most trustworthy face, four wheels and at least two doors, we set off from the airport on our quest for those stretches of calm, idyllic palm-lined beaches. Women don't need to worry especially about using public transport; if a journey is dangerous it probably won't have anything to do with gender. More people die in road accidents than by other means, but once you see how many people can fit into a car you realize that the number of deaths isn't necessarily related to the number of actual accidents. Jamaican taxis are known as the eighth wonder of the world. This could either be because at least eight drivers will be vying for your custom or because eight is the average number of passengers. You might not see any need to lose weight before exposing all in a bikini, but if you haven't the money to rent a car to yourself, a diet merits serious consideration.

Having found a cheap hotel we decided to take a walk and get our bearings. Unwanted attention comes in many well-rehearsed, usually good-humoured forms and it doesn't take long to work out that in Jamaica you have to deal direct. Apologetically, we tried telling the women who wanted to braid our hair "Not now", which means later on. We tried just walking by and nodding a smile, which means you want to talk, preferably business, and we tried laughing and saying our hair was too short. If you're not interested in what someone has to sell, just say no and say it firmly. It is actually possible to braid short hair. The unfortunate consequence of an over-polite attitude can be seen on cropped and braided tourists on beaches island-wide.

Depressed by the recommended tourist option of private beaches, we headed for a secluded cove on the way into town, planning to relax and catch up with some sleep. A group of dreadlocked men and small boys waded in the sea with a large fishing net. The late afternoon sun still beat hot on the otherwise deserted beach and just as we were enjoying our guidebook moment a boy appeared from nowhere brandishing an aloe vera leaf and pouncing enthusiastically on my leg. "Yuh wan some aloe?" he piped.

"Um, well not really, no", I replied.

I was too late. The pace in Jamaica is generally slow except when it comes to cash transactions. "Got some dollars for me?" he asked, pronouncing the magic word which summoned five of his friends who all kindly offered to relieve us of our Western burdens such as cigarettes and money. George, the oldest of them at nineteen, warned us that the town was seething with thieves and "nuff bad bwoys". We needed a guide, he told us in a tone which managed to convey both menace and concern. Noting our scepticism, he pointed to the scar around his neck and chatted merrily about his recent stint in prison by way of proving how dangerous the town is. It wasn't so bad inside, he said, because most of his spars had all been in there at some point too and anyway, he shrugged, it was just part of life. Suitably impressed by his scar, we decided that our first day maybe wasn't the best time to accept George's offer to see more of his life, and headed back to the hotel.

The next morning we accepted the offer of a lift to Negril from a hotel resident. With its seven miles of white beach, the reddest sunsets and a renowned laid-back attitude left by the 1960s' hippies who favoured the town, we were convinced that tranquility was finally within our grasp. When Leon, our driver, dismissed our destination as a "ruff spot" we shrugged it off as another display of over-zealous tourist control.

The hour-long ride took in a technicolour landscape of cane fields, colonial relics, ramshackle huts and random, roadside traders who appeared for work from no apparent nearby town. The combination of heat, blue skies and lush, vividly coloured fauna was overwhelming. Corrugated iron houses sprung up here and there and a young girl walking through a fishing village had handwritten "Gun girl dunnomess" on her T-shirt. Jamaica's contrasts were certainly striking.

From sixteen to sixty, female tourists are bombarded with lyrical sweet talk.

Negril's parish of Westmoreland is a lively farming region with more than its fair share of pot-holed roads and booming sound systems. Leon dropped us off to catch the bus to one of the cheap, rented huts which line the beach. "Your destination blow-job city", wisecracked the bus conductor. Another undue warning, we thought, and laughed.

Most of our time in Negril was spent laughing; it was the best strategy for dealing with what would otherwise be infuriating. A human free-for-all (except everything has its price), Negril is home to one of Jamaica's most popular tourist souvenirs. This is where the walking, talking and frequently dancing male dolls, commonly known as "rent-a-dreads" or "rastitutes" make their living by patrolling the beach and "entertaining" unattached visiting females. From sixteen to sixty, female tourists are bombarded with lyrical sweet talk. This was something we were unprepared for and it took me several looks in the mirror to check that I hadn't turned into a Kim Basinger clone before I realized what was going on.

Being in Negril must be something like experiencing a twenty-four hour Chippendale extravaganza. Madonna may have coined the phrase vogueing, but these boys have claimed it as their national dance, breaking into a move every time a fresh female opportunity presents itself. "I have children in France, one Italian an' I have one in Germany. I an' I a good father, seen", belched Desmond, Rasta of thirty-something years and one of Jamaica's leading export agents. Perched by the bar, keeping a keen eye out for future female investments, Desmond took a swig of his cocktail and explained his theory of paternal responsibility. "Dis Jah a say, I an' I have control over my life an' de youth they 'ave theirs." Exactly how a six-year-old is responsible for their own life somehow got lost in the mesh of Rasta soundbites and rum. "Dis place like Sodom anyhow", he belched, another cocktail and a good few rejections later.

Male prostitution differs from female prostitution in that the men remain in control. "We run t'ings seen," said one disgruntled man who wasn't going to take a rejection standing up. The number of female tourists who are happy to play the game can make it difficult when you're trying to persuade someone that you didn't just come to Jamaica to sample the "big bamboo" they are

"Rassclat! That woman went with three different men last night. She act like a one woman Oxfam show!"

offering – a situation which is exacerbated by the high profile of resorts like *Hedonism*, where American students spend their holidays dressed in strategically placed tassles and fuelled on intravenous rum.

Respect has to be earned and while women will be implored to "go natural" by countless sweet-talking men who are all pitching a "positive t'ing", women who concede will be branded for "running around". When I said how good it was to see a German woman out partying with her daughter one night, one of the men who hung around our rooms shrieked with laughter, "Rassclat! That woman went with three different men last night. She act like a one woman Oxfam show!"

Despite everyone's warnings we were still determined to reach Kingston and decided to head back to Mo' Bay for the weekly train through the Blue Mountains. Peace and tranquility still eluded us, but something had obviously woven its magic because we didn't bother to check the timetable. The train wasn't running. There's a saying about travel in Jamaica that getting from A to B is no problem; it's what happens in between that can throw you off track.

Our diversion took us via a funeral party at St Anne's on the north coast, in completely the opposite direction to Kingston. Leon, who had originally driven us to Negril, assured us that we would be welcome and that there would be lifts to Kingston from the party. Keen to see more of the island and its people, we accepted without reservations. Leon was at least sixty years old and his friends were all respectable, middle-aged businessmen with whom, we reasoned, we must be safe.

Set in a million-dollar mansion on the top of a hill, surrounded by acre after acre of verdant land, the party was hosted by ex-ministers, businessmen and general cronies of the Jamaica Labour Party leader, "don" Edward Seaga. Most of the people there lived in North America, coming back to their Jamaican playground at weekends. The women were mostly light-skinned or Syrian and the men's main concern was money, with which they could buy and use anything – us included.

The house came complete with a dark-skinned family who had a yard in the gardens and their own bit of patio to dance on, marked out by a white line. It was apartheid in our faces and taking the first lift out, we fled. When we came across an overturned truck in the village at the bottom of the hill, our accountant driver beeped his horn impatiently and the female passenger shouted out for a "nigga ghul" to come tell her what had happened. The thought that these village people had inconvenienced them by having an accident outraged them. The thought that someone might need help just didn't occur.

The party prepared us for Kingston, which spread out like another bad traffic accident at the base of the Blue Mountains. Our bus route had taken us through the heartland of Jamaica, past small towns and huts where images of poverty were countered with land for subsistence and breathtaking scenery. The ramshackle huts crammed together along the freeways under the city smog had not even this appeal. I couldn't help wondering what had happened to make it go so wrong.

The disparity between rich and poor which we had glimpsed in St Anne's was magnified in Kingston, where a sharp divide separates the uptown gentry from the downtown ghettos. Denham Town and Jones Town were like embers around the blitzed debris of Trench Town. Market women piled up their fruit on the cracked slabs of paving stone and the people trying to scratch out a living far outnumbered those who had come to buy. Meanwhile, the middle classes in new Kingston spoke with American accents, ate in American diners, watched satellite TV and kept their eyes firmly averted from life at the bottom of the hill.

Without any contacts and feeling too voyeuristic to walk around town alone, we cut our stay in Kingston short. Heading out of town on a bus, we made the mistake of asking fellow passengers what all the graffiti about Jim Brown meant. The bus went suddenly silent and the faces froze aghast. We'd involuntarily raised the issue of politics and no one was prepared to risk a comment.

Our return to Westmoreland was a relief. The rent-a-dreads knew by now to leave us alone and once that barrier had been overcome we were free to enjoy their friendship and accept their invitations to homes in nearby villages. We spent surreal afternoons watching *Scarface* and Kung-fu videos in a yard full of Rastas and rudeboys, went on overnight drives over mountains and past lakes under skies of the clearest, brightest stars, sang along to calypso and Madonna at the top of our voices and spent endless heated hours discussing the position of women in Jamaica. "I like you ragga English", said a self-styled bandalero after one such verbal wrangle, "You take the bait every time, but you think I dunna know the score, huh?" Slapping me round the backside with the fish he was preparing for tea, he ran off giggling.

Our journey back to the airport was a day later than planned – we'd totally forgotten the date. A friend agreed to drive us and in true Jamaican fashion we set off with a car crammed full of people who came along for the ride. Running into a police roadblock, we were asked to get out and spread ourselves over the car to be searched. The police found a fingernail-sized amount of ganja at the bottom of my bag and vindictively fined Tony, the driver, five hundred Jamaican dollars for "failing to stop". It was obvious that we weren't travelling with a family of official guides and the authorities apparently felt that such unsanctioned mixing should be punished.

Leaving Jamaica was the first time I have cried at an airport. Our time had been frustrating, hilarious and eye-opening. Even with the most blood-boiling kind of hassle, the humour at least, was hard to resist. "Hey strong English", shouted one man as we took our bags out of the car, "Yuh wan come use your leg muscles an' chop off my balls?"

T R A V E L N O T E S

Languages Most people speak patois or "Jamaica talk" among themselves, but people can easily switch into English. Katy Noakes found listening to the banter one of Jamaica's "biggest, unmarketed pleasures".

Transport Buses are inexpensive, but slow, and the driving can be pretty wild. Mini-buses operate on all the main routes, always jam-packed since they only set off when full. Some taxis have meters, but it's wise to sort out the fare before you set off. Hitching is definitely not recommended.

Accommodation Hotels tend to be expensive and it's usually better to try to find a room for rent. Lots of houses on the beach at Negril offer inexpensive rooms.

Special Problems There are varying reports about the safety of Kingston – the shanty-town areas in the southwest of the capital are certainly to be avoided – but provided you feel confident and carry very little money it's worth a visit. Market prices shoot up one hundred percent at the sight of a white face, so if you are white, be prepared to bargain.

Standard medical care is very dubious and medicines expensive, so make sure you are insured and, as far as possible, take your own supplies. Ganja or marijuana is widely grown and smoked, but it's illegal. It's also very, very strong.

Guides *Caribbean Islands Handbook* (UK, Trade and Travel/US, Passport Press) includes a reasonable section on Jamaica.

CONTACTS

Sistren Theatre Collective, 20 Kensington Crescent, Kingston 5. Founded in 1977, Sistren is a theatre collective for working-class women who use drama, workshops, pamphlets and screenprints to explore how women see themselves and how they can improve their lives in relation to issues such as sexual violence, work, relationships with men and with other women. The group works mainly in the shanty towns and in rural areas, but it's worth getting in touch to try to see them in action.

BOOKS

Ziggi Alexander and Audrey Dewjee (eds), *The Wonderful Adventures of Mrs Seacole in Many Lands* (1957; UK & US, Oxford University Press, 1990). Mary Seacole, who was born into Jamaican slave society, writes about her life and travels.

Sistren, *Lionheart Gal – Life Stories of Jamaican Women* (UK, The Women's Press, 1986; reprinted 1994). Edited by Sistren's long-standing artistic director, Honor Ford-Smith, this book is based on testimonies collected in the course of the theatre collective's work with ordinary Jamaican women.

Pat Ellis (ed), *Women of the Caribbean* (UK, Zed Books, 1977/US, Humanities Press). This collection of essays provides a good general introduction to the history and lives of Caribbean women.

Leonard E Barratt, *The Rastafarians: Sounds of Cultural Dissonance* (UK & US, Beacon Press,

1988). Enlightening book on the cult of Rastafarianism.

Jamaica in Focus (Netherlands, Kit Press/Jamaica, Ian Randle Publications, 1993). Authoritative guide to the history, politics, economy and people of Jamaica.

FICTION

Lois Battle, *A Habit of Blood* (UK, Star Books, 1988, o/p/US, St Martin's Press, 1989). Exuberant novel focusing on Jamaica's politics and drug subculture.

Erna Brodber, *Jane and Louisa Will Soon Come Home* (UK, New Beacon Books, 1981). The author's first novel, written in the form of a long prose poem about life in Jamaica.

Michelle Cliff, *Abeng* (US, Penguin, 1992). Explores the life of a young girl growing up among the contradictions of class, colour, blood and Jamaica's history of colonization and slavery.

Pamela Mordecai and Marvyn Morris (eds), *Jamaica Woman* (UK, Heinemann, 1982). Exciting anthology of poems by fifteen Jamaican women.

Olive Senior, *Arrival of the Snake Woman and Other Stories* (UK, Longman, 1989). Lively collection by one of Jamaica's foremost writers.

Also look out for the work of Jamaica's best-known woman poet, Miss Louise Bennett.

Japan

For some years now Japan has been asserting its power as the world's richest nation, the pivotal force of international commerce, technology and fashion. There are signs of this changing: the prolonged recession of the early 1990s, aggravated by fear of competition from China's galloping economic growth, has begun to crack some of the country's confidence. However, the nationalistic pride that accompanied the boom years and relegates visitors from less successful nations to a second-class status has yet to be dented. This is not so much a problem for white Westerners, who tend to be treated with traditional hospitality and courtesy, but Black or Asian visitors (of whatever nationality) face blatant discrimination.

Japan is an expensive country to visit and most travellers staying any length of time look for work. Teaching English can be a surprisingly lucrative business and, though positions in Tokyo are becoming harder to find owing to a growing influx of unemployed graduates from overseas, persistence will usually be rewarded. Another option open to Western women is hostessing (see below) – not as seedy as

it sounds but you have to be pretty desperate to stick it out for long.

The crowds and hectic pace of Japan's cities can be hard to adjust to. Tokyo, in particular, with its pulsing energy and high-tech façade can be quite overwhelming. However, Japan does have a reputation for safety. Sexual harassment and violence are relatively rare (at least on the streets or in the countryside) and, even wandering around at night, you're unlikely to feel personally threatened. It is however, easy to feel isolated. People might be curious about you, and want to question you about Western culture or practise their English, but few follow this up. Especially among older Japanese, Westerners have a reputation for being clumsy, unclean, confrontational, ignorant of etiquette, and very much out of step with the country's peaceful and harmonious way of life. Even if you speak Japanese you'll find it difficult to cross the cultural divide.

Living and working in the country you'll also come up against a deeply entrenched sexism and conservatism. Pornography is evident and available everywhere – in newspapers, advertisements, even early evening television – and prostitution is a well-established industry.

Women in Japan are expected to take a subservient role. The renowned male work ethic, the devotion to a company and a job, is greatly dependent on women's unpaid labour as house-wives. Women are heavily discriminated against in the work-place and are often only taken on by companies as temporary, supplementary labour with lower pay and none of the security and benefits available to full-time workers. It is also quite common for female employees to be pressurized to retire "voluntari-ly" when they reach thirty. Much the same level of discrimination has existed in education and, until relatively recently, in almost all levels of government.

Mama-san's Babies

Sarah Dale, in her late twenties, works as a solicitor in the south of England. She began travelling relatively recently when, driven by the need to escape the cloisters of law, she gathered up her savings and flew to Thailand for an extended holiday. Two months later, running out of money but reluctant to fly home, she heard about "hostessing" in Japan; the last of her savings went on a flight to Tokyo and a bright red silk dress.

The hostess, I learned, was the modern equivalent of the geisha, a centuries-old and highly venerated profession that attracts Japanese girls like a vocation. Geishas are the embodiment of that enduring Japanese icon: feminine perfection. They exist to serve men and preserve the traditional arts such as singing, dancing and playing classical instruments like the *samisen*.

Her modern counterpart, the bar hostess, has exchanged silk kimonos for cocktail dresses, and the *samisen* for a karaoke box. She is considerably less expensive than her predecessor yet she shares the same values: to be the feminine ideal, to entertain, to listen, to be serious, to dazzle with her wit and charm. It is not considered a demeaning job. Certainly no sexual favours are expected – just mild flirtation, perhaps a glimmering eroticism. Many Japanese girls claim to be proud to serve men in this way and be recognized for their "skills". The pursuit of this feminine ideal is revered in Japan like an art form.

Hostess bars, I learned, abound in their thousands in Japan. Each bar has a manageress, always called "Mama-san", who will set the particular, and distinctive character of her establishment. Western girls, particularly of the blonde-haired, blue-eyed variety, are considered a special treat and a myriad bars boast them like a range of exotic fruit. I was enchanted. This would be much more fun than writs and wills and I set out for Tokyo in search of a dissolute life.

As soon as I arrived I found myself a room in a cheap hostel known as a "*Gaijin* House". These are always full of foreigners working as hostesses or English teachers who usually have good job hunting tips to offer. "Just walk into bars on spec and ask for work", they told me. So that same night I staggered out in a haze of jet lag, to the hostess Mecca: "the Ginza". It was impossible to decipher what was and was not a bar, so I took pot luck. My enthusiastic smile and carefully articulated "hostess" was met each time with a horrified hiss of "gaijin", arms arranged into a cross in front of the face and a closed door. Clearly crossbones meant

> "*Gaijin*", I realized was Japanese for foreigner. Literally "outside person", it was the first Japanese word I learned.

"no" and "*gaijin*", I realized, was Japanese for foreigner. Literally, it means "outside person". It was the first Japanese word I learned.

Perhaps I kept walking into private parties that night or perhaps I was just damned ugly. I didn't understand and I didn't find work. I crawled away from the Ginza and headed back to the "outside person's" house.

By Monday morning I was freshly resolved. I scoured the ex-pats' newspaper, *The Japan Times*, and found several bars advertising for Western girls to work as hostesses. I made some calls, had an interview and got a job at a bar called *San Michel* in Akasakamitsuke. Not quite the Ginza but nevertheless a thriving business district.

All dolled up in a silk dress I'd had run up cheaply in Bangkok, I tottered off on high heels to my new life. On entering the bar I was immediately faced with a full-length portrait of Mama-san reclining in a cocktail dress that she had thrown on. Mama was a middle-aged lady, petite, shrew-like and a bit tawdry. She had been born in Japan but was third-generation Korean and so still considered *gaijin*. Starting life herself as a bar hostess she had saved enough money by whatever means and started her own enterprise. She spoke no English and used "Boy" as her interpreter. Boy was a girl – or at least that was the consensus of opinion – and her job was to greet customers, bring drinks to the table, and fire hostesses.

> **Mama called me her baby, plucked a hair out of my chin and barked at me to sit.**

Mama called me her baby, plucked a hair out of my chin and barked at me to sit. A posse of women gathered round, all sporting that ubiquitous silk dress. There was Danielle, a skinny American with flaming red hair. She had just graduated and was hostessing to repay college loans. Anna and Femka, two marvellously tall Dutch girls saving for another season of going gaga in Goa. Sophia, a sexy Swede, with an unrealized dream to be a model and legs that undulated from beneath her skirts, and Domarra, an Italian linguist perfecting her Japanese. Completing the group was a loud fat woman from Manchester, whom I got the distinct impression I had been chosen to replace. All these gorgeous girls and then us two.

Our guests arrived. A group of Japanese salarymen, that is business-men, on a corporate razzle. Prohibitively expensive for the individual, hostess bars are mostly frequented by salarymen on the obligatory evening out with the boss. The company foots the bill and all the salaryman has to do is drink himself into oblivion and remain there until his boss says he can leave.

We jumped to attention and in concert squealed: "*Irrashaimasse*", meaning welcome. High heels scurrying, we fetched whisky and water, glasses and ice, bowls of sweets and hot wet flannels . . .

The flannels, *"oshibori"*, were for the guests to wipe their hands with, a Japanese ritual unfailingly observed before eating or drinking. Mama pointed to where each of us should sit and the party began.

Assiduously we catered to their every need; we topped up drinks and clinked ice cubes in glasses, we lit their cigarettes, and intermittently, unwrapped a sweet to delicately pop into a guest's mouth.

The usual questions and small talk commenced. You know, the subjects that always surface when people don't know each others' language very well. Then gradually as the whisky unlocked our guests' tongues and inhibitions took flight the conversation became increasingly bawdy. Each hostess's innuendo was met with admiring guffaws from the guests while more serious comment was politely listened to and ignored.

We were perfect young ladies. Never so inelegant as to cross our legs, lean back in our seats, bite our nails or play with our hair. Never so rude as to divert our attention for a second, our admiring gaze for an instant from these latter day Samurai who, weary from another day fighting for Japan's economic miracle, would look to us adoring *gaijin* girlies to ease away their tensions. Departures from this strictly observed code of etiquette were met with a public shriek from Mama and a whispered interpretation from Boy.

Domarra felt that hostessing was the perfect opportunity to practise the Japanese language and exchange cultures. I found there was a limit to how much you could discuss with a middle-aged Japanese man who has worked for Mitsubishi all his life, cannot speak a word of English and is four sheets to the wind. The salarymen I met were more interested in exchanging saliva. Like little boys they would giggle and tell me their hobby was "girl-hunting". Tentatively they would try to touch our legs but the gentlest of reproaches, such as a clucking no, a surprised giggle and a firm push or a wiggle of the hips and a motherly slap, was enough to bring an immediate retraction and a resumption of that blank expression, as if nothing had ever happened. Femka believed in preventative measures and employed the beguiling tactic of "lovingly" clinging onto her guest's hands so that she knew exactly where they were. Mama was approving. This was a "decent" bar. We were all her babies. The only thing we were to massage was ego.

The art of hostessing we learned was mere coquetry. Never yes, never no, but a tantalizing maybe. To our guests it was the stuff of dreams. It kept them coming for months.

For me the evening's climax was certainly before the guests' arrival. We would sit around swapping travellers' tales and talking about our lives back home and what we planned to do next. There was a strong sense of togetherness and we rallied each other along. I don't think any of us could quite capture the reality of the job we were doing. Our bizarre placement seemed more and more hysterical.

Our guests frequently asked us to sing karaoke. These requests were met each time with some moments of feigned modesty, as was required by Mama-san, and then a rather undignified scramble for the microphone as we each sought a three-minute retreat from wandering palms and inane conversation. Microphone firmly in hand I yelled out "Sonny" and everyone danced. The guests were at their wooden best and the girls were not much better. No one had their heart in it, no one had the beat and a domino of glances passed through us. I remember it like a framed picture.

> *Throwing away such girlish things as make-up, heels and Bic razors I claimed back my sanity and decided to be myself.*

San Michel closed at a quarter to midnight. Depending on the caprice of their boss, the salarymen would either stagger hiccuping to another bar or to their homes for a few hours' sleep before doing it all again the next day. After bowing to our guests the other girls and I would leave the bar. Once around the corner we threw off our heels, and like a fleet of Cinderellas ran in stockinged feet through the streets of Tokyo for our last trains home.

I suppose what really got to me about hostessing was that I had put a price on my freedom. Ordinarily, when faced with a slobbering old man with a red face and a preoccupation with asking "How big is your boyfriend's dick?" one might shout some abuse, turn away, and leave. In this situation, however, I had relinquished such rights; I had sold them to Mama-san. It was mental prostitution.

So I decided to "empower" myself. Throwing away such girlish things as make-up, high heels and Bic razors I claimed back my sanity and decided to be myself. Openly flouting the rules of decorum, I recklessly crossed my legs, deliberately leaned back in my seat; heedless, I unwrapped those sweets and popped them, horror of horrors, into my own mouth. Most offensive of all I offered opinions, disagreed, argued, behaved just like the owner of a pair of Doc Marten boots should. I played the raconteur and clowned around, but in my own way and not in the freeze-dried, vacuum-packed fashion they expected. Curiously they responded with laughter and fascination. Perhaps they were bemused to see this in a woman.

Something would just not let me quit. I suppose I was curious to see how long I could last being me: two weeks basically, and Boy was sent to fire me. She gave me a big hug and my wages up to date; £50 for each night I turned up and an inexplicable £15 deduction for the use of toilet paper!

A lot more money than this can be earned! The sleazier the bar, the more Japanese you speak, the longer you've been around and, of course, the longer your legs, the higher the rates. You can double, triple this basic with tips earned for anything from being wined, dined or complimented to singing a soulful ballad or performing an exotic belly dance. The job can be as risqué as you want it to be and consequently you can earn as much money as you like. A woman able to handle the masquerade and approach the whole affair as some peculiar brand of performance art can make a killing. I got my fifty quid for just turning up!

With the hostessing mystique shattered, I found myself a job as an English teacher, which is an option open to anybody with a degree and English as their native language. Within weeks I was wearing a suit again, even carrying a briefcase. I had been sucked back into respectability despite myself.

I later met up with Anna, one of the Dutch girls and she told me that she had been fired a few days after me. It seemed Mama thought she smelt. Anna didn't care. She shrugged and told me, "Nobody care zat I smell in India. Oh well, tonight I go for job as bunny girl." Mama-sans do hire and fire indiscriminately, but there is always another hostess job just around the corner. Femka, meanwhile, was doing famously holding court to a string of admirers. Somehow she was able to slip on the mask more comfortably than I, the deodorant more successfully than Anna. Danielle like me took a teaching job and no doubt Domarra is there to this day, exchanging cultures.

> *In the most sinister privatization of all, the chemistry in human relationships has been set apart and sold as a service.*

The loud fat one from Manchester left a few days after I arrived. Hostess with the Mostest, she had been at *San Michel* the longest. Six months of hostessing had made her enough money to do an overland trip to Israel. On her last night she gave a sonorous rendition of *My Way* on the karaoke and then gave me all her old clothes in exchange for a packet of condoms.

About ten months later, when I was living in a different part of Japan, I was waiting for a train and spotted Sophia pasted up on a billboard – all legs, she was modelling shoes. She had realized her dream.

The women I met who hostessed throughout their stay developed a jaundiced view of the country. I could see how this could happen; working at night and sleeping in the day meant that it was easy to miss some of the fragments that make up Japan. As a teacher and through living with a Japanese family I saw women treated in a different way. Marriages, which are often arranged, are an economic necessity. The family is like a small business, producing the next generation of mothers and salarymen. In the most sinister privatization of all, the chemistry in human relationships seems to have been disentangled, set apart and sold as a service. Instead of relaxing at home with their families, Japanese salarymen go out in droves to relax with strangers. When I was teaching, my students bowed and called me *"sensei"* in hushed tones. This was refreshing after the hostess bar, but eventually the rigid formality seemed almost ridiculous – it had a sterility about it. Accustomed to living in a melting pot of emotions and responses it was difficult to find my role.

I'm glad I had a short stint at hostessing. It gave me first-hand experience of an aspect of Japan that is often missed by travellers. I was surprised to see how deeply rooted and unshakeable were my principles. My need to be appreciated for everything I am as a woman, rather than just one feminine façade, was more intense than I had ever really known. Hostessing helped me to work out what I don't want with my life.

Finding a Place in Kyoto

Riki Therivel went to Japan on an American scholarship to study civil engineering. She lived for almost one-and-a-half years in the country – including some time with a Japanese family – did a variety of teaching jobs to boost her savings and travelled extensively throughout the country and into China.

When I left the US for an eighteen-month stay in Kyoto, I knew almost nothing about Japan. But I planned to rectify that by living as much like a Japanese person as possible. In my fantasies this involved spending long hours cross-legged in a remote Zen monastery and communicating predominantly in *haiku* verse.

This vision faded more or less as soon as I arrived. I was taken, at 10pm, from the airport to the university, where my fellow students (all men) were waiting to greet me. Over the next few weeks I set about learning how to read and speak Japanese. The other students were pleasant and polite, and we got on in very slow and simple sentences. I noticed, however, that they seemed uncomfortable with direct questions and invariably called to their friends to confirm their opinions. No one seemed willing to express a personal view or even enter into a discussion on their own, although they asked me many questions, especially about my views of Japan. At that point I started understanding how very group-oriented the Japanese are, and also how easily the group casts out members who do not conform. As a foreigner, I wasn't expected to understand the group "rules", but, equally, I couldn't expect to be completely accepted.

People in Japan work long hours, usually six days a week, and generally take only a few days' holiday a year. In the evenings, the men often go out to dinner and then to the bar with their fellow workers, spending little time at home. This leaves little space for other things, like travelling around the country, which I also wanted to do. So after a month of living Japanese-style I started going to lunch with other friends and taking Saturdays off to travel around. Unfortunately this seemed to alienate the other students, and the tentative friendships that had begun chilled quickly. Luckily the university soon matched me up with a host family who had volunteered to help a foreigner to adapt to Japan; the Sueishis took me to festivals, taught me to cook Japanese meals, lent me their sewing machine, and really did become my "family".

I had been provided with an apartment in a foreign students' housing block, a modern Western-style affair, and very luxurious considering that Japanese students usually live in tiny three metres by three metres rooms. But three of us soon tired of what we considered to be a gilded cage, so we moved to a Japanese-style house. The move itself was an exercise in formality and ritual: the house had been rented by friends-of-friends who were willing to recommend us, then my host mother and I visited the landlady with presents, and the negotiations reached a crescendo of innumerable phone calls before we were deemed acceptable tenants.

Living in a Japanese neighbourhood was a wonderful way to learn about everyday life. Each morning the women would wave off first their husbands then their children. On my morning shopping trip I would see them all in the street, sweeping the already-clean tarmac; by the time I returned they would all be in their houses again. The recycling truck would come by with blaring loud-speakers and we would scuttle out with our newspaper bundles. The garbagemen, in turn, were greeted with beautiful piles of neat blue plastic bags. According to a Japanese proverb, "the wife is happy when her husband is healthy and out of the house"; the women in my neighbourhood must have been happy most of the time.

What struck me was the uniformity of the women's lives. Girls are expected to finish high school and perhaps study English or cooking or fashion during a two-year stint at college. Then they work for a few years and marry. The usual age for marriage is between 23 and 25 and about half are arranged. This initially shocked me, but my host mother reasoned that people from similar backgrounds who have the support of both families will develop love, or at least what she called "warm currents between them".

The first child comes a few years after the marriage, and the second a few years after that. There is a lot of social pressure to stick to this format. My host mother said that, despite her agreement with feminist principles, she would still suggest this traditional path to a daughter, simply because not conforming would lead her into so many difficulties.

Women in Japan hold their cups and food bowls differently from men, bow more deeply, and use different verb endings. I learned, only after several collisions, with much subsequent apologetic bowing, that women walk through doors after men. Women rarely wear shorts or sleeveless blouses, or even anything very colourful; black and white were definitely *de rigueur* while I was there. Traditional events like tea ceremonies, visits to temples, or trips to the bathhouse also involve etiquette that is best learned from someone who has been before. Foreigners can get away with almost any infringement of the rules and are not expected to master more than the simplest Japanese words. But this only serves to confirm preconceptions that they are invading barbarians.

During my stay I met a lot of Japanese people, but the cultural differences were so strong that I made few friends. The Japanese express themselves predominantly in allusions, ritual phrases and body positions; very different to the more verbal and confrontational style of communication I was used to. Also I was brought up with an entrenched belief in egalitarianism, whereas Japan is very hierarchy-oriented, so we had different preconceptions of what friendship should be. Foreigners have their place in the hierarchy, usually at one of the extremes. White Americans are treated with a mixture of admiration and contempt; admiration, strangely enough, because of their victory in the war, and contempt because Japan is now beating them economically. The Germans are widely respected because of their own post-war achievements, while Blacks and Asians are seen as inferior; if Japan could rise from economic obscurity why couldn't they?

Foreign women, with their strong opinions and aggressive mannerisms, are considered threatening.

Women in Japan are trained (externally at least) to buttress, build up, and coddle their menfolk, and are simply not expected to have any opinions of their own. My conversations with women of my age (mid-twenties) consisted of their questions and my answers, or my questions and their deflections. Of course, there were exceptions: the open-minded and incredibly charming Japanese woman who joined me on a journey through China; the woman I met in a crowded and steamy cafeteria who involved me in a wonderful and unintelligible discussion about nuclear war (I think); and my host mother who is one of the most energetic, self-assured and lovable people I have met. But generally the women I met treated me deferentially, tentatively, and often shied away, as though I were a tall and unpredictable extra-terrestrial.

Foreign residents in Tokyo and Kyoto have founded women's groups, where meeting times are listed in the English-language papers. Japanese women's organizations exist, but these are more like special interest clubs than support groups. Because foreign women tend to be viewed primarily as foreigners and only secondarily as women, I don't think that they would provide much help for the woman traveller in Japan.

Because Japanese women are expected to be so submissive, foreign women, with their strong opinions and aggressive mannerisms, are considered threatening, especially by men. On the other hand, foreign women are also attractive because they are different, and possibly because they are thought to be more sexually available than Japanese women. A Japanese male friend said to me "You're American which puts you above me, but a woman which puts you below me, so we must be equal." One man used to send me and several Western friends an endless stream of postcards and presents, as though we were movie stars. My supervisor asserted his control over me shortly after I arrived by insisting that I go home with him after a drinking party. He woke up his sixty-year-old wife at midnight so that she could prepare snacks for us and then politely insisted that I stay the night as a guest; from then on I avoided the office drinking parties.

However, as unpleasant and frustrating as the sexual discrimination often was, it was never translated into physical harassment. Japan prides itself on its low crime rate, and one can walk around safely anywhere at any time. Public transport is invariably clean, punctual, and safe. The occasional drunken man may mumble "you are beautiful" or "speak English to me", but I never had to go beyond a polite "no" to stop it. Because crime is so rare in their country, many Japanese see other countries, and especially America, as highly dangerous places where drug abuse is rampant and gun-toting hoodlums lurk on every street corner. They were much more afraid of me than I was of them.

I travelled around a lot, predominantly by bicycle. Japan is dotted with beautiful rural villages tucked between steep mountains, and I spent many pleasant afternoons sweating my way up to them and careering back down. The roads are clogged with cars near the cities, making cycling dangerous, but an hour's ride got me away from the traffic and into as much countryside as Japan still has. There aren't many cyclists in Japan, and even fewer women cyclists, but those that I did see were friendly and always yelled out a greeting as they sped past.

Hitch-hiking in Japan is easy and safe, even for a lone woman. The difficult part is explaining what is wanted, since few Japanese hitch-hike themselves. We made big signs, in Japanese, "please take us with you", and never had problems getting picked up, even with a bike. In fact, once they picked us up, the drivers seemed to feel responsible for the outcome of our journey, and often drove us directly to our destination. We finally learned to ask the drivers where they were going first, and rearrange our journey to save them the sometimes very lengthy detour.

Finding a job in Japan was easy, especially once I had made a few connections. I taught English to schoolchildren, office workers and doctors, corrected translations of Japanese articles, and worked as an assistant at an international Zen Buddhism symposium. English teachers are in high demand and the pay is quite good.

The Zen symposium took place only a week before I left the country and somehow fulfilled my initial romantic vision of Japan. I had worked for the symposium committee for several months, so that when the foreign scholars arrived I felt like a host rather than a visitor. We all went to a traditional tea ceremony and, kneeling to be served by a kimono-clad woman, with a view of a rock garden and pond, I felt that maybe I had learned a lot in Japan after all. I still didn't feel at home and would probably always be treated as a foreigner, but I had learned how to cope with loneliness and a thoroughly foreign culture.

TRAVEL NOTES

Languages Japanese. Little English is spoken outside the cities.

Transport Extensive, efficient and expensive. Most travellers opt for the excellent train network on which you can save money by buying a Rail Pass in your country of departure. Hitching is very unusual but fairly safe.

Accommodation Japanese-style hotels (*ryokan*) are difficult to cope with and, unless you have knowledge of the language, it's best to go to the tourist office for advice. Look out for "business hotels" which can be up to fifty percent cheaper than normal ones. "Love hotels" are best avoided although they are not only used for illicit sex; privacy can be hard to come by in Japan's overcrowded cities and people are willing to rent rooms by the hour.

Guides *Japan – A Travel Survival Kit* (Lonely Planet) packs in a wealth of detail.

CONTACTS

All the following are in Tokyo.

TWIN (Tokyo Women's Information Network), c/o BOC Publishing, Shinjuku 1-9-6, Shinjuku-ku, Tokyo 167 (☎358 3941). The best source of information on feminist groups in Japan (both Japanese and English-speaking). Organizes feminist English classes and produces a biannual journal, *Agora Agoramini.*

International Feminists of Japan, Fujin, Joho Centre, Shinjuku Ku, nr Akebonobashi Station, Exit 4a (meets the first Sunday of every month). Aims to forge better links between Japanese feminist groups and their counterparts abroad. Publishes monthly newsletter, *Feminist Forum.*

Fusen Kaikan (Women's Suffrage), 21-11 Yoyogi 2 Chrome, Shibuya-ku, Tokyo 151 (☎370 0238). Centre for education, research and publishing, with a library and a good permanent exhibition of the life of journalist and political activist Ishikawa Fusae (1893–1980), who was active in the Women's Suffrage League in the 1920s. The staff speak some English.

Gayon House Bookshop, next to Tokyo Union Church (nearest station Omote Sando). Feminist and anti-nuclear books.

LESBIAN GROUPS

There is a fairly well-established lesbian network in Japan, but Japanese and foreign women tend to organize separately. The main meeting points are lesbian weekends arranged every public holiday. For information, write to **Lesbian Contact**, CPO Box 1780, Tokyo 100-91 (send an International Reply Coupon). The group publishes a regular newsletter, *DD*, with articles, listings and events. Japan's few lesbian bars are concentrated in the Shinjuku Sanchome area of Tokyo.

BOOKS

Liza Crichfield Dalby, *Geisha* (US, University of California Press, 1983, o/p). Contemporary study of a living phenomenon. The author, an anthropologist, became a geisha during her stay in Kyoto.

Lesley Downer, *On the Narrow Road to the Deep North* (UK, Sceptre, 1990, o/p/US, Summit Books, 1989, o/p). Slightly smug, but very readable account of the author's journey in the footsteps of Japanese poet, Matsuo Basho, which, like Isabella Bird, led her to the remote northern provinces of Japan.

Sachiko Ariyoshi, *Letters from Sachiko* (UK, Sphere, 1984, o/p/US, Atheneum, 1982, o/p). Letters to the author's sister in the West highlight the constraints faced by women in contemporary Japanese society.

Isabella Bird, *Unbeaten Tracks in Japan* (1880; UK, Virago 1984/US, C E Tuttle, 1971). Includes fascinating descriptions of the remote wildernesses of northern Japan by one of Britain's best-loved and prolific Victorian women travellers.

Shizuko Go, *Requiem* (1973; UK, The Women's Press, 1986/US, Kodansha, 1985). Diary narrative of the last months of World War II, as experienced by the "daughters of military Japan".

Yukio Tanaka (ed), *To Live and to Write: Selections by Japanese Women Writers 1913–1938* (UK & US, Seal Press, 1987). Essays by the first major women writers in Japan, dealing with subjects traditionally taboo for women.

FICTION

Alison Fell, *The Pillow Boy of the Lady Onogoro* (UK, Serpents Tail, 1994). Set in eleventh-century Japan, this novel tells the story of a Lady who, unable to find sexual satisfaction with her aristocratic lover, employs a blind boy to whisper cruelly sensual tales to her from behind a screen, thus inflaming her passions.

Junichiro Tanizaki, *The Makioka Sisters* (UK, Picador, 1983/US, Putnam). A very well-known novel in Japan, with a quintessential heroine struggling between passivity and self-will.

Yuko Tsushima, *Child of Fortune* (UK, The Women's Press, 1986/US, Kodansha, 1992); *The Shooting Gallery and Other Stories* (UK, The Women's Press, 1988/US, Pantheon, o/p). Lucid pictures of the lives and aspirations of contemporary Japanese women and the pressures they face to accept a subservient role.

Michiko Yamamoto, *Betty San: Four Stories* (1973; UK & US, Kodansha, 1992). Again addresses the subservient domestic roles of Japanese women – and also East-West incompatibilities.

Special **thanks** to Sandra Mori for additional background.

Kenya

K enya's image of Westernization, affluence and stability, so effectively developed since independence from the British in 1963, has been somewhat tarnished by recent years of political turmoil, but its attractions – from big game parks to mountains, lakes and mile upon mile of magnificent sandy beaches – continue to draw thousands of tourists every year.

Though Kenya's tourist trade has always been mainly geared toward expensive safari packages and sun-and-sea holidays, plenty of facilities exist for independent travellers. Most women, however, tend to travel in pairs rather than alone. Sexual harassment is a fairly persistent problem, especially along the predominantly Muslim coastline where the experience of mass tourism has fuelled stereotypes of Western women as "loose" and "available". The continual comments and propositions can at times feel personally threatening, and on the beaches it's never a good idea to isolate yourself. Statistics for violent robbery are also high, and carrying any symbol of wealth (in fact anything but the bare necessities) can make you a target. As always, mounting crime goes hand in hand with poverty and deprivation, of which Kenya undoubtedly has its share – evident in the vast urban slums that stretch north from the capital, Nairobi. A major commercial centre, buzzing with vitality, Nairobi is a convenient base for travel, but the prevalent street hassle can detract from its appeal. You'll find life altogether more relaxed – and people most easy-going – away from the city and major resorts. Western Kenya, incorporating Lake Victoria, is particularly recommended in this respect. With its landscape of rolling hills, jungle and low-key national parks this is an area virtually untouched by tourist development.

It's clear that by and large the economic benefits of tourism have failed to filter down to the majority of the population. Though the country is supposedly moving towards a multi-party democracy, against a backdrop of political corruption together with a disturbing rise in ethnic conflict, it is hard to see this happening. President Daniel arap Moi, meanwhile, holds onto power amid mounting accusations of human rights abuses and state repression.

Women are active in local community organizations and there are numerous women's groups throughout the country. Many are associated with *Maedeleo ya Wanawake* (Progress of Women), a popular autonomous organization responsible for setting up multi-purpose centres for health education, skills training and literacy groups. In addition, the National Council of Women of Kenya, partially funded by the government, campaigns to abolish the practice of female genital mutilation, reform legislation on abortion, and increase women's knowledge of contraception. A continuing scandal is the extent to which untested contraceptives (or those banned in the West) are being foisted on Kenyan women.

Knowing Nairobi

Lindsey Hilsum is a journalist and foreign correspondent for the BBC. When she wrote this piece she had been working in Nairobi as a freelance writer and Information Officer for the United Nations Children's Fund.

I t was my first solo walk through the streets of Nairobi. Having just arrived from Latin America, where I learnt that streetwise means ready to run or ready to fend off catcalls, comments and unwelcome hands, I was on my guard. But in Nairobi no man bothered me. I was proffered the occasional elephant-hair bracelet, the odd batik, but no one tried to touch or waylay me. Some months later, a Norwegian woman friend arrived on her first trip outside Europe. As I showed her around Nairobi that afternoon, men shouted and stared at her. Talking to other women later, I understood the problem; because I had already learned to walk with confidence and aggression, no one perceived that I was vulnerable. But my friend gave off an aura of uncertainty – she was obviously a newcomer, a tourist and, as such, was fair game.

It is possible to travel widely in Kenya using public transport. There are hotels and campsites scattered throughout, and people usually go out of their way to help. A lone woman is something of a curiosity in small towns and rural areas but people are more likely to be sympathetic than hostile. "Isn't it sad to be without a husband and children?" I have been asked. My reply, that I prefer it that way, has started many good conversations. People like to talk – a smattering of Swahili helps, but there are many Kenyans who speak English.

For most visitors, getting to see a game park is a high priority. The most comfortable way to go is on an organized tour. I went on one to Masai Mara, and found myself ensconced in a Volkswagen mini-bus with two cowboy-hatted Texans who were "in oil" in Saudi Arabia, an American couple plus toddler also from Saudi, and a lone geriatric British bird-watcher. Other people have found themselves crushed on these tours, straining for a glimpse of a lion through the forest of telephoto lenses, and my sister ended up in the Abedares with a busload of Americans who turned out to have won the trip by being "workers of the year" at a Coca-Cola factory.

> *Hacking my way through the undergrowth at night I realized how threatening the forest can be.*

It's more fun to go independently, but only with a reliable, preferably four-wheel drive vehicle. I spent one hot, frustrating, exhausting week trying to get to Lake Turkana in an ancient Landrover, the remnants of a long-since discarded Ministry of Livestock Development Sheep and Goat project. Accompanied by a friend as mechanically incompetent as myself, I never made it to the lake, but now know all the amateur motor mechanics between Baringo and Barogoi.

If you want to explore the natural rainforest, however, that lies just an hour's drive from Nairobi, you should definitely go with a guide. It's easy and very dangerous to get lost. Hacking my way through the undergrowth at night, in search of two friends and two small children who had not returned from a walk, I realized how threatening the forest can be. One moment it is luxuriant and enticing; the next, when every cough could be a leopard and every thud an elephant, it becomes sinister. We would never have found our friends – who had lit a fire and tucked the children snugly into the forked foot of a tree when they realized at dusk that they were lost – without the local Forest Rest House warden, who searched with us as a guide.

One place that has become popular with low-budget tourists is the largely Muslim island of Lamu. With its white sand beaches and curious melée of backstreets, downmarket restaurants and mosques, it is closer culturally and historically to Zanzibar and Ilha de Mozambique than to the rest of Kenya. Sometimes I think I'm just prejudiced against it. The first time I went, my friend Laura and I took the sweltering eight-hour bus ride from Malindi, and then the boat. The sun blazed as we left the shore, my period started, and I passed out. Stumbling to the quay at Lamu, I collapsed in the dirt. Laura, pursued by a young man informing her of a nice cheap hotel he was sure she'd like, went in search of liquid. She found a bottle of bright orange Fanta. I took one glance and then vomited. All around me were male voices, saying things like, "get her to hospital" and "why don't you go back to your own country?" Needless to say, it was two women who helped us find a place to stay.

Personal experience apart, Lamu can be difficult for women. The traditional Muslim culture has been sent reeling by the advent of beer and bikinis, and while women tourists bathe topless, Lamu women walk the streets clad in black robes from head to foot. Concerned about the corruption of local youth and the rising numbers of "beach boys" who hang around tourists, the local authorities are reported to have forbidden young local men from talking to visiting women. The clash in culture has found expression in sexual violence, and there have been several incidents of rape on the beach. Never bathe topless, and never lose sight of other people on the beach, however solitary and tempting it may appear.

Back on the mainland at Malindi the beach is fringed with luxurious hotels, complete with bar service, butler service, air conditioning, chilled wine and four-course meals. Not so far away, the town crumbles into ramshackle mud-and-wood dwellings where sewage runs along open drains, and household electricity and water are just promises the municipal council has yet to fulfil.

Personally, I avoid staying in tourist hotels, not only because the luxury jars alongside such evident poverty, but because guests are alienated from experiences as alive in a tourist town like Malindi as in any upcountry village where *mzungu* (white people) are rarely seen.

Generally, I stay in a *hoteli*, a small guest house found in any town. They are cheap, occasionally clean, and almost invariably run by friendly people. But single women sometimes have problems with men knocking on their bedroom door (this happens in upmarket hotels too), so I always make sure that my room can be firmly locked from inside.

I think the only way I've come to understand anything about "ordinary" Kenyan women is by frequenting local bars. In many countries, bars are a male preserve, but in Kenya there are usually women about –

Opening gambits like "Tell me about free love in your country" are irritatingly common.

barmaids, prostitutes, and in some places women doing their crochet over a bottle of beer. Not many *mzungu* women go into bars, except in tourist hotels, so those that do attract a fair amount of attention. "People say it is dangerous to come here", said the proprietor of one bar in Kisumu, "but you are safe." I agreed with him, and he bought me a beer simply because I'd dared to be there. As I left, some Asian youths cruised by in their Mercedes. "Wanna fuck?" they called. That was when I felt nervous and wished I could find a taxi back to my hotel.

The women tend to assume a protective role. In one bar in downtown Nairobi, a woman kept me by her side all evening. "No one speaks to my sister without my permission!" she insisted, glaring at anyone, male or female, reckless enough to look at me. As I entered a bar in Kisumu, Jane the barmaid, came to sit with me. A young man slouched towards us from the counter. "My friend is talking to me", said Jane, and he shrugged and walked away.

Women like Jane have interesting stories, and they usually like to talk. Many came from rural backgrounds, left home to look for a job in the big city, got pregnant, and have been trapped in the circle of barmaiding and prostitution ever since. Options for women are few once you leave the village; with no education and no money, and with children to support, prostitution is often the only way.

These women may ask you for an address, hoping for a job as a housemaid, or some money to pay school fees, or some clothes. They're not talking to you because they want something, however, but because it feels good to talk, and they're curious. There is a sympathetic link between women of different cultures, and it is somehow comforting to find common ground with a stranger. "You can so easily end up in a maternity", lamented one woman I know, who hangs around the same bar in Nairobi every evening. "I could be pregnant again. So could you." Later she took a male friend of mine aside. "Don't you get my sister pregnant", she admonished him, "That would be a very terrible thing to do!" Kenyan men do tend to look upon foreign women as an easy lay, and opening gambits like "Tell me about free love in your country" are irritatingly common.

If you have any problems, women around will usually help. But beware "big" men in small towns. If it's the local police chief or councillor who is making advances, it may not be possible for other local people to help out, because of his power and influence. If in doubt get out; preferably accompanied, preferably in a vehicle. I never walk alone at night in Nairobi; mugging and rape are quite common, and it's always worth the taxi fare to be safe.

I don't think that Kenyan men are intrinsically any more sexist than men from my own country, England. As a person unfettered by family, educated and employed and travelling unaccompanied, I get treated in some ways as an honorary man. But underneath it all, a woman is a woman is a woman, and most Kenyan men I've met agree with their president, who announced in September 1984 that God had made man the head of the family, and to challenge that was tantamount to criticizing God. Certainly when I've expressed my doubts, the response is generally that in my culture we may have different notions, but their women like it that way. I'm not so sure about that.

Throughout Kenya large numbers of women's groups have banded together to earn some money; making handicrafts, growing crops, keeping bees or goats, or running other small-scale businesses. Their success is variable. Some groups have made profits and shared them; in other cases men have sabotaged the group when they felt threatened by the women's success or have even appropriated the money. In others, lack of organization, inexperience, or simply time among women already overburdened by the day-to-day tasks of survival have built in failure from the beginning.

Women do want better healthcare, contraception, education for themselves and their children, and a higher income. But their needs and wants come a poor second to the concept of "development" which a male-dominated government and which predominantly male-dominated aid agencies promote. The rhetoric of the UN Decade for Women has resounded throughout Kenya, and we all know that small-scale water projects, reforestation, support to women as farmers and access to credit are important. But agricultural extensionists are still men; although it's women who dig the land, women are rarely consulted, and there is a tendency to start "women's projects" as a sideline to the more serious business of "nation building".

Women leaders in Kenya tend to take the attitude that gentle persuasion works better than protest. Many of them are middle-class and urban, their ideas and problems often seen as divorced from the reality of ordinary Kenyan women. With their emphasis on education, welfare and income-generating projects they have been criticized for supporting the status quo and denying the possibilities of radical change.

A Western feminist is often resented. There is good reason for this – many Western women simply do not know about the issues which affect Kenyan women, but nonetheless push their own priorities. On the other hand, the widespread denunciation of feminism (which finds its most outrageous expression in the letters pages of the newspapers) is a way of keeping women down, by telling them that any change is "un-African". I have come to believe that issues such as accessible clean water and getting more girls into school are more important to most Kenyan women than free abortion on demand or the acceptance of lesbianism – indeed, many Kenyan women oppose the latter two. Other issues, such as male violence and access to health-care and contraception are as important in Kenya as in any Western country, although the starting point for pushing to achieve these things is different.

> *The widespread denunciation of feminism is a way of keeping women down, telling them that change is "un-African".*

Foreign women who have lived in small towns and villages, usually as anthropologists or volunteers, have a deeper understanding of Kenyan women than I do. Many leave the country thoroughly depressed, as they see Kenyan women, year after year, accepting violent husbands, one pregnancy after another, children dying, endless work and little reward. Most visitors can't see all that, because it takes time, and nor do they get to see the other side of things, such as the sense of community amongst women and the strength of character that outward acceptance and apparent submissiveness belie.

It's not possible to understand so much on a short visit, but I think that many women coming to Kenya could see and understand a lot more if they dared. It took me a year to pluck up courage to travel Kenya alone, on *matatus* (collective taxis) and buses; hitch-hiking, going to small towns, being open, talking to people. There's no need for every woman to take a year to do all this – it's fun, it's interesting and it's worth it. I haven't had nearly enough yet.

TRAVEL NOTES

Languages Swahili is the official language; also Kikuyu, Luo and Maa. English is widely spoken.

Transport Public transport (buses and a small train network) is reasonable and safe. On well-worn tourist routes there are also collective taxis, usually big Peugeots. *Matatus*, impromptu communal trucks, need more confidence. Hitching isn't advisable.

Accommodation Along with simple *hotelis*, establishments known as Board and Lodgings (B&Ls) can be found in any town and are good value. In gameparks there are very expensive lodges but also *bandas* (small wooden huts with cooking facilities; you bring your own food and sleeping bag) and "tented camps" (tents provided and set up within lodge compounds).

Guides *The Rough Guide to Kenya* (Penguin) gives an excellent run-through of just about everything you'll need to know about the country.

CONTACTS

Maedeleo ya Wanawake (Progress of Women), PO Box 44412, Nairobi (☎02/222095). Largest and best-known women's organization with numerous local groups.

National Council of Women of Kenya, PO Box 43741, Nairobi (☎02/224634). Publishes *Kenyan Women* and co-ordinates groups throughout the country.

BOOKS

⊠ **Dervla Murphy**, *The Ukimwi Road* (UK, Flamingo, 1994). *Ukimwi* is the Swahili word for AIDS, a unifying if harrowing theme in Dervla Murphy's 3,000 mile journey by bicycle from Kenya through Uganda, Tanzania, Malawi, Zambia to Zimbabwe.

Cindy Buxton, *Survival in the Wild* (UK, Collins, 1990, o/p). Photographer's account of travels around Africa, including an assignment in Kenya.

Elspeth Huxley, *The Flame Trees of Thika* (UK, Penguin, 1994/US, Penguin, 1982); *Nine Faces of Kenya* (UK, Harvill, 1991/US, Penguin,

1992). The first, an unremarkable account of life in an area popular with big-game hunters earlier this century, became a best-seller. Huxley's more recent work is an anthology of writings on war, exploration, local legend, poetry and wildlife – still with a colonial flavour.

Beryl Markham, *West with the Night* (UK, Virago, 1984; illustrated edition 1989/US, North Point Press). Highly evocative account of life in the inter-war Kenya colony by the woman who, in 1936, made the first east-west solo flight across the Atlantic.

Cheryl Bentsen, *Maasai Days* (UK, Collins, 1990). Readable anthropological account of the Maasai.

Anonymous, *In Dependent Kenya* (UK & US, Zed Books, 1982; US o/p). A strident book which you shouldn't take with you, condemning the status quo and Kenya's involvement in the neo-colonial web.

Look out, too, for *Viva*, a monthly magazine combining feminism and fashion in a glossy, appealing package.

FICTION

Karen Blixen, *Out of Africa* (1936; UK, Penguin, 1986/US, Modern Library). A best-seller and cult book covering Blixen's experiences on a coffee farm in the Ngong Hills between the wars. Evocative, lyrical, sometimes obnoxiously racist, but a lot better than the film.

Toril Brekke, *The Jacaranda Flower* (UK, Methuen, 1987, o/p). A dozen short stories, most of which touch on the lives of women.

Martha Gellhorn, *The Weather in Africa* (UK, Eland, 1985/US, Avon, 1981). Three novellas, each set in Kenya and dealing absorbingly with aspects of the European-African relationship.

Muthoni Likimani, *Passbook Number F 47927: Women and Mau Mau in Kenya* (UK, Macmillan, 1986/US, Praeger, 1985). Describes, in ten fictionalized episodes, the impact on women's daily lives of the 1950s Mau Mau revolt in Kenya.

Rebeka Njau, *Ripples in the Pool* (UK, Heinemann, 1978). Novel, full of myth and menace, about the building of a village clinic.

Marjorie Oludhe MacGoye, *Coming to Birth* (UK, Virago, 1987). Acclaimed story of a young woman's arranged marriage, its failure and her new life in post-Uhuru Kenya. Set during and just after the Mau Mau emergency.

Also look out for the stories of Grace Ogot, including *Land Without Thunder* and *The Promised Land* (both Nairobi, East African Publishing House, 1968).

Malaysia

F or many years Malaysia featured mainly as a stop-over destination, with tourists spending a few days in the sprawling capital Kuala Lumpur or the beach resorts along the west coast, before heading on to Singapore, Thailand or Australia. Increasingly, however, travellers are opting to spend more time in the country, exploring the astonishing natural landscape of mountains and dense rainforest within the peninsula or crossing the four hundred miles of South China Sea to visit the north Borneo states of Sarawak and Sabah. The widespread use of English (this was a former British colony) and plentiful transport and accommodation make this an ideal place to ease into Southeast Asian culture.

Owing to the extraordinary economic development of the last few decades, Malaysia now ranks among the richest nations in Asia. Its population of some sixteen million is characterized by a racial mix of roughly fifty-five percent Malay, thirty-five percent Chinese and ten percent Indian, plus a tiny minority of indigenous communities, with the Chinese holding on to the bulk of economic power. In terms of religion, Buddhism, Hinduism and Christianity are all recognized by the state, but Islam is the official faith adhered to by most Malays.

Kuala Lumpur is an ethnically mixed, solidly cosmopolitan capital. Without business deals or serious shopping to consider it would be hard to justify spending much time among the skycrapers, commercial bustle and intersecting highways. It is, however, a fairly easy and safe city for women. You might discover that the cheap hotel you found doubles up as a brothel, or the bar you've wandered into is lined with erotic dancers, but this has nowhere like the sleaze of Bangkok and rarely feels threatening.

Travelling in predominantly Chinese areas you'll find that relatively little interest is shown towards foreigners, and, apart from economic dealings and a cursory curiosity, you are left mainly to your own devices. The likeable Chinese-dominated island of Penang and expensive west coast resorts have a fairly cosmopolitan and relaxed atmosphere. In predominantly Malay and Muslim areas, especially along the eastern coast where fundamentalism has begun to take hold, you can feel more uneasy. Malaysian **women**, though they maintain a high profile in public, dress and behave with great modesty – a long white headscarf and baggy trousers and tunics are standard dress. By comparison Western women are considered loose and immoral (a notion fostered by the sight of half-clad tourists and a thriving Western pornography trade) and although men rarely approach or touch the constant stares can be oppressive. As everywhere it's important to show respect and hold back in dealings with men until you feel sure you won't be misinterpreted. That said, many women do travel alone without encountering major difficulties. Trekking is now popular, especially in the national parks of Sabah and Sarawak, and in Taman Negara (literally "National Park"), the peninsula's main area of protected rainforest, described by Madeleine Cary below.

Despite the country's relative prosperity, Malaysian women's lives are by and large dominated by the restraints of Islam and oriental traditions. Only a small number of girls go on to higher education as marriage and child-rearing remain the focus of most women's expectations. Malaysia has a burgeoning women's movement but, as Irene Fernandez, founder of a group promoting women's rights, points out, "faced with the increasing use of religion and culture to justify women's low status within the family, community and society", theirs is very much an uphill struggle.

A Natural High

Until 1990 **Madeleine Cary** juggled her life as a single parent with a career as a media producer. That year her son Ky, aged sixteen, was killed in a tragic accident. After some time trying to recuperate and heal with family and friends she decided it was time to seek life-affirming experiences again. With a backpack, a few savings and no clear itinerary in mind, she flew to Bangkok, marking the beginning of ten months' low-budget travel through Southeast Asia. She has also contributed pieces on Thailand and Canada to this book.

The river journey to the jungle's base camp echoed every dramatic image I had of jungle adventures, from Vietnam movies to *The African Queen*. The muddy brown river widened and the jungle on either side became denser, trees and shrubs stretching higher. Suddenly it looked as if the scale of nature had shifted. Every living thing seemed larger. The scents from the myriad shrub and plant life wafted past and changed constantly, from sweet jasmine-like fragrances to pungent, almost menthol scents. Occasionally tribal inhabitants of the jungle, the Orang Asli ("Original People"), would appear from behind bushes to watch us. Scaly creatures would bob to the surface of the water. The birds darted by in flashes of vibrant colour.

I was experiencing a child-like excitement about this adventure. After four months of travel in Southeast Asia, I had failed to undertake a jungle trek. For every guided tour on offer there would be a story concerning inexperienced guides, rapes, thefts, obnoxious travelling companions and the inevitable Western insensitivity to the local environment. There were tales of stoned tourists staggering down jungle trails, chanting Bob Marley songs at high volume and frightening off every bit of wildlife in the area. It had not held much appeal. I was also embarrassingly aware of my fear of the demands of a trek. Then I met a traveller whose frequent treks had left him something of a self-styled afficianado of jungle lore. His enthusiasm about jungle living was infectious. When he asked if I would like to accompany him on his foray into Malaysia's Taman Negara jungle, I saw it as a welcome chance to finally experience the adventure of trekking. With that intuition that develops after months of lone travel, I had decided that he was a good sort and had already reached an uncomplicated level of friendship with him. It was really down to whether his claims to knowledge and experience of jungle life were genuine.

The Taman Negara jungle in central Malaysia is one of the richest in Southeast Asia. Being home to such a variety of animal and plant life, including the tualang, the tallest tropical tree in the world, it is considered a magnificent example of unspoilt tropical rainforest. As the wooden longboat sputtered down the murky river, I revelled in my good luck at being able to spend a week in this renowned jungle with an experienced trekker. But we had not yet escaped civilization. Suddenly, a huge holiday complex loomed out of the tropical mist as we turned a corner into the base camp. Here, luxury chalets were available for the rich and cautious who could take walks on small, safe paths in the jungle area around the site. We had to register, pay a nominal fee and I also needed to hire a tent from the supplies office. My friend was content to simply sling a hammock in a tree, but I was not so hardy as to shun insect and waterproof shelter. His fluent Malay and hard bargaining got me an old tent for a pittance. Its poles, string and pegs were missing, but he was confident that we could improvise with twigs and vine.

Feeling enervated and intrepid, and not wishing to be accused of holding us up, I insisted I would be all right alone.

My only trepidation about the trek concerned the nine-mile hike we would have to undertake to our campsite. My companion had already planned the route and warned me that after six or seven miles of fairly easy trekking, there would be a steep uphill climb for the last two miles that would be backbreaking. I am not afraid of a bit of hard work when necessary, but I knew that I would be carrying a week's supply of food and a tent and was beginning to question whether I would stay the course.

When we finally left the base camp with rucksacks efficiently packed and strapped to our backs, with every available bit of skin covered to fend off the leeches and full water bottles hanging round our necks, I was too excited to feel the weight of my pack or to notice the cloying, damp heat of the jungle we were taking a trail into. In his khaki clothes and jungle boots, bandana tightened round his forehead and machete at the ready in his belt, my partner looked like he had been brought in from central casting. I had to hide my amusement when I first saw him as his usually buoyant mood had given way to a serious, almost nervous state. I decided it must be the remnants of some primordial male pre-hunt ritual.

As expected, I started to feel exhaustion after the first two hours and we were still nowhere near the dreaded steep climb. My companion, used to the demands of a trek, was blazing a trail at full steam. By comparison I seemed to be moving like a snail. However, I found myself ahead of the game when we came to a small river with a fallen log across it. I have a good sense of balance and managed to walk the log effortlessly whereas my companion confessed his fear of walking logs and had to remove his footwear and wade thigh deep through the unpleasantly opaque water. As the

I wondered how I must look bent over like a harridan, crawling on hands and knees, spluttering expletives.

sky slowly darkened with an impending rain cloud, we had to decide on a course of action now that we were falling behind schedule. We agreed that he should charge on ahead in order to set up camp before evening rains and darkness. Feeling enervated and intrepid, and not wishing to be accused later of holding us up, I insisted I would be all right alone so long as my energy held out. Here was not a man to treat a woman like a "lady". He gave me clear instructions about which trail to stay on, promised he would come back and look for me if I had not arrived at the camp by nightfall and with that dashed off into the distance like a gladiator.

That is how I ended up breaking the number one rule in the trekker's safety code: never travel alone. I did not see that we had any choice but to operate in this way. And, strangely, I felt no fear as I continued alone on the trail in this magical environment. There were supposed to be tigers and elephants in the area, but local people had stressed that they usually keep clear of human visitors. Naturally, there would be snakes and other reptilian creatures, not to mention the millions of different insects. Yet, as I did not know what to look for, I plodded on regardless. I could hear the monkeys high up in the gigantic trees and the hornbills with their "hoo-hoo, ha-ha" laughter. My only real cause for panic was whether I had sufficient stamina to complete the journey. Energy levels were running dangerously low. Every minute I would stop to give my back and shoulders a rest from the overwhelming weight of my backpack. And this was still relatively flat territory.

When the uphill climb started, I had reached zero energy and was staggering around like a drunkard. I stopped to eat provisions, drink water and rest until I felt refreshed. Later, I could only manage half a minute of the upward haul before I had to stop again. The hill turned out to be an almost vertical climb with tree roots for steps and stalks and trailers to hang onto for support. At every point where I arrived at what I thought was the summit, I looked up to see yet another stretch of several hundred metres reaching skywards. Counting, swearing out loud and concentrating on anger helped spur me on. I thought of *Pilgrim's Progress* and wondered how I must look bent over like a harridan, crawling on hands and knees, spluttering out expletives and panting as if close to death.

I think it was a near-death experience, looking back. Now, whenever I have to try to achieve something which I think I cannot do, I always remember that nightmarish trip up that steep jungle hill where sheer willpower got me to my goal against all odds. When I finally reached the summit and saw camp-fire smoke curling up through the trees in the valley, I felt ecstatic, switched gear and ran downhill, leaping over fallen trees and sliding on carpets of dead leaves. The reward for this arduous expedition was the sight of our arboreal home, an idyllic clearing by the river. In an adjoining stream a smooth rockpool with a light waterfall above formed the perfect bathing area. The first thing I did when I arrived was fling off all my sweat-soaked, muddy clothes and plunge my aching body into the pool. I lay exhausted in the cool, crystal water but on the most incredible natural high I have ever experienced.

My friend already had his hammock set up in a tree with a small shelter made of tarpaulin. My tent was soon erected by improvising with twigs and vines. Then, before I could think of having a rest, the trees started to sway in ominous winds, announcing the imminent arrival of our first major jungle downpour. By hanging tarpaulin over the fire we kept sufficient flame going to boil water for tea and rice. After such an exhausting day, even lumpy rice with cold tinned goat curry tasted sublime. As the rains subsided we fell into a state of almost comatose relaxation and sat back to enjoy the evening chorus. It was the cicadas who started the symphony, providing the base maraccas rhythm. Another cicada joined in with a sustained, almost electronic-sounding, haunting trumpet pitch which rose through one slightly mournful key and died out on a rapid staccato. As one trumpet sound faded away, another would start up, sometimes nearer, sometimes further away. Then the counterpoint of monkey chatter and birdsong would bring the performance to its crescendo. In the

It took a couple of days before he realized that I was not impressed with his display of survival techniques.

mornings, the same creatures would provide a wake-up call that was remarkably different in tone and key. If the evening symphony was slightly ominous, the dawn chorus was full of life and promise.

Our week in the jungle soon fell into a routine based around the frequent and predictable rainstorms and the survival needs of cooking, cleaning the utensils, washing clothes and gathering wood. The reward at the end of each day would be an hour or two of the weird concert provided by our unseen companions. We divided the chores of cooking and washing, but nearly came to blows over the most effective way of starting a fire when all available tinder was sodden with rain. I was probably asking for trouble trying to tell this overgrown boyscout how to play the survival game, but I have never been able to keep quiet when I think I have a solution to a problem. It took a couple of days before he realized that I was not impressed with his constant display of survival techniques and I realized that this was not the most suitable place to make an issue over my right to prove my competence. Every day we would have to start the fire around three o'clock as the rains would come by six, which gave us enough time to get a good flame going for boiling water and cooking rice. Even though it was a daily occurrence, it was still alarming as the light dimmed and the gigantic trees swayed threateningly in heavy gales which always preceded rainstorms. One of the most dangerous aspects of jungle life concerns the frequency with which large trees topple over in the gales or under the weight of the rain. Sometimes we could hear them crashing around us and were never sure, when we heard a nearby crack, if a huge tree was about to collapse onto the camp.

We spent hours discussing how we would respond if a hungry tiger wandered through or a herd of elephants rampaged.

I felt a strange combination of peace and serenity with an underlying sense of danger in the jungle. It was a stunningly beautiful environment in which to contemplate and reappraise life and, once really settled in, to leave the past behind and live life on an immediate level. The dense cathedral of trees and shrubs that surrounded us formed a spectrum of green, gold and brown shades with patterns of light filtering in as the sun moved across the sky. The fragrances changed throughout the day as the various shrubs and plants opened out in the baking sun and then the steaming damp. All day, fascinating insects and butterflies hovered, particularly attracted to any gaily coloured items we had lying about. I did not think it was possible for living creatures to have such vivid colours and patterns: dayglo orange, turquoise, lime green, stripes, dots and even some eccentricities like dangling pom-poms or long tail-spikes to aid camouflage. Some butterflies liked to sit on my hands and taste the salt, allowing me a close view of their beauty. Spotting stick insects as they played at a variety of disguises became another favourite pastime.

The only real hazard came from the minuscule leeches which would somersault at high speed across the leaves to attach themselves to your skin or clothing. The tiny, thread-like creatures could worm their way through fabric unnoticed, so body checks became necessary rituals throughout the day. One morning we were invaded by wasps and another by a troop of large stinging ants. On both occasions my friend was impelled by testosterone to take action rather than stay sensibly and patiently in the zipped-up tent. The result was that he managed to get stung and bitten and did not even

I felt I was tapping into some unknown strength and determination as I stumbled through the crashing water.

succeed in getting rid of the pests. Once insects decide to investigate in large numbers, you just have to wait in shelter until they have scouted and then moved on. There was evidence of larger creatures in the area, too: the occasional wafts of animal urine scent on the air, the mounds of recent elephant dung and the large cat prints we saw in the mud by the river bank one day. One night we heard what sounded like a feline growl in the distance. We must have spent many hours around the evening campfire discussing how we would respond if a hungry tiger wandered through or a herd of elephants came on the rampage.

On one of our daily explorations away from the camp, we found an abandoned Orang Asli settlement with its bamboo shelters, the remains of old fires and herbs dried out in the trees. Bunches of flowers, which tribal girls wear in their hair, were hanging from the shelters. I was hoping we might meet some of these people, but we only managed to hear the laughter of their children one day echoing through the jungle.

I was just getting used to being so blissfully cut off from civilization when, one day, a telephone engineer from Ipswich wandered into camp. His legs, covered with leeches, were bleeding profusely. We welcomed him and got a pot of tea going. He was a real loner and seemed disappointed to be in the company of other humans. He pitched his tent and stayed the night but had disappeared by dawn, giving rise to a few sick jokes about hungry tigers.

After a week our food supplies had run out and we reluctantly packed up and began our return journey to the base camp. The trek back was much less tiring; our load was a lot lighter without the food and we were both refreshed and fit from our week of getting back to nature. For most of the journey we were pelted by torrential rain.

When we got to the river which we had crossed easily the previous week, it was flowing rapidly and was clearly several metres deeper because of the rainfall. This time, as we discussed all the options, I noticed my companion was not so keen to play leader. Either he had run out of steam or had realized that I was worth listening to when it came to bright ideas. Or perhaps he had never tackled a dangerous river before. I wandered along the bank until I saw a part of the river which looked shallower where the water was bumping over stones and forming patterns. I reported back and we decided to give it a try. When he insisted he go in first to test the depth, I did not argue; he was taller and stronger than me. The water at the deepest part came up to his knees which meant that it would reach my thighs. We formed a cortege of legs and walking sticks to ford the waters. I battled against the flow and more than once was nearly knocked over. As with the pilgrimage a week before, I felt I was tapping into some unknown strength and determination as I stumbled slowly through the crashing water. When we finally reached the safety of the bank on the other side, we both collapsed, exhausted and dripping wet. Like a couple of kids, we fell into hilarity and self-congratulation about our boldness. Then we looked back across the river to the dense jungle territory we had left behind and a sad silence fell. Leaving this temple of nature to return to society was a hard wrench. The first sight of civilization we saw was the rear end of a panicking tourist, naked from the waist down, desperately trying to pick leeches out of his bleeding groin. As we began to pass the well-heeled tourists from the base camp, the artificial scents of cosmetics and toiletries hit our noses with a nauseating impact. They, in turn, stepped aside with expressions of disgust as we passed. No doubt we smelt as wild as we looked by now.

One more week in the jungle and I might have wanted to adopt it as a permanent lifestyle. The experience had left me spiritually high, emotionally calm and in superb physical shape. I had learned not just practical survival techniques, but also how two people must stave off bad humour and competitiveness in order to co-operate for the mutual good. Most importantly, I had shown myself that I could achieve something which I previously thought was beyond me. I now had a new perspective on my own capacity for bravery and determination, not to mention living on wits and intuition. I was looking forward to continuing my lone travels into other parts of Malaysia, but I had great difficulty refraining from inviting myself along when my friend started to plan his next trek. As we waited for the boat which would take me out of the jungle, he chatted in Malay to an Orang Asli tribesman. They spoke animatedly for some time and then he turned to me with a look of anguish. "This man is telling me about his wife", he said. "He says she was eaten by a tiger in the jungle last year!"

TRAVEL NOTES

Languages The national language is Bahasa Malay, an easy to learn rudimentary language which uses latin script. Most Malaysians also speak good English, especially at an official level. There are also tribal languages still used by the Orang Asli.

Transport Malaysia offers every form of transport, with three national airlines, a railway line of limited use, an excellent bus network and a long-distance taxi system, whereby you can travel in a car so long as there's a full complement of four passengers. The roads are in good condition and hitching, especially down the western side, is an acceptable form of travel for foreigners, though as in most places, not advisable for a woman alone. In some towns and villages, bicycle rickshaws (trishaws) are cheap and plentiful for short distances.

Accommodation You'll find every type of accommodation, from luxury to low budget. The many Chinese hotels offer cheap, spartan rooms and often come with their own restaurant. Hostels, YMCAs and Rest Houses are popular for low-budget travellers. Beach resorts usually have some relatively inexpensive grass hut accommodation, often with meals included.

Special Problems This is a Muslim state, and although no particular dress codes and behaviour are compulsory, it's advisable to respect local custom: avoid wearing scanty clothes and never bathe topless. Malaysia has a deceptive veneer of Westernization, but outside Kuala Lumpur tourism is relatively recent.

Guides *The Rough Guide to Malaysia, Singapore and Brunei* (Penguin) is packed with up-to-date information.

BOOKS

Isabella Bird, *The Golden Chersonese* (UK, Oxford University Press, o/p /US, Century, o/p). Lively, amusing letters from early adventuress Isabella Bird in Southeast Asia.

Mary Turnbull, *A Short History of Malaysia, Singapore and Brunei* (Singapore, Graham Brash). A study of the history of the area.

Special **thanks** to Elizabeth Bunning for background information.

Mali

O nce the cultural and economic centrepiece of West Africa, linking trade along the great Niger River to the caravan routes of the Sahara, Mali has become a cross-roads for travellers in the region. Until recently the bulk of tourist traffic was the overlanders, heading south from Algeria in truck convoys or jeeps along the trans-Saharan route to Gao on the banks of the Niger delta.

Serious civil unrest in Algeria and the Tuareg uprising in Mali's northern areas have since cut off this option, although plenty of independent travellers still arrive using the road, rail and air links with neighbouring capitals.

Given its historical status as a gold-rich seat of learning and culture, the sheer poverty that confronts you when you arrive in the country can be disorientating. Political

instability, a staggering national debt and a series of devastating droughts have left few resources for development and even in Bamako, the capital, symbols of prosperity are scarce. Tourism is one of the country's few profitable industries, and the costs, for state-run hotels, excursions and guides can be comparatively high. Bureaucracy is far more intrusive than in any of the neighbouring states and in some towns you still have to register on arrival with the police.

As a predominantly Muslim country this can be a difficult destination for women travelling alone or with other women. Although the atmosphere is considerably more tolerant than in the North African states, women are expected to keep in the background and initiating conversations with men can be easily misconstrued. Although there are no rigid dress rules, it's considered respectful to cover arms and legs (breasts are far less of an issue). It's unlikely that you'll face any actual sexual threat, but it can feel oppressive to be continually scrutinized and commented on by men. In the medieval towns of Djenne and Timbuktu, where hustlers congregate, the hard-sell tactics and continual harassment can take on a menacing edge. Life is undoubtedly easier if you are travelling with a man or in a mixed group (especially in the male-dominated bars and cafés) although when with a male companion all conversations and transactions will be directed through him — it can be unnerving to find yourself treated as an appendage, sometimes even blatantly ignored. Outside the tourist areas the atmosphere changes. People greet strangers with open hospitality and friendliness — it's important to carry gifts with you as a means of reciprocating.

Unlike in the Islamic states north of the Sahara, Malian **women** have a high profile on the streets and dominate market trading. A clear feminine pride is displayed by women shouldering the massive burdens of supporting children and homes while scratching a subsistence income through trading or cultivating small plots of land. The *Union Nationale des Femmes du Mali*, a predominantly urban, middle-class organization, has for some years been campaigning for women's rights, the most contentious and sensitve issue being the high incidence of female genital mutilation. Malians are concerned to debate and resolve these issues within an African context, counteracting what is seen as sensationalist and irrelevant interference from the West.

Eyeless in Mali

Melanie McGrath, a freelance writer, had already travelled for some months in West Africa before meeting up with her boyfriend for a trip into Mali. Their stay in Bamako, the capital, became dominated by the friendship they formed with a Malian student, who introduced them to the popular culture of his country and the shadowy life of street politics. McGrath's latest book, *Motel Nirvana* (published in the UK by HarperCollins) charts her stay among the religous cults of the American Southwest, and she has also contributed a piece on Burkina Faso to this book.

Bamako begins where the desert ends, just at the place where warted stumps of baobab trees give way to a scatter of adobe huts, sheeny in the sun. These are the suburbs. From here the brown minarets of mud mosques at the capital's centre are as distantly grandiose as the World Trade towers might be to Coney Islanders. There is water in this dust, which is why the huts are here. Women with babies lassoed to their chests stroll along the side of the road forming caravans, each with an enamel bowl balanced on her head. Wherever the pump is, it is not visible to us. There are fewer swollen bellies here than in the savannah villages to the east and north, but the life is a country life all the same, which is to say that the men sit cross-legged in the dust and wait for the rainy season, when it comes, if it comes. No one bothers to protect themselves from the tornadoes of flies.

When I first arrived in West Africa it was the fly-blacked faces of country children with their runny eyes which most disturbed me. I took the triumph of insects to be a metaphor for despair. At some point between the Biafran war and the 1990s images of big-bellied infants had become so much a slogan that I could no longer see them and be horrified. So, it was the sucking mosquitoes, the blackflies and bluebottles and sandflies bloated with blood and sweat that spoke to me most eloquently of the interminable

> *Behind the leathern tan there I am, bloodless and weak. I imagine that my mother would have told me I had aged.*

heat, and the impermanence of resistance. I realize now that patience and stoicism play a greater part in African life than they do where I grew up, but I did not see that then. When I look at photographs of myself from that time, I realize how beaten I was. There is a kind of tension on my face, which makes me look both quizzical and anxious, as if I had spotted something strange beyond the eye of the camera. Very often I am squinting, merely, I suppose against the heat haze and reddened dust. But always, always my arms are in a furious blur, whirring round and round in a hopeless, avenging war against the army of insect life.

At the bus station we take a taxi to the *Grand Hotel*. Since leaving Ouahigouya in northern Burkina Faso, I've lost about a stone in weight. Behind the leathern tan there I am, bloodless and weak. I imagine that my mother would have told me I had aged. Paul is more or less unrecognizable; rope thin and with a flame red scab across his face where the midday sun reflecting off the River Niger caught the tender skin and branded it. It was not until he had paddled to the far river bank that he felt the burn. As if that were not enough we are both scraping at a rash of blisters where desert sand has eaten into the skin of our limbs and buttocks. We are agreed that it is time for some luxury, for sanity's sake, and at any price. It is early afternoon. The temperature is in the late 40s and the air heavy with greasy Harmattan dust, which colours the town rosy rust and gives camouflage to the pink painted balustrades strung along the boulevards. Some Muslims hold that the Harmattan winds are God's way of reminding the faithful to keep fast over Ramadan. Whatever their cause they bring the Sahara a little closer each year. In the dust grow date palms, the first greenery we have seen in weeks. They give the city of Bamako a kind of ramshackle elegance, not unlike the more tawdry parts of the French Riviera.

It is Ramadan, so no one has eaten or drunk since sunrise and the streets are empty of pedestrians. Yet every time the taxi slows a gaggle of children appear from some alleyway or door and rush towards the vehicle shouting "Il faut me cadeauteur!" or simply "Donne-moi!" You hardly hear them before they are upon you. Neither of us dares wind a window down lest we are sucked from the car by a thousand marauding infant hands. The driver turns on his air-conditioning system, and the air begins to broil nicely. We swing off the main Avenue de Fleuve by the Cathedral onto the rue Gourand which leads down past bakeries and motorcycle repair shops towards the central market. All at once a crowd appears from our left and we find ourselves in the midst of some kind of ceremony or demonstration along with much of the rest of the city's traffic. The driver switches off his engine and we wait. The air-conditioning carries on autonomously, converting the car into first sauna then steam bath as the condensation of our breath evaporates from the vinyl cladding of the seats. I am painfully aware that when I walk out of the car and into the lobby of the most expensive hotel in Mali I shall be sporting a large soaking stain on my buttocks.

We can see militia now, managing the protest, if that is what it is, and moving people along. Some kind of bottleneck must have formed, because people are pressing against the cars in the middle of the road and all of a sudden there are bodies squashed against the windows of the taxi, blocking out the light. The car in front begins to sound its horn in time to a drumbeat up ahead. Our taxi driver joins in, then winds down his window and gesticulates enthusiastically in the air with his fist. It could be Naples in the rush hour, but it isn't. The taxi driver thinks these are students demanding that some soldiers responsible for firing on an earlier demonstration be brought to justice. The civil servants are out too, on strike in support of the students. The government hasn't paid them for a couple of months and they are running out of food and patience. "So you support them?" asks Paul. The driver shrugs in reply "I just don't want my car to get damaged. You know, it's all I've got."

The night at the *Grand Hotel* breaks a cherry or two; our first hot water (as opposed to the tepid, peppery stuff we've lived with for two months); an ancient copy of *Time* magazine, the only English read in weeks. Never mind that we already know the stories. Better in fact, because it removes the need to concentrate. Paul orders a club sandwich, and what arrives is a tower of sweet bread curled about the edges and teased with intimations of processed cheese, the whole sweating rather grimly in the air-conditioning. No ham, of course. A bite or two on and we realize it was the "club" rather

> *We looked to him to give us a part to play and put an end to the outsider's unease.*

than the "'sandwich" which provided the initial appeal, being redolent of "luncheon clubs" and "country clubs": all those kinds of clubs we shake off contemptuously at home but are secretly drawn to abroad as symbols of mindless, guilt-free indulgence.

I suppose we should have seen from the beginning that Issa was an opportunist. He wore his aspirations on his sleeve. There was no pretence to it. What Issa dreamed of was to be rich and Western, maybe even white. Most young Africans, who have grown up in independent states and never travelled beyond, cannot conceive of the strength of the racism so rife in the developed world, but Issa, I know, had his suspicions. We should have seen from the clothes he wore, which spoke of his aspirations, the hopes he nurtured through his acquaintance with us, and other travellers before us. Where those around him paraded in magnificently embroidered tunics, Issa wore white polo shirts; where others were prone to dramatic displays of friendship, anger or joy, Issa was reserved and cool. What Issa wanted, I see now, was to be like us. And if I am honest, all we asked was that he enable us, somehow, to fit in. We looked to him to give us a part to play and put an end to the outsider's unease. Issa saw this, I think, and it explained his exquisite patience with our pitifully stumbling French, the way he oiled our conversation with helpful little turns of phrase and eased us gently into menu Bambara. In this respect he was a go-between, passing messages from the world he knew and despised to the world of his fantasies and in seeking to reconcile the two had perhaps himself become lost in the interstices.

Nonetheless, we thought him breathtakingly romantic; educated, self-assured, a student radical fighting for a multi-party democracy in a country where the people, had we stopped to consider it, were in truth disenfranchised less by politics itself than by poverty. Still, he made us feel privileged to be in on all the inside stories. He took us to the places where marches were held, he told us of arrests and beatings, he led us into whispering alleyways full of discontented youth. It was a true alliance of students and workers, he said, who had pressed Moussa Traore into promising a free vote in parliament which would herald the beginning of multi-party democracy in Mali.

> *Looking back, I can see that his political world was so alien we resisted intimacy with it.*

For fifteen years Traore had stood before the crowds and cursed the International Banks, the Western loan sharks, the great conspiracy of wealth, while at the same time embezzling from the shrunken coffers of his own country dollars sufficient to build new towns, or end the water crisis. Malians were beginning to grow bored of the same old tales of World Bank chicanery and CIA scum and soon there remained no one else to blame except Traore and his entourage because, aside from a few development agencies and a scattering of Christian missionaries, no one else took the slightest interest in Mali. Almost imperceptibly, over a period of months, the rich diplomats, landowners and bureaucrats stopped attending cocktail parties at the Presidential palace and shed their friends in government and the military.

Issa pointed all this out to us, but we just didn't absorb its implications. Looking back, I can see that his political world was so alien we resisted intimacy with it. We were willing to take on only the most superficial kind of integration – a cult handshake, the correct way to tie a turban, which bakery to patronize. It is the convention in our world that there is only one effective political act – the act of voting. Between times we are content to become talkers, whingers, mere observers of a political scene which carries on, secure in its mandate, entirely without us. In Mali, by contrast, there are very many political acts – demonstrations, strikes, protests, even criticism is an act of great political significance because the government knows it has no mandate and can have no mandate while it fixes the vote and a part of its people starve. So instead it watches. The people and the government circle round each other watching, until one or other strikes. It's a game of reflexes.

We moved from the *Grand Hotel* to the *Pension Djoliba*, where Issa was staying. Our room was painted navy blue and had no windows. A fan flickered on and off with the electricity supply, then died. It was a kind of eyeless prison. I got sicker and we moved out, to a tiny shabby little room with a sunken bed and a window looking out over leafy boulevards. Our days passed on the balcony, watching the rose coloured sun dive beneath the slate rooftops and corrugated iron shacks of Bagadaji district. Issa sang us songs, which we taped and whose rudiments we picked up by demanding repeats,

When I became too ill to get out of bed, Paul rang the British consul, who found our situation ludicrously mundane.

and more repeats after the first. Issa spoke a dazzling array of languages; Bambara and Wolof, Fula, Malinke and a little More, the language of the Mossi people from the South. Most of these are unrelated; the African equivalent of speaking Russian, Magyar, Welsh, English, Portuguese and modern Greek. And Issa knew the songs of each, from fast-paced Wolof dance tunes to spiky, edgy Malinke ballads.

Now and then we would venture out to eat, taking Issa along as a kind of guest-cum-guide. He wove for us a path through the *Grand Marché* so that people would let us by without insisting on a Polaroid or some other "*cadeau*". I wished we had more to give, but a gift for one meant a gift for all, and to single people out would have been seen as an act of gross discourtesy. We would spend hours in the market, absorbing the smells of dried fish and pineapple, and poking about among the food stalls, challenging each other to identify hairy manioc from sorghum, pounded yams from millet flour. The women would compete for our attention and we would amuse them in turn by admiring their woven hair, or the whorl of African fabric some knotted round their heads whose tip would reach nearly a metre into the sky. As payment for our intrusions we would buy mangoes or tiny red bananas to distribute among the children around our feet, and so the show would continue.

After the market Issa would take us to a restaurant, warning us on the way about who to avoid, what to hide, which conversations never to begin. Bamako is an expensive place, and I remember that Issa would make a habit of choosing the most expensive dish on the menu, usually steak or lamb brochettes. Afterwards we resented this, although at the time it seemed a small price to pay for his company. Looking back, one can hardly blame him. Burkina Faso and Mali produce the most delicious beef and lamb I have ever eaten; but livestock is so prized that people taste it, if at all, only at the most important of religious festivals, living in the meantime on rice and yams and millet cous-cous. There are few green vegetables. A ubiquitous sauce made from palm oil and chili renders the grain palatable. Richer families may throw a guinea fowl or scrawny chicken into the sauce pot, feathers and all. Nothing is ever wasted here. Animals convert into calories, old tyres into shoes and buckets, rusted piping into musical instruments.

When I became too ill to get out of bed, Paul rang the British consul, who evidently found our situation ludicrously mundane. Naturally we should expect to be sick, travelling through the Sahel in the heat of the dry season, in any season. He congratulated Paul that he, too, had not succumbed and urged us to be grateful for that, at least. "It's not a good time to be here, anyway, it's unstable", he said, without expanding. "Try the American Embassy", he added and hung up. This was good advice, at least. Dr Joel K Reismann proved embarrassingly welcoming. In truth, I think that embassy life was so cut off from the everyday actuality of West Africa − diplomats lived in a sweep of breezeblock houses with special shops to provide homesick American palates with a supply of potato chips and salsa sauce, air-conditioning of a strength to defeat the African heat, sealed windows to block out the Harmattan dust − that no one ever succumbed to the endless round of malaria, hookworms, river blindness and bilharzia that blighted the lives of thousands of Malians. So the doctor spent his days alone and welcomed any opportunity to talk. He sent me away to produce a stool sample.

A month in the Sahel had hardened us. Where we had been open we were self-enclosed, dry and taciturn.

I never found out what it was that had made me ill because when I went back to the Embassy the next day, the place was deserted and padlocked up, for reasons that were obscure to me at the time, but are now quite clear. It is sometimes difficult to believe that anyone could have missed the signs of disquiet during those days in Bamako, but miss them we did and it was quite by accident that we were saved from the consequences of our own short-sightedness. But I am fast-forwarding and I want to tell you what happened exactly and how we came to know about it.

There is a single plane that leaves Bamako for Burkina Faso. Otherwise it is a twenty-four to thirty-hour drive along pitted dust roads in a *taxi-brousse* to the border. Sometimes, in the wet season, there is no passable route at all. Since I was too ill to contemplate such a journey, and the heat and dust had become unbearable, Paul and I decided to fly out on the next plane. As it turned out ours was the last plane to leave the country before the troubles began. But it was not the heat and dust which forced our hand in the end. Nor did we leave because of demonstrations and Issa's insistence that there would be trouble, or even because of what the British consul had, in his disengaged way, hinted at. As for the increasing presence of soldiers on the streets, we didn't notice them.

No, we left to save what remained of our respect for each other. A month in the Sahel had hardened us. Where we had been open we were self-enclosed, where we had delighted in conversational intimacies we were now dry and taciturn. I suppose we were little more than wary interlopers each on the territory of the other, with Issa the only connection between us. Later I saw that he had sensed this tension and capitalized on it, playing the role of conduit between us. This may not have been a conscious act on his part, but there is no doubt that he benefitted from it. It was to him we turned for our laughter, in him we confided our impressions, to him we confessed our ignorance. He was our temporary saviour because he saved us from the baldness of our relationship. It was not that Paul and I had ceased to care for one another's company altogether, but I think that whatever feeling remained between us was merely the memory of warmth. The heat of the desert had simply sucked out the rest.

If we felt betrayed, it was merely because we had not wished to understand that poverty puts a value on everything.

Issa helped us pack and we rode together in a taxi to the airport. He was withdrawn and a little sullen, understandable in retrospect. Our minds were already too much in another country to take much notice. We exchanged kisses, embraces, addresses. Issa promised to come and stay. We wished him luck with his student agitations. You'll get there in the end, we said, because you deserve it. I recall that we gave him a present, but I can't remember what it was. We were in the air when we realized that Issa had stolen the most valuable piece of equipment we had – the professional tape recorder on which we had recorded our diary over the past months and our conversations on the balcony of the *Djoliba* hotel. Most of the tapes went too. So much for the kisses, the exchanges of confidence, the promises of friendship; even his songs were lost to us. And yet, how could we have expected otherwise? He had paid us, after all, with his company. For a short few days he had made us feel that we fitted in. What we had chosen not to see was entirely our own responsibility. If we felt betrayed, it was merely because we had not wished to understand that poverty puts a value on everything.

We found out about the coup two days later, in the marketplace at Bobo-Dioulasso in southern Burkina Faso. I was bargaining for a length of cloth and a scarf with a picture of Moussa Traore emblazoned across it. I remember that the cloth was printed with purple shells and that I wanted it a good deal because it reminded me of the sea. That always puts you in a weak position, wanting something badly. The owner of the cloth knew this too and was intransigent about the price. Eventually she gestured to the scarf and said she'd throw it in for free. She said that it wasn't worth so much now that Traore had been toppled. Paul and I looked back at her in astonishment.

Under a shade by the hotel swimming pool that afternoon we learned the details from the World Service. The army had put down a student protest with tear gas and rubber bullets. This brought others out until there were mass demonstrations on the streets of Bamako. Moussa Traore responded by ordering in more troops who were armed this time with heavy artillery. In the furore Younnussi Toure used his influence with parts of the army to stage a coup closing the airport and all borders. No foreigners were allowed in or out and there were curfews night and day. At least forty people died in the protest, mostly students. We do not know to this day whether Issa was among them.

TRAVEL NOTES

Languages Although French is the official language, only a small percentage of the population speak it fluently. Most use Bambara, the main African language. Only a few students in the city are likely to speak much English.

Transport You can travel by boat from virtually one end of the country to the other – an exciting, but tiring and uncomfortable option. Trains, buses and the overcrowded *taxis-brousse* (bush taxis) cover a reasonably wide network although roads are fairly rough, often giving way to sandy tracks.

Accommodation Mali has few of what you could describe as luxury lodgings and accommodation prices seem inordinately high for what you get. The choice tends to be limited to the goverment-operated *campements* (small, often fairly shabby, hotels). Outside the towns it is possible to stay with local families but you do need to be sensitive to the burdens involved in any form of hospitality. Be ready to offer money/gifts in return.

Special Problems Bureaucracy has long been one of Mali's specialities. Happily, with the demise of SMERT, the unfortunately named state tourism company, you are no longer forced to go on guided tours by the tourist police. But the days when you had to report to the police on arrival in every town are not long gone, and Mali is still big on roadblocks. Beware that due to the ongoing Tuareg rebellion, the region north and east of Mopti is *zone sécurité* – making Timbuktu and Gao all but no-go areas at the time of writing.

The main tourist areas are thick with hustlers. The chances of getting ripped off are quite high although for most women, it is the harassment underlying the hard-sell approach that causes the most unease. Given the gross inequalities in wealth that enable you to travel to Mali you should expect to pay over the local rates. Bars and cafés are men-only, and uncomfortable places to wander into alone. Public swimming or sunbathing are ill-advised.

Guides *The Rough Guide to West Africa* (Penguin) includes a chapter on Mali.

CONTACTS

Union Nationale des Femmes du Mali, BP1740, Bamako. Formed in 1974 to fight for women's rights, the Union organizes literacy programmes, promotes the participation of women in development work, and campaigns against female genital mutilation.

BOOKS

Bettina Selby, *Frail Dream of Timbuktu* (UK, John Murray, 1991, o/p). Selby's lively account of her bike ride along the banks of the Niger River from Niamey to Bamako. A wealth of descriptive detail, along with the colour photographs make this a riveting read.

It's also well worth looking out for any **films** by Souleymane Cissé, the most famous name in Malian cinema. His 1986 film *Yeleen* ("Brightness") uses the theme of conflict between old and young to illuminate his idea of African values. Justly, an international hit.

Mexico

Mexico is a chaotic and exciting country with a tremendous amount to offer the traveller. Between the highly developed resorts lie miles of beaches, but most of the interest lies inland. Quite apart from the country's magnificent scenery and fascinating Spanish colonial history, large areas of central and southern Mexico are rich in Indian traditions and the relics of extraordinary ancient civilizations. An extensive

bus network makes it easy to get around and, depending on the exchange rate (Mexico is in a permanent state of economic crisis), there's plenty of inexpensive accommodation.

After a very stormy past, Mexico has long been regarded as one of the more stable countries in Latin America. This stability is based more on its strength as an advanced industrial power than on just or democratic government. In early 1994 an indigenous uprising in the wealthy southern state of Chiapas sent shockwaves through the nation and there are currently signs of mounting social unrest elsewhere. Despite efforts to present a radical face to the outside world, the Institutional Revolutionary Party (PRI), in power for nearly fifty years, is deeply conservative. Having persistently denied the need for land reform and other measures to help alleviate widespread poverty, especially among the Indian groups who make up roughly thirty percent of the population, the PRI is finally meeting the challenge many Mexicans feel it deserves. The odd gesture of reform was made in the run-up to recent elections (won by a narrow PRI majority amid outcries of corruption) but, by and large, little has ever been done to implement the kind of social changes symbolized by the famous 1911 Revolution which inspired the Party's name.

The high level of poverty endured by most Mexicans has led to considerable resentment of the affluence of their northern neighbours in the United States. This is sometimes focused on tourists and can be hard to contend with. Gringas (Western women), representing wealth and a type of sexuality denied to Mexican men, are easy targets for ill-feeling. Approaches from men tend to be aggressive, so you need to feel strong. It's also worth making a great effort to learn at least some Spanish before you go.

Not only foreigners need to arm themselves against machismo. Mexican feminists have long recognized it as a deep-rooted obstacle in their struggle for equality and freedom. However, as in the rest of Latin America, more urgent concern is given to the denial of basic economic and social rights. Since it began in 1970, a large section of the **women's movement** has had close

423

links with various political parties of the Left. At the same time there is an autonomous movement, for which abortion is a central issue, and there are several organized lesbian groups. Although certain reforms, such as the elimination of discriminatory laws, have been passed on paper, Mexican women see themselves as having a lot more to fight for.

A Matter of Adjustment

Bella McGuinness spent six months in Mexico as part of a degree course in Spanish and Latin American Studies at the University of Portsmouth. She so fell in love with the country that she decided to take a year out from her studies and returned to Mexico, supporting herself by teaching English.

I arrived in Mexico City drunk with jet-lag and wearing the only clothes I had – my bags had been left behind in Amsterdam. Stepping out into the streets that sprawl off the main square or *zocalo* was one of my biggest thrills. I liked Mexico City instantly, although it was often difficult to imagine why.

The capital is a landlocked metropolis and host to a ferocious complexity of man-made and natural elements. Blasting sunshine and gargantuan tropical downpours tip an already precarious balance. The tide of people, traffic and vast roads to cross seems endless and, at an altitude of 2261m, climbing up steps can be unbearable, however fit you are. The pollution, too, can make you irritable, especially when it obscures the mountain range, creating a towering gloomy sky that leaves you feeling almost marooned. On clear days though, the city is vibrant with a fragile and chaotic beauty and an intensity that is infectious. The stall-holders on the *tanguis* (market) commandeer the city's pavements. The shoe-shiner and the chewing gum vendor jostle for space amid stalls of US candy bars, tacos from the basket and outmoded perfumes. Over half of Mexico's inhabitants live on the borderlines of extreme poverty and street selling (fascinating for the tourist yet little tolerated by the authorities) is a vital means of survival.

Initially, I felt exposed and vulnerable, but this was more a result of scare-mongering than anything else. On my first night, terrified of the dark unfamiliar streets, I ran full pelt down the Cinco de Mayo avenue to my hotel. It was only 7pm. The metro was daunting too; I was touched up, talked to and stared at in turn, something I eventually learnt to deal with by reading a newspaper, leaving no opportunity for eye contact. At peak hours barriers are erected to divide men and women. One day, without thinking, I walked into a men-only carriage – nothing happened, but I panicked momentarily nevertheless. Looking confident when you're feeling scared is a vital, if difficult, knack to acquire. I was also robbed at the beginning of my stay. I wasn't holding onto my bag securely enough, it was rush-hour and I was riding on the now obsolete, yellow "school" buses that used to run in ribbons along the capital's central avenues –

> *It can be easy to fall for compliments about "amazing green eyes", especially spoken in Spanish.*

prime conditions for theft. By comparison, I always liked and felt most at ease travelling in *collectivos*. These are VW transit vans, often customized with names such as *Montezuma* or *Azteca*, and rocking with *Radio Tropical*. Inside they are adapted to seat eight or nine people facing each other and, perhaps due to the seating arrangement, men tend not to grope. In fact great trust is assumed between passengers and drivers alike, who pass fares and change front to back, Chinese-whisper style.

My first six months were spent in The National Autonomous University of Mexico (UNAM), a vast conglomeration of battery-farm style faculties, interspersed with buildings of great beauty, among them the mosaicked library. My British university enjoyed an educational exchange with UNAM and I could enter any class as an *oyente* (listener). I found the university impressive, both for its enormity (250,000 students) and its setting, straddling seven miles of black volcanic rock, mingled with flashes of brilliant colour. The three-dimensional murals by Siqueiros embellish the Faculty of Science. Scarlet Jacaranda trees shimmer against the backdrop of the inky mountains.

This used to be the most prestigious university in Latin America, notorious as a hotbed of student activism in the 1960s. Today it faces severe problems from under-funding, high student drop-out rates and poorly remunerated teaching positions, as well as competition from the private universities that are springing up all over the city. But with its deeper roots, and its own vigilante police, radio station, cinemas, theatres, publishing house and film company, UNAM still has many advantages. I didn't attend classes solely to learn about a particular subject, but also to listen to Spanish, meet people, explore the grounds and generally soak up Mexican culture.

When I first arrived in the city I put an advert in the newspaper, *Segundo Mano* (Second Hand), to exchange English conversation for Spanish. I received thirty phone-calls from men eager to meet me, but not one woman. Needless to say, I suspected an ulterior motive.

However, while machismo's ugly side is omnipresent, there is an aspect that adores, reveres and idolizes women. Feeling vulnerable in a new city, it can be easy to fall for the superficiality of flattery and compliments about "amazing green eyes", especially spoken in a language like Spanish. In the end you have to rely on instinct and remember that your greatest asset is flexibility. Arriving in Mexico City armed with a series of male deterrent strategies won't necessarily ensure you the best time.

Finding somewhere to stay is not difficult for exchange students, but given that ninety percent of young Mexicans live with their families, student-type accommodation is limited. Family accommodation did not appeal to me, but I was lucky to find a hostel which catered for foreign students in the township of Coyoacan, in the of south of the city.

We were eleven in total, of various nationalities, including Italian, Argentinian, Nicaraguan and Mexican. It was an inexpensive, easy-going place with humming birds in the garden and housemates as alternative family. Most Mexicans will tell you that Coyoacan isn't the true Mexico. Others claim this home of Trotsky and Frida Kahlo (whose family house has been turned into a fascinating museum) is the intellectual heart of the city. Film directors and university lecturers line the open terraces, swilling *café Americanos* and brooding over chess games. The district's traditional, colonial grace, intimate appeal and washed-lavender *tortilleras* (tortilla shops), alongside the newness of *Burger Boy*, also make it the coveted home for Mexican *guerros* (white skins).

My two women students were extremely diligent. Men, on the other hand, were happy to sit back, drink coffee and flirt.

I often went out in the city centre. Many enjoyable nights were spent at the *Bar León*, a cramped and steamy dive tucked away in the corner of a seedy hotel facade and easy to miss. Here salsa stars give virtuoso performances, providing the perfect night-out for *quinceaneras* (fifteen year-old-girls who in Mexico enjoy special birthday celebrations) and ageing playboys alike. The more formal dance halls, like the *Los Angeles*, are eye-openers too, where the doyennes of danzon, cha-cha-cha and *merengue* take to the floor. Mexicans tend to dance in twosomes, but I never managed to capture the grace and style of my Mexican friends, who were happy to leave me dancing alone.

Cantinas were another option, though I rarely went without a crowd. In the city centre, they can be fairly heavy: my friend and I were once launched upon by a boy with a set of false eye-lashes and a flick-knife nestling in his groin. Luckily, the owner told him to leave us alone. At other – more salubrious – bars, guitarists serenade the tables while overweight businessmen dole out the chat-up lines. I met many Mexicans who preferred not to drink but see a film, a great Mexican pastime.

I eventually found work through my newspaper advert. Officially, you're not allowed to work without a permit, but all my employers waved this aside. My first job was in a bank, giving English classes to executives. The work was pleasant and hassle-free and the standard of English excellent. My only two women students were extremely diligent. Men, on the other hand, were happy to sit back, drink coffee and flirt, though quite politely. Dress code was all important and women tended to pile on the make-up, sometimes to the point of looking quite ridiculous. In a silk shirt and white jeans I was just about acceptable, but one day made the mistake of wearing sandals from Oaxaca, a famous market town in southern Mexico. As people in the elevator looked down at my feet and sniggered, I realized such sandals are regarded as indigenous footwear, beneath the "dignity" of bank executives.

> *I saw no one from dawn to dusk until the last day when, coming out of my room, I noticed forty men waiting for the collectivo.*

I also worked in a private university, teaching elementary English. The job was more informal but by no means a pushover. The students were wealthy, sulky and couldn't wait to get out of the class, mine being the last of the day. Fortunately I was paid quite well so it was worthwhile. In contrast, a group of novice priests I taught started out by being charming, only to end up crying if I failed to give each student my undivided attention. Luckily the atmosphere was eventually eased by the arrival of two girls in the class.

At one stage I did some voluntary work for Amnesty International, mainly on the administrative side. This was run by *extranjeros* (foreigners) who failed to take into account that all the events they organized were beyond the financial means of most Mexicans. A far more rewarding voluntary project was teaching a six-week English course to refugees. These were mainly Central Americans who, as part of a United Nations scheme, were preparing to fly to New Zealand to start a new life. Some had only functional literacy, so the classes were very slow but marked by great solidarity, courage and good humour. Typically, on the last night they organized a party for all the people involved, with El Salvadorean food and *Cuba Libres*. I was also engaged in a similar project for South American exiles. The women in all these classes were, without doubt, the heads of household, and considering the level of stress they were suffering appeared remarkably strong. It was a period that greatly moved me.

427

I did travel during my time in Mexico – always alone though sometimes meeting a friend at my destination. The exhilaration of reaching a soft tropical beach after weeks or months in the city was hard to beat. My first trip, however, was totally disorienting. I hadn't been a week in Mexico City and was still in the throes of culture shock when a young woman invited me to stay with her family in Juchitan, which turned out to be a small, rather sleazy tropical town down south, beyond Oaxaca. After more than twelve hours on the bus, I finally arrived in the town square in the searing midday heat. The market was in full swing: people were selling bundles of knobbly iguanas, gasping for breath; mangy dogs scavenged from meatstalls; and swarthy women wielded giant vanilla pods, the sweet, heady scent of which was almost overwhelming. Luckily my friend arrived and led me to the semi-abandoned house, hung with the essential hammocks, where she lived with her parents and grandmother. Cool pineapples were hacked open. The grandmother, a Zapotec (from Oaxaca), had snowy-white hair and a face crinkled like a walnut – she had lost count of her age yet swung dangerously high on her hammock, wafting only a hint of cooled air through the soupy haze. I felt my most vulnerable and clumsy during those first few hours as I flailed about against a merciless sun. One week later I was loath to leave.

Another time I went to Tabasco in the southeast, to a deserted beach. I saw no one from dawn to dusk until the last day when, coming out of my room, I noticed as many as forty men waiting for the *collectivo*. "Ah, we were waiting for you", one of them announced. I looked a bit surprised. "We have been staying in the huts behind yours. We have been your guardian angels." A few of the other men grinned sheepishly. Next minute the *collectivo* arrived. "After you, my queen." Solicitously, they ushered me into the van.

A Place to Return to

Valerie Walkerdine is a psychologist, writer and artist living in London. Fascinated by Mexico, she has visited the country five times in recent years to travel, work and extend friendships she has made there.

I first had the idea of going to Mexico when I was working for the summer in Canada, from which (like the US) it is possible to get very cheap flights. Although clear that I wanted to see America's so-called back yard for myself, I found it difficult at first to work out where to go. This being the first real solo trip I had made, I suppose I was also slightly afraid.

Cheap flights from North America to Mexico all tend to focus on very Americanized holiday resorts, which are not the best places to go unless you like observing imperialism at work in a particularly obnoxious way. A Mexican woman in one airline office was helpful and found me some literature, but other travel agents just wanted to shunt me off to the beach resorts.

People also suggested that it would be too hot for me in the summer – I have very fair skin – as Mexico is chiefly known as a winter resort. Basic knowledge of the Mexican seasons, however, would have cleared up this mistake; it rains a lot in July and is certainly no hotter in the summer than in winter or spring, though the climate varies according to region.

Men will ask outrageous questions about your sex life.

In the end I decided to start with the city of Oaxaca, some 500km south of Mexico City. My guidebook made it sound interesting, not too full of gringos, off the tourist beach scene, and with a strong, relatively intact Indian heritage. It turned out to be a very attractive town, though not exactly off the tourist trail. The surrounding state of Oaxaca was stunning, offering a combination of pre-Columbian remains, tropical forests, mountains and a beautiful coastline. Visiting some of the more remote coastal areas with a friend, however, I felt that, while they looked inviting, they might well prove dangerous for a woman on her own.

Getting around Mexico is relatively cheap if you have a European or North American income. For Mexicans it is very expensive, as is the general cost of living. I travelled by plane and bus – trains are very slow, rental cars extortionate. It helps considerably to speak Spanish. On my first trip I spoke none, but can now hold a reasonable conversation, which really repays the effort of learning. I found people on buses eager to talk. Unlike Europeans, who hide themselves in books on journeys, Mexicans like to sit together and chat.

A woman alone, however, is considered an oddity in this patriarchal country and everyone wants to know if you are married and have children. Men will ask outrageous questions about your sex life. It's easy to pass this off as proof of the blatant sexism only to be expected of a macho culture, but it's not as simple as that. Attitudes to gringos and gringas are also about the hate and envy felt by an oppressed and exploited people.

White women, especially with fair hair, are about the most hated, envied and desired of all. Any glance at the television screen makes it immediately obvious that white skin equals wealth and class in the Mexican popular imagination. Hence many Mexican men's desire to "have" a white woman is matched by their secret (or sometimes not so secret) contempt.

As the Canadian film, *A Winter Tan*, demonstrates, Mexico can feel like a place to let go of the strictures of European morality, but the relationship of the gringa tourist to Mexican patriarchy requires some reflection. The film painfully documents the "adventures" and eventual death of a North American woman looking for sex in Mexico. In quite a racist way, it presents the pain of a white woman in search of sexual freedom and, unable to find what she is looking for at home, she is left to pursue the fantasy through another of escape and Otherness. Of course, tales of the promiscuity of gringa women abound in Mexico and it is important to try and reflect upon the complex relationship between not only capitalism and patriarchy, but of power and powerlessness between white women and Mexican men.

> *I let go of some of my attachments to work and recognized that I could relax, that there were other things in life.*

I have to say that these are issues which I have thought about as I have got to know Mexico and Mexicans better. I was not actually frightened by the harassment at any time, but I do advise caution, for instance when travelling on the metro in Mexico City. The public transport system is stunningly efficient in carrying millions of people at low cost: consequently the trains are always crowded. Where they are available it's wise to travel in women's compartments. You also need to hold on very carefully to your money. In this respect it obviously helps not to go around saying loudly in English (or Spanish for that matter) how cheap everything is: it is only cheap to us.

Mexico exists with an overt level of corruption and danger in its political and everyday life which can be frightening and shocking. To gain more insight into this complex country it is well worth trying to make contact with feminist groups and to find out what is going on politically. The strongest current is socialist feminism, but the talks I went to were overwhelmingly run by white, middle-class women. However, in both these discussions and the political meetings I attended, people were friendly and more than willing to talk about what was going on. On my last visit, feelings were running especially high in the aftermath of yet another round of corrupt elections. Zapatistas (supporters of the politics of Emilio Zapata, principal hero of the Revolution) marched in the streets of Mexico City and beyond. Elsewhere ordinary people laughed at the very mention of the word *revolución*. "We call it *robolución*", was a common remark.

Mexico is beautiful in a way that makes you never want to return to northern winters (or summers). There is something about the quality of light and the big skies that is easy to romanticize – as it is to exoticize the country's rich and varied culture. The mixture of indigenous and Spanish cultures can quite take your breath away and makes the West seem horribly obsessive in its post-modernist hype and materialism. I remember stopping in New York on the way home from my first visit, having been relaxing with friends north of Mexico City. It was perhaps the first time in many years that I had actually felt able to let go of some of the attachments to work and begin to recognize that I could relax, that there were other things in life. New York after this seemed gross.

> *The women in the market wanted above all not to be photographed in the humiliation of their poverty.*

For all these reasons and more, it didn't take long for me to dream up an excuse to return. This was provided a few months later by the chance to do some research for a short film about the Mexican painter, Frida Kahlo. My Spanish had improved and I found it fairly easy to wander alone around Mexico City – even with a Super-8 movie camera complete with tripod! I also travelled to Guanjuato and Patzcuaro to the north. The former is a colonial town of great beauty where, in my memory, the golden yellow walls of houses blend with the winter sunshine. In the glorious December light, Patzcuaro, built on the shores of a huge lake, was spectacular. Many Mexicans were on holiday, eating meals of freshly cooked fish overlooking the water. The boat trip out to the central island is lovely, though everything, from the fishermen lifting their nets for the tourist cameras to the souvenir stalls on the island itself, shows how tourism has become a central means of survival for local inhabitants.

I was fascinated by Mexico and yet, as an academic and visual artist, I was aware of how much writing about and seeing of Mexico through European eyes there had already been. D H Lawrence, Malcolm Lowrie and Graham Greene have all set novels here, and all, in one way or another, use the country to explore the fascination and exoticization of European "man" for the "other" – the uncivilized and primitive, the hot passion against civilized European coldness.

It is all too easy to see Mexico like this, as well as the other version, the big holiday playground south of the border. Of course, there are also writers and artists who want to see and to document oppression and poverty. But this is equally problematic in its way. The role of voyeuristic observer, looking to report to the affluent West, does nothing for, say, the women I met in a street market picking through the thrown away rotten produce; they wanted above all not to be photographed in the humiliation of their poverty.

In the end I made a tape-slide about the relationship between my geographical journey, the problem of the voyeuristic aspects of observing and reporting on other cultures' oppression and poverty, and my own history and personal journey towards liberation. Mexico is an exciting country which makes you look again at all those things most of us take for granted in Europe. The diversity of its cultures, the stunning remains of pre-Columbian civilizations, the wonderful revolutionary artistic heritage, mixed with the complexities and oppression of its present, make it seem both wonderful and terrible. I will keep on going back.

TRAVEL NOTES

Languages Spanish and various Indian dialects.
Transport Buses are the best means of getting around. Trains are cheaper but limited and very slow. Hitching is more hassle than it's worth, with the additional threat of police harassment, and is definitely not recommended.
Accommodation Cheap hotels are usually easy to find and it's worth haggling.
Special Problems Many women have enjoyed travelling alone through Mexico, in spite of sexual harassment. Self-confidence and some knowledge of Spanish help.

Don't get involved with or ever trust the police. Police bribery is a common racket (especially if you're driving). Also, don't even think of touching drugs. It's usual for a dealer to sell them to someone, sell the information to the police and then get half the drugs back once his victim has been arrested.
Guides The Rough Guide to Mexico (Penguin) is informed and often amusing. Mexico (US, The Resource Center, 1992), edited by the centre's founder, Tom Barry, is a useful guide to Mexican politics, society and environment – distributed in Britain by the Latin America Bureau (LAB).

CONTACTS

Movimiento Nacional Para Mujeres, San Juan de Letran 11-411, Mexico DF (☎512/58 41). National women's organization, useful for contacts throughout the country.
CIDHAL, Aptdo 579, Cuernavaca, Morelos. Women's documentation centre primarily concerned with popular education among working-class women.
For information on the lesbian scene in Mexico, contact *Ferrari's Places for Women: Worldwide Women's Guide*, PO Box 37887, Phoenix, AZ 85069.

BOOKS

⭐ **Mary Morris**, *Nothing to Declare: Memoirs of a Woman Travelling Alone* (UK, Penguin, 1988, o/p/US, Penguin, 1989). This highly readable account of living and travelling in Mexico and Central America successfully combines travelogue with an exploration into the writer's own self.
Katie Hickman, *A Trip to the Light Fantastic: Travels with a Mexican Circus* (UK, Flamingo, 1994). Hickman describes a year spent with Circo Bell's Circus, initially as an observer but eventually as a performer in her own right on the circuit around Mexico. Circus anecdotes are interwoven with rather lengthy retellings of folktales and photos taken by the writer's husband.
Sybille Bedford, *A Visit to Don Otavio* (1953; UK, Eland Books, 1982/US, Hippocrene Books, 1989). An extremely enjoyable and surprisingly relevant account of travels in 1950s Mexico.
Hayden Herrera, *Frida: A Biography of Frida Kahlo* (UK, Bloomsbury Press, 1989/US, HarperCollins, 1983). Biography of the extraordinary Mexican painter who died in 1953.
Elena Poniatowsla, *Tinisima* (UK, Faber & Faber, 1995/US, Farrar, Straus & Giroux). Novelized biography of Tina Modotti, the silent-film star, photographer and revolutionary who was a friend of Kahlo's and equally extraordinary.
Augusta Dwyer, *On the Line: Life on the US-Mexican Border* (UK & US, Latin America Bureau, 1994). The author, a Canadian journalist, uncovers the stories of dozens of ordinary Mexicans struggling to survive in the dirty cities of the border.

Gisela Espinosa Damián, "Feminism and Social Struggle in Mexico" in Miranda Davies (ed), *Third World – Second Sex 2* (UK & US, Zed Books, 1987). This article, by a former CIDHAL worker, discusses the experience of co-ordinating workshops on sexuality in a poor neighbourhood of Mexico City.

FICTION

Carmen Boullosa, *The Miracle Worker* (UK & US, Jonathan Cape, 1994). Compelling tale of a woman who can make dreams come true, heal the sick and solve mysteries, beginning with a murder in the backstreets of Mexico City.

Ana Castillo, *The Mixquiahuala Letters* (UK, Bilingual Press, 1993/US, Doubleday, 1992). Chicana novel charting the friendship of two women, one white and wealthy, the other poor and Mexican American, on a trip through the Yucatan. Together they battle self-doubt, mutual mistrust and the unwanted advances of every man they meet.

Denise Chávez, *Face of an Angel* (US, Farrar, Straus & Giroux, 1994). By another Chicana writer, this is the engaging story of a gutsy New Mexico chile-parlour waitress and her sexual adventures.

Harriet Doerr, *Consider This Señora* (US, André Deutsch, 1994). A wise and gently thoughtful novel based around three American women's experiences in Mexico.

Laura Esquivel, *Like Water for Chocolate* (UK, Black Swan, 1993/US, Doubleday, 1994). Best-selling love story with a hint of magical realism. Esquivel skilfully draws a world of strong, complex female characters: the main protaganist wields power by preparing splendid meals, while her sister becomes a revolutionary general. Beautifully written, with some great Mexican recipes.

Joanna Labon (ed), *Storm 7–8: New Writing from Mexico* (UK, Jonathan Cape, 1992). Part of a ground-breaking series of literary magazines promoting new writing in translation. Hard to track down but well worth the effort.

James O'Reilly and Larry Habegger (eds), *Travelers' Tales: Mexico* (US, Travelers' Tales Inc, 1994). A selection of stories, anecdotes and quotations aimed at reflecting the country's essence through the eyes of travellers and writers, including Alma Guillermoprieto, Mary Morris and several more women.

Thanks to Jennifer Accettola for her comments on these Travel Notes.

Morocco

O nly an hour's ferry ride from southern Spain, Morocco is easily the most accessible and popular of the North African states. The fact that it is so close to the well-trodden Mediterranean routes, however, and its French colonialist feel, can be misleading and disadvantageous, leaving you little time to adjust to an Islamic, essentially Third World culture. In line with the precepts of Islam, women keep a low profile, particularly in urban life and travelling alone (or with other women) it can come as a shock to find yourself continually surrounded, scrutinized and commented on by men.

These pressures are at their most stifling in the main resorts and cities where sexual harassment easily merges with the continual and persistent approaches from hustlers and "guides" (many Moroccans depend on tourists for economic survival). Tangier, the main point of entry for most travellers, is perhaps the hardest to contend with, and it's not uncommon for women to manage only a few days before taking the ferry back.

To do this, however, would be to miss a great deal. The Moroccan tradition of hospitality towards strangers runs far deeper than the mutual exploitations of tourism, and just as you can experience harassment you can also experience great friendship and generosity. It's essential to remain polite and even-mannered in all your dealings. At its best – in the high Atlas mountains, in Marrakesh and throughout the southern desert routes – Morocco can be a great country to visit.

Since Morocco's independence from the French in 1956, **women** have looked to the state to take over the traditional functions of providing welfare and educational services for the family. A small proportion of women have managed to gain access to higher education and – despite intense discrimination – professional employment. For the majority, however, modernization has brought only the erosion of traditional networks of support, with few alternatives provided. This has very much increased women's vulnerability to isolation and poverty.

The official government women's organization, the Women's Union, has centres running skills training classes in most of the large cities. More recently, a feminist group, linked to the Left opposition movement, has also emerged in Rabat, printing a women's paper *The 8th of March*; distribution is increasing and the group has also organized various conferences, seminars and events in other cities.

Running through Fes

Margaret Hubbard, who works as an English teacher in Scotland, set off to Morocco for a month's holiday. Although she had long been interested in Islamic culture and had already travelled in the Middle East, this was her first trip alone to a Muslim country.

I knew that there were likely to be difficulties in travelling as a woman alone around Morocco. I'd been warned by numerous sources about hustling and harassment and I was already well aware of the constraints imposed upon women travellers within Islamic cultures. But above and beyond this I knew I'd be fascinated by the country. I had picked up a smattering of Arabic and the impetus to study Islamic religion and culture during trips to Damascus and Amman (both times with a male companion). Also I already had enough experience of travelling alone to know that I could live well with myself should I meet up with no one else. So, a little apprehensive but very much more determined and excited, I arrived at Tangier, took the first train out to Casablanca and found a room for the night. It was not until I emerged the next morning into the bright daylight of Casablanca that I experienced my first reaction to Morocco.

Nothing could have prepared me for it. Almost instantly I was assailed by a barrage of "Voulez-vous coucher avec moi . . . Avez-vous jamais fait l'amour au Maroc . . . Venez avec moi madame . . . Viens m'selle". Whatever I had to say was ignored at will and wherever I went I felt constantly scrutinized by men. Fighting down the panic I headed for the bus station where, after a lot of frantic rushing to and fro (I couldn't decipher the Arabic signs), I climbed on to a bus for Marrakesh.

It wasn't that the harassment was less, in fact it was almost as constant as in Tangier. But wandering through the Djemaa el Fna (the main square and centre of all life in Marrakesh) amongst the snake-charmers, kebab-sellers, blanket weavers, water-sellers, monkey-trainers, merchants of everything from false teeth to handwoven rugs, I became ensnared to such an extent that my response to the men who approached me was no longer one of fear but rather a feeling of irrelevance.

Marrakesh proved to me that I was right to come to Morocco. There was too much to be learned to shut out contact with people and I heard myself utter, as if it were the most normal reply in the world, "Non, monsieur, je ne veux pas coucher avec vous, mais pouvez-vous me dire pourquoi ils vendent false teeth/combien d'années il faut pour faire des tapis à main/pourquoi les singes [monkeys]". That first night I returned to my room at 2am more alive than I had felt for months.

I'd also stumbled upon a possible strategy for pre-empting, perhaps even preventing, harassment. Moroccan hustlers know a lot about tourists and have reason to expect one of two reactions from them – fear, or a sort of resigned acceptance. What they don't expect is for you to move quickly through the opening gambits and launch into a serious conversation about Moroccan life. Using a mixture of French and Arabic, I developed the persona of a "serious woman" and from Marrakesh to Figuig discussed the politics of the Maghreb, maternity rights, housing costs, or the Koran, with almost anyone who wanted my attention.

It became exhausting, but any attempt at more desultory chat was treated as an open invitation and seemed to make any harassment more determined. That isn't to say that it's impossible to have a more relaxed relationship with Moroccan men. I made good friends on two occasions with Arab men and I'm still corresponding with one of them. But I think this was made easier by my defining the terms of our friendship fairly early on in the conversation. As a general rule whenever I arranged to meet up with someone I didn't know very well, I chose well-lit public places. I was also careful about my clothes – I found it really did help to look as inconspicuous as possible and almost always wore loose-fitting blouses, longish skirts and occasionally also a headscarf.

"Is it true that women are opened up by machine?" is a question that worries me still.

After exploring Marrakesh for five days I took a bus out over the Atlas mountain range to Zagora. The journey took twelve hours and the bus was hot and cramped but, wedged between a group of Moroccan mothers, jostling their babies on my lap and sharing whatever food and drink was going round, I felt reassured, more a participant than an outsider.

This was also one of the few occasions that I'd had any sort of meaningful contact with Moroccan women. For the most part women tend to have a low profile in public, moving in very separate spheres to the tourists. There are some women's cafés but they're well hidden and not for foreigners. For me, the most likely meeting place was the *hammam*, or steambath, which I habitually sought out in each stopping place.

Apart from the undoubted pleasures of plentiful hot water, *hammams* became a place of refuge for me. It was a relief to be surrounded by women and to be an object of curiosity without any element of threat. Any ideas about Western status I might have had were lost in the face of explaining in French, Arabic and sign language to an old Moroccan woman with twenty-four grandchildren the sexual practices and methods of contraception used in the West. "Is it true that women are opened up by machine?" is a question that worries me still.

I arrived in Zagora on the last night of the festival of the King's birthday. It was pure chance. The town was packed with Moroccans who had travelled in from nearby oases, but I met only one other tourist – a German man. We were both of us swept along, as insignificant as any other single people in the crowd, dancing and singing in time to the echoing North African sounds. At the main event of the night, the crowd was divided by a long rope with women on one side and men on the other, with only the German and I standing side by side. I felt overwhelmed with a feeling of excitement and well-being, simply because I was there.

From Zagora I headed for Figuig and the desert, stopping overnight en route at Tinerhir. It's possible that I chose a bad hotel for that stop but it was about the worst night that I spent in the entire trip. The men in and around the hotel jeered, even spat at me when I politely refused to accompany them, and throughout the night I had men banging on the door and shutters of my room. For twelve hours I stood guard, tense, afraid, and stifled by the locked in heat of that dismal hotel room. I escaped on the first bus out.

Further south I met up with a Danish man in a Landrover and travelled on with him to spend four days in the desert. It was a simple, businesslike arrangement: he wanted someone to look after the van while he slept and I wanted someone to look out for me while I slept. I can find no terms that will sufficiently describe the effect that the desert had on me. It was awesome and inspiring and it silenced both of us. On the rare occasions that we spoke we did so in whispers.

The men who had hustled me in the morning looked on with respectful interest as I hurtled by in the cool of the evening.

I also found that the more recent preoccupations that I had about my life, work and relationships had entirely slipped from my mind, yet strangely I could recall with absolute clarity images from over ten years ago. I remain convinced that the desert, in its simplicity, its expansiveness and its power changed me in some way.

At Figuig I parted company with the Dane and made my way in various stages to Fes. I tended to find myself becoming dissatisfied after travelling for a while with a male companion. Not because I didn't enjoy the company, which was more often than not a luxury for me, but I used to feel cheated that I was no longer at the forefront and that any contact with Moroccans would have to be made through him. This is often the case in Islamic countries where any approaches or offers of hospitality are proffered man-to-man, with the woman treated more or less as an appendage. I was prepared to go on alone however uncomfortable it might become as long as I was being treated as a person in my own right.

In Fes I discovered yet another, perhaps even more effective, strategy for changing my status with Moroccan men. I am a runner, and compete regularly in marathons and I'm used to keeping up with my training in almost any conditions. Up until Fes I'd held back, uncertain of how I'd be greeted if I dashed out of the hotel in only a track-suit bottom and T-shirt. My usual outfit, a long skirt and blouse, was hardly suitable for the exercise I had in mind.

After seriously considering confining myself to laps around the hotel bedroom, I recovered my sanity and sense of adventure, changed my clothes and set off. The harassment and the hustling all melted away. I found that Moroccans have such a high regard for sport that the very men who had hustled me in the morning looked on with a respectful interest, offering encouragement and advice as I hurtled by in the cool of the evening. Furthermore I became known as "the runner" and was left more or less in peace for the rest of my stay. After this I made it a rule to train in all the villages and towns I stayed in on the way back to Tangier. Now when I run I conjure up the image of pacing out of Chaouen towards the shrine on the hillside, keeping time with the chants of the *muezzin* at dawn.

Returning to Tangier I felt as far removed as it is possible to feel from the apprehensive new arrival of the month before. I felt less intimidated by and more stoical about my status as an outsider and I had long since come to accept the fact that I was a source of income to many people whose options for earning a living are sorely limited.

Walking out of the bus station I was surrounded by a group of hustlers. I listened in silence and then said, in the fairly decent Arabic that I had picked up, that I had been in the Sahara and had not got lost so I didn't think I needed a guide in Tangier; furthermore, that I had talked to some Tuareg in Zagora who told me that it is a lie that Moroccans buy their women with camels; please would they excuse me, I had arrangements. I spent the next few days wandering freely around the town, totally immersed in plotting how soon I could return.

Three Kinds of Women

Pat Chell lived for two years in Fes, teaching English at the university. She has since returned to Norwich in the UK where she works almost exclusively with travellers and gypsy communities.

"In Morocco, there are only three kinds of women", I was often told, "virgins, wives and whores". It is as useful a proverb as any to keep in mind when you visit, and a start to understanding the core of the country's culture – Islam and the family.

A woman in Morocco must be a virgin when she marries, and usually — she is expected to prove this on consummation of the marriage by showing evidence of hymenal blood. I have known "Westernized", bourgeois women, no longer virgins but about to marry, who have gone to a doctor in Casablanca to have the hymen restitched. This has not necessarily been done to deceive their prospective husbands, with whom they may have been sleeping in any case, but to "observe form" and keep the two families happy.

I have also known of liberal families who have given their consent for a couple to sleep together, after the marriage contract has been made but before the wedding ceremony, yet have "satisfied themselves" that the woman was a virgin upon the first occasion.

The only legitimate reason for a woman not being a virgin is if she is a wife. If she is known to be neither, then she will be considered a prostitute. Indeed, once a girl's virginity is lost and her marriage prospects become virtually nil, without family support she may well have to resort to prostitution as a means of making enough money to live.

Many students equated feminism with danger because they saw it as anti-Islamic.

Prostitution is very common in Morocco. All unmarried Moroccan men whom I spoke to about sex had had their only experiences with prostitutes (apart from those who had been "lucky" enough to meet tourists who would oblige).

On the first occasion this was almost always as an adolescent with a prostitute known for her experience in dealing with "virgins", though Moroccans would laugh at that expression, as the concept of male virginity does not exist. Indeed, many regard childhood circumcision as equivalent to the taking away of virginity. A bridegroom is tacitly expected to be sexually experienced and one who is not is seen as something of a joke.

Homosexuality, though it does exist as a sexual preference, is more likely to be thought of as a substitute for the "real" thing; tourists sometimes misinterpret Moroccan men's show of physical affection for each other as sexual, but this is simply a cultural norm. As for women, I'm not so sure that the concept of sexual satisfaction (let alone sexual preference) even exists. Amongst my students at the university, presumably an intellectual elite, the idea of choosing lesbianism, either for physical or political reasons, was inconceivable. If anything, it was regarded as another example of Western decadence.

Some of my students did have relationships with men but this was a very risky business indeed. If the relationship was "known about" and then ended, the woman could be branded as a whore and her life made a misery. I have met female students who have been beaten by fathers or brothers simply for being seen talking to a man. Another, who had been raped, did nothing about the attack even though the assailant was known to her, because she was sure that if her family found out she would be taken from the university. Many families are reluctant to allow their daughters to go to university, not because they don't want them educated – they often do as job prospects for women continue to improve – but because they don't want them to be at risk by being in a situation where they can have contact with men.

A number of students, male and female, were obviously dissatisfied with the status quo. A married student I knew attempted to help his working wife with chores until he was forbidden to do so by his mother, and his wife was severely reprimanded for failing in her wifely duties. They, like most young Moroccans, were not in a financial position to have a home of their own, even if the family constraints against doing so had not been there. Others of my students wanted to marry Europeans, not so much to have a more equal relationship, nor for the financial benefits, but because there was more likelihood of their being able to free themselves from family restraints.

I was only ever aware of one student who did not want to marry. This was Saloua; she was very intelligent and studious, determined to further her studies, which would have meant leaving Morocco, and then returning as a university teacher. She saw this as the best way in which she could help the women of her country.

Although Saloua had a very supportive family, she knew that she had to have a strategy to allow her to carry out her plans. She dressed in Western clothes but very demurely – rather middle-aged "Marks and Spencers". She was rarely seen alone, thus denying any man an opportunity to talk to her. When with women, she avoided the usual "gossip" and *No father would put his daughter at risk by letting her travel unless she was already "worthless".* "scheming". In a mixed teaching group she spoke only when invited to do so. If she did become involved in a classroom discussion with males, she would be pleasant but distant, humourless and polite. In other words, she always kept a low profile. She was aware of walking a very tenuous tightrope to freedom. She was the most courageous Moroccan woman that I met and I wish her well.

Many students, however, equated feminism with danger because they saw it as anti-Islamic. Some of the most politically active women that I came across were involved in Islamic fundamentalism and wanted nothing to do with Western decadence and therefore nothing to do with me.

Moroccans form their ideas of Western women from two main sources, the media and tourists. The cinema is very popular and there is an abundance of European soft-porn films. I have heard great cheers in the cinema when the "macho" hero has torn off a woman's clothes or physically abused her prior to her becoming a willing sexual partner.

One of the biggest culture shocks I had in this respect occurred in a very poor home with no running water, toilet or electricity. There was, however, a television and a wire would be run over the roof to a neighbour's when we wanted an evening's viewing. Every Wednesday, neighbours would gather to watch *Dallas*. It was the first time they had spent time socially with a European and so naturally they were curious. My host had to go to great lengths to explain that I was not a "Pamela" or a "Sue Ellen" and that neither were the majority of Western women. I don't think they were very convinced.

If a woman is alone or only with women, what kind of woman can she be? No father would put his daughter at risk by letting her travel unless she was already "worthless". Her nearest equivalent in Moroccan society is the prostitute. She sits in cafés, drinks alcohol, smokes cigarettes or hashish and will even comb her hair in public. She often dresses "indecently" – not even a prostitute would do this. Why should a woman want to "flaunt" her body? She will also often be prepared to have sex if you can charm her into it. These are the kinds of attitudes I heard so frequently.

And, as a traveller, these are the attitudes which you can expect to meet. The inevitable sexual harassment comes in a variety of forms, from the relatively innocuous to the absolutely obscene. The most persistent and annoying is a clicking noise made with the tongue every time you walk past a café, for example. Not terribly serious, you might think, but the cumulative effect is very degrading.

Then there are more direct, verbal approaches. I would strongly advise against confronting anyone who pesters you, as your remonstrations only provide unexpected entertainment. I've never yet seen a woman come out of one of these confrontations without feeling foolish and humiliated. Your anger will simply not be understood. You are unlikely to receive much sympathy from Moroccan women, either. They will either disapprove of you and think that you must be prepared to accept the consequences of being out in public (i.e. in the man's world) or they will fail to understand your annoyance as there are many young Moroccan women who seek this kind of attention. It is proof of their attractiveness and may be the only kind of contact they have ever known with men.

I don't think as a tourist you can ever avoid sexual harassment completely, but there are certain compromises that reduce its extent. You can dress "appropriately", in skirts, rather than trousers, and in sleeved, loose-fitting tops. You should avoid making eye contact too, and not start up a "casual" conversation with a man – there is no such thing in Morocco. Above all, be as polite and even-tempered as possible. Moroccans have a highly ritualized, elaborate etiquette, which you will not be able to learn in a short time, but they do respect politeness. Loss of temper equals loss of face, no matter what the provocation.

What I have written are generalizations. There are Moroccan men and women who do not share these attitudes. There are many students who genuinely want to practise their English and can only do so with travellers. Unfortunately, on a short stay, the Moroccans you're most likely to encounter are street hustlers only after your money or your body. Sometimes, particularly if you are feeling threatened or insecure, it is difficult to tell whether people are being genuine or "hustling". But if you are cautiously optimistic and rely on your instincts, then you might find, as I did, that Moroccans are incredibly hospitable people, many of whom love to have Westerners to stay.

I hope that I haven't put you off travelling to Morocco. Too often, sadly, I met travellers who judged the society with Western values: they saw the men as villains and the women as martyrs.

With a Toddler in Tow

Jo Crowson, a single mother, travelled to Morocco from Britain with her two year old daughter, Merry. While most of the Moroccans she met seemed very positive in their attitudes towards her and her child, she found that fellow male travellers could be surprisingly critical and unsupportive.

I had already spent some time in Morocco with a group of friends, both male and female, and had a pretty bad time – entirely our own fault. For a start we went in July (temperatures at 31°C plus) and we went straight to the Rif mountains where one of our party immediately got caught with hashish. We spent the next two weeks trying to get him out of prison and virtually all our combined funds on his fine. So I had a good idea what not to do in Morocco.

Six years later, I found myself a single parent in great need of a winter adventure and my thoughts turned again to Morocco. It was not too far (in case Merry, my two-year-old daughter got ill), it was accessible over-land (I wouldn't have to pay for two flights), it was inexpensive and it was definitely different. I decided to go for it, but with so many doubts, fears and reservations, that I thought I was probably completely mad.

In the following weeks I read as many guidebooks and travel books on Morocco as I could find in the library. This did little to ease my fears. All included warnings about sexual harassment, and the incredibly persistent street hustlers, and they all, without exception, advised women against travelling alone. I decided that if, after a couple of days, I found that travelling with a child was just as difficult as travelling alone, I would go back to Spain and spend my time there. Having established this "escape clause", I felt a lot better.

I managed to get a lift with friends as far as northern Portugal, which I thought would make the journey cheaper. I'm not sure that it did in the end, but it is good to see the land you're travelling over and watch the gradual changes as they happen. (As a result of this journey I have many tips to pass on to anyone planning to spend three days in the back of a car with a two-year-old.) I was also lucky enough to get a letter sent poste restante from some women friends who were already travelling in Morocco with their children, suggesting a couple of good places to visit and saying what a wonderful time they were having.

Feeling very brave and excited we boarded the ferry, had our passport checked, and kept a look out for dolphins.

After we left our friends in Portugal we had a great journey into Spain and down to Algeciras, from where there are ferries to Morocco. It gave us a chance to get adjusted to our new lifestyle and to gain confidence. It also gave me a bit longer to feel apprehensive about how we'd cope. Finally the great moment arrived and feeling very brave and excited we boarded the ferry, had our passport checked, and kept a look out for dolphins.

I'd decided we'd go to Tangier as it's better connected than Ceuta and I could get a train straight out to Rabat. The south is supposed to be slightly easier for travellers than the north and Rabat sounded like the least problematic (as well as the least exciting) place to acclimatize in.

Despite all my fears, arriving at Tangier was astonishingly easy. We were waved through customs, while most of the other people were emptying out their luggage, shown where to buy our train ticket and pointed in the right direction for the station. There, two unofficial porters grabbed my bags and charged five dirhams for help I didn't need. Ah well. I'd managed the first obstacle although I was still pretty nervous – what if my carriage fills up with men?

At the next stop three young men got on, followed by two women. I began to relax a bit. One of the three started talking to me in English, eating away at my reserves of confidence (not difficult) by saying that we wouldn't be getting to Rabat until very late, it was a terrible city, all the hotels would be full and so on. He was attempting to persuade me to get off at his home town, which he described as a beautiful seaside resort full of tourists. This put me off. I looked it up in my guidebook and was put off even more. It was when he insisted that the youth hostel where I planned to stay at Rabat would close at 6pm that I suddenly realized

I was having my first encounter with a dedicated "hustler". He left the compartment and the women seated opposite me warned me that he was a "bad Moroccan" – a phrase I heard frequently during my stay.

From then on I communicated with my fellow passengers in abysmal French, with the help of an exchange of bananas for biscuits. They were delighted by Merry but seemed very anxious when she fell asleep that she should keep her legs fully covered. I'm not sure if it was fear of her catching cold or the glimpse of bare flesh that particularly disturbed them, but I covered her anyway. Moroccan girls wear loose trousers under their skirts from babyhood onwards and although I had thought about keeping myself covered up, I hadn't considered Merry. From then on I made sure that she wore trousers and/or longish skirts everywhere except at the beach and no one else ever commented.

Their attitudes ranged from praise for my bravery to criticism of my mothering instincts.

When we arrived in Rabat I stomped off, trying to look more confident than I felt. I was a bit worried that the youth hostel might not let us stay as, according to the handbook, children under five were not admitted. Either the manager didn't know that or didn't care and we got a place for only a few dirhams a night. The bunk beds were a great hit with Merry and I wanted an uncomplicated place to stay with contact with other travellers for first-hand, up-to-the-minute information. There were no women staying at the hostel that night. The other residents seemed shocked that I was travelling alone with a small child. Their attitudes ranged from praise for my bravery to criticism of my mothering instincts. More than one warned me of the danger of Merry being stolen and sold into slavery. I treated this prejudice with the contempt it deserved, but I did wonder how they could bring themselves to travel in a place where they believed such things were common. At this point I was still wondering myself what I was doing there, but then one man went too far in his criticisms and I retreated angry but fortified.

Rabat was indeed a mellow city and we wandered around the Medina without hindrance or offers of a guide. At the Kasbah, however, a man approached us and offered to show us around although he said he wasn't a guide. "Good," I said, "as I'm not going to pay you." It was all very amiable and the Kasbah was lovely, like a village within the city, and everyone seemed to know my "not a guide". I relaxed into chatting while he showed me where he lived and we drank mint tea. He invited me to an evening meal of couscous and after I accepted it he went off.

Left to my own devices I began to regret having accepted as I didn't feel completely happy about going to his house alone after dark.

I decided to leave a note for him saying I couldn't make it and hoped he would get it. I felt pretty bad about not trusting him, but, with Merry there I had become more than usually cautious and was simply not prepared to launch into any situation where I felt our safety was in doubt. I still felt bad though.

All the time I was in Morocco I masqueraded as a married woman. I felt there was nothing to gain in explaining my real circumstances as they would inevitably be misunderstood. Over the course of my stay my "husband" got ever closer. Whilst in Rabat he had been working in England, but on the advice of my Moroccan friend I moved him to Tangier. Later on I occasionally said I was meeting him in a café. (I met a woman who pretended she was pregnant whenever she felt harassed and said it worked.)

Back at the hostel I was happy to meet a woman who had been travelling around Europe on her own. Before coming to Morocco, however, she had gone to a youth hostel in Malaga to find someone to travel with. She found a man who was also travelling alone and seemed to have enjoyed her stay. Also at the hostel was a young Moroccan visiting Rabat in order to get a US visa. He was a devout Muslim and we had a friendly and completely uncomplicated conversation about America, the country he was aiming to visit, before he was suddenly and quite aggressively thrown out by the manager. This was despite his being there at the invitation of one of the guests. It seemed to me he was thrown out because he was a Moroccan.

The best part of travelling with my daughter was the contact she brought with Moroccan women.

As I spent more time in the country I became more relaxed, told "lies" more readily, became better tempered and began to learn who to avoid. Sexual harassment is a problem for women in Morocco, but I seemed to experience less than a lot of other women I met who were travelling with men. I think perhaps having a child labels you as some man's property. "Hustlers", however, still made approaches – and proved incredibly persistent, innovative and subtle. It is important to remember that it is need that spurs them on to such great lengths to part you and your money. Tourists in Morocco are viewed as rich, and in many ways it's true. We're certainly privileged.

Both Merry and I loved Marrakesh immediately. We found a room in a cheap but fairly clean hotel just off the Place Djemaa el Fna, from where we could wander out amongst the stalls, entertainers, travellers and bus-trippers or climb up to the terraces to look out at the views and sip mint tea. I found it fascinating and enjoyed the anonymity of the crowds, while Merry adored the snake charmers and other entertainers. She also loved stopping to buy fruit here, nuts there, and freshly made egg sandwiches from the woman who ran the hard-boiled egg stall. She soon, however, began to miss the freedom to run about and play, and wanted to go to the coast – whilst I would have preferred to stay longer.

We went on to a small village just north of Agadir called Taghazoute and rented a room from a Berber family; a mother, grandmother, two sons and two daughters. Although communication was hard – I couldn't speak Berber and they had very few words of French – we smiled a lot at each other. They seemed especially pleased with Merry and would take her out to show her their animals or bring small children in to see her, and every now and then Yasmina, the mother, would offer us food. It was an ideal place to stay and the beach itself was wide and fairly empty.

Somehow we managed to communicate about our kids and school just as I suppose women all over the world do.

I was worried about how safe it would be to swim alone, but resolved this by asking a couple if we could join them for a bit. Later on I became more confident about swimming alone and was happy just to site myself near family groups. I tried to make sure that I was never completely alone with no one in sight, as a woman friend had earlier been assaulted on an isolated bit of beach not far up the coast.

The best part of travelling with my daughter was the contact she brought with Moroccan women. In Essaouira I met a woman called Barka who offered me a room in her house. Again communication was a little difficult but we seemed to manage well on a mixture of French, Arabic, and empathy. She lived alone with her eight-year-old son – her husband was working somewhere in the north (fishing, I think) and didn't come home very often. Eating meals and watching TV together, we soon became very close. Her son Mohammed loved Merry and wanted us to stay much longer than we could. The only problem I had with Barka was that she would refuse to let me help with any chores and wanted to do all of my own work as well. I ended up having to hide in the toilet to wash my clothes.

When it was time for us to leave, she came with us to say goodbye at the bus station. On the way we dropped her son off at school where she introduced us to some of her friends. It was a scorching day and all the women were covered from head to foot in thick white blankets with just their hennaed hands and feet showing and their eyes peeping through above the black veils they wore. I was hot in my light clothing.

We were so different in our dress, customs and language, and yet somehow we managed to communicate about our kids and school just as I suppose women all over the world do. Later Barka kissed me goodbye through her veil at the station and made me promise to come back and visit her. I felt I didn't want to leave.

We spent a couple of days exploring Tangier before catching the ferry. For part of this time, we joined up with a couple of English men and I was surprised to find that, with them, I experienced more harassment than I'd ever encountered alone with Merry. I also had my first and only offer to buy hashish.

In the end leaving Morocco wasn't so much of a wrench as Merry caught some sort of stomach bug which made her sick and incredibly tired. Travelling back through Spain to Portugal was awful for us both, although marginally worse for me (she slept through a lot of it). One of the worst aspects was the amount of criticism I got from other travellers just when I could have used a little support. I'm not sure why I encountered so much unhelpfulness, especially from male travellers, but fortunately there were exceptions. And Moroccan, Spanish and Portuguese people have a great attitude towards children.

Travelling with a child, I found I couldn't live on as tight a budget as I'd planned, due mainly to the need for odd, expensive, treats. I also felt pretty isolated at night when Merry was asleep but I still wanted to be out and about. Before I went I didn't expect night-time to be a problem as at home Merry is capable of staying up till all hours. I don't know if it was the fresh air and excitement but her pattern certainly changed and she was asleep by eight every night. I took a pushchair with me so that I could push her around if she slept but this wasn't practical. The roads and paths anywhere other than in the cities were so bad that I would have to carry the pushchair as well as Merry most of the time. Even in the cities there are usually many steps to negotiate. Her pushchair was only useful for carrying our stuff from the bus to the train station.

Overall, I think it's a great idea to travel with a child in Morocco, though I wouldn't recommend it to someone wanting a "holiday". It's an adventure above all else and requires a certain amount of work. Other women I know have travelled in Morocco with their children and all agreed that they had a great time. One friend managed to borrow someone else's daughter as well as take her own and so travelled with two ten-year-olds – that has to be the perfect arrangement. And in a way all my earlier fears have left me feeling that I have really accomplished something. When I wasn't feeling a bit scared about what I was taking on I felt incredibly strong and extraordinary – it's not often women get to feel that in their lives.

TRAVEL NOTES

Languages Moroccan Arabic (a considerable variant of "classical" Egyptian/Gulf Arabic) and three distinct Berber languages. French is widely spoken and is taught in schools.

Transport There's a small but useful train network. Travel otherwise is by bus (plentiful and cheap) or collective taxi (*grand taxi*), which run between towns according to demand. In the Atlas and sub-Sahara you can negotiate lifts on trucks – some of which operate like buses. Hitching is inadvisable, though fellow tourists are sometimes worth approaching at campsites.

Accommodation Very rarely a problem – there are all categories of hotels graded by the state and other (even cheaper) options below them.

Special Problems Arrival can be daunting at both Tangier and Tetouan, where you'll find the country's most persistent, aggressive and experienced hustlers. If it's your first visit it makes sense to move straight on – it only takes a couple of days to get used to things. Many tourists come to Morocco to smoke hashish (*kif*). Although officially illegal, the police tend to turn a blind eye: the main trouble lies with the dealers, who have developed some nasty tricks (like selling you hash then sending friends round to threaten to turn you in to the police unless you pay them off). It's best to avoid the *kif*-growing areas of the Rif mountains and the drug centre, Ketama.

Guides *The Rough Guide to Morocco* (Penguin) is a well-deserved classic.

CONTACTS

Centre de Documentation et d'action Féminin, 46 Rue Aboudest-Agdal, Rabat. Recently formed and very small feminist group.

BOOKS

Nancy Phelan, *Morocco Is a Lion* (UK, Quartet, 1982, o/p). Ordinary, lightweight travelogue – but well observed and includes a variety of interviews/experiences with Moroccan women, both rural and urban.

Edith Wharton, *In Morocco* (1920; US, David & Charles, 1988). Elegantly written tavelogue by the author of *The Age of Innocence*.

⭐ **Fatima Mernissi**, *The Harem Within: Tales of a Moroccan Girlhood* (UK, Doubleday, 1994). Fascinating insight by Morocco's leading sociologist into the closed community of women in Muslim culture, including the intimacy and sense of fun that binds them together. Mernissi's *Beyond the Veil: The Sexual Ideology of Women* (1975; UK, Al Saqi, 1985/US, Indiana University Press, 1987), is an enlightening study, while by the same author, *Doing Daily Battle: Interviews with Moroccan Women* (UK, The Women's Press, 1988/US, Rutgers University Press) features eleven Moroccan women, from a range of backgrounds, talking candidly about their lives. Finally, *Islam and Democracy: Fear of the Modern World* (UK, Virago, 1994) provides a thoughtful overview into the complexities of contemporary Islam, gratifyingly free of polemic.

Vanessa Maher, *Women and Property in Morocco* (UK & US, Cambridge University Press, 1974; both o/p). Respected academic study.

Nepal

For the first half of this century Nepal was an isolated mountain kingdom, virtually untouched by the outside world. Since the 1960s it has been caught up in a full-scale tourist boom, with travellers pouring into the capital, Kathmandu, and, accompanied by local guides, out along its spectacular Himalayan trekking routes.

As a primarily rural and Hindu society – with a large Buddhist minority – Nepal is a relatively safe place to travel; Kathmandu

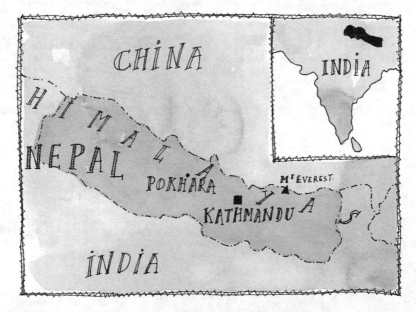

has its share of hustlers, eager to gain custom, but they are rarely aggressive in their approach and violent crime, even theft, is uncommon. You'll find that you are treated first and foremost as a foreigner rather than a woman, and that the atmosphere is generally tolerant. However, it is important to be sensitive to local customs – shorts and skimpy clothes are considered offensive.

A growing number of women trek alone and on the well-trodden, shorter treks this is considered reasonably safe; it's advisable, however, to have company if you're planning anything longer or more adventurous. What is disturbing, however, is the pattern that tourism is creating. The Kathmandu and Pokhara valleys are being transformed by package tour operators into timber lodge and breeze-block enclaves for foreigners (causing serious environmental damage), and the trekking industry, for all its supposed "contact with local people", is as prepared as any other to exploit workers, offering the lowest of wages and poor conditions. If you want to feel good about trekking, you'll need to choose your tour with care.

At present Nepal's political and economic future is highly uncertain. The spirit of idealism that gripped the country in 1990, when King Birendra's government was overturned by a wave of popular protest, has since waned, leaving mounting discontent at the continuing economic hardships and the compromised policies of the new government. The leading Nepal Congress Party, having squeezed through the 1993 election by a slim margin, faces accusations of selling out to Delhi (over major aid, development and trading policies) and provoking the power-brokers of Beijing by providing asylum to thousands of Tibetan exiles. It seems likely that the government will be forced into coalition with the leading Communist parties, who made massive gains in the elections, leading to an unstable few years of government reshuffles and hectic electioneering.

Until the recent restoration of democracy, **women's groups** were forced to work underground. The few officially sanctioned bodies – notably the All Nepal Women's Organization – were oriented mainly towards providing educational and social welfare services. Their campaigns, on issues of property rights, polygamy, and child and forced marriages, were criticized by Nepalese feminists as being largely tokenistic. The bulk of Nepalese women (predominantly Hindu) live in rural villages where their lives are dominated by the demands of subsistence farming and the traditional roles of domestic work and child-rearing. In the eyes of the law they are entirely dependent on male relatives, who have the right to determine their occupation, marriage partners and the fate of their children. A growing scandal has been the numbers of girls sold by their families into prostitution in India, many of them only allowed to buy their release after they have become "damaged" (increasingly meaning infected with AIDS). Sherpanis and other Buddhist women have far greater power and status within their communities and high-caste Hindu women may flout convention, but the majority of Nepali women have to struggle against extremes of exploitation.

The View from My Courtyard

Alison Murdoch has made several visits to Nepal over the last decade, to trek, spend time with Tibetan friends and deepen her knowledge of Tibetan Buddhism. Most recently she returned to the country with her seventy-year old friend Pen. She has travelled extensively in neighbouring India and Tibet, as well as China and parts of Southeast Asia. Back in London she works in housing, research and campaigning projects with the homeless.

Many people go to Nepal to trek, but my personal preference is to stay in one place and simply sit still. My favourite place for doing this is a small stone–flagged courtyard high up in the Solu Khumbu, or Everest region, open on one side to a backdrop of thousands of mountains.

Much of the time you can't see the mountains. You just sit like a theatregoer watching the sweep of the clouds as they gradually move up from the river below, constantly rearranging themselves in magisterial patterns. Now and again a porthole of blue opens, spotlighting a snow-covered peak lit neon by the sun.

However, you have to trek to earn this view. It does not come easy. From the comforts of the Kathmandu Valley the high mountains are generally not even visible. Just sometimes, on a clear day, you suddenly spot their snowy contours where you'd normally expect the sky to be.

Kathmandu is a mass of bustle, noise, confusion and commerce, its medieval squares and narrow streets draped with tourist gifts, videos and cheap electrical goods. Well-to-do locals now wear jeans and mis-spelt pirated T-shirts: "Gwcci" or "University of Los Angels". Range Rovers are the status symbol for a new moneyed elite.

For most travellers, Kathmandu is a necessary stop, a place to sort out a trekking permit and book an onward flight. The Thamel area, a previously undistinguished northern zone of the city, has newly equipped itself to cater for the 1990s traveller in pre-trek or post-trek relaxation mode. Featureless breeze-block hotels and ethnic clothes shops line up alongside an endless array of new cafés selling Italian, Mexican, Japanese food – whatever the latest culinary fashion happens to be. The Nepalese are swift to adapt to a changing world, and are adept at providing the comforts sorely missed in the rest of Asia.

"Freak Street", a decaying medieval enclave where the hippies used to hang out is now a ghost town. Only a few curious foreigners stray down the dirty wooden alleyways or stop for a break in the 1960s cake shops, still housing collections of well-thumbed paperbacks and grimy-cased rock cassettes. Banana milkshakes, lemon meringue pie and dope were the Nepalese response to that generation of homesick visitors. Every now and again you notice a thin white-faced survivor of that earlier era in the back of a dark shop hung with dusty brass and hand-blocked cotton prints.

Apart from in the main squares and markets, the history of Kathmandu rots away unseen. Children shriek at play in 500-year-old wood-carved courtyards, the statues draped with washing. In the early morning mist devotees make private offerings of incense and flowers to tiny streetside shrines daubed with layers of orange and red pigment. The affluent are now moving out to beyond the ring-road, leaving the decaying city centre to its sewerage and pollution problems.

The high mountains of the Everest region are a separate world. By land, they're a full week away: one day in a jarring metal bus, and six on foot. Four river valleys have to be traversed. You can travel the route in an hour by air, but still have to trek for three days to get to my favourite spot. On my fourth visit, I offered to share what I'd discovered with one of my best friends, a seventy-year old woman called Pen.

It was Pen who had encouraged me to buy my first single air-ticket to Asia, and one-and-a-half years later, on my return, I moved into the basement of her London home. She always maintains that our most interesting conversations took place late at night sitting on the stairs, and this is where we first had the idea to trek together to the village of Lawudo, the site of my courtyard. I didn't realize at the time what an adventure it would be for her, and what a challenge for me to reverse roles in a relationship where she had always been the more experienced and resilient. Six months later under a blue Kathmandu sky I met her off the plane from London.

Trekking in Nepal is mostly about people. This often takes visitors by surprise, especially if they're expecting a wilderness experience. These mountains are lived-in. The indigenous people of the region are the Sherpas, who came over the passes from Tibet about three hundred years ago, and still preserve most of the traditions of that culture. Their name was immortalized by the early ascents on Everest, and the arrival of the mountaineers and tourists has changed their society dramatically.

Grey hair crosses all boundaries and brings natural respect in traditional cultures.

Although many Sherpas still scrape a living from steep terraced slopes, others make disproportionate earnings from their foreign guests. Shiny new lodges along the tourist trail, depleting an ever-dwindling supply of local timber, look like Monopoly hotels in comparison to the tiny stone huts perched higher up the valleys.

The linkmen are the porters, the lifeblood of a region too rugged for roads. Baskets bearing unimaginable loads are carried on straps around their foreheads, making a pretty picture, if you can bear to stare at people under such physical stress. Up and down they move, like a line of ants, shod (if at all) in flimsy Chinese canvas shoes. Full bottles of Coke are their profit margin on the way up, and the non-biodegradable empties on their way down. Foreign tourists will pay more than the porter's entire weekly wage for a glass of Coke to quench their high-altitude thirst.

Travelling with Pen intensified the people-experience. We moved more slowly, partly for health reasons (altitude sickness is a daily danger) but also because of her endless curiosity about every new plant by the path, and every village family. Grey hair crosses all boundaries and brings natural respect in traditional cultures, and I experienced new levels of hospitality that I never received as a lone woman in her thirties. This was partly due to having a "chaperone", but also to something more intangible. Everyone related to Pen as the grandmother that she is.

Her excitement was catching. The vistas at the bends in the path, the ropebridges and the smiling children became even more vivid images to treasure. I had forgotten how satisfying is the combination of walking steadily up a river valley all day and eating by firelight in a wood-lined lodge kitchen at dusk, swapping life stories with fellow trekkers of every nationality.

Pen's sense of achievement in reaching Namche Bazaar, the long-standing pit-stop of the Everest expeditions, even overcame some of my customary resistance to this place of Swiss chocolate and high-tech mountain gear. "Jimmy Carter and Robert Redford slept here" proclaims the most affluent lodge.

We spent an extra rest day in Namche, with me fighting my impatience to reach our destination – only four hours away up the Thame valley. I had foreknowlege of the contrasts in store, and above all of the intense privilege of being embraced by a lifestyle that has hardly changed over the centuries.

We stopped again and again, but her heartbeat didn't lessen or her head stop spinning.

Lawudo consists of a tiny cluster of buildings built around the cave where a hermit lived and meditated earlier this century. At the heart of the village, perched vertiginously above the trodden path, stands the Tibetan-style *gompa* or temple, its brightly fringed windows looking out over the river valley far below. The last time I reached Lawudo I stayed for over two months, and the family who live there have become cherished friends. I longed to relive the view from my favourite spot.

The next morning we set off early for the final stretch of our uphill journey. At first the track winds its way on an even gradient through the rhododendron forests, then suddenly, at a turn in the path you catch sight of Lawudo, straight ahead but impossibly far above.

The last hour is a heart-straining climb up a mountainside so steep that even a yak track has hairpin bends. We set off uphill, slowly, then even more slowly, until Pen was reduced to only a few steps at a time. We stopped again and again to drink and to rest, but her heartbeat didn't lessen or her head stop spinning. Was it altitude sickness, cheating us on the final ascent? I felt overwhelmed by my anxieties and responsibilities, and the thought of Pen's family so far away in England. There was no sound but the cawing of ravens and the roar of the river far below. We were utterly alone.

Finally, in desperation, I made the decision to leave Pen under a bush for shelter and race uphill to find my friends and get help to carry her down again.

Usually one of the family spots the visitor on the path and runs down in greeting with a thermos of welcoming tea. This time there was no one in sight. The painted wooden door creaked open onto the court-yard where the yaks and cows graze. A twenty-foot prayer flag hung listlessly in the thin air. Gasping for breath I hardly noticed my surroundings.

I hadn't seen my friends for nearly two years, nor even been able to send news of my coming. I found them in the kitchen, and tumbled the story out, struggling also to control my grief at a visit that wasn't to be. One person gathered up tea and food, another harnessed the yak, and we all hurried out to descend the mountain and take Pen back to the medical facilities and relative comforts of Namche.

Lawudo is a vantage-point, and much time is spent observing the tiny figures in the valley below. Glancing down I saw an amazing sight: a frail elderly Englishwoman with boots, hat and stick determinedly climbing the final stretch up to the door. It was Pen. Maybe she had needed to complete her journey alone. She entered the courtyard in quiet triumph.

Hospitality is a sacred ritual among the Sherpas, who welcome every visitor as if they were the Buddha. In this case it was a particularly powerful experience. Bending our heads to pass under the wooden threshold we stepped into the tiny dark kitchen and collapsed on the bench next to the kitchen fire. We remained there for hours in the comforting semi-darkness, sharing and absorbing the ordeal that we had gone through to arrive.

The only light filtered down dustily through a hole above the clay cooking range: Lawudo is above the tree, electricity and even water line, the nearest spring being a half-hour round trip away. Man-made things are rare and precious, and dwarfed by the landscape all around. Even a length of string has to be brought in from somewhere, and is used and reused in every conceivable way. Ordinary daily life feels like a stubborn gesture in the face of raw nature.

The stranger's first meal is usually a precious omelette – the egg brought from someone, somewhere down in the valley who keeps a hen – washed down with sweet milky tea from the thermoses that keep the Himalayas going when the kitchen fire has gone out. The oil for frying and the dried brick of tea and powdered milk are from India. Tibetan traders come over the high

Nawang Samten claims that she knows no English but after a few days had the vocabulary to enquire "Do you have diarrhoea?".

passes bringing butter, dried yak meat, and an extraordinary object that looks like a haggis, made of hardened compressed animal fat that can be grated into soups and stews.

All that can be grown here are potatoes and the strong-tasting "greens" of my childhood. Potatoes are stored in a pit in the ground, a natural deep-freeze, or else dried in flakes in the summer sun. Many of the recipes that result are inconceivable to the Western palate. Think of potatoes boiled in a wok, then mashed to a pulp on a corrugated stone flag that has been in the family for generations, then kneaded into balls and recooked until stretchy like Play-Doh in a soup made of vegetables that have been preserved for several months in a blackened wooden tub of milk. Butter tea, the Himalayan visitor's best-known horror story, is a walkover by comparison.

The people who live this life of extraordinary adversity are as strong as you can imagine. The women are assertive and broad-shouldered, wearing tracksuit trousers beneath their traditional long woollen skirts. They hold power as equal workers, childbearers and keepers of the family's disposable wealth, in the form of their big turquoise and coral jewellery. Whether at parties or monastic rites, women and men face each other down opposite sides of the room, finding a strong and healthy companionship within their own gender. Humour is rough, ready and extremely coarse.

This particular household is run by a Buddhist nun called Nawang Samten, or just Ani-la (literally "the nun") for short. She frequently breaks out into expansive and intoxicating laughter, but is also capable of a disconcerting directness. Nawang Samten claims that she knows no English but a few days into my first visit had the vocabulary to enquire "Do you have diarrhoea? I'm so sorry". We have had some wonderful moments, sharing our mutual concerns about our contrasting life situations. She struck an immediate sympathy with Pen, intuitively attending to her need for some extra comfort and support.

Two quiet and, for me, magical weeks passed. The mists swirled around us like a barrier from the outside world, as we settled down into the main Sherpa activity of simply surviving the elements. Pen borrowed extra clothes against the cold that she felt so much more than I, but also suffered badly from the fleas that lived undisturbed in the animals and pelts and are part of everyday Himalayan life. I spent my early mornings in the courtyard, just watching, and my afternoons helping to mend the roof. Returning to the kitchen I would find Pen ensconced in the comforting warmth of the range watching Nawang Samten at her daily tasks.

Our departure was timed for just after the biggest festival of the year, the Tibetan Buddhist celebration of the Buddha's birthday. Annual festivals are of inconceivable importance when life is so harsh, and dominated by the cycle of the seasons. Everyone in the community contributes to the festival in some way. Women from the neighbouring villages began to arrive in a steady stream, bringing offerings of provisions and labour, and laying out their bedding rolls wherever they could find some floorspace.

The day before the festival felt like Christmas Eve. Amid much laughter everyone lent a hand in rolling dough for traditional cookies, while the chief monk fashioned extraordinary sculptured offerings out of coloured butter. Toddlers watched in shy amazement as the unaccustomed goodies piled up in the shrine room.

On the first day of the ceremony itself, just as the dawn light began to creep over the peaks, we were woken by the eerie and unfamiliar sound of a conch shell being blown. In contrast to the darkness outside, the temple interior was a warm blaze of butter lamps and colour. Silk paintings were suspended from the decorated beams, hung with tassels of multi-coloured brocade. The monks and nuns were snuggled into great capes of rich red wool, and the Sherpa participants arrayed in their finest clothes.

The three-day ceremony is dedicated to Chenrezig, the Tibetan symbol for compassion, and involves a mixture of chanting, silent prayers, fasting and physical prostration, punctuated by the sounds of ancient drums, cymbals and bells. It is an ancient set of rituals that, inevitably, has a profound and mesmerizing effect. Time drops away, to be replaced by a rhythm of musical crescendos, leg-stretching in the courtyard outside, and endless steaming cups of tea. Sharing inspiration, weariness and jokes, the strangely assorted crowd of people gradually and silently grew closer.

At the end of the ceremony the custom is for each participant to offer their fellows a white scarf and gift of money, which represent both a tribute to the shared experience and to each person's inner divinity. Pen and I sat humbled, embarrassed and extremely touched to receive the equivalent of a few British coins from people who had almost no material wealth compared to us.

Two hours later we set off down the mountainside on the slow walk back to the West, each carrying our different experiences back to the outside world. We were reversing our footsteps in one sense, yet we both felt that a part of us remained.

TRAVEL NOTES

Languages Nepali and regional dialects: some English is spoken on tourist circuits.

Transport Within the Kathmandu Valley there are buses; further north trekking is the only option, other than a small network of flights (expensive, though if time is tight you can fly out into the Himalayas and trek back). The recent introduction of fuel rationing has meant that buses are more irregular and crowded – be prepared for long waits.

Accommodation Plenty of cheap places to stay in Kathmandu and surrounding areas; also small hotels on regular trekking routes. On more remote routes, there are virtually no tourist facilities and you'll have to carry your own tent or join a trekking party with porters. The Nepalese are incredibly hospitable and often invite foreigners to sleep in their homes – you should reciprocate with a small gift or some money.

Special Problems Although many tourists wear short summer gear, this is seen as disrespectful. In the more orthodox Hindu areas you may be asked – as a foreigner (and therefore untouchable) – to sleep outside the main living room. Everywhere you should try to avoid touching cooking utensils or food that is being prepared, and if you're given water to drink from a communal vessel avoid any contact with your lips.

For trekking, proper clothing and equipment are absolutely necessary. Altitude sickness is a common problem and should be taken very seriously. There is little clean drinking water, so infections are rife; the numerous stool test laboratories in Kathmandu are an entrepreneurial innovation and have a poor record for reliability.

Guides The Rough Guide to Nepal (Penguin) gives the best overall view of the country, with information about the many different ethnic minorities and current environmental issues. Best

of the specific trekking guides is *Trekking in Nepal* (US, Mountaineers).

CONTACTS

Centre for Women and Development, PO Box 3637, Kathmandu. A non-governmental organization established by a group of professional women, which collects and disseminates information on women's issues and development projects.

BOOKS

Dervla Murphy, *The Waiting Land: A Spell in Nepal* (UK, Arrow, 1990, o/p/ US, Overlook Press, 1989). A personal account of working with Pokhara's Tibetan refugees in 1965, written in the author's usual entertaining, politically astute and sensitive style.

 Monica Connell, *Against a Peacock Sky* (UK, Penguin, 1993, o/p/US, Viking Penguin, 1991). Beautiful, impressionistic rendering of life among the *matawaali* (alcohol-drinking) Chhetris of Jumla District, capturing the subtleties of village life in Nepal.

Lynn Andrews, *Windhorse Woman* (US, Colorado University Press, 1989). One woman's spiritual quest in Nepal; decidedly New Age.

Lynn Bennett, *Dangerous Wives and Sacred Sisters* (US, Gallery Press, 1976). Good insight into the life and position of Hindu women in Nepal.

Lynn Bennett (ed), *The Status of Women in Nepal* (Nepal, CEDA, Tribhuvan University). Lengthier, more academic study.

FICTION

Karuna Kar Varilya, *Nepalese Short Stories* (US, Gallery Press, 1976). A collection of stories by some of Nepal's best writers, on a wide variety of themes.

Pacific Islands

T he South Pacific is an immense area, dotted with thousands of mostly tiny islands. The main exceptions are the vast island of New Guinea, north of Australia, and the two principal islands of New Zealand in the southeast. The many clusters which lie in between make up the countries of Fiji, Western and American Samoa, French Polynesia (the largest island of which is Tahiti), Tonga, Vanuatu and New Caledonia, to name just a few. Until recently, inaccessibility and

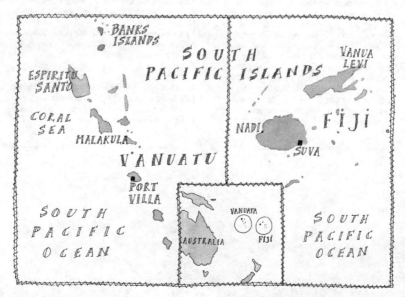

limited facilities have kept these smaller Pacific nations relatively unknown to package tourists and independent travellers alike. Inevitably, however, commercial interests have begun to exploit the appeal of idyllic island scenery (with its combination of rainforest and glorious white beaches fringed with coconut palms) and Tahiti, for one, has already been virtually transformed from a Pacific paradise to a tourist nightmare.

Some countries, most notably Fiji, New Caledonia and Papua New Guinea, have seen a reversal of this trend owing to political unrest, rooted in the effects of colonization. Vanuatu (featured below) was colonized both by the British and the French, from whom it only gained independence in 1980; yet it has managed to maintain an unusual degree of political stability. This string of lush green Melanesian islands is also relatively free from the ravages of mass tourism. Cruise ships regularly disgorge parties of Australians to spend a day in and around the attractive capital, Port Vila, but elsewhere visitors – especially women on their own – are a comparative rarity. People will generally treat you with friendly, if sometimes disarming, curiosity and provided you're careful to respect local customs, sexual harassment is unlikely to be an issue. There are plenty of places to stay in and around Port Vila, a lovely town built up several hillsides around a curved bay (and incidentally, famous for its gourmet French cuisine), but away from the capital, and certainly on remoter islands you'll have to rely largely on village hospitality. Similarly, finding transport is very much based on people's good will.

The key political issue in the Pacific, alongside colonialism, is the implementation of French and American nuclear tests and the dumping of foreign nuclear waste into the ocean. In recent decades a vast network of nuclear bases, ports and airfields was set up throughout the region with little, if any, consultation with the indigenous people. Today, inspired by the example of Vanuatu, there is an impressively united and growing movement for a nuclear-free and independent Pacific, a movement in which women play a leading role. Much of the work of the Pacific's strong **women's movement** is co-ordinated by the Pacific Women's Resource Centre, which links up groups and spreads information between islands with the help of a satellite communications system. As well as the vital nuclear issue, the concerns of the movement include violence against women, racist and sexist use of experimental contraception, tourist exploitation, women's rights legislation and the need for a feminist approach to development projects.

Adventures of a "Snail Woman"

Linda Hill, a forty-year-old New Zealander, spent two months in the Pacific islands of Tonga, Samoa and the Cook Islands, before travelling on for another seven weeks to Vanuatu: "nuclear free, independent, and a different world".

Vanuatu is a scattering of Melanesian islands between New Caledonia and the Solomons. It is too far from the rich tourist markets of the First World to get many visitors. A few package tourists arrive to stay in the overpriced hotels, and regular cruise ships stop for day visits, releasing a flood of very white Australians over Port Vila or Champagne Beach. But backpackers are still virtually unknown – in a six-week stay, I met one Japanese guy waiting out his visa renewal for Tuvalu, and two Australian nurses exploring Vanuatu largely by trading ship, as I was myself. And I would say, from the way news of their later movements reached me through the locals, we five were the only ones in the country at that time.

The crews of the trading ships seemed familiar with the ways of back-packers. Outside Vial and Sano, however, people stopped what they were doing and came over to investigate. "Where are you going? Who are you visiting? Are you a teacher, a nurse or a missionary? And where is your husband?" The Australian women told me that in Hogg Harbour the village women had gone into a huddle at the sight of them and come out giggling. "You are snail women", they were told. "You carry your house on your back and you walk slow!" Though my pack was light and I carried no tent, I was delighted to think of myself as a snail woman too.

My standard answer to the recurrent question, "Where is your husband?" was "No husband, they're too much work." The women would laugh and agree. It seemed acceptable that, having no family responsibilities, I should be free to do as I pleased. There don't seem to be possible penalties attached to a woman walking or travelling on her own, as in, say Samoa, where a woman who doesn't take her sister along might meet difficulties, especially after sundown.

Certainly, I always felt very safe and welcome – a pleasant novelty for the locals rather than an intruder. The women I met were friendly and generous and the "house on my back" slowly filled with beautiful hand-made baskets and grass skirts. The best I could do in return was to take addresses and photos, inevitably posed, and send copies when I got home.

As in Polynesia, hospitality is given on the assumption that it will be returned. Where this is unlikely it is important to try and redress the balance of obligation, and not to leave people the poorer. Take enough food with you: tea, sugar, coffee, rice, tinned beef or fresh meat from the town are suitable gifts to offer if you are invited to visit someone's family or village for a few days. If you're uncertain you can always ask another ni-Vanuatu (literally, "born Vanuatu") to advise you on what is appropriate.

If you're exploring on your own, you'll soon find somewhere to stay in one village or the next if you ask around. A church may have a room for guests or there may be a women's committee house, perhaps doubling as their kindergarten, where visitors can be put up. There may be a fixed charge for an overnight stay, but where this is not specified, it is appropriate to make a donation of about the going rate, say, 200–300 vatu, to the women's committee, church or chief.

Interest in you will include concern that you are eating. If you have your own food, it is advisable to make that clear or someone will turn up with a plate of *taro* and "Vanuatu tinned fish" (land crab!). You could share your supplies or contribute some from the village co-op store, or accept whatever arrangement will be made for you and make sure your donation redresses the balance. Someone will show you where women and men go to wash. If camping, it is nearly always proper to check with the nearest village about a campsite. Perhaps safest, too, to be in a way under the villagers' wing, since people will certainly come to see what you are up to.

The 105 languages spoken in Vanuatu present a problem to locals rather than to the traveller, but it is quite usual for totally "uneducated" people to speak two or three languages besides their own. Those with schooling will speak either French or English, as well as the lingua franca preferred by independent Vanuatu – Bislama.

Bislama is largely a corrupted English vocabulary on a Polynesian grammar base, and can be learned easily enough by English-speakers with the aid of books available in Vila. People tend to ask standard questions about background and family, and I was soon able to conduct the basic social conversation in Bislama and understand a remarkable amount on more complex subjects. I speak French and met many English- and French-speaking ni-Vanuatu with whom I could communicate at a very satisfactory level. I found that I learned a great deal about the country and current opinions and politics.

Choice of language is a political question in modern Vanuatu. Under the old colonial condominium there were areas of strong French (Catholic, Francophone) and British (Anglican in the north, Presbyterian in the south, Anglophone) influence which still structure politics today. The present Vanua'aku Party government reflects mainly the Anglophone communities, while the gradually consolidating main opposition comes from Francophones.

But large areas are still *kustom*. These villages should not be regarded as "backward" or merely left behind by modernization. Theirs is often a deliberate political choice, reflecting condemnation of both sides for undermining age-old conventions and traditional forms of leadership by introducing the colonial system of electoral government. There are various expressions of this view, but it has been associated with rejection of churches and education, always the thin edge of the colonial/imperialistic wedge. A recent solution by less remote *kustom* villages has been to send most children to a French-speaking school since the present government is Anglophone, but a few children to an English-speaking school, just in case. This may be supplemented with a *kustom* school to preserve the old ways.

> *I very quickly had to revise any notion that this society was less socially advanced than my own.*

I very quickly had to revise any notion that this society was less socially advanced than my own. Most of the people I met lived in communal, non-cash, village economies, still only peripherally connected zto the money economy of capitalism through need for tools, kitchen equipment, clothes, modern building materials, transport, fuel and – even here – tinned goods, tailor-made cigarettes and Fosters lager. Most village needs, however, are still provided by food and materials from gardens, sea and bush. "We don't have to pay money for everything, like you", my friend Ernestine told me. "We can take two or three weeks' holiday anytime and there'll still be plenty to feed the kids."

Other criteria of supposed "backwardness" stem from simple lack of access to information and knowledge that our world takes for granted. Access to radio is recent and battery- (cash-) dependent. Books and even writing materials are largely non-existent outside Vila and Santo. Take copies of the government newspaper with you from Vila and pass on any spare magazines, maps, or other material in English or French.

My church affiliation was something I was asked about constantly. Each Sunday I was in Vanuatu I seemed to go to a different denominational church with the different people I met. I had resurrected a brief Anglican background for conversational purposes, but then found myself very embarrassed at being the only person at a service who didn't know the Anglican prayerbook responses by heart, especially as I was the only mother-tongue English speaker.

In the past, bits of information, missionary teaching, and such bizarre experiences as the sudden arrival and equally rapid departure of Uncle Sam with World War II, led to some ingenious philosophical explanations of the world, such as the still popular Jon Frum cargo cult in Tanna. Cargo cults mushroomed throughout Melanesia with the arrival of European-manufactured goods,

The sisters were still talking about a German woman who turned up in 1978 and stayed a fortnight with them.

which, inexplicable according to local technology, were understood in spiritual and millennial terms: "Our ancestors must be sending us things. These Europeans try to make us pay but one day our ship will come." The Jon Frum (*frum* means American) variation on this theme seems to have been sparked off by a US pilot's decision to redistribute goods meant for the war front to Tanna locals.

In the more remote islands and villages, people just don't get to hear about things and have no way of checking what they do hear. You will meet with some fascinating opinions and you yourself will be a source of information for people. One thing ni-Vanuatu like is a "good story" and I had to repeat again and again the different things that had happened to me on my trip.

I was able to relate first-hand news of the devastation still being caused to villages by the volcano in East Tanna. I told about going to the Friday night Jon Frum cargo cult service at Sulphur Bay and dancing with the women to the wonderful funky music, in a grass skirt that they gave me. Then there was the walk home in pitch dark across an eerie moonscape of black ash, lit only by thunderous flashes from the volcano, and the deaf man who nearly jumped out of his skin when I tapped him on the arm and pushed my white face into his to ask directions.

My white face often had a similar effect on toddlers, who no doubt associated me with doctors, nurses, injections and nasty tastes. Smiling didn't help – they all do that before they hurt you.

Another very popular story I told was about dancing at a Vanuatu wedding in North Ambrym. I had arrived by trading ship at Ranon and walked up to the French-speaking villages around Olal. When I asked about accommodation, I was offered a bed in the New Zealand-donated leper hospital at St Jean's Mission, now just a clinic. But I should just drop my things and hurry, I was told, because the entire village was going to a wedding nearby.

The male teacher from the mission turned me over to some women my age, who talked to me in French, translating for others. With them I joined the line to kiss the beflowered bride and groom sitting under a canopy, leave a small present in a growing pile and have my head sprinkled with talcum powder. With Ernestine, her sister and her four children, I shared a large banana leaf parcel of earth-oven cooked *taro*, *kumara*, pork and beef, flavoured with fern leaves. The sisters were still talking about a young German woman who had turned up in 1978 and stayed a fortnight with them, just "doing what the women do".

That evening there was a wedding disco, with Western pop music, reggae and the local bands in Vila, tea with bread and butter, and *kava* out the back. Everyone was there; men and women danced in separate groups and I got up with the women I had met earlier. When I teased one for dropping out before I did, a man sprang over from the other side of the floor to sweep me off in a foxtrot. My tired partner at once started to beat him about the legs for the impudence of dancing with a woman, and everybody roared with laughter. This was a story that delighted ni-Vanuatu elsewhere: that I should have been dancing "Vanuatu-style" with the women. Europeans danced "modern-style" with a man, like people did in Vila. I tried to tell them their way suited me very well.

The "men's house" culture recorded by ethnographers and anthropologists throughout Melanesia seems to be paralleled by an unrecorded but strong culture of women who tend to work together and interact socially in groups. Women approached me very easily and small groups of girls wanted to accompany me and show me everything. This women's culture is being supported by the liberal Vanua'aku Party government, with a few strong women's rights advocates such as Grace Molisa. Feminism, still in its early stages, will, I hope, like the rest of Vanuatu's development, be a home-grown product.

I came back from Vanuatu with a strong desire to go back in a couple of years, not to be a "snail woman" again but to stay in one of the villages for a month or so, just "doing what the women do". In the meantime I have a plan for subsistence agriculture in my Auckland garden!

TRAVEL NOTES

Languages More than 700 languages are spoken throughout the South Pacific. The main language in Vanuatu is Bislama.

Accommodation Away from the main tourist resorts you will often have no choice but to accept village hospitality. Such invitations are a privilege and require at least some understanding of local culture and traditions.

Transport A limited selection of trading and cargo ships, and domestic airlines will carry you between the islands. Of the two domestic airlines, *Dovair* is slightly less expensive. Travelling by cargo ship costs about half the price of an airfare and includes meals. Take a radio to check the shipping news and keep your fingers crossed. They go by cargoes, not schedules. Transport on land varies from place to place, but anywhere of any size has a mini-bus service.

Special Problems Be careful not to offend local customs by your dress. A woman's thighs are considered more erotic than her breasts and should not be exposed in public, so shorts are definitely out.

Guides *South Pacific Handbook* (US, Moon Publications) is very practical and covers even quite remote places. Lonely Planet have individual *Travel Survival Kits* to Vanuatu, Tonga, Samoa, New Caledonia, Raratonga & the Cook Islands, Tahiti & French Polynesia, Fiji, Micronesia and The Solomon Islands.

CONTACTS

The Pacific Women's Resource Centre, PO Box 534, Suva, Fiji. Provides information about women's activities all over the South Pacific. Also publishes a magazine, *Women Speak Out.*

The main contact for Vanuatu is the *National Council of Women*, Box 975, Port Vila (☎2318), which co-ordinates thirteen island councils with 75 smaller branches.

BOOKS

Charlene Gourgechon, *Journey to the End of the World* (US, Charles Scribner & Sons, 1977). Fascinating account of the author's daily life with traditional tribes in Vanuatu.

Jan Dibblin, *Day of Two Suns: US Nuclear Testing and the Pacific Islanders* (UK, Virago, 1988, o/p/US, New Amsterdam Books, 1989). Account of protest amid the atolls and in the international courts against the inhuman appropriation and use of land by the US military. Draws widely on the personal experiences of women and men of the Marshall Islands.

Grace Mara Molisa, *Colonised People* (Vanuatu, Port Vila, Black Stone Publications, 1987). Poetry plus statistics on women in Vanuatu.

Margaret Sinclair, *The Path of the Ocean: Traditional Poetry of Polynesia* (US, Hawaii University Press, 1982). Fascinating transcription of traditional oral verse.

Pakistan

Since the demise of the overland route to India relatively
few travellers, let alone solo women, have visited Pakistan.
More than a decade of dictatorship under General Zia, the
strict Islamic rules that he ushered in, and the subsequent communal violence that has erupted under three successive changes
of government in six years,
have left the country with a
disturbing reputation for
intolerance and instability.

Benazir Bhutto's rise to
power and international fame
in 1988, as the first woman to
head an Islamic state, raised
hopes of unity and
liberalization that soon sank
under scandals of nepotism
and corruption, exacerbated
by fierce fundamentalist
opposition. By the time of
her 1993 re-election victory, she had emerged as the figurehead of
a political dynastic family in the tradition of Asian women rulers,
her media image transformed to that of a more conventional wife
(she accepted an arranged marriage) and mother. Promises of
repealing discriminatory laws against women were issued, this time
in more muted tones.

Travelling around Pakistan as a woman on your own is a struggle. At best you'll be seen as an oddity, at worst a symbol of decadent Western values, immodest, available and a fair target for harassment. Away from the luxury hotels it takes resilience to cope with the continual propositions, leering and comments on streets crowded with men. Sometimes hotel-keepers will even refuse rooms for single women, for fear of encouraging immoral behaviour. Travelling with a man helps, as does dressing with extreme modesty – for instance wearing the traditional *shalwa camise* (loose fitting trousers and tunic) with a *dupati* (shawl) covering your hair. But unless you're escorted by Pakistani friends, your chances of avoiding unpleasantness are pretty slim. That said, however, while you are more vulnerable as a lone woman, you are also far more likely to be offered protection and help from strangers, being drawn into the safer confines of the extended family group or offered seats among the women in seg-regated areas on buses and trains. Once you cross the line into becoming a guest, or become well-known in one particular place, harassment melts away. For most, the frequently unlooked-for acts of kindness and hospitality, together with a magnificent, diverse scenery spanning desert, jagged mountains and deep, dark ravines make it all worthwhile.

The Islamicization programme introduced during the late 1970s brought with it a wave of legislation that very clearly limit-ed the freedoms of **women** and undermined their security at the heart of the family. These rules are still being implemented, most forcefully against working-class women, who cannot protect themselves with bribes or family influence. Under the notorious Hudood Ordinance, women cannot secure a rape conviction without four *male* witnesses and, unless rape is proved, run the risk of being themselves imprisoned, flogged or stoned for the crime of *zina* (adultery or unlawful sexual intercourse). Opposition to these laws remains strong. The Pakistan Women's Action Forum (WAF) acts as a network for groups in all the major towns, spearheading campaigns for the laws to be repealed.

Large demonstrations were staged in Lahore and Karachi even under Zia, though they were dispersed by mass arrests and a brutal show of force. One of the saddest aspects of Bhutto's compromised politics is that, having initially endorsed the WAF charter of demands, she failed to either prevent or condemn further use of police force in breaking up demonstrations by women.

Back to Lahore

Maria del Nevo first went to Pakistan in 1986, when she lived for two years working as a volunteer with the Christian community in Lahore. Eager to learn more about the country, she later returned as a journalist for, among other publications, the radical weekly news magazine, *Viewpoint*, and the British-based *New Internationalist*.

The Pakistan experience begins before you've even touched down on Karachi soil. It starts at Dubai, or Bahrain, or at one of the other Arab states where most flights to Pakistan stop to refuel. One minute you're listening to a well-fed, inebriated ICI engineer who's regretting having agreed to an extension of his contract and yet another year in the heat and dust; then suddenly he's disembarked and you find yourself not only the sole single woman on the plane, but the sole foreign female. Awkwardly I looked out of the corner of my eye, only to meet either innocent wonder or savage lust in the eyes of almost an entire jumbo-load of men, many of them tweaking massive moustaches – a well-known seduction technique.

Having survived Karachi airport with its contemptuous immigration officials and hundreds of porters grappling to get a hold of my trolley, I finally reached Lahore, a frenzied mass of lorries, cars, rickshaws, motorbikes, cycles, donkeys, oxen and camels. And men. Men everywhere. Men and eyes. That's the first thing I notice when arriving in Pakistan.

It was imperative that I live in a flat where there was a family below or above. To do otherwise would not have been culturally correct.

Living alone in the heart of the city, I quickly had to learn the basic rules of survival for Western women. A foreigner could spend their entire life in Pakistan and still be guilty of the most appalling cultural blunder. As a single woman, it was imperative that I live in a flat where there was a family below or above. This was mostly for safety, but also because to do otherwise would not have been culturally correct.

For five months I lived in a first-floor flat with a family below, in a road so narrow that in the evenings when I opened my shutters I could have a quiet chat with the woman in the house opposite. It was a lower middle-class neighbourhood, which meant that for the most part the women remained in their homes, and when they did go out were unrecognizable in their heavy black *burqas*. Ragged, barefoot children played all day in the dusty lane, at marbles or a noisy game of cricket.

I was an enigma to them because I had chosen to live in that dusty, narrow, cramped alley.

Everyone seemed to live on top of one another. Our houses had no sound-proofing, and the whole street was woken in the mornings not by the *azan* (call to prayer) from the little mosque nearby, nor by the cocks crowing in the street below, but by the family directly next door to me, who had a ritual argument over breakfast, the husband and wife screaming abuse at each other in rapid Punjabi until the mother-in-law had had enough and pushed her son out of the house, telling him to come back at night in a better mood.

I had been told that I wouldn't last long living in such a neighbourhood, that the water flow would be intermittent, the noise and pollution intolerable, that the local boys would pester me and eventually drive me out, and that I'd face hostility from the women or alternatively find my life taken over and controlled by them. The water was scarce. It either came at dawn or late at night, or not at all and I had to spend much time storing it in large metal drums and kettles. The noise I got used to. Indeed, I wanted to hear the bustle of the bazaar just at the end of my road and the overflow of domesticity from other houses. The dust was bad, but in Pakistan it's everywhere anyway, in rich and poor neighbourhoods alike.

Yes, the boys did bother me. They gathered at nine every morning, when I was due to leave for work. They'd watch as I wiped the windscreen of my battered old Volkswagen and snigger when it didn't start. They posted love letters through my door, and Valentine cards in the middle of May. But they never harmed me. They were never unpleasant. They were just young boys who lived in a society where contact with women outside the family was denied them. I suppose I was a novelty.

The women in the neighbourhood were neither hostile nor interfering. We chatted as we hung our washing out on our roofs, and exchanged greetings as we passed one another's front doors. But we all had other business to attend to. Money, for all of us, was scarce; we all had to work hard and had little time for idle social gatherings. I was an enigma to them, not because I was a foreigner, or a woman who wanted to live alone. But because I had chosen to live in that dusty, narrow, cramped alley.

The community eventually got used to me. They were protective and looked out for me. Just as I knew their daily routines, they came to know my movements. It was comforting to discover that the entire neighbourhood knew what time I was due home every evening from work. It was comforting to know that if I ever had any problems, I could go and knock on a door and be sure of help. This feeling of being protected wasn't limited to the area where I was living: I felt it, and experienced it, frequently, wherever I was.

> *While one man might be harassing me, a hundred more would come to my rescue.*

Moving around a city like Lahore can be intensely stressful. Women have little public presence; and therefore any woman who does venture out is a spectacle, whether local or foreign. Foreign women are especially vulnerable, basically because men in Pakistan see us as fair game. The little they know about us is learned from the James Bond films occasionally shown at the cinema houses, or from smuggled pornographic magazines and videos.

As if being stared at wasn't enough, I was followed when on foot and even when driving my car. Men would bump into me deliberately, stick their tongues out, and noisily smack their lips. I had my bottom pinched and my breast grabbed; I was harassed like this by young boys and elderly men alike. Sexual harassment, referred to locally as "Eve teasing", is considered a social evil in Pakistan, but is common nevertheless. I never found a set response to this harassment, but reacted according to my mood at the time. When two young boys once roughly pulled at the bag on my arm I turned and fired a volley of filthy Punjabi abuse at them: they looked horrified and ran off. At other times when I tried this the boys just laughed and decided I was game for more.

One thing I learned about the streets of a Pakistani city – though at first I was too outraged to be consoled – was that while one man might be harassing me, a hundred more would come to my rescue. I only had to point a finger and the accused would be lynched. On the one hand women are vulnerable if they venture out; on the other they claim an automatic right to protection. Basically, although the harassment was unpleasant, I never once actually felt in serious danger.

Working in a local newspaper office gave me an altogether different insight into Pakistan. In my office were men and women of all ages, mostly from middle-class families, some of whom had been partly educated abroad. On the surface it seemed as though the sexes worked alongside each other as they do in any office in the West, but after a time I became aware of the level of discipline required in a country where the sexes interact so rarely outside the immediate family. Gossip is a national pastime. If I talked to one man more than to another, rumours spread like wildfire, a situation made worse by my status as a foreigner and therefore supposedly open to developing personal relationships.

The honour of the Pakistani family is dependent on its women. Their reputations are guarded with zeal.

It started with offers of a lift home whenever we worked late or when my car had broken down. Before I knew it they were popping round to my flat for tea – tea that would last the entire evening. It took me a while to refuse kind gestures in such a way that wouldn't cause offence. I had somehow to get it across that although in my own country I might well socialize with male colleagues after office hours, in Pakistan the rules were different and I had adapted to them. Most effective was to tell them that I didn't think my neighbours would be pleased if I had male visitors. This they understood.

Essentially I had to come to terms with the fact, that while dealings with men might always be problematic there were times when things couldn't be done without their assistance or influence. Once I had learnt this I was in a far better position to really enjoy the many pleasures of living in Pakistan.

For one thing, I was never lonely. Among the many inhibitions I had to shed in order to appreciate the country was a natural desire for privacy. To begin with I thought the reason whole families – and I mean three generations – slept so close together was lack of space; they often only have two or three rooms, sometimes only one. Later, when I went to stay with a friend at her family home in a nearby village, I realized there was more to it than that.

It was the middle of summer and after a gruelling journey on the treacherous Grand Trunk Road I found myself sitting in a yard, trying unsuccessfully to balance a runny *dal* (lentils) in a fold of wafer-thin *chapati* (bread) under the mesmerized gaze of twelve children. My friend's mother and aunt giggled from the shadows of the kitchen, while her father sat with his *hookah* pipe across the yard, glaring at me from beneath heavy eyelids.

Hot, tired and irritable, I couldn't wait for the day to end. However, come night-time the father ordered one of his sons to bring a *charpoi* (string cot) for me and I watched, horrified, as the small boy placed it alongside all the others. Coming to my rescue, my friend told her father that I'd be much happier sleeping in one of the living rooms. He was shocked. "My God", he said, shaking his head, "If I went to stay in someone's home and they sent me off to sleep alone I would think I had been punished!"

I did sleep alone that night, but soon afterwards I was not only sharing beds with my friends but with most of their children as well, while husbands were duly sent to look for sleeping arrangements elsewhere. By the time I left Pakistan I, too, would have felt sorely rejected had I been sent off to sleep in a separate room.

It wasn't easy getting to know women. Purdah makes them elusive, added to which they are very much preoccupied with family pressures and the burden of being mother, wife and housekeeper. I found this frustrating and longed for female company. I couldn't help feeling hurt and annoyed that the women I did meet didn't seem as eager as I to build up a relationship. I eventually realized that this was partly due to my approach.

Once acquainted, women invited me to their houses for tea or dinner and there I would sit, like a guest of honour in the most comfortable chair in the middle of the room while children silently and deftly served me sweetmeats and cold drinks. Husbands always dominated the conversation and if I occasionally caught a woman's eye it was only to exchange a shy, embarrassed smile. I invariably left feeling disappointed and irritated with myself and with them.

Only when I overcame an irrational fear of being sucked into domesticity did those tedious tea parties come to an end. Then I was barging into kitchens to stir enormous cooking pots of *dal,* carrying a child on each hip around the house so that their mother could attend to the youngest, lounging across a bed on a July afternoon with half a dozen other exhausted women, talking and fanning feverish babies, wandering for hours through narrow, congested and noisy bazaars, haggling for an hour over a kilo of carrots, and spending an extraordinary amount of time talking about husbands and mothers-in-law.

When I moved into the female world of Pakistan it was as if I had hit the core.

The honour of the Pakistani family is dependent on its women and their reputations are guarded with almost obsessive zeal. I don't think I ever saw a group of women strolling aimlessly in the street, chatting and laughing. I never saw a woman running for a bus – she would wait for the next one. I never saw a woman riding a bicycle or doing anything that would look even remotely undignified. When I once asked a friend why she never visited any of the neighbourhood women, she looked shocked. "I could never do that!" she said. "Everyone in the neighbourhood would say I was lazy and that my mother-in-law had picked a useless woman for her son."

The burden of being a family's symbol of honour, and the stereo-typical image of the passive, docile Eastern woman greatly contribute to the hardships experienced by Pakistani women. They are also the ones to suffer most from the Islamicization first imposed by the Zia dictatorship. Yet I came across female force on a number of occasions. When I marched down the Mall in Lahore with several hundred feminists, shaking their fists in the air and shouting in unison to abolish the Hudood Ordinance. I saw it again in a small fishing village south of Lahore where the literacy rate was nil until a local adult literacy organization came along and over half the women fought tooth and nail with their husbands and fathers until they were allowed to attend classes for two hours every afternoon. And I saw it when I was at a friend's house and the women gathered together to discuss what to do with an errant son who spent all his money on heroin.

When I moved into the female world of Pakistan it was as if I had hit the core. The attachments I made seem even now unbreakable. Once I showed a genuine willingness to join in, I found there was a place reserved for me in their life behind the curtain.

My most lasting impression is of a people struggling to survive – a struggle that only differed slightly among villages, sprawling urban slums or the city wastelands where village migrants and the homeless are forced to pitch makeshift tents. Despair is evident almost everywhere, a despair over the appalling, obscene wealth of a tiny elite while the majority live in near abject poverty. Despair, too, over widespread corruption and power-crazed politicians. Despair that even the first step to development and progress looms on a distant horizon like an unconquerable mountain.

Yet amid this feeling of hopelessness there is a visible determination and strength, a fierce patriotism. With their strong sense of community and close relationship with the land, the people of Pakistan struggle with a grace and dignity which seemed to me almost spiritual, and which changed my entire perception of the so-called developing world.

While the fact that I wore traditional dress, ate the local food, earned a local salary and put up with the hardships of lower middle-class urban life initially created disbelief, it didn't take long for that disbelief to turn into genuine pleasure. "She was a Pakistani in another life", my friends would tell each other proudly. Whenever I met anyone there were barriers to be broken; I was white, and a woman alone. In order to prove that I was neither raving mad nor a harlot I had to be careful about my behaviour, the way I moved, looked, talked. It paid off. When a friend's mother-in-law once came and kissed me on both cheeks, stroked my hair and told me that if she had been lucky enough to have had a third son she would have wanted me as a daughter-in-law, I knew I had received the ultimate compliment.

When it came to finally leaving the country, I don't know how I managed to walk away from Lahore. But I cried all the way to Karachi and continued unabashedly throughout the two-hour wait in the international departure lounge. I sobbed loudly and didn't stop, even when a man approached with a glass of water which he passed to me before sitting down opposite, from where he watched me intently and with obvious amusement.

Alone on the Overland Route

Wendy Dison has been travelling since 1980 when she realized that a career in administration was not for her. Since crossing through Pakistan on her way from Iran to India she has lived in Mexico, and has also spent time in Guatemala.

Where the eastern Iranian desert meets the Baluchistan desert of Pakistan a wire fence runs across the sand to mark the border. In the Pakistan frontier town of Taftan, a warm wind whipped up the dust in the main street where goats chewed pieces of cardboard and wild-looking men with dark skins squatted in the shade. Proprietors of shops made of packing cases watched me with friendly interest. One man with a gold-embroidered pill-box hat and a ready smile that revealed large white teeth invited me to rest in his shop until my bus left. During the afternoon he brought bowls of stewed meat and potatoes from the cookshop over the road and showed me how to eat using only a *chapati*. I found it difficult but he encouraged me, ignoring the mess I was making.

A loud two-tone horn announced the departure of the Quetta bus waiting in the bazaar, brilliantly decorated with coloured lights, chrome, plastic cut-out shapes and rows of chains dangling from the bumpers. Men swarmed up and down the ladder at the back to load boxes and bundles on the roof while inside I scrambled for a seat, climbing over enormous quantities of luggage and stools in the aisle. The men stared at me and I was too overwhelmed to do more than stare back.

We travelled east on a dirt road with bone-rattling ridges across the vast stony Baluchistan desert where everything – rocks, bushes, people – had been bleached and burnt to the colour of the earth. The sun set spectacularly and as soon as it touched the horizon we stopped for prayers. The men dispersed, purified themselves with a symbolic "wash" in sand, faced Mecca and started the ritual of praying – bowing and touching their foreheads to the ground, kneeling in the last rays of the sun with their shoes beside them and their loose clothing blowing in the wind.

After three days in the country I saw my first Pakistani women.

Around midnight we stopped in a small village. In a pool of lamplight outside a restaurant groups of people squatted on rush matting around teapots and bowls. Huge pans simmered on a mudbrick fireplace and unglazed pots of water stood on straw rings with drinking bowls balanced on top. Two men wearing wide Afghan turbans invited me to join them and we ate in a friendly silence, dipping our *chapatis* into a communal dish of meat and drinking bowl after bowl of green tea.

In Quetta, the capital of Baluchistan, the broad avenues lined with plane trees and houses set in walled gardens are unmistakably British but the bazaars, I was relieved to find, are colourful, bustling and very much Asian. On the pavements men are shaved, tailors work at sewing machines and cooks stir smoking pans of *samosas* and sell them in bags made from used school exercise books. Lorries decorated with exotic paintings of tigers and mosques trundle past raising clouds of dust and heavy black bicycles, carrying three people, weave among camel-drawn carts and buses groaning under the weight of men clinging on to the outside. I ate in a restaurant with smoke-blackened walls and a choice of either tables and chairs or a raised platform for those who preferred to squat. Men watched me curiously and when I looked up from my spiced spinach they held their gaze. Pakistani men look each other in the eye without embarrassment but I found their steady gaze disconcerting.

After three days in the country I saw my first Pakistani women. Travelling in the ladies' compartment of the Quetta Express the women emerged from their sombre veils and the carriage was filled with glittering colourful fabrics, gold earrings, jewelled nose studs and smiling faces. Delighted to meet a foreigner they spoke to me in Urdu, teasing me when I couldn't understand and enjoying my attempts to pronounce their names. My photos from home fascinated them and one woman, married only two months, showed me her wedding album. They offered me *pan* – a mixture of spices and mild intoxicants wrapped in a betel leaf – and laughed when I screwed up my face at the bitter taste and then, in my ignorance, swallowed it with watering eyes. At the stations we reached through the windows and bought hard-boiled eggs, bananas, and tea in disposable clay cups. Later, when it grew dark and sleeping shapes draped with shawls sprawled on the hard wooden seats and carriage floor, the women offered me a turn on the luggage rack and I slept.

Multan, a traditional religious city, came as a shock. Women wore the *burqua,* a garment that fits tightly round the crown of the head, completely covering all but the woman's feet. She sees the world through a net visor. In traditional society women turn their backs on male strangers. Hurrying along the back streets of the towns they turned away as I passed, mistaking me for a man. My behaviour rather than my appearance was to blame for the misconception; I was doing things that Muslim women didn't do. It saddened me to see them pull their veils over their faces and retreat into the shadows.

The men were clearly unused to seeing Western women. Youths trailed me, giggling and jostling, leering rickshaw drivers kerb-crawled, men followed me making kissing sounds and suggestive comments, and boys nearly fell off their bikes in their efforts to turn and watch me. I felt so uncomfortable that I returned to my hotel.

That night, lying awake with men peeping at me through knot holes in the door, my spirits were low. It seemed that the dire warnings I'd been given about Pakistani men were justified. How could I hope to travel in this country? I was heading for the mountains and experience led me to hope that it would be different there. Yet my guidebook gave the disheartening advice that it was dangerous to travel alone in the Himalayas – for women, of course. I left for Lahore early in the morning, hating myself for giving in but unable to face another day in Multan.

That night, lying awake with men peeping at me through knot holes in the door, my spirits were low.

Lahore felt much more European. Unlike their drab veiled country sisters the women of Lahore wear brilliant colours and their *shalwa camise* are more tightly fitting – some even have short sleeves, though legs are always covered. However, it was difficult to look around the city. I attracted whistles and leers even though I was modestly dressed. Men stood close to me, staring, oblivious to my feelings, and everybody asked questions, always the same, about my country, my name, my age, my occupation, my qualifications. Few people bothered to listen to the answers.

By the time I left for the mountains I loathed men. The *chai* shop at the bus station smelt of diesel fumes and was crowded with men sheltering from the rains. The wails of a baby came from behind a curtain where women could sit in private. The waiter, confused by my anomalous status, did not seat me with the women but cleared a table for me and protectively kept away any man who tried to sit with me. Outside the rain poured, streaming from the plastic sheeting that vendors rigged up over their stalls and filling potholes in the bus yard through which motor rickshaws lurched. People struggled in the mud in plastic slip-on shoes.

> *Maybe the men weren't unfriendly, just ill at ease when a woman invaded their preserve.*

After a twenty-hour bus journey up the Indus gorge we emerged in Gilgit, isolated among the high mountains of the Karakorams. In the dusty bazaar swarthy men wearing dun-coloured blankets over their *shalwa camise* stared at me curiously. In tiny shops bargaining sessions were conducted over glasses of tea, the customers sitting on sacks of lentils or squatting against piles of rock-salt, smoking cigarettes through clenched fists. If the draped figures of women were seen at all they disappeared quickly.

In the *chai* shop, men lounging on string beds turned to look as I entered. The sight of a foreigner, let alone a female one, was enough to attract attention and it was impossible for me to break through the barrier of staring eyes and speak to anyone. Maybe the men weren't unfriendly, just ill at ease when a woman invaded their preserve. But the result was the same; I drank alone.

Away from the town it was different. Walking on tracks between villages I was stared at by children and tongue-tied youths and young women giggled at me, but everyone greeted me with "Salaam". In the villages so many people invited me in for tea it was difficult to choose one house without offending.

At the end of the day the smell of wood smoke heralded a settlement. Children came whooping down the terraces shouting "angrezi" (foreigner) and led me to an old man sitting outside his house, presumably the headman. Inside, orders were given to his wife and daughters and a meal of *chapatis*, chillied potatoes and rice was prepared on the stove. The women held a water jug for the man and I to wash our hands, then served the meal to us, waiting until we had finished before they ate. I hated the deference they showed me. As a foreigner and an honorary male I felt I was betraying these women.

These women had little variety in their lives and seemed to enjoy my visits as a break in their routine. Away from men they relaxed. Though we had

PAKISTAN

no common language they managed to ask many questions: "Was I alone? Why did I have short hair? How many children had I?" In a land where children are highly valued, I was pitied for being childless. Once I was admonished for my immodesty and advised to roll my sleeves down and button my shirt higher at my neck. Often I was gently teased and it didn't matter that I couldn't understand. It was frustrating however, not to be able to talk to the women other than in sign language. The Urdu I was learning was of little use when every village spoke a different dialect, and as girls have only recently started to receive education, few women spoke English.

Being invited into people's homes, forbidden to men outside the family, was one of the privileges I enjoyed in Pakistan. But it didn't outweigh the disadvantages. In many areas I felt threatened. Probably there was no real danger although once I was forced to turn back when a man blocked my way, masturbating. Conflicting emotions confused me as I left. In this country I had felt oppressed even while I was humbled by the hospitality. And three months of being treated as a second-class citizen, albeit often graciously, had left me resentful of being a woman. This was the hardest thing to bear.

TRAVEL NOTES

Languages Urdu, Punjabi, Pushtu, Sindhi and numerous others. Many people speak English in the main towns.
Transport Buses, ramshackle and cheap, will always get you to your destination. Mini-buses are faster, more comfortable and only slightly more expensive, with the advantage that you can book a seat. Trains are frequent, but tend to be unreliable, slow and very crowded. Most buses and trains have special seats or compartments for women and children, recommended if you're travelling alone. There are also separate queues for women to buy tickets.
Accommodation Places to stay range from top-class international to small, locally run hotels. When using the latter, it's worth checking the room and sanitary facilities before signing in. Some of the smaller hotels are reluctant to let out rooms to single women.
Special Problems Harassment can become restrictive and oppressive. It helps to dress conservatively in long, loose clothes or the traditional *shalwa camise* (long-sleeved tunic and trousers). It's also possible to rent a guide from a hotel. If you ever feel uneasy you should seek help from Pakistani women.

Guides *Isobel Shaw's Pakistan Handbook* (The Guidebook Company) is well-researched with plenty of maps, good historical and cultural background and sound advice on what to do and where to go, including trekking.

CONTACTS

Shirkat Gah, 19F Block 6, Pechs, Karachi. Useful source of information about women's campaigns and activities throughout the country.
Simorgh (Women's Resource and Publication Centre), 1st floor, Shiraz Plaza, Main Market, Gulberg 2, Lahore (postal address: PO Box 3328). Women's centre providing resources, documentation, research etc, for the women's movement.
Women's Action Forum (WAF), 103 Basement Raja Centre, Main Market, Gulberg 2, Lahore (postal address: PO Box 3287, Gulberg, Lahore). Holds monthly public meetings, and organizes workshops, seminars and discussion groups in both Urdu and English.

BOOKS

Kathleen Jamie, *The Golden Peak: Travels in Northern Pakistan* (UK & US, Virago,

1993). One of Scotland's most accomplished new poets, Kathleen Jamie describes her journeys along the Silk Route of Pakistan with fluency and precision. Her unconditional sympathy for the people she meets, her facility for detail and dialogue create new standards in travel writing. The old *Golden Peak Hotel* at Gilgit forms the base and reference point for her travels on foot, in jeeps and by raft to the most remote regions of the country.

Dervla Murphy, *Where the Indus Is Young* (1976; UK, Flamingo, 1995/US Transatlantic Arts, 1978). Lively account of a journey through the more remote parts of northern Pakistan which the author made with her seven-year-old daughter.

Emily Eden, *Up the Country: Letters from India* (UK & US, Virago, 1983). Fascinating collection of letters recording the author's experiences as "first lady" to her brother George who, in 1835, was appointed governor-general of India. She describes in vivid detail their two-and-a-half year tour up the country, part of which is now Pakistan.

Christina Lamb, *Waiting for Allah: Benazir Bhutto and Pakistan* (UK, Penguin, 1992). Informative, if sometimes heavy-going, journalistic account of Benazir Bhutto's accession to power in December 1988, through the events leading to her equally dramatic departure less than two years later.

Emma Duncan, *Breaking the Curfew* (UK, Arrow, 1990, o/p/US, Viking Penguin, 1989, o/p). Well-researched, highly readable introduction to power and politics, finished shortly after General Zia's death in 1988.

Benazir Bhutto, *Daughter of the East* (UK, Mandarin, 1988/US, Simon & Schuster, 1989). Benazir describes her fabulously privileged upbringing in Pakistan, her Oxford years and the traumatic events surrounding her father's death. There's little that could be considered self-revealing, but it's worth reading as a loose chronicle of the more obvious influences on her life.

Khawar Mumtaz and Farida Shaheed, *Women of Pakistan* (UK, Zed Books, 1986/US, Humanities Press, 1987). Concise account of women's determined resistance under the Zia regime.

★ **Katia Antonopolou**, "Daughter of the East", in Mike Gerrard and Thomas McCarthy (eds), *Passport to Travel* (UK, Serpent's Tail, 1994). A choice extract from a Greek travel writer renowned in her own country but sadly not published in the UK or US. Here she recounts a meeting with Benazir Bhutto's campaign cavalcade. A feast of evocative images.

Paraguay

Rarely visited, Paraguay is something of a backwater. This fact is entirely to your advantage. There is little of the "gringa" mentality, and, even as a woman alone, you are unlikely to be intimidated by men. The kind of violence and theft against tourists associated with, say, Colombia, Peru or Brazil, is also virtually unknown.

Two bitter wars and several autocratic dictatorships have, however, left their scars on this remote, landlocked country, whose population of three-and-a-half million includes a high proportion of people of Guarani Indian descent. During 34 years of military rule under the notorious General Alfredo Stroessner, when hundreds of political dissenters were killed, imprisoned, or disappeared, indigenous peoples faced extinction as their lands were seized to make way for cattle ranching, intensive agriculture and foreign speculators. At the same time Paraguay became known as a tax haven for infamous right-wing pariahs, including the deposed Nicaraguan dictator Anastasio Somoza and several Nazi war criminals. It also became known as an important staging post for drug traffickers.

Stroessner was finally overthrown by a faction of his own army in 1989, since when opposition parties have had more say and there has been a reduction in the scale of corruption and human rights violations. Genuine democracy, however, remains as elusive as concrete reform.

Paraguay's backwardness and isolation is reflected in a set of outdated, patriarchal laws that discriminate blatantly against **women**. A woman found guilty of adultery receives a prison sentence twice as long as a man in the same situation, and, in the eyes of the law, rape of a single woman is a less serious crime than that of a married woman. Women were only accorded the right to vote in 1961 and in 1987 the government passed a law prohibiting women from working outside the home without their husband's permission. The number of women's groups campaigning for change has greatly increased in the last five years, especially in the field of trade-union and peasant organization. But as long the vast majority of Paraguayans remain condemned to poverty, issues such as land redistribution are likely to overshadow more specifically feminist demands.

"Land of Peace and Sunshine"

Mary Durran spent two months in Paraguay at the invitation of a missionary friend, towards the end of the Stroessner dictatorship. On returning to Britain, she worked for the London-based Central America Human Rights Committee before setting off again on her travels, this time to the United States.

I n spite of the claims in official tourist leaflets, there wasn't a great deal of sunshine when I arrived at Asunción airport. But the city was bathed in a wintry haze, dusk was approaching, and there was certainly an air of tranquility, if not peace, about the place. Bored-looking officials stood around leaning on airport counters, grunting to each other in Guarani, Paraguay's indigenous language. Two of them welcomed the diversion of a thorough search through my rucksack.

I hadn't chosen Paraguay for any specific interest in the country's culture or politics. I had simply followed up the offer of a friend, Paco, who was sent there as a missionary shortly after being ordained as a priest. Caught up with sitting final exams and with my last long summer before me, I had vaguely suggested visiting him to "help with whatever I could", but had made no definite plans as to how I'd spend my time.

As we drove from the airport through the cobbled streets, swerving to avoid potholes, toward the suburb of Lambare, dishevelled-looking barefoot children approached us at traffic lights to sell us newspapers, crying their wares in the curious nasal tones that only a Guarani speaker could utter. I caught a glimpse of a weather-beaten old Indian woman, her wrinkled face blackened by constant exposure to the elements, her headdress a sad mass of flopping, dirty feathers. Cows grazed placidly on grass verges and squalid tumbledown shacks stood beside spacious white houses with gardens and swimming pools. Every street corner displayed the regulation poster of the ailing president of the republic with the slogan "Peace and progress with General Stroessner".

I did later discover the Asunción depicted by the tourist leaflets: the grandiose white government palace, home to the president and a few dignitaries, which stands only a few yards away from the mosquito-infested shanty town on the edge of the River Paraguay; the impressive *Hotel Guarani* and its fashion shows featuring the latest European collections for the Paraguayan jet set; exclusive discotheques where elegant bow-tied waiters address customers in the indigenous language, yet a beer would cost the average Paraguayan at least a day's wages. There was something faintly ridiculous about the sombre grandeur of the dark and cool interior of the Heroes' Pantheon, where the bodies of former dictators are interred.

> Judging from the advertising and television, European women and lifestyles are presented as the models to aspire to.

A few days after my arrival, we drove along a dirt track road, pitted by ditches and potholes. Red sand flew everywhere. I was on my way to Yhu, a small town in the east of the country and home to about 1500 people. As we passed the *ranchitos* (wooden huts with thatched roofs) of the smallholders, old men raised their ruddy hands in greeting, their palms reddened by seasons of contact with the dark soil. The red sand contrasted with the verdant green of the surrounding *estancias* and beautiful brightly coloured butterflies basked in the hot sun.

Having done my homework, I knew that about 80,000 people, mainly smallholders and their families, lived in the district surrounding Yhu. There were only two doctors in this area, about the size of Wales, and I had been invited to stay with a family who were determined to improve the standard of healthcare in their community. Chiquita was a 23-year-old voluntary rural health worker living with her family in the small community of San Juan. Trained by missionary sisters in basic first aid and preventative healthcare, her main task was running the health club which had been set up to encourage villagers to take measures to prevent disease.

As I was introduced to Chiquita's parents, her numerous brothers and sisters and in-laws, I took in what were to be my immediate surroundings for the next few days. The family was housed in four straw-roofed wooden huts in the middle of a plot of land where bananas and manioc (a starchy root crop) were cultivated. A couple of black piglets ran around squealing and several hens pecked at the ground. A crackly old wireless set played the latest American disco sounds alternated with the inimitable strains of Paraguayan polkas – popular folkloric music brought over by German settlers at the beginning of the century. Most of the lyrics were in Guarani, and sang of the beauty of the Paraguayan countryside and the charms of the indigenous *cunatái* –

The family insisted on providing one of the younger brothers as a chaperone every time I went anywhere.

young women. There's some irony in such eulogies, since judging from the advertising and television I saw in Asunción, it is European women and European lifestyles that are presented as the models to aspire to.

A log fire in one of the huts served as the kitchen. To prepare a meal (often manioc and cornflour omelettes), water had to be drawn from the well and food was cooked in a pot hanging over the fire. There was no chimney. The fire burned from dawn to dusk providing light, warmth and comfort during the long winter evenings. Its earthy smell permeated everything – clothes, hair and sleeping bag – and remains one of my most vivid impressions of the few days spent with Chiquita and her family.

I was made to feel very welcome. Although not speaking Guarani was a distinct disadvantage (as it is everywhere in Paraguay), Chiquita's parents made sure that their Spanish-speaking children translated their greetings and questions. Her teenage sisters and brother were intensely curious about me and never seemed to tire of staring while I wrote letters or read. This made me feel rather uncomfortable, though I tried to bear in mind that, for them, to stare was simply a natural expression of interest and curiosity.

I very quickly became aware that I was an object of absolute fascination for most of the villagers too, many of whom had never been any further than Caaguazu, the main provincial town some sixty miles away. "Did I have a husband?" No, I answered patiently, to at least twenty different people. "Why then, was I not accompanied by at least one of my parents?" (I had to smile at the idea of my ageing parents accompanying me over gruelling dirt tracks to a hamlet where there was neither post, newspapers nor electricity!)

Since I was unaccompanied, the family insisted on providing one of the younger brothers as a chaperone every time I went anywhere, even if it were only a few yards away. I found this quite amusing if sometimes irritating, but realized that the family were genuinely concerned about my welfare and simply couldn't understand the notion that I didn't mind, and sometimes even preferred, going out on my own. Norma, Chiquita's sister, explained to me that women who went out alone were generally badly thought of, considered by men to be trying to attract their attention.

Eighteen-year-old Norma had a boyfriend from a nearby village, who would come to visit her on the traditional courting days: Tuesdays, Thursdays, Saturdays and Sundays. Why such a rigid code? "Normally, the girl's parents would think badly of a *novio* (boyfriend) who disregarded tradition", she explained. The young couple would often sit in the dusk outside the huts, but always within sight of Norma's mother or one of her older brothers. And for them to go to one of the travelling dances without a chaperone was unthinkable – mother or older brother had to go too. I was surprised to learn that in spite of this strict moral code, there were several single mothers in San Juan and the surrounding area. But it did seem that most families required their daughters to adhere to this convention.

Although Paraguay is unquestionably a male-dominated society, I actually felt very safe as a lone female traveller. I found most Paraguayans gentle and softly-spoken, and if there is a grain of truth in the myth propagated by Stroessner that Paraguay is an "oasis of peace", it lies in the fact that the traveller in Paraguay does not have to be obsessive about devising ingenious methods of hiding money and valuables in their shoes and underwear. The violence and theft that tourists experience in many other Latin American countries are virtually unheard of in Paraguay. Neither are women travellers likely to be intimidated by men on city streets or in the countryside. Paraguayans welcome travellers, who are generally treated with friendliness and curiosity, and foreign women receive probably far more respect than their Paraguayan counterparts.

Almost inevitably, during my stay in San Juan I never once saw a man do any of the traditionally female household tasks. On top of housework, the women seemed to do most of the backbreaking work in the *chacra*, each smallholder's plot of land, a lifeline for the survival of the family.

Chiquita's family were lucky enough to possess title deeds to their land. I met a family who had no documents proving "ownership" of the tiny plot of land that had housed and fed their ancestors for centuries. Their peace had been shattered one day by the agents of a foreign absentee landowner who had bought the land from the government. Some of the neighbours had refused to move from their plots and were subsequently continually harassed by agents of the landowner. One man had been shot dead in a violent scuffle.

I later found out that Paraguay's land distribution problem is acute. Although vast expanses of land are available for cultivation, there are approximately 300,000 landless families in the country and eighty percent of the national territory is owned by just one percent of the population. Many people in eastern Paraguay had been driven to occupy uncultivated land owned by absentee landlords, and these occupations, although legal under Paraguayan law, have led to several violent conflicts between squatters and army or police-backed landowners.

Lesson one began: "William Shakspeer borned in Stratford-upon-Avon". I could at least do better than that . . .

Malnutrition is also a severe problem. On my first day in San Juan, I woke to the din of cocks crowing and the smell of the fire. I itched all over from mosquito bites. We rose at 6am and walked three miles along the red sand path to the health centre. Already, a queue of patients had formed – old men, mothers with crying children, a man whose arm was in a makeshift sling. I watched Chiquita administer a salt and water solution to a scrawny baby with chronic diarrhoea. She then recommended a simple diet to the mother.

Chiquita explained that many families lived for several months of the year just on manioc, especially if the price of cotton had been low at harvest time. This explained why most of the children were undernourished. Attempts by local farmers to organize to beat the middlemen's price monopolies on cotton had been met with brutal government repression. Several peasant leaders had been imprisoned and tortured for their efforts.

I left San Juan amazed at Chiquita's dedication and commitment to what was a never-ending task, with few rewards. I returned to Yhu, and spent three weeks living in relative luxury, in a house belonging to missionaries, which had running water, and electricity for a few hours in the evening! During the day, I taught a variety of subjects to some of the 165 pupils at the only secondary school in the district.

Not having come prepared to teach, I felt somewhat daunted by the prospect – until one of the sisters showed me a 1950s-produced, dog-eared English-language textbook. Lesson One began: "William Shakspeer borned in Stratford-upon-Avon". I reckoned I could at least do better than that and decided to have a go. I tried to organize my lessons on an exchange basis: I would teach my class an English or a Spanish song, then I'd ask the pupils, aged between 13 and 27, to teach me a Paraguayan song in Guarani. This way, I hoped to place equal value on their culture, and to make the point that things European weren't necessarily better, as many of them believed.

Many were intensely curious about the lifestyle and material goods I had in England; they were very disappointed to discover that my parents lived in an ordinary semi-detached house and not a *Dynasty*-style mansion which they assumed was the norm in Europe. I often asked the young women about their feelings about the status of women in the Paraguayan countryside. What did they think of the fact that the women did all the work in the house, often on the *chacra* and looked after the children as well? Most shrugged and said, "that's the way things are". One girl of about fourteen said, "women are lucky, because if there's a war, it's the men who've got to do the fighting".

There is one image of the national school in Yhu that has stayed with me. Every day, before school began, the pupils would line up outside the building and halfheartedly sing the national anthem. One of the lines referred to Paraguay as the republic "where union and equality reign". I thought of the Asunción elite and their white houses with swimming pools and contraband Mercedes, and then of the peasant families in their cramped huts who eked out the year with a meagre diet of manioc. That was the reality behind the veneer of the "land of peace and sunshine". There was a very hollow ring to that anthem.

TRAVEL NOTES

Languages Although Spanish is the official language, most people express themselves more fluently in Guarani. Seventeen Indian tribes speak variations of another five different languages.

Transport Buses run between all major destinations, but the more remote parts of the country are very hard to get to, even if you rent a jeep. Hitching, though probably marginally safer than in other Latin American countries, carries the obvious risks and is not recommended.

Accommodation Good cheap accommodation is plentiful in Asunción and, apart from some of the *residenciales* around the railway station, hotels are generally clean and safe. The same applies to the hostels which you'll find along all major roads. It's more difficult to find somewhere to stay once you get off the beaten track.

Guides *The South American Handbook* (UK, Trade and Travel/US, Passport Press) has around 25 pages on Paraguay.

CONTACTS

For more information write to the **Paraguay Committee for Human Rights**, Latin America House, Kingsgate Place, London NW6 4TA, UK (☎0171/372 5244).

The only women's organization we have been able to locate in Paraguay is the women's studies group, *Grupo de Estudios de la Mujer Paraguaya*, Eligio Ayala 973, Asunción, who produce a publication, *Enfoquer de Mujer*.

BOOKS

Gay Küppers (ed), *Compañeras* (UK, Latin America Bureau, 1994/US, Monthly Review Press). This compilation of interviews and articles featuring "voices from the Latin American women's movment" includes a small section on women leading the Paraguayan Peasants' Movement.

Poland

P olish images flooded the world media throughout the 1980s. Strikes and riots at the Gdansk shipyards and elsewhere were the harbingers of the disintegration of Communism in Eastern Europe, and the decade closed with Poland's first democratic elections since the 1920s. Half a decade on, the media spotlight is off as the country enjoys what is, by its own peculiar standards, a period of political calm and economic prosperity. Inflation is under control, the zloty is a fully convertible currency, the queues and shortages are a thing of the past, and the government has come full circle: Lech Walesa, autocratic and increasingly unpopular, hangs on as President, while the government, contrary to all expectations, is a left coalition of rural interests and post-Communists.

Economic and social changes have been intense throughout the decade, as Polish entrepreneurs have moved to recreate their own local visions of the West. The changes are visible and upfront, with a building boom, and shops groaning under the weight of consumer goods for those with the money to buy them. And that, of course, is the down side. Chronic unemployment (currently around fifteen percent) is an established part of Poland's brave new capitalist world, and all the triumphal talk of market-led transformation can't hide the continuing struggle of large sections of the population to make ends meet. The security around jobs, homes, education, healthcare and pensions, has all gone with the dismantling of the old state, and in many small towns the local factory – the main provider of jobs – has closed down. Crime has rocketed, too, amid a sense of alienation and dejection among the young and old and unemployed.

Overall, though, Poland has never been easier to visit, with a new infrastructure of privately run hotels and restaurants, and active promotion of tourism – to the beautiful city of Krakow, to the ancient waterside towns along the Wisla or the Tatras mountains and the national parks and forests. Western tourists, especially second-generation Polish immigrants, are flocking to all these areas, and there are plenty of opportunities for contact. Polish hospitality is legendary and there's a natural progression from a chance meeting to an introduction to the extended family.

In general terms Poland is a safe and friendly country to travel around alone, and, the big cities apart, where you should exercise usual caution after dark, encounters rarely feel threatening or intrusive. That is, so long as you are white. As Sylvia Okopu explains below, Poles are often insulting in their reaction to Black or Asian foreigners. Theirs is a very homogenous society – almost exclusively of Polish and Catholic ancestry, since the devastation of the age-old Jewish community in the Holocaust – and it has a lot of learning to do. As a casual visitor you are likely to find yourself socializing mainly with men; women tend to have far less time to spend entertaining strangers, and often seem distant in their dealings with Westerners. Some may find it hard, too, to cope with the old-style gallantry, hand-kissing and giving of flowers that are the veneer of a deeply macho society.

Polish men tend to consider themselves exempt from domestic work, while women are expected to marry young and take on full responsibility for home and family. Dropping out of the workforce to become a full-time housewife is viewed as a positive "Western" option, with considerable social cachet. While **feminism** is a problematic concept in Poland, carrying echoes of former indoctrinaire politics, the country has seen an upsurge in political activism over the last few years focused on campaigns for a more liberal abortion law. Poland currently has some of the most restrictive laws in Europe: voted in by parliament, with huge pressure from the Catholic Church after the collapse of Communism, then amended to a more liberal measure by the left coalition. Recently Lech Walesa has stepped in to veto the abortion amendment, threatening to use all means possible, even unconstitutional ones, to prevent it being passed. The issue remains the focus of impassioned controversy.

More Images than Words

Lucy Kimbell arrived in Poland in 1991, aged 24, and stayed for two years, working as a freelance journalist, and travelling throughout the country. She had already travelled extensively, living for a year in both Barcelona and Sudan. At present she is back in London working as a journalist and writer.

E ven after two years in Poland, I found it hard to work out which symbol on a toilet door indicated the ladies' – the circle or the inverted triangle. Some doors had cute pictures of males and females, a few had the Polish words, but most had the geometry.

It was symptomatic of my time in Poland, a country which left me with many more images than words. Indeed, it was Poland's most archetypal image, the Black Madonna of Czestochowa, that had brought me there in the first place. Although firm about being an ex-Catholic, I had become fascinated by this fourteenth-century icon of a Madonna and child, and its hold on a nation, and I wanted to observe the ritual of her festival. Like so many others, I also wanted to see the changes in Eastern Europe at first hand.

On that initial 1991 visit, I fully expected to see the images we had been fed in the West: long queues for basic goods and foods. Instead, I found Mars bars and Tampax on sale in the kiosks dotted around the streets: the longer I stayed, the fuller the shops got as reforms opened up the economy and the rich got richer.

Joining the annual pilgrimage from Warsaw to Czestochowa – ten days of walking through the ripening fields, along with thousands of others – gave me a glimpse into the traditional Poland of wooden-slatted farmhouses and religious liturgy. I wanted to see more, so I stayed on.

The following two years, which I spent working as a journalist and occasional English teacher in Warsaw, were challenging and rewarding in almost equal measure. I stood in the cold at tram and bus stops, struggling with the language and holding on to my sense of self as a person, as a woman in an often uncomfortable environment.

Getting to grips with the place as a journalist was hard, too. Poland, I found, was a country which through its history of war, invasion and occupation had hidden itself away somewhere. From my grasp of the language I could gradually get the gist of things from newspapers and overheard conversations on buses, though mostly I relied for information on friends who spoke English, and on just using my eyes.

I looked in the dirt cheap and often dirty restaurants called milk bars where ageing men and women in overcoats huddled over soup at plastic tables. I looked in grandiose marbled museums and found a Communist-inspired representation of the past. I looked in the new tacky nightclubs of Warsaw and found young women in makeup and microskirts dancing to bland Europop.

I found repeated and often painful references to the past in conversations with friends and in films and newspapers as I watched Poland try to throw off its Communist past and rejoin what it sees as its rightful Western heritage. After a while I realized that what I had been brought up to call Eastern Europe was a fraying label stitched into a raggedy suit. I now describe Poland as being in Central Europe, having learnt that for many Poles, that distinction is crucial.

During my two years, and on subsequent visits, I have travelled widely in Poland, sometimes with friends on ramshackle local buses or overheated dawdling trains, sometimes on my own. Many towns felt provincial and cold, with barely a pizzeria to distinguish their drab streets as pre- or post-1989. One place that made an immediate impression was Krakow, a warm-stoned, southern city built round a medieval square. It was Warsaw, however, where I got established, and to which I owe a grudging affection.

Warsaw is a dour city that seems not to have come to terms with its suffering. Its walls bleed history. The plaques commemorating the victims (Catholic – rarely Jewish) of the last war, for example, are always freshly adorned with red roses or with newly tied ribbons representing the Polish flag.

The city's inhabitants are in large part recent immigrants, from the countryside and other Polish cities, and the houses and apartment blocks are predominantly modern. I only met a couple of Warsaw families who predated the Nazi occupation. None of them were Jewish. The town's large Jewish population had almost all been murdered or deported to death camps by 1943. By chance, however, both of the flats I ended up living in were built before the war.

My first flat was in a 1930s building on Poznanska Street, close to the junction of Jerozolimskie and Marszalkowska, the city's main shopping streets. In contrast to friends who lived in utilitarian concrete blocks built in the 1960s and 1970s, I had heavy dark furniture, wooden floors that bred dust balls, and "double glazed" windows: meaning two windows that opened on to the building's courtyard. Inside the yard a few plants grew in earth so fine it was almost a dust. Unlike the blocks, there was a sense of neighbourliness – a sense which had survived the bleak days of informers.

My second apartment was in a three-storey house in a garden of roses and sweet peas, across the Vistula River in the greenery of Saska Kepa. Like many cities divided

I found the frost in the early morning at the tram stop in minus 15°C almost unbearable, no matter how many layers I wore.

by a river, Warsaw has its own snobbery about which side you live on. The north bank, known as Praga, is often portrayed as dangerous, where the Red Army sat and watched as the Nazis defeated the insurgents of the Warsaw Uprising in 1944, and then destroyed the city. When I told people where I lived in Warsaw, they almost always asked if I knew about this piece of their history.

In the post-war rebuilding, the planners neglected to make use of the river, which now slides through the city unnoticed, unexplored. On my daily tram and bus journeys back and forth, I developed a fondness for the dark, almost oily waters beneath the heavy bridge. The dusty, sandy riverside beach was a favourite cruising spot for gay men, which was about as far as the Vistula went in terms of romance. There are no human-scale bridges to cross holding hands with your lover, no peaceful embankments to linger on in the evening. Just one summer concession, when a heavy iron-hulled boat is moored next to the highway under the Old Town and becomes a floating bar for the city's floating youth. Otherwise the Vistula was wasted as a feature, and the city felt dry.

Warsaw has other city virtues: a manageable, compact place, with around one and a half million people, frequent buses and trams, and relatively safe to walk around at night – if you are white. I got to know it well, and felt pleased when a Polish friend from Lodz visited for a weekend and commented that I behaved like a "citizen".

By then, I had my network of favourite bars, cafés and cinemas: I knew where to go to buy second-hand English-language books or silver jewellery and knew what time to go to a hotel to buy my copy of *The Guardian* before it ran out. Like many Poles, I was hooked on ritual porcelain cups of rich hot chocolate, which I consumed in the café next to the *Wedel* chocolate shop. This has two chambers, one pink, one green, with eighteenth-century decor, and a waitress who comes to your table and asks what you would like – though the only thing they serve is hot chocolate. Served with Wedel wafers, it is the best I have ever tasted, and on cold, dark early evenings, when the snow was turning grey and the city had a metallic bite in the air, the choice was simply one cup or two.

> *I never worked out how they could wear heels on frosty, pitted pavements nor short skirts in the bitter cold.*

Getting to know a place, and developing your own routines, is of course part of any new city experience. But, for me there was a sense of achievement in negotiating the Polish language, in having made good friends; in knowing I could manage what could often be a difficult environment – without being able to say exactly what made it so difficult.

There were, of course, the everyday struggles. I found it depressing to go into a shop and ask a simple question in Polish – a question like "Have you got any yoghurt?" – and for the assistant, usually an older Polish woman who was sick of her job and underpaid, to bark back what became almost a joke response under Communism: "Nie ma." There isn't any, and don't bother asking when there might be some. Three of these barks on a cold morning left me demoralized, yet aware how soft I was having been brought up in a culture where your custom was sought after.

I also found it irritating to spend half the morning on the phone trying to arrange an interview and get three wrong numbers because of an old-fashioned telephone exchange which you can hear clicking round the dial. I found the frost in the early morning at the tram stop in minus 15°C almost unbearable, no matter how many layers I wore. Sometimes I found the pale orange of the street lights at night not strong enough to soothe my fears when walking alone.

Often I was angry at being stared at for no reason, as far as I could see. I found, when I got back to Britain, that I had changed my appearance to avoid attracting much attention. In Poland I took my nose ring out after a few months but kept my leather jacket and clompy shoes that few

Polish women wore. I never worked out how they managed to wear heels on frosty and pitted pavements nor short skirts in the bitter cold.

In my day to day life, rushing from the English-language newspaper where I worked to a private English lesson to an interview to a film opening to a snatched sandwich from a kiosk on the street, I could not have managed dressing as many Polish women did. One difference was that I knew I would have to get the bus or tram home on my own at the end of the day. I rarely saw Polish women out on their own. Sometimes they were out and about with other women, but most often they were with husbands or boyfriends or in large groups.

There was I, no husband or boyfriend, wending my way between Warsaw's nascent gay community and the straight pubs and clubs. I did not find myself making friends easily with Polish women, and instead my closest friends were Polish gay men and Sylvia, a woman from London (whose particular experience follows below). During nights out we swayed through the streets from Warsaw's trendy, Polish-yuppie *Harenda* bar to nightclubs where if you were lucky the DJ might have some rare groove, mixing it badly into Polish rock.

Two years went by and it began to feel right to leave, and start again in London. Parts of Poland, of my time in Warsaw, remain strong, and especially the images. I remember standing at midnight during the jazz festival on the steps of the monstrous Palace of Culture, Stalin's gift to the Poles in the 1950s, catching the first snowflakes on my fingers. Or creaky old ladies lined up on their knees in the chapel by the shrine of the Black Madonna. Or the handsome soldiers with pert behinds and mean boots guarding the tomb of the unknown soldier where one of my gay friends told me he went cruising. The pink triangle, the Black Madonna, the circle on the toilet door. The circle, or the triangle, I can never remember.

Fame and Hassle in Warsaw

Sylvia Okopu, from south London, worked in Warsaw at the same time as Lucy Kimbell, teaching business English and customer sevice training. Here she adds a note on the different perspective she had as a black woman.

Bizarre though it seems in retrospect, I went to Poland for a holiday and ended up staying there to work after being offered a job in Warsaw. I accepted readily, as London was offering me very little in the way of prospects. I returned to England, worked out my notice at British Telecom, packed everything (including black hair products, which you won't find in Poland) into an enormous suitcase, and got on a plane back to Warsaw.

I had hoped there might be fewer obstacles to life and work in Warsaw than in London, but my ideas of the practicalities of day to day living were not so naive. I knew I would have to get accustomed to stares at my colour whenever I ventured out, and I felt this was understandable. If an Eskimo walked down my local high street I would surely do a double take. But I was not quite prepared for the blatant verbal abuse levelled at me, and the sneers that accompanied it. This, I was to learn, was a common feature of my life in Poland.

Taking a bus or tram around Warsaw, away from the office enclaves of Western companies, the experience was most intense. People on the street had no reservation about shouting out "Black devil" or other such abuse as I went on my way to work at seven in the morning, or, more alarmingly, if I was returning from a night out. There were nights when I was taunted with racial abuse by groups of thugs, and, after a while, I always took taxis to and from bars or nightclubs. They weren't expensive by Western standards and they cut out the unpleasant middle man – racial hassle.

Polish men saw me as "dusky exotica"; an experience and challenge that they could impress their friends with.

As for my treatment as a woman, I felt it was impossible to divorce my racial origin from my sex. Polish men tended to see me as "dusky exotica"; an experience and challenge that they could impress their friends with. It was hard to blame them for their ignorance, especially coupled with the Polish media's sensational depiction of Blacks, expecially in the prevalent porno mags. My advice in the dating game is to suss out any guy who makes advances. They may not be after your personality. Surprise, surprise.

However, I wouldn't want to give a completely negative image of life as a Black woman in Warsaw. It had its major plus points – recognition and all the other trappings of "fame". People immediately thought that as a Black chick from London I was hip and trendy – and I could deal with that. If you are not offended by the concept of tokenism, TV and radio can be your oyster. I ended up gaining experience in researching and presenting a weekly rap and hip hop radio show, and getting in front of the cameras judging a male beauty pageant. Not bad for a Sarf London girl.

Freight to Krakow

Daisy Scott is a freelance writer from Brookline, MA. She journeyed to Europe by Polish freighter in the summer of 1992, and made her way on by train to Krakow.

I got my first taste of Poland on the Atlantic Ocean, aboard a merchant ship sailing from Port Newark, New Jersey to Bremerhaven, Germany. The ship, the *M/S Kazimierz Pulaski*, hailed from Gdynia, and her officers, crew, navigation charts, life jacket instructions, entertainment videos, courtesies, and *kielbasa,* a grey pink sausage omnipresent at meals, were all Polish. My plan had been to continue from Germany only as far as Prague, but my ship experience – with the sole exception of the *kielbasa* – made me curious enough to go on to Krakow.

What sense of place could I get from a working ship with five passengers, thirty-four officers and crew, mammoth containers of toxic chemicals and frozen chickens, tractors – and somebody's Porsche tied down in the hold? Plenty. The ship seemed like Poland itself, changing the old ways, adjusting with heavy effort to the new. On the one hand the Captain had thirty years' worth of merchant marine stories, told with passion, grace and a rich dollop of philosophy. On the other, our third officer – a young, successful mariner – complained about the slow pace and boredom of shipping. He didn't find it romantic. He wanted to get into computers. Talk of home was full of old-fashioned pride, but included the pain and harsh effects of current economic reforms. Even the ship was feeling it. She was overdue in drydock, but the company, fearful they might need to sell her off for cash, delayed it. So she was "weeping": her portholes bleeding rust down her sides.

I had heard a couple of horror stories about sexual harassment on ships, so I asked the company rep about it before I booked the crossing. She assured me, a little indignantly, that nothing like that had occurred on this line. In any case, the captain would deal severely with any hint of a transgression. As one of three women on board (the others were the elderly wife in an Irish couple, and the young daughter of a crew member) I felt uncomfortable only once. A sailor discovered that I was sleeping in a double-single, that is, with no cabin-mate. He didn't speak much English, but managed "That's good to know", with a universally understood leer. I avoided the guy, and stuck a chair under the door-knob at night. After a few days, the feeling passed. For the most part, the crew was courteous and friendly – and busy, too, working.

The few English-speaking mariners were happy to talk, particularly on the bridge during watches. Discussions with my impatient third officer were lively and blunt, full of opinions about the follies of his homeland: the politics, the economy. But he could wax rhapsodic with the best of them about the hills surrounding his hometown. Wroclaw (pronounced "rrohswuhf" – go figure). In the end, it was he who yelled after me, as I debarked in Bremerhaven, "Visit Krakow!"

I did. In fact, I left my original destination of Prague in a run. Prague, in its tenure as the hottest spot in Eastern Europe, has become a tourist mecca, every other guy wandering about with a videocam glued to his eye. Particularly during the summer, "entrepreneurs" multiply at a dizzying rate. The hammers and saws of the reconstruction trade are a constant accompaniment, as is the hard-edged energy of new, very efficient capitalists. I escaped to the slower, more grinding rhythms of Poland.

Differences declared themselves right away. The good trains were reserved for travel to and from Frankfurt, Vienna, the West. Travelling from one former Eastern Bloc country to another were the old trains. Carpets coughed up dust; head pieces were rubbed to a sheen with use; covers went missing. The toilet rivalled some I'd seen in China. We rumbled slowly through farmland. I watched soil being tilled by hand and horse. Women in skirts

In Krakow the pews were full of the praying. If there was no room, they knelt on the cold, stone floors.

and dresses bent over hoes, working long furrows. Factories sat in the middle of fields, concrete reminders of everything I'd heard about Poland's legendary pollution.

A young family from the compartment next to mine stood in the breezeway, leaning against open windows. In stifling heat, this at least allowed the dust and dry air to move. The husband, naked to the waist, snuck looks at me. Surly or curious? He left the car. I made a friendly overture to his wife, with a map, asking where we were. When he returned, his wife spoke with him, and his attitude changed. We worked out a conversation of sorts, all pointing and nodding and maps and a stolen word or two. He took his leave. A few minutes later, he reappeared in a neat, blue, buttoned shirt. He gestured formally, asking if he might sit down in my compartment. Then he pulled out a fistful of Czech money and, moving one hand, then the other back and forth between us, said, "Dollars?" He had changed into his good clothes for a visit to the bank.

Once in Krakow, I encountered the omnipresent dust, the smell of diesel and leaded fuels, and a fog of shabbiness on anything made in the last fifty years. Pollution gouged out the city, eating away at masonry and statuary, staining stone, poisoning the air and food. I was warned not to eat anything grown within eight kilometres of the city, and to ask, in the markets, where the produce was from. A university student I met told me the safest bet was to eat what doesn't grow in Poland at all: kiwis, bananas, pineapple, if you can find them.

As oppressive as that could feel, the city had not yet been franchised into sameness – oppression of another kind. There was no McDonalds – then, at least. I loved Krakow's quirks. There seemed to be dozens of tiny, independent shops selling women's hats. The smell of cooking cheese was ubiquitous – the national bread-and-cheese dish, *zapiekanka*, cheap and sustaining, with a dozen variations. I thanked a man for his help and conversation, extended my hand for a handshake, and found it kissed instead – an old custom that

Anything actually written on a menu looked like Welsh on drugs.

hasn't quite died out. I heard the clop of horses' hooves, the omnibus's bell, the surprisingly loud rumble of wooden wheels on street, conversation in Polish, in French, in English, the whoosh of a truck's airbrakes, a hammer hitting wood, a tour guide explaining something over the scrape of heels, laughter. I heard a trumpet blare from the tower of Saint Mary's on the Rynek Glowny, the vast market square in the center of Krakow. The tune halted abruptly. A mistake? No. Just a reminder of the thirteenth-century look-out who tried to warn the town of a Tartar onslaught. An enemy arrow found its way to, and through, his neck, ending his trumpet-playing days. Seven hundred years later, the solo is cut off every hour, on the hour. In the rush toward the new, the Western , the commercial, I could feel tradition's strong undertow.

For instance, to me, what separated Krakow's churches from many churches in Western Europe, was . . . the Church. Most everywhere else, it seems the sightseers outnumber the prayerful. In Krakow the pews were full of the praying. If there was no room in the pews, they knelt on the cold, stone floors. Nuns and monks were a common sight, even young nuns and monks. The last time I'd seen a young nun, I was thirteen, in parochial school. These days, in the States at least, it's something like spotting an endangered species.

New entrepreneurs were a little hesitant, not very aggressive. And while the person on the street might go out of his or her way for you, the people charged with helping you might well not. In the main *Orbis* office (*Orbis* is the state tourism agency for foreigners), a backpacker came to the head of a very slow line, only to have a wooden "This window is closed" sign put up in his face. He took out a Swiss army knife and calmly carved into the wood: "I waited 110 minutes for this".

At Krakow Central Station, having already bought my train ticket, I stood in the information line, the domestic tickets line, then a special line I believe was for international travel, then for a bit in another domestic tickets line. I waited a couple of minutes in the wrong reservation line, then the right one. Then a mistake in my ticket was discovered, and it was back to domestic travel. The clerk did not understand what I wanted – not necessarily her fault, mind you – but her method of dealing with it was to slide the money back under the counter window, and turn calmly to the next person in line. This was my cue to start behaving like a deranged person, per the squeaky wheel theory. But the next person in line was a nun. I couldn't act out in front of a nun. Damn wimples.

Not many people spoke English. Signs were in Polish, then Russian. For transportation, I found xeroxed maps indispensable. Other times, I relied upon the kindness of strangers. In the main post office, where I signed up to have a phone call to Germany placed, they announced "Niemcy" ("Germany" in Polish) over and over. I blissfully ignored it, until a woman leaned over and asked, "Deutschland?".

In my full complement of Polish, learned on the ship, only "please", "thank-you", and "beer" were helpful in restaurants. Anything actually written on a menu looked like Welsh on drugs. One night, I dimly recognized a meal's elements. *Pomodor* was probably a tomato, something else sounded like french fries. Only the main dish remained a mystery. I hailed a waitress, pointed to the word and shrugged, what was it? She told me, in Polish. I shrugged again. She hailed a colleague, who also explained it in Polish. That's when I started to cluck. They nodded emphatically. *"Najlepszy*! The best possible" I crowed, triumphant. It really was very good roast chicken.

I found myself grimacing at it, but I boarded the bus – the perfectly normal, refurbished bus – for Auschwitz. *Orbis* offered their regular, arranged tours to the site of the largest Nazi death camp, but I called one of the independent guided groups that go out there. It's in two parts, Auschwitz I, and Auschwitz II, known as Birkenau. I'm not sure why I went. I thought it was important. I was also afraid of feeling sick. But to be honest, Auschwitz I was preserved like a park. There was grass; there were trees; you could buy a soda; there were trash cans, exhibits, informative signs. I found it very bizarre that, in the guides' talks, camp inmates were referred to as "victims of Fascism", not as Jews. How could that be? I talked to a young man, Andzej, who worked there, asking if this was an example of Poland's own brand of anti-Semitism. His answer was sincere enough, about how the Slavs were on the list of under-races, too; that they were the next to go, and how it wasn't only the Jews. But just the week before,

Andzej had been assailed by a former inmate, now an old man living in New York. "Why aren't you saying Jews?" the man had cried, "Jews died here". It shook the young man up. Later, I heard him say to his group, "And of course we must remember that ninety percent of the victims here were Jewish".

Much of what's displayed in the buildings was disintegrating slowly with time and lack of funds to preserve it. There was a room filled with hundreds of suitcases, each one marked with a name and address, waiting for its owner to reclaim it. There were piles and piles of eye-glasses. There was a glass case filled with infant clothing. There was the women's hair. We were recited number after number after number until they washed over me, incomprehensible, and certainly unreconcilable with the soft, warm day outside. At Birkenau the preservation work lagged far behind. Things have literally rotted, leading to one artist's suggestion that a fitting memorial would be to let the camp rot right into the ground. I came upon a tiny cluster of flowers, violets, I think, laid on a long bench in a barracks. There were large groups, big tours, gaggles of youngsters going through these places. The sun was strong. We were all on holiday. Days later, sitting at coffee on the ul Francueska, I realized how gloomy my journal writing had turned, how I was thinking about the children I knew, how in a different place and time my gangly 12-year-old brother, now struggling with adolescence, would not have stood a chance. Such thoughts left me staring into space.

TRAVEL NOTES

Languages Polish. Almost everybody over twenty has learnt Russian at school, although most don't like admitting to it. Some people speak English and older people often speak German.

Transport Mostly by train: make sure you take the *expresobowe*, as other services can be incredibly slow. Hitching is uncommon and you should expect to contribute towards (rationed) fuel. Public transport in towns is inexpensive and frequent, as are taxis.

Accommodation You no longer have to stay in the state-run "international" hotels, although these can be booked with no fuss through the official travel agency, *Orbis*, if you can afford rates of £70/$100 a night for a double room. "Local" hotels, graded from one to five stars, are not too luxurious and prices fluctuate with no apparent call to reason; however, they're okay, and tend to work out at around £10/$15 for a double. Private rooms, offered through agencies in most cities, are cheaper still but are often in high-rise flats on the city outskirts.

Special Problems For Westerners, the biggest hassles are hotel room thefts, pickpocketing and car break-ins – all growth industries. Most of the old shortages are history, though you may still need to revert at times to the *Pewex* "hard currency shops", remnants of the bad old days. Found in all major towns and in *Orbis* hotels, they sell Western goods and medicines.

Guides *The Rough Guide to Poland* (Penguin) is written with enormous enthusiasm and knowledge. If you're interested in meeting locals, supplement it with Jim Haynes's wonderful **People to People: Poland** (UK, Canongate Press/US, Zephyr Books): basically an address book of Poles interested in meeting (and sometimes accommodating) Western visitors. The idea is that you strike up friendships and reciprocate hospitality at home.

CONTACTS

Women's groups, active in campaigns for wider availability of abortion and contraception, among other issues, include the *Liga Kobiet Polskich* (Polish Women's League), ul Karowa 31, Warsaw 00324 (☎48 22/26 88 25).

BOOKS

⭐ **Eva Hoffman**, *Lost in Translation: Life in a New Language* (UK, Mandarin, 1991/US, Penguin, 1990). An autobiography of immense power and depth. Eva Hoffman writes of a post-war Jewish childhood dislocated by her parents' decision to finally leave Poland and emigrate to Canada. The empty spaces of uneventful Vancouver form the backdrop of her yearnings for Krakow's rich cultural heritage. In her more conventional travel narrative, *Exit into History: A Journey through Eastern Europe* (UK, Minerva, 1994/US, Penguin), she returns to her native Poland as part of her wide-ranging travels through post-Communist Eastern Europe. A literary *tour de force* – erudite, lucid and knowing.

Lynne Jones, *States of Change – A Central European Diary* (UK, Merlin Press, 1990). Travels – mainly in Poland – in the late 1980s, paying special attention to the alternative political scene of peaceniks, punks, greens and the like.

Jnina Baumann, *Winter in the Morning, A Young Girl's Life in the Warsaw Ghetto and Beyond* (UK, Virago, 1991/US, Free Press, 1986). Account of resilience and courage during the Warsaw siege and Nazi occupation.

Susan Bassnett and Piotr Kuhiwczak (eds), *Ariadne's Threads – Polish Women Poets* (UK, Forest Books, 1988/US, Dufour). An anthology of eight contemporary poets.

Portugal

O ver the last decade Portugal has been busy shrugging off its image as a rural backwater in Europe. Under a period of extraordinary economic growth, fuelled by European Community subsidies, a new order is emerging based on industrial and urban wealth. Lisbon, the capital, a disarmingly attractive city with a buoyant multi-cultural atmosphere (owing to decades of immigration from Brazil and former African colonies) is rapidly gaining status as a major European cultural and cosmopolitan centre. Beneath the veneer, however, there remain entrenched pockets of poverty; illiteracy and infant mortality are higher than any other country in the north; and just beyond the main cities you still come across villages steeped in tradition, with women dressed in black (for husbands absent in France, Germany or at sea) struggling to live off the land.

For holiday-makers the country's attractions are the wide, long beaches of the

PORTUGAL

Atlantic coastline, lush countryside and good, inexpensive food
and wine. Most tourist development is concentrated along the
southern Algarve, and travelling alone in these parts you can
feel lost among the endless couples sipping *vinho verde* and
watching the sun set. As with any major resort there are men
hanging round the bars and discos in search of the easy tourist,
but they rarely pose much of a threat. Portugal is a relatively
straightforward country to travel around; prosperity has brought
with it an efficient rail and bus network, and the atmosphere
generally feels safe and relaxed. Machismo is less rampant than
in other Latin countries: men may occasionally hiss and make
comments on the streets of Lisbon (train stations and the Bairro
Alto – the main area for clubs and bars – are uneasy places
to wander around alone at night) but elsewhere traditional
courtesy is accompanied by a welcome male restraint. The
Portuguese talk of themselves, with some justification, as a
country of *brandos costumes* – "gentle ways".

Despite positive legal reforms and the high profile of women
in higher education, old attitudes die hard and the Portuguese
women's movement has had difficulties mobilizing on any
large scale. Nonetheless, there are a couple of central organizations in Lisbon which can put you in touch with what's
happening around the country.

"What You Do and What You Don't"

Elizabeth Mullett has lived and studied in Lisbon, and has travelled throughout the
country. She found it justified its reputation as one of the easiest countries in which to
travel alone.

Lisbon is one of the most attractive capitals in the world: a breezy,
dazzlingly white city which has somehow escaped the worst of
urban expansion. I lived there for a while, with a thesis to
research, a long list of archives to visit and an irredeemably student
income on which to do it. Not quite a resident, nor quite a tourist,
I rented a room and traipsed between libraries and the city sights. I
explored the frantic covered market on the river front in the early

mornings and, from my landlady, learned to cook the sweet rice desserts and the rich stews, brimming with pigs' ears and calves' shinbones.

I also learned to duck the harassment experienced by most young women in the city, finding in museum gardens and monastery cloisters the perfect places to read or write letters undisturbed. Following the example of other students, I used to take my books and newspapers to one of the big town cafés in the evenings and sit there with a coffee, half-studying, half-watching the world. Local incomes are low but the habit of an evening out universal. I acquired an ability to stay up until four in the morning to listen to the city's *fado* music (a kind of national blues — worth hearing), to eat breakfast standing up in the busy *pastelarias,* to look people back in the eye and to take lunch seriously.

I was so energetically absorbing a new culture that it took me some time to feel a foreigner's isolation. It wasn't that most Portuguese women of my age were locked into family life, married with several children already; more that, despite the relaxing of social attitudes since the 1974 revolution, women are still essentially seen in the image of their family relationships — somebody's

Talking to feminists, I found that the most highly valued opportunity had been to travel, either through work or study.

daughter, wife, mother or widow. Acute housing shortages in Lisbon and Porto and a national minimum wage of less than £100 a month mean that most children leave home only after marriage and often not even then.

To be sure, women achieved paper equality within five years of the revolution, but male socialism has tended to view women's needs and aims as secondary and feminism has had little institutional and popular support. A liberal family background makes more difference than legislation and if the corridors of the universities are full of women students, access to higher education (gained by under two percent of the population) is still largely a privilege of the middle classes. Talking to feminists, I found that the most highly valued opportunity had been to travel, either through work or study, and that way gain a sideways look at their culture and sense of themselves as individuals.

My work took me to Evora, a whitewashed Moorish town in the Alentejo, a region which seemed to me one of the most fascinating. Since Roman times it has been an area of vast rural estates, most of which were seized from landowners and transformed into collective farms after the revolution. Governments responded first by extending, then restricting, agricultural credits needed by these new farms, and now big families are being allowed to return to parts of their estates.

The towns are therefore a focus of both the region's poverty and its provincial bourgeoisie. The narrow convoluted streets have mostly escaped redevelopment and are still lined with sixteenth- and seventeenth-century houses; if the sky on summer nights has more stars than you've ever seen before, it's because electricity has not reached every house in every town.

Every Tuesday, Evora's main square is full of livestock farmers in dark suits and black hats, negotiating business. At lunchtime they swarm into the local restaurants and fall upon the goat stews, dishes of pork cooked with shellfish, and great steaming plates of salt cod boiled with chickpeas. This is a profoundly masculine society – the characteristic music of the region is that of the male voice miners' choirs – and if you travel from Evora to any of the medieval towns beyond you will find cafés full of men meeting after dinner. It's rare to see women on the streets after nightfall.

As I moved around the north, to the granite and down-to-earth city of Porto and to Vila Real and the castellated hill towns of the Spanish frontier in Tras-os-Montes, I was confronted with a quite different world. This is the area of the great vineyards, but also of small subsistence farms. On the terraces of the River Douro and in the handkerchief-sized plots, there are jumbles of cows, cabbages and vines, each holding infinitely subdivided among families by the inheritance divisions of the Minho district. For the visitor, it's an area which repays a good eye for changing styles of domestic architecture – from the granite boulders of the Beiras to the drystone walling of Tras-os-Montes; a stomach for the egg-yolk and sugar confections, different in each town; and a taste for the Dão wines and the delicious semi-sparkling *vinhos verdes.*

The gentle and courteous social attitudes make Portugal one of the easiest Latin countries in which to travel alone.

To the east of the Douro, the journey from Chaves to Bragança takes you through some of the most spectacular scenery in the country, wild and empty. From time to time you pass through villages desiccated by emigration; communities of old people, women and children, whose men work in the cities of Central Europe, returning only for visits in the summer months. It's the most conservative area of Portugal, where adherence to the Church and respect for authority have remained strongest. As "widows of the living", the wives remain rigidly subject to popular criticism of their social behaviour – as one woman put it, "what you do and what you don't".

What you do and what you don't, as a visitor, is very much up to you. There are excellent detailed guidebooks and the tourist offices are friendly and helpful about all sorts of requests – where to go to find the country's remarkable wild flowers, for example, or where to nurse a particular ailment or allergy at a spa. Whatever you can learn of this strangest of the romantic languages in advance will help immeasurably, though many Portuguese do speak some English or French and understand Spanish. And the survival of gentle and courteous social attitudes make Portugal, beyond Lisbon or the busy beaches, one of the easiest Latin countries in which to travel alone.

Family Life in the Alentejo

After travelling by Landrover around Africa with her husband and three young sons, **Jan Wright** settled in a remote part of the Alentejo where she has been living since the late 1980s. From the beginning the family threw themselves wholeheartedly into the local peasant life.

A gust of hot air singes my eyebrows and I duck back before swabbing out the clay oven and beginning to shovel in the loaves. One after the other: ten three-pounders, a pizza, a flan, a couple of cakes and a dozen sweet potatoes. Get them in as fast as possible before the oven cools and then relax. Relax? I'll be lucky! Sometimes the weekly bake is a disaster, bread charred on the outside or soggy on the inside. But I'm learning, and the disasters are the exception now and not the rule. A small handful of flour on the oven floor – if it goes dark brown the oven's too hot; a knowing tap on the bottom of the first loaf out – if it's too soon pop it back in for another ten minutes. Even the neighbours have to agree it's good.

The neighbours love to help and advise. Even more they love us to be wrong. We are doubly strangers: foreigners and city people. We are ignorant of everything that to them is basic knowledge, learned in the early years of life from father or mother. Or more likely grandfather or grandmother, for in this society child-rearing is usually passed back to the older generation to free the parents for the relentless toil which all too often leaves them old beyond their years. "Kill the pig next Saturday?" They look at us in horror. Have we offended some religious festival? We look at each other, at a loss, and eventually they deign to explain: "It's the waning moon." We all look at each other, time travellers, by some fluke caught in the same place at the same time.

Portugal, in the twentieth century. Closer to Africa than to Northern Europe, the Alentejo was, up to fifteen years ago, a semi-feudal society where most people were too poor to afford shoes, where the old starved if they had no family to support them. It's one of the last examples of the peasant society in Europe – and one that is unlikely to survive among the red tape of EC grants and the glitter of the world on the other side of the TV screen.

Five miles from the west coast and just north of the border with the Algarve, we have a valley to ourselves. Its elements are a continuing wonder to me: native Portuguese trees, Imperial eagles circling overhead in spring, wild flowers, and lots of butterflies. There are no main services and no prospect of ever having them. A track deters all but the most determined visitors. Our building has thick clay walls and a tiled roof; small windows to keep out the sun; an open fireplace and, outside, the great clay bread oven.

The prevalent machismo can turn male children into strutting, demanding brats.

There's a stream which runs dry in the summer and spills out in furious flood once or twice a year, when we get half the annual rainfall in a few hours. "The worst rain for forty years", they assure us as we all huddle in the local bar. They said that last time, too.

We've been here three years now, myself, my husband and our three children. We drive the boys four kilometres up to school in the morning because it's a long steep hill, and who wants to go to school? They make their own way home, stopping to play with friends, getting a freshly baked bun from the old couple who live in the last house of the scattered village, spotting wild flowers and butterflies, birds of prey, the occasional snake. We are a significant minority in the school. There are only ten children, aged from six to ten, including our three. There is just one teacher, an unwilling exile from Porto, who responds to her enforced sojourn in the back of beyond with frequent absences "on business in Odemira".

Predictably it is Sam, our eldest, who has had the most problems settling into our life here. He knew the greater stimulation of primary school in England. He's a great reader and took a long time to develop the skill in Portuguese sufficiently to be able to read the books that interested him. He has had several confrontations with the teacher. "Copy out this passage." "What does it mean?" "I'll tell you later. Copy it out." "I won't copy it out until I know what it means." A sudden reminder of how authoritarian a society Portugal was, and therefore is. After fifty years of fascism many people had forgotten, or had never learned, to think for themselves.

Now, fifteen years after the revolution, the same attitudes and ideas persist, even though the physical compulsion has disappeared. We can only explain both points of view: that he is right, but that while he is in the school he must learn to compromise. The other two boys always have the stimulation of their older brother. Sam suffers from our isolation. Eddie, the youngest, is almost more Portuguese than English. He takes his imaginary cigarettes out of his imaginary breast pocket and taps them on the table: the stance and gestures are completely Portuguese. He was under three when we came here. When we help him with his homework, it's usually in Portuguese. We hope they will all be fully bilingual when they are older and, in their turn, exercise the choice we made of where we would live. Can we also protect them from or show them an alternative to the prevalent machismo that can turn male children into strutting, demanding brats?

My neighbours, Edite and Ze, started with nothing but a couple of goats and a rented house.

In choosing the Alentejo, we chose a pre-consumer and almost pre-money society. We all have plastic carrier bags, but the shops charge for them and so we wash and re-use them. There is practically no visible rubbish: anything edible goes to the pig; anything organic disappears in the manure heap; oil cans and paint tins reappear as plant pots. The council provides big square bins at strategic places on the road and we drop off the few bits that are left. Our neighbours usually have one or two money-making lines: peanuts, maize, beans or potatoes, goats, pigs or cheese.

If there is a surplus of something, it is for giving not selling. Giving to family, giving to visitors, giving to those amazing English who are so incompetent that they don't have cabbages coming out of their ears when everybody else does. In return we give the one thing that we have and they don't: transport. Recently I was hailed by one of the ladies of the village and told there was a funeral that afternoon and would I take some of them. Eight elderly women in black chose the Landrover in preference to the taxis that were taking the rest of the villagers. I felt rather flattered.

The poorer of our neighbours have very few cash outgoings: they live entirely on their own produce. When they kill a pig, of which every scrap is used, they eat meat; the bulk is salted down to keep them going for months. Potatoes, beans and bread are eaten in quantity and so are vegetables in season. The cool dark back rooms of the clay houses are ideal for storing vegetables. We were astounded to be given tomatoes in February – they had kept perfectly since the previous October. Cash is spent on alcohol, occasional clothes, and very little else. In the house of our nearest neighbours up-valley there is a bed, a rough wooden table, and a crate for a chair. They cook over an open fire and the only light is a candle.

There are Alentejo jokes, just as England has Irish jokes. The rest of Portugal sees the Alentejans as stupid and lazy. Lazy perhaps, because they might have seen the Alentejan farmer from their cars, sitting with his back against the cool white walls of his house, looking at the distant sea. They were still in bed when the peasant did half his day's work before breakfast.

My neighbours, Edite and Ze, started with nothing but a couple of goats and a rented house. In a lifetime's work, during which their holidays can be counted on one hand, they increased the herd to 150 goats and 50 cows. The kids and calves are sold once a year; Edite sells goats' cheese of high repute. By local standards they are now wealthy people. Over the years they paid for two daughters to go to university and now, in their fifties, have bought and paid for the house and acres to which they will retire when a few more calves, a few more goats have added to the security in the bank. The only machine that assists their farming operation is a petrol pump; they do not own a vehicle. A black-and-white TV runs off a car battery; a gas light and the open fire illuminate the kitchen around which the life of the family revolves. In an unusually hopeful sign for this way of life, the youngest daughter, after trying several city jobs, has come home to work alongside her parents.

True, the trend is away from the country. The young people want electricity and the tarmac road, and the government encourages moves to pull people into the money-spending, tax-paying economy. Portugal as a whole is poised between the past and the EC dream of the future. In the early 1990s car ownership increased by eighty percent in twelve months, but with a high cost in people defaulting on credit, which was all too easy to arrange.

The older people, though, do not simply hold to their way of life through ignorance of any other. Antonio, the local contractor, worked for several years in France to pay for his tractor. Mario, who runs the local garage as a sort of semi-charity for the usually decrepit vehicles around, can afford to do so because of the money he made in Africa and the Middle East. Like in many other Mediterranean countries, there are few families who don't have someone working abroad, providing for the present or the future.

The women collect and stir the blood for black pudding and the men burn off the hair with a gas burner.

When the emigrants return they don't want to bring back the ways of more "advanced" countries: they appreciate the way of life here, the importance of the family and friends, the simple pleasures of good company, the beauty of a countryside largely unscarred by man.

It's half-past eight. Still cold at this time of year, and as we mutter greetings to our neighbours, one of the grandmothers, less than five feet tall and dressed in black (she is a widow and widows wear black for life), comes forward with cake and a tiny glass of the local *medronho* spirit, distilled from the fruit of the strawberry tree which grows wild over the hills. Down it in one, and give the ritual exhalation as the spirit burns. We are here to help our neighbours kill a pig: an excuse for a two-day celebration of eating and drinking, music and dance.

The pig is enticed out of the sty, seized firmly by six men and walked to a low table. The fearsome jaw is tied. The pig is lifted bodily on to the table. Two men hold each back leg and one the front against the death throes. The knife goes in deep, twists, and within three or four minutes of leaving the sty the pig is dead. We pause for another glass of spirits; nobody enjoys the act of killing and few of the local *matadores* will kill more than once in a day. The women collect and stir the blood for black pudding and the men burn off the hair with a gas burner. (Edite and Ze use burning gorse, but here we are modern.) Then the men scrape the skin white again with the razor sharp penknife that every countryman carries. The pig is opened and the women take the guts and organs for sorting and grading and making into sausages.

Cassimira found herself insulted by some men at the well. She took her father's shotgun and fired two rounds over their heads.

My stomach turns as I wash out the intestines, turn them inside out and wash them again. The balance of the work is with us now. Great cauldrons steam over the open fire as the pork fat is rendered down and the skin cut into pork scratchings and the sausages prepared. Meanwhile, since early morning, a separate group of women have been preparing the feast that marks the first major stage of the job; the pig has been halved and the sides separated from the head and the spine. The men lounge around drinking and smoking. Until the meat sets and they can joint it they have nothing else to do.

As in many rural societies, the division of roles is very marked: women tend to socialize with women, men with men. Some jobs are women's jobs, others men's. The women are strong and often run the families and the farms while the men go away or abroad to work. Cassimira, Edite and Ze's daughter, found herself insulted by some men at the well. She walked back up the hill, took down her father's shotgun and fired two rounds over their heads. She was fifteen. She describes with relish their hasty retreat to their car. Having seen the ease with which she hoists a hundred-weight sack of animal food on to her shoulder, I would prefer to be on her side in any fight!

Interestingly, both men and women are known by their Christian names, with or without the equivalent of Mr or Mrs. So I am Jan or

Senhora Jan and my husband is Chris or Senhor Chris, an external sign, perhaps, of the degree to which people keep their own identity.

Alanteja society is poised at a crossroads, firmly divided between the generations. At the moment it's a land of windmills and watermills, of cobblers and cartwrights, blacksmiths and coopers. A way of life very close to nature and based on the village. With a lifetime of immense hard work, the older generation have scraped together a sufficiency and in many cases considerable wealth. The fruits of that thrift are now being lavished on their children.

Our neighbours down the valley have bought their son the car they never allowed themselves. Next they will buy him a plot of land and build him a house. It is almost certain that the son will never return to till the family land.

The alternatives for the future are all too obvious. The paradise that the Algarve once was has been destroyed by piecemeal development, soaking up easy foreign money. The danger is very real that this development will spread up the more austere but totally unspoilt west coast. Inland, as the people move away from the land, the eucalyptus trees move in: mile after mile of monoculture – the fastest growing tree in the world which, after three crops and thirty years, totally depletes the soil. Many of the plantations are there to guarantee IMF loans, providing secure hard cash in terms of pulp for Northern Europe.

Our own property is an island in this sea. We feel privileged to be experiencing and sharing this life. It seems likely that soon the waves will close over a way of living that has been self-sustaining for the last two thousand years.

TRAVEL NOTES

Languages Portuguese is a difficult language, especially when it comes to pronunciation, but if you know some French and/or Spanish you shouldn't find it too hard to read. English and French are quite widely spoken in cities and most people understand Spanish (albeit reluctantly).

Transport A slow but reasonably inexpensive and efficient network of buses and trains covers most of the country. Taxis are cheap and reliable; everyone uses them all the time in Lisbon, though outside city boundaries you should negotiate fares in advance. Bicycle rental is a good, if exhausting, way of exploring the countryside.

Accommodation Reasonably inexpensive hotels and pensões are widespread, and there's little problem finding somewhere to stay, even at the height of summer. In smaller towns it's quite accepted to ask advice from the nearest friendly-looking woman, who will know who lets rooms. Staying in youth hostels is cheaper (there are about a dozen in Portugal, most of them open all year round), but you won't meet Portuguese people that way. There are also about a hundred authorized campsites, mostly small and attractive.

Guides *The Rough Guide to Portugal* (Penguin) is reliable and up-to-date.

CONTACTS

There are relatively few **women's organizations** in Portugal. The following addresses, all in Lisbon, are good initial contacts.

Comisão da Condicão Feminina, Avda de República, 32-1 Lisbon 1093. Researches and maintains a watching brief on all aspects of Portuguese women's lives; organizes meetings and conferences, and is very active in areas of social and legal reform. Also a good library and connections with feminists throughout the country.

Informação Documentação Mulheres (IDM), Rua Filipe de Mata, 115a (☎720598). Women's centre incorporating a small library and the one women-only café in Lisbon. Run by a collective of lesbian and heterosexual women, very keen to welcome foreign travellers and publicize the activities of the centre. French, German and English spoken.

Editora das Mulheres, Rua da Conceição 17 (4th floor). Feminist bookshop right in the centre of town.

Espaço-Mulheres, Rua Pedro Nunes 9a. Art gallery and meeting place for women (daily 3–7pm).

BOOKS

Maria Velho da Costa, Maria Isabel Barreno and Maria Teresa Horta, *The Three Marias: Portuguese Letters* (UK, Paladin, 1975/US, Doubleday). Collage of letters, stories and poems by three feminist writers. Hard to obtain, but worth the effort.

David Birmingham, *A Concise History of Portugal* (UK & US, Cambridge University Press, 1993). Very readable account of Portugal's history from the earliest days up to 1991.

Mike Gerrard and Thomas McCarthy (eds), *Passport to Portugal* (UK, Serpent's Tail, 1994). A selection of Portugal's finest contemporary writers. Well worth tracking down.

Thanks to Elizabeth Mullet for supplying much of the information for these Travel Notes.

Russia

A wariness is beginning to set in about travelling to Russia. The surge of optimism with which the West greeted the fall of Communism in 1991 looked set to turn the newly independent country into a major destination, with visitors, for the first time in seventy years, being able to travel and explore on their own, without being shepherded around by the state tour operator, *Intourist*. A few years on and St Petersburg has made a limited appearance on the tour circuit, as has Moscow, but few Westerners travel beyond these cities other than for

business or academic exchange. And for those that do, *Intourist* remains the dominant (and easiest) option, with its network of tours still in place in Russia and the new repubics of the old Soviet Union. Even the Trans-Siberian railway has failed to capture new business.

The reasons for this are all too familiar from news reports on the state of the "new Russia", as the hard realities of transition from Communism to "enterprise" culture have taken shape, accompanied by a rapid descent from superpower status to a country cap in hand for economic aid. Russia for travellers is, simply, a lot less safe than in the old days and equally problematic. Stories abound of mafia racketeering, a rocketing crime rate, child gangs roaming the streets of St Petersburg and Moscow, and a society polarized by massive disparities of wealth. A new elite has swiftly emerged, creaming off foreign deals and taking their pickings of the overpriced western products flooding the market, while the vast majority of Russians have found themselves impoverished by the shifting economy, and a new strata of society has to contend with real destitution. Just as it was hard to grasp what life constrained by a totalitarian regime could really be like, it's difficult now to get a measure of the insecurity and hardships flung up by a society in such a severe state of flux.

Street crime, muggings, theft and robbery on trains are all part of the new reality, even if actual violence against tourists remains no higher than in American or European cities. It's ironic that with a freedom to travel unimaginable only five years ago – you can step on and off trains in formerly prohibited areas, talk and stay with whoever you like – the main deterrent is a sense of unease, not knowing what to expect in a society where the rules keep changing. There's also the problem of expense. The new services – including most joint venture hotels, restaurants and shops – gear their prices way over the heads of ordinary tourists (and the majority of Russians), catering to the free-spending *nouveau riche* or Western businessmen. Although it's a relatively simple matter to arrange private board and lodging once you arrive, self-sufficiency is hard without a street sense that involves knowing how and where to get basic foodstuffs or do *blat* (private deals).

With the exception of the Trans-Siberian route (see below), travellers tend to keep to the Russian heartland west of the Urals, their attention fixed on the grandiose, cosmopolitan cities of Moscow and St Petersburg and the monuments of Russia's Imperial, Orthodox and Soviet past. The splendours are much as they ever were, although an air of urban decay has recently taken hold, at odds with the bright new shops and hotels. Trolley buses pass with windows smashed, ancient buildings crumble for lack of repair, the streets are poorly lit, and street markets have sprung up with stallholders trying to palm off the odd packet of cigarettes or pair of winter boots to supplement another week's income. If you like your travel tinged with an encounter with history in transition, the experience is fascinating, but – St Petersburg aside – modern Russia is no holiday.

Although most Russians now wear Western fashions, you are bound to feel conspicuous and quite vulnerable outside the tourist areas. For women, there are additional problems posed by the economic crisis, especially in the hotel bars, where many students and professionals work as prostitutes to boost meagre incomes; sitting alone over a drink can easily be misconstrued as soliciting. Sexual harassment on the streets is rarely much of a problem for tourists, and certainly no worse than in other major Western cities, though it's not considered safe to walk alone at night and Russian friends wouldn't dream of letting you do so.

In the main the old clichés of Russian hospitality, with men acting the part of old-fashioned *gallants*, still hold true – the flower-giving, the flattery, the hand-kissing, the vodka flowing freely at the merest excuse – and if you stay any length of time you will be overwhelmed by the extraordinary lengths to which people will go to entertain a guest. It's important to keep in mind the practical needs of your hosts and try to reciprocate where you can.

For many Russian women the collapse of Communism also meant dispensing with the worn-out rhetoric of sexual equality. **Feminism** had long become discredited as state propaganda, masking the realities of women foisted with low paid, low status jobs while struggling to cope with the exhausting logistics of keeping home and family together. Since 1991 a backlash has been underway, and the institutionalized sexism that lay beneath the official party line has surfaced in force combining with the need to forge new images for women. In the early days of *perestroika*, Gorbachev called on women to "return to their purely womanly mission", and as unemployment escalates, working women have become easy scapegoats, facing increasing discrimination in higher education and employment. The debunking of the heroic Soviet worker myth has led to a new emphasis on glamour: microskirts are standard interview gear, with the role of pampered housewife (for most women unobtainable) acquiring huge social cachet. The reality this time, however, is that more women are under pressure to stay at home, without the added income to make this viable and even less social assistance than previously existed under the Soviet system. Few families can get by on a single wage. As in the West, the blame for society's shortcomings is being conveniently shelved onto single mothers.

Out in the Russian Boondocks

In 1978 **Caroline Walton**, a writer living in London, took a tourist trip to Moscow. It was to be the beginning of a long involvement with the country, that led her to study Russian language, history and politics and, after the break-up of the Soviet Union, return to live and work in Samara, an obscure provincial town. She is currently completing a book about those aspects of Russian life that have endured the upheavals of the last eighty years.

I have been fascinated by Russia since my teens. I thought that a country which could produce Dostoevsky and the Bolshevik revolution must be quite extraordinary. After taking a degree in Russian politics and history I began to tackle the rich and subtle language.

My teacher in London was a Russian refugee from Samara, a city of one-and-a-half million lying on the Volga 1000km east of Moscow. It bristled with military installations which kept it closed to Westerners from 1946 to 1991 – the city was so "secret" that Volga cruise-ships carrying foreign tourists could only pass at night. When the Soviet regime collapsed my teacher arranged for her family back home to send me a personal invitation. This got me a private visa that allowed me to travel independently within the country.

I jumped at the chance to explore the mysterious deep and hidden Russia where few people would speak English. I had already visited Moscow and St Petersburg as a tourist and found their citizens fairly used to Western visitors. Provincial Russia, exemplified for me by Samara, would have a very different feel. My teacher described it as living on the edge of civilization.

I was one of the first Westerners to set foot in the region for nearly half a century. People were astonished to meet an English woman. With my fair colouring, different clothing and strange accent they assumed I came from one of the Baltic republics. My hairdresser convinced herself that I was really Polish, insisting that no Westerner in their right mind would want to live out in the Russian boondocks. Once over their initial surprise, people bombarded me with questions about what we in the West thought of them. They were embarrassed by the attempted coup in October 1993, and anxious to know how it had been portrayed on British TV.

When I first arrived in Samara, in the summer of 1992, I fell in love with the old town; its crumbling Art Nouveau mansions and elaborately carved wooden houses. It seemed untouched by the last fifty years. Beyond the centre, however, lie miles upon miles of identical twelve-storey apartment blocks, interspersed with great grey concrete bunkers which turned out to be shops and schools. I rented a flat in this region in the winter and spring of the following year and found work teaching English.

As a native speaker I was in high demand; no mention was ever made of a work permit. My greatest problem was finding out where to get hold of the basics of life. The huge local supermarket offered a selection of twelve different food items. For six weeks I combed the city for toilet paper. Staggering home over the treacherous, icy pavements clutching my three rolls, I learned the meaning of triumph.

The first room I rented was in an ancient communal flat, a wonderful, atmospheric place, but not one I should like to spend my life in. Two toilets, two cold water taps and three gas cookers served eight families. My next-door neighbour, Baba Tonia, took charge of me. She had lived for decades in the one room with her many cats and alcoholic husband and her main joy and solace was the American TV soap, *Santa Barbara*. She fell in love with my *Sainsbury's* bag, which I gave her. Two days later she came to me crying, saying she had lost her pretty little bag. I fished out another for her. Thereafter, if I ever threw rubbish out in a carrier bag, she would open it, pick through the waste to see if anything was salvageable, and return the bag to me, carefully washed.

In order to survive, Russians weave a labyrinthine web of friends and acquaintances around themselves. This network is used to obtain the unobtainable. I was sometimes mystified by the wheelings and dealings going on around me – until I considered that the money economy does not have the pre-eminence that it has in the West. The Soviet system worked in two ways: things were either bought or obtained through *blat*, power and influence. There is an old joke that if you want something the shops are the last place you look. This still holds true. When I needed a train ticket from Samara to Moscow, for example, I found every berth booked for a month in advance. Even the tourist office, which sells tickets to foreigners in hard currency at five times the rouble price, could not sell me a ticket. Baba Tonia's best friend, however, used to work on the railways and she had a friend in the local government offices . . . I received a first-class ticket for roubles for the date I wanted, and I presented the ladies concerned with drums of imported tea and *Sainsbury's* bags.

> *Sometimes I felt I played the twentieth-century "general at the wedding", seated beside the host at a dinner.*

Russians invest great effort in cultivating potentially useful contacts. A foreigner opens up a whole new bag of possibilities and that is partly why so many people will fall over themselves to make friends. On my first visit I was bowled over by kindness and attention; on my second I sank into depression when I realized how calculated some of this hospitality was. The third time around I understood that people were being practical rather than cynical and found it amusing trying to guess the significance of each friendly overture.

Occasionally I was completely off the mark. One businesswoman stuffed me with caviar, took me to the opera, and even bought presents for my parents. I guessed that I had been earmarked to chaperone her teenage daughter on a trip to London. I was wrong. My closest friend in Samara worked for this woman. One day he told me that she had summoned him into her office and asked him to lend her a million roubles. He was obligated to her because of her generosity to me, apparently. My friend said he had never realized how grasping his fellow countrypeople were until he saw them around me. I saw that my presence altered the equation of relationships between people.

Sometimes I felt I played the twentieth-century equivalent of the "general at the wedding", seated beside the host at a dinner in an attempt to lend prestige to the gathering. I discovered that three hours is the minimum length of stay, however casual the invitation. Drinks have to be downed in one and being female is no excuse. I found it easier to refuse all alcohol than to start drinking and then bow out. I said it was on doctor's orders and was deliberately vague about my ailment. Vodka will be recommended as a cure for everything, including cystitis.

I was often asked for practical help, such as an invitation to England. I was happy to comply with such requests, but expectations of me could be absurdly exaggerated. For example, a former KGB Major invited me to dine at his home. Friendly and garrulous, he told me he had shadowed Mrs Thatcher in a Tblisi theatre. A blimpish MI6 agent had approached him, "KGB I presume?" I laughed, and he went on to explain that he was tired of his country; could I help him find a job with our security services?

Women my age looked years older. Daily life in Russia exhausted me – and I had no family to look after.

After a while I made it a rule never to accept invitations unless I felt I knew what was expected of me in return. I did not like being taken by surprise and felt embarrassed at refusing impossible requests. Despite my guardedness I made genuine friends. I mainly mixed with women and very young men; from their twenties onwards most males devote themselves to pickling their brains in vodka. My female friends were bawdy, boundlessly kind and intellectually curious.

I have never had so much fun with women anywhere in the world as I have in Russia; it is one of the reasons I keep returning. I have travelled alone in many countries and grown used to questions about what I am doing without a man to protect me. I have even been annoyed by women who suggest I have ventured so far from home in order to find a man. Russian women, on the other hand, were curious rather than judgmental. They wanted to know what I did, how much I earned, how much it costs to travel and where else I had been. A Russian woman in her thirties without husband or children is a rare exception and subject to heavy social pressure. But they have heard that many forms of behaviour are possible in the West and they were tolerant of my eccentricities.

I was stunned by the conservatism of provincial Russian society. Racism, particularly directed against gypsies and Muslims from the former republics to the South, is overt, as is homophobia. Young girls want to be married by 21. "If we leave it till 26 or 27 no one will have us", a student told me. Higher education makes no difference to girls' aspirations: if they are really lucky they might marry one of the new breed of businessmen and then not have to work at all.

The economy of every country in the world would collapse if female labour were withdrawn; nowhere is this more apparent than in Russia. They shoulder the double burden of work in the home and (usually) low-paid outside jobs. I knew of few men who helped with household chores. Despite myself, I must have swallowed some Soviet propaganda about the equal status of women. In reality I was shocked by the drudgery of their lives. Women my age looked years older. Daily life in Russia exhausted me – and I had no family to look after. Shopping and cleaning and washing everything by hand took hours. Sometimes water or electricity was cut without warning. Women complained to me that they were tired out. So was I, but I had the option of going back to England for a rest.

Strolling along the Volga one balmy May evening, it dawned on me that everyone else was pissed out of their brains.

Russian women drink more than their British counterparts, but still hold their lives together far better than their men. On Easter Sunday I watched a magnificent procession of drunks pass down the road from the cemetery. People came by in threes: a man in the middle supported on either side by his wife and mother. I thought each trio made a perfect representation of Russian family life.

Some women refer to their husbands as a second child. They will resignedly tuck him up in bed when he staggers in drunk. It seems that the main reason why so many women tolerate their dire relationships is low wages. On average they earn thirty percent less than men. They are concentrated in low-paying "female" professions such as health-care or teaching. I knew a university lecturer who earned fifty thousand roubles a month, for example, and a young male police constable who earned more than double her salary.

Most divorces are initiated by wives and the chief reason given is the husband's alcoholism. A few young women opt for single motherhood. An acquaintance told me she had decided not to marry the father of her son. As a single mother she would move up the housing queue and qualify for an allowance for the child (equivalent to a dollar a month, which buys four litres of milk). There is worry in high circles about this tendency (sounds familiar . . .) and much is made of the danger to the child of the absence of a male influence while growing up. Although the good of this influence if the male is a raving alcoholic, as is so often the case, seems dubious to say the least.

My social life centred on the hut of a Ukrainian wise-woman called Lina Ivanovna. She dispensed herbal remedies to people distrustful of conventional medicine or too poor to buy it. She had learned her skills from her grandmother during the Nazi occupation of their village. There had been no doctors for the civilian population; the villagers relied on the herbs and incantations of Lina's grandmother. Lina also reads futures in the cards; all sorts of people used to come for readings, including Communist Party officials.

I would sit in Lina's foetid hut with dogs, kittens, and rabbits playing around my feet. Her cronies were a vivid hotch-potch of nationalities. Zhenya, the raddled old gypsy, was a refugee from Moldova.

> *Russian male friends shared my feelings of unease; some had bought guns as "protection".*

Resplendent in purple lurex, she would heave with laughter at my accent. Zuzanna the Georgian girl was worried by her family's threats to send her home, marry her off, and force her to give up her studies in favour of domestic duties. Vera the Cossack dyed her hair a violent red and dripped with jewellery. She complained that her neighbour had denounced her for selling vodka without a licence. "Well it's true I was selling vodka, but what can I do, I have an invalid son to support?"

"Who is in gaol for GBH", whispered Lina Ivanovna. One day a shy, pregnant woman arrived, asking for a card reading. She was desperate to find out where her husband was; he had been missing for five days. Lina gently sent her away, then told me she was sure the man was dead. A week later his body was found with face and hands sliced off. He had been murdered by the local mafia for a debt of four thousand dollars.

The rebirth of capitalism in Russia is brutal and has led to a massive upsurge in crime. A few people have become very rich while hyperinflation has impoverished the majority. Wages buy so little that more and more people turn to robbery, extortion and all sorts of racketeering. Despite all the talk of banditry I only felt uneasy at night, when the streets are empty of all but the drunk and the villainous. Strolling along the Volga one balmy May evening, it dawned on me that everyone else on the street was pissed out of their brains. Groups of extremely dodgy-looking men hung around expensive cars parked on the embankment. Russian male friends shared my feelings of unease; some had bought guns as "protection". It made me sad: the Soviet Union used to feel safer than any other country I knew.

Another ominous change is the flooding of the market with Western products. I was surprised at the quality of Russian food: at one time, lack of choice was made up for by taste and freshness. In the course of a year I noticed local produce disappear from the shops to be replaced by expensive Western foods bursting with chemicals. Excellent chocolate is made in Samara, for example, but this became harder and harder to find, while Mars and Snickers were everywhere. Television zaps out a constant stream of adverts for Western goods.

Returning to Moscow after five months in the provinces was a culture shock. Feeling like a home-coming exile, I had to readjust my mind to different sights and conversations. In Moscow women drive cars, and at dinner parties they discuss the influence of Zen Buddhism on the works of J D Salinger. I had grown used to discourses on the price of Mars bars.

Samara and its environs had shown me the quintessential Soviet land of industrial cities and collective farms. My time there was pre-

A friend is joining a seventeenth-century sect of religious flagellants. Another is waiting for a big strong Western man.

cious and unforgettable, but if I were to live in Russia again I would choose Moscow. As a person who prefers London to the rest of England, and New York to America, I tune into the pace and freedom of Moscow's cosmopolitan atmosphere. There I no longer feel like a fish out of water or, as the Russians say, a white raven. I am at home in Moscow; it functions as a great city should, and in some respects is a gentle introduction to the rest of the country. It has a veneer of sophistication, transport is logical and nowadays the shops are crammed with imported food and clothing. However the Westernization process has begun to take its toll; among other excrescences the city now boasts a "British Pub".

More than anywhere else, Moscow reflects the nation's changing economy. Extremes of wealth and poverty have become blatant. In places the capital sports a *nouveau-riche* facade, while the mainline stations have a Third-World aspect, to put it mildly. Yet it remains a fascinating and surreal city. At the Architects' Union a friend tells me she is joining a seventeenth-century sect of religious flagellants. Never mind the economic crisis, she is worried about saving her soul. Another friend is waiting for a big strong man from the West to sweep her off her feet. In a co-operative restaurant decorated with pink plaster pregnant ladies I overhear a woman extol the wonders of corsetry. In the Novodevichy cemetery for the glorious dead a *babushka* peers at the photo on the tomb of a general. She invites me to join her in counting the hundreds of medals on his chest.

Moscow has always enticed me with the beauty and drama of its past. I would take long solitary walks within the inner ring road, recognizing the old haunts of the heroines of Pasternak and Bulgakov and letting the city unfurl its history in the courtyards, stucco mansions and tiny onion-dome churches. Moscow's seven brooding grey Stalin towers seem oddly reassuring after the Asiatic wilderness of the provinces.

Despite the rising crime rate I find Moscow no more dangerous than London. The city centre is better policed than elsewhere in the country. After dark it felt safer than Samara, and there were plenty of women on the streets. Muscovite friends shared my confidence, although they advised against late-night forays into the suburbs. In Samara women hardly go out after dark because there are almost no public places to go to. When visiting friends in the evening I would stay the night if they could not arrange a lift home.

While Westerners are still a novelty in the provinces and are feted accordingly, Muscovites are growing used to foreigners. I heard some Americans complain about hostility from locals who resent Western economic interference. On the other hand Russian friends have complained of condescension from certain Western teachers and technical advisors. As always, a visitor's reception will depend on her attitude. In my experience, those who are willing to have their preconceptions shattered will reap the greatest rewards.

The collapse of the Soviet Union has made a big difference to me, for it means I can travel more or less freely within Russia and talk to who-ever I like. Three years ago this would have been inconceivable. However, so-called democracy has done little to improve the quality of life of the majority of Russians. They still need internal passports, and know that bribery is the only way to get things done. I am always sobered when I reach my first port-of-call in Russia: the foreign visitors' registration office. There, in a little office on the banks of the Volga, sits a faceless bureaucrat with great power. A portrait of Lenin hangs over her head just as it has always done. The country is run by people who have simply swapped their hammer-and-sickle badges for the double-headed eagle .

Each time I leave Russia my spirits soar. Back home I stand in super-markets gawping at our overstocked shelves. It still amazes me to watch people board a London bus in rush hour without a punch-up. But after a couple of months I start to miss Russia. It must be like having a baby. Memories of the sheer physical discomfort recede: the cold, the crush on the buses, frustration with the idiocy of daily life. As I recover from exhaustion I feel nostalgic for the existence that is so much more intense than the one I know at home.

Passing Time on the Trans-Siberian

As a young child **Katharine Nicholls** moved with her family to Bulgaria for two years. She would gaze across the Black Sea trying to imagine the vast mass of land on the other side. Years later, as Communism and the USSR began to collapse, she collected her savings and brought herself a ticket on the Trans-Siberian Railway. She currently lives and works in London as a freelance illustrator.

The Trans-Siberian Railway from Moscow to Beijing, I had decided, was the kind of experience that one could have without actually doing too much and yet would fulfil all the normal requirements of a real adventure. I therefore went for a first-class berth on a Russian train (there's a Chinese one too) with a two-night stop-over at Lake Baikal, easing myself in gently by first doing a package tour of the Baltic State capitals.

When the two-week tour suddenly came to an end in St Petersburg, I was devastated. My sister kissed me goodbye early in the morning before setting off for the airport with all our other jolly tour companions. I hadn't anticipated that I would feel so emotional. It was the best holiday I'd ever had, so why did I have to spoil it all by heading off across Russia on my own? The *Intourist* rep was hardly reassuring: "I think it is very uncomfortable to travel on the Trans-Siberian Railway", she said, "I would never want to do it myself". Why should she? Why should anyone want to go on such a long and tiring journey? My diary entry for that morning was splattered with cowardly tears.

I checked out of the hotel and with my bags in the cloakroom, spent the day wandering dreamily around the icy streets of St Petersburg, peering closely at the Rembrandt portraits in the Winter Palace, contemplating the history of October Square and pushing my way through the crowds on the Nevsky Prospekt. As the light faded I stood stroking the gravestone of Dostoevsky in a cemetery packed with famous men.

Later, on my way back to the railway station, a thin, blond man offered me a bunch of red carnations. In cynical, London style I refused them, sure that otherwise he'd follow and hassle me. We boarded the metro train together and he sat next to me, all the time insisting that I take the flowers. An old lady, plumped opposite, weary with shopping, seemed to disapprove of the whole charade so, after a few more attempts to refuse, I decided to give in gracefully, beam my hearty thanks and accept his offering. My suitor handed over the flowers with a wounded nod of acknowledgement. That was all. He didn't want to talk after that, though I tried, and we sat for the rest of the journey in glum silence, the flowers awkwardly between us. He showed no desire to follow me off the train.

The attendant on the overnight journey to Moscow ushered me into a two-berth compartment almost entirely filled by a huge, bearded man wearing a skimpy, white vest that displayed his hairy chest to full advantage. Despite his welcoming, gold and white smile, it seemed like a good idea to take up the attendant's offer of another berth, for a small fee, all to myself. Sleeping peacefully that night it never occurred to me that the recipient of my two dollars would be spending the hours bolt upright on a wooden seat. In the morning he appeared with a cup of tea and I offered him a pack of Marlboro, hoping to compensate for the dark pouches under his eyes.

When we stopped at our first station, Yaroslavl, where Anna Karenina had first met Count Vronsky, I was decidedly unwell.

This prompted him to disappear and return with a bag full of souvenirs and the inevitable military hats to flog. The red carnations were lying limp on the table and I idly dropped some water on the stems. That evening, in a tourist hotel in Moscow I arranged them in a vase, bemused by how much I now wanted to keep them alive. Outside a thin fall of snow had begun to transform the grey rooftops.

At breakfast I shared a table with two elderly Canadian women who, having just completed a six-week tour of Central Asia, were tucking into some dry black bread and fatty sausage and showering praise on the "fine service and wonderful guest care" of the hotel staff. It was good to hear such positive words after our indulgent wrinkled up noses and endless complaints about food on the tour.

The *Intourist* guide who had taken us bravely on her last "Baltic Capitals" tour, fending off the anti-Russian sentiment that she'd encountered along the way, had asked me to spend the day with her. We met that morning on the outskirts of Moscow and hugged each other like old friends. Arm in arm we wandered around an enormous craft market on an icy piece of wasteland, gazing at the paintings strung up on washing lines between the silver birches. By evening the beginnings of a raging temperature had taken hold and I had to summon up all my reserves of energy for the evening's big occasion, a huge dinner in my honour, with all her relatives. She had spent the previous two days shopping and cooking for the occasion.

Twenty-four hours later I was sitting in a first-class compartment on the dark-green Trans-Siberian train, dosed up with aspirins and smiling apprehensively at the Russian businessman sitting opposite, wondering whether or not he spoke any English. He didn't, and with my ten or so words of Russian, our conversation didn't exactly sparkle. The train began to slide quietly out of Moscow in a pink, winter dusk. I looked out and noted with mixed feelings that the snow was really getting quite thick. When we stopped at our first station, Yaroslavl, where Anna Karenina had first met Count Vronsky, I was decidedly unwell. By eight o'clock my companion and I were tucked up in our respective berths. We'd given up trying to communicate, with final snorts of disgust at the phrase book, some time ago. Now, as the train clanked steadily into the night, we slept, he snoring softly just inches away from me and our heavy sliding door firmly locked against the other passengers.

The solid fuel stoves in our carriage belted out heat all night long and the next morning I woke up sweating and exhausted, with a severe headache and a parched mouth. I dressed as secretly as I could and rushed out to drain the samovar. Two cups of tea later, some body fluid had been replaced but I still felt very weak. As I looked out at the little blue and green houses dotted among the snow-covered pine trees, I resolved to obtain the forbidden window key for that night, reassuring myself that if necessary I would use "dollar power" to achieve this.

"Nyet" said the *provodnitsa* (carriage attendant), and again with a firm shake of the head, "Nyet". She didn't appear open to negotiation at that moment, so I decided to try again later. I knew that this was not supposed to happen, according to Eric Newby's *The Big Red Train Ride*. I should be able to make friends with her and charm her into giving me the key. The trouble was that she had a shrill, military-like authority that didn't invite immediate friendship.

I sat back and thought about the previous day, when Olga had not only fed me with what was probably a week's supply of precious fresh food – vegetables, cheese and sausage – but had also laden me with presents. On being shown round her apartment I'd made the mistake of admiring a large Chinese vase in an otherwise bare room, only to have to spend the next ten minutes begging her not to give it to me. Luckily I had the excuse of travelling light, but it took descriptions of hoped-for mountain climbing expeditions before she reluctantly accepted that the vase should stay where it was. However, I did walk away with a large bag full of baked black breadsticks, a jar of strawberry jam, a packet of Indian tea, a bottle of vodka and a painted egg. In return, my sister and I had given her some French cosmetics and perfumes with which she had been gratifyingly delighted.

In faint wintry sunshine I saw young boys skating on frozen ponds, dark pine woods looming behind rickety wooden houses with white gardens and ice-covered haystacks. I fancied a nice cup of hot tomato soup. My companion watched with fascination as I pulled open a plastic telescopic glass, the one my boyfriend had lovingly equipped me with on my departure. I emptied the contents of the package into the extended glass, smiled briefly at my audience and hopped out of the compartment to fill it with freshly boiled water from the samovar. He did have the grace to turn away when I re-emerged two minutes later in some pain and smelling strongly of tomato soup, the collapsed glass in my hand.

> *My companion left the train. I wasn't terribly upset: it had felt a bit like a failed arranged marriage.*

The *baboushka* could be heard shouting outside our door while I cowered inside, convinced that the whole carriage was being told of my folly. The telescopic glass, I noted, was for cold drinks only.

It was getting dark when we stopped at Perm, home at that time to the last remaining political prisoners of the Soviet Union. I jumped enthusiastically onto the black ice covering the platform, but it was not my feet I landed on. I looked swiftly up and down, told myself there was little point in risking my health by standing in a deep-freeze and hopped gratefully back to the tropical heat of our compartment.

We trundled on towards Siberia, metal searing through ice as we approached the Ural Mountains. At this point, the guidebook informed me, excited crowds would gather in the corridor to witness the "puny white obelisk that marks the border between Europe and Asia". There probably was another tourist on the train somewhere, I thought, although I hadn't seen one on the platform and my carriage was made up solely of Russian men, bored long-distance commuters, who obliviously read their newspapers and checked their watches. I asked someone the time and was surprised to learn that we'd already crossed two time zones. At Sverdlovsk (1818km from Moscow) my companion left the train. I wasn't terribly upset: it had felt a bit like a failed arranged marriage.

A comfortable plump woman came in next, showing lots of metal teeth in a large smile and clutching paper bags full of sweets and little biscuits. She hung up a very stiff fur coat and mopped her streaming eyes. On discovering that I didn't speak Russian she shook her head in disbelief, made a few more attempts to try and jolt my brain into action and then finally, threw up her hands in despair and gave in to the dreadful situation. After that we relaxed and smiled at one another a lot. I was grateful to her for being a woman and for putting bags of sweets at my disposal.

The daylight hours were so short that it was dark by 4.30pm and I read in the guide that we were crossing the "dreary Great Siberian Plain" and that it was time to get one's book out. I had two to choose from: Dostoevsky's *Brothers Karamazov*, carefully chosen to intensify the "Russianness" of the experience, which I firmly rejected in favour of Jane Austen's more escapist *Persuasion*. I became lost in the minutiae of English society.

At Omsk my woman left the train and I watched her walk down the platform towards the dusty, windy city where quite a few of the political exiles had ended up, including Dostoevsky himself. My sadness at her departure was diminished immediately by the attractiveness of the young man who took her place. Something wonderful happened to my sign language skills: he spoke no English, French or German but together we drew pictures, sang Beatles songs and ate Siberian meat pancakes. He was a military aircraft pilot stationed in Novosibursk. His name was Dmitri and I know little more than that about him; but I do have some excellent sketches of watermelons and some temperature charts in my diary that he made in response to my questions about Siberian agriculture. We made full use of the much despised phrasebook and at one point I saw him hesitate over the "chatting up a girl" section, athough neither of us asked the question that was in the air – "Are you attached?" Outside the sky glowed pink over luminous snow and ramshackle villages. Clumps of silver birches flashed past the window and solid white streams ran like ribbons alongside the train. We were crossing the Barbara Steppe and clattering towards a very red sunset.

Suddenly we were at Novosibursk. The past five hours had whizzed past and there was Dmitri putting on his coat and hat. A blast of freezing air swept through the carriage as we shook hands and then suddenly he was gone, lost among the crowds on the platform. I returned glumly to my seat, wishing we'd exchanged addresses and knowing it was extremely unlikely I'd ever have a reason to visit Novosibursk. The guidebook confirmed this by saying there was very little architecture from before the revolution; nevertheless I told myself I would surely have to verify this one day – after all, these guidebooks can often get it wrong . . .

We passed an old man trying hard to extract one of the logs from a dishevelled pile half buried in the snow. Nobody had replaced Dmitri in my compartment and I was alone as we forged our way in deepening snow from Western into Eastern Siberia.

Later that evening, feeling quite well again and having tested the dining car and found, contrary to expectations, that it served some very edible food, I heard a knock at the door. I opened it and recognized a

> *He walked in, closing the door behind him, and asked in almost polite sign language whether I would sleep with him.*

young soldier whom I'd noticed hanging around outside my compartment and whose silent attentions had recently begun to make me feel uneasy. He walked straight into the room, closing the door behind him, and asked in almost polite sign language whether I would sleep with him. I asked him to leave but he made it clear that he had no intention of doing so. I'm quite proud of what I did next: I calmly leaned towards him and put my arms around his neck as though to kiss him. Surprised by this, he allowed himself to be pushed far enough backwards for me to slip open the door behind him. It had been a risk, but I had made it out into the corridor where his friend was standing, and began yelling my head off in English, anything I could think of. His friend finally put a restraining hand on his shoulder to lead him away and I retreated to my room in a flurry of tears and wrote furiously in my diary all evening.

We stopped for fifteen minutes at Krasnoyarsk, the city where Lenin was exiled before the revolution. I put the previous incident behind me and jumped out onto the platform. A peasant woman was selling cabbage *blinis* (pancakes) and people held them in bare hands as they ate, which amazed me as I'd just been informed that the temperature had now reached minus 20°C. A few scarlet-faced passengers boarded the train, hoisting up children bundled up in furs like little round teddy bears.

The next morning we entered deep pine forests and, catching occasional glimpses of dark wooden cottages among the trees, I decided this must have been the homeland of the witches of my childhood. My new, rather domineering, travelling companion was playing his tinny radio at full volume and tapping his foot contentedly to the high-pitched voices belting out tuneless songs. I glowered at him. His coat and hat had been tossed cheerfully onto my bed and I realized how territorial I had become. Lest I should develop "cabin fever", I walked out into the corridor to gaze at the rocky foothills of the Sayan mountains on the other side of which lay Mongolia. The shady figure of the soldier who had caused me grief the previous day, sent me back to the carriage, glad, suddenly, of the large physical presence of my new companion and quite happy to accommodate his hat and coat. My protector, it turned out, was a military doctor with lots of merry vodka-drinking friends on the train who shortly piled into our compartment and poured me out a large glass of the potent Russian spirit. Well-oiled, we spent a pleasant few hours attempting to beat down the language barrier, competing with the radio which was periodically turned up to the deafening volume that they all seemed to enjoy immensely.

My personal stereo had caused some interest in our carriage. A very beautiful Russian girl with long dark plaits and rosy cheeks appeared (to the delight of the military doctors), having heard about this piece of equipment, and I was asked to repeat several times the price I'd paid for it, translated into roubles. She was disappointed, however, with my choice of tapes; to attempt to make up for this I sprayed her wrists with Rive Gauche perfume which she also disliked, wrinkling up her small freckled nose in disgust.

> *The cold was quite a shock, having sweated my way through the past four days in a T-shirt.*

It was my last evening. That night I was due to leave the train at Irkutsk and I was looking forward to spending two nights in a hotel, to having a shower and to seeing Lake Baikal. There were varying opinions throughout the carriage as to what time we'd arrive and at one point, anxious not to miss my stop, I carried my possessions down the steps and onto the platform only to be called back by a group of giggling people: I had got the wrong time zone. When we did finally arrive in Irkutsk the cold was quite a shock, having sweated my way through the past four days in a T-shirt. I slithered around on the platform trying to look confident, while kind women pointed me in the direction of the exit. With clothes and rucksack proclaiming me a tourist, I was eventually found stepping over sleeping bodies in the crowded station by the Irkutsk *Intourist* representative and led to a waiting minibus.

Ten minutes later we were speeding along the hilly roads that led towards Lake Baikal. The "we" now included a Swiss girl of about twenty, very bright, who spoke fluently in English, French, German, Italian and had just learned Russian on the train, the language in which she now chatted to the driver. I told myself that I had other qualities. There was also Jane, English and my age, who hadn't yet mastered the native tongue, I was pleased to discover. They had met on the train in second-class and told me they'd had a "fantastic time", having met loads of "fun people" and that there had been a party every night. I replied that I had had a similar time and smiled convincingly; but they looked doubtful. As we talked the mini-bus, gathering speed on the black-iced road, suddenly veered towards the verge. I shot out a hand and shook the driver on the shoulder who woke up with a start and saved us from the ditch by a dramatic skid. For the next seventy kilometres we sang loud clapping songs in order to keep him awake. Having hardly communicated with anyone for a few days except in mime, it felt a little odd to be now stamping my feet, clapping my hands and singing, often solo, at the top of my voice.

In my wonderful hotel room later that night I opened the French windows, put a blanket around my shoulders and stood on the balcony overlooking Lake Baikal. It's the oldest and deepest lake on earth and contains a fifth of the world's fresh water. It's also home to some otherwise extinct species because of the high oxygen content. There was a strange rhythmic sound floating across the water that night and the atmosphere was made even more eerie by the smoky gases rising from the lake as it prepared to freeze over for the winter. I had yet to cross Mongolia and to see some of China; but at that moment I was sure nothing could be more impressive than this. Surrounded by mountains, it was described by the writer Valentin Rasputin as "the great cathedral of nature". Standing in its pulpit, immersed in splendour, I pondered some of the most trivial thoughts that could possibly have come to my mind: would I have had a better time had I met the two girls on the train? Answer: Yes . . . but I'm glad I didn't. I had met them now, though, and was infused with contentment at the sheer security of it.

TRAVEL NOTES

Languages Russian. It's worth learning the Cyrillic alphabet to decipher maps and street signs. Outisde the main tourist areas relatively few people speak English.

Transport Trains are the main form of transport (flights are expensive and have a poor reputation for safety). City metros run till the early hours, though in Moscow and St Petersburg these can feel unsafe late at night. Most Russians get about their cities by flagging down passing cars (breadvans, ambulances, any vehicle will do) and negotiating a paid lift. This is not advisable on your own.

Accommodation Moscow and St Petersburg offer a range of places to stay, from outrageously expensive international-class hotels, to seedy Russian joints, stamping grounds of pimps and racketeers. Few tourists can afford more than the low-budget, rudimentary, but reasonably safe travellers guest houses, although the new youth hostel in St Petersburg promises to be a big hit. Another option is to take a package tour and have accommodation sorted out in advance or to arrange a private room with Russian contacts.

Red tape is still a problem if you want to stay in the provinces. Your best bet is to contact provincial schools and colleges who are often willing to make visa and accommodation arrangements in return for some language practice with a native English-speaker.

Special Problems Bureaucracy is still the biggest hurdle. If travelling by private invitation your visa must state the areas you wish to visit. Once in that area you are supposed to register yourself at the office which supplied the invitation. In practice, it is quite possible to visit other cities without showing your visa and get visa extensions without too much trouble. As regards safety, the usual rules apply – hide cash and valuables and don't flaunt your relative wealth. This is made easier by the fact that urban Russian women generally dress extremely well. Russians are deeply conservative, especially in the provinces, and unconventional clothes, ripped jeans, nose rings etc, are frowned upon. Drinking in Russia is in a stratosphere of its own and many people think a party tame without a brawl. Drunks are a constant nuisance, and sometimes a threat, for men as well as women.

Guides *The Rough Guide to Moscow* and to *St Petersburg* (Penguin) manage not only to encapsulate two cities in flux, but handle the history, culture, politics and practical information with verve and precision. For wider Russian travels, there are useful sections in the now dated *USSR – A Travel Survival Kit* (Lonely Planet).

CONTACTS

Moscow: *Lotus*, c/o Anastasia Posadskaya, Institute of Socio-economic Studies of Population, Academy of Sciences, Krasikova 27, Moscow 117218 (☎129 0653). Small feminist research group that welcomes books, articles or research papers from the West.

St Petersburg: *The Women's Centre*, ul Stekhanovsteva 13 (☎528 18 30). Founded by Olga Lipovskaya, the centre publishes a journal called *Zhenskaya Chitenie* ("Women's Reading").

BOOKS

★ **Mary Morris**, *Wall to Wall: A Woman's Travels from Beijing to Berlin* (UK, Flamingo, 1993/US, Penguin, 1992). Includes a journey across Russia in the late 1980s. Her easy prose style and light touch with dialogue make this an engaging, often moving, read.

Susan Richards, *Epics of Everyday Life* (UK & US, Penguin, 1991). Having made four trips to Russia between 1988 and 1990, in this book Richards manages to encapsulate the anachronistic, sometimes surreal aspects of Russian life, poised between the new and old order.

Christina Dodwell, *Beyond Siberia* (UK, Sceptre, 1994/Can, Remploy Press). A byword for intrepid journeys, Christina Dodwell this time crosses the vast territories of eastern Siberia towards Alaska, herding reindeer, driving dogsleds and skiing frozen rivers en route.

Anastasia Posadskaya (ed), *Women in Russia* (UK & US, Verso, 1994). Contributions from a range of Russian women provide a powerful indictment of women's oppression under the Soviet system, with a clear-sighted appraisal of the new pressures and challenges being faced.

Anna Lina Bukharina, *This I Cannot Forget* (UK, Pandora, 1994/US, Norton). These memoirs by the wife of the charismatic Bolshevik leader and revolutionist, Nikolai Bukharin, give an extraordinary insider's view of the revolutionary elite that created the Soviet Union.

Christine Sutherland, *The Princess of Siberia* (UK, Robin Clark, 1985/US, Farrar, Straus & Giroux, 1984). Follows the life of Russian socialite and politico, Princess Maria Volkonsky, who accompanied her husband into exile after the

failed Decembrist uprising of 1825. With fellow exiles they exerted a subtle but enduring influence on the life of their frozen outpost.

Larissa Vasilieva, *Kremlin Wives* (UK, Wiedenfeld & Nicholson, 1994/US, Arcade). From Lenin's widow to "the Raisa phenomenon", Vasilieva charts the often tragic lives of the women who teamed up with the Soviet power-brokers.

Irina Ratushinskaya, *Grey Is the Colour of Hope* (UK, Sceptre, 1989/US, Vintage), *In the Beginning* (UK, Hodder & Stoughton, 1990/US, Knopf, 1991). The first describes the dissident poet's experiences in a labour camp, the second explores her childhood and faith.

FICTION

Maria Khmelik, *Little Vera* (UK, Bloomsbury, 1990). The book of the film (including a fascinating appendix of readers' letters), considered far-fetched and melodramatic by some, an accurate portrayal of Russian family life by others.

Alexandra Kollontai, *Love of Worker Bees* (UK, Virago, 1977/US, Academy Chicago Editions, 1978) and *A Great Love* (Ayer, reprint of 1929 edition). One of the most remarkable figures of the revolution, Kollontai was the only female member of the Boshevik Central Committee. She fled to Norway at the height of Stalin's purges, where she wrote these two collections.

Tatyana Tolstoya, *On the Golden Porch* (UK, Penguin, 1990/US, Vintage). Highly acclaimed collection of short stories that draw on a wealth of Russian characters and settings. Also look out for her latest collection, *Sleepwalker in a Fog* (UK, Penguin, 1993/US, Vintage), a novella and several short stories, again celebrating the lives of her people.

Julia Voznesenskaya, *The Women's Decameron* (UK, Quartet, 1986/US, Holt, 1987). Combining humour with blunt realism, Voznesenskaya sketches the lives of ten women brought together on a Russian labour ward. An immediate best-seller when it was launched in the West.

Thanks to Caroline Walton for help in compiling these Travel Notes.

Saudi Arabia

I slam of the stern Wahabite tradition dominates all aspects of life in Saudi Arabia. Although Western technology is welcome, its culture most clearly is not. The country permits no tourism. With the exception of Muslims, who can obtain pilgrimage visas to visit the holy sites of Mecca and Medina, foreigners can only enter the country on work or family visas.

However, due to Saudi's oil industry – the country is the world's leading exporter – foreign workers make up a significant part of its population. Among this large community, the vast majority migrant workers from the Arab world, are several thousand Westerners. Most women among them are on family visas, accompanying their husbands, but a significant number come independently as teachers, doctors, nannies and nurses.

Western women living in Saudi Arabia are faced with numerous restrictions. It is illegal for a woman to

drive; it is essential to dress extremely modestly and to keep to the areas marked out for women – the rear of buses, the "family section" of a restaurant and so forth. Failure to observe these and many other practices (see the *Travel Notes* at the end of this chapter) can lead to severe reprimands or arrest by the *mutawa*, the religious police. At the same time, Western women, particularly single workers, are vulnerable to harassment – both from Saudi men for failing to conform to the role expected of women, and from the large numbers of foreign bachelors.

Westerners are usually housed in special compounds, often luxuriously equipped; however, with strict curfews for women, these can become stiflingly insular. Reports are that the various rules and regulations have an infantalizing effect and many foreign wives, like their Saudi counterparts, complain of abject boredom. It's not easy to explore the cities, let alone travel around the Kingdom on your own. Most women join up with other ex-patriates for trips around the country.

Saudi **women** are expected to lead traditional, secluded lives, their roles strictly confined to that of wife and mother. On the rare occasions when they go out, they are heavily veiled and accompanied by their husbands, fathers or brothers. Their participation in the open labour force is one of the lowest in the world, though, with the widespread introduction of female education in the 1960s, changes have started to take place. Women are now encouraged to work in segregated female sectors (as teachers, doctors, social workers, nurses, etc), and the government has also begun to consider the economic advantages of employing women outside of teaching and social services instead of relying on a large foreign workforce. Moves in this direction provoke much opposition from the conservative Muslims in the country, but at the same time there is a growing movement among Saudi women, backed by liberal men, advocating women's greater participation in economic and social life.

Back Behind the Veil

Alice Arndt first went to Saudi Arabia in 1975, on a two-year teaching contract; she returned ten years later to live, with her husband.

I first arrived in the Kingdom nearly two decades ago, washed in on the wave of modern technology, foreign workers and petrodollars. If you had asked me then, I would have told you that, of course, in a few years Saudi women would be driving cars, veils would gradually disappear, and that the shops which closed their doors at prayer times would constitute an ever smaller minority. I noted the increasing educational opportunities for women, and felt certain that they would soon lead to demands from the women for further work opportunities and ultimately for emancipation. And the large number of young Saudi men who were being sent to other countries for advanced degrees would surely be infected with more liberal attitudes towards the women at home. I assumed without question that the East–West gap would gradually close, and took it for granted that exposure to Western customs and values would lead inevitably to their adoption.

Well, it hasn't turned out that way at all. It is still illegal for a woman to drive or own an automobile or to ride a bicycle. Today, virtually every shop closes up tight during the several daily prayers, and any shopkeeper who's slow to lock his door or pull down the shutters is likely to find the *mutawa* brandishing a long stick in his direction. Even television programmes are interrupted by a prayer intermission.

Women in the Kingdom must dress more conservatively than they did during my first stay – and that includes foreigners as well as Saudis. My husband's company issues regular bulletins about the "Dress Code" for employees and their families. The long skirts which I used to wear are now considered to be too form-revealing because they have a waistband; a long, loose dress is preferred. For the same reason, trousers must be covered by a long tunic top. Did I really wear sleeveless blouses in the summer heat one and a half decades ago? Not today.

A man lectures a class of women from behind a one-way glass, which functions like a veil: they can see him but he cannot see them.

Recently, with my family and friends, I ventured into a very old market area of a conservative town in the centre of the peninsula. Although I wore a black silk *abaya,* a long cloak that extends from the top of my head to my feet, covering all but face and hands, the local residents – both men and women – were not satisfied until I was peering out at them in astonishment through three layers of black gauze which hung before my face.

When I first arrived in Saudi Arabia, I got a job teaching English and mathematics to young Saudi men in an industrial training school. Although it was somewhat remarkable for them to have a woman teacher, my skills were needed at that time and most of my students accepted me with friendly good grace. Today, women are not permitted to teach in that school. In some women's colleges, there is a shortage of qualified instructors similar to the situation at my training centre years ago. When it is necessary for a man to teach a class of women, he lectures to them from behind a one-way glass which functions just like a veil: they can see him but he cannot see them.

This is how the Saudis always said it would be. They insisted from the very beginning that they would take Western technology without taking Western culture. They warned that they would hire foreign workers when they needed them and send them home the minute they had trained Saudis to do their jobs. Today, with oil production at a twenty-year low, thousands of foreigners are leaving the Kingdom every month, returning to homes all over the world.

In addition to preserving their traditions and customs in the face of modernization, the Saudis are participating in that broad political and religious conservatism which has swept across both East and West. Fundamentalist Muslims, within and without the Kingdom, are urging the Saudi government, as Guardian of the Holy Cities of Mecca and Medina, to be ever stricter in adhering to and enforcing Islamic principles.

Most of the Saudi women I met were disapproving of their sisters in the West. They see Western women as unprotected, living in dangerous cities, and unable to rely on the men of their family to escort them on the streets. A strong sense of sisterhood has always been a part of Arab culture, and constant familial support buoys Saudi women throughout their lives. In contrast, Western women's lifestyles seem full of risk – of loneliness, promiscuity, and abandonment by their children in their old age.

In public, Saudi women and men are separated. Schools are segregated by sex. All museums and public exhibits have men's days and women's days during the week. The few women who venture to worship in a mosque are confined to a special section. Even weddings are celebrated with a men's party and a women's party.

Education for females outside the home is a new phenomenon, which began only 35 years ago. Today there are girls' schools at every level, including women's programmes at several universities. Older women are included in a national literacy campaign. Opportunities exist for women to study abroad (usually with their husbands). A woman may become a teacher (with female students) or a doctor (with female patients) or a businesswoman (whose brothers provide the interface with the male world). Several banks have established branches just for women. The government has recently begun to consider whether putting their own women to work would be less disruptive to their society than bringing in masses of foreign workers, and is looking for ways to create more "women's jobs".

I am acquainted with a few Saudi women who refuse to wear the veil – they are fortunate in that their families support them in this move – and a couple who rankle at government censorship and what they see as religious coercion. I know of several who feel depressed by the numerous restrictions placed on them. But they all consider themselves to be good Saudis nonetheless, and are devoted to their families, culture, religion and country. There is no political action group in Saudi Arabia, male or female. Women are not agitating for "liberation" or "equality". Change in Saudi society will come from the inside, within individual lives, homes and families, and at a pace consistent with the Middle Eastern concept of time – one profoundly different from the Western concept.

There is no political action group in Saudi Arabia, male or female.

Thanks to the oil boom of the 1970s, the Saudis' material needs are basically met. The country is now self-sufficient in food production; electricity has reached a large number of towns and villages; education is free and available to anyone who wants it; hospitals are well-equipped and their number is growing as fast as the staff can be found; even the nomadic Bedouin have access to new water wells drilled here and there in the desert. These material advances can free the people to turn their thoughts and energies to the larger questions of life, to contemplate, perhaps, among other things, the role of women in this modern manifestation of their ancient culture. And that has to be good for Saudi women, for their men, and for both halves of the earth.

TRAVEL NOTES

Languages Arabic. English is widely spoken and understood.

Transport There are frequent and reasonably priced air services between the main cities and a good network of roads. Rental cars are available in all areas, but single women wishing to take trips further than 30km have to obtain a driver (it is illegal for a woman to drive) and written permission from their employer. The larger cities have a public bus service, with special women's compartments, closed off from the rest of the vehicle and entered by a separate door. In addition, employers of Westerners usually operate a private recreational bus service for shopping and beach trips.

Accommodation Special compounds have been built for foreigners. Women are subject to curfews and need a written invitation from a married couple in order to stay out overnight. Cohabitation is absolutely prohibited. Hotels are often reluctant to register single women and, although it is not legally required, you may be asked to produce a letter of permission from your employer, husband or father. During the *Hadj* (pilgrimage) hotels become very full and you'll need to reserve a room well in advance.

Special Problems Visitor's visas are usually only given to workers travelling to a job already obtained in the Kingdom, to women and children on family visas, and to visitors attending a conference or invited by an academic or commercial institution. Tourist visas are not available and it is becoming increasingly difficult for single women to obtain a work permit. Customs officials search luggage thoroughly for alcohol, drugs, medicines and pornography. Penalties for attempting to bring any of these items into the country can be severe.

Western women, in particular single ones, are subjected to a wide array of both verbal and physical abuse – cars hooting, kerb-crawling, staring and touching. However, penalties for all crimes are very harsh and actual physical attack (in public at least) is incredibly rare. If you feel uncomfortable you should make a fuss; few men would persist if confronted. It is illegal for a woman to spend time alone with a man who is not a relative. Dress codes are strict and rigidly enforced. Any woman considered immodestly clothed faces severe treatment from the religious

police. Many foreigners find it simplest to wear the *abaya*, which covers the body from head to toe.

Guides *The Green Book; Guide for Living in Saudi Arabia* (US, Middle East Editorial Associates), edited by Madge Pendleton, is useful to prepare yourself for the regulations. *Saudi Arabia: A MEED Practical Guide* (UK, Middle East Economic Digest) gives a good overview and details of sights.

CONTACTS

Saudi Arabia Women's Association, BP 6, Riyadh. The association provides information about Saudi women's organizations, most of which are for social and charitable purposes.

For general background, contact the *Saudi Arabian Information Centre*, Cavendish House, 18 Cavendish Square, London W1M 9AA, UK (☎0171/629 8803).

BOOKS

Freya Stark, *The Southern Gates of Arabia* (1936; UK, John Murray, 1971/US, J P Tarcher, 1983, o/p). Classic tale of explorations of the wild desert mountains, palaces and cities of Hadhramaut and South Arabia by one of Britain's most famous women travel writers.

Lydia Laube, *Behind the Veil* (Aus & UK, Wakefield Press, 1991). Amusing account of an Australian woman's experiences working as a nurse in Saudi Arabia.

Soraya Altorki, *Women in Saudi Arabia* (US, Colorado University Press, 1988). An analysis of life in the rich Jeddah elite. Focuses particularly on Saudi women's efforts to improve their status working within traditionally defined roles.

Arab Women's Solidarity Association, *Women of the Arab World* (UK & US, Zed Books, 1989). With an introduction by Nawal el Saadawi, this collection of essays brings together feminist writings from the entire Arab world.

FICTION

Hilary Mantel, *Eight Months in Ghazzah Street* (UK, Penguin, 1989). Gripping, often funny novel centring on a woman who joins her engineer husband in Jeddah, only to find herself embroiled in a mystery based on her investigations of the empty flat upstairs. Full of insights into the restrictions of being an ex-pat wife.

Senegal

S enegal was the first West African country to be colonized by France, and the continuing French influence is immediately apparent in the smooth road networks and transport system, and in the exclusive coastal resorts, restaurants and private beaches. The country draws around 200,000 French package tourists a year – and it is also one of the most popular West African destinations for independent travellers.

Beneath the French veneer, however, Senegal has a profoundly African Muslim culture and the precepts of Islam are widely practised and felt. In comparison with the North African states this imposes relatively few restrictions on women, who maintain a high profile in public life – especially as market traders. Politically the country is run as a multi-party democracy and although there has been serious conflict in the southern Casamance region, where secessionist demands have given way to a guerrilla war of independence, the country is still considered one of the more stable in the region.

The capital city of Dakar is perhaps the worst introduction to the country. Many people compete to make a living from the tourists and French ex-pats, and the constant pressure and hard-sell tactics of the street vendors and "guides" can give it a coercive atmosphere. The only real danger, however, is in the wealthy commercial centre where muggings are now common. Elsewhere in the country you experience few problems, though you will need to get used to being a symbol of affluence and to having people constantly approach you for money. How you cope with this is a personal issue; most Senegalese routinely give something to beggars and it's vital to remain friendly and polite. Sexual harassment is far less evident. It's advisable, though, and certainly more comfortable in the hot climate, to wear long, loose clothes.

Travelling around the country is fairly easy, although some areas south of The Gambia, where fighting occurs, are out-of-bounds to tourists. Transport is good, there's a fair amount of accommodation, and the Senegalese people are renowned for their hospitality to strangers. It is quite likely that you will be invited to stay in some-one's house, in which case be aware of the burdens you are imposing. There's no offence in paying for as much as you can and it's polite to offer gifts.

The main **women's organization**, the *Fédération des Associations Feminines du Sénégal* (FAFS) was founded by the *Parti Socialiste* and retains close links with the government. Its chief emphasis is on development and the provision of social welfare and educational services. Although it has a wide membership and has set up a range of local groups, its impact in the rural areas is still small. A more radical group is the Association of African Women in Research and Development (AAWORD), created by a group of African women dedicated to feminist research from an African perspective. Over the last decade they have assisted in numerous schemes, emphasizing the need for direct participation of local women in development projects. One of AAWORD's central concerns has been to place the issue of genital mutilation firmly in context as an African problem to be resolved by African people, counteracting Western outrage and sensationalism.

Life with the Diops

Daphne Topouzis, a founder editor member of *Africa Report*, an American bi-monthly magazine of African affairs, spent six months in Senegal researching a PhD; she lived with a Senegalese family on the outskirts of Dakar.

My original purpose in going to Senegal was to research the impact of French colonial rule on the development of Black politics during the 1930s and 1940s. I also wanted to collect material on the women's movement in the cities and on the role of women in rural development. Yet, by far the most valuable experience I had in Senegal came through living with a Senegalese family.

A friend who had also researched in West Africa helped me make contact with a Muslim family in Dakar. Though we had never met before, the Diops borrowed a couple of relatives' cars and came to meet me at the airport like an old friend. Hospitality (*teranga*) is central to Senegalese culture and hosts will go to great lengths to provide their guests with everything they possibly can, often exceeding their means.

My first days at the *Keur Diop* (Diop household) in Liberté VI, one of Dakar's suburbs, were overwhelming. Not only was this my first time in Africa but it was also the first time I had lived with a family of twenty. I shared a tiny room with two other women my age and was at once deprived of all privacy and independence, both of which had until then seemed essential to me. Differences in lifestyle and culture initially seemed both fundamental and insurmountable.

Curiosity and shyness on both sides made conversation awkward for the first couple of days, until the youngest children broke the ice. They taught me my first words of Wolof, reminded me of everybody's names, gave me directions to the bus stop and involved me in family activities. Within a week or so I had settled into a daily routine and had learnt a great deal about my host family and its expectations of me.

Marianne, aged 56, was a secretary in a Dakar hospital, the second of four wives and mother of three daughters and five sons. Just under half of all marriages in Senegal are polygamous (Muslims can have up to four wives), which is a harsh reality and nightmare for many women. It involves economic hardship, neglect of the older wife, favouritism of the younger one, jealousy (wives often share the same bedroom), oversized

After remarking jokily that my long, straight hair looked dull and ugly, they set about plaiting it.

families and overcrowded households. We spent long hours discussing polygamy, men, and the lack of choices for women. What impressed me most was her good humour, which invariably meant that conversations about grief ended with hearty laughter.

Marianne's daughters (aged 16, 22 and 23) were insatiably curious about me and soon became constant companions. One particular incident a few days after my arrival brought us together. After remarking jokily that my long, straight hair looked dull and ugly, they set about plaiting it. "Plaits can make anyone look good", they reassured me. But, however graceful they looked on them, plaits made me look worse than before (not to mention the fact that the children became afraid of me). We laughed about it for hours, and later in the evening, fearful that my feelings had been hurt, my closest friend, Fatou, offered me a *pagne* (square patterned fabric tied around the waist). It felt comfortable and looked good – or so was the general consensus – and I began wearing it regularly.

My relationships with the men in the family were friendly and comfortable except for an isolated misunderstanding with the eldest son. But being always a little uncertain of my status I tried to maintain a safe distance. I rarely saw Mr Diop (a retired postman) as he spent almost all of his time with his third wife. However, I always looked forward to his weekly tea gatherings with his comrades from World War II where colonial politics were passionately discussed. They never quite understood how I knew so much about this relatively obscure period of African history, but greatly appreciated my avid interest in their accounts as well as my endless questions and occasional contribution to the discussion.

On the whole, everyone in the family was discreet, never asking personal questions which might have been difficult to answer (on religion, politics or sex). Part of the explanation might be that I was much more curious about them than they were about me. But, like most Senegalese, they were far more tolerant of me than I had expected. For instance, though visibly puzzled by the fact that I did not have children (but less concerned by the fact that I was single), they never pressed the issue.

As a devout Muslim family, the Diops had assumed I also would be religious (the fact that I was Christian did not make us all that different in their eyes) and when I first arrived they gave me directions to the local church. I never went there, and although they realized I did not practice my religion they never held this against me. Similarly, they were perplexed by the fact that despite being white, which meant rich, I dressed relatively casually while they, despite their very tight budget, were always elegant and graceful. In this case, I began to take more care with my clothes as a result of living with them, but again, they never tried to talk me into it.

In fact, two months after living with the Diops, the differences in culture which had at first seemed so radical began to wane and I was treated like a member of their family: they encouraged me to learn Wolof, dance the *sabar*, wear *pagnes*, and help with the cooking and shopping.

The only two things I found difficult to cope with were the lack of privacy and their unshakeable belief that, being white, I had an inexhaustible supply of money. The lack of privacy meant that I did not have a quiet half-hour to relax, read, or write letters. But there was no way around it as the family was large and the house overcrowded. The real challenge for me, however, was that the women with whom I was closest seemed unable to understand my professed need to be alone once in a while or my occasional spells of gloom and loneliness. I was gently scolded for my self-indulgent attitude and forced to confront why privacy and independence as I understood them were so important to me.

I found to my surprise that it did feel lonely and painfully silent without the usual commotion.

One particular incident has crystallized in my mind: on the last day of Ramadan, all but three young children and a couple of adults had gone to the local mosque to pray. At once, the compound which was full of activity and the noise of many children became unusually quiet. Marianne came to me and said anxiously, "I cannot stand it when the house is empty. It feels so lonely." While in the past I would have relished this rare moment of peace and quiet, I found to my surprise that it did feel lonely and painfully silent without the usual commotion. When the children returned, Marianne was visibly happier and proudly said to me "Now you see why my children (which virtually meant the whole extended family) are my fortune."

This is not to say that I resolved the problem of privacy, but I learnt a lot from doing without it. The problem of money I never fully resolved. Even though I contributed a weekly sum to the family income, regularly bought treats, took the children to the cinema, etc, etc, I was regularly asked for cash. If there was an emergency such as medical expenses or school fees, I gave what I could. But often it was for luxuries like cosmetics, which seemed essential to them but not to me. I learnt to say I did not have money but that always created some tension. In retrospect, I believe it is wiser to give something, even if only a fraction of the amount, rather than refuse altogether and appear insensitive to their needs.

Except for those relatively minor problems, my life with the family ran smoothly once I had established a routine of my own. My day began at 7am when after a cup of *kenkilabah* (local herb tea) I would take the bus to the "Building Administratif" where the government archives are held. After work I would return to Liberté VI, often stopping by on the way amid the tiny, dark market stalls, loaded with vegetables and colour.

Marianne's daughters would start to prepare the food in the courtyard while there was still daylight. Evening entertainment consisted of either visiting friends or dancing to the haunting tunes of Dakar's musical superstars Youssou N'Dour and Super Diamono. Social life around the family was so enjoyable that I never went downtown to discos, restaurants or bars. I knew they existed, and they are popular amongst the Senegalese, but it never seemed worth the trip. Liberté VI was relaxing after a hectic day in Dakar. Everybody knew each other, little French was spoken, and no whites lived there. At first I felt uncomfortable being stared at in the streets but gradually people got used to me. As soon as I learnt some Wolof the barrier was broken and I began greeting neighbours regardless of whether I knew them or not.

My first trip outside Dakar was to Fatik, a small town four hours south of the capital. Marianne's son took me to visit his grandmother and her family. The further away we got from Dakar the more we could see the effects of the drought: long stretches of land with dried-up baobabs, cotton trees and abandoned villages. Around Fatik the dry earth had cracked and dead cattle in different stages of disintegration baked in the sun. We visited the local market to get *gris-gris* (protective amulets) and then went to a wrestling match. Wrestling is Senegal's national sport and worth seeing. On a Sunday afternoon you can catch up to thirty matches. They last only a few minutes each and involve mesmerizing ritualistic movements.

I began having all the symptoms of malaria: chills and flushes, headaches, hallucinations and diarrhoea.

A second trip to Touba was a little disappointing. Touba is the birthplace of the Mouridyyia – Senegal's fast-growing Muslim brotherhood. A great mosque and Koranic university dominate the town, which itself is very poor. The contrast between the incredible wealth of the mosque and the poverty surrounding it is quite disturbing. Touba has its own militia who can (and do) arrest people for drinking alcohol or smoking cigarettes within the boundaries.

On another trip, with two women friends, I took the Casamance express boat down to Ziguinchor and visited the US Peace Corps house, which is situated right behind the port. (The Peace Corps is an American voluntary development agency.) Even though I initially had reservations about the organization and its approach to work in Africa,

I found the volunteers friendly, hard-working and eager for company. Travellers can stay at the house for a small fee. Also, the volunteers are usually delighted to take travellers to their assigned villages. Their knowledge of the local languages and the fact that they are well-integrated in the local community were a positive contrast to the Canadian missionaries nearby who seemed totally estranged from their surroundings.

After Ziguinchor I went to Diembering, a small village off Cap Skirring. Villagers were drying fish in the sun, mending fishing nets and repairing pirogues on the beach. I had originally planned to stay for a few days at the government *campement*. But the same evening I began having all the symptoms of malaria: chills and flushes, headaches, hallucinations and diarrhoea. Usually, the first 72 hours of malaria attacks are the worst and after that a large dose of Nivaquine begins to work. I was helped on to the boat back to Dakar and went to the Peace Corps doctor. (They usually only treat volunteers but made an exception in my case.) It took ten days for me to recover and when I returned to the Diop family they treated me as though I had been long lost, showing very real relief and concern.

Soon after that episode I was stopped in the centre of Dakar by a gendarme who wanted to check my passport. As I didn't have it on me I was taken to the station, where I encountered at least twenty whites picked up for the same reason. (I was later told that every once in a while the police go out on such raids to show foreigners who's boss.) After sitting for hours in the waiting room I began to feel uncomfortable and frightened. The Chief of Police asked me a long series of questions and then calmly assured me that I would be there all day. A few moments later someone offered me a cigarette and I thanked him in Wolof. Suddenly the atmosphere changed, the police became warm and apologetic and I was inundated with invitations and offers of hospitality.

These problems did not cast a shadow over my stay. They were part of the challenge of trying to lead an integrated life in a very different culture and climate to my own. I've kept contact with the family in Liberté VI, whom I consider now part of my extended family, and am returning soon for another six-month stay.

TRAVEL NOTES

Languages French and several African languages – Wolof is the most widely spoken.

Transport The basic transport throughout Senegal is the bush taxi (*taxi-brousse*). Each passenger pays for a seat, and the taxi leaves only when it is full. Try to travel early in the morning to avoid long waits for other passengers, especially in villages. Prices are government-fixed and fairly low. In Dakar there are more conventional taxis and buses.

Accommodation Dakar's tourist hotels are generally expensive, though you can stay in *campements* (inexpensive, comfortable accommodation in simple buildings) at Casamance, outside the city. In rural areas it is likely that you'll be invited to stay in people's homes. You should offer some money or gifts towards your keep.

Special Problems You will often be approached for money by hustlers, beggars and other people who need it and have none. People have their own ways of dealing with this – most give coins or small gifts.

Guides *The Rough Guide to West Africa* (Penguin) has a major section on Senegal.

CONTACTS

Association of African Women in Research and Development (AAWORD), Codesria, B3304, Dakar. A pan-African women's federation that carries out research, publishes a journal, and campaigns for women's rights throughout Africa.

Council for the Development of Economic and Social Research in Africa (CODESRA), BP3304, Dakar. Research centre that works, among other themes, on women and development in Africa.

BOOKS

Christina Dodwell, *Travels with Pegasus – A Microlight Journey across West Africa* (UK, Sceptre, 1989/US, Walker & Co, 1990). Intrepid, lively travelogue in which Dodwell journeys from Cameroon to Senegal not only in a microlight but, among other things, by camel and motorbike.

Mariama Ba, *So Long a Letter* (UK, Virago, 1982/US, Heinemann, 1981, o/p). Brilliant portrait by a Senegalese feminist of a Muslim woman living in a society of transition. Ba's second book, *The Scarlet Song* (UK, Longman, 1986), focuses on the relationship between an educated French woman and a poor Senegalese man.

Nafissatou Diallo, *A Dakar Childhood* (UK, Longman, 1982, o/p). Autobiographical account of growing up in Dakar.

Aminata Sow Fell, *Beggars Strike* (UK, Longman, 1987/US, Longman, 1981). Fictional tale of a beggars' uprising in Dakar by Senegal's leading woman novelist.

Spain

Propelled by the extraordinary economic growth of the last two decades, Spain has emerged as a new player in Europe. The slick sophistication of the towns and cities, the fast trains, the vibrant cultural scene (with film, design and music at the cutting edge) all seem a far cry from the isolation, poverty and bigotry of the Franco years. Recession, however, is biting and the socialist government – the new establishment – is struggling to cling to power amid corruption scandals and spiralling unemployment. The complicating factor, beyond all this, is regionalism. With a dozen autonomous regions claiming their own language, culture and legislation, a journey across Spain, from Galicia to Catalunya, or the Basque Country to Andalucía can in many ways feel like a pan-European hike.

Amid all the post-Franco transformation, Spain's macho image has noticeably faded. Women have a high profile in most aspects of public life (the extremely well-developed tourist industry included) and there are few parts of the country where a woman travelling alone is likely to feel threatened or attract un-wanted attention. At least,

that is, if you're white. Black visitors of either sex have to contend with frequent stares and comments and very often get harassed by the police (see Maureen Mckarkiel's piece below).

In general terms the big cities, like others in Europe, have their no-go areas where street crime and drug related hassles are on the rise, but there's little of the pestering or propositions you come up against in, say, Paris or Rome. The outdoor culture of the *terrazas* (terrace bars) and the fact that crowds mill around the streets until late at night helps you to feel less exposed. The major resorts of the *costas* have their own artificial holiday culture. The Spanish men who hang round the discos or at fiesta fairgrounds pose no greater or lesser threat than similar slick operators at home. The language barrier simply makes it harder to know who to trust.

Predictably, it is in the more isolated regions, separated by less than a generation from desperate poverty (and often still starkly poor), that more serious problems can occur. Over the last ten years, we have had two reports of women being followed and attacked in remote parts of Andalucía. It's important to know a bit about the land you're travelling over – in some areas you still find shepherds sent into the mountains with nothing but the wine and food they take with them for payment. Such practices, however, are dying out and even in relatively isolated regions you'll find a fairly knowledgeable and sophisticated approach to tourists. Hiking is popular in the country as a whole and many women happily tramp the footpaths, especially in the Pyrenees and along the pilgrims' way to Santiago (for more on which see the chapter on France).

The **women's movement** in Spain burst into action during the Civil War – the *Mujeres Libres*, a branch of the anarchist movement, boasted 30,000 members in 1938 – but their efforts were short-lived. The Franco dictatorship (1939–75) effectively suppressed all feminist activity, peddling in its stead the ideology of the family and traditional Catholic values. A small number of writers in Barcelona and Madrid managed to reawaken the debate in the 1960s and early 70s, and presaged an explosion of activism that followed Franco's death and the return of democracy. By the early 1980s women's groups had sprung up in all the major cities, pushing for reform on issues of birth control, abortion, divorce and discrimination in work and pay. Pro-choice abortion rallies were staged with women, some of them well-known figures, declaring publicly that they had undergone illegal abortions and defying the courts to run show trials.

Following the election of the socialist government in 1981, and subsequent entry to the EC (opening access to supreme court rulings), important legislative reforms have been achieved. Currently new laws are under discussion to further enlarge the right to abortion and provide equal legal rights to cohabiting couples (homosexual as well as heterosexual). As in Britain and North America, however, there's a widespread feeling that the women's movement is languishing. The setting up of a new government body to debate women's issues (the *Istituto de la Mujer*) has gained less support than predicted and is widely criticized as a cosmetic exercise with little political clout.

Madrid and Around

Natania Jansz, a clinical psychologist, writer and editor, has spent numerous holidays in Spain, visiting friends whom she has known since her early twenties. In 1993 she organized three months' unpaid leave from work and drove to Madrid.

It was hot even by Madrid standards, well into the forties. For most of the afternoon I had slouched around the apartment of a close friend, barely dressed, reading fragments of novels and listening to the sounds of neighbours erupting from the ventilation shaft. The five o'clock clatter of forks against bowls marked the beginnings of tortilla-making and the end of the most stultifying part of the day. An hour or so more and I emerged from the shower to try on some brand new items I'd picked up in the Madrid sales, toy with the make-up and get ready for the slow gathering evening. It had taken nearly a fortnight to shed my London shabbiness but now I was off, *Madrileño* style, among the cars, taxis and shoppers of Quevedo, central Madrid. Venturing out earlier had been a mistake. A brief foray to join the siesta insomniacs at a nearby tourist bar had left me zig-zagging between the air-conditioned blasts of shop doorways. Now I strode out across the three-lane junctions ignoring the press at the pavement's edge, the horns, and the clammy August heat; gliding, I hoped, like a vespa. Down Fuencarral, with its cinema hoardings, shops and cafés, down narrow streets of stucco tenements with high ironwork balconies decked in faded awnings and geraniums, and out onto a bar-lined square. Amongst the plastic tables of the *terraza* I found Pilar and two of her colleagues. "Hola, guapissima" ("Hello beautiful") she exclaimed, leaving just enough teasing in her voice to show that for her also Madrid's glamour was optional, only for fun. I had arrived.

Madrid was not a city I took to easily. Brief visits had always been frenetic affairs, emerging in the different parts of my metro map by day to pick off galleries, squares and parks and then leaping in and out of taxis for a nightly round of bars and clubs. They were exciting but befuddling times, which often left me feeling just slightly out of focus, attending to the wrong details – standing at a bar looking around for a chair instead of savouring my exquisitely marinaded tapas of anchovies; scanning for grandiose facades rather than enjoying the whimsical tilework of bars and shopfronts; leaning forward in the taxi to catch a view of the city when no real panorama exists. Madrid is a city in close-up. Like any capital you need to know what to look for and where to find it, but *Madrileños* are startlingly precise in their choices.

Evenings involve a series of rendezvous, nodal points for groups to form, merge or fragment. Choosing where you eat a few tapas, down some *cañas* (glasses of beer), maybe have a meal, or the sequence in which you move from one bar to the next, is complex, involving anticipating the movements of friends, knowing the scene. Yet it's managed with gregarious ease by most of the *Madrileños* I know. And the city is small enough, and taxis cheap enough, to range around freely. It seems to me that only Londoners resort to a map the size of a large paperback and a weekly listings magazine when they contemplate a night out in their city.

It was friends who had brought me to this country, a small group of Spaniards whom I'd met years ago at a university in England and kept in touch with through reciprocal visits, augmented by friends sent abroad armed with each others' addresses. Odd samples of the Spanish scene would filter through; fly posters of rock and flamenco concerts sponsored under the heady days of Madrid's first post-Franco socialist mayor, the philosopher poet Tiero Galván; pronouncements on Almodóvar and the Movida – the scene which revelled in excess amid the new freedoms; anger at the corruption of the socialist government (a sign that Spain had become truly West European). Meanwhile I was a bystander, happy to pick my way through the odd week's holiday in the city, a southern town or beach, leaning on the simultaneous translations of Spanish friends or losing myself in the thick of the well-developed holiday industry.

At first it was the outdoor life of *terrazas* that played on my mind – that accomplished holiday atmosphere that even the most ambitious Spaniard can summon up over a beer in the sun. And the way people would greet each other, kissing and spinning off pet-names unselfconsciously in ways only camp friends could get away with in this country (hello fatty, skinny, beautiful, redhead, blondie).

Grannies scoured the ground for syringes dropped by the junkies the night before.

In Britain you run the risk of people toppling back in surprise or sticking out a foot if you so much as lean towards them. Spain was different. It was noticeable too how incurious people seemed about work status on a first meeting. That inevitable question that frames all introductions, "And what do you do?", barely arose.

It took nearly twelve years before I decided to make a break for it, take three months unpaid leave from work and point the car south. Pilar had offered me a spare room and the self-imposed rigours of an English-free zone while I embarked on an intensive language course. The thrill of my first days of minimal fluency waned as I became submerged in the mysteries of the subjunctive, Madrid slang and the new dependency of relationships based on Spanish. It was an easy matter, however, to establish my own routines in the city. For an early morning *café con leche* there was the bar on the corner of the street, where I would squeeze between the line of office workers standing at the counter, dunking *churros* (large sticks of fried dough) into glasses of coffee and brandy, cigarettes smouldering behind their newspapers. Returning later I could enjoy a more sedate drink among the well-coiffed elderly ladies taking their mid-morning break and flirting, or discussing ailments, with Luís the barman. Lunch, if there was time or money enough, had the potential of a regional tour – a Galician bar for *pulpo* (octopus), an Andaluz bar for paella, a Basque restaurant for the ultimate blow-out meat feast, for which recovery is measured in days. If inspiration was lacking I would end up at the local square munching a *bocadillo* and watching toddlers play on the gritty centre while grannies scoured the ground for syringes dropped by the junkies the night before. And the night – well the night was many different places, varying around the theme of food, drink, films and lingering on balconies.

It seems odd to me now how safe I felt in Madrid. Crowds thronged the streets late at night and taxis were everywhere. For some reason the signs that would normally make me flinch and quicken my pace failed to register: a couple of teenagers shooting up on a park bench; a woman hurtling round a corner and clattering down a dark street; an indistinct group ambling a few yards behind me. Somehow I'd been lulled by friends who felt secure in their city despite its dangers, who talked about having bags snatched or street muggings with indulgence, as anecdotes. Perhaps I was carried away by their ease but I felt relaxed on my own and nothing ever did happen to dispel this.

As much as I enjoyed the gregarious outdoor culture of the city – the ready way that groups of men and women would form – there were linguistic and cultural snags to all this easy sociability. In Britain you don't learn how to be intimate in large mixed groups and the concentration it took to find and keep up the thread drained me. Either I found myself launching into too intense discussion with a neighbour or would spin centrifrugally to the outside of the circle. I was struck by the familiarity between the men and women I knew – a sense of knowing each other and an ease in each other's company that seemed stronger than I'd experienced at home. Yet there were times when I found myself missing the exclusive company of women. Perhaps I just missed the assumption that I might want to spend the odd evening alone with women friends. Symptomatic of this was when I was invited to a women-only bar, only to find myself once again in a large mixed group.

Moments like these threw me back

> *If a deep, dark machismo was still smouldering in a corner of Spain, I had yet to find it.*

into reveries about the late 1970s and 1980s – the experiments (often flawed, crude but also joyful) made in Britain and America to marginalize the power of men and place women at the centre, proclaiming a solidarity. According to Spanish friends who knew those times, feminism in Spain had taken a different course. The deeper radicalism (and comradeship) spawned by the Franco years had been harder to shake and, while women, as always, leaned on each other for emotional and practical support this was largely a private matter. Competition, they reckoned, had had a freer rein. It was a small difference, and against the background of the generally insecure and competitive 1990s, it seemed to me a slight one.

I recognized too that I was moving among friends, people who were warm, sophisticated and considerate and perhaps not representative. Also I was on holiday: by definition only skimming the surface. In general, the men I came across seemed to censor their comments less and were a little more dependent on the attentions of women. It also struck me that the glamour/style ethic could get a bit imperious at times. Yet if a deep, dark machismo (something beyond the conservatism of rural Europe) was still smouldering in a corner of Spain, I had yet to find it. A policeman called me *chica,* while writing out a speeding ticket, and a man hissed obscenities in my ear while I pressed through the crowds at the Rastro (Madrid's largest street market). But mostly the men I met – barmen, street traders, even garage mechanics (who in Britain could run courses on the ritual humiliation of women) treated me in a manner relaxed, and free of reserve. In general there's an informality to dealings in Spain that cuts across divisions of class and money. People chat to each other. I found it a relief.

In August, *Madrileños* began to speak nostalgically of mountain villages, the greenery of the north, particular wines, citrus groves, the sandy beaches and coves of the south. Suddenly regional affiliations, dormant for much of the year, spring up, complete with childhood summer memories. Like all Spanish pleasures, these have the ring of the connoisseur and a practical edge; somebody, somewhere, knows some-

These places, which might have been threatening if I was stuck there at night, seemed innocuous enough.

one with a free room in an apartment by a beach. Not any beach, but a particular beach, close to a bar that sells sea anenomes or goose barnacles to be savoured at their peak of perfection in the third week of the month. This type of precision, as uncanny as their city knowledge, thrilled and baffled me. So far removed was it from the indiscriminate pleasures of a sun-sea-sand package on the costa del somewhere. I settled for a drive south into Andalucía to a seaside cottage without water or electricity near Almería, stopping off en route in the Alpujarras to stay with some British friends who had a farm.

It was mirage weather on the the plains of La Mancha south of Madrid, flat pans of intense heat that gushed through the open windows. The monotony of the landscape didn't help. Long vistas were punctuated occasionally by colossal barrels, signalling the local wine *bodegas.* Windmills, in Don Quixote land, were in plentiful supply but most of them were painted on the front of bars in a bid to inject some romance into the hot dreariness all around. On the horizon stood a lone black bull. So did a guitar-playing sherry bottle – both of them advertising hoardings from the 1950s, now elevated to the status of protected monuments.

In an attempt to stave off heat stupor I bar-hopped along the *autovia,* sometimes stopping at village bars, filled with teenagers playing fruit machines, sometimes at truck stops to perch on a stool nibbling tapas. These places, which might have been threatening if I was stuck there at night, seemed innocuous enough, and the barmen and truck drivers were helpful about directions. The gorge of Despeñaperros, the

Andaluz border, was a welcome sight, giving way to the olive groves of Jaen. I made a mental note to return in a loop through Extramadura, renouncing windmills for the refinements of *conquistador* towns and storks floating down from the sky to perch on main square turrets.

After eight hours of hard driving I reached Granada. I had been there almost a decade before with my sister, arriving by bus from Malaga for a whistle-stop tour of the Alhambra Palace. It was Corpus Christi, not that we understood the significance of this at the time, and we planned to loiter away a day amid the pleasures of Moorish art. Instead we squinted into the "serene" coutyards

Should she go to a pig-killing, or get a shiatsu massage from someone she'd met at an ex-pat women's group?

through a wall of bodies and snatched glimpses of intricate ribbon-tile mosaics and wondrous stalactite vaultings in the camera-clicking instant allowed us before the next onrush of sightseers. Eventually we gave up, retreating to a quiet, if obscure, corner of the lemon and rosemary-scented garden. Over the river crowds were milling around platforms erected in the main squares. Adolescent couples sped past on motor-bikes, leather jackets tailing off into the flounces of rented Sevillana costumes while older folk sat around, similarly bedecked, sipping *fino*. Even babies were kitted out for the festivities, lying in a nest of frills in their pushchairs, flowers stuck to their heads. It was our first *feria*, a night of carousing, foot-stomping, raucous singing and couples endlessly twirling around the wooden planks. We sat on the edge fielding inclusive smiles and nods from the large family groups around us. Later I discovered this barely ranked as a warm-up in the Andaluz calendar. *Granadinos* are famously restrained.

This time I stopped only for a coffee in a square overhung by the cathedral before heading on towards the mountains. Annie and Chris had sent me a scrawled map of the Alpujarras with instructions, ones that had proved irresistible in Madrid. "Park at the fourth bend on the track under the olive tree just past a pigshed overhung with bougainvillea and honk for a lift across the river." Honk I did. Three dogs barked back. Below me a fast-drying river bed gave out onto a soft green pasture where sheep stood clumped in the shade under orange trees. A stone farmhouse merged into the scrubby hill directly opposite, with the corner of an alfalfa field, startlingly green, behind it. Before long, puffs of dust appeared above a long line of oleander bushes announcing the arrival of Chris and two-year-old Chloe in their ancient landrover, dogs scampering behind them. Annie and Chris had lived in the mountains for five years, carving a farm out of the interstices of three rivers with help from Mateus, a neighbouring shepherd and farmer and now a close friend. They were part of a growing band of foreigners (mainly British but with a sprinkling of other West Europeans and Americans) who had ditched familiar urban pressures to try a new life in the sun-drenched south. Peasant farmers had meanwhile been migrating in the other direction, selling up land and cottages (as prices edged up they could hardly afford not to) and moving to new flats in provincial towns. It left a strange, anachronistic mix. On my first night Annie was hovering between two invitations. Should she go to a pig-killing with Alpujarran neighbours or take up the offer of a shiatsu massage from someone she'd met at an ex-pat women's group? She settled for a night swopping tales of England and the Alpujarras gazing out over the dim valley contours. Mateus walked up for a beer and to return a couple of scythes but was too shy to linger long with a stranger.

Resentments occasionally surface about the foreign take-over (particularly the latest crop of new age travellers blamed wrongly for the spread of heroin abuse in the mountain towns) but mostly the atmosphere is tolerant. I was surprised, however, to find Annie and Chris clambering into a demure dress and long trousers for a trip into Órgiva, the nearest town. I didn't need to, they explained, the town is swamped with passing tourists in shorts, but living there they had chosen to make their own compromises with conservative provincial life. Small details like this, coupled with the fact that both of them worked incredibly hard to cultivate their land and ensure a living, set them apart from the holiday cottage set. They were farmers *en serio* (who took it seriously) I was told by Mateus' cousin; high praise in those parts.

For six days I picked oranges, joined Chloe's entourage of dogs and a chewed Barbie doll on trips to the river, and searched for ways that a consummate townie like myself could help out on a farm. Chris and Annie laughed at my excesses of plant-watering and bread-making (a triumph for a first-timer) but I simply wasn't up to the harder grind of building walls. (Under the August sun and well into the second month of drought the everyday routines could be staggering.) They talked to me of the pressures to revert to a traditional division of labour and the invidious effect this could have – the influence of the Alpujarras unravelling the newer ground of relationships. A couple of ex-pat friends of theirs had separated under the strain, not much liking the men and women they had become. For Annie and Chris the main worries were focused on Chloe. What ideas about herself would she imbibe at the local school? At present she mixed happily with a typical Alpujarran blend of local Spanish children, a family of Dutch Muslims, and various new-age toddlers at a makeshift nursery. I too hoped that she would forge on in a style of her own.

I left for Órgiva (my return planned), stopping for a snack at a chic new patisserie to ease myself back into tourist Spain. As I drove east, the rolling arid landscape gradually gave way to the desert of Almería, still used for location shoots for Spaghetti Westerns. The cottage was in the tiny hamlet of Sopalmo, no more than a few buildings grouped loosely around a small bar and fountain, 2km from the coast. The woman who ran the bar handed me the keys to the cottage along with a note left for me by Pilar, Esteban and Victoria. They were at the beach. Not any beach . . .

The Barcelona Look

Maureen Mckarkiel spent eight months living and working in Barcelona. She had visited the city once before on a holiday as well as travelling to other parts of Spain. Since returning home she has begun full-time studies in London.

I arrived in Barcelona not knowing anybody. All I knew was that two women whom I'd met the Christmas before at a friend's house in London had kindly invited me to stay in their flat and that one of them was due to meet me at the airport.

I remember walking into the arrivals lounge to see Lydia beaming at me. She was with another woman – I guessed it was Menti whom I had heard so much about. A friend in London had given me the low-down on this Spanish crowd who lived in an old working-class but now gentrified district, called Gracia. If his descriptions were right then I was going to be staying with some exceptionally nice people.

We arrived at Lydia's flat after a fairly speedy journey by metro to find a crowd of her Gracia friends waiting to greet me. Lydia explained that everyone had wanted to come and meet the new visitor. By now I was beginning to feel quite overwhelmed and very nervous. I needn't have worried. I went through the customary "Hola! Qué tal?" and two kisses on the cheeks with all of them. I'd only been in the country for a matter of hours and already I'd kissed more people than I would normally have done in a year. It was nice – I liked it!

Everybody wanted to know if I spoke Spanish and if I had a job lined up and nearly everyone was able to give me some positive advice which I found genuinely helpful.

My nervousness eased considerably under such encouragement, everyone was so warm and hospitable. But most of all I did not sense any awkwardness with these new friends or see signs of that distant "look" that is almost invisible to anyone who isn't black. It is something that is difficult to describe to those who have never experienced it, but is all too graphic to someone who has to deal with subtle forms of racism everyday of their lives.

I was relieved. A lot of worries had stemmed from how I would be received once living and working in the city. I knew that Spain itself was a very "white" country and, coupled with the alarming rise in racism and fascism in all parts of Europe, including Spain, I felt I had good cause to feel concern.

They seemed to be asking "How can you be an English teacher? You're Black!"

My first week was spent going round to different English schools armed with a clutch of addresses and my qualifications. I wasn't really surprised to find that there were no jobs available. The teaching term had started in September and it was now March. I'd arrived six months too late.

However, I was slightly taken aback by the return of that "look" on the faces of the people who were interviewing me – something between incredulousness and disdain. They seemed to be asking "How can you be an English teacher? You're Black!".

How I reacted to this varied with my mood. Sometimes I'd feel optimisitic and good about the city. After all, hadn't I been taken under the wing of some wonderful people? But during weaker moments I would succumb to depression and wonder what had happened to the Barcelona I had fallen in love with on holiday two years before.

One of my most disturbing experiences in relation to finding work was with a well-known school that Menti had taken me to, absolutely certain that they were looking for teachers.

We arrived and asked to speak to the director. Menti explained that I was a qualified English teacher and was looking for a job. He went away for a few minutes and then returning, ushered us into a small office saying that someone would be along to take my details. Menti looked at me reassuringly as we waited, but I wasn't too sure.

Another man appeared. He introduced himself as the head of studies. I must admit he seemed quite pleasant, albeit in a slightly "customer services" kind of way. He asked me how long I had been in the country and how long I planned to stay. After I had replied politely to his questions he turned to Menti and started speaking in Spanish. I could tell there was a problem. Finally, Menti turned to me and asked if I had a work permit. I knew that I didn't need one because of the EC regulations. I explained that I was born in England and was a British citizen. His reply was to insist that I fill in what can only be described as an immigration form.

I couldn't believe it. I looked at him in amazement and asked why I had been given this piece of paper. Menti added that she had accompanied another British woman to the school months before and that she had not been asked to fill in any form. By now it was crystal clear. I stood up and stormed out. I think Menti was more angry than I was and kept on apologizing profusely.

Fortunately, my luck soon changed. With an amalgamation of part-time work in a school just outside Barcelona, supply teaching at

I realized that people were not out partying every waking moment. It is a myth that I'd really believed.

the school where Lydia's sister worked, and private lessons, I was able to support myself financially without too much of a problem. It also meant that I could take a full and active part in the vibrant social life of the city – a crucial part of my well-being. On holiday I had spent a few glorious days and nights of non-stop clubbing, looking at arty buildings and eating. It surprised me when I found that Lydia and her friends were reluctant to go clubbing every night of the week. However, I soon realized that people were not out partying every waking moment. It is a myth that I'd really believed.

People in Barcelona work very hard under pretty poor conditions – long hours and short contracts – many finishing work as late as nine in the evening, usually followed by an hour or two studying at "school". Even my own situation prevented a life of relentless boogying. I was having to get up at 5.30am, three mornings a week, to get to a small town outside the city in time to give an English class at eight. The weekends were therefore sacred and almost always packed with celebrations. If it wasn't someone's birthday, then it would be their "saint day", or else a festival.

Anyone lucky enough to be in town for a visit would be given the "treatment". This meant a weekend of non-stop partying – usually beginning with a meal at someone's house, followed by a club or tapas. This would all be conducted in the company of about thirty people, an amalgam of Menti and Lydia's friends, a large number of whom were supporting my sometimes extravagant lifestyle by paying for private English classes.

My favourite evenings began in a bar, were followed by tapas at the port and then on to the beautiful old music hall called "La Paloma". Dizzy from the mixture of beer, dirt-cheap champagne and the buzz in the atmosphere, we would dance until we dropped. (By the time I left Barcelona I had refined my versions of the waltz and paso doble.) The night would be rounded off by an early morning *churros con chocolate* (fried dough and a cup of thick chocolate), picked up on the way home. Heaven!

SPAIN

Nights like this easily surpassed my holiday. Then I was a consumer of Spanish culture rather than someone included within it. A fairly reserved and fiercely independent person, I felt myself drifting easily and happily into a life of physical and emotional dependence upon this big happy family I'd become part of. Their support and understanding acted as a buffer against the harsh realities of the outside world, although it never managed to ease all the worries I had.

In my day to day life I was continually having to cope with the fact that people saw me as "different". The Spanish are famous for their, let's say, "up front" approach. On the metro you don't find people staring at their shoes or huddled behind a newspaper, or finding any means possible to avoid making eye contact with the person sitting opposite. Oh no! In Spain people look you straight in the eye, only removing their gaze when they are ready.

This was something that I never really got used to during my eight months in the city. In the beginning I found it stressful just walking down the street. At first I wondered if I was being uptight and just imagining that everyone was staring at me. Yet people would literally stop what they were doing and just stare as I headed towards them. A discreet look over my shoulder would confirm that they had turned 180 degrees to catch every moment of the amazing sight.

I longed for someone who would be able to understand without it always looking as if I were over-reacting.

For the first two months or so this was extremely wearing. Most people want to go about their business as comfortably and, for me, as anonymously, as possible. This was something I had become accustomed to in London and there were times when I longed for that freedom.

As far as I was concerned the main reason that people were looking at me was because I was black. Discussing this issue on a number of occasions with Lydia and Menti, they agreed that my colour was an aspect but were both adamant that the main reason was because I was so attractive. Rather than making me feel better this only served to increase my frustration. I longed for someone who would just be able to understand without it always looking as if I were over-reacting.

I found the general attitude towards racism trying at times. But I was able to put it down to ignorance. Spain has never had a large black population and debates about racism have been less than central to left-wing politics. All my Spanish friends were definitely good anti-racists and outraged about the blatant discrimination I faced. They were truly humanitarian people. Lydia personified generosity and honesty, was easy-going and sociable. We could talk about anything and everything. The same was true for Menti, who inspired me with her resilience and courage. It just used to piss me off having to go through the more subtle issues and arguments again and again – ideas that people in London would have readily understood.

Just to choose one example from many, Menti's brother had a habit of addressing me as *"negrita"* (little blackie!). One night at Menti's house, while I was re-filling my cup of coffee, he made a comment and began to laugh. My ropy Spanish prevented me from understanding and I asked Menti to translate. Apparently he had decided that my vast consumption of coffee was the reason for my being so black! Picking up my irritability she quickly added that people in Spain always made these kind of jokes and nothing was meant by it.

I was lucky enough to have a pretty steady stream of friends coming out to visit me while I was there, although Steve, a Black friend of mine, was constantly harassed by the police on suspicion of being an illegal immigrant. This lasted the whole week he was there. After having spent so long establishing a kind of equilibrium it was deeply upsetting to find the old feelings crashing back.

On my days off I liked to go to the Ramblas and just wander around. It was the nearest thing to London I could find, in terms of the racial mix of people – Moroccans, Peruvians and West Africans were just part of the crowd – and it would ease my homesickness whenever it came.

People often speak about the sexism of Spanish society and, from my own experiences of sexual harassment I would agree that this is a problem. However, I never felt threatened by sexism in the same way as I did by racism. I think the difference was that I could find solace and empathy with the many Spanish women I had got to know.

I decided to flee the city before the start of the Olympics and spend a month-and-a-half in Girona. I left Spain under the pretext of going for a short holiday in London. I'd been offered a full-time job with a flat for the next term but the moment I was back in London, I knew that I wouldn't return. It was time to get back in the shade.

TRAVEL NOTES

Languages Spanish; also Catalan, Basque and Gallego (in Galicia) and an array of dialects.

Transport An extensive bus and train network covers the country. Taxis are plentiful and fairly inexpensive in the main cities.

Accommodation Plenty of choice, covering the range from basic *hostals* to luxury hotels.

Guides *The Rough Guide to Spain* (Penguin) is a wonderful tome that catches the vibrancy and diversity of the country. *The Rough Guides* also have volumes on *Andalucía* and *Barcelona and Catalunya*.

CONTACTS

Madrid: *Librería de Mujeres*, c/ San Cristóbal 17. A women's bookstore with feminist and lesbian literature. A good place to pick up local information.

El Barberillo de Lavapies, c/Salitre 43. Bar and café with an eighty percent female clientele.

No Se Lo Digas a Nadie, c/Ventura de la Vega 7. Women-owned and -managed bar – mixed and relaxed, with a bookshop and library.

Barcelona: *Proleg Librería de Mujeres*, c/Daguería 13. Women's bookstore with feminist and lesbian titles in Catalan and Spanish.

Daniels, c/Cardona 7. One of the few women-only disco-bars.

Sevilla: *Librería Fulmen*, c/Zaragoza 36. Sevilla's women's bookstore.

Asamblea de Mujeres de Sevilla, c/Alberto Lista 16. Lesbian group with feminist information for all of southern Spain.

Café Sureñas, c/Guadiana 9. A women's café, though men are welcome.

BOOKS

Rose Macaulay, *Fabled Shore* (UK & US, Oxford University Press, 1986; o/p in UK). The Spanish coast from Catalunya to the Portuguese Algarve as it was in 1949. Read it and weep.

Nina Epton, *Grapes and Granite* (UK, Cassell, 1956, o/p). One of the few English books on Galicia, full of folklore and vistas of rural life.

George Sand, *A Winter in Majorca* (UK, Academy Press, 1979, o/p/US, Academy Press, 1992). Sand spent a winter with Chopin at the monastery of Valldemossa. Her attempts to inspire the locals with a sense of intellectual and moral freedom went unappreciated and she left with this embittered and dark account in mind.

David Parker (ed), *Vision on Fire: Emma Goldman on the Spanish Revolution* (UK & US, Commonground Press, 1983; o/p in UK). Feared in her native America as an incendiary Communist, Goldman gets to grips with the Spanish revolution, appearing in Spain at various times between 1936 and 1938.

FICTION

Ana María Matute, *School of the Sun* (UK, Quartet, 1991/US, Colorado University Press, 1989). Tells of lost childhood innocence in a Balearic island as old scores get settled under the cover of Civil War.

Mercé Roderada, *The Time of the Doves* (UK, Graywolf Press, 1989, o/p/US, Graywolf Press, 1986). A working-class woman in the Barcelona suburb of Gracia struggles to survive the poverty and chaos of the Civil War. Lucid and lyrical, the book was highly acclaimed when it emerged in the 1970s. Well worth tracking down.

Maruja Torres, *Desperately Seeking Julio* (UK & US, Fourth Estate, 1991). The Julio of the title is Iglesias, Spanish icon and international phenomenon. An enjoyable romp of a novel from a popular journalist (and regular columnist for *El País*), who is famous for keeping a finger clamped on the nation's pulse.

If you can read Spanish (or Catalan) look out for works by Montserrat Roig, one of the country's foremost feminist writers.

Sweden

S weden is approaching something of a watershed in the mid-1990s. With the end of the Cold War, its identity as a peace-mongering, neutral state has diminished, while recession is threatening to undermine its high standard of living. Since 1990 unemployment has risen from three to fifteen percent and, for the first time in nearly half a decade, the rule of the Social Democrats was interrupted by a brief foray into right-wing government and free-market economic measures. Now, as the country moves towards membership of the EU, there are fears that its unique and laudable aspects – enlightened welfare policies, environmental protection, asylum for refugees – will be dragged down by the less scrupulous (and poorer) European states.

These concerns, however, barely impinge on travellers getting to grips with the enormity of the landscape (with a tiny population that dwindles as you head north) and the extremely high cost

of living. Expense apart, Sweden is a remarkably relaxed and hassle-free destination. The trains and buses run with bewildering regularity and most people, even in quite remote areas, speak some English. Swedish women think nothing of travelling around their country alone, and taking long solitary walks has almost the status of a national pastime.

The appeal of the country lies primarily in the outdoors: hopping off the inland railway to walk through lakeland and forests, journeying farther north to catch the midnight sun, or rambling around the tiny resorts of the Bothnian coast. However, Swedish city life, such as it is, has its attractions, too, with historic ports such as Gothenburg, Helsingborg and Malmö, and Stockholm, one of the most stylish and liveable European capitals. Even if you've read about it ahead of a visit, it can come as a surprise to boat and swim off the Stockholm waters, or take a local bus out to unpopulated outskirts of lakes and woodland.

If there's a negative side to all this, it lies in an introspective Nordic outlook on life that can be hard to cut across on a holiday trip, and in the over-regulatory Swedish state. Alcoholic drinks have to be bought, guiltily, at a state-run outlet; bars and restaurants, outside of the main cities, are lacklustre affairs: it's hard to resist a feeling that, compared to its southern neighbours, Sweden lacks a spontaneity and *joie de vivre*. You need to be sufficiently self-contained, know what you want to do, and be prepared to spend, to get the most out of a trip.

Over the last forty years, a wealth of **pro-women legislation** (anti-discrimination policies, good health-care, maternity and childcare provisions) has been passed. In line with this, a younger generation has emerged confident of their rights and with the expectation of full participation in all aspects of social and public life. Swedish women, however, are only too aware that there are many corners still to fight and that the uncertain economic future leaves little room for complacency. After decades of vigilance and activism, feminists are beginning to mobilize again against a political backlash. When the proportion of women representatives in government dropped after the 1991 election, campaigns and lobbies sprang into action. The main feminist network at present, *Stödstrumporna* ("support tights" after the earlier Scandinavian feminists "red stockings") rallies under the slogan "The Whole Wage" – their demand is for an equal share of the political and financial power of their country.

Jazz in the Snow

The jazz singer **Kate Westbrook** has travelled all over the world. She began her career as singer/instrumentalist with the Mike Westbrook Brass Band, a group of versatile musicians who played anywhere from concert halls to city parks. She subsequently married Mike and has since earned her living performing and touring. For two decades she has gone back to Sweden every other year or so, in all seasons and in all musical guises.

V ery early on in the life of the Westbrook Brass Band, before they had a manager, I wrote to the *Kulturhuset* arts centre in Stockholm suggesting that we might play there. The director of music, Johan Etzler, sent back a charming letter, inviting us to come. Over the decades Johan has become a close friend, and Sweden one of my favourite countries. The Swedes, though apparently so reserved, really respond to our music and I have the warmest feelings for the people and the countryside.

My most recent visit was to perform with a southern Swedish Big Band, the Tolvan Band, playing a piece that Mike and I had created using themes and arias from the work of Gioacchino Rossini. I had toured with the Tolvan before. They are excellent musicians and great people to work with (even if they do chew gum a lot, only removing it to eat or to put their instrument in their mouths). On this occasion the band was joined by soloists from other parts of the country – a cellist, a bass player, an accordionist, a percussionist, as well as Mike and myself from England.

I was the only woman in the band. Not unusual in a country like Britain, but slightly surprising in Sweden, where I have come to expect more enlightened attitudes. Nevertheless, I was never made to feel uncomfortable as the sole female. It may well have been an advantage that I only speak a few words of Swedish and so have no idea what people are saying to each other. Usually when travelling I at least make an attempt at the native tongue – I speak French and Italian fairly well, and sing in several languages (including a Swedish dialect song) – but I've barely made any progress in Swedish since my first trip. It's all too easy to become lazy when everyone, even in the most remote corners of the country, speaks English so well.

On this trip with Tolvan we had a rehearsal period in Lund, at the southwestern tip of the country, before setting off on tour around Scandinavia in a fine big bus. It was autumn, my favourite season in Sweden. The silver birches had turned, along with all the other deciduous trees, and harebells lingered in the scrubby heath and flat grey rocks. Farms dotted the landscape, many of them painted a marvellous deep terracotta red, reminiscent of parts of New England. I've been told that the red paint was originally used for the boat bottoms of fishing fleets, and was taken up as a cheap protective cover for wood-frame buildings, proofing them against the severities of the climate. A white line painted around the doors of barns points up the entrance in the dark, and the window frames of the houses are usually painted white too.

In the windows, above the ubiquitous gingham and lace cotton curtains, hang coloured hearts made from wood, or small glass ornaments, or dried flowers in bunches. The Swedish love arranging domestic trivia like this, and really go to town at Christmas, when small children wear crowns of evergreen studded with lighted candles. Travelling round Sweden at Christmas time I have seen moose in a snowy landscape, and skiers hiking across the flat countryside on short skis. I have

Travelling in the coldest part of the winter in a mini-bus is the equivalent of going to the North Pole in a cotton frock.

seen people pushing sledges bearing children, or wood, or groceries. On reaching a downward slope the "driver" steps onto the long runners at the back and rides down. When the ground is level again the tall handle at the rear of the sledge serves to steady the person pushing, rather like an elegant wooden zimmer frame.

Once, we were travelling in the coldest part of the winter with a small band, in an English mini-bus. This is the equivalent of going to the North Pole in a cotton frock. The inside of the windows towards the rear of the vehicle were caked with ice, and our skimpy tyres skated about on the surface of the road. At one point we were driving along a straight stretch beside a frozen lake when suddenly the bus performed a graceful pair of revolutions in the face of an oncoming truck, and landed in snowbound reeds at the lakeside. Within seconds an ambulance arrived out of nowhere, made sure that no one was hurt and disappeared again into the white empty landscape. Eventually we were helped by passing motorists to push the bus back onto the road and, miraculously, made the gig that night.

In such severe weather it's always good to have what's known as a "suede shoe gig", where the performance space and sleeping quarters are under the same roof or have inter-connecting doors so you don't have to mess up your suede shoes by going out in the street. A few years ago our trio (Mike and I and saxophonist Chris Biscoe) went to play in Härnösand on the east coast – not as far north as the Arctic Circle but north enough. Again it was winter, with the temperature at minus 24°C and falling. We were booked into a hotel only a short walk from the club, but during these few steps the moisture in our noses froze, tickling uncomfortably, and every breath hurt. The water in the inlet was iced over, leaving tankers and boats stranded like beached whales. Upstream a factory emitted a vile smell, made sharper still by the intense cold. There was a large illuminated print out of the temperature and time over the other side of the bay, and I spent much of the night staring out of the window in fascination as the recorded temperature dropped, and numbered minutes and seconds ticked by. The only other lights in view were the appallingly clear stars.

After Chernobyl, the region received one of the highest doses of radioactive fall-out outside Kiev.

With these long, dark winters, the suicide rate is high. During interminable journeys on the road, and in spite of myself, I frequently found my thoughts turning to death. There's a skeleton in the city museum in Stockholm, dating from two thousand years ago or more: a small person, buried in the foetal position. Oddly enough, I found this a very comforting image. Having summoned that creature to my mind's eye I could return to my book or get into conversation again.

After the long winter come the welcome signs of spring and the big thaw. Great icicles fall from the eaves of buildings, creating a real hazard in town for pedestrians. Everywhere there is deep slush, and the streams, rivers and lakes are full. Water is never very far away in Sweden.

Swimming in the summer is a bracing experience, with no Gulf Stream to take the cold edge off the sea. Inland lakes aren't much better, but the sun can feel wonderfully warm, shining late at night and coming back after only a few hours. The Härnösand promoter told us that she hates the summer. It is so short that she feels under tremendous pressure to get a tan, to have barbecues, and to relish the fact that it never quite gets dark. And the weather is not all the people of Härnösand have to be concerned about. The concert promoter also told us of the terrible effect the Chernobyl disaster has had on the region, which received one of the highest doses of radioactive fall-out outside Kiev. Local people are still bitter. They're no longer able to supplement their tables by gathering berries, fungi, and roots, and won't be able to again for many years.

On the autumn trip with Tolvan we were booked to play towns and cities in the south of the country before heading on to Gothenburg, a town which I find reassuringly familiar. Over the years I have been to the same hotel, the same clubs in Gothenburg and, on the whole, they change very little. I was outraged on this occasion when "our" Chinese restaurant, where the waitress used to expect to see us every year or so, had been transformed into an anonymous Japanese place. Although Gothenburg has a jazz club, the *Nefertiti*, for some reason we have never played there. We have, however, played in the rather grand theatre, the university, and in the art gallery flanked by sculpture and fine paintings. For several seasons we did concerts in a shambolic private museum/club owned by Sven, a dear friend. Touring as we do, we make friends along the way and intense bonds spring up, kept alive with occasional letters and postcards and rare visits. Sven was ancient and tall, immensely cultured and gracious, living with the cancer that made him as pale as Swedish porcelain and with his hair dyed brick red. He has since died and the venue has closed down.

From Gothenburg we travelled north to Stockholm. This time, instead of icing up, the bus overheated badly. We watched videos in the sweltering atmosphere until we could stand it no longer. In a rainsoaked industrial wasteland, we unloaded our gear and waited while relief buses were summoned, both inadequate. The original bus was fixed at last; the journey took eleven hours in all and we turned up at the club, tired, damp and late for the soundcheck.

Stockholm's *Fasching Club* has been host to all the great American and European jazz musicians. The room is long and narrow with a balcony round one end, and the management are forever trying to make the space work, in spite of its awkward skinny shape. They've tried putting the band below the balcony so that those above look down on the tops of the musicians' heads. They've put the stage on one side of the room, flanked by two blocks of audience. It was like this the night I sang there with Tolvan, meaning, in effect, that I spent the evening turning from one side to the other, or else looking straight into the eyeballs of the sound engineer who had his desk against the wall opposite the bandstand.

Almost all our Stockholm friends turned up for the concert. Poor Frippe, with his clean-shaven upper lip and chin, and wispy beard below, and emphatic be-bop talk that keeps him just this side of madness, clutching an alto saxophone and forever waiting to "sit in". Lovely deaf Gunilla, who spends all night driving taxis after the *Fasching* closes, was there, fragrant and in peach silk. One of her delights is to feed *surströmming* to the many jazz musicians she knows. Considered a great delicacy by the Swedes, *surströmming* is rotten herring and, as one musician so elegantly put it, "makes a bad fart smell like a breath of fresh air".

These days the *Fasching* can only afford to put on jazz a couple of nights a week, though one of my favourite Swedish singers, Monika Zetterlund, can still be heard there at regular intervals. She has performed with the best Swedish and American jazz instrumentalists. At the Memorial Concert for the assassinated prime minister, Olaf Palme – a champion of the arts who had many close friends among the artists and intellectuals of his country – she sang a politicized Swedish version of *As Time Goes By*, lamenting the country's loss to an audience mute with shock.

Apart from *Fasching Club*, Stockholm has a number of small jazz clubs, and a Radio Station concert hall where we once played a lunchtime concert. With the Radio Band, and various other groups, we have performed at the handsome concert hall in the *Kulturhuset*, an arts complex in a modern shopping mall, overlooking a fine example of 1950s' fountain design. Despite the drug addicts who inhabit the underground pedestrian area outside, I feel quite safe walking round here on my own. Indeed Stockholm is a lovely capital in which to wander. A great sweep of water reaches right into the heart of the city, where the public and commercial buildings are situated, bringing with it a glorious light and all the attendant bustle of a port. The old town is quaint and well-heeled, while the newer parts are spacious and clean, if a little soulless. There's a delightful sculpture down at the water's edge, of a person, apparently below ground, raising the lid of a manhole cover and poking his nose out into the air. He has been there, fooling passers-by, for at least twenty years.

It was like stepping from the cold north air into a painting by Delacroix or Matisse.

The Museum of Modern Art, jutting out on one of Stockholm's many promontories, is one of my favourite haunts. The collection is good, and they occasionally host concerts in the main gallery. It's a splendid thing to listen to music with a backdrop of Matisse's massive collage of "Apollo". You can get a good cup of coffee in the café, too, along with those strange bright green cakes that appear in every Swedish eatery.

With Tolvan we went to Västerås, stopping off several times to eat in motorway cafés. The menu never varies at these places, and the choice, though limited, is good. There's *Pytt i panna*, hash with an egg on top, very tasty nursery-type food. Or *Köttbullar*, which are meatballs served with Lingon berries (cranberries). I like the large flat wheels of crispbread that hang on specially designed wooden spikes, that never seem to go stale and that go with absolutely anything. The Swedes boast that country people eat bread made from the bark of trees but I've never come across it.

On reaching Västerås, we drove into an industrial estate, totally deserted and cloaked in darkness with warehouses towering between vast areas for loading and unloading. In the centre of this concrete park stood a small single-storey building, entirely on its own. Inside this odd venue there turned out to be a restaurant with a stage at one end, a manager who loves the music, and, later in the evening, a packed house and a terrific reception. It was all very Swedish.

At the end of a tour we often move on with the band to Finland. Though in the aftermath of two ferry disasters it will never feel the same again. I used to love taking the overnight boat from Stockholm to Turku or Helsinki, especially in the depths of winter with the sea frozen over, the small islands of the archipelago standing out dark against the glistening whiteness, and a great roaring noise of ice being riven by the prow of the ship. After the *smörgåsbord*, we would go up to the main lounge where there was invariably a singer with electric keyboard and rhythm box churning out ABBA songs (even the most sophisticated Swedes are proud as punch of ABBA). Then we would take a last look out on deck before turning in. Stepping back inside from the darkness to the light, it was always startling to be confronted by the sight of lots of gypsies. Many of the travelling people have family in Sweden and come from right across Russia and Finland to take these boats, bedding down for the night on the elaborately patterned carpet in all their finery. The women wear massive crinoline skirts, layer upon layer, each shot with gold or silver on vibrant colours. Small girls in elaborate dresses are festooned with ribbons and cloth flowers, while the men and boys wear tight-fitting waistcoats and flamboyant shirts. It was like stepping from the cold north air into a painting by Delacroix or Matisse.

TRAVEL NOTES

Languages Most people speak good, often perfect, English.

Transport Quick, efficient bus and train services connect most of the country. Cycling is popular, especially in the south.

Accommodation The great number of youth hostels and campsites means that finding a place to stay can be much less expensive than you might expect. It's also worth checking out private rooms, bookable through most tourist offices.

Guides The Rough Guide to Scandinavia (Penguin) has a good section on Sweden.

WOMEN'S ACCOMMODATION

Kvinnohöjden, Storsund 90, 78194 Borlänge (☎0243/22370). A feminist study centre and guest house in rural Sweden with room for fifty women. The centre has a sauna, a small sailing boat, library and darkroom. Week-long summer courses are held with residents sharing the cooking and chores. This is Sweden: no alcohol or drugs allowed.

BOOKS

Mary Wollstonecraft, *A Short Residence in Sweden, Norway and Denmark* (UK & US, Penguin, 1987). Searching account of Wollstonecraft's three-month solo journey through southern Scandinavia in 1795.

Agneta Pleijel, *The Dog Star* (UK, Peter Owen, 1992/US, Dufour). Powerful, emotive tale of a young girl's approach to puberty, by one of Sweden's leading writers.

Taiwan

Not least among the many anachronisms of Taiwan is its pretensions to be the legitimate Republic of China. At the end of the 1949 revolution the defeated Nationalists fled the mainland for the island and took full political and economic control. Their party, the Kuomintang, has remained in power ever since and, under the guise of securing the country from Communist invasion, held it under martial law for close on four decades. But, following the ending of martial law in 1986, this already economically advanced nation has seen dramatic changes. The increasingly rapid pace of industrialization has been accompanied by a steady move toward liberalization, evident in the leadership's tolerance of the main opposition Democratic Progressive Party (DPP) whose very existence would have been unthinkable not so long ago. The DPP rejects reunification in favour of establishing an independent Republic of Taiwan. In reality, as the restrictions and obstructions imposed by both sides continue to fall away, it seems more likely that the two Chinas will come closer together.

Political rights have never been a predominant issue in Taiwan. This is first and foremost an entrepreneurial society – money is an abiding obsession and consumerism rampant. Visitors expecting a harmonious and gentle taste of the East will be sorely disappointed. The massive overdevelopment of the main cities, crowded with ugly high-rise blocks and choked with traffic and pollution, can come as a shock, as can the incredibly high cost of living. Taiwan is second only to Tokyo in expense.

Travelling alone, however, is relatively safe. The strong military presence has meant that street crime is uncommon and Western foreigners are generally treated with great courtesy and kindness. Although the country has a fairly large community of ex-patriates (mainly American businessmen and itinerant English teachers), most of them tend to lead rarefied and isolated lives. Thus, in the less commercial districts of the main cities and all over the countryside you are likely to attract a great deal of attention. People may well stare and point at you but this rarely leads to more than a friendly, if sometimes too avid, interest.

As in Hong Kong and South Korea, **women** in Taiwan are caught between the conflicting demands of a modern, Westernized and highly competitive culture, and traditional Confucian values. In constitutional terms they are supposed to have equal rights in work and education, and indeed the numbers in higher education and the professions is rising all the time. Taiwan also has the highest proportion of female politicians in Asia. Yet women still face entrenched discrimination, are ghettoized in poorly paid jobs and expected to take a subservient role within marriage. Not surprisingly, reforms in employment and family law are the main priorities of the country's burgeoning women's movement. Another key concern is prostitution which, though illegal, exists on a massive scale (you'll be warned against wandering alone in the red light district of Taipei), making Taiwan a popular destination for Japanese businessmen in search of cheap sex.

Taipei without Maps

Kate Hanniker travelled to Taiwan to stay with a friend who was working there on a temporary contract. She spent a month exploring the capital, Taipei, and made a few trips to the south of the island.

Taiwan is a little island with big ideas. Physically it is half the size of Ireland, with a population of only nineteen million, yet the Nationalist Kuomintang Government still considers itself the only legitimate ruler of the vast mainland and it convenes regularly to pass legislation for the Peoples' Republic. In spite of, or perhaps because of, its exaggerated sense of self importance, it is extremely successful in other ways.

Within the last forty years the country has leapt from rags to riches. Its people are a disconcerting mixture of those men and women who have been caught up in the whirlpool of moneymaking activity and of those – largely the older generation – whom this frenzied activity has utterly passed by. Life for this latter category is noticeably more comfortable than it was thirty years ago but essentially their lifestyles remain little altered by the new wave of consumerism.

The bulk of the wealth is concentrated in the five major Taiwanese cities, and especially in Taipei, where the women are streets ahead of their country cousins in their Western dress. For the *nouveau riche*, life in Taiwan is luxurious and massively consumer-oriented with all shops open daily until 10pm. Unemployment stands at two percent and beggars, touts and pimps are noticeable by their absence. Towards the end of my visit I was thrown by the sight of a beggar and the word suddenly reeled back into my vocabulary (though squalor had not left it).

The cost, inevitably, of this surge of economic growth is overdevelopment, scant accommodation and appalling pollution. In Taipei, apartment blocks stand high and virtually back to back. On the outskirts of the city, homes are little more inviting than chicken shacks and three generations of a family are often crammed into one flat. Traffic is choking and anarchic. The Taiwanese prefer to call it "flamboyant" and the surprisingly low level of road accidents indicates that they employ not a little skill in getting about as quickly and as economically as possible. They use the same sixth sense when conducting their business affairs.

Since I was possibly the only redhead in Taipei, I caused something of a stir.

What struck me most during my four-week stay was how immediately secure I felt, despite the fact that I had only a limited Chinese vocabulary and a roughly sketched street-plan in English characters which at times impeded, rather than guided, my progress. Being able to roam freely and unaccosted was something I had not expected in Asia.

On one of the numerous occasions when I lost not only my way, but also all sense of direction, I felt safe enough to accept a lift from a man I had asked for directions. He spoke no English and was kind enough to leave his work and drive me to my destination on the other side of Taipei.

Whenever I asked the way (most people speak Chinglish to match my Englinese) I would be drawn into a lengthy confab and on occasions an entire family joined me on the street to mull over my map. At times the sense of obligation the Chinese showed towards me as a stranger transcended my (cynical) belief. Finally they would point me in any direction to save the important Chinese "face" and I would embark unknowingly on a vast detour. Yet again I'd have to hail a taxi, defeating my purpose of familiarizing myself with the city. With time I came to accept this as simply the most reliable method of getting from A to B without travelling via C and D.

My novelty value as a foreigner was seemingly endless. And since I was possibly the only redhead in Taipei, I caused something of a stir. Children ran up to me grinning as if I was a long lost friend. "Hey, Okay, Number One", they would holler. All foreigners are American to the Taiwanese. "*Ingwor*" ("I'm English") was a phrase I soon mastered, but it made no odds, their reaction was still as fervent.

Westerners seem to embody some kind of utopia for the Taiwanese. Fashionable Chinese women have rejected their traditional clothing, opting instead for bolstered shoulder pads. And Western images and models are used to promote even the most oriental of products. It's easy to see how this emulation is interpreted as adulation by the resident ex-pats, who live in isolated splendour in the north of Taipei. Their arrogance translates itself into maudlin attempts to recreate mini-Europes and USAs, epitomized by the disconcerting appearance here and there of a pub or *bierkeller*.

> **I was a street away from the notorious Snake Alley, where women are sold to Japanese businessmen for $1.25 a day.**

As a European woman I seemed to inspire respect and admiration, especially since I was negotiating the city by myself, unescorted. This is quite contrary to Chinese custom, rooted as it is in Confucianism and chauvinism. Attitudes, I'm assured, are gradually changing, but beyond the more sophisticated work places, sexual discrimination and harassment are still everyday problems. Women may rule over the home, traditionally a power base in Taiwanese society, but they have far less status in public life and double standards are very obvious. For example, it is accepted that men will have "other women" – prostitutes or mistresses – but a wife will be reviled and cast out if she is found to be "unfaithful".

In custodial cases the children will automatically stay with their father. And even where a woman has been subjected to domestic violence, she is ill-advised to seek a divorce, which may result in her social ostracism. Although Taiwanese businesswomen wield considerable power, they are often paid less and work longer hours than their male counterparts and many working-class women suffer harsh conditions in the nation's sweatshops.

The only time that I felt ill at ease in Taiwan was on my final morning when I visited the Lungshan Temple area. There was no obvious threat but the atmosphere unnerved me. A dog twitched to death on the sidewalk and a crowd of old men looked on and shouted useless encouragement. Younger men in string vests stood entranced around a streethawk who measured up a white powder in brass scales. Schoolgirls hovered half-naked in doorways. Later I learnt that I was a street away from the notorious Snake Alley, where women are sold to Japanese businessmen for $1.25 a day and where turtles are tortured for their blood, which is guzzled by the same men to increase their virility.

The sex industry is big business in Taiwan. All except the most expensive hotels increase their profit margins by letting out rooms by the afternoon and by transmitting soft porn day and night. Hairdressers and tearooms often operate as hostess-type joints, not necessarily brothels, but places where the lonely businessman can fork out large sums of money in exchange for a few hours of female company.

My great joy in Taipei was looking around the temples. The Confucian Temple seemed to be the only public place to have escaped the rest of the city's haphazard development. The Taoist temples on the other hand were home to the same bedlam to be found in the streets. Chickens, children and dogs run amok through the endless passages, up into the small sub-temples. The tiered levels offer panoramic views of the city.

The temples throw up constant surprises to the Western eye accustomed to uniform architecture and solemn devotion. On one floor multi-coloured puppets rotate in a perpetual electronic parade, offering gifts to the gods. Somewhere in the grounds an opera may break out. Old men sit around a table playing cards and watching a TV rigged up precariously on an altar. A businessman waves joss sticks and throws crescent-shaped pieces of wood to find out if he should change his car.

The state is just beginning to invest money in tourism but as yet there are few concessions to the Western traveller. This has its advantages and its drawbacks. It is pleasant to find areas of natural beauty still unspoilt by the commercialism which has so ravaged the cities. But it can be frustrating when travelling to be faced with the options of a state-run tour or of getting lost trying to decipher Chinese town names. The tours are blatantly commercial, whisking you from site to site with a final compulsory stop at a local factory, where you will be assailed by pretty girls hoping to persuade you to part with your money.

Initially I was irritated by the persistence of the sales people, not only in the tourist shops but also in the village stores, where the shopkeepers wave excitedly and shout at any foreigner passing within ten metres of their shops to come inside and spend. Finally I learnt to laugh at the unashamedness of it all.

Getting around by public transport is cheap and efficient but you're restricted in where you go and what you see. I rented a car which is relatively inexpensive. Cheaper are the mopeds which clog up the streets of Taipei (often with an entire family aboard one bike), but you have to be brave to contend with the traffic. Driving down the east coast I found wild and untouched beaches. Central Taiwan was a visual feast – the tranquility of the huge mountains chilling the lakes and paddy fields by night gave way to the intense heat of the March sun and lizards and creepers and luscious foliage.

TRAVEL NOTES

Languages Mandarin is the official language but most people use Taiwanese. English is widely taught although people tend to be shy of trying it out in public.

Transport An efficient bus and train network covers most of the island, and taxis are abundant and relatively cheap.

Accommodation The international hotels are very expensive, but there are plenty of cheaper and reasonably comfortable youth hostels.

Special Problems Expense. You'll have to fork out for accommodation and food. Harassment is rarely a problem, although few women wander alone into the red light districts of Taipei and Kaohsiung, where drug-peddling and prostitution breed their own violence.

Although the government is now toeing a softer political line, you should be very careful not to compromise others in political discussions. The Taiwanese are still exhorted to inform on potential "Communist agents".

Guides *Taiwan – A Travel Survival Kit* (Lonely Planet) is the best general guide.

CONTACTS

Women's Research Programme, Population Studies Centre, National Taiwan University, Roosevelt Rd, Section 4, No 1, Taipei. A resource for information on women's issues, although most of the literature published is in Chinese.

The Mandarin Training Centre, National Taiwan Normal University, 162 Hoping East Rd, Section 1, Taipei. The common-room noticeboard is a useful place to look for contacts, information about jobs, language courses, accommodation etc.

BOOKS

Ching-Hsi Pserng and Chiu-Kuei Wang, *Death in a Cornfield* (UK, Oxford University Press, 1994). Illuminating collection of stories by Taiwan's leading contemporary writers, three of them women.

Tanzania

Compared with Kenya, its northern neighbour, tourism in Tanzania is relatively low-key. Few travellers venture beyond the "northern circuit" of the capital, Dar-es-Salaam, the island of Zanzibar, Arusha (for the ascent of Mount Kilimanjaro), the Ngorongoro crater and the Serengeti. The highest mountain in Africa, Kilimanjaro in particular attracts thousands of trekkers each year, eager to conquer its snow-capped summit. Yet Tanzania is a huge country and it's well worth heading beyond the famous tourist sites simply to take in its vast landscape of plains, lakes and mountains, and visit wildlife reserves such as the Gombe Stream National Park (featured below). Though conditions are improving, independent travel – without

the money to rent a jeep or a small plane – can be slow and arduous. However, once outside the capital which, like most large cities, has definite no-go areas, most women find the country reasonably relaxed. As a general rule you should dress modestly, especially in predominantly Muslim areas such as the island of Zanzibar.

Tanzania's population is made up of a diverse range of tribes and cultures – Muslim, Christian, Animist, Hindu. No single group dominates, and the language of Kiswahili affords a very tenuous communal link. Since gaining independence from the British in 1961 life for the Tanzanians, beset by shortages of everything from fuel to vital medical supplies and foodstuffs, has not been easy. Implementation of the socialist policies of President Julius Nyerere, in power for over twenty years, was fraught with difficulties, dominated by a flailing economy further crippled by war with Uganda. Recently, however, conditions have begun to improve. When Nyerere stepped down in 1985 (he remained chairman of the sole political party for another five years), Ali Hassan Mwinyi took over as president: his policy changes, among them a shift away from reliance on collective farming, appear to be working. Today the country is attracting aid money from Western countries, tourism is on the increase, new roads are being built and there's food in the shops. An air of optimism surrounds the build-up to the first multiple-party elections in 1995.

The last few years have also seen progress in the development of the **women's movement** in Tanzania. In addition to the National Women's League, *Umoja ya Wananwake wa Tanzania*, which has a branch in nearly every village, the Tanzania Media Women's Association (TAMWA) is an excellent umbrella organization, based in Dar es Salaam. Among other things, in 1991, TAMWA helped to start the country's first ever crisis centre dealing with sexual harassment, domestic violence and discrimination against women and children. It also broadcasts radio programmes, organizes workshops, and produces popular education material and a regular newspaper, *Sauti ya Siti*.

Thirty-six Hours to Paradise

Lori Reich spent some time doing development work in southern Tanzania before she decided it was time to explore the western part of the country. She was especially interested in visiting Gombe Stream, a national park and research area for Jane Goodall's famous studies of chimpanzees. Her visit to the park, which lies on the shore of Lake Tanganyika, began with a 36-hour train journey.

A sorry looking heap of scrawny chickens with their legs tied together was pushed under my seat while someone dumped a gunny sack of dried maize kernels in a corner. A woman outside the train was trying to cram some cloth-tied bundles of baskets and cooking pots, rims sticking out at awkward angles, through the window. Welcome to the women's second-class compartment 18 B on the Tanzania National Railway. Thirty-six scheduled hours from Dar-es-Salaam on the Indian Ocean straight west to Kigoma on Lake Tanganyika.

Sharing the sauna-like compartment with me, besides the chickens, were two women. Judging by their carefully braided hair and the shimmering polyester fashions beneath their *kangas*, the pair were office workers on a holiday to their family home. Three more women, also with *kangas* over their dresses, held young children, quietly squirming, and babies sucking contentedly at their breasts. There were quite a few older children too. These compartments were designed to sleep six, as the men's compartments still do. But children of school age don't count as passengers and always travel with the women, along with all the baggage.

I was conspicuous, not only for my white skin, but also as the only woman not wearing a *kanga* over my skirt. These colourful rectangles of cotton have hundreds of uses: head-

> *She didn't need to point out the toilet. I could smell it, a reeking hole in the floor of a dark closet without a door.*

scarves, dresses, shawls, baby slings, baggage holders, towels, dressing gowns, bed sheets . . . there's an old saying about Tanzanians being born into them and buried in them when they die. I regretted having packed mine so far down in my backpack – I should have known better by now.

Just as our compartment was beginning to cool down with the evening breeze, one of the women wrestled the only window up, shutting off the cooling draft of air. She then deftly wedged a green flip-flop into the sash to secure it in place.

I let out a yelp. With all the children, the bundles and bags piled up all around us, the compartment was only made bearable by that whisper

579

of air. The woman looked at me in surprise. Thieves ride on the roof of the train, she explained. At night they lower themselves into the carriages, grabbing watches, money, and anything else they can get before disappearing. This method effectively locks the window against them. She explained other things, too, such as the water situation. "Use it now, while there still is water in the tiny sink under the window", she advised, "by tomorrow it will be finished".

She didn't need to point out the toilet. I could smell it down the corridor, a reeking hole in the floor of a dark broom closet without even a door. If I hadn't already been dizzy from the smell, the rushing of the track under my bottom as I squatted would have done the trick.

The train stopped at every station, village and railway worker's shack along the track. With the prolonged deceleration for the stops and the gradual starting up again, progress was painfully slow. I got out my packed supper and shared some of it with the children. At first they were very shy, then amazed that I could speak Swahili (most of the farmers I'd been working with in the south spoke no English) and ate the same food as they did. Soon we were laughing and chatting away, playing traditional riddle games which they nearly always won.

Eventually we pulled down the beds and slept fitfully in the airless, cramped carriage. To the slow rhythmic clacking of the rails I debated silently with myself which was worse, the heat or the thieves. Or was it the mosquitoes that made themselves known as soon as someone turned off the single, dim bulb which was our only light?

In the morning when the train stopped yet again, the woman retrieved her flip-flop and opened the window to start haggling with a boy outside selling boiled eggs. She shouted at another who had roasted maize. Women with baskets of guavas and bananas balanced on their heads caught the coins thrown down to them. Farther down the line you could buy souvenirs, such as carved wooden whistles, nodding birds on a stick, and wild honey mixed with water and poured into old gin bottles.

We reached Tabora Station in the early afternoon where, with an endless shunting of carriages, the train was divided. Passengers bound for Mwanza and Lake Victoria shuffled off with their baggage and kiddies. The woman with the flip-flop and her friend waved a cheery goodbye. Meanwhile the women who, like me, were staying on board, took their babies and washed them under the standpipes to remove the accumulated effects of not having nappies. Adults demurely washed hands and faces, brushing their teeth with twigs bought from yet another boy at the side of the train. Once chewed, this particular type of wood becomes quite bristly, making an effective toothbrush.

When the shunting had finally finished my flip-flop companion came back to find me. There'd been a mix-up and no second-class carriages were going to Kigoma. I would have to move to third-class and if I didn't hurry I wouldn't even get a seat. I humped my pack over to the new train and joined the general scramble for space. Probably more out of the Tanzanians' kind attitude to foreigners than the force of my elbows I managed to secure a seat, right next to the toilet. No more comfy segregated compartment with pull-down beds, sink (with or without water) or dim light bulb here. No glass in the windows to stop the cooling breeze. Third-class is distinctly "open plan".

This time, just as I'd been warned, hands began to reach down from the outside roof of the train.

Facing me were two guys from Zaire. As the train slowly started on the long straight stretch to Kigoma, they talked about their musical tour of Dar-es-Salaam. At first I thought they were bluffing, trying to chat me up, but once the train was more or less rolling they got out a guitar. One played while the other beat amazing rhythms on the hard guitar case.

Despite the stench from the nearby toilet, and the crowd of people lurching in the aisles, with their infectious music the two men held the entire carriage's attention. They got us all laughing, clapping and even joining in the choruses – a mixture of French, Swahili and Lingala, the main language of Zaire. Had there been room we would have got up and danced. Meanwhile the train continued as before, more often stopping than going. In the vast dry plains I occasionally spotted antelope, the loping shape of a giraffe running through the dappled heat or sunlight glinting on buffalo horn. Then, at dusk, the train stopped, yet again in the middle of nowhere.

This time, just as I'd been warned, hands began to reach downward from the outside roof of the train. To shouts of protest from the victims, they grabbed at anything they could; watches, glasses, caps, small bundles and baggage disappeared up through the open windows. I ducked my head in my lap in an instinctive reaction to danger. Suddenly the indignant cries became focused on my Zairean companions and I raised my head to see their guitar – our collective sanity – being stealthily removed. Anger quickly overcame fear. With a protesting growl and one movement, the Zaireans and I pulled it back from those grasping hands. Cheers rang out. Individual losses were forgotten in the sheer joy of saving "our" music. We sang until darkness became complete.

At midday, the train finally lurched into Kigoma, on the shore of Lake Tanganyika, at the end of the line. My aching muscles felt every one of the 36 hours I had travelled so far. Not wanting to lose anymore time,

I headed off on a local bus to nearby Ujiji where I was to catch the water taxi to Gombe Stream.

Being early, I amused myself by talking to the fishermen who were mending nets in the shade of their boats. I joined some children splashing in the warm, clear water of the lake in which tiny fishes nibbled at my toes. I took the opportunity to wash off some of the worst dust from my face and arms, and with it all the lingering strain of the train ride.

An old wooden boat, surprisingly large, finally chugged into sight. As I waded out to it with my backpack on my back, I felt envious of the Tanzanian women who calmly balanced their colourful bundles on their heads, hitched up their *kangas* and, with children strapped to their sides, sashayed gracefully after me through the knee-deep water.

There being no roads to the villages along the shoreline, the water taxi serves as a kind of local bus. Like the train, it stopped at every tiny village that clung to the steep hillsides of the lake, unloading sacks of maize and rice, and disgorging passengers along the way.

It was late afternoon when we pulled in nearly to the shore and I was able to "walk the plank" to dry land. The plank was very narrow and with the boat rocking unsteadily and a heavy pack on my back, I was glad that there were few passengers left to witness my wobbly progress.

After asking them to pick me up in a couple of days, I waved goodbye to the friendly crew. As the chugging of the engine receded I felt an overwhelming peace. The only sounds came from the soft lapping of the water on the sandy beach, and birds singing in the forest.

Gombe Stream, like all the villages along the lake, has no roads, no electricity, and sees very few visitors. The park ranger and the chimp researchers live in a small secluded area away from any tourists. I was disappointed that Jane Goodall herself was not there.

I was to stay in a simple cement building, grandly called a "lodge", which was divided into narrow individual sleeping cubicles and a communal living area. The only windows consisted of heavy iron grillwork backed with mosquito screening and the door was secured by a massive bolt. The blackened cookhouse just down the path had an ancient cast-iron stove and doors with similar stout grilling over the windows. Ernest, the park ranger,

> *It was eerie being the caged animal with thirty free-roaming baboons watching my every movement.*

showed me around, completed the inevitable paperwork and fee collection, made arrangements for the morning and left me alone.

I had just got the fire going in the cookhouse and put the rice on to boil when I heard the loud snap of a twig outside. Ernest had warned me, but until that moment I could never have understood what it was really like to be living in a zoo. A troop of baboons had quietly surrounded the building and were observing me. It was eerie being the caged animal with thirty free-roaming baboons watching my every movement. Soon the smell of the fruit and onions got the better of their shyness and they were scrambling on the grillwork, screeching and trying to reach my food through the bars. Luckily I was safe inside, and by the time I had finished the dishes they had disappeared.

I had good reason to believe the numerous warnings personally penned by Jane Goodall and posted all about the lodge. In her succinct style, she wrote about not feeding the baboons and chimps, describing the potential danger of crossing their path (chimps are three times as powerful as the average male human). When studying the

> *He longed for the fast city life of music, discos and cold beer.*

chimps she used to put her young son in a cage for protection. Nowadays no children under seven are ever allowed into the area of forest where the chimps roam – some years earlier a group of chimps killed a child who'd been out collecting firewood.

Towards dusk I went for a swim in the lake. Stars were beginning to appear as I walked back up the sandy beach to the "lodge" and fishermen out on the water had hung huge lanterns on their boats to attract the fish. Their glow echoed the starlight on the otherwise inky black surface. All night the sound of the men's singing drifted through the still air like a lullaby. By sunrise the fishermen had disappeared, their nets full of slim silver fish which would be dried before being "shipped" to all parts of the country as a popular delicacy.

That morning, as Ernest and I climbed up the steep hills of the rainforest to the main chimp observation hut, I was soon gulping for breath. The lush, tropical vegetation hides an unforgiving terrain. We finally arrived to meet the chimp researchers who, trained by Jane, carry on the day-to-day observations while she's away. But for their tape recorders, dictaphones and camcorders, these men looked like typical village farmers, often barefoot in their threadbare trousers and ranger hats. With minds as sharp as their equipment, they knew the name and family history of every chimp we saw that day.

It's hard to describe the first chimpanzee I saw in the wild. Majestic, awe-inspiring, nonchalant? It was one of those magical moments: she looked at me long and hard, straight in the eye, before deciding I was simply another researcher and continuing on her way. That day I watched chimp babies having a rough and tumble, and a big male drumming on an empty barrel. In the rainforest clearing the sound reverberated off the dripping trees. My Zairean friends would have been jealous of his volume if not his skill. Then I noticed a female's rear end. It was a deep red, very swollen and painful looking. Assuming she had somehow injured herself, I pointed her out to Ernest. He grinned at me and euphemistically explained that the red swelling was a sign she was ready to mate.

The chimps eventually wandered further away, trailed by the researchers who were still meticulously recording every interaction. Tourists aren't usually allowed to follow researchers or chimps away from the observation hut, but despite my earlier struggle I managed to convince Ernest that I was fit enough to make it through the forest to explore the animals' habitat.

After what felt like hours of clambering up and down steep slopes we stopped for a short rest beside some water. By that time Ernest seemed like an old buddy. Most Tanzanians are easy to talk to and endlessly curious about life abroad. I answered the standard questions: "No, I am not rich. No, I am not married. Perhaps one day I may have children, but not now. Yes, my parents are alive and I miss them." I told him how envious I was of his position, living and working with nature. His life seemed rich in all the right ways, uncomplicated and very desirous. Needless to say, he vehemently disagreed. Being well-educated (he spoke perfect English), he longed for the fast city life of music, discos and cold beer. Because there was no local school his wife and children had to live in town so he only got to see them once a month. Nor was there a hospital. He hated being so isolated and wanted to transfer to another park – somewhere with lots of tourists. His words made me stop and think. Perhaps I was being hopelessly idealistic. We laughingly decided to exchange lives.

In between the slipping and the sliding, the rocks and the streams, and the aching calf muscles, I had glimpses of the forest canopy, alive with colobus monkeys with their distinctive white shoulder pads. The dense undergrowth was also filled with birds and buzzing insects. We even spotted a bongo, a rare species of antelope.

By the time we circled down to the lake again for the long trek back along hot sand to the lodge, I had fallen in love with this peaceful, beautiful place where, in spite of Ernest's longings, there are no cars, no discos and no clocks to tell you how long you've been gone.

TRAVEL NOTES

Languages Kiswahili, English and numerous tribal languages. Learning a few standard greetings in Swahili will get you a long way.

Transport Bus services, though erratic, cover much of the country and are likely to improve with road repairs. Also useful are the mini-buses (*matutus*) and shared taxis. Trains are slower and timetables notoriously unreliable, but can be more comfortable, especially if you travel first-class.

Accommodation The YMCAs are cheap, friendly and admit women too; the YWCA in Dar is a good and secure meeting place. Hotels and guest houses are similar to those in Kenya though less developed. All "tourist" hotels require payment in hard currency, not Tanzanian shillings.

Special Problems Entry to any of the national parks is quite expensive and again payable in hard currency, preferably US dollars. Theft is mainly a problem in the capital and in and around bus or train stations.

Guides *East Africa – A Travel Survival Kit* (Lonely Planet) has thorough chapters on Tanzania.

CONTACTS

The Tanzania Media Women's Association, described in the chapter introduction, can be contacted by writing to PO Box 6143, Dar es Salaam.

BOOKS

⭐ **Dervla Murphy**, *The Ukimwi Road: From Kenya to Zimbabwe* (UK, John Murray, 1993). *Ukimwi* is the Swahili word for AIDS, a unifying if harrowing theme in Dervla Murphy's 3,000-mile journey by bicycle from Kenya through Uganda, Tanzania, Malawi and Zambia to Zimbabwe.

Jane Goodall, *Through a Window: My Thirty Years with the Chimpanzees of Gombe* (US, Houghton Mifflin, 1990). Sequel to Goodall's *Shadow of Man* (1971), continuing her perceptive study of Tanzania's chimp population.

Thailand

Thailand's tourist boom shows little sign of abating. For many years the pre-eminent Asian tourist destination, the country caters for over five million visitors a year. Backpackers, trekkers and veteran hippies are now mingling with well-heeled tourists and families on package deals, attracted by immaculate beaches, ancient ruins, Buddhist temples and tiny unspoilt islands. With its well-established tourist infrastructure, Thailand easily sells itself as an exotic yet manageable taste of the East.

Bangkok, a city of sky-scrapers and highways, dotted with old temples and market-places, is the commercial and cosmopolitan hub of the country. Although regarded as a success story of South Asian industrialization, its fame (or notoriety) still largely rests on the red-light district of Patpong Road, which together with the beach resort of Pattaya to the east, forms the nucleus of Thailand's sex

industry – a legacy of the country's role as a "rest and recreation" area for GIs during the Vietnam War. For most travellers the sex industry is an irrelevance but, like the sweatshops and homeless kids roaming the streets, it's hard to ignore this aspect of the capital, even though just a few blocks away from the neon lights and massage parlours most people continue to follow a traditional Buddhist way of life. If you choose to explore the city's seedier side it's as well to be sensitive and avoid asking too many questions, however well-meaning. Not that you're likely to feel threatened by men – women travellers are of little interest to punters and pimps alike – rather that, as Lucy Ridout points out in her piece on Pattaya, sex workers are understandably angry and tired of being interrogated by "concerned" Westerners.

From the point of view of harassment, Thailand comes as a welcome respite after the hustle and restrictions of much of Asia. Although lone travellers are always the focus of attention, and subject to curious questioning, the atmosphere is generally tolerant and relaxed, and the interest rarely feels threatening. Added to this, there are always other travellers to team up with, or Western comforts to indulge in, if the going gets hard. As anywhere, it helps to show respect for local customs, to return the politeness of your hosts and dress modestly. Theft is a growing problem, although given the extremes of poverty in many of the areas frequented by tourists, it's surprising how low-key this is.

Thailand's tourist explosion has in many ways widened the gap between rural and urban economies. Droughts, floods and government indifference conspire to make a subsistence livelihood untenable for four months of every year, forcing thousands to migrate from their farms to the city. Among them are the bulk of women who work in the service and sex industries, often earning minimal wages while the government cashes in on a potential billion dollars in foreign-exchange earnings. A number of **women's organizations** have been campaigning to improve the conditions for Thailand's sex workers, mirroring similar efforts in the Philippines. One such is the Women's Information Centre of the Foundation for Women, based in Bangkok, which is committed not only to providing immediate assistance to those exploited by the industry, but targets the initiators of organized sex tours, lobbies politicians and campaigns for international support and media co-operation in not sensationalizing the issue.

A Familiar Charm

Until 1990 **Madeleine Cary** juggled her life as a single parent with a career as a media producer. That year her son Ky, aged sixteen, was killed in a tragic accident. After some time trying to recuperate and heal with family and friends, she decided it was time to seek life-affirming experiences again. With a backpack, a few savings and no clear itinerary in mind, she flew to Bangkok, marking the beginning of ten months' low-budget travel through Southeast Asia, including Malaysia (see p.403).

I awoke on my first morning in Bangkok to the quickening rhythm of bells from the neighbouring Buddhist temple. At five in the morning there were no travellers or tourists to be seen; only the local Thai community, the saffron-robed young monks, the crisply uniformed schoolchildren, the street vendors and peddlars going about their business. The overnight rainfall had left a fresh damp air that was being injected with the dawn aromas of incense and smoking woks. Petrol fumes and the chaotic blasts of horns and revving engines announced the frenetic city life starting up just streets away.

Fourteen years earlier I had awoken in this same city about to embark on a 1970s drop-out adventure. I thought of where life had taken me since then and how, having just turned forty, I was now embarking on a year's lone travel in Southeast Asia. A deep personal tragedy had brought me to a watershed. I gazed at the activity on Bangkok's bustling streets and promised myself to use this year to find confidence, purpose and peace again.

Why I chose Thailand as the place to start owes much to my distant memories of the place. I was acutely aware of how tourism and the backpacker trail had brought about a major transformation. Others had warned me that I would not recognize the place. However, something enduring and comforting about the Thai culture and people had lured me back. It was at least a relatively familiar place to begin and I refused to believe that the entire country had been over-run with foreign businessmen, lager louts and hippies looking for cheap thrills.

Millions of visitors pass through Bangkok every year and yet I was still startled by their sheer numbers when I arrived in the city. I felt conspicuous with my squeaky-clean rucksack and my general demeanour which vacillated between naive excitement and a novice's paranoia. The majority of younger travellers had a uniform appearance of tie-dyed baggies and beaded hair. This was no surprise but I was taken aback by their "cooler than thou" attitude. In areas developed to cater to the needs of the back-packer, like Koa San Road, the local people have adopted all the fashions and manners of their Western counterparts. I stayed for two nights in this area and found few people approachable. During the day I explored the city; when I entered the old Thai suburbs, enjoying a spicy soup at a street market, or taking tea at an old shack by the river, I began to remember the familiar charm of Thai life.

As soon as my jet lag lifted, I took a train heading south from Bangkok, intent on finding my own way through the southern peninsula, trying, like many a lone wanderer, to plot a route away from the tourist and hippie trail. My first port of call was to be Hua Hin, a town on the eastern coast which the guidebook described as a "delightful seaside resort the Thais are keeping for themselves". When I arrived I drove through the quiet back streets in a rickshaw and was delivered to an old-style guest house where two young Thai women received me warmly, offering me a cheap, clean room. I settled in and felt at peace for the first time since leaving England. Until, that is, I set out to investigate the place at dusk and found that, beyond the old town, bars, neon lights and discos flooded the street and everywhere I looked, lithe young Thais, both male and female, were accompanied by large, well-heeled Western men. I was angry at first at the ill-researched guidebook and then felt amused by the irony of the situation. In trying to escape the backpackers, I had ended up in a beach resort where prostitution was veiled behind the guise of holiday romance.

I never felt harassed but frequently felt I was being looked after.

Later that evening I sat on the guest house balcony with the two young Thai women and discovered they were both from rural farming communities and had come to the place to seek a fortune. One had a young baby and the three of them shared room and board in the lodgings in exchange for looking after guests. Their real earnings came from foreign "boyfriends" and much of their money was sent home to their village families. They clearly saw themselves as following a path which meant freedom from poverty, but it left a disturbing impression of the nature of Western exploitation.

For the next few weeks I travelled on public transport from one small town to another, trying to avoid the coastal "resorts". Thai bus and train travel was cheap, regular and reasonably comfortable. I rarely met other Westerners on these trips as most of them used the network of air-con tourist buses which shipped them en masse from one popular resort to another. Obviously, buses packed with wealthy Westerners make good targets for bandits and pickpockets and it was no surprise that tales of unfortunate incidents usually involved this expensive and exclusive means of transport.

I enjoyed the rhythm of those first few weeks of travel. Every day I would make a journey by bus or train alongside amiable Thais and enjoy the fantastic views unfolding through the windows: rice paddies, rubber plantations, jungles, rolling hills and sharp, jagged mountains. I watched the pattern of daily life in remote farming settlements, villages or small towns. Everywhere, Buddhist temples adorned the environment. I never felt harassed but frequently felt I was being looked after. It was hard to feel lonely when a toothless old lady would offer me some rice cake or a helpful bus driver would go off his route to deliver me to suitable accommodation. Often I would leave the bus and have a host of concerned, smiling Thai passengers waving to me. After finding a cheap place to stay, I would wander out to watch the magical transformation on the Thai streets as dusk fell. Night life is almost as bustling as day life in Thailand. Street food stalls appear and serve up delicious steaming concoctions within minutes. House shutters are open revealing tableaux of the family life within. Markets are a sensory delight, their cornucopia of exotic produce and domestic goods displayed together in incongruous partnerships; pigs' heads hang next to haberdashery; mounds of tobacco are flanked by dried fish; flowers and strings of sausages sway together from overhead rafters.

Although I had learnt the power of contact through just a smile and a few gesticulations, I was aware that my inability to speak their language was becoming a problem for me. Thai is tonal and very difficult to grasp and I had failed to pick up more than a rudimentary collection of words. I started to feel inadequate; was I so conditioned by Western verbosity that I was incapable of relinquishing the need to verbalize and intellectualize for a while? Then an incident occurred which acted as a catalyst.

I had crossed the peninsula to the western coast and was coming into the province of Phang-Nga, which was reputed to have unique geographical features: huge limestone rocks rose up from the sea in remarkable formations, some of which housed ancient caves with pre-historic drawings. Interested in exploring the area, I arranged to go on my first organized tour, a cut-price expedition that promised a guided boat trip to the rocks and caves and, later, a visit to a floating village built on rafts. On the morning of departure, however, it turned out I was the only low-budget traveller in town and so I had to take the tour alone. For some reason, the English-speaking tour guide failed to appear. Thus I was chauffeured round the magnificent sights by a taciturn old Thai boatman who chewed on his cigarette and gazed out to sea the whole time. I felt a childish disappointment and sat in a sulk as we sailed around the weird and beautiful seascape. I had been secretly hoping that I would meet other travellers on the tour, or, at least, have a tour guide to converse with in English. I realized then that my capacity to take joy from the experience was being hampered by my inability to share my impressions and sensations verbally. I surrendered to my Western conditioning and decided to go on the backpacker trail.

Travellers' tales were becoming predictable; ideas and impressions were hackneyed; attitudes were often reactionary.

It was not difficult. I was close to the area where the impact of tourism is mushrooming at an incredible rate out from over-developed Phuket to the surrounding islands and coastal resorts. On a boat crossing to the island of Ko Lanta, I was approached by several young Thai touts. Already English was the common language again. Each tout brandished photo albums of their resort, usually the same Polaroid visions of grinning guests, palm-lined beaches, grass huts and sunsets as the next. I took pot luck with a place named "Paradise" and was herded into a pick-up truck with several other travellers when the boat docked. And so I finally got to experience the pleasures and pains of mingling with other backpackers. I indulged in verbal diarrhoea for days, incessantly articulating everything that had happened on my travels so far. I was not alone. Others would arrive, dump the rucksack, order a coconut shake and be off on a three-hour monologue before they even asked where you were from. The rapid turnover rate meant that different people arrived every day – I probably met at least fifteen different nationalities in the space of five days. Eventually, however, it all started to feel repetitious. Travellers' tales were becoming predictable; ideas and impressions were hackneyed; attitudes were often surprisingly reactionary. One evening a Swiss hippie waxed lyrical, claiming that the song *Message in a Bottle* said it all about the state of the world. When he started quoting Phil Collins lyrics, I went to my hut to pack. It was time to return to my previous lone travelling routine.

I headed back to the mainland and travelled down to Satun, the mainly Muslim Thai province that borders Malaysia. In the evenings the Thai national anthem was pumped out over the streets on loudspeakers just to remind these traditionally rebellious people of their Thai citizenship. I relished the varied and fascinating Thai culture with renewed enthusiasm and intended to get the best out of my last two weeks before my visa expired. In an effort to get to the nearby island of Ko Tarutao, a national park of reputed stunning beauty, I stumbled across a bizarre place that gave my sojourn in Thailand its final fling. Boat trips to Ko Tarutao were over for the season but there was a small vessel heading out to Ko Bulon, an island which was not even mentioned in the guidebook. I thought I had finally found an untarnished gem, an authentic, unspoilt Thai island.

Ko Bulon was a complete surprise. The island consisted of a small Thai community in transition from living off the fishing and farming trade to developing the place for low-budget tourism. It was all in embryonic form when I arrived yet already there were several

It was necessary to be vetted by these two strong women before you could be accepted into the community.

Westerners encamped, almost permanently, in self-made beach huts and tree houses. Mostly they were exiles from Europe and North America who, for love of the country, or addiction to its drugs or lifestyle, had worked out the best way to reside longterm in Thailand. Ko Bulon was close to the island of Langkawi in Malaysia which meant the two-month Thai visa could be easily renewed in a twenty-four hour trip across the border.

In a sense, Ko Bulon was a microcosm of modern Thailand. Local people seeking a livelihood and security were prepared to cash in on the Westerners who sought an escape into a free and sensual lifestyle. It was a strange synthesis and helped me understand more clearly how the onslaught of tourism had occurred in the country at large. What was different about Ko Bulon was the fact that the foreigners at least made some attempt to adapt to the Thai community. Many knew fluent Thai and some even lived and worked with the Thai families. I was staying in an area owned by the patriarch Bang Lee and his huge extended family. One of his daughters-in-law ran the local store, a bamboo-stilted platform with shelves of produce and hardware. She had befriended a Thai-speaking Icelandic woman who helped her with the store and the children. I got the feeling it was necessary to be vetted and passed by these two strong women before you could be accepted into the community. I was lucky enough to be invited to dine in the storeowner's living quarters on my first evening and she liked the way I amused and entertained her children. I was offered a tent to sleep in on the beach. Later, when the crushing heat made it too hot for a tent even overnight, I was given floor space in someone's treehouse.

Bang Lee had already built a few basic beach shacks and a spartan restaurant for the occasional travellers who, like myself, found the place almost by accident. He was planning a major conversion to cope with a future influx of backpackers and tourists and was already chopping down the beautiful trees which lined the beach so that there would be timber for bulding. Ironically, it was the Westerners who lived in the community who took greatest offence at this development. They bombarded Bang Lee with eco-conscious arguments but he, naturally, was irrevocably caught up in visions of future fortune and power.

As I passed a window, a young woman with a glowing tan and confident gaze stared back at me. I was looking in a mirror.

Not all the Westerners saw Bang Lee's plans as a threat, however. One, an enterprising American who, despite mastering the Thai language and donning a sarong, still hung on to his cultural roots, was planning his own free market profit-making scheme. He had bought an old Thai fishing vessel and converted it into a "tour boat" to provide island cruises. Keeping investment risk to a minimum, he had "converted" the boat by installing a curtain around a hole in the floor for a toilet and nailing a canopy of tarpaulin onto the top of the captain's cabin as the sleeping quarters. The maiden voyage was due to take place while I was there. It was only when I saw the motley collection of backpackers the American had roped in for the tour that my curiosity got the better of me. Some New Age West Coast Americans, an Australian environmentalist, a French academic and two Swiss secretaries made up the passenger list. Meanwhile, the American's partner and Captain, Mr Chang, had recruited two young island boys and a local boatman for his crew. The combination of these characters convinced me that, if nothing else, the boat tour would provide a psychologist's dream of group dynamics. I talked myself into a free trip in exchange for help as a deckhand.

As expected, the journey offered more excitement in the shifting dynamics between the people involved than in the experience of touring the tropical islands. My role as "social director" was quickly established as I acted as a buffer between the increasingly annoyed guests and the churlish American who had overestimated his skills in handling people. They felt they had been overcharged for the experience of living in cramped and primitive conditions for five days at sea. He felt they were expecting too much. Before long there was rivalry and conflict on board. The environmentalist was upset by the Thai crew's behaviour as they threw beer bottles and cigarette butts into the sea. He would sit cross-legged chanting to the ocean for forgiveness. The Europeans fell out with the American; the women joined forces against the men. In time, however, after a few outbursts of temper, moods settled and group bonding occurred. Relationships shifted, a New Age couple decided to split up and a romance blossomed between the boatman and a Swiss secretary. In only five days we had undergone an intense experience which left most of us more in touch with ourselves and our companions. I had discovered a role that would be given to me many times in the forthcoming months: playing "agony aunt" to all and sundry. I had also learnt how to cook Thai food in a dangerous and noisy engine room, how to swim against the tide, how to remove sea urchin spines from a foot. Ultimately, we all seized the moment and took delight in the beautiful island locations we visited. We befriended monkeys, snorkeled in coral reefs, bathed in crystal waterfalls and all took turns at night fishing hauls. We visited communities of nomadic sea gypsies and learnt Thai songs from Mr Chang, whose only English consisted of "I love you" and Elvis Presley lyrics. Finally, on our last night at sea, we held a wild singing and drumming party, raving on deck under a full moon as the old boat creaked over the Andaman sea.

I was so reluctant to leave Thailand that I overstayed my visa time by two days, incurring a small fine at the border. It was hard to believe that only two months earlier I had started out from Bangkok in a defensive shell. As I passed a shop window, a young woman with a glowing tan and confident gaze stared back at me. I was stunned when I realized I was looking in a mirror.

Just One Big Service Industry

Lucy Ridout is co-author of the award-winning *Rough Guide to Thailand*. While researching the book she spent five days in Pattaya, heart of the country's sex industry.

I'd never felt particularly comfortable strolling through the red-light districts of London, Paris, or Amsterdam (alone or in company), always unsure whether to smile at the prostitutes in a sisterly and compassionate fashion, or instead to march shyly past, head down and eyes averted. In Pattaya, however, you can't just look the other way.

Selling sex is Pattaya's *raison d'être*, and the former fishing village is now packed with go-go bars and massage parlours. Metre-high neon signs adorn every shop-front, flashing "Pussy Galore", "Love Nest", "Sexy Ladies" and the like, morning, noon and night. Touts patrol their sidewalk patches outside, thrusting menus detailing "acts with ping-pong balls, bananas and razors" at you as you pass the open doorways. Inside, young Thai women in bikinis and G-strings jiggle unenthusiastically around fireman's poles, to the appraising stares of a (mostly) white male audience. Upstairs, said "acts with . . ." are performed in a slightly more clandestine arena. All in all, hardly the kind of town a single woman traveller would choose to spend a week or two.

Perhaps I was most shocked by the artificiality of it all. Because it's common practice to buy a "wife" for the week, everywhere you look you see couples play-acting at being couples: cuddling and petting and snogging and fondling – performing all the usual mating rituals, but without the affection or tenderness. Sure, there are relationships like that all over the world, but in Pattaya they were repeated *ad nauseam* – and so publicly – that at times I felt like I was attending some kind of kissagram's convention in a Hall-of-Mirrors.

> *There is something gross about a sweating, beer-bellied European man with his hand clamped to the breast of a Thai teenager.*

There is something undeniably gross about the sight of a sweating, leering, beer-bellied European man, in shorts three sizes too small, with his hand clamped to the breast of a svelte and sprightly Thai teenager.

I met one such European punter lying by the hotel pool one afternoon. In fact he didn't look typical at all (Swiss, in his late twenties, and not unattractive), and turned out to be a teacher. When he told me he was in Pattaya for the sex, I was amazed. I should have been surprised at my own naiveté, but he seemed such a normal twenty-something, and he'd already told me about his nurse girlfriend (safely back in Geneva). Would he tell his girlfriend when he got back home? No, but he'd certainly try out a few new tricks he'd picked up in sin city. Such as? Well, body-to-body massage for definite, in which participants smother themselves in soap lather and then writhe all over each other.

Sounded appealing, I had to admit. But appealing enough to override feelings of guilt, fear of disease – and, the big one – qualms about the exploitative nature of the whole business? Could I ever pay for the privilege of being pampered and flattered and serviced by a young Thai man: all cheekbones, tanned muscles and come-to-bed smiles?

A few days earlier, on the tiny nearby island of Ko Si Chang, I'd met a Portuguese woman who obviously had no worries about paying for *her* fantasies. Travelling with her was just such an attractive Thai man – a university student of about her age – whom she was paying to accompany her for her last five days in the country. That was the first and only time I encountered this type of sexual role reversal in Thailand (although Pattaya has a large population of male prostitutes, they nearly all work with gay men).

Why was it that paying for sex seemed so much less unpalatable to me when it was the foreign *woman* doing the buying? Certainly, it was encouraging to witness women at last recognizing and doing something about their own desires, but surely the economic exploitation is no different, whatever the permutation? Would these women buy sex at home? Would these men? If not, which was the bigger incentive to try it here in Thailand: the availability, the feeling that while on holiday normal behaviour did not apply, or the price? Sex is cheap here, and sex-trade wages low. But not as low as in a lot of other industries.

In some villages, money sent home by prostitutes far exceeds financial aid given by the government.

Like prostitutes the world over, Thai sex workers are for the most part economic refugees from the poorest parts of the country. Compelled by meagre harvests, large families and paltry wages to leave their rural homes in north and northeast Thailand, they're easily drawn into an industry where they can make in a single night what it takes them a month to earn in the rice fields.

The luckiest ones make enough to be able to send money home: in some northeastern villages, money sent home by prostitutes far exceeds financial aid given by the government. Women from rural communities have always been expected to contribute an equal share to the family income and it's hardly surprising that many opt for a couple of lucrative years in the sex bars and brothels as the most effective way of helping to pay off family debts.

Noi's situation was typical, though none the less shocking for that. I got chatting to her one evening in a wooden beachfront café on the island of Ko Samet, several years ago, on my first ever trip to Thailand. Hers was a sobering story to hear in such a paradisal setting.

Seventeen years old, she was on the island with her boyfriend, an Austrian some twenty years her senior, who flew to Thailand two or three times a year to see her. In the intervening months she worked shifts in Bangkok's sex bars. If she needed extra money while he wasn't around, she'd write and ask, and he usually wired some over.

He was a good man she said, and treated her okay. She didn't feel free, she didn't love him, but with the money she earned from being his temporary wife, she'd been able to support her younger sister through dressmaking school. The girls' mother had died about ten years earlier, and their father was too ill to work, so Noi was unselfishly determined that her sister should become the family's success story.

Later, I started to get wary of interrogating the working women in Bangkok and Pattaya about their lives. It was obvious conditions weren't exactly rosy, and by then I'd seen enough documentaries and read enough true-life accounts to have formed a fair idea of the uniform grimness of their breadline existence. Noi had wanted to confide, but in some of Pattaya's bars I got a strong sense that the women were getting fed up with the constant prying and outraged questionings from well-meaning, right-on foreign sisters. Who wants to talk about work all the time, especially work that's so unremittingly unpleasant?

That said, of course, there have been some tremendously positive projects initiated by Thai and foreign women, aimed at improving working conditions and helping raise the aspirations of Thailand's sex workers. One such is a Bangkok organization called "Empower", whose projects include regular English classes (the more English you understand, the less likely you are to get ripped off), and frequent medical check-ups.

Perhaps in some ways sex tourism was no more or less exploitative than other kinds of tourism.

Although there are an estimated 700,000 prostitutes in Thailand and it's common practice for men of all ages to visit them, prostitution is actually illegal, and has been since 1960. This means that sex workers also live in constant fear of arrest. While sex industry bosses easily circumvent the law via legal loopholes and substantial payoffs, sex workers have no legal rights at all and will often endure exploitation and violence from both pimps and customers rather than face fines and imprisonment.

According to a group of Bangkok students I met, a typical lads' night out will invariably end with a few hours in a brothel. I couldn't say whether this easy availability of sex makes Thai men more or less aggressive towards Thai women (though it certainly endangers their partners' health: there are currently over 200,000 reported HIV infections in Thailand). I personally encountered very little harassment anywhere in the country, except for once being flashed at, in the grounds of a ruined temple, by a man whose behaviour was far more ridiculous than threatening.

In Pattaya I was, thankfully, invisible to the Western men, who kept their wolf-whistles and gropings for the Thai women. But I did appear something of an oddity to the Thai men there, and as such was treated with curiosity – and generosity – but never intimidated. In fact, solo women travellers arouse curiosity in all parts of the country, not least because Thais themselves very rarely go anywhere alone, and can't understand why anyone else would want to. A number of older women I met on buses and trains would also be perturbed at my being so old (26), and yet having neither husband nor babies to keep me company.

Being confronted by all facets of Pattaya's sex industry for an uninterrupted period of five long days turned out to be a surprisingly thought-provoking experience. I had anticipated being sickened and disturbed by what I saw, but my observations and encounters there threw up a whole lot of unexpected questions as well: questions on personal, political, and professional issues.

I came away with the uncomfortable notion that perhaps *in some ways* sex tourism was no more or less exploitative than other kinds of tourism (say hill-tribe trekking or budget beach-bumming) in Thailand. That as a tourist you are, on one level, obliged to treat the whole country as one big service industry. However, as the author of a guide book to the country, I obviously maintain that relationships between tourists and indigenous people can and should be mutually beneficial, and that a sensitive and informed guide book can only help achieve that end.

Back in the UK now, I sometimes feel like a part-time spokesperson for Thailand, and have to admit to pangs of guilt at having chosen to write here about the sex industry. Thailand's sex industry has become hot media material over the last few years, and the Thai government has, not surprisingly, reacted with indignation to such one-sided coverage; recent international flare-ups have been ignited by Time magazine's decision to use a photograph of a Thai bar girl and her foreign client for their cover story on sex for sale, and by Longman's definition of Bangkok as "a place where there are a lot of prostitutes" in their latest dictionary. I realize that in some ways I'm helping to exaggerate this lop-sided profile of the country and so I should emphasize here that most travellers to Thailand have absolutely no contact with the sex industry unless they choose to do so. Thailand's flesh trade is pervasive, but it is rarely intrusive, and as such constitutes a single aspect of a complex and multi-faceted culture that has for over two thousand years adopted, adapted and assimilated a broad range of foreign influences and will undoubtedly continue to do so.

TRAVEL NOTES

Languages Thai, the national language, can be difficult to master. One word may have five different meanings, according to the tone in which it is pronounced. Hill-tribe languages are spoken in the north, while regional dialects are strong in the northeast and far south. Most Thais concerned with the tourist trade speak some English, as do students; otherwise a few stock phrases usually suffice.

Transport Generally cheap, efficient and fairly safe. Buses are the fastest way of covering long distances, and you often get the choice between plush air-conditioned coaches and the cheaper fresh-air and hard-seated variety. The train network is not as extensive, but generally takes you along more scenic routes. In towns, shared taxis work like small local buses and follow fixed itineraries, the infamous three-wheeled *tuk-tuks* are excellent value for medium-length taxi rides, and bicycle rickshaws are a good way of covering the shortest distances. In rural areas with sporadic public transport, Thais of both sexes hitch, and will sometimes pay the driver for the ride.

Accommodation Accommodation is varied and caters to every travelling need from the luxury hotel to the cheap and basic grass hut. Chinese hotels often provide the best value in small towns. Guest houses, "bungalows" and youth hostels are also popular.

Special Problems It is important to observe certain rules of behaviour when visiting Thailand. As well as being polite, it is important to avoid touching the head (considered the holy part of the body) or pointing with the feet (a reviled part of the body). Clearly, it is only sensible and respectful to dress modestly, making sure legs and arms are covered. Harassment can be an issue in popular resorts where some foreign women indulge in romantic liaisons with the local men.

Drug-smuggling carries a maximum penalty of death, and possession can also result in heavy sentences: it's not unheard of for tourists to be framed by their suppliers. Border areas are volatile (though most are impenetrable jungle anyway) and fighting sometimes breaks out on the Burmese border in particular. Theoretically, Buddhist monks are forbidden to have any contact with women, which means, as a female, you mustn't sit or stand next to a monk, or even brush against his robes. Topless sunbathing is not illegal, but it is deeply offensive to most Thais.

Guides *The Rough Guide to Thailand* (Penguin) is packed with useful information.

CONTACTS

Friends of Women, 49 Phra Athit Rd, Bangkok (☎02/280 0429). Runs a counselling service and takes up women's rights issues.

BOOKS

Sanitsuda Ekachai, *Behind the Smile* (Thailand, Thai Development Support Committee, 1990). The collected articles of the *Bangkok Post*'s (female) social affairs correspondent, highlighting the effect of Thailand's sudden economic growth on the country's rural poor.

Thanh-Dam Truong, *Sex, Money and Morality: Prostitution and Tourism in South-East Asia* (UK & US, Zed Books, 1990). Hard-hitting analysis of the marketing of Thailand as sex-tourism capital of Asia.

Tibet

ore than any other destination, Tibet has captured the imagination as a remote and inaccessible Himalayan realm, suffused with mystical significance. Before the Chinese invasion of 1959 only a few travellers had entered the country, trudging recklessly on across dizzying mountain passes, inured to frostbite and xenophobia in their bid to enter the once forbidden city of Lhasa, seat of the Dalai Lama. With the Chinese occupation the Nepalese and Chinese borders were sealed, the Dalai Lama escaped into exile in India, and for two-and-a-half

decades only fragmentary images emerged of a country and culture systematically wrecked and impoverished by Chinese expansionism. Before even the terror of the Cultural Revolution spread to Tibet, thousands of monasteries had been destroyed. Large numbers of the population have since been executed, imprisoned and exiled, while under a massive Sinoization progamme Chinese citizens have been encouraged to move to the region by tax, work and housing incentives.

The Autonomous Region of Xizang (Tibet), its borders shrunk by annexation of the eastern and northeastern regions, remains occupied territory, administered by the Communist Party Committee under five prefectures. It is no longer, however, a closed state. In the much-vaunted new era of tolerance (and in a bid to prop up a collapsing economy with tourist dollars), the borders were opened to foreign tourists in 1984. At first visas were only granted to tour groups on expensive flight deals to Lhasa, but independent travellers soon followed, entering the country by any means possible – in disguise, hitching lifts in Chinese trucks, posing as tour groups. Arranging a visa for independent travel is now routine, and with new direct flights from Katmandhu and tours operating across the Nepalese border to western Tibet, oportunities for travel within the country are widening. However, officials within Tibet have their own way of interpreting visa regulations and you can never be sure which areas or activities are currently proscribed. At the first signs of civil unrest, such as the Lhasa uprising of 1988, the borders have swung shut again, although a hard core of independent travellers (for some reason women have always been at the forefront) have always managed to smuggle themselves in. Meanwhile, from his base in Dharamsala (increasingly more Tibetan in atmosphere than Lhasa), the Dalai Lama continues to promote a negotiated peace settlement – though with little response from the Chinese authorities.

Lhasa itself has changed beyond recognition. Although a renovation and rebuilding programme is under way, often only the facade of the capital's cultural and religious monuments have been saved, while traditional Tibetan areas are still being demolished as part of "slum clearance". The Chinese population more than outnumber Tibetans within Lhasa (also in Shigatse and much of eastern Tibet) and large Chinese compounds have sprung up alongside army barracks and Chinese businesses. With the rapid growth of tourism the city now boasts a few international-class hotels, a range of hostels and restaurants – even yak burger joints and satellite TVs. The easing of religious repression has meant that prayer flags are again flying and pilgrims mingle with foreigners on the circuit around the Jokhang temple and Potala Palace. Monasteries and monastic schooling are, however, still tightly regulated, with monks and nuns among the first targets of state crackdowns. Many Tibetans consider the recent reforms to be little more than a cynical public relations exercise, aimed at promoting tourism and calming Western concern about continuing occupation and repression within the country.

For all the country's guarded isolation in the past, the Tibetan people are very welcoming toward foreigners, whose presence signals some degree of security from more blatant human rights abuses. And tourists are clearly partisan, seeking out Tibetan businesses to patronize. In reality many of the dealings will be with the Chinese; truck-drivers, shopkeepers, hotel staff, check-point guards and state officials. Within either community it's unlikely that you'll come across any particular problems as a woman travelling alone. Harassment is rarely an issue and, unlike in neighbouring Nepal where memories of the hippy trail and Western pornography have left powerful impressions, there are few negative stereotypes to contend with. In rural areas Western travellers are still a rare sight and it's not unusual for children to run away in fear. You'll need to learn a few words of Tibetan to get by. The main concerns, however, are the rigours of the journey. Nights can be bitterly cold – stories have circulated about foreigners freezing to death on the back of trucks over the high mountain passes – and altitude sickness has to be taken seriously. A growing number of women cross the country alone, trekking, hitching, renting four-wheel drive vehicles or a yak to carry the backpack, but you need to be certain of your health, stamina and survival skills to even consider it.

Tibetans still face considerable discrimination in education, employment, health and housing, and opportunities for **women** to enter the professions are few. Within the main cities Tibetan women have a high profile on the streets as independent traders, manual workers or in the Tibetan-run tourist facilities. The majority, however, still live in the rural areas and continue to work alongside their extended families, ekeing out a subsistence living in the harsh, frost-bitten terrain. The strength and independence of these women are easily mythologized; reinforced by encounters with nomadic women crossing the vast plateaux with their families and livestock, and nuns completing lengthy pilgrimages with little more than a few bags of *tsampa* (grain) to sustain them. Tibetan women have played an active role in the resistance movement – the 1959 uprising was launched exclusively by women – and nuns have frequently featured in the frontline of demonstrations, risking imprisonment and torture. In an attempt to reflect the political and cultural role of women, the government in exile has initiated a quota system for women and attempts are being made to raise the status of nuns in the Buddhist hierarchy.

"Om Mani Padme Hum"

Wendy Teasdill spent fourteen years travelling and working as an English language teacher in Europe, Asia, South America and Japan. Her cherished plan had always been to explore Tibet alone and on foot, and, when the country opened up to individual travellers in the mid-1980s, she moved to Hong Kong as a base for her Tibetan travels. For the next six years she made several solo journeys into the country and is currently completing a book about her marathon trek to Mount Kailash in the west.

Tibet. The very name evokes a misty uprising of hidden secrets and psychic revelations. I had read Heinrich Harrer's best-seller, *Seven Years in Tibet*, at an impressionable age and could not shake off the dreams it had stirred in me of travelling to this most sacred and inaccessible realm. At 21 I headed overland on my own to India and Nepal. My yearnings, could I have followed them, should have led me scrambling over the Himalayas in Heinrich Harrer mode, but instead I was stuck in a neighbouring country with no other outlet for my feelings than coveting a pair of brightly coloured Tibetan boots made of felt with soles four inches thick.

It was to take ten more years before I was finally able to enter Tibet. In 1984 the country began to allow in tourists and by 1987 was receiving large numbers of independent travellers. Because of the Chinese invasion of the 1950s, it was to Beijing that I went to apply for a job in Lhasa, but my hopes were disappointed. In September and October of 1987 the Tibetans staged mass demonstrations calling for independence and Chinese withdrawal, and all foreigners, including those working in the region, were kicked out. Only tourists on expensive, short-stay package tours – the sort who would be herded around and so have little contact with the people – were allowed in after the unrest. Then in March 1988 came more trouble. I perched in Hong Kong, teaching English, listening to the BBC World Service and waiting for things to relax.

In June 1988 I arrived alone at Golmud, the godforsaken town which is the springboard to Tibet, and left with eighteen others. It was a face-saving device by which we paid a hundred dollars each to rent a bus and be driven as a "tour group" to Lhasa. For two days and nights we made our way in relative luxury up through the wide desert tracts to the Tang La Pass, the border area of the Tibet Autonomous Region. The only vegetation for miles around was a low-level cushion growth of greeny-brown, dotted with tiny flowers. Vultures and eagles circled overhead in the wide, thin sky and once or twice we passed a small herd of gazelles or a flock of wild geese or ducks waddling about on a marshy desert patch. Few manage to make a living in this desolate area and the only people we came across in the dreary compounds along the route were hollow-eyed, Chinese truck-drivers sucking up bowls of noodles.

Once in Lhasa everyone disbanded and went their separate ways. I made straight for the Barkhor, the stall-lined circuit around the Jokhang temple, the hub around which Tibetan society revolves. It was here that the anti-Chinese demonstrations erupted. Pilgrims arrive from all over the region to walk clockwise around the circuit, swinging their prayer wheels, chanting and begging alms. The stalls alongside are stacked with an amazing variety of goods: prayer flags, hairslides, kerosene, walnuts, musk (sadly too, the skins of endangered species like snow leopards — Tibetans love to edge their long coats with a piece of pelt) and almost as soon as you step into the area you are besieged by the women street vendors. Many of these are Khampa women from Kham in eastern Tibet, recognizable by their hair plaited into 108 thin strings fastened at the ends with turquoise beads.

Out in the mountains were nomad camps run completely by women who looked after the yaks and sheep.

"Hey! Changee money? How muchee?" they call out, thrusting strings of coral, turquoise or silver bracelets under your nose while watching your reactions from behind their luminescent smiles. Their sense of humour is infectious, laughing good naturedly both with you and at you at the same time — a combination you rarely see in the desperate vendors who throng most tourist circuits the world over. On the whole, Tibetans prefer to laugh and be positve than dwell on their misfortunes and bartering becomes a great excuse for a joke with a foreigner. Western men with beards are a source of wonder and amusement, because Tibetan men have smooth, hairless faces. I've seen the women around the Barkhor point at a man's beard, and ask a price — to everyone's delight.

At night time the Barkhor was a completely different place. White cotton blinds with blue appliqué crosses lidded the black-edged windows of the sleeping temple. The only people you would meet would be a dedicated pilgrim or two measuring the circuit in prostrations in the dust around the holy site, undisturbed by the daytime clamour; or perhaps a group of lads lounging against some of the upturned trestle tables, smoking and joking. "Hey! *Inji!*, Changee money?" they'd call out and laugh, *Inji* being the generic word for foreigner. There seemed nothing to fear although Tibetan woman are rarely seen hanging around the Barkhor at night.

Traditionally, the structure of Tibetan society is patriarchal, based on the idea that the male principle is active and wise while the female principle is passive and compassionate. The male is the bone, the female the flesh. One cannot exist without the other and this understanding permeates all strata of Tibetan life, from the banal to the esoteric. If you go into a Tibetan home, the woman always serves the tea. Surprise, surprise.

Women are also regarded as inherently more sinful than men. When a man wants to become a monk, he must take a couple of hundred vows. When a woman wants to become a nun she must take over a hundred more. Whenever I stayed the night at a Tibetan monastery, I would have to sleep in the kitchen, as women are not allowed to stay within the monastery walls. I met some wonderful women in these places although I did wonder what went on in the *makakala* shrines in the temples to which women are denied access.

> *Others would tell me that there was another big river coming up and that I was bound to die soon.*

Some women do, however, hold high office and progress through different reincarnations, such as Yeshe Tsogyal, consort of the great magician Padmasambhava, and the Thunderbolt Sow who, in her present incarnation, has married and is a dedicated Communist functionary. And one must not forget the *Dakinis*, the magical sky-dancing females who can be seen painted on temple walls wearing nifty rainbow-striped leggings, and whose function it is to reveal hidden wisdom.

The female principle may be passive, but there was little passivity about the women I met in Tibet. They walked with confidence, their heads held high, their shoulders back and seemed strong. It is amazing to hear laughter bellowing out from a woman trying to manouevre a massive sack of barley flour or butter on her back. Out in the mountains I often came across nomad camps run completely by women – the men were off trading for months at a time – who looked after the yaks and sheep, herding and milking them as well as making all the cheese, butter and yoghurt, and taking care of half a dozen children at the same time. In days of old, women would ride into battle beside their husbands as a matter of course, and there are several instances where women have led the men. One of these is the Khampa queen, Chime Dolma, who led two successful campaigns against the Chinese nationalists in 1936 and 1939.

I was told that the women who haunt the Barkhor are often prostitutes, yet the sleaziness usually associated with this type of work was quite absent. Several years later I found myself drinking beer and smoking cigarettes in a Lhasa brothel; apart from the fact that every so often a woman would disappear with a male guest for twenty minutes at a time, everything was pretty much the same as an evening in an English pub, except a good deal merrier. Only the fact that the women drank and smoked betrayed their profession. It is, however, a sad reflection on the economic limitations for

Tibetans in Lhasa that prostitution is a growing trade. The fact that it is tolerated and not clamped down upon, as in "other parts of China", suggests that the Chinese are happy to allow what they would otherwise see as moral decay to continue in Tibet.

Back in 1988 I left Lhasa quickly and set off alone to Mount Kailash, 1500km to the west. I hitch-hiked half way and walked the rest, taking the southern road because it was closed to traffic. The whole of western Tibet was out of bounds to individual travellers and I reasoned that there would be less chance of being caught that way. It was also easier to shake off the various other tourists who wanted to come with me; when I insisted I was going by the southern road they decided it was too crazy and dropped out of their own accord. They were of course quite right to back away. The road was closed on account of the monsoon-swollen rivers that cut up the track and made it impassable in the rainy season. Indeed there were a few dodgy river-crossings, culminating in a nasty little episode involving a swift flowing river. It was chest high, I lost my balance and was dragged along the boulder-strewn floor by ice-cold water, convinced I'd drawn my last breath. But three weeks of walking with a month's supply of food on my back had made my legs stronger than I'd realized, and I survived to tell the tale.

> The witch had pink skin, a large nose and long golden hair. Just like me, they pointed out.

Western Tibet is very remote, and it took a month of walking to reach Mount Kailash. There are no buildings for hundreds of miles, and sometimes I wouldn't see anyone for a week. Occasionally I met nomads. The first thing they always wanted to know was where my male friend was. They were also puzzled about how I had got there with the road being closed. When they grasped that I was alone and on foot, the kind and polite among them would exclaim with admiration, pour me endless cups of butter tea and invite me to stay with them until the end of the rainy season. Their generosity and sophistication were astounding. The not so polite ones would tell me that there was another big river coming up – there was always a big river ahead – and that I was bound to die soon. I will never forget the vivacity with which one woman made cut-throat gestures while shrieking with laughter, at which the whole tent load of people collapsed in mirth at the thought. All the same, they kindly fed me a dish of fresh yoghurt for my "last meal". Though the rivers tried to get me, I never felt personally threatened by any Tibetans.

On the occasions I did meet nomads, I rather enjoyed smoking their green tobacco in rolled up newspaper. This was disapproved of. It was not good for a girl to smoke, they said. The only hostility I ever encountered on that walk was when I was foolish enough to ask the first person I'd seen for several days if he had any tobacco. He shouted at me that he was a Lama and I a woman, and set the dogs on me. I scarpered to be alone under the stars.

I loved those days of being alone. At first, when the weight of my rucksack bore down on me, more and more painfully at every trudge; or when I sat river-sodden in my tent listening to the rain with only a few cold biscuits filling my stomach, I would regret my folly. It was then that I yearned for safe restaurants with plates of spinach and cheese and jolly companions, and was appalled at myself for doing so. Wasn't that just what I was trying to get away from? Yet, even in my direst moments, I never considered turning back. The vision of Mount Kailash ahead was too vivid, too compelling. Every morning I would lay out my wet things to dry in the sun, eat some muesli with water and read uplifting words from the *Bhagavad Gita*. Then I'd hoist up my pack and plod, one foot after another until mid-afternoon, when I'd break for some hard tack army biscuits. At nightfall I'd stop and pitch my tent. Occasionally, if I was lucky, I'd find dried yak dung and cook noodles with seaweed. Otherwise it was just more of those wretched biscuits. After a week or so I was acclimatized. My pack had become a little lighter, my muscles were toned up and I began to think less about what I had left behind and became more absorbed in the horizon, the mountains and the boundless beauty of clouds and light. Nothing gladdened me more than the fact that I was alone, saturated in spacious happiness.

The nuns fell again to measuring the lengths of their bodies around the sacred mountain.

I came first to Lake Mansarovar, the holy lake of the sun to the south of Mount Kailash. Walking round it I ran out of matches and begged a box from the kitchen of a monastery. Grinning novices gave me a box on which was depicted a witch. She had pink skin, a large nose and long golden hair. Just like me, they pointed out. It was true. To Tibetans, foreign women are incredibly ugly, with flanks like horses and eyes like dead people. It's the blue eyes that are really scary. Brown-eyed *Inji* girls may, if they're very clever and lucky, catch a Khampa man. I should perhaps have felt flattered that once, while waiting for a lift along the northern road from Kailash, a Khampa man shared his beer with me and made improper suggestions. He was drunk and easily dissuaded. And it never happened again. At times I have had fights, forgotten five minutes later, and at others made great friends with the Khampas. But no more improper suggestions.

Mount Kailash is generally regarded in the East as being the mystical centre of the world, the meeting place of heaven and earth. It richly deserves this sacred reputation. Though western Tibet is officially a closed area, I was, after I had paid my fine, given permission to stay a month. During that month I explored the mountain and lakes, visiting monasteries and other holy places, and meeting pilgrims. I even met a Dutch girl, Purnina, who, though physicaly frail, was mentally strong. She had managed the trek to Kailash by arranging lifts for her rucksack from anyone with a yak and vegetables from anyone with half a potato to spare. We walked around Kailash together, reading to one another from books about the mountain and meditating on its ice-capped dome.

The most remarkable people in Tibet are, for me, the nuns, who have to take so many vows. One day, while Purnina and I were walking, we met a group of six who had hitch-hiked together from Lhasa and were prostrating around the mountain. While it took us three days to circum-ambulate, their feat took them a month. They carried with them their tents, pots, tea, bags of barley flour, their prayer beads and very little else. Joining them at their fire one night, they insisted on sharing their food and drink with us despite having almost nothing to spare. We were able to decline the meal on the basis of being vegetarian – it had a few bits of dried yak meat in it – but the tea we could not. I managed to press on them some of my own powdered milk, an expensive luxury in Tibet, but it was hard to make them accept.

The following morning, after prayers and tea, the nuns set out again. Walking back to the stones which marked the limit of their previous day's protestations, uttering the eternal mantra "Om mani padme hum", they fell again to measuring the lengths of their bodies around the sacred mountain. When they came to streams, they would simply tuck in their skirts and fling themselves across the water. I was privileged to know them. Their generosity and laughter were humbling, their stamina astounding.

Wherever I have walked in Tibet, I have come across groups of nuns, swinging along with the same cheerful good humour. Yet their lives are not carefree. As often as not, it is the nuns who are arrested for demonstrating for independence and who put themselves at risk of imprisonment and torture for doing so.

Hitching back from Kailash via the northern road I teamed up with a little old nun who I had met in one of the monastery kitchens around the lake. Like all nuns she was called Ani-la. She had a stumpy gait and swung her prayer-wheel wherever she went, chanting "Om mani padme hum" very carefully and seriously. I'd give her a leg-up onto lorries and we'd lay out on the same sheepskin under the stars at night, and, though my Tibetan was not very good, she always managed to communicate with me however complicated her story. When one truck

> *My companion, who was becoming more and more irritated with our driver, finally lost all control and punched him.*

abandoned us in the middle of nowhere early one morning, she set about borrowing a teapot and some wood. Soon we had tea. Chanting "Om mani padme hum" and polishing the teapot with her charred and leathery fingers, she laughed at

our situation. "fancy that!" she kept on exclaiming. "They got us to pay them last night, and we never suspected a thing. And now they're gone. Ha ha ha!" And the salt-flats laughed back.

In March 1989 there were more demonstrations for independence followed by the bloodiest crackdown yet. Martial law was imposed and it took another year before Tibet was declared once more open to tourists. And again – it was the high-paying tourists that they wanted, not low-paying, long-staying backpackers like myself. Still, I lived in hope, and after three months hovering around the outskirts of Tibet, successfully hitch-hiked into Lhasa.

Again, I did not enter the region alone. Seeing me buying my disguise of a long, black Tibetan coat and wide-brimmed felt hat, an English man, who had just decided to give up and go elsewhere, changed his mind and tagged along. Woe the day. It was a hellish journey.

We left Golmud in the back of a small *put-put* and went another fifteen kilometres or so face down in the back of a tractor before flagging down a lorry driven by a bedraggled, half-Chinese Tibetan, who seemed a little slow-witted and couldn't stop smoking Golden Monkey cigarettes. It took three days and nights to reach Lhasa. The poor driver was risking his licence and heavy fines by taking us, and, to avoid being spotted by the checkpoints, we hid under a tarpaulin on the back. It was burning hot by day and freezing cold by night. The lorry kept on breaking down and my companion, who was becoming more and more irritated with our driver, finally lost all control and punched him, sending him running off into the snowy night in his hole-ridden socks. I seemed to be expected to play a maternal role and comfort them both, feeling the bumps on our driver's head on one side and mollifying my embarassed countryman on the other. The whole experience was a poignant reminder for me of how much better it is to travel alone.

Once in Lhasa we were surprised to find our presence tolerated by the Chinese and welcomed by the Tibetans who, despite a long history of xenophobia, touchingly believe that we will tell the world about their troubles and so be instrumental in bringing back the Dalai Lama.

It turned out that we were among the first individual foreigners to stay in Lhasa since the beginning of martial law. Each day we would meet one or two others who, by some wild chance or determined cunning, had slipped into the traditionally forbidden city. For some reason most of these were women. It is always a challenge to enter Tibet as an individual, and so the sort of foreign women who manage to go there are generally resilient individuals with a lot of character and a streak or two of crazy wisdom – not unlike the Tibetan women, in fact. I love them all.

The last time I did this journey, at the beginning of last year, I was pregnant. The Tibetans I met were delighted to hear it and, although they prefer to have a girl first, who will be of more use around the house, they told me they would pray I had a boy. They meant well. As I write, I am packing to return. This time with my ten-month old baby daughter.

TRAVEL NOTES

Languages Tibetan and Chinese (Mandarin is the official dialect).

Transport A wide range of options from helicopter tours or renting a jeep, to more basic bussing and hiking. However, there are no trains, and buses are erratic and rudimentary. Independent travellers have tended to hitch lifts on trucks. At present this is illegal; drivers risk a hefty fine and you could be sent back to the border.

Accommodation Lhasa has a range of hostels and hotels. Beyond this the options are limited to guest houses, truckstops and army camps (not a good idea if travelling alone). At present travellers are required to stay in "approved" accommodation though many just hike off with their tents.

Special Problems Sudden border closures or tightening of restrictions within the country add an element of chance to the business of independent travel. Physical hardships: the bitterly cold nights made worse by wind and rain, and the high altitudes, must be taken seriously. You're unlikely to find much medical help at hand.

Guides *Tibet – A Travel Survival Kit* (Lonely Planet). Reasonably comprehensive and very practical, with some useful background sketches of the country's history, politics and culture. Stephen Batchelor, *The Tibet Guide* (Wisdom

Publ) offers a more in-depth view of Tibetan society.

BOOKS

★ **Mary Morris**, *Wall to Wall: A Woman's Travels from Beijing to Berlin* (UK, Flamingo, 1993/US, Doubleday, 1991). The journey begins for Morris at the Mongolian Embassy in Beijing and takes her in stages through Tibet, Mongolia, Russia and Eastern Europe. Her deceptively light prose style and polished images make this book an evocative, often delightful, read.

★ **Catriona Bass**, *Inside the Treasure House: a Time in Tibet* (UK, Abacus, 1992). Highly readable and informative account of Tibetan life in the mid-1980s, based on a year spent teaching in Lhasa. Sadly, Bass's optimism about Chinese reform proved unjustified.

Alexandra David-Neel, *Journey to Lhasa: The Personal Story of the Only White Woman Who Succeeded in Entering the Forbidden City* (1972; UK, Virago, 1983, o/p/US, Beacon Press, 1988, o/p). At age fifty-five, Alexandra David-Neel crossed into northeastern Tibet from China, dressed as a pilgrim with her maps hidden in her boots and revolver tucked into the folds of her rough coat. An inspiring account of endurance and the quest for knowledge, by one of this century's most indomitable travellers.

Helena Drysdale, *Alone through China and Tibet* (UK, Constable, 1986). Following the route of Alexandra David-Neel (see above), the author travels from Xian to Lhasa.

Dorje Yudon Yuthok, *House of the Turquoise Roof* (UK & US, Snow Lion, 1990). Autobiography of a Tibetan noblewoman describing the life of the Lhasa elite before the Chinese invasion.

Heinrich Harrer, *Seven Years in Tibet* (1953; UK, Paladin, 1988/US, J P Tarcher, 1982). Interned by the British in India during World War II,

Harrer escapes over the mountains to Lhasa and a new life amongst the Tibetans. An instant best-seller.

Carol Devine, *Determination: Tibetan Women and the struggle for an Independent Tibet* (Canada, Vauve Press). Charts the participation of Buddhist nuns and ordinary women in the Tibetan resistance movement.

Thanks to Alison Murdoch and the Tibet Information Network for help in compiling this chapter.

Turkey

For the last fifteen years or so, Turkey has been in the grips of a tourist boom. Tour companies, turning their attentions from over-exploited Greece, have transformed vast stretches of the Aegean/Mediterranean coast into a concrete mass of hotels and holiday apartment blocks catering for thousands of tourists – largely European – each year. Yet the carefree, Westernized image of the tourist enclaves can be misleading. You don't have to venture far to discover a deeply traditional and predominantly rural way of life. Nor do you have to spend long in the country to gain a sense of political instability and repression. The government is democratically

elected but fiercely repressive in its response to Islamicists and to the Kurdish insurgency in the east. As in the years of military dictatorship that ended in 1980, the government is once again being criticized for arrest without trial, torture and the use of death squads in dealing with political opponents. Visitors are, however, largely screened from such matters – although parts of eastern Turkey are virtually out of bounds and there have been bombing campaigns in Istanbul, Fethiye and Marmaris.

Although Turkey is officially a secular state, women are expected to conform to Islamic customs and values. Westerners who flaunt these by asserting their freedom to wander about unescorted and mix freely in public with men are stereotypically viewed as "immodest" – an idea reinforced by the portrayal of bikini-clad tourists in the popular press. Travelling alone you are likely to have to contend with persistent, though not particularly threatening, sexual harassment. As usual, this is at its most oppressive around the main tourist areas – the coastal resorts, circuit of ancient sites, and the commercial districts of Istanbul – where men collect in search of the "easy" tourist. Yet to close yourself off or react suspiciously to all approaches would be to miss a great deal. The Turkish people have a reputation for hospitality and many will go to great lengths to make you feel welcome.

While you can't completely escape unwanted attention, it can help to follow the lead of more Westernized Turkish women and adopt a conservative style of dress and behaviour. Similarly, if you sufffer from any overt harassment you should make your predicament clear to passers-by or fellow passengers. You'll find that Turkish women will be only too happy to take you under their wing.

Women in Turkey are well-used to walking the tightrope between meeting the demands of a modern, secular state while upholding the cherished traditions of a suppressed Islamic culture. The contradictions this involves were highlighted in 1988 when feminists marched with veiled students to demand their right to wear headscarves in the classroom. With the success of Islamic fundamentalists and ultra-nationalists in the 1994 election, the balance has now shifted and women's groups are preparing to defend their civil rights against manifestos that demand further restrictions for women.

In at the Deep End

Rosie Ayliffe spent three years working in Istanbul as a university teacher, freelance writer and tour leader. She has since returned numerous times to research and write the *Rough Guide to Turkey*.

I went to Turkey because I couldn't think how I had finished my formal education without knowing quite where Istanbul was. I was in the university careers library, wondering if I could get one out on loan, when I happened on an advertisement for jobs teaching English in Istanbul. I thought the best way of discovering where the place was and who lived there would be to answer the advertisement.

That same day I was given a job and found myself surveying the prospect of going to Turkey. I "knew" more about Istanbul than I had realized. I knew that it was a Muslim city, and that it was therefore inhabited by people with a sympathy for the Iranian revolution. I knew that the Turks or "infidel" had failed to conquer Vienna in 1683 and that this had been a great relief to the civilized West. I knew from my wide-ranging knowledge of Turkish cinema that Turkish men beat their wives, and from British cinema that you would be arrested and made to walk around a pole indefinitely if you irritated Turkish customs officials.

I arranged accommodation before I went out. A friend who had been living in Istanbul offered to put in a good word with Zahide and Mustafa, who owned the house he was living in. I thought he was joking when he warned me to keep a bottle down the toilet against rats.

September was blistering hot but I sweated cold terror on the flight over. Was I carrying anything that

> *I kept a bottle in the hole in the floor which served as my toilet, but it didn't stop the rats from coming through the roof.*

could possibly cause offence to the customs officials? Would the university give me a job if they knew of my political sympathies? At the time I didn't know that I would have to work for over three months before I saw my first pay packet, not because there was really any serious vetting procedure in operation, but simply because of the sheer inefficiency of a bureaucracy that makes our social security system look like the Starship Enterprise.

I arrived on the anniversary of the 1980 military coup. I wasn't surprised to be greeted by machine-gun-toting soldiers, I was only surprised to be allowed to walk freely through passport control. Again, it would be a matter of time before I realized that Western visitors to Turkey are nowadays treated with care and respect by the officials, in a cosmetic attempt to improve a deservedly unprepossessing image.

My new home was situated on the Asian side of the city in the hills overlooking the Bosphorous. One rusty tap sometimes gave me cold clean water. More often it jetted forth a stream of shit-coloured fluid, thick with oxidized iron, or didn't work at all. I did always keep a whisky bottle in the hole in the floor covering an open drain which served as my toilet, but it didn't stop the rats from coming in through a hole in the roof.

> *I was quite happy to be assimilated to such an extent that I became harem, "forbidden territory".*

The house was what is known as a *gecekondu,* a home "built in the night". An ancient law states that when a roof is put on a house it becomes a legal dwelling place. Contractors have devised methods of building apartments so that the roof is virtually on before the walls are up, and shacks spring up all over the city, literally overnight, before the authorities have time to interfere.

I learnt some Turkish through necessity. None of my neighbours or my landlady spoke any English and nor did the local shopkeepers or restaurateurs. Rather too proud to use sign language, I was hungry by the time I mastered "Could I have a . . . ?" and "Have you got any . . . ?"

Mustafa and Zahide were ancient siblings celebrating their approaching dotage in occasional outbursts of screaming, resembling either song or rage as best suited the prevailing circumstance. She was as mean as he was foolish, but they were kind enough to me, and screamed with laughter and "Masallahs!" every time I learnt a new Turkish word.

A rather more interesting companion was the doctor, their older brother, who lived in another wooden house in the same complex. While I watched him go crazy, he had moments of lucidity which seemed to suggest that insanity was a kind of refuge from the glaring injustices of the society in which he had found himself.

He sometimes spoke to me in guarded terms about torture in Turkish prisons and I learnt from him what had happened to the radicals and intellectuals in Turkish universities. Periodically he would rush out while I was doing my washing and implore me not to use detergent in the water since it would do untold destruction to the food chain. I ignored him until three years later, when the press exposed the scandal of phosphates in Turkish detergents.

About eight months after arriving I was told that new neighbours were moving into the compound and was delighted when a young and friendly couple turned up to clean the tiny wooden shack which I had previously taken for an outhouse. The woman, Cybele, was eighteen, and a friend of the doctor's. They had met at English classes in the military academy down in Cengelkoy.

We became friends, helping each other with housework, brewing up pots of tea together and sometimes, when two of her old-crone aunts came to visit from a neighbouring village, we would put on a tape of jangly arabesque music and us two youngsters would be forced to dance while the old women banged on drums, shook tambourines and cackled.

I went to visit her family home one day, in order to take photographs of a new baby for its father who was doing his military service. Three families and countless children appeared to live in a two-bedroom shack and off less than an acre of land. Although it was Ramadan and they were all fasting except Cybele, I was proudly served with a large meal. According to Islamic tradition a guest is given the best food in the house, and I have no doubt that as elsewhere in Turkey this rule was rigidly adhered to in that household, but the food was still virtually inedible.

On the way home I asked Cybele why she wasn't fasting. She was evasive, and it was only when she began to discuss babies that I realized that she was pregnant. Not long after this she came to my house clutching at her stomach. Her aunts arrived and took over, and throughout the evening issued a running commentary on her miscarriage. Cybele and her husband left and I never saw them again. Many of the women I met subsequently stated that they had been forced through the pain and humiliation of one or more abortions before marriage and that this was an accepted form of birth control.

Despite the fact that I was living off the beaten "Stamboul" tourist track, I provoked no more than a passing interest in the village. Perhaps Zahide and Mustafa kept the inhabitants so well informed of my day-to-day activities that there was little left for them to learn from source, but I also suspect that I had developed a well-deserved reputation for haughtiness.

For the first few weeks I seriously expected that unless I behaved with the utmost decorum my house would be surrounded by lusty youths until the early hours of the morning; and I stared rigidly ahead of me at all times rather than risk giving someone an excuse to talk to me. In time I began to realize that my attitudes to Turkish men were shaped by the same degree of unfounded prejudice that served to inform their attitudes toward Western women.

The first incident to bring this home to me happened within a few days of my arrival. Completely lost and miles from home in the street around the covered bazaar in Cagaoglu, I went into a workshop to ask directions. A boy came out with me, and I imagined he would start to point and gesticulate. Instead he accompanied me down to the ferry port, boarded the ferry with me, then found me the right bus and took me to the bottom of my hill in Cengelkoy. Before I had found any of the words to tell him that I really didn't think it would be terribly wise of me to invite him up to my house, he had grinned, said goodbye, and set off on the two-hour journey back to his workplace. That was the last I saw of him but the first of countless occasions when I was party to acts of altruistic kindness from Turkish men.

Most foreign women I met were rather less fortunate in their experiences with Turkish men.

While I never felt relaxed enough to make friends with men in the village, this was as much a result of their own personal taboos as of any misconception on my part, and I was quite happy to be assimilated to such an extent that I became *harem,* "forbidden territory".

When I travelled around Turkey I think I was afforded some protection by my appearance. As I learnt more Turkish my manner must have become more confident, and this combined with a dark complexion meant that I was continually mistaken for a Turk, or at least, cast enough doubt over my nationality to evoke the possibility of a spectral elder brother in the minds of would-be aggressors. My short hair, masculine dress and "boyish" figure further added to the confusion and I was often treated to the familiar epithet of "Agabey" or "big brother".

Only on one occasion did I feel at all threatened by a man, and that was in Trabzon bus station at three in the morning, when I was put into the care of someone who was evidently less than psychologically stable. After escaping from his clutches I took refuge in the company of a group of bus drivers, who realized what was wrong and demanded to know what he had done. They must have taken the matter into their own hands, and a few weeks later some friends travelling through the city returned with the news that my would-be molester had lost his job as a result of the incident.

Most foreign women I met were rather less fortunate in their experiences with Turkish men, and the only advice I could give was to seek the company of women at every opportunity, simply by showing and responding to friendliness. I found I was more comfortable in the company of Turkish women – to whom sisterhood seems a natural concept – and I was especially grateful for the matronly protection I received from older women wherever I travelled in Turkey. While they questioned me about my marital status and wondered at such freedom of movement afforded by independence from any family, I rarely felt that this curiosity had a pejorative edge and by the end of my stay I had been adopted into several Turkish families.

During the first year of my stay I taught English to students of Islamic theology at the university. I had been disappointed in my belief that Turkey would be peopled with religious zealots screaming for their own Islamic revolution, since most people seemed only too happy with the secular state and access to Western commodities and culture. I was warned by teachers in other faculties, however, to expect the worst of my new students.

These people, I was told, wished to annex Turkey to Iran. They were enemies of the Republic and the only English they would ever need would be the vocabulary required to hijack an aeroplane. Islamic fundamentalism is regarded with distrust and distaste among the middle classes in the big cities in Turkey. Most of my students were from villages in the east, from backgrounds of extreme poverty. For many of them, the only form of education they had known to date was religious instruction: rote learning of the Koran, the life and teachings of the Prophet and some Arabic.

I arrived on the first day to find that the students had voluntarily segregated themselves by sex, the women seated in two silent rows on the furthest side of the classroom. Contrary to the rules of *Yok,* the controversial Higher Education Council established after the coup in 1980 in order to depoliticize the universities, their heads were covered in long silk scarves, and most of them wore thick woollen stockings and calf-length coats buttoned at the neck and wrists.

I rapidly discovered that the Western textbook I was using was not suited to the task in hand. There was no way these people were going to mill around a classroom shaking hands with each other. When one of the male students presented me with a picture of Chris Evert Lloyd on which he had biroed a *carsaf* (the black garment worn by fundamentalist women throughout the Islamic world), I conceded that it was time to forego the trendy TEFL teaching text and work on material which might prove more relevant in the prevailing atmosphere.

Pointing to a picture of Ataturk, founder of the Turkish Republic and official national hero, whose picture must be displayed in all public places, I asked the students what kind of man he had been. My question was greeted by silence and I concluded that this was a taboo subject.

I learnt later that even among devout Muslims there is divided opinion concerning Ataturk and his efforts to Westernize Turkey. Some say that he destroyed Islamic intellectualism and rendered their cultural heritage inaccessible by changing the Turkish alphabet. Others felt that there was no contradiction between Islam and economic and cultural progress. The students were naturally wary of expressing their feelings on such controversial issues since some classrooms retained bullet holes as a result of fights that had broken out before the military coup in 1980.

> *I found nothing to argue with in their determination not to be regarded as sex objects.*

The majority of the women were serious academics, and some intended to continue their education in other faculties when they had finished their religious studies. They were proud of the emphasis that Islam places on education for men and women, and they didn't feel that Western feminism had much to offer them.

I found nothing to argue with in their determination not to be regarded as sex objects (the reason they gave for covering their bodies in public), nor with a justifiable pride in their academic or artistic achievements. A couple of years after I left the faculty, it was Ilahiyat women who staged the biggest political demonstration since the coup at Istanbul university, when they protested against a ban on covered women in the classroom.

The only aspect of their lives that I couldn't agree with was that the women refused to attend services in the mosque. This was a reaction against feminism in Turkey. By staying away they reaffirmed that the mosque, the traditional forum for political as well as religious debate, was male territory.

I stayed another two years in Turkey after I left my *gecekondu* slum-dwelling and my similarly humble teaching post. I found jobs that required rather less explanation among the leftist and cultural elite, and apartments which required rather less housework.

Most visitors to Turkey opt as I did for a lifestyle that is somewhat more comfortable than that experienced by the majority of Turks. With the possible exception of decent plumbing, all modern conveniences and European commodities are now available in the major resorts and the cities in the west of Turkey. The Turkish people who service and maintain the tourist industry have a better grasp of Western values and behaviour than most of their visitors have of Turkish attitudes.

The people who make money out of tourism may have more time for driving jeeps and drinking Coke than for reading the Koran. The veneer of Western liberalism in Turkey's cities and the process of rapid cosmetic change to which this new generation of Turks is a party, cannot however disguise from them that poverty, year-round physical discomfort, sexual tension and Islamic fundamentalism are the basics of Turkish life for the majority of its population. Most Turks welcome tourism as their most valuable growth industry, but many young people also see tourists as their most valuable allies, as they attempt to improve their country's record on human rights and bring about lasting social change.

TRAVEL NOTES

Languages Turkish. Some English is spoken but German is more common.

Transport Most people travel by bus; the service is extensive, efficient and cheap. Trains tend to be slower and cover less ground. Shared mini-buses (*dolmuses*) cost little more than buses and go to even very remote villages. Hitching is not recommended.

Accommodation All main resorts and cities have plenty of inexpensive accommodation. Some women carry their own padlocks to secure hotel doors. In the east, you'll be able to find places to stay but the choice is far more limited.

Special Problems Sexual harassment – especially in the east, which can be dangerous for women travelling alone. Anywhere in Turkey it helps to dress reasonably modestly: cover your shoulders and don't wear shorts. A recent worrying trend has been the rise in tourist muggings – it's wise to avoid any display of wealth. Also steer clear of drugs; severe penalties are enforced even for possession of a small amount of cannabis.

Guides *The Rough Guide to Turkey* (Penguin). A guide through the labyrinthine world of modern Turkey, co-researched and co-written by Rosie Ayliffe.

CONTACTS

Kadin Cevresi Yayincilik (Women's Circle), c/o Handan Koc, Klodfarer Caddesi 41/36, Servet Han Cagaloglu, Istanbul. A group of radical feminists, and the main point of contact with other autonomous groups. They have a publishing house and produce a magazine called *Feminist*. The group welcomes the donation of international feminist literature.

Demkad (Union of Democratic Women), Tiryaki Hasanpasa Caddesi 60, Toprak Han Kat 4, Akseray, Istanbul. Part of the Turkish left and hostile to radical feminism. They work with women in the shanty towns and with the prisoners' support group *Tayad*.

Bilsak (cultural centre), Siraselviler Cad, Sogaci Sok 7, Taksim, Istanbul. Regularly hosts feminist events.

Committee for Defence of Democratic Rights in Turkey (CDDRT), 84 Balls Pond Rd, London N1, UK. Publishes the *Turkey Newsletter* which includes news of women's campaigns and demonstrations.

BOOKS

Rose Macaulay, *The Towers of Trebizond* (1956; UK, Futura, 1981/US, Carroll & Graf, 1989). Beautiful, quirky novel of camel-travelling and High Anglican angst.

Freya Stark, *Alexander's Path* (1956; UK, Century, 1984/US, Overlook Press, 1988). Classic travels in Asia Minor.

Sirin Tekeli, *Women in Turkey* (UK, Zed Books, 1993). Feminist collection of interdisciplinary articles challenging the status quo and women's position in contemporary Turkey.

Uganda

Gradually, as confidence in the leadership of Yoweri Museveni's National Resistance Movement has grown, Ugandans are beginning to put behind them the nightmare of nearly two decades of slaughter, corruption and chaos. The task is a hard one. Nearly 300,000 were killed under the Amin dictatorship, the entire Asian population was summarily thrown out of the country, and under Uganda's "liberation" by the Tanzanian army (and subsequent rule by Obote and Okello), death squads again had free reign. Now, after a hesitant period of readjusting to Museveni's reforms, foreign aid and investment is flooding back, business in Kampala, the capital, has almost returned to normal and tourists are welcomed. More than anything else, it is the sight of backpackers or tour groups wandering around Kampala or taking buses to the country's gameparks and beauty spots that convinces Ugandans that times are changing.

For travellers Uganda has once again been declared safe to visit. Road blocks still litter the highways, but they are no longer staffed by gun-toting drunks in uniform. Museveni's army is one of the most disciplined Uganda has known and approaches to foreigners are almost always courteous. Downtown Kamapala still shows the ravages of war in its potholed roads and bullet-scarred facades but restoration is well under way. Electricity is reliable, water runs from taps, and the markets are well-stocked hives of activity. Most visitors keep to the affluent suburbs where aid agencies, international business headquarters and plush hotels are concentrated, although there are few dangers for women in venturing out alone around the capital by day. It's crucial, however, to follow local advice about no-go areas at night and be careful not to flaunt your wealth. Pickpocketing and burglaries are a risk, just as in any major capital, but violence towards Westerners is rare. In general terms there's a refreshing absence of the hustle and harassment you get from men in the neighbouring East African countries. People tend to be curious and helpful and while some might ask you for money – poverty remains an endemic problem – there's rarely any pressure.

Travelling around the country to the gameparks, lakes and mountains is relatively straightforward although accommodation is basic and journeys tend to be slow and arduous (matatus or shared mini-buses are the main form of transport and, though relatively inexpensive, are packed and driven at breakneck speed. Buses are safer). You may well be warned against travelling in the north, along the border with Sudan or the northeast border with Kenya where outbreaks of fighting still occur.

For most visitors, the risk of illness and the physical hardship of long, tiring journeys in the heat have become the biggest deterrents. Death by malaria or drought has recently been overtaken by the AIDS crisis that is sweeping East Africa. At least a third of the population of Kampala is believed to be HIV positive and although the goverment has responded with innovative education campaigns, it will take years to judge whether these have any effect. This is a beautiful country but you need to take care.

Women in Uganda have long borne the brunt of war and famine, struggling to maintain village and family life in the wake of massacres and shortages. Polygamy, although now officially frowned upon, remains a fact of life with women left to bring up parallel families with little material help from the father. Museveni's government is attempting to enhance the status of women and improve access to education and employment by bringing in positive discrimination policies and encouraging the work of women-oriented NGOs. Working against the traditions of a staunchly male-dominated society is, however, proving an uphill task.

Living without Fear

Anna Borzello, a British journalist in her late twenties, moved to Kampala to work as a correspondent for a news agency. At the time of writing she had been in the country for three months.

It would be hard to imagine a more undignified departure. The day before I left I rang up my friends and whined: "What am I doing?" I clung to my boyfriend and cried: "Why am I leaving?" I rushed to the toilet with diarrhoea and threw up instead. My parents took a bleached-out, red-eyed wreck to the airport.

Six months earlier I had written to ten sub-Saharan newspapers, looking for work. Uganda had answered. All I knew about the country was that Amin had killed a lot of people and that it had perhaps the worst AIDS problem in the world. The image was made worse by meeting an Asian whose family had been thrown out of Uganda in the early 1970s: "My friends went back last year", she told me. "They were shot".

I would probably have been scared off were it not for the ex-patriates. Their voices were tinged with envy when I told them what I intended to do. "I think", said one returned volunteer, "that you will have the most wonderful time".

I realized they were right the minute I saw the red flowering tree at the entrance to the airport. The car passed green banana plantations, wooden shacks, the wide blue of Lake Victoria and swerved to avoid strolling villagers and men scything grass by the side of the road. There was none of the grey concrete normally associated with airport environs. There wasn't even a street light.

David, the news editor of the paper, had offered me a room in his house. I was rather apprehensive about this, fearing that I would be trapped way out in the ugly suburbs with a predatory man. I couldn't have been more wrong. The house was beautiful – a porched building up a quiet mud track, with a six-foot statue of St Jude in the bedroom cupboard – and David a gracious host. In fact, David and his brother Mike turned out to be unusual for Ugandan men. Both were vegetarians, in a culture where every meal must have meat, and cooked for themselves in a land where a mother is shamed if her married son enters his kitchen.

Kampala was also a surprise. I had been warned it was a "pit". But I liked it instantly, mainly because the countryside is never further than a fifteen-minute drive from the city centre. The centre itself is small (small enough to walk across in half an hour); trees line empty roads; large storks, as big as children, perch on roofs and weigh down branches; buildings are shabby, though through the dirt and peeling paint it is possible to make out grander days.

Their caution was infectious. For the first weeks I couldn't sleep as I listened to the guard dogs howl below my window.

The area around the taxi park is a different, poorer world. Hundreds of identical white vans, carrying the scars of their numerous accidents, gather in a large crater and form a bowl of noise reverberating with the shouts of conductors, beeping horns and the curses of pedestrians as they narrowly avoid being run over.

The taxi park spills over into the encircling market which is filled with piles of padlocks, fake leather briefcases, passion fruit, bottles of home-made bed bug lotion and piles of dead *muzungus'* (white peoples') clothes. At night business continues, lit by a hundred home-made lanterns.

My office, despite being in the calm centre of town, is as crowded and chaotic as the taxi park. The newsroom is a small windowless hole with far more people than desks and a network of computer cables which people regularly trip over, deleting the forthcoming edition of the paper.

Initially I was frustrated by the disorder (a basic disorder which means that press releases are given to reporters the day after the event), not because it made my work hard, but because the staff are talented and the paper could have been so much better with a fraction more discipline.

It took me a few weeks to realize that disorder is a feature of Ugandan life. Part of this is simply bad organization; but another part is because people are aspiring to standards which presuppose conditions that can't, as yet, be met. It is pointless, for example, to expect appointments to be kept in the rain when nobody has raincoats, just as it's naive to expect journalists to check their stories when the phones never work and nobody will speak to you unless the Minister clears it first.

Kampala has an easy-going atmosphere which is why I couldn't understand it when everyone warned me not to take a taxi home alone at night or walk on the streets after dark. Their caution was infectious and for the first few weeks I couldn't sleep as I listened to the guard dogs howl below my window and counted the gunshots of the neighbourhood patrol.

It was only when I realized that much of Uganda's fear is a hangover from the recent civil turmoil rather than a reflection of real danger, that I began to calm down. Whenever I am in a car with a Ugandan at night they will inevitably marvel that there are people on the streets: "Four years ago you couldn't do that. You'd have been shot". Now, like the handful of other *muzungu* women without a car, I feel confident taking "special hire" taxis home late at night, though I still feel uncomfortable walking after sunset.

> *A recent news report told of a Ugandan woman in Bermuda shorts being stripped by men for "being indecent".*

My fears of sexual harassment, based on a fax which my editor had sent me which warned that reporters might make "gender sensitive" comments, were, thankfully, ill-founded. Once a boy said: "Will you play sex with me?" as I walked home at dusk. Otherwise, nothing. Conversations with men have been free of leery looks and innuendo. Perhaps I have been lucky: my friend had her breast groped in the market and her bottom pinched in a disco. I have been crudely propositioned in a late-night bar – but by ex-patriates, not by Ugandans.

There are ways to minimize the chances of any unwanted attention: a recent news report told of a Ugandan woman in Bermuda shorts being stripped by men at the taxi park for "being indecent". While shorts, short skirts and sleeveless T-shirts are politely tolerated when they're on *muzungus,* I wouldn't wear them. Having walked behind a European wearing tight red shorts, I know that every person on the street will stare.

Despite the poverty (and Uganda is one of the poorest nations in the world), there are very few beggars in Kampala. "Beggars are hated", I was told. "There's so much land around that people think they should find some and develop it." The only exceptions are people with disabilities, who have no other means of getting money.

This doesn't mean that Ugandans aren't generous to the poor. Wage-earning Ugandans are like mini social services, supporting large numbers of family and friends. David, for example, pays for two of his brothers to go through school, one through university, and is building his mother a house. Despite this acceptance of patronage, I have never been asked for financial help – a stark contrast to Ghana where whites are treated like a walking World Bank.

Nor are visitors hassled by touts. In central Kampala people don't even look, let alone make personal comments. The only exception is the taxi park, where a white person will attract endless cries of "hello, *muzungu*". These are usually just conductors trying to fill their bus. I am now so used to it that I can blank out, and the more I look as though I know where I'm going the less "*muzungus*" I get.

Probably the key to it all is that Ugandans are incredibly polite. When I had to break down my bedroom door because I'd lost the key, a group of boys stood behind me murmuring apologies. When I've been lost, people have helped me find the way. Most of the men who have struck up conversations simply want to know what I think of Uganda. The corollary to this politeness is that people only voice their dissatisfaction behind your back. Outrageous gossip is part of life.

In most countries, people assume that whites are tourists. In Kampala, which has a poorly developed tourist industry, whites are assumed to be

> *So many people are dying [of AIDS] that the café next door has to stop giving its employees time off to attend funerals.*

ex-patriates. There are many grounds on which ex-patriates could be hated (many are under-qualified and overpaid), but I've never heard any criticized simply for the colour of their skin. Racist attitudes are reserved for the Asians: white Ugandans associate their return with prosperity (the economy plummeted when they were thrown out in the 1970s), and they are also disliked for failing to integrate.

In general, the disadvantage of being a *muzungu* in Uganda is that everyone assumes you are rich. The unfair advantage is that they also assume you are powerful, making it far easier for a white person to demand authoritatively to see the person in charge.

Backpackers form a slightly different class and are regarded with amused tolerance: amused because, by Ugandan standards, independent travellers are appallingly scruffy, and tolerance because Ugandans, who are fearful of being dependent on coffee exports, believe unequivocally that tourism is a good thing.

Despite the courteous people and the green, hill-ringed city, my predominant impression in the first few week was of death. It was everywhere. I kept on meeting people with histories which in Europe would have made them trauma victims, labelled and defined by their suffering, but in Uganda were considered just part of life.

Everyone seemed to be going to funerals of people who had "fallen sick" and left behind flocks of small children. The old lady staying in my house was too scared to go to her village because someone had threatened to kill her. Car crashes filled the papers. Our guard had lost his son. "Why do you have only two children in Europe?" he asked me. "If you have ten, you know if five die you have five left."

AIDS adds to the numbers: as many as one third of people in Kampala are HIV positive. So many people are dying that the café next to my office has to stop giving its employees time off work to attend funerals. Despite the fact that Uganda is known for its open attitude to AIDS, being HIV positive still carries a stigma. People lie about their status and I have heard many stories of women who have been persuaded by their boyfriends to have unprotected sex, only to discover that the man knew he was HIV positive all along.

I was also unsettled by the attitude towards children. Six-year-olds haul jerrycans as big as themselves up muddy paths. Street children rummage in the rubbish skip. The papers are full of stories of the defilement and beating of under-tens. The comment of one father after his young son had his penis bitten off by a pig is particularly illuminating: "What use is he to me now?"

Women are only marginally better off. While the Ugandan government is pro-women (positive discrimination in the universities, numerous NGOs working for women's rights) and the educated Kampalan woman, strong, funny, politically aware, often outspoken, may not initially seem as though she needs to have her rights fought for, women – in particular those in the villages – have a long way to go.

In my office, for example, there are no senior female staff, and while the male reporters talk to the editors as equals, the women approach them as subordinates. It took me a while to notice that even though everyone was friendly there were few deep cross-sex friendships: women stick together and there is a separate, and supportive, female community.

Uganda is still, unofficially, a polygamous society, but unfortunately educated women now have modern expectations. They want faithful men, but the men are loath to give up years of sexual freedom. The bulk of the traditional healers' customers are women keen to lure back their errant husbands with a love potion. Men frequently get their girlfriends pregnant, then leave, rarely contributing to the child's support. Affairs are the norm, fondly referred to as "away matches". "That's just how we are here; you can't change it", a Ugandan journalist told me.

While women complain that the men are liars, cheats and chronically unfaithful, men complain that women are too materialistic, trading in the good guys for the rich ones. Young Ugandan girls hanging off middle-aged ex-patriates are a common sight. I recently talked to a ravishing 21-year-old Ugandan about her

British boyfriend. "He's old", she said, casting her eyes down, "but I hope he will take me to England".

Equally, many ex-patriate women date Ugandans, though I have only met one who doesn't bitterly regret her experience. Their complaints are always the same: the charming man, having wooed successfully, starts to come home late, drunk and, inevitably, to sleep with other women. One British girl had adapted so well to her Ugandan boyfriend's behaviour that she is now content to be his "number one wife".

Recently, as I've listened to the progressive announcements of the Ugandan government, and on the same day watched a woman being dragged topless through a village street to be taken to a witchdoctor, I have felt that the international donor community has imposed an order on Uganda which is totally alien to its nature: as if a neat pattern has been pressed down onto an unwieldy substance.

Uganda is two worlds: there is the English-speaking, Kampala-based, IMF, development-set world which has four-wheel drives, affluent ex-patriates and lengthy development plans featuring "networking", "cost-sharing", "task forces" and a lot of talk about "sustainable development".

And then there is Uganda as it is lived by most Ugandans: not a nation at all, but a collection of rural-based tribes, with their own languages and customs, who live a subsistence life in many-wived families and inhabit a world of witch doctors, ghosts and rain-makers. This, combined with the power of the Church and the bawdy behaviour of many of the priests and nuns, makes rural Uganda a must-see for the medieval scholar.

Nobody lives purely in one world. Kampala heaves on a swamp of magical beliefs which constantly bubble into modern life: first division footballers urinate on the goalposts in the hope that it will help them win, while a policeman I interviewed recently let off the attackers of a badly beaten man because he believed the wounds could be satisfactorily explained by witchcraft.

Kampala, despite being the size of a small town, is a roaring metropolis compared to the rest of Uganda. I didn't realize this until I saw the country from the air. From 2000ft there is no sign of development, just round mud huts in circles of scratched earth surrounded by a small broccoli forest which stretches to the horizon. Villages are connected to trading centres by red dirt roads which cut their way through swamps and trees.

I have only been up-country a few times, but each time I visit a village I realize how partial my view of Uganda is. My friend took me to visit his mothers, all six of them, in their compound shaded by fruit trees and fringed by coffee plantations. None spoke English, though one ululated in greeting; the children knelt to say hello and chickens were slaughtered as a welcoming gift. Kampala was as far away as London.

Although I have travelled and worked in developing countries before, Uganda has been my education. It took the aerial view, for example, for me to realize what "poor infrastructure" means, and to understand why it took the Ugandan press two weeks to find out that victims of the Rwandan civil war were drifting into Lake Victoria only 150 miles from Kampala.

It is also the first time that I have really examined my Western preconceptions. I arrived expecting a war-ravaged, oppressed land full of dying people, and discovered that my image was years out of date. Ugandans, despite their many problems, admire their president, are proud of their country and are optimistic about their future.

Uganda is one of the most rewarding countries I have ever visited, and I am sure this is partly due to my privileged position. Not only am I working with thirty intelligent, committed, interesting and funny people, but I am paid to hitch rides on trucks to refugee camps, watch *Miss Uganda* competitions and listen to the president speak. On top of this, I am spared the barrier of having to relate to people across a financial divide. I am not a traveller, dealing only with people who make their living from my money. I am not a volunteer, which means I don't have to pretend I'm doing anyone a favour by working for free. And I am not an ex-patriate receiving a salary twenty times higher than the people in my office. Perhaps this, more than anything, is the crucial difference.

TRAVEL NOTES

Languages English, the official language, is widely spoken. Outside Kampala, people also speak Luganda and Swahili.

Transport *Matatus* (mini-buses) and shared taxis ply all the main roads but tend to be incredibly cramped and uncomfortable. Buses are a safer, if slightly more expensive option. Domestic flights and cross-country train journeys are notoriously unreliable and often cancelled at short notice.

Accommodation While there still exists a circuit of guest houses and cheap hotels, these tend to be in a desperate state of disrepair. In Kampala renovation work continues apace on the main hotels and there's a well-run youth hostel.

Guides *East Africa – A Travel Survival Kit* (Lonely Planet) provides good, practical coverage on Uganda.

BOOKS

★ **Dervla Murphy**, *The Ukimwi Road* (UK, Flamingo, 1994). *Ukimwi* is the Swahili word for AIDS, a unifying if harrowing theme in Murphy's 3,000-mile journey by bicycle from Kenya through Uganda, Tanzania, Malawi and Zambia to Zimbabwe.

Bettina Selby, *Riding the Desert Trail – By Bicycle to the Source of the Nile* (UK, Abacus, 1989). Selby's extraordinary 4,500-mile journey took her through Uganda and Sudan, with lively accounts of her adventures from being arrested to flying over the Sudd swamps in a bi-plane.

Ukraine

For centuries the fortunes of the Ukraine have been inextricably linked with those of its neighbour, Russia. A "second among equals" in the hierarchy of Soviet states, its importance was fixed as a border area (Ukraine literally means border-land) and an agricultural and industrial heartland. Kiev, the capital, dotted with Byzantine monuments, was the centre of the first Russian state from the ninth to the eleventh century and is still known as the mother of Russian cities. Yet, for most non-Slavs Ukraine was little more than a side show to the Imperial

and Soviet power bases of Russia. In 1986 Chernobyl – the traumatic images of clouds of radiation drifting from a blazing nuclear reactor – focused minds more sharply.

Since gaining independence in the wake of the failed 1991 Moscow coup, Ukraine's relations with Russia have become increasingly tense. Disputes are escalating over the sovereignty of the Crimea and the fate of the large ethnic Russian minority – nearly a fifth of Ukraine's population. The country's transitional economy, already in crisis, was sent reeling towards hyperinflation by Russia's moves to cut off cheap supplies of oil and gas. Food shortages and blackouts are now common, even in the capital; industry is floundering; and the fabric of the main cities – transport, roads, houses, historic monuments – is beginning to crumble for lack of repair.

As in most of the former Soviet Union, the financial chaos of the last few years has provided a breeding ground for new mafia gangs – a minority soaking up immense wealth from racketeering, while the majority are left struggling to cover the basics by taking on multiple jobs and doing unofficial deals. For women, who also have to contend with the full weight of domestic chores, life can be relentlessly hard.

Tourists to the Ukraine still tend to rely on state-backed package tours, although once you arrive there are plenty of options for making alternative private arrangements. One sign of strained diplomacy with Russia is that the border between the two states has become one of the trickier crossings in the region – it is currently easier to arrange a visa on to Moscow before you set out than by applying in Kiev. Travelling around the country still involves a fair amount of bureaucratic hassle although state officials tend to be more flexible (and unpredictable) than in former Soviet days – bribes are the key to most transactions. Safety is also a growing concern for travellers. Street muggings are on the increase in all the main cities – Ukrainian women are now as uneasy about walking alone along unlit streets as we are in the West – and tourists are considered easy targets. You do need to plan carefully your return journeys at night and, generally, avoid flaunting any expensive Western goods.

As a visitor it can take a while to adjust to being part of a privileged elite, feted and sometimes resented for your spending power. The Ukrainians have a tradition of open-handed hospitality that remains a matter of pride, and even minimal encounters can lead to invitations, unlooked for acts of kindness and endless rounds of vodka-toasting. However, you do need to be aware of the practical needs of your hosts. Few Ukrainians can afford to go into the joint-venture cafés, shops, restaurants and hotels that now cater for foreigners (and the mafia): if you want to share a drink with friends, be prepared to foot the bill.

Decades of Communism have done little to challenge the very rigid sexual stereotyping that persists in Ukrainian society. Unless elderly or travelling with children, **women** tend to be addressed as *"dievushka"* (girl) or *"dievchunka"* (girly). It is usual to marry young, and remaining single into your thirties carries serious stigma (it's also hard to get by on a single salary). Glamour is *de rigueur* for women, while men tend to assume a chivalrous role – flattering, flower-giving and escorting you home. Travelling alone you are likely to receive a fair amount of attention from men, although this tends to be more flirtatious than threatening. In the tourist- and mafia-frequented bars and hotels the situation is heavier. Many women – including students and professionals – are resorting to prostitution in the tourist areas as a means of coping with hyperinflation and, sitting alone, it will be assumed that you are soliciting.

Muddling Through in Kiev

Helen Buhaenko, daughter of Ukrainian and Welsh parents, grew up in the Welsh town of Abergavenny. Just over a year after Ukraine gained its independence she followed her father on a visit back to his homeland, arranging a three-month permit to help set up a new language school in Kiev. She is now studying Russian at the school of East European and Slavonic Langauages in London.

I n all, my dad waited forty-nine years before returning to Kiev. He swore to go back only when the Motherland was free; so on the first anniversary of Independence he joined the dancers of the Krushchatick and telephoned home with the folk tunes playing in the background. Inspired, I arranged in his absence to work in Kiev myself that next month, helping to establish one of the city's first language schools. Dad's second call is memorable for his descriptions of his swollen feet – squashed on a trolley bus on the way to market. By the last week he vowed never to travel by train again after a nose-on collision with a moving toilet. When he got home he said it would be better if we didn't visit Ukraine for a while. Too late: I was off in two weeks. Dad gave me some dollars and a bumper pack of travel wipes.

My emigré friend says the thing she misses above all about Ukraine is the horizon. Here she feels as though she is living in a pocket. Over there, the vast expanse of the steppes serves to remind you of how insignificant the small details of everyday life really are, leaving you more open to the unexpected and inexplicable. At least that's how I came to explain the Ukrainians' ability to shrug off with weary detachment events that left me open-mouthed, beggaring belief.

Tables and chairs flew, the room was filled with mace gas and everyone was shouting "mafia!"

Time and again the incongruity of situations quite threw me. Visiting a teacher training institute, we came across a small room on the third floor guarded by a man wielding a club, wearing what looked like a Nazi uniform. Inside, the room was packed with icons and aristocratic memorabilia for sale. A small man sitting on a chair in the corner waved a hand towards the merchandise saying, "There is no catalogue. I know all the prices by heart".

Behind a white unmarked door on the fourth floor was a teeming market trading in Italian boots and bags, marked up in dollars way beyond Western prices. Only the very elite could possibly have afforded such items – for elite read mafia. Instantly recognisable, these burly, swollen-faced youths in their black leather jackets would spend their time patrolling their patch of bars and restaurants.

After work, in the evening, a group of us used to head off to a joint venture Swiss-Ukrainian café opposite the market. Once, while we were deep in conversation, a man rushed in past the police guards on the door, and made for the heavies at the bar. Suddenly a fight broke out. Tables and chairs flew, the room was filled with mace gas and everyone was shouting "mafia!" while scrambling for safety to the toilets and out onto the pavement. There was another man lying unconscious outside. The paid-off police had quickly disappeared, while the original attacker was dragged into the kitchen.

This was the only violent incident that I witnessed in Kiev, the only time that the murky undercurrents of the mafia world broke to the surface. Just as memorable were the many acts of everyday kindness, such as the women carrying bones in their pockets to throw to the hungry dogs in the street, or the seated woman who insisted I place my shopping bag on her lap when standing one day in a full to bursting bus.

Living in a world where the parameters move daily, it is easy to feel insecure and vulnerable. Sometimes it felt as if we were living in Wonderland, unable to predict what event would befall us next. Once I was teaching in my classroom when the lights went out and a dog rushed into the room. The café downstairs stopped selling coffee for a month as it found jumpers were a more lucrative market. Why was it necessary to have a gynecological examination before joining the swimming pool? Luckily the doctor forfeited the check-up for a bottle of vodka, the ubiquitous bribe.

During any one day you will find yourself making an awful lot of double takes – at the women selling ice cream out of their pockets in the dead of winter; the man in the sports stadium holding up a sausage he wanted to sell. Once a Russian friend and I needed to hitch a lift to get home. No cars stopped, but eventually a scheduled bus drew up. The driver didn't have any passengers so he agreed, for a negotiated fee, to turn the bus round and drive us home instead. Time and again doors that remained resolutely blocked for months on end would swing effortlessly open in their own good time.

A lot of patience is needed when trying to sort out any bureaucratic negotiation – buying train tickets, renting a flat or trying to organize a visa to Russia involves hours of queuing, waiting, bribing, name-dropping and ultimately resignation in the face of hopelessness.

As a group we seemed to muddle along, lurching between fortune and misadventure. Our pay, at the time, was partly in dollars, partly in local currency (coupons), which meant that we had to change some money each week on the street. No one could be sure if this was illegal or not as the code of law was in the process of being rewritten. (Incidentally, I met the Canadian woman who was helping to draw up the new bill – it's amazing who you meet at parties in Kiev!) One Saturday afternoon a colleague was changing money on the Krushchatik (the main street of Kiev) when he felt a hand on his shoulder, swung round in a panic and was wrestled to the ground by a pair of policemen. They bundled him into a car and locked him in a cell for three hours, insisting that he was a Russian acting as a foreigner. Eventually an interpreter verified his credentials and he was released with the parting words: "The next time you want to change money, first come and see us at the station."

Visiting the Bulgakov Museum with the temperature outside at minus ten and not a soul on the horizon, I found myself ushered in by the curator. "As we are alone, let's close the museum and have tea upstairs", she suggested. We climbed Bulgakov's stairs and entered the kitchen, which is normally sealed from the public. There the lady gave me biscuits and tea and talked about her visitors and their interest in the novelist. It was a rare moment, as was my meeting, that same afternoon, with an American theatre director who was talent-scouting for his production of *Othello*. Together we watched a production of *The Master and Margarita*, swopping ideas for a likely Iago. I never saw him again.

> *"You can buy what you want, go where you will, and what's more, take the man with you out of this country."*

Slowly I was learning to expect the unexpected. We had been set the task of making an inventory for the staff room and after honing down our original list, which included a photocopier and coffee machine, we settled, more realistically, for just paper, chalk and books. Delivery day arrived, and what faced us on the staffroom table was a row of twenty red plastic beakers and some white ice cream bowls. Our director said that he'd bought up all he could find in the stationer's.

I specifically asked to share a flat because I wanted to learn the language. My flatmate was Oksana, a slim-built woman who I always picture in a voluminous fur coat ("from Brezhnev's time, you can't get these now").

When I arrived, she was standing in the kitchen, waiting for me with a bowl of soup. She'd been expecting me for the last four evenings and had made something each night. We never managed to get to know each other really well, partly because of the language and partly because Oksana worked so hard I never saw her. She spent from Monday to

Friday hurtling between her three accountancy jobs, completing work quotas in coffee breaks. Up at six, she came in at nine and went to bed at ten. For some time I thought she must be enjoying herself at the weekend because she never spent Friday or Saturday night in the flat. But over a bottle of vodka she told me she spent the weekend with her husband in his house out of town. She cooked him all his weekday meals on Saturday and cleaned his house on Sunday. Her family didn't like him, and she didn't seem to like him much either. "But he will die if I don't feed him, and it is better to be married than single."

Although extraordinary for having a flat of her own, Oksana was typical in tolerating an unsatisfactory marriage. A Belorussian friend of mine says her husband considers he is fulfilling his duty by making love to her once a week. The other nights of the week he spends stun fishing with an electric rod. To overcome her isolation and depression from being alone all day with small children, Olena rings any man she knows to be in the village to come over for a chat. I met no one who professed to be faithful, and very few who were seeking divorce. With the breakdown of so many structures in society, a fluidity pervades all arrangements. Women cling to marriage for the social status it affords. Foreign women receive a lot of unsolicited attention. The dichotomy of the situation was best summed up by my friends Natalka and Michael: "Here you are a princess", said Natalka. "You can buy what you want, go where you will, and what's more, take the man with you out of this country."

Michael, a Georgian, had a different opinion of Western women: "I would never marry one. They are too feminist. That means they sleep with everyone."

On our arrival, the teachers were issued with (illegal) mace guns for protection while walking home at night. The only time I used mine was accidentally in the staffroom, to great effect; but those guns put our nerves on edge. The streets are unlit, even in the heart of the city, and with the shortage of fuel the situation can only worsen. After dusk Oksana always found someone to walk with her, because she was particularly afraid of opportunist muggings. I finished work at ten and had to change trolley buses three times before walking home alone along an unlit leafy avenue. Often teachers stopped over at each others' houses to avoid the walk home alone.

There are no organized taxi companies in Kiev, only private individuals who pick up hitch-hikers for a fee. Katy, a teacher friend, and I found it was generally safe to stop cars if we stuck together, as long as a price was established at the outset. Another problem was that the car could break down in the middle of nowhere or, as happened once to us, that the police stop and haul away the driver after finding he has no licence or papers.

In fact it was not on the streets that I experienced any harassment, but in hotels and restaurants. Ukrainians like to eat in large jazzy restaurants, accompanied by a glitzy band. The music booms, the vodka flows and flowers appear mysteriously at the table. Then two burly men loom over the table with a "Dance, please – yes?" and no amount of cajoling will deter these suitors from their conviction that two women at a table must be petrified with boredom and just screaming out for a jig.

Once I was taking a bite of beetroot when a man yanked my elbow, landing my plate, fork, beetroot and the two of us on the floor. The manageress threw him out amid something of a skirmish. I was certain he would be waiting for me in the car park.

Being a regular woman customer at a bar or restaurant involves a quiet act of diplomacy. The resident prostitutes were at first worried about competition and needed reassurance that we were not after their clientele. Easier said than done when the majority of Ukrainian men will instantly interpret two independent women with spending power as being on the game. Fairly representative was one night when an enormous Belgian man sank, drunk and incoherent, into the circular plastic seat beside us. His official interpreter, a young female student, patiently ministered to his needs. Then a man poked my arm, said: "Oh, may I?" and plumped himself in the seat on the other side.

The closer I came to people, the more complex and mystical they revealed themselves to be.

"I am a general", he announced, "I have a son that tall". He pointed to the fluorescent lamp. "Nuclear, I am, very big." Then out shot his fist with a hundred dollar bill, which he placed in Katy's drink. "I want you now."

Luckily he was so drunk it was all he could do to remain seated. As we hastened to leave, the girl with the Belgian said: "So nice to meet you. My name is Lena. I am studying at Kiev State University in the faculty of Science and Engineering. I have taught myself to speak English. Do you think I have a good accent?"

Many students are turning to prostitution as a means of financing themselves at a time of hyper-inflation. The only way to avoid being taken for one is to go out with a male companion, or stay in and wait for an invitation to a private party. These are great fun and go on all night, with a lot of stomping, drinking and dancing. In fact most activities in Kiev involve drinking. Although socially very difficult to bow out of a toast, women are allowed to substitute champagne for vodka. This news was gratefully received after a week of welcome parties, when I thought I was not going to be able to stay the course.

The paucity of material life in Ukraine seemed to be counterbalanced by an aspect not immediately apparent to the visitor. Most people have a very intense spiritual outlook. In 988 Prince Vladimir brought Byzantine Christianity to Kiev-Russ. When the Turks sacked Constantinople, the Orthodox Church moved its centre of faith to Kiev. The city has always felt itself to be a special, mystical place. Now the people are experiencing a huge re-awakening of their belief. Or rather, beliefs. For, following the general principle that with the collapse of the old order all general guidelines flew out of the window, true faiths and bogus sects are being adopted without discrimination. The closer I came to people, the more complex and mystical they revealed themselves to be. For example, my teaching partner Irena, a quietly-spoken woman in her early thirties, working on her thesis entitled "The

Oksana made me take off my shoes when entering the flat, then wash the soles to remove the radiation.

Idiom in English", had sought help from a monk to rid herself of voices that were bothering her at night. They had started after her boyfriend had emigrated to America, rejecting her "for a couple of bananas", and leaving her to take care of his grandmother. The monk had successfully grappled with her evil demons, covering himself with bruises in the process. He instructed her to turn her thoughts from her boyfriend to Jesus. She happily complied.

Her story initially surprised me, but then I discovered that a Belorussian friend had applied to study theology at the Vatican University and that Natalka, our school secretary, practised levitation and believed that she was paying in this life for her sins of adultery in the last one. (Incidentally, it was said that in my former life I had been a woman who gathered herbs on the steppe.)

It may be that the incredible pressures placed on individuals at the moment are catapulting them into finding consolation in the nether world. Certainly our director resigned to pursue more fully a Buddhist way of life. And some students were torn between continuing classes or having lessons through the medium of the *Book of Mormon*.

A continuing pressure that people face is living with the legacy of Chernobyl. The official line is that after the disaster in 1986 the streets of Kiev were washed clean of radiation. The population was advised to drink a glass of vodka a day or, alternatively, a glass of red wine, to help purify the blood. It is said that some people had geiger counters, but threw them away because they kept on bleeping. The reality of the situation is that no one can afford to be fussy about potentially irradiated foodstuffs when so many goods are in short supply and shopping is so time-consuming.

A girl at the British Embassy told me they had been given three green discs to attach to their windows: if they turned red then radiation levels were high. They had never done so. But then a woman from the US Embassy said that radiation hot spots were dotted in confidential locations around the city. Obviously the air is rife with rumours about the actual situation and its effects on the population. But hard facts are hard to find. Reports on levels of radiation in the city are unalarming, but their findings are based on Soviet data and few people are willing to believe the figures. Certainly, for the visitor there seems nothing to worry about. Long-term guests are recommended to follow local guidelines and leave the city once every three months for some fresh air. I definitely do not feel qualified to give an opinion about radiation in Kiev, but it would be very wise for the long-term visitor to sort out how she feels about this subject before settling in.

I found it slightly unnerving that Oksana made me take off my shoes when entering the flat, then wash the soles under the tap to remove the radiation.

This is certainly a time of opportunity in Ukraine. To sit in a joint venture café is to be seated next to Hungarian geologists, film directors from Canada, French booksellers and German retail agents. Each day unfolds its own surprises. Generally, it was easier for the couples who could share the shopping and the bus rides home; but being a single woman was to be open to the most extraordinary adventures and receptive to many confidences.

I left after three months, scared off by the worrying reports about radiation. I can't wait to return – the lure of the fascinating over-rides such fears, especially as I only experienced Ukraine in the winter. A friend of mine explained this exciting, inviting country very well when he said he'd travelled far and wide and never been to anywhere more foreign than Kiev. I just hope it'll take less than my father's forty-nine years to go back.

TRAVEL NOTES

Languages A sensitive issue amongst Ukrainians. Moves to institute Ukrainian as the official language of education, politics and commerce have stoked tensions with the ethnic Russians and Russified Ukrainians. Ukrainian nationalists in Kiev and Lviv take a dim view of being addressed in Russian. In the tourist areas of the main cities you are bound to find some English- or German-speakers.

Transport It is now possible to fly direct to Borispol airport from a number of European cities. Kiev has a clean, inexpensive and efficient metro system and there are plenty of trolley-buses, buses and trams. It can be hard to get hold of tickets for long-distance train journeys. Touting around different ticket agencies, waiting in line and jostling are the norm.

Accommodation Kiev and most other main cities have a range of tourist hotels. It's often easiest to book through a tour company. Once in the country you can make your own arrangements to rent a flat – via one of the many new agencies – or you could take a private room with a family (where you get treated like a prodigal daughter).

Special Problems Visas. You should apply for a visa from the Ukrainian embassies before setting out – you can't rely on buying one at the airport. It's usually fairly straightforward to extend this once in the country. Safety is becoming a major concern, with a real danger of opportunistic muggings on the city streets at night. It's best not to wander around alone after dark. Much is said about the violence of the mafia but this rarely impinges on tourists.

Guides There's little that's bang up to date. *USSR – A Travel Survival Kit* (Lonely Planet) has reasonably good maps and cultural details.

BOOKS

There are few books specifically about the Ukraine available in English (but see *Russia* on p.533).

USA

Anyone travelling to the USA from Europe will feel a sense of familiarity about the place: all the exposure to American film, TV and culture does form a preparation. However, it's equally likely that, on a first-time visit, this will be accompanied by considerable culture shock. It takes a while to get to grips with a country that is, genuinely, a continent. A continent where extremes of wealth and poverty can be just a couple of blocks apart – and where whole neighbourhoods, even whole towns, are formed by particular and highly diverse ethnic populations.

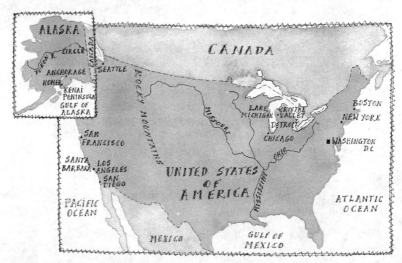

The hardest place to arrive, by general consent, is New York City, whose pace and hustle (all part of its appeal) can leave you feeling too vulnerable and too small. The West Coast – Washington state, Oregon and California – is perhaps the gentlest place to adapt, with its more relaxed and laid-back ethos an enduring (but true) cliché. But this is only to scratch at the edges. The vastness of Mid-America, the distinctiveness of the Deep South, the remarkable desert scenery of the Southwest, the quieter East Coast cities: all this adds up to just a fraction of the USA's staggering variety. Off the mainland lie the tropical islands of Hawaii and the icy wildernesses of Alaska, a stone's throw from Russia – no wonder many Americans don't feel the need to go abroad. There's a lifetime's worth of travel at home.

As far as issues go, it's important – especially if you're travelling coast-to-coast – to get a grip on the strength of regional chauvinism. Each state has its own legislation as well as political affiliations and, between them, attitudes towards women (and God) vary greatly. On sexual issues, the Moral Majority and associated groups such as the Pro-Lifers are continuing to strengthen and extend their base, proving effective as an anti-abortion lobby, and in the simmering climate of hysteria over the spread of AIDS, receiving growing support for their tough line on "sexual deviance". In terms of race, colour discrimination remains an enduring fact of life, not just restricted to the rural South. Black and Hispanic urban ghettos tend to be the poorest, most deprived in the country, and the rehabilitation of Native American culture has done little to halt the erosion of Indian territories and lifestyles. Considering the size and number of America's ethnic minorities, integration remains a reality for comparatively few.

Travel presents few problems. Only in situations where you really stand out as a tourist is there likely to be persistent trouble from hustlers. In this case the main thing is to look confident, be firm and at least seem to know where you're going. Big cities can sometimes feel unsafe – all have definite no-go areas – and travelling anywhere in urban America it is always wise to avoid carrying more cash than you need for the day. It clearly depends on the going exchange rate, but the USA does tend to be expensive for foreign visitors. On the plus side, the American reputation for hospitality is well-deserved and even the briefest encounter can lead to offers of floorspace or a bed for the night. Anyone who can afford it drives, and a good network of buses will usually get you to whichever town you want.

There is a feeling, shared by many women in the US, that the **women's movement** slumbered its way through the dead weight of the Republican years. While an embattled group of activists tried to tell women that their rights – reproductive freedom, equal pay, the Equal Rights Amendment – were under threat, many American women, feminists and non-feminists alike, experienced the 1980s as an era of private reassessment and reappraisal. It was a defiantly "me-oriented" decade in which activism in any form was unfashionable, and in which personal and independent struggles for success and fulfilment were a priority.

By contrast the 1990s have seen something of a reawakening. At the turn of the decade an estimated 600,000 Americans took the streets to oppose an impending Supreme Court ruling that threatened women's consitutional right to abortion. More recently, under the changing fortunes of the Clinton administration, women are holding on to and asserting their full lobbying powers. Organizations such as the Washington-based Centre for Women's Policy Studies have been at the forefront of calls to have gender-based crimes (from threatening phone calls to murder) enshrined in the statute books while date-rape has been established as a national concern. It's hard to know how much ground will be lost by the mid-term Republican victories, but it seems clear that women in America are not easily going to submit to a political backlash.

Just Jump in and Get Cracking

Deborah Bosley and Melanie Jones have made several trips to the States, travelling around and occasionally working. This account by Deborah concentrates on their experiences of New York. Back in England she is currently working on a novel.

Perhaps the most maligned and the most adored city in the world, New York is forever on the discussion table. The plethora of information on the city, the media exposure, and stories from friends who have visited, will give you at least a sense of it. Nothing, however, can ever prepare you for arrival.

Reactions vary, so expect every and any: to our minds there are two ways of approaching New York and between us we tried them both. Either, like Melanie, you can remain closeted in your arrival bubble, that haze of defences that is not the result of neurosis but simply the fear of a city whose reputation eclipses the possibility of ever meeting it on neutral ground. Or you can, like me – and I was also scared to death – just jump in and get cracking.

Our experiences were shaped by circumstances; in a perfect world you would be smack in the middle of Manhattan and able to stay in a roach-free zone in one of the racier neighbourhoods. The outer boroughs may at first seem a more economical option, but commuting back and forth to Manhattan will be a drain on both your time and resources.

Fortunately Americans (even New Yorkers) have a well earned reputation for extending offers of a place to stay to friends and friends of friends, and we were not about to turn down

> *Resigned to a long night, we camped in the lobby, cracked open the Jack Daniels and decided to ride it out.*

the promise of a bed in Greenwich Village, even if the offer was third-hand by the time it reached us. An address to head for can make the first few hours in New York infinitely more reassuring. Bearing this in mind, we would definitely recommend that, in the absence of a friend or contact, you book a hotel ahead. Don't just turn up and hope for the best; for women especially this can be a recipe for major headaches and a safe place to stay is vital until you've reached a degree of acclimatization and are feeling less overwhelmed.

That said, our own advance arrangements did not make the first few hours in New York any easier. We arrived around midnight to our pre-destined apartment block only to find a note pinned to the door saying: "Back at 8am – Sorry, Frank". Resigned to a long night, we camped in the lobby, cracked open the duty-free Jack Daniels and decided to ride it out. Bemused apartment dwellers nodded us cautious hellos on their way in and out, and one chap, having walked past us six times or so, heard our story and invited us up to his place to finish the JD in comfort.

We crept back down at the appointed hour and finally met Frank, our host. He was a walking contradiction – at once a man of stifling geniality and, equally, acerbic bitchiness. Only the fortuitous circumstances of immediate shelter; employment (working the stalls in the SoHo flea markets of which Frank was a proprietor) and free food (he was also a catering manager at New York University), caused us to pause and reconsider our immediate inclination to get the hell out.

> *One of my more useful acquisitions at the time was a fabulous cliché named Buddy.*

Fifty dollars a day for as long as we liked – we couldn't believe our luck. Not that working, living, eating, sleeping and socializing with Frank wasn't about to test us to our limits. But we believed that his condition, as with many New Yorkers, was symptomatic of where he was and of the survival skills he had acquired in order to exist without being completely discordant from New York's perverse scheme of things.

Our two months with Frank exposed us to a New York we might otherwise have missed and almost certainly steered us away from simpler experiences we might have enjoyed. Gay club fiends, though common enough in Manhattan, do nonetheless live in a somewhat self-contained world. For me this was New York at its best: highly strung, living completely beyond my means and energies and feeling (falsely) secure in the company of strangers who cared little or nothing for my welfare beyond novelty value.

I flourished, using every dexterous social skill at my disposal to charm my way into the circle of New York's terminally trendy and inevitably transient night-time life. One of my more useful acquisitions at the time was a fabulous cliché named Buddy, who was manager of New York's then hot-spot, the *Palladium*. Like the unfolding of some tacky movie, his character was revealed in all its ungloriousness when he opened the cupboard above his bed and produced a 26-foot python. Too much.

Meanwhile, Melanie was finding the city a little harder to swallow. Ever the realist, she arrived defensive and bristling with indignation at the rudeness and hostility of New Yorkers she had tried and sentenced before arrival. It's hard to take a back seat and feel easy about things in New York unless you're heavily sedated, and for Melanie the experience proved too crushing. Her belief in human sincerity was obscured by too many five-minute friendships: intimacy on contact, and then goodbye. It was all too fast, furious and unfriendly, and she took to adopting a foetal position in the centre of the only air-conditioned room in Frank's smelly apartment for much of the two months.

Indeed, New York is weird. Unless you've lived there for years, you can't even really trust your friends. On one particular occasion we were carousing in the Lower East Side's *Pyramid Club* and could only look on in amazement as Frank removed his shoes and socks and, with both hands full, gently manoeuvred his agile feet to the back pocket of a nearby pair of 501's and from an innocent night creature softly prised a $100 bill with his nimble toes. Not that his altruistic nature didn't surface occasionally; but even the sight of Frank thrusting $20 bills into the outstretched palms of passing tramps did little to redeem him in our eyes.

Violent crimes against women are high, but your bearing and approach will determine much.

So, seeking some less hurried, more meaningful social contact, we decided to try out New York's women's scene. At the end of our street was a lesbian bar called *The Cubbyhole*, which strictly prohibited men. It had been recommended to us several times and we arrived with high hopes. But on arrival we found that even getting through the door was a test. Squeezing past the massive, glaring woman who was guarding the entrance shook our confidence, and it wasn't much better inside.

Rather than finding here a good-humoured, supportive and relaxed environment in which to sit and get ploughed with impunity, we found instead a tense gathering of seemingly competitive women pitched against each other, sitting steadfastly in the groups or couples with whom they had arrived. There was little cross-group chit-chat and banter such as you would expect in a place of this kind. Maybe we went on an off-night, but our experience of other women's bars in New York wasn't dissimilar and we were later to find them diametrically opposed in attitude to their far more relaxed (and to our minds superior) counterparts in California.

But New York is known for its extremes, and again we believed that, all things being symptomatic and circumstantial, fear for one's safety surely plays a part. It's a fact: you do have to watch out. Violent crimes against women are high, but your bearing and approach to New York will determine much. The usual rules apply: never walk alone after dark in unfamiliar places; look people straight in the eye, etc – but don't make too much of an issue of it. "There's nothing to fear but fear itself" is pretty applicable here. It really is no more menacing than other large cities and you should be aware of the confidence-destroying vibes of paranoia. Having said that, go on your hunches; everything happens so fast in New York that you'll have to assimilate many of your experiences in so few moments that your instinctive reactions will be important.

It won't take much to knock your confidence. I'd been riding high for months in New York, felt I had it sussed and knew how to handle myself. Working in the markets in SoHo and on Broadway had opened up contacts and engendered a feeling of belonging until, on the day before I left, I took a subway from Broadway alone. Nothing heavy at four in the afternoon, but across the platform from me stood, or rather staggered, a rangy, thin black boy, staring at me. Behind him was a huge poster giving information about AIDS. Suddenly he screamed across at me: "Suck my dick and die." Of course he was completely smashed, or cracked out of his head, and couldn't get to me because of the track between us, so there was no immediate danger. But the experience was chilling and one that has stuck.

To me this typifies some of the completely unbridled aggression that runs beneath everything in New York. Naturalness seems in short supply in the city. Maybe it's not the fault of the people. The madness which surrounds them is absolutely to blame for the rise of neuroses, which feed neuroses, and so it goes on. So don't let it get to you; put yourself in the driving seat and treat New York as an adventure. Lose yourself for a while, and be somebody else.

The Dating Game

A co-author of The Rough Guide to California and San Francisco, here **Deborah Bosley** goes on to write about living in the city.

Searching for something to say about San Francisco, only one thing prevails and that's sex. Blame it on circumstances, state of mind or any other unspecified personality disorder but I cannot divide the two in my mind. Without its attitude to sex, San Francisco would be just another place on the West Coast – certainly not the gay capital of the world, not the place where the nuclear family began to melt down. Paris may be for lovers, but San Francisco is for the seriously randy. Call it liberation if you like.

As the dark clouds of puritanism settle over California; as drinking is largely discarded as a social lubricant in favour of the non-addictive Prozac, and smoking is treated as a murderous dependency, sex at least has stabilized its currency and remains one of the few forums for experimentation and adventure. If you're thinking that I must have been getting laid a lot to come out with such a statement, think again.

My time in San Francisco coincided almost perfectly with one of the most distressingly celibate periods of my life. But it was my exposure to a "singles" culture that taught me most, giving me an unparalleled opportunity to polish my courtly skills and refine the art of dating. This is not a town in which to shop for husbands. Save that for when the party's over. San Francisco is a finishing school for flirts.

Don't be fooled by casual attitudes; everyone's on the make. This is evidenced not only by total strangers who strike up conversations with you at random, but also the sheer physical attractiveness of its inhabitants. In San Francisco, there is an importance placed on personal appearance that I relished. Inevitably so much preening is narcissistic, but coming as I do from a nation of pasty-faced sartorial slapdash, it was refreshing to witness such impressive grooming. Of course San Franciscans are blessed with just enough sunshine for a year-round, fashionably light, West Coast tan, but they also have the bonus of an immigration pattern that has resulted in some intriguing and beautiful racial mixes. The competition is stiff, and you'll have to take measures to stay ahead of the game. Don't pack in haste; include one or two absolute killer outfits. This will help you to distinguish the woman from the canvas mountain, adorned with rucksacks, sensible clothing and stout footwear that usually constitutes your average female traveller. Save your earnest tie-dye for the Third World. San Francisco is a sophisticated, world-class city with a barely concealed snobbery in all things alluding to taste. Dress up.

Next comes the sheer physical allure of the city itself. I refer not to its gently rolling hills, phallic downtown towers or the tidal forces of the Pacific pushing in and out of the bay, but to its actual layout. As well as being (for the most part) a beautiful and well-kept city, it is arranged into a series of distinct ethnic and social neighbourhoods, each with its own restaurants, bars and clubs that will help you narrow down your hunting ground to a comfortable area. So, for example, if you like the kind of men who are cadaverously good-looking, hang out in clubs and usually carry a respectable quantity of cocaine, South of Market is the place for you. You can spot them early, taking in a game of pool, lounging moodily at the bar before following them into any of the legion of SoMa's night clubs. If you're on the lookout for a preppy, well-educated Ivy League high-flyer with pots of cash, the oak-panelled singles bars of the Marina and the Pacific Heights will give you a good taster of what you can hope to find. Or perhaps the idea of dancing in the Mission district with slightly dangerous looking Latin boys, who don't speak English, is more your speed.

If I don't address the needs of gay women, it is not because I don't consider their adventures to be of equal importance, but because they don't need any help from me. The majority of women I saw in the lesbian bars and clubs of San Francisco had that gorgeous, silicone-free, lived-in look that distinguishes them from the sculpted, scalpelled, dream-babe image that their southern Californian counterparts cannot quite get away from. Just pick out the relevant listings from any guidebook or local magazine and you'll have a field day.

No, it is the poor, tormented straight woman, persecuted by legions of beautiful men who do not want to sleep with her who needs all the advice she can get. Because despite my best efforts to find a nice straight man, I would find myself again and again hanging out with the queens.

Your walk will change to more of a studied, slow stride, perhaps with a hint of a swagger.

San Francisco is a fruit-fly heaven. Bored, perhaps, by the ease with which they can find men in general and sex in particular, I found gay men particularly keen to escort straight women around town. It can be a frustrating charade, but think of the advantages. You get to step out with men who know how to dress, open doors, pick up tabs, hail taxis, admire your outfit, make you laugh and listen to all your tedious anxieties about life. He may not want to go to bed with you, but the people who see you out together don't necessarily know that. They can usually cook, and in my experience throw the best parties; they talk to you with an abandon that most straight men, if they are playing their typically guarded game, cannot afford.

Don't be put off by the doom-mongers who complain that there are no straight men in San Francisco. As I've said, you're not looking for a husband and you don't have to be straight to spoil a woman, flatter her, make her feel she is riveting company and generally add to her self-esteem. What you must be wary of, however, is the time-honoured trap of falling in love with your best gay friend. Fascination lies that way, but so does heartbreak and, speaking as one who fell in love with, married and eventually buried hers, I must offer a warning.

So free your mind of any ideas you may have about love – the lasting kind at least. San Franciscans with whom I became acquainted regarded long-term relationships as something to be avoided for as long as possible – an attitude that results in scores of thirty-somethings wondering why they're on their own. But hopefully you won't be around long enough to uncover the drawbacks and can simply enjoy the society of a city that delights in seduction in its many forms. When the AIDS crisis hit San Francisco there was never a question of abandoning sex or reverting to some bogus code of monogamy. Instead people came up with ever more imaginative uses for the humble condom, handed out leaflets that clearly defined safe and unsafe practices and strongly urged the former. Tragedy notwithstanding, the fun continued.

But the biggest kick for me was the dirty talk. In common with their propensity to discuss themselves at length, San Franciscans are not afraid to talk about sex in any social situation. I frequently overheard descriptions of acts that would leave me pondering their plausibility for days, and indulged in abandoned, drunken discussions the like of which I had not indulged in since the sixth form. It is difficult to fully do justice to the palpable sense of sex all round. Maybe it's the way you find men and women blatantly cruising you as you step out for groceries; or it could be the sexual aid shops for women (*Good Vibrations*, 17th St), staffed by fresh-faced assistants with their matter-of-fact approach to things you wouldn't tell your best friend. You'll notice that your walk will change to more of a studied, slow stride, perhaps with a hint of a swagger creeping in.

Whatever form the change takes, you become aware of yourself in a way you would never allow yourself in normal circumstances. I suppose that applies to travel everywhere in the world; but not everywhere in the world is sex in all its many guises so blatantly in your face. Whether you're between lovers or just bored with the one you have, I cannot recommend strongly enough the restorative properties of a couple of weeks in America's most beautiful city and the boost to a girl's confidence that it will provide.

Routes West

A researcher on issues connected with child protection and women's health, **Cathy Roberts** spent eighteen months travelling and working between England and the US – mainly southern California, home of her best friend. During this time she also gave birth to a son, Sam, who spent the first year of his life accompanying her on her travels.

Southern California is not a place you get to know easily first time round. And nor are Californians easy to get to know quickly, though you would never be made to feel a stranger or unwelcome. An odd mix of roots and transience permeates all the cultural and social groups which make up the region's incredibly diverse population. It's as if the westward migrations only really stopped because the sea began, while the northward flow of peoples continues to fill space which is really a continuation of home. Spritually, everyone is still on the move. As a foreign working woman with a new role as a mother and a desire to get to know this unfamiliar land I seem to fit in.

Other than the cross traffic to and from Central America, most visitors to southern Calfornia will come in through a major metropolis like Los Angeles – not an easy place to love. Created by an industry devoted to fabricating unreality, LA as a city doesn't really exist; there is a downtown, but I had been visiting for years before I found it. Instead, it is made up of a series of city states (as I think of them) that together sprawl over two valleys between the mountains and the sea. Each city state, whether Hollywood, South Central, Westwood, Santa Monica or Glendale, has its own wealthy, middle-class and poor districts, its own rules and regulations. If you can find a patch to fit your temperament and pocket, it's perfectly possible to burrow in and become part of the community. You'll soon discover the good shopping, eating and entertainment places, and how to get around on foot or by bus.

LA has a bewildering array of galleries and museums, which Sam and I haunted, along with my friend and her five year-old son. Anything that has ever sparked off anyone's imagination is on display to the public somewhere in or around LA. We visited botanical gardens, the original Spanish mission sites, sculpture galleries, model farms, vineyards and towns; we went to huge municipal museums and one-room local showrooms. We also "did" the great shows of Universal Studios and Disneyland. And loved every minute of it.

Sitting down to feed in a shopping mall or park, I'd find myself the focus of an instant women's group.

Getting to know other women seemed to me less easy in LA than in other parts of America, notably San Francisco, but it's still not hard. Bookstores are a good source of information on women's groups and organizations, while several districts have women's cafés or clubs. Travelling with a baby is a help: sitting down to feed in a shopping mall or park, I'd find myself the focus of an instant women's group, with the odd father sometimes joining in too.

When it comes to outdoor activities, apart from the advantages of warmth and light (in fact, we were drenched in Disneyland, having chosen unwittingly to visit on the day the flood rains started), almost all public places are accessible in structure and attitude to children. I found few places in California that I couldn't easily get into with a baby in tow, or where I wasn't instantly helped if there was any problem. Back in England, I miss that spark in people's eyes as I approach with stroller and accompanying baggage. The cheery "have a nice day" is not necessarily as hollow as it sounds.

Another aspect of access is less positive. Despite the recent arrival of a metro system, the only real way of moving between two parts of the city is by car. I couldn't leave hospital with Sam until the staff had checked that a car was there, complete with approved babyseat in the back. Until the summer of his arrival I had never driven in America, but within weeks the freeways were part of my living space. I appreciated the freedom of being able to load the car and go, and confess that I liked the image of myself driving with the top down, rock on the radio, beautiful baby in the back, making the roads my own.

I got to know certain places – where my friends lived or where we were going to play or eat, or where I needed to work – but I couldn't tell you anything about the lives in between. That was LA though, and LA is not the whole of southern California. Get out of the sprawl (and it takes some time and miles) and you'll find an incredible range of landscapes and communities. I had the chance to move up the coast a way and explore the area between LA and San Francisco: specifically, Santa Barbara County.

The obvious way north is the Pacific Coast Highway, which bursts through the mountains just before Oxnard, going on to hug the coast in a gorgeous ride through Ventura. Along this route Sam and I would pull into the only mainland banana plantation and sample the incredible variety on offer; a little pink one tasting of pineapple was a big favourite. We'd also sometimes do a northeastern approach or re-entry to LA through the avocado and orange groves, so that we'd arrive at our destination with all the ingredients for guacamole, but already too full to eat it.

In many ways Santa Barbara is the living image of the California of the movies and there's nowhere quite like it. It's a beautiful area and, owing to the lie of the mountains, enjoys its own ecosystem of weather and seasons; when LA was shivering and mopping up after the storms, Santa Barbara maintained a pleasant 21°C with a decent mix of sunshine and showers. February 1993 saw me sitting on a rock by a babbling brook, up in the hills of Montecito, baby kicking in the shade in his Moses basket, while I drowsed like a lizard, supposedly reading but actually soaking up the memories to carry back home.

The town of Santa Barbara slides down the hills to the coast over a small fertile plain and, thanks to determined planning, retains a distinctly Spanish look and feel. The cost of living generally matches the place's wealthy appearance, although there are low-budget areas, and the University, perched on the hills outside town, provides a student community with a student lifestyle to go with it.

The Pacific Coast Highway runs close to the beach, while the train provides a vital link for anyone without a car (but you do miss the roadside stalls). A free bus travels up and down the main street from the hills to the coast (free public transport is always memorable in the USA). I considered buying a bicycle – very popular on the waterfront – but wasn't convinced my car weakened muscles would cope with the gradients. Along the ocean, cafés and a Sunday market provide good opportunities for meeting people and seeing what's going on. Although the middle-class lifestyle is fairly suburban here, and communities tend to be built around people who know each other through work or schools, a significant New Age presence makes for a certain openness. There are strong Central American communities too, reflected in the shops and the cuisine. There's also a sense of trying to retain the shadows of the native American presence, with several recognized sites in the area.

The old-style cowboy with old-style attitudes still lurks in the hearts of many a small town male.

During my stay, I made some forays beyond the hills away from the coast. The westward migration up to the turn of the century is still alive in the very stylized communities around the vineyards and farms of the Santa Ines mountains and valleys. Again, access is mainly by road, but one year I'm determined to pile family and friends into a Winnebago (a kind of motorized covered wagon) and set off to explore further. For anyone who likes wine, the area is a wonderland of small vineyards – never too pushy to let sales pitches get in the way of appreciating their efforts, and with no stereotypical attitudes about men being the wine buffs of the world. In fact, I was reminded of how, since prehistory, women have been the cultivators and the brewers. Other memories of Santa Barbara involve visions of evenings sitting in the open, sharing with friends the wine and the stories collected that day, smelling the pine, the redwoods (and the skunk!) and knowing why people from far and wide made the struggle to California.

Despite being in LA through the riots, and despite knowing its general crime rate and sense of alienation, I felt safe enough there, both on my own or with friends. There are areas I wouldn't go to; some never, some perhaps only in the daytime. But I feel exactly the same in England. In some of the smaller places too, you may have to be careful who you talk to or what you say – the old-style cowboy with old-style attitudes still lurks in the hearts and minds of many a small town male. If your face doesn't fit you may not get support from some of the women either. A conservative strain runs through white, small town California which I wouldn't have relied on for help had I ever needed it.

From the point of view of travelling, I felt no better or worse in southern California than I would in any other US state, or indeed Europe. Owing to my work, I am very aware of the problems of violence against women and children. Among my colleagues, I came across a vital energy and commitment and a refreshingly radical, feminist approach to understanding violence and how to deal with it. I also experienced sullen cynicism and blatant sexism but generally speaking, in California I found an acceptance of me as a woman which I do not have at home.

A Trip to the "Last Frontier"

Lorna Menzie works as an advertising copywriter in London. Inspired by a magazine article about "the greatest dog race on earth", she flew to Alaska with the aim of witnessing the race for herself. This was the first time she had travelled alone.

"Alaska. Where men are men and women win the Iditarod." So read the headline of a Sunday supplement article about the gruelling sled dog race that takes places every year in Alaska. Launching off from the state capital, Anchorage, the competitors travel on six-foot long sleds pulled by up to twenty husky dogs for over a thousand miles through the earth's most inhospitable territory. It's the ultimate test of Alaskan machismo; it was therefore somewhat galling when a petite woman called Libby Riddles swiped the first prize from under the men's noses in 1985. Since then a woman called Susan Butcher has won on three occasions.

Reading about the Iditarod and Libby Riddles' cunning win I became hooked. I decided to write off to The Race Organizers, Nome, Alaska, and see what happened. To my surprise I received an unbelievably enthusiastic letter back from a dog racer, or musher, called Matt, describing the excitement of racing and insisting I had to come and see it for myself.

I had no other contacts, but with three weeks holiday ahead I felt I could do something a bit more adventurous than drink *glühwein* in the Alps. With the incredulous laughter of my friends still ringing in my ears, I boarded the plane to Anchorage. The month was February, not a time of year recommended by the American Tourist Board.

If Anchorage hadn't been a strategic refuelling spot on the way to the Far East, I doubt whether the plane would have bothered to even set down. Glancing at the cabinload of Japanese businessmen, I got the distinct feeling I would be disembarking alone. I settled down in my seat to see what I could learn from the few guidebooks I'd managed to find.

After a few pages I began to sweat. Layers of thermal underwear didn't help (I was convinced I'd be walking off the plane in a blizzard), but more uncomfortable were the statistics. Long dark nights, cabin fever, alcoholism and lawlessness provide conditions for the highest incidence of rape and murder per head in the United States. Alaska is nearly half the size of Europe; I reasoned that it couldn't be homicidally dark everywhere and, with a population of only 460,000, I might not bump into too many people.

We eventually touched down in Anchorage in brilliant sunshine at a warm 0°C. The town was definitely low on charm. The airport bus meandered past standard issue shopping malls and empty office blocks, testimony to the oil, gold and mineral rushes that have come and gone. Having found out the high cost of hotel accommodation, the only pre-planning I'd done was to reserve a youth hostel bed. The uninspired grid system of 1st, 2nd and 3rd Avenue and A, B, C Street meant that at least the bus knew where to drop me off.

> *Travelling alone you get to do things and be with people that normally you might choose to avoid.*

I arrived at lunchtime, when the hostel was as eerily empty as the malls we had passed, but by early evening the place began to fill up with the long-stay residents. Many of them were sitting out the winter here, waiting for the lucrative summer season when they could get jobs in the tourist trade or the canneries. By mid-evening things were definitely looking up. Mavis "all my exes live in Texas", myself and five others from the hostel went on a spot of bar-hopping to *The Buckaroo Bar*, *Fly-by-Night* and *Chilkook Charlies*.

Yes, this is ten-gallon hat "good ol' boy" country. The atmosphere wasn't over-friendly, but then again neither was it at all threatening. It was great fun and a good way to get to know the people I'd be living with for a while.

It was quite a night, especially for Bonnie, my Mormon room-mate who was on orange juice only. It wasn't until after quite a few drinks in several bars that I realized Bonnie was missing. We'd driven about twenty miles and I was beginning to get worried as she was good fun but fairly unworldly. Some of us retraced our steps, only to return in the small hours, still Bonnie-less. To my amazement, there she was waiting outside the locked hostel. She'd fallen asleep under the table in *The Buckaroo Bar* and a friend of the barman had given her a ride into town. I realized that although it doesn't hurt to be a little circumspect, you shouldn't judge everybody by a few statistics you might read. I discovered, too, that travelling alone you get to do things and be with people that normally you might choose to avoid. It didn't have to change my personality, but I did have to dump some of my preconceptions.

Two days later, I was beginning to wonder what the hell I was going to do in Anchorage for a week before the race started. Then, over the telly and a jumbo bag of corn chips, up came the offer of a ride north.

Having left at home my boyfriend and travelling companion of seven years, it was weird to be with a couple without being part of one. Doug was from California and his partner, Kumi, was Japanese. We agreed we'd share the petrol and visit some of his friends along the way.

The ride north was spectacular. Frozen lakes and towering rock-faces gave way to snow-drenched forests. First thing in the morning, the ice froze into delicate lace patterns hanging from the trees. It was a magical, totally silent landscape. Occasionally the stillness would be broken by the sight of caribou deer or an eagle overhead. The scarcity of civilization and the sheer scale of Alaska makes it staggeringly remote and beautiful. So far I hadn't seen a husky dog team, but I'd experienced more than I could ever have imagined. The trip was already worth it.

Reaching the outpost of Circle, fifty miles from the Arctic, took two days. Still not an igloo or polar bear in sight – just plenty of sunshine and, thirty miles down the road, Circle's answer to a health farm.

It was during the Klondike gold rush that Circle first appeared on the map. Conditions for the gold prospectors were appallingly harsh, so when natural hot springs were discovered nearby they were well-used. Bearing in mind that the mighty Yukon River at Circle is frozen solid at that time of year, you could see why the springs are still popular. The gold rush brought thousands to this desolate spot, where brothels and gambling dens soon sprang up to relieve the miners of their hard-earned cash. Nowadays all that is left is the *Hot Springs Hotel*.

I took myself off for long sessions in the outdoor pool. The natural heat of the water at 59°C served the dual purpose of keeping me very happy and heating the greenhouse, from which you can enjoy fresh tomatoes even when the outside temperature hit minus 31°. Floating on my back, and looking up at the cloudless blue sky with huge overhanging icicles just visible through the steam, I felt extremely content. As nobody visits the hotel mid-week, we had the undivided attention of the backwoodsmen running the place. Bobble hats glued firmly on, both indoors and out, they were very gentle hosts and revelled in telling tales of harsh Alaskan life to us wet-behind-the-ears townies.

My return to Anchorage was a huge anti-climax. Not having checked the dates Matt had given me a month earlier, I'd missed the pre-race meeting. This is where details of the thousand-mile route are given and the rookies, or novice racers, receive tips from the old timers. Basically, it's a big get-together and sounded fun. The hostel seemed stark and boring and no place to nurse my abject disappointment.

As the going had suddenly got tough, I headed straight for a shopping mall. I'd seen in an advert that Libby Riddles, the first woman to win the race, was going to be signing at a bookstore. Libby Riddles was surprisingly interested in my quest and kindly fixed me up with the vital transport to a couple of race checkpoints. She was charming, and so affable that it made the thought that she'd trounced the competition even sweeter. Lasting two weeks, the going is physically and mentally exhausting. Libby had made a calculated but extremely risky final push, mushing through a blizzard in temperatures approaching 15°C below, to win the title with a two-and-a-half hour lead.

Among the potential hazards are frostbite, blizzards, losing the trail and – possibly worst of all – encountering moose.

Not having done my homework, I hadn't taken in that being in a wilderness you wouldn't be able to watch the race beyond the first few checkpoints; and that transport was needed, even to those. When they say wilderness in Alaska, they really mean it, so I was particularly grateful for Libby's help.

At 8.30am downtown Anchorage was packed out with spectators, stewards, helpers and wagons unloading hundreds of feverish huskies onto the slush. The atmosphere was electric. While the dogs were barking and slavering to be off, the mushers were in a frenzy, packing and repacking their sleds, since every extra pound carried can cause trouble later on. Each team has up to twenty dogs and separating and sorting them into their harnesses was quite a feat. At the start of the race the mushers, one to each sled, were allowed some help, but once they'd passed the first two checkpoints they were completely on their own. Among the many potential hazards are frostbite, blizzards, losing the trail and – possibly worse than anything – encountering moose which, despite their dopey appearance, won't hesitate to savage a dog.

Libby had fixed me a ride to the checkpoints with an old friend and race enthusiast called John Kelly, who'd spent his working life on Arctic ice stations in the American navy. His ambition, which he'd eventually achieved at the age of sixty-two, had been to walk the Iditarod trail alone. As the last team disappeared through the woods, we repaired to the Chinese restaurant to swap stories.

The next morning I woke with the nagging feeling of "Now what?" The fanfare of the race was gone and I was at a serious loose end. After only one morning of pacing the hostel, the answer came in the form of a Swede called Lars. Another passionate racing enthusiast, he thoughtfully suggested that I could go south with him, to Homer on the beautiful Kenai Peninsula, and stay with the friends he'd made the previous year. At the same time we could follow the racers' progress on TV and in the papers. That very afternoon we took off for Homer on a scheduled flight.

These people still adhere to the doctrine that if you disobey your husband, he has a right to beat you.

Putting up a stranger at a moment's notice didn't seem to bother Liz, Edwin and Michael at all. They were all escapees from the softer mainland states of Washington and Oregon, enjoying the less pressured lifestyle of mending fishing nets in winter and working as lifeguards at Homer's indoor pool to pay the bills. They had also started up and were voluntarily running Homer's answer to marriage guidance counselling.

Unemployment, alcoholism and depression brought on by the short daylight hours combine to bring trouble to the lives of the townspeople. The native Indian population has the difficult task of trying to survive in modern Alaska while maintaining their traditions. There are also three Russian villages in the area which have staunchly resisted the outside world. The original inhabitants came to the Kenai Peninsula long ago, having been expelled by the Tsar for their extremist views. These people still adhere to the doctrine that if you disobey your husband, he has a right to beat you. If your disobedience continues, the same task falls to the local priest. Seeing the freedoms enjoyed by other women, some of the sect had become a little disaffected and had sought help. It was part of my hosts' task to put the women in safe houses while the couple found a less violent solution to their marital troubles.

Not only did I have great admiration for these new friends, but they were brilliant company as well. By day I took myself on long walks, for which they lent me snow-shoes so that I could explore the vast wood behind the house. I found them very unwieldy and preferred to stick to the well-beaten tracks which afforded a wonderful view of the mountains without any danger of running out of road to walk on.

Walking the ten miles into Homer, I gave up counting the number of people who stopped to offer me a ride. People thought it rather odd that I was walking all the way for enjoyment. I suppose you get used to anywhere if you live there long enough, but trudging along, taking in the white peaks and glaciers surrounding Kachemak Bay, was quite something to me.

In the evenings after work we all hung out together. I cooked Liz, Edwin and Michael a full works roast dinner one night – they amazed me by going totally crazy over the roast potatoes. It was nice to share something so ordinary from our culture that they thought was positively exotic.

On my last night the three of them asked me to take part in a quasi-Indian ritual, something they did partly in reaction to the over-whelming number of devout Christian sects in the vicinity. After dark we climbed through the deep snow at the back of the house until we reached a mound, a good half-mile from any neighbours. They stood me on the mound of snow, which was decorated at four corners with moose bones and a crow's wing, and we stared up at the night sky, thick with stars. Then, shaking their home-made moose-hide rattle, they slowly began to encircle me, chanting good wishes for my journey home to England.

"I Saw You Naked in Michigan"

Nancy Stender writes about her first ever trip to the famous international Michigan Womyn's Music Festival which takes place every August in the middle of a forest in northern Michigan. An American currently living in Ann Arbor, she works as a buyer for a national bookstore chain in the US.

I had wanted to attend the Michigan Womyn's Music festival for several years, and I finally got my chance in the summer of 1993. A combination of adequate finances, suitable transportation and free time made the trip possible. I had heard wild tales of naked women dancing and singing and showering together, of great music and bland vegetarian cuisine and of the opportunity to meet women from around the world in a comfortable, communal setting. And, of course, there was the famous bumper sticker plastered across the bumpers of cars everywhere, emblazoned with the phrase "I saw you naked in Michigan".

To many women in the lesbian and feminist community, the one word says it all: "Michigan". There is no need to explain any further. When I'd hear women talking together, asking "Are you going to Michigan?" or "Did you have a good time at Michigan?" I knew they weren't just talking about one of the fifty states.

The event itself, as well as the year-round planning that goes into it, sounds like the ultimate utopia. The flyer, available at feminist bookstores and through the mail, gives ample descriptions of the history of the festival, and details about accommodation, fees, activities and rules. The fun always starts on a Monday in August and ends on a Sunday. The longer you stay the cheaper it gets per day. The entire festival is disabled-accessible – with shuttles run by DART, as well as sign language interpreters for all events and numerous other offerings. There is a 24-hour sober support area, first aid on hand at *The Womb* and peer emotional support can be found at *The Oasis*. A Womyn of Color support tent also has constant events going. Help seems to be available no matter what your problems or needs may be.

A number of transsexuals had set up camp outside and were protesting their exclusion from the event.

One must be prepared to rough it at Michigan. The festival site, stretching over 650 acres, lies deep in the heart of the Northwoods. It's a camping experience to remember; you need a tent and sleeping bag (unless you have your own RV, for which there is a separate campground), and the festival organizers recommend a change of shoes, rain gear, sun clothes, water container, paper plates, utensils, towel, flashlight, soap and shampoo. I would also add sunglasses, insect repellent, sunscreen, toilet paper and a small mirror to that list. A pamphlet entitled *First Timers Camping Tips* is available on site.

There are many ways to get there. The small airport nearby runs a festival shuttle, or you can come by bus or car. I chose to drive, setting out early on Saturday morning on what was supposed to be a four-hour drive. Unfortunately, I found the directions on the flyer to be less than helpful, and got sidetracked several times. I had eagerly expected a veritable caravan of women to be clogging up the roads and so confidently assumed that I wouldn't get lost, which was a mistake. However, none of my problems were too serious and I got there with few hassles in the end.

My festival experience started on a high note, with smiling, shirtless, tanned women directing traffic at the gate. Unfortunately, the front gate was also host to some controversy, as a number of transsexuals had set up camp outside and were protesting their exclusion from the event. Michigan is advertised as being only for "womyn born womyn" and transsexuals are excluded. This issue has been an ongoing debate for the past few years, as transsexuals have been ejected from the grounds. I have no idea where the debate is heading, but it was the subject of much conversation while I was there.

I was eventually pointed to a parking area for registration. Advance registration is available, with a sliding fee scale and scholarships for women who need them. I decided to just show up and charge it on my Visa card. (No personal cheques are accepted and there is no instant cash machine on site, so get your cash before you enter. The nearest small town is miles away.) I was immediately asked whether this was my first time – a question continually asked by the women running the event, and which got a little annoying after a while. I got a green plastic wristband as proof of admission (and first-timer status), and then went to drop off my belongings and park. Being thus identified as a first timer, I was shown to the Orientation tent. Frankly, I thought this was a big waste of time. A video was running: its subject was how wonderful the festival is, and how many great volunteer opportunities are available. A woman at Orientation, spying my green band, excitedly led me over to the volunteer workshift schedules and crowed to the woman in charge, "We have another virgin here!" I was too cowed to protest about such a sexualized nickname, however, and immersed myself instead in studying the work rosters.

> You haven't lived until you've seen a group of naked women Country and Western line dancing.

The system appeared to be incredibly disorganized. It was suggested that you sign up for two workshifts of four hours each but all the rosters – under headings such as Kitchen, Child Care, Traffic, Security, and so forth – were already filled. We were told to sign up anyway, so I dutifully added my name to the list under Traffic. I never did figure out the difference between Traffic and Parking, which no one could explain. All this information got transferred to index cards that ended up Goddess-knows-where. The area had an aura of chaos about it, with women scurrying around looking for lost ballpoint pens and paper. I trekked back to my stuff, and waited for a shuttle to take me to my campground.

I ended up at Amazon Acres, which seemed to be a pretty general camping area. There are also chemically free, noisy and quiet camping areas, as well as sites for those with children. Since it was the last couple of days of the festival, good camping spots were hard to find, but I hiked back pretty far into the woods and set up camp. (The farther back into the woods you are, the longer the distance between "Port-o-Janes" and your tent.)

I was feeling pretty victorious about getting my tent set up as I caught the shuttle to "Triangle", which is the hub of activity for the festival. Warning: the shuttle buses consist of flat-bed trucks and assorted wagons towed by tractors, and are crowded, slow and irregular. I finally learned to skip them and just follow the pedestrian path.

The weather was warm and sunny, and reports had it that 7,500 women were on "The Land", as it's referred to. I saw women completely nude, women with shirts and nothing else, with pants or shorts or skirts with no shirt, women wearing nothing but their underwear, and women who were completely clothed. There was such an incredible mix of ages and colours and body shapes – it was truly amazing. Everyone looked happy and excited to be there, and music was everywhere. I really think that you haven't lived until you've seen a group of naked women Country and Western line dancing. I eventually shed my own shirt and settled down to watch some concerts. There are three stages, with many different kinds of music being performed. The musical end of things was organized in an extremely professional manner. Practically every event was on schedule, large posted signs clearly identified the running order of musicians, and disabled and non-smoking seating was available. The bands were all excellent: I saw a Japanese drum band called Sawagi Taiko, a children's concert, gospel singers, rock and roll. The lighting and sound were superb. Many women had brought lawn chairs that are very low to the ground, and I wish I'd done the same. It would have made sitting much easier.

I could wear a bag over my head and no one would give me a second glance.

Be sure to bring your plate and utensils with you wherever you go, so you don't have to walk all the way back to your campsite at mealtimes. I learned the hard way and decided to shower en route. The showers were cold, and there was a little bit of a line, but it sure felt wonderful. The facilities are outdoors and quite rough, but I don't think anyone really cared. It was just so great to have water. The food at Michigan is legendary for being pretty tasteless and repetitive and in short supply, so arrive early if you want to eat something edible. It's nothing really horrible, just a lot of sprouts and peanut butter and beans. For those who truly can't deal with the food situation, junk food is now for sale; last year was the first time they tried this experiment, and from the lines of women waiting for candy bars, cookies, ice cream and potato chips, I would judge this a success.

All day and evening the artists are around, signing CDs and cassette tapes of their music. The musicians are very accessible and friendly.

I felt the safest I have ever felt in my life, which was a remarkable experience. As I tramped back to my tent Saturday evening after seeing Linda Tillery and the Cultural Heritage Chorus I wasn't the least bit afraid of the all-encompassing darkness. I also felt free to look any way that I wanted – I could wear a bag over my head and no one would give me a second glance.

I have heard reports from friends that the festival is a good place to pick up women, but I have no such tales to report. I did meet many wonderful women from around the world though. I also saw women engaged in pretty explicit sexual activities, so if public displays of affection freak you out, this probably isn't the place for you.

Sunday morning it was overcast and eventually started to rain. The weather kept getting worse, so I decided to pack up early and head home that afternoon. Since the shuttles were running ninety minutes late, I resigned myself to hauling all my gear, in the rain, the mile or so to my car. I was cursing feminist bureaucracy as I loaded my stuff, but had to smile when a woman handed me a rose at the exit gate.

Next time I shall go earlier, stay longer and go with a friend. That way I'll be able to get the maximum amount of enjoyment out of my stay. Altogether, Michigan was a wonderful, energizing and (dare I say it?) empowering experience.

TRAVEL NOTES

Languages English – but there's a significant first-generation immigrant population who don't necessarily speak it. This is particularly true of the Spanish-speaking Americans in California, New Mexico and New York.

Accommodation Generally inexpensive, and with high standards. Most places have toll-free numbers which you can use to book rooms in advance. Chain motels are safe, clean and can be a great bargain: beware, though, of seedy, budget-price hotels in "unsafe" parts of of town. Across the country, youth hostels, which don't usually require membership, are a good bet. There's also a well-organized network of campsites. If you've got a little more money to spend, it's well worth trying the new, flourishing breed of Bed and Breakfasts, often in rather grand, nineteenth-century homes.

Women's Holidays *Alaskan Wilderness Programmes for Women*, PO Box 773556, Eagle River, AK 99577, USA (☎907/688 2226 or 1-800/770 2226) offers year-round activity trips and wilderness retreats for women, including mountaineeering, glacier travel and dog mushing with some of Alaska's top female mushers. Includes adventures for children.

For backpacking trips in the wilds of California and Utah, open to women of all ages and experience, contact *Cloud Canyon Wilderness Experience*, 411 Lemon Grove Lane, Santa Barbara, CA 93108, USA (☎805/969 0982).

Qui Travel, 165 W 74th St (☎212/496 5110) is a women's/gay travel agent based in New York City.

Those interested in attending the *Michigan Womyn's Music Festival* should write to PO Box 22, Walhalla, MI 49458, USA.

Transport It's generally agreed that the best way of getting around the USA is to drive. A car gives you mobility and independence – not to mention the chance to hear some great radio stations – and it can be the most economical way to travel. Car rental and fuel are inexpensive, while the cheapest places to stay, the chain motels, are usually strung out on the interstates on the edges of town and not accessible by public transport. Non-drivers have the option of *Greyhound* and *Trailway* buses, which cover all major destinations; the alternative *Green Tortoise* is more limited, but efficient, fun and a great way of meeting people. For long distances, domestic flights are worth considering – there are always a range of special deals and, by European standards, they can work out to be fairly inexpensive. Hitching is extremely dodgy for both sexes and not recommended under any circumstances.

Special Problems The cost and bureaucracy of US healthcare is horrific. You must take out medical insurance and if there's any chance you may need gynecological care, be sure to double-check your policy. Some don't cover it and it's very expensive (as are contraceptive pills).

Guides The Rough Guide to the USA (Penguin) is detailed and lively, and as invaluable as ever, and there are separate guides to *California, Florida, San Francisco, The Pacific Northwest* and *New York*. Also recommended are *The Woman's Travel Guide to New York* and *San Francisco* (UK, Virago/US, RDR Press), which combine practical information and advice with some great, often entertaining, insights into women's contribution to the history, art and culture of the cities.

CONTACTS

The Index/Directory of Women's Media, published by the *Women's Institute for Freedom of the Press*, 3306 Ross Place NW, Washington DC 20008 (☎202/966 7783). Lists women's periodicals, presses and publishers, bookstores, theatre groups, film and music groups, women's news services, writers' groups, media organizations, women's radio, special library collections, and more. Invaluable and updated yearly.

The National Organization for Women, 15 W 18th St, 9th Floor, New York 10011 and 425 13th St NW, Washington DC 20004. With groups all over the country, this is a good organization to get referrals for specific concerns: rape crisis centres and counselling services, feminist bookstores and lesbian bars.

WOMEN'S BOOKSTORES

Necessarily a select listing of feminist bookstores, which are nearly always a good source of other local contacts/activities.

Washington DC: *Lammas Women's Bookstore*, 321 7th St SE (☎202/546 7299); and 1426 21st St NW. Bookstore and information centre, with two branches.

Anchorage: *Alaska Women's Bookstore*, 2440 E Tudor Rd, No. 304, Anchorage, AK 99507. Also a resource centre and music store.

Austin: *Book Woman*, 324 E Sixth St, Austin TX 78701. Feminist books, records and posters.

Los Angeles: *Sisterhood Bookstore*, 1351 Westwood Blvd. Bookstore and resource centre.

A Different Light Bookstore, 4014 Santa Monica Blvd, Hollywood 90029 (☎213/668 0629). Lesbian and gay books.

New York: *Womanbooks*, 210 W 92nd St (☎212/873 4121). Bookstore, record shop and community centre run by women and stocking a wide range of feminist and lesbian titles; pick up the city's monthly feminist paper, *Womanews*.

Oakland: *Mama Bears*, 6536 Telegraph Ave, Oakland CA. Bookstore, coffeehouse and arts and crafts gallery.

A Woman's Place, 4015 Broadway, Oakland CA. Women's art and bookstore.

San Francisco: *Old Wives' Tales*, 1009 Valencia St. Feminist, lesbian, Third World books.

San Jose: *Sisterspirit*, 1040 Park Ave, San Jose CA. Non-profit women's bookstore and coffeehouse featuring live entertainment every other week.

WOMEN'S CENTRES AND RESOURCES

Washington DC: *Bethune Museum and Archives National Historic Site*, 1318 Vermont Ave NW. Archive of educational resources on black women and organizations.

Chicago: *North-Western University Women's Center*, 619 Emerson, Evanston, IL 60201 (☎312/492 3146). Information about local women's groups.

Detroit: *Women's Liberation News and Letter* (branches throughout US), 2832 East Grand Blvd, Room 316, MI 43211.

Los Angeles: *Lesbian Political Action Center*, 1428 Fuller Ave, Hollywood 90046 (☎213/874 8312).

New York: *Barnard Center for Research on Women*, 109 Barnard Hall, 3009 Broadway (☎212/854 2067). Clearinghouse for information on women's organizations, studies, conferences etc. *The Saint Mark's Women's Health Collective*, 9 Second Ave (☎212/228 7482). One of the foundations of the New York women's community, offering traditional and alternative medicine at sliding-scale prices.

Lesbian and Gay Community Center, 208 W 13th St (☎212/620 7310). Major centre for events and information, used by over 250 groups.

San Francisco: *Women's Needs Center*, 1825 Haight St, (☎415/221 7371). Provides free healthcare and contraception advice, charging only the cost price of any medicine prescribed and asking for donations from those who can afford it.

BOOKS

This is inevitably more an idiosyncratic dip into the pile than any sort of "representative sample".

Linda Niemann, *Boomer – Railroad Memoirs* (UK, Pandora Press, 1993/US, University of California Press, 1990). Spirited and raunchy account of one woman's experiences of five years travelling and working on trains in the American West.

Josie Dew, *Travels in A Strange State* (UK, Little, Brown & Co, 1994). Entertaining account of the author's experiences of cycling for eight months right across the US.

Christian Miller, *Daisy, Daisy: A Journey Across America on a Bicycle* (UK, RKP, 1980). Wonderfully funny accounts by a not-so-old English granny who cycles from coast to coast on a small folding bike, camping out along the way.

Mary Shields, *Sled Dog Trails* (US, Pyrola Publishing, 1984). Low-key account of the 1974 Alaska Idiatrod by the first woman to complete the race, as well as descriptions of many other sled dog trips in Alaska, taken with her partner John.

Isabella Bird, *A Lady's Life in the Rocky Mountains* (UK & US, Virago 1982). Entertaining account of a Victorian woman's adventures on horseback in the Rockies, written in the form of letters home to her beloved sister Henrietta.

Agnes Morley Cleveland, *No Life for a Lady* (1941; US, University of Nebraska Press, 1977). Wonderful stories of growing up on an open range cattle ranch in western New Mexico in the late nineteenth century.

Marianna de Marco Torgovnick, *Crossing Ocean Parkway* (UK & US, University of Chicago Press, 1994). Enlightening collection of essays combining memoirs with analytical theory to reveal what it was like to grow up as an Italian American woman in Brooklyn, crossing cultural boundaries to marry a Jew and become a scholar and literary critic.

Jill Ker Conway, *Written by Herself* (US, Vintage, 1992). Anthology of American women's autobiography over the last 150 years. Written by scientists, African-American women, pioneers, reformers and artists, the accounts range from the writings of the fugitive slave Harriet Jacobs to Margaret Sanger, founder of the American birth control movement.

Joanna Stratton (ed), *Pioneer Women: Voices from the Kansas Frontier* (US, Simon & Schuster, 1981). Splendid collection of excerpts from diary entries and letters written by the unsung women pioneers. Vivid, lively and gripping.

Susan Faludi, *Backlash* (UK, Chatto & Windus, 1992/US, Crown, 1991). Pulitzer Prize-winning journalist exposes the myth that feminism's battles have been won. Highly readable.

Angela Davis, *Women, Culture and Politics* (UK, The Women's Press, 1990/US, Vintage). Recommended collection of essays by one of America's leading black activists. Davis's *An Autobiography* (1975; UK, The Women's Press, 1990/US, International Publishers Co, 1988), reissued with a new introduction, is also fascinating.

June Jordan, *Moving Towards Home* (UK, Virago, 1989/US, Virago, 1994). Powerful political essays

by yet another multi-talented Black American woman activist and writer.

Maya Angelou, *I Know Why the Caged Bird Sings* (UK, Virago, 1984/US, Bantam, 1979). First and arguably the best volume of this ongoing (six volumes so far) autobiography by one of America's most extraordinary multi-talented Black women writers. The latest, *Wouldn't Take Nothing for My Journey Now*, was published in the UK by Virago in 1994.

Gloria Steinem, *Outrageous Acts and Everyday Rebellions* (1983; UK, Flamingo, 1985, o/p/US, NAL-Dutton, 1984). Illuminating journalist/feminist writings of 1960s and 1970s. Her most recent book, *Revolution from Within* (UK, Corgi, 1993/US, Little & Brown) illustrates a growing national preoccupation with personal fulfilment and success.

Betty Friedan, *"It Changed My Life"* (UK, Gollancz, 1977/US, Dell, 1991; both o/p). Collection of influential writings, and now historic speeches, that provides a first-hand account of the development and continuing impact of the American women's movement.

Camille Paglia, *Vamps and Tramps* (US, Vintage, 1994). Collection of essays by controversial feminist whose bestsellers *Sexual Personae* (1990) and *Sex, Art and American Culture* (1992) caused an international stir. Priding in her "raging egomania and volatile comic persona tending toward the loopy", here Paglia brings her searing intelligence to bear on Bill and Hillary, Madonna, D H Lawrence, Lorena Bobbitt and Barbra Streisand, among other subjects.

Feminist magazines include: *Womanews*, *New Directions*, *Quest*, *Sappho's Isle* (all New York); *Off Our Backs* (Washington); *Sojourner* (Boston), and *Plexus* (San Francisco). The almost mainstream *Ms* is available nationwide.

FICTION

Tama Janowitz, *Slaves of New York* (UK, Picador, 1987/US, Pocket Books, 1989). Engaging soap opera-style novel set in the trendiest areas of the city.

Audre Lorde, *Zami* (UK, Sheba, 1984/US, Crossing Press, 1983). Powerful evocation of what it's like to be Black and lesbian in a white heterosexual society.

Tina McElroy Ansa, *Ugly Ways* (US, Harvest, 1994). Lively work by one of the USA's leading new African-American writers, about three sisters who come together for their domineering mother's funeral.

Lorrie Moore, *Who Will Run the Frog Hospital?* (UK, Faber & Faber, 1994/US, Knopf). Marvellous novel, chronicling the lives of two friends growing up in small-town America. The frog hospital refers to their habit of trying to rescue the frogs which had been shot and left to die by local boys in the swamp next to their village.

Toni Morrison, *Jazz* (UK, Picador, 1993/US, NAL-Dutton). Morrison's most recent award-winning novel, set in Harlem in 1926, tells the story of the wife of a door-to-door salesman who shoots his lover. *Song of Solomon* (1970; UK, Picador, 1989/US, NAL-Dutton) is a complex, beautifully told fable set in the Deep South of America, but probably her most extraordinary book is *Beloved* (UK, Picador, 1988/US, NAL-Dutton), a prize-winning ghost story centred on the tragedy of slavery.

Joyce Carol Oates, *The Oxford Book of American Short Stories* (UK & US, Oxford University Press, 1992). A mix of classics and contemporary writers, including Amy Tan, Louise Erdrich, Ursula Le Guin, Eudora Welty and Katherine Anne Porter.

Tillie Olsen, *Tell Me a Riddle and Yonnondio* (1960 & 1974; UK, published in one volume, Virago, 1990/US, both Dell, 1989). The first is a collection of four short stories exploring some of the "pain and promise of fundamental American experience"; the second, her only novel, tells the story of a working-class family struggling to better their lives in the Midwest during the Depression.

Jane Smiley, *A Thousand Acres* (UK, Flamingo, 1992/US, Fawcett). This gripping saga, set on a farm in the Midwest, centres on three sisters and their relationship with the father who stands to bequeath them his land. Highly recommended.

Betty Smith, *A Tree Grows in Brooklyn* (UK, Mandarin, 1992/US, HarperCollins, 1968). Classic tale set in pre-war Brooklyn of a courageous Irish girl making good.

Amy Tan, *The Joy-Luck Club* (UK, Mandarin, 1991/US, Ivy Books, 1992). Best-selling novel based on a Chinese American woman's experience of growing up in San Francisco.

Alice Walker, *The Color Purple* (UK, The Women's Press, 1983/US, Pocket Books, 1985). Engrossing, deservedly prize-winning novel about two sisters growing up in the Deep South between the wars. Walker's other works include two volumes of short stories and four novels.

Velma Wallis, *Two Old Women* (UK, The Women's Press, 1994/US, HarperCollins). Alaskan legend of two old women, abandoned by their migrating tribe as it faces starvation brought on by an unusually harsh winter.

Other women writers to look out for include Joan Didion, Louise Erdrich, Rosa Guy, Paule Marshall, Grace Paley, Marge Piercey, Susan Sontag, Anne Tyler and Edith Wharton. Finally, crime fiction fans should read the novels of Sarah Paretsky (published in the UK by Penguin), and Marcia Muller (UK, The Women's Press).

Vietnam

For some years now the Communist regime of Vietnam has been prising open relations with the West through a series of foreign policy changes (notably stepping into line over Cambodia) and instigating internal reforms through its policy of *Doi Moi* or "economic renovation". The result of this has been the lifting of a Western trade embargo, imposed with crippling effect in the aftermath of the Vietnam War and punishingly maintained throughout most of the ensuing decade.

Under this new era of liberalization, tourism quickly took root. An initial flow of backpackers and business travellers forged the way for what is now a full-blown and increasingly mainstream industry. In America and Europe alike, Vietnam is perceived as one of the most in vogue Asian travel destinations. It is inexpensive and beautiful,

and its terrible recent history has lent a powerful if ambivalent fascination, witnessed by a spate of articles and books by returning Vietnam vets, their friends, daughters and sons.

What travellers find in Vietnam is a mix of traditional Southeast Asian attractions – the lifestyle, the markets, the supposedly "gentle" people, a rapidly expanding economy – and an infrastructure and society still scarred by the war years. The devastation wreaked by first the French and then the Americans is all too apparent, and Western fascination with the war years has lent a mythic element to the locations of offensives and even massacres: a visit evokes complex emotions. As tourism becomes more and more routine, however, those factors will presumably fade. Vietnam has a strong enough appeal in its own right.

The basics of travel in Vietnam are simple enough – and becoming more so by the day. Getting there is routine, so too are visas, and there are fewer and fewer restrictions on areas that can be visited. As a foreign woman travelling independently, it is likely that you'll be treated as a novelty, petted and looked after rather than face any harassment or hostility. In general people are eager to meet Westerners, Americans included, and treat their presence in the country as a sign that the worst days of shortages and restrictions might be over.

Vietnamese **women**, known as the long-haired army, were active as soldiers in both the Vietnam War and the battle against French occupation which preceded it. In fact their history as warriors goes back to pre-colonial times. But only since 1975 has their status improved and their achievements gained full recognition. Largely through the efforts of the Women's Union, the years immediately following reunification saw great progress in work and education opportunities, better healthcare and general women's rights. As the official national women's association, the Union (formed in 1930 and now with ten million members) continues to organize at all levels, from supporting village co-operatives to advising the Prime Minister on new policies for implementing women's rights. But like everything in Vietnam, theirs is a hard struggle. Women continue to bear the brunt of the "American war" with many still suffering miscarriages or giving birth to children disabled by the effects of dioxin and Agent Orange and other chemical weapons.

Nothing Ventured

Roz Williams set off for Vietnam with her husband in the early 1990s to carry out a new life among the entrepreneurs of Saigon. Both have stayed on in the country that they now consider their home, and she works as a journalist.

It was Daniel's suggestion, but I agreed wholeheartedly because I couldn't imagine either of us coming up with a similar idea again. The alternative was a London I was tired of, or a lingering half-life in some rural backwater. So, without reading a guidebook, or even dragging those confused memories of news footage from the recesses of my mind, we packed slim suitcases and flew to Ho Chi Minh City, Vietnam. To make our fortune.

If I had imagined anything, it was a rural society: streets filled with rice and baskets and smiling peasants "longing to be my friend". Instead I found the urban confusion of a rapidly developing Asian city, beset by noise, dirt and an interminable mass of people.

Our first month was more ordeal than pleasure. I experienced life as an interested bystander, detached. It was when we returned after a brief trip to England that I realized how happy I was to be back in these familiar streets. Determination rather than love had triggered our return, but we couldn't stop smiling as our bumbling old Peugeot braved the bicycles to take us "home".

We spent our first three months in the *Prince Hotel*. The claustrophobia in that room drummed in the frustrations we both felt in trying to "get started" in an Asian society. You do need to be able to escape Vietnam, and being forced to work and play in one room kept us in a perpetual state of tension.

Saigon has a pace all to itself. We would set up appointments, shouting in pidgin English at the telephone box on the corner, only to be stymied time and again. The attitude to meetings is more relaxed than in Europe but, surprisingly, while being late is understandable to Westerners, the Vietnamese can just as easily be early. Many times I would return to our hotel, steam into the lobby sweating from my bicycle only to be told that my friend had left although the appointed hour was some time ahead. I also found it hard to remember that absolutely everything closes at lunchtime, which lasts from 11.30am until 2pm. Somehow this can seem to last for most of the day if your timing is wrong. That is the point, of course: it is you who got it wrong.

One of the bittersweet joys of living in our backpacker hotel was getting to know the street children. Anh and her brother "Scarface" (he fell on a sheet of glass as a baby) would

> *She will try to sell the baby, or maybe give it to an orphanage; but nobody likes half-Caucasian babies here.*

always join us in the restaurant. We now know them very well, and have learned how the street mafia works (in their case, they give their mother all their earnings). We discovered that we could not buy from one without incensing several others and had to develop ways of being fair: a pack of postcards from one today and a map from another tomorrow. This is endearing fun until something turns sour and you realize how vulnerable they are. An eighteen-year-old (she looks twelve) recently became pregnant. I was surprised to find that the others all despised her for it and thought she'd been stupid. She is the "happy hooker" on our street, and seeing her swell each day amid the disapproval of her mates was disheartening. She will try to sell the baby, or maybe give it to an orphanage; but nobody likes half-Caucasian babies here.

My first real truck with socialist red tape came when we wanted to rent the house we now live in. Housing is increasingly problematic in Saigon, particularly at the upper end of the market. We weren't at the upper end, which has already been cornered by large international corporations with equally large expense accounts, but there were certain things we required and were prepared to pay for – privacy and security being the most important.

The first few places I saw were rooms in slum quarters, always full of Chinese and with evil-smelling kitchens. Living here would have meant waking your landlady and half her family each night, as they slept in the front room. It would have been almost impossible to lock our rooms, as many walls do not extend to the ceiling. I imagined the computer I am now writing on disappearing in under a week.

I have rarely felt safer in terms of sexual or criminal aggression. For the moment, the only thing to worry about is your wallet, which is quite likely to be stolen; violence is rare, although there might be a "mishap". A friend nearly met his maker when his camera was ripped from him as he drove his Honda down a main thoroughfare. You have to be sensitive about how you display your wealth: a camera may be worth a year's salary.

Sometimes it is hard to understand how a Vietnamese mind works. We had our suitcases stolen on a train to the beach resort of Nha Trang.

They were flung from the moving train, followed by the desperate criminal who returned the contents to us several weeks later, asking us to teach him English and help him emigrate. He had asked an English-speaking friend to write a letter from him, apologizing for his actions and saying the temptation had proved too great.

Our search for a house finally ended and we found our magical home – not everybody's idea of magic (and some of our ex-pat friends laugh when they come here), but many Vietnamese peoples' idea of what a house should be like. We live in a *nouveau riche* Communist area, full of customs officials who have earned lots of money from unmentionable sources.

Communism, even a watered-down Asian variety, has certain constraints. To have the correct papers you must fulfil certain criteria, which budding young writers and entrepreneurs do not. It took eight weeks of trailing round officialdom before we discovered a tenuous loophole, inevitably involving a large handout. Of course, if the authorities wished to get tough they could; but as Vietnam struggles towards its market economy we cross our fingers and doubt they will.

There is an unspoken idea that pioneering in a developing country is "man's work".

Time is increasingly important to us as the pace of the city steps up. Time together, to keep a relationship alive is one of the hardest things to find. Working as a journalist inevitably leads to spending much of your life alone. I enjoy this, but when you add it to frequent business trips for both of us, there are problems. Vietnam seems to have a bad effect on foreign marriages, principally because you may both react differently to your environment, but also because in an atmosphere where so many marriages break up it's all too easy to follow the trend. By realizing that things were getting bad, we have managed to make them better and to make time amid the chaos.

My work for a Vietnamese newspaper has been hard work, and offers little financial gain, but is nevertheless enormously satisfying. The Saigonese are just beginning to get used to foreigners, but a foreign woman alone constantly takes them unawares. Vietnamese women may have significant roles in many spheres, but this is not necessarily expected of foreigners. I had to interview the managing director of a progressive company at one of its factories several kilometres from Saigon. It was difficult to find, and I had to lend a paddy worker my portable phone to listen to intricate directions in Vietnamese. It was a wonderful moment. I am not sure she had ever used a normal telephone before (you sometimes find people dialling with the receiver down). When I arrived at the factory I looked like Biggles as I removed my glasses, shaking off dust from the track, to be met with gaping mouths and confused looks, followed by broad grins. While they expect foreigners (certainly foreign women) to be shut away behind an invisible wall of money, the reaction I have universally received from the Vietnamese has been delighted encouragement. It has only been within the ex-patriate community that I have felt the steely edge of sexism.

There is an unspoken idea that pioneering in a developing country is "man's work", and with compliant Asian women to cater for every foreigner's whim a questioning Caucasian woman is seen more as a threat than anything useful. I often find myself at the butt end of jokes about being domineering, but I allow my skin to thicken and get on with my main task, trying to understand the Vietnamese way.

It is inspiring how well I am treated here and I hope I will never take it for granted.

It is only by diving into the mercurial waters of Saigon that you begin to understand its intricacies. Daniel once imported a shiny piece of industrial equipment which took six trips to the airport to retrieve. On each attempt we had been told that nobody knew where it was, that it had already left, or finally that we had not got a license to use it. Eventually, after learning each official's name we managed to take it home with us, only paying a few dollars and waving goodbye to our new friends.

That is the way to success in Vietnam: patience and humour. The Saigonese have waited a couple of decades for a new life, and they relish seeing the rebirth of their city. We have some elderly friends. Alain (a Francophile), well-versed in Chinese medicine enjoys identifying all his friends' ailments. He is not, however, allowed to open a practice because, as a member of the former regime, he is not eligible for the right papers. He is constantly inviting us to his house, where his long-suffering wife prepares traditional feasts. Only three years ago Alain could have been arrested for having foreigners in his home, so he's overjoyed to see us come and go as we please.

The first time I invited Alain and his wife to our house I was very disorganized, having only just moved in. Any Vietnamese woman would have made lengthy preparations to produce something memorable for their honoured guests. It was with pangs of guilt that I hopped onto my Honda and sped to Cholon to buy a few groceries. It took me twenty minutes to buy a kilo of onions at a market stall: the seller was so amazed at this unexpected foreign spectre. I had met almost everybody in the market by the time I left, exhausted and late. Now my Vietnamese is a little better and some of them know me, it is as easy as going to a European supermarket, and infinitely more pleasurable.

It is inspiring how well I am treated here and I hope I will never take it for granted. A foreigner is almost always treated better than someone Vietnamese. You are loved for being a sign of the times, a part of the Vietnamese dream coming true. Several times I have walked into packed rooms filled with people queuing for a vital stamp for their papers, only to be swept to the front desk with willing translators trying to assist me.

Once, after touring a factory site with a foreign friend, I found myself locked in conversation with him on its pros and cons. After a few moments a smiling boy appeared and gave us an umbrella to shade us from the midday sun.

Alain's wife and I embarked on a short cookery course at the Women's Institute, hoping to improve my Vietnamese as much as anything. The poor teacher found herself battling for the attention of the class as they all wanted to feel my clothes and ask me about myself. My cooking skills were a source of great embarrassment. I was not dextrous with my chopsticks, or with the razor blade they used for transforming carrots into goldfish. At least I did amuse almost the whole school, and kept my class in fits of giggles for much of the time. The other women would all help me, telling me how beautiful I was (more an expression of how exciting it is to have you here than based on any aesthetic judgement), and holding my hand through the more complicated descriptions of how to kill a chicken. I often think of Vietnamese people arriving in London, and imagine how they feel about their reception there.

Living abroad for the first time as a married woman has brought with it some surprises. Vietnamese people are very conscious of family hierarchy and whether you are married or not is of great importance. When I use my deplorable Vietnamese to say that I have been married for five years and have still not produced any children, people's faces fall. They drop the subject out of sympathy for my awful physical complaint and move on to questions about my job. Working for a worthy Vietnamese newspaper, I usually achieve a relieved smile. Being married means respectability, however, or in the case of my unmarried foreign friends, a need to be looked after. Because of the Asian attitude to sex – men need to have it all the time, wives don't – Vietnamese men will not pester you unless invited. I was once kissed by a drunken individual, but it was a case of mistaken identity since I was in a brothel at the time. Sadly, this form of chivalry is just beginning to change, and blondes, especially, sometimes find themselves surreptitiously kissed or fondled unexpectedly.

The biggest surprise has been with the ex-pats. When I first thought of life abroad I assumed I would be spending all my time with the

Vietnamese, or with Daniel. This has not happened; it would be impractical for my job. International conglomerates usually choose single men for so-called hardship postings and Vietnam is, amusingly, one of these. Consequently, foreign men outnumber foreign women by at least ten to one. This puts independent women, whether married or not, overly in demand and prone to sexual advances.

Many of the foreign men are lonely. The type of Vietnamese girl who pursues foreign men is often on the make, and many relationships emerge, doomed to die when the man returns home (or his wife reappears). I often find it difficult to deal with these quasi-mistresses and their menfolk: on the whole they do not wish to form relationships with foreign women anyway.

Saigon is still an erotic city – just. It is not beautiful, nor even French, but it pumps with such vitality. Every morning at dawn the street vendors begin to hawk their wares, sounding the first rhythmic reverberations of the city. I feel both free and happy to straddle my Honda and join the mêlée of the early morning rush hour. Russian trucks vie with thousands of bicycles and increasingly larger motorbikes. It is a form of live "space invaders" bound to get your adrenalin going. I know I stand out, but I can shout back in Vietnamese now and not worry about being approached and asked all the usual questions about my age, marital status and children.

More than a year after we flew here we have not made our fortune, but we still might. We think we know a bit about what's going on, we feel at ease and can give newcomers their welcoming lecture and introductions. We tell them we know Vietnam but we will not really understand it, even if we live here for ever. But that is part of the magic that keeps us here.

A War That Can't Be Forgotten

Sarah Furse went to Vietnam en route from Britain to Australia. It was a brief visit at a time when tourists were only granted short-stay visas for an organized tour. As a result of a meeting with the Women's Union of Ho Chi Minh City, on arrival in Australia she and two travelling companions raised several thousand dollars towards funding a gynecological research centre for the treatment of women and children still affected by the deadly chemicals used in the Vietnam War.

Day 1: 6.30am. Toula and I are sipping weak coffee and chewing on rubbery omelettes in the coffee shop of our downmarket hotel in Bangkok. We are interrupted: the Diethelm mini-bus is here to whisk us away to the airport en route for Ho Chi Minh City. We trundle off through the already bustling streets of Bangkok, picking up the four other members of our tour – two German bank clerks, a Scottish farmer and an Australian psychologist – from their decidedly more upmarket hotels, and check each other out for potential camaraderie over the next week.

Two hours later, the ravaged defoliated land west of Ho Chi Minh City is a shocking sight. Alongside the runway the wrecks of military planes sit like rusting cadavers. Customs clearance takes an eternity, with umpteen forms to fill out detailing personal "luxury" effects, the purpose of the visit, etc.

Eventually we are ushered through to the exit area, to be met by our guide, Hinh, a beaming smile lighting up her face. She makes the customary welcome speech in perfect English, which she delivers to every group of Western tourists who arrive here at reasonably regular intervals. We clamber into a minibus and head off into the heart of the city (still known as Saigon), to the *Doc Lap Hotel*, our home for the next week.

We are immediately surrounded by a mob of children, tugging at our sleeves, calling us "Mama, Mama".

First impressions are of an exhausted, dilapidated city: peeling paintwork on the facades of French colonial buildings; rusty iron gates and railings; rising damp; and thousands of Vietnamese in conical hats, riding all manner of bicycles – two-wheelers, three-wheelers, four-wheelers (with incredibly large loads precariously balanced) and *cyclos* (bicycle taxis). Everyone looks in a hurry to get somewhere.

On the sidewalks French baguettes are sold and bicycles are being mended: nearly everything happens on the dusty, cracked pavements of this city. Faded billboards advertise movies and political propaganda. Old women and men, dressed in the customary baggy black trousers, squat down, talking, thinking, chewing betel nuts and absent-mindedly brushing flies from their faces.

We arrive at the *Doc Lap*, are given room keys and instructions to meet for lunch in the *Rooftop Restaurant*. Then we head off upwards in the rickety lift. A brass plaque showing the floor numbers indicates that the Australian Embassy was once lodged on our floor. After a brief glance from our tiny balcony, over the rooftops of Saigon, Toula and I are eager to step out and wander the streets for an hour or two.

Clutching our map of Ho Chi Minh City, written in Vietnamese, we emerge from the hotel to be immediately surrounded by a mob of children, tugging at our sleeves, calling us "Mama, Mama", and talking ten to the dozen in broken English about fathers in Australia and the United States. Many of these children are Amer-Asian or Austro-Asian street kids. Unwanted and undisciplined, they eke out a living by begging tourists for cigarettes to sell on the black market, and soap, towels, shampoo, disinfectant or pens to trade with. They are eager to show us their city, to tell us their stories and to receive affection and attention from us.

The traces of war are so visible in their faces looking intensely up at us. A little boy, Deng, whose father was a black GI, laughs nervously but does not come as close as the others. Later we learn that he sees himself as "bad, unclean, no good", because he is black. Racism is prevalent, even here. Feeling distraught by this, our first encounter with the children of Vietnam whose lives have been totally shaped by being born out of war, we quickly retreat to the hotel.

A wave of nausea suddenly takes over, leaving me weeping inwardly at the horrors and perversions of this war.

Half an hour later we re-emerge. This time there are fewer children and some of them have brought along "souvenirs" for us, carefully wrapped, with little notes of friendship written in shaky English. Nguyen has given me a beautiful black lacquerware vase with a goldfish on it; Thi, a gaudy plaster cat and dog ornament. They slip thin arms through our own rather fleshy ones, and take us for a walk around Saigon, telling us to look after our bags because "bad people will steal". A woman pedals up and asks if we speak French. I say "yes" and she proceeds to tell me that her fifteen-year-old son's father is called Harry Miller and lives in California. She wants to send her son over to him. Can I help? I can't and she pedals resignedly off into the crowded street.

Now the sun is setting and it is time for us to eat and retire, so we say our farewells and go back to exchange experiences with the others over a sumptuous Vietnamese dinner. There is a Russian circus staying in the *Doc Lap*, and on several occasions in the lift we are spoken to in Russian. I dredge up what little I can remember from my school studies fifteen years ago, to tell them that my mother is Russian but I don't speak or understand the language very well.

Day 2: In the morning we visit the enormous, ugly Imperial Palace which once housed the South Vietnamese Government. It is now a museum and the venue for occasional Party conferences. It feels eerie to stand on the rooftop where the helicopters landed to fly the generals, ministers and other top officials off to safety at the fall of Saigon in 1975.

Then on to the Imperial War Museum. Outside it, a large group of "Young Pioneers", proudly wearing red kerchiefs and reminiscent of Boy Scouts, clamber over each other in their eagerness to be photographed next to an old tank. Inside the museum the history of Vietnam's occupation by the Chinese for a thousand years, and more recently by the French, Portuguese and Americans, is vividly displayed in blurred and dog-eared photographs with accompanying texts written in Russian, Vietnamese and English. A display of guns, bomb shells and the containers used for spraying Agent Orange and other chemicals stands close to the grotesque guillotine which was used by the French right up until 1960. Paintings depict various methods of torture used on suspected revolutionaries. There are photographs of babies horrifically affected by Agent Orange, and a distorted foetus in a jar. An American anti-war pamphlet shows a group of GIs grinning at the camera, surrounded by the dismembered bodies and heads of captured Vietcong guerrillas, the caption reading something like: "This is what they don't tell you about the war. You can come and try just to survive and get home in one piece. Or you can come and be turned into a psychopath like the GIs in this photo. They will fuck you over, whatever you do."

> *The Vietnamese are ingenious at turning abandoned articles of war into tools of peace and productivity.*

A wave of nausea suddenly takes over, leaving me weeping inwardly at the horrors and perversions of this war. We leave the museum emotionally drained and return to the *Doc Lap* for a subdued two hours at the hotel. Afterwards we are taken across town to a lacquerware factory, an industry which has survived in Vietnam since the fifteenth century. But my mind is still full of what I have just seen – images that will haunt me forever – and I can't take anything in.

In the evening we wander out to buy some books and walk by the river. An Amer-Asian boy of about thirteen, his emaciated spine bent over and twisted so badly that he can only crawl on his hands and feet, follows us, begging for cigarettes. I give him my packets and feel anger and sorrow mounting as I see yet another victim of Agent Orange struggling to survive.

Day 3: Up early, and off in the mini-bus through the crowded streets where syringes are sold openly to the city's thousands of heroin addicts, and out into the lush green countryside towards My Tho on the banks of the Mekong River delta. Water buffalo, harnessed to antiquated wooden ploughs, plod through the rice paddy fields that flash by the windows of the bus. Lorries pump noxious black diesel smoke from their exhaust pipes; old buses carry a hundred bicycles on top, a hundred passengers inside; neat oblongs of rice line the side of the road, drying in the humid sunshine.

At My Tho we board a tiny boat and are ferried downriver at high speed, to an island bursting with palm trees, grapefruit, coconuts and bananas. Here it is extremely fertile, indicating how the whole of South Vietnam must have looked before wartime defoliation. The islanders make a very good living from fishing, and from farming tropical fruit and vegetables in carefully irrigated jungle.

On the way back to My Tho we see a half-sunken US Navy battleship which has been turned into home for scores of Vietnamese people, their huts clinging precariously to the hull of this floating war memorial. The Vietnamese are ingenious at turning abandoned articles of war into useful tools of peace and productivity. GIs' helmets are used as wash basins and watering cans; bomb shells are hammered out and melted down for use in light industry on the communes; brightly coloured plastic electrical wire is woven into beautiful padded tea-cosies — it seems nothing is wasted.

On the way back to Ho Chi Minh City we stop at a Buddhist monastery to hear about the many monks and nuns who performed public self-immolation in protest at the war. In the evening, Hinh takes us to have dinner at *La Bibliothèque de Madame Dai*, an exclusive restaurant lodged in the former library and law office of Suzanne Dai. A former senator in the South Vietnamese government, she now runs evening classes for illiterate women and children, as well as making visitors to her establishment aware of her love of Vietnam (despite her disagreement with Communism) and the needs of her people.

Day 4: Today we are going to Vung Tau, a fishing village and beach resort some two hours' drive from Saigon. On the way we pass an area of scrubland where one of the biggest US Army bases now stands empty and useless on a bleak hillside. Vung Tau itself feels like any seaside town, with its souvenir shops and cafés along the promenade, women mending reams of fishing nets and the ubiquitous Soviet tourists sporting straw hats and sunburn. The Vietnamese are drilling for oil in the South China Sea, with the aid of Russian and Norwegian experts, and a big refining plant – Sovietpetro – sits prominently at the entrance to the village.

After lunch, it's on with the bathers and off to the beach, at one end of which, on top of a high hill, stands an enormous statue of Jesus on the cross, arms outstretched to the heavens. Despite Communism, the Vietnamese are still very religious: sixty percent are Buddhist, twenty percent Catholic, and the rest hold an assortment of beliefs. All seem to be free enough to practise their varying creeds unhindered.

In the evening, Toula, Di (the psychologist we have befriended on our tour) and I head off for coffee on the promenade and end up having a fascinating, largely mime-based, discussion about politics with a group of young Russian sailors.

The next morning, armed with paracetamol to temper our diabolical hangovers from one too many Vietnamese brandies, we are taken up a steep rocky track to the old lighthouse, to look out over a spectacular view and see the remains of what was the largest Australian base in Vietnam.

Day 6: Another trip out of the city, this time westwards to the barren defoliated area around Cu Chi, centre of the extraordinary 300km network of underground tunnels, built and maintained by the Vietcong despite numerous attempts to destroy them. Many children were born underground. Running beneath villages and even American army bases, these tunnels contained rest areas, kitchens, arms caches, booby traps and latrines.

They measured only 60 x 40cm in the connecting sections; Toula and I crawl through a 50m stretch, slightly enlarged to cope with the size of Western tourists. It is a frightening experience: the guide's torch goes out; it is overwhelmingly hot and claustrophobic, with huge cockroaches, rats and mosquitoes clambering up the walls that we can't see, only feel. It gives us some idea of what it must have been like to spend weeks, even months underground, and we emerge gasping for air and water. We are then introduced to a woman whose husband, a Vietcong guerrilla, had been stabbed to death and disembowelled and who herself had helped build a section of the tunnel during the war.

It is estimated that women exposed to dioxin have six times more chromosome breaks than survivors of Hiroshima.

In the afternoon we go to Bamboo Shoot 1 Orphanage, where the children learn skills such as weaving, carpentry, embroidery and dressmaking to help them obtain jobs when they leave. They seem to be well cared for and loved, but there is so much more that they need: simple things that we in the West take for granted such as pens, notebooks, milk powder, medicines, shoes, cotton thread, books, and so forth. How will those needs ever be met in a country that is struggling so hard with a besieged economy and enormous social problems? There is a policy not to send Vietnamese children for adoption outside Vietnam any more. It is very hard to suppress idiotic desires to take half a dozen of them home with me!

Day 7: Today is the big day for Di, Toula and myself. We have written a letter to the Womens' Association of Ho Chi Minh City, asking to meet with them to exchange information about women in Vietnam and women in Australia and England. Our request has been granted, and we leave the men in our group to amuse themselves while we spend a fascinating and very productive afternoon hearing all about life for women in Vietnam since 1975.

The Women's Association comprises women from every walk of life and is dedicated to fighting for women's rights in all areas and at all levels. Though linked to the government Medical Health Department, it remains an independent, self-funded body. Its work includes running rehabilitation programmes for drug addicts and prostitutes; classes for illiterate women and children; medical centres for women and children; creches, orphanages and kindergartens.

One of its greatest needs is the means to try and combat the terrible long-term effects on women and children of Agent Orange. The wartime spraying of this deadly chemical has caused – among other things – a variety of congenital cancers, miscarriages, and babies born with severe mental and physical disabilities resulting in limblessness, severe cleft palate, lack of spine, kidneys, and tear ducts. There have also been cases of women going through a seemingly normal pregnancy only to give birth to their own cancerous reproductive systems and it is estimated that women exposed to dioxin (a highly toxic component of Agent Orange) have six times more chromosome breaks than survivors of Hiroshima.

The Women's Association asked us to try and help them to set up a gynecological research centre in Ho Chi Minh City to research these affects and attempt to find solutions to a huge problem that does not end simply because the war is over. So we decide to take up their request and set up "Orange Action", with the aim of raising at least some of the US$100,000 they need.

We left Vietnam on the eighth day, our minds full to bursting with experiences, images, ideas and emotions. More than anything, we left determined to continue the links we made with women in Vietnam and to make "Orange Action" a success.

TRAVEL NOTES

Languages Vietnamese, though quite a few people speak some English picked up during the American occupation. French is also quite widely spoken.

Transport Most visitors are still expected to take organized tours; independent travellers wanting to visit different regions need special permits, available from the state tourist office Vietnamtourism. However, restrictions may well be lifted in the near future. For those who manage to get around independently, express buses, mini-buses and the more basic local buses connect most of the country, though many roads are still desperately in need of repair. A main

railway runs between Hanoi and Ho Chi Minh City, and several smaller lines head out of Hanoi. A variety of boats ply the many waterways. The main transport in cities is the cyclo, a form of pedal bicycle rickshaw.

Accommodation Apart from the odd new or recently refurbished hotel at the top end of the market, the standard of accommodation has yet to catch up with the recent tourist boom. Westerners are expected to use "tourist" hotels, and to pay in hard currency. It's still not really acceptable to stay in more authentic places – generally cheap and pretty basic – though you may succeed with persistence.

Special Problems All foreigners require visas, obtainable from Vietnamese embassies and consulates around the world. Bureaucracy inside the country can be very trying, as *Vietnamtourism* likes to try and control all tourist movements.

Vietnam has only minimal health facilities, so be sure to bring your own medicines, tampons, contraception, etc.

Guides *Vietnam – A Travel Survival Kit* (Lonely Planet) is probably the best of the recent wave of guides. *Guide to Vietnam* (Bradt), may be a bit scanty in places, but is written by a photographer who really knows and loves the country and its people.

CONTACTS

Organized tours are increasingly popular. **British operators** include *Regent Holidays*, 13 Small St, Bristol BS1 1DE (☎0117/921 1711), and *Bales Tours Ltd*, Bales House, Barrington Rd, Dorking, Surrey RH4 3EJ (☎3016/885 991). *Vietnamtourism's* representatives in Britain are *TBN* (Vietnam), 7 Palmerston Close, Chester, Cheshire CH1 5DA (☎01244/374915) – useful for an update on travel restrictions.

In the US try the *Indochina Consulting Group*, 844 Elda Lane, Westbury, NY 11590 (☎51/633 36662); or *Viet Tours*, 8907 Westminster Ave, Garden Grove, CA 92644 (☎714/895 2588).

BOOKS

Sue Downie, *Down Highway One: Journeys through Vietnam and Cambodia* (US, Allen & Unwin, 1993). From 1988–90 the author travelled by bus and truck the length of Vietnam and in to Cambodia, interviewing a wide selection of people. Good accounts of the countryside and the cities, but somewhat depressing about the devastation caused by misguided US policies.

Arlene Eisen Bergman, *Women of Vietnam* (UK, Monthly Review, 1980, o/p/US, People's Press). Interesting material on the history of women's participation in Vietnam's centuries of struggle for liberation.

Michael Herr, *Dispatches* (UK, Pan, 1978/US, Random House, 1991). Journalist's acclaimed account of the Vietnam War.

FICTION

Marguerite Duras, *The Lover* (UK, Flamingo, 1986/US, HarperCollins, 1992). Set in the pre-war Indochina of the author's childhood, this is the story of an intensely passionate affair between a young French girl and her Chinese lover, and the hatred it inspires all around them. A huge success in France, where it went on to win the *Prix Goncourt*, and a great deal better than the film of the same name.

Zimbabwe

Despite its share of internal conflict and economic problems, Zimbabwe exerts a powerful pull on Africa travellers. Beautiful landscapes, game parks, great music and easy transport are attractions enough, but it's the spirit of the place, its lively upbeat feel that brings visitors back.

For British travellers there's an odd familiarity in many aspects of the country's infrastructure – the legacy of a century and a half of colonialialism that was brought to an end in 1980 after a long, bloody war of liberation. Despite this history, little antagonism has ever been shown towards white travellers. Women on their own are likely to be approached with offers of a "good time" but this is rarely threatening. You can say no. Street harassment otherwise is negligible. Harare and other towns have no-go areas that you'll be warned about and it's best to avoid going to nightspots and bars alone. The most negative aspect of the

country is likely to be white Zimbabweans; though you'll find them outgoing and generous, the hospitality and lifts they offer too frequently carry penalties in the form of having to suffer impassioned racist monologues.

The early years of independence were dogged by sporadic outbreaks of violence between the Shona (largely supporters of Robert Mugabe's ruling ZANU party) and the minority Ndebele (who mainly supported the rival ZAPU). Towards the end of the decade tensions were greatly reduced by a Unity Agreement, signed by both parties in January 1988. Optimism, however, soon gave way to disillusionment as unemployment and the cost of living continued to rise and President Mugabe failed to deliver his promises of land redistribution. At the beginning of the 1990s Zimbabwe was pushed to the brink of disaster by the worst drought in living memory, but the dangers of famine passed with the arrival of rain in 1993. In terms of raising people's living standards, the future now rests largely on the success of the government's much-vaunted Economic Structural Adjustment Programme.

Spurred by the experience of women fighting side by side with men, the post-independence government has made efforts to improve the position of **women**. Several laws have been passed, the most significant being the Legal Age of Majority Act whereby a woman, like her male counterpart, ceases being a minor at eighteen. However, laws have limitations and women have a hard time battling against centuries of tradition and custom. The Ministry of Community Development and Women's Affairs has made inroads through its focus on literacy and self-help projects in rural areas, apparently met with great enthusiasm by the women concerned, and various other organizations encourage income-generating projects with the aim of strengthening women's economic power. But the tendency is still to concentrate on traditional home-based activities, which do little to change fundamental attitudes about women's inferiority. Signs of a growing women's movement, illustrated by initiatives such as the

Musasa Project, dedicated to tackling the problem of violence against women, indicate the possibility of deeper, lasting changes in the future.

To Harare by Truck

After a spell of casual work in London, **Jo Wells** and her friend Emma, both in their early twenties, visited Zimbabwe as part of a low-budget trip to Africa. Five months later they returned, "different people"; Jo went on to study African history, while Emma used her experience in textile design.

I knew Zimbabwe would be good as soon as we arrived at Lilongwe. By this point the oppression of Malawi and its people was getting to us, and the Africans we met from Zimbabwe and Zambia seemed to have a free spirit in comparison. Having originally decided to fly to Harare, we eventually opted for a lift through Zambia with an obliging trucking company. This route was the long way round; most overlanders cut through Mozambique, but Emma and I weren't interested in challenging our bravado by facing that sad, war-torn country amid a barrage of armoured vehicles. Besides, we hoped our passage via Zambia would enlighten us on the sheer massiveness of the continent.

Our driver, aptly named Steady, had the job of transporting a gigantic oil container each week from Harare to northern Malawi. We had caught him on his return run, so he was inclined to travel at a leisurely pace. We spent three days in his truck, sleeping, eating, talking, and all the while watching the vast African landscape spread out before us. I suppose *It was as if we'd left the so-called Third World and crossed back into the West again.* as two white women we were a bit of a novelty, sitting up there in the cab of a young black trucker, and therefore bound to generate attention as Steady stopped at small villages to trade packets of soap powder or bottles of Malawi gin. But everywhere people came out to greet us with the never-ending warm friendliness of the Africans; men and women alike called out "sisters, you're welcome!"

Zambia is a poor country, its people crying out for essentials like bread, meat and vegetables. Throughout the country, we heard endless tales of crime, mainly theft, and every Zambian we met was a "businessman", indulging in various petty dealings simply to earn a crust. Despite all this, we found people to be generous, kind and trustworthy, guidebook rantings about their "dodginess" to be taken with a pinch of salt.

After a three-day diet of Pepsi and popcorn, and the potholed Zambian roads, it was a relief to cross the Zambezi into Zimbabwe. The contrast is remarkable: the first thing we noticed being the abundance of wildlife — baboons careering around the customs buildings and large grey elephants casually strolling in the background. Poor old Zambia is a devastated place. Nothing has been able to restrain the ruthlessness of the poachers who have deprived the countryside of its natural population. There's not even a bird in the sky. The richness of Zimbabwe, on the other hand, is luxurious; the roads are straight and smooth and even have cars on them, but wait . . . the people in these cars have white skin.

The entry of two whites into the crowded enclosure was an event in itself.

We stopped at a motel to find ourselves in the grip of yet another culture shock: toasted cheese sandwiches and hamburgers on the menu. It was as if we had left the so-called Third World and crossed back into the West again. Whites were very much in evidence with their big, affluent cars, grand-looking farmhouses, and money. I turned to Steady: "What's happening here? Hasn't the situation changed between black and white since independence?" "Oh", smiles Steady, "we're all friends now; you'll see soon enough". I did see, that night in fact. It takes a while for bad memories to die.

We decided to spend the night outside Harare, so we could arrive fresh and clean in the morning. The clientele of the motel's restaurant was African, an environment in which we had begun to feel at home. As I sat there, wilting over my soup, an old man came over and began to mutter at me in Shona. Being exhausted, I hadn't the energy to try and be enthused by his attention and thought he was drunk. Before I knew it, he was abusing me in English: "White trash, scum", he said. Steady immediately leapt up and led him outside.

It was the first time that I had been insulted on racial grounds. It didn't offend me. On the contrary, I felt fortunate to have avoided it for so long. Steady and the manageress of the restaurant were unbearably apologetic over the whole scene, while I wished desperately that I didn't belong to the race that provoked these people to behave in this way.

The next morning we entered Harare, which, with its colonial mansions and wide tree-lined avenues, again exuded an air of comfort and wealth. This spacious city with its modern planned centre was more what I'd expect of Australia. We began our stay at the youth hostel, a fusty old house complete with batty old warden, clinging to her lost youth in Yorkshire with the aid of a few dusty mementoes. Our fellow travellers here were unfortunately fairly obnoxious, all white, and mostly consisting of strapping Afrikaaner women "doing Africa".

To their obvious disapproval, we managed to evade their company that first night by escaping to a township outside the city, accompanied by the hostel cleaner, Geoffrey, and his band of musicians.

The township of Chitungwiza lies about thirty kilometres from the centre of Harare. Aesthetically, it's a depressing hole, the portaloo-type dwellings bearing no relation to the leafy avenues of Harare. However, despite its inaccessibility by public transport, the place is teeming with atmosphere and undoubtedly the capital's life blood.

It was Sunday afternoon and Geoffrey and his crew were due to perform an eight-hour marathon in the local beerhall. The entry of two whites into the crowded enclosure was an event in itself. We stepped out of the van into silence as people turned in genuine astonishment. Feeling uneasy, I almost climbed back in but a middle-aged woman waddled up and with drunken assertiveness purred "Relax, sisters. You're welcome." From then on we had the time of our lives. Never before had I commanded so much attention; in eight hours there wasn't a minute to collect my thoughts, let alone talk to Emma, though she too seemed to be enjoying herself.

The African crowd at a social gathering is wonderfully uninhibited, no doubt partly due to the endless buckets of *Chibuku* (African beer) that they pour down their throats. People, men and women alike, certainly know how to "get on down". As the band played a steady rhumba, I could have watched those women swing their hips around for hours, but there were friends to be made, beers to be drunk and spliffs to be smoked.

As night set in it got pretty cold, for this was wintertime below the equator, and we gratefully accepted Geoffrey's offer to take us to warm up at his family's home. Inside the single-storey house it was warm and cosy; people sat in the living room watching *Dynasty* on a large colour television while Geoffrey's mother leapt up to fetch us tea and biscuits. We were introduced to a sister, Gladys, who worked in the city for *Air Zimbabwe*. Aged around nineteen, her ambition was to save up all her money and emigrate to Dallas the following year. "It's so much better there for black people", she told us, "They can earn a lot and buy nice houses." It was a bizarre dream – she in fact knew no-one who had visited America.

After we returned to the hostel, I found time to collect my muddled thoughts. This experience of Zimbabwe had touched me in a curious way. Eight years since independence, the persevering divide between races was still very much in evidence and, to a European, appeared both antiquated and crude. I remember my hackles rising when a former South African (intelligent) friend of mine once said: "A revolution could never succeed in South Africa because all the servants who work for the wealthy whites have seen the scope of money. Everyone wants their piece of the cake, even if it means depriving someone else . . ." The occasion in Chitungwiza and Gladys's words rang out in my mind. If there's one thing about Zimbabwe, it makes you think.

Caught Between Two Worlds

Kate Kellaway spent three-and-a-half years living as a schoolteacher in Zimbabwe. After a painful period of readjustment, she finally settled back in London where she now earns her living as a writer.

Independence in Zimbabwe has meant important legal gains for women. There is a Ministry of Women's Affairs, several women's groups and a steady, growing interest in the women's movement. But it is hard to connect these facts to the women I've known and the girls I've taught in Zimbabwe. Only a small educated minority are active in women's affairs – or able to protest – and it is still the exceptional woman who can define her oppression.

The closest I came to Zimbabwean women was when I was living and teaching in St Mary's, a black township outside Harare. The difference between Harare the town and the Harare townships, now euphemistically renamed "high-density suburbs", is so extreme that they shouldn't really share the same name. The luxurious "low-density" suburbs of Zimbabwe's capital are reminiscent of Britain's wealthy stockbroker belt, the style an inheritance of colonialism. The townships, made up of vast complexes of tiny houses, are crowded with people deprived of adequate amenities, a colonial inheritance of another kind.

I wasn't really lazy so much as frightened by the routine of housework that shaped the women's day.

When I went to live with a family in St Mary's, I was congratulating myself on breaking away from the "British" Zimbabwe to experience the "real thing". But it is terrible to make of someone else's hardship an interesting experience for yourself. Besides it wasn't as simple as that. I was there because it was the home of Moses, my boyfriend. Throughout my stay I felt a conflict between accepting hospitality and looking at what was around me.

St Mary's is the oldest of the Chitungwiza townships, 25 miles from Harare yet still without electricity. Imagine row upon row of ramshackle houses, squashed together between miles of dusty streets. You are surrounded by people all day long. There are so many babies that at any given moment one will be crying. Cocks crow dementedly in the middle of the night.

Before I got a job at the local township school my days were spent at home with the women. Moses' sister, Rutendo, had three little girls. She got pregnant at fourteen, her husband treated her badly, and she was glad to be home again. Unlike many women in her position she managed to get custody of the children, whom she brings up with her mother. Moses' father worked far away and, apart from a brother, it was a predominantly female community. Moses' mother was a professional mother. She was my Zimbabwean mother for a while: she accepted me, welcomed and joked with me, and tried in every way to make me feel at home.

What was I doing here? What image was I trying to create with all this knitting, sewing and cooking of sadza?

I didn't speak much Shona then, just enough to say a few essential things like "Ndipeiwo mutsvairo" (Give me the broom) or "Ndine usimbe" (I'm lazy) or "Ndaguta" (I'm full). I wasn't really lazy so much as frightened by the routine of housework that shaped the women's day. Zimbabwean women keep their houses immaculately clean, but in St Mary's it was an unending fight against dust and dirty feet. Rutendo would rise at dawn and sweep the yard with a broom made of twigs, making beautiful patterns in the dust. Moses' second sister, Musafare, applied strong-smelling wax polish to the kitchen and dining-room floor. The day was punctuated by a trickle of water as children, clothes, floors, pots, shelves, everything, was washed.

Most tasks involved bending. I picture Rutendo and Musafare bending from the hip. Rutendo taught me how to cook *nhopi*, a delicious pumpkin porridge made with peanut butter. She showed me how to scour a pot with sand and how to cook *sadza* – not easy over a wood fire, as it becomes stiff and hard to stir. Zimbabwean women have good strong arms; I felt puny and ridiculous struggling to stir a pot of *sadza* for fifteen, my eyes streaming with tears from the smoke. "Crying for *sadza*", Rutendo used to call it.

I was the only *muzungu* (white) in the township but people soon became openly friendly, shouting greetings when I passed. The men were often easier to talk to, partly because they spoke more English. I also think they felt a freedom to talk to me about subjects they wouldn't discuss with their own women.

One day Rutendo and I went to see her sister, Elizabeth. She was very pregnant – so pregnant it would have been tactless to ask when the baby was coming – and explained that she wanted to be a policewoman after the child was born but her husband was against it. She asked me to check that her application form was correctly filled in. (Later she became a policewoman and her husband beat her up because of it.)

I went to talk to Rutendo in the kitchen:

"Matimati", I stated.

"Matimati", Rutendo confirmed.

"Mafuta ekubikisa?" I asked.

"Yes, cooking oil," said Ruteno, adding it to the pan. In the small black saucepan the *sadza* began to thicken. Using the *mugoti,* a special stick, I stirred. Rutendo was delighted: "I'll tell Moses you are a good housewife now."

Later we sat outside Elizabeth's house, eating *sadza* and sour milk. The sun burnt my calves. I surveyed my pink espadrilles and the pumpkin leaves swaying in the breeze and was suddenly filled with panic. What was I doing here? What was life like for these women? I watched one of them idly stitching a border of little green checks onto a loosely woven yellow tablecloth. "Have a go," she indicated, thrusting the material into my hands. I didn't, afraid of ruining it or showing myself up as an inept needlewoman.

What sort of image was I trying to create with all this knitting, sewing, and cooking of *sadza*? By the time I reached home I felt exhausted from the strain of trying to communicate without enough words. I was so pleased to see Moses' mother, she must have sensed it for she unexpectedly reached for my hand and kissed it.

Women like Rutendo and Moses' mother are authoritative and powerful in the home. One of the most popular subjects my students asked to debate was "Who is the most powerful, the father or the mother?" There was no foregone conclusion. Other popular subjects included bride price, polygamy, and "a woman's place is in the home". Students tended to be reactionary, the girls being the most timidly conservative, although seeds of protest often lay beneath the surface. Most of them, at least, were prepared to express a distaste for polygamy, though few questioned the concept of marriage or women's domestic role in the home. I remember a boy named Launcelot saying: "Women should not go to school. I want a nice fat wife who'll keep me warm in winter and feed me *sadza* all the year round – that's all she will do." The day was saved by a boy, aptly named Blessing, who stood up and spoke passionately and eloquently in favour of women's freedom from the slavery of domesticity and cruel husbands. I'm sure that many girls will eventually gain the confidence they need to express their views themselves.

TRAVEL NOTES

Languages English is the official language. Shona is most widely spoken, followed by Sindebele.

Transport A good railway network connects all major cities. Buses are slow and usually very crowded, but they're cheap and travel almost everywhere.

Accommodation All hotels tend to be expensive. Lodges, to be found in all the national parks, are cheaper but nearly always self-catering.

Guides *The Rough Guide to Zimbabwe and Botswana* (Penguin) has full, practical coverage.

CONTACTS

Women's Action Group, Box 135, Harare or 127 Union Ave, Harare. Formed in 1983, in response to a massive and widespread police round-up of women apparently suspected of being prostitutes, the group acts mainly as an advisory body for women on legal rights, health, hygiene and nutrition. It also publishes a quarterly magazine, *Speak Out*.

Zimbabwe Women's Bureau, 43 Hillside Rd, Hillside, Harare (☎734295). Aims to promote the economic self-sufficiency of women outside the formal waged sectors of urban and rural areas. Helpful if you're interested in visiting various projects; try asking for Mrs Chikwavaire.

Voice, 16 Samora Machel Ave, Harare. Co-ordinating body of non-governmental or volunteer organizations. Not a women's organization but very useful for gathering information.

BOOKS

★ **Dervla Murphy**, *The Ukimwi Road* (UK, John Murray, 1994). *Ukimwi* is the Swahili word for AIDS, a unifying if harrowing theme in Murphy's 3,000-mile journey by bicycle from Kenya through Uganda, Tanzania, Malawi and Zambia to Zimbabwe.

Doris Lessing, *Under My Skin* (UK, HarperCollins, 1994). Highly regarded first volume of autobiography, recounting Lessing's early years in Rhodesia.

Sekai Nzenza, *The Autobiography of a Zimbabwean Woman* (UK, Karia Press, 1986). Sekai describes her life and shows the issues facing black Zimbabweans amid the contradictions resulting from the long oppression of white minority rule.

Ellen Kuzwayo, *Call Me a Woman* (UK, The Women's Press, 1985). This remarkable autobiography movingly reveals what it's like to be a black woman in South Africa. Much of the book, notably about life in the townships, can be related to Zimbabwe.

FICTION

Tsitsi Dangaremga, *Nervous Conditions* (UK, The Women's Press, 1988). Set in colonial Rhodesia during the 1960s, this excellent first novel tells of a young black girl's longing for education which, she soon learns, comes with a price.

Zimbabwe Publishing House has a fast-expanding women's list in fiction and non-fiction. Also look out for short stories and/or novels by Nadine Gordimer and Doris Lessing.

FURTHER READING

⭐ *Journeywoman*, 50 Prince Arthur Ave, Suite 1703, Toronto, Ontario M5R 1B5, Canada (☎416/929 7654). This "networking magazine for female travel enthusiasts" features letters, news, stories, medical tips, contacts and any other information relevant to women on the move. All profits go towards breast cancer research.

⭐ **Mary Morris (ed)**, *The Virago Book of Women Travellers* (UK, Virago, 1994). Published in the US as *Maiden Voyages* (Vintage, 1993). A selection of women's travel writing ("the best and bravest") covering three hundred years. Idiosyncratic, as any anthology of such scope is bound to be, this book nonetheless contains some rare gems. See also the bibliographies in the chapters on Mexico and Russia for Mary Morris' own highly recommended travel writing.

⭐ **Dea Birkett**, *Spinsters Abroad: Victorian Lady Explorers* (UK, Gollancz, 1993/US, Blackwell, 1989, o/p). A concise and well-researched look at the button-booted spinsters who launched themselves across the further reaches of Empire. In unravelling the motives and perspectives of these women, amid a rich store of impressions and historical detail, Birkett allows us to judge for ourselves if these are the role models we wish to follow abroad. For one of the best examples of contemporary British travel writing, read also Birkett's ⊟ *Jella: From Lagos to Liverpool* (UK, Gollancz, 1994), her award-winning debut travel book. She charts her journey as an honorary crew member, and only female, on board a merchant navy ship bound for Liverpool from West Africa. *Jella* ("boy") is the name given her by the Sierra Leone sailors on board.

⭐ **Jane Robinson**, *Wayward Women: A Guide to Women Travellers* (UK & US, Oxford University Press, 1991). Very readable annotated bibliography covering sixteen centuries of women's travel writing from the Abbess Etheria, who journeyed to the Holy Land in the fourth century, to such modern adventuresses as Dervla Murphy and Naomi James. Her second compilation, *Unsuitable for Ladies* (UK & US, Oxford University Press, 1994) is an anthology of extracts featuring some two hundred of those listed before.

Mary Russell, *The Blessings of a Good Thick Skirt* (US, Collins, 1988). Accounts of women travellers from early pilgrims through sailors, climbers and aviatrixes, backed up by political analysis covering topics such as following versus leading, duty, risks and dangers. A ground-breaking book that helped relaunch some of these earlier travellers.

Travelers' Tales: A Woman's World (US, O'Reilly & Associates, 1995). A new anthology of contemporary writing, featuring fifty authors, from established names like Dervla Murphy to the previously unpublished.

Marion Tinling, *Women into the Unknown* (US, Greenwood Press, 1989). Biographies of more than forty women travellers, both contemporary and historical. Also contains a huge, partially annotated bibliography.

Thalia Zepatos, *A Journey of One's Own: Uncommon Advice for the Independent Woman Traveler* (US, Eighth Mountain Press, 1992). Comprehensive discussion of every travel topic imaginable, emphasizing the positive aspects of travel rather than its risks. Good resource for details on organizations that provide specialized services such as homestays and educational travel, while dealing with such topics as sexual harassment, visiting remote areas, haggling and so forth.

Thalia Zepatos, *Adventures in Good Company: The Complete Guide to Women's Tours and Outdoor Trips* (US, Eighth Mountain Press, 1994). A comprehensive and invaluable resource that discusses various sports with first-person accounts of trips, specialist resources (for people with disabilities, lesbians, women on spiritual quests etc) and a list of every company that offers women-only trips.

The Virago Woman's Travel Guides (UK, Virago/US, RDR Books). Ambitious series combining practical advice and information with fascinating material on women's contributions to the history, art and culture in each city's museums, galleries and monuments. Guides to Rome, Paris and New York were published in 1993; London, Amsterdam and San Francisco in 1994. Virago have sadly dropped the series, but several more books, including country guides, are planned for publication in the US.

⭐ **Lindsy Van Gelder and Pamela Robin Brandt**, *Are You Two . . . Together? A Gay and Lesbian Guide to Europe* (UK, Virago, 1992/US, Random House, 1991). An engaging, wittily written, mix of historical detail, anecdote and practical information is used to explore fourteen destinations, among them Amsterdam, Berlin, Copenhagen, London and Venice.

⭐ **Marianne Ferrari (ed)**, *Ferrari's Places for Women: Worldwide Women's Guide* (US, Ferrari Publ Inc, PO Box 37887, Phoenix, AZ 85069). An excellent country-by-country directory of listings for lesbian travellers on the lookout for the best bars, clubs and accommodation. Useful also for straight women who want to find some women-only space abroad.

Women Going Places (UK, Business Factory, 1994/US, Inland Books). New, British-based directory aimed at carrying on the spirit of the discontinued *Gaia's Guide International*. Lists resources relevant to women travellers, emphasizing women-owned and operated ventures, including tour operators, accommodation, women's centres, helplines and bookstores. Difficult to get hold of, but worth tracking down. Available in the UK direct from The Business Factory, 141 Praed St, London W2 1RL (☎0171/706 2434); in the US from the Inland Book Company, PO Box 120261, East Haven, CT 06512 (☎203/467 4257).

Maggie and Gemma Moss, *Handbook for Women Travellers* (UK, Piatkus, 1995). Practical guide, divided by theme not country, with general advice on what to wear, staying healthy, travelling with children, personal safety and more. The travel tips, impressions and advice are particularly useful for women confronting the issue of travel for the first time.

Christina Dodwell, *An Explorer's Handbook – Travel, Survival and Bush Cookery* (UK, Hodder & Stoughton, 1984). Solid survival kit listing everything the intrepid traveller might need to know. Published in the US as *An Unconventional Guide for Travelers to Remote Regions* (Facts on File).

Paula Snyder, *The European Women's Almanac* (UK, Scarlet Press, 1992/US, Columbia University Press). Useful reference guide to the status of women in 26 countries. Statistics cover everything from employment, education, health, political representation and childcare provision to immigration and residence rights.

★ **Charlotte H Brunen (ed)**, *Unwinding Threads* (UK, Heinemann, 1994/US, Heinemann, 1984). Excellent anthology of modern African women's writing, covering wide geographical range, including the Islamic Maghreb areas. Good introductions, both general and to each region and author, updated for this latest edition. Contributors include Ama Ata Aidoo, Mariama Ba, Buchi Emecheta, Doris Lessing, Nadine Gordimer, Bessie Head, Assia Djebar and Latifa el-Zayat.

FURTHER CONTACTS

Women Welcome Women, in the **UK**: Frances Alexander, *Granta*, 8a Chestnut Ave, High Wycombe, Bucks, HP11 1DJ (☎01494/439481); in the **US**: Betty Sobell, 612 Penfield Rd, Fairfield, CT 06430 (☎203/259 7832); in **Australia**: Gloria Hodgson, 7 Maron St, Speerspoint, Lake Macquarie, NSW 2284 (☎049/508 648). Non-profit-making organization dedicated to fostering international friendship by enabling women of different countries to visit each other. There are currently 1600 members, from the age of 18 to 80, in more than sixty countries worldwide.

Women's Travel Advisory Bureau, "Landsdowne", High St, Blockley, Glos GL56 9HF, UK (☎01386/701082). Service aimed at encouraging and informing women on all aspects of travel, from where to go to how to build the self-confidence to set off alone. They provide tailor-made advice as well as publishing a general information pack for women.

Marco Polo Travel Advisory Service, 24a Park St, Bristol BS1 5JA, UK (☎0117/ 294123). Friendly, reliable service offering specific tips for women travellers as well as first-hand knowledge of travel to many destinations, mainly outside Europe.

Travel Companions, 110 High Mount, Station Rd, London NW4 3ST, UK (☎0181/202 8478). Non-profit-making organization, started by two women with the aim of putting people who prefer not to travel alone in touch with other like-minded travellers. Open to anyone from 25 to 75. A flat fee covers at least three introductions as well as general advice towards planning every kind of holiday.

Rainbow Adventures Inc: Adventure Travel for Women Over 30, 15033 Kelly Canyon Rd, Bozeman, MT 59715, USA (☎406/587 3888 or 1-800/804 8686). Worldwide adventure travel;

everything from African safaris to horseback trips through Yellowstone.

Outdoor Vacations for Women over 40, PO Box 200, Groton, MA 01450, USA (☎508/448 3331). Adventure trips that require no previous experience to a number of destinations including Costa Rica, France, Alaska, Canada, Mexico and Turkey.

Womanship, The Boathouse, 410 Severn Ave, Annapolis, MD 21403, USA (☎301/269 0784 or 1-800/342 9295). Live-aboard learn-to-sail cruises for women of all ages, no previous experience required. Destinations include the Bahamas, Maine, Greece, New Zealand and Tahiti.

Women in the Wilderness, 566 Ottawa Ave, St Paul, MN 55107, USA (☎612/227 2284). Specializes in canoeing and water travel to the Arctic and the Amazon for women of all ages.

Woodswomen, 25 W Diamond Lake Rd, Minneapolis, MN 55419, USA (☎612/822 3809). Outdoor adventure trips – some of which include children – in the US, Mexico and Latin America, for women of all ages.

Call of the Wild, 2519 Cedar St, Berkeley, CA 94708, USA (☎510/849 9292 or 1-800/742 9494). One of the oldest outfits in the US offering hiking adventures for women of all ages and abilities. Most are in California and the Midwest, but they also do occasional trips to Hawaii and Austria.

Frauen Unterwegs, Potsdamerstr. 139 1000, Berlin 30, Germany (☎030/215 1022). Long-established women's tour operator organizing anything from city tours and European activity holidays to trips to non-European destinations such as Egypt, the Gambia, Kenya, Thailand and Jamaica. Usually led by German-speaking female guides but open to every woman.

Stay in touch with us!

ROUGH*NEWS* **is Rough Guides' free newsletter. In three issues a year we give you news, travel issues, music reviews, readers' letters and the latest dispatches from authors on the road.**

direct orders from

		UK£	US$	CAN$
Amsterdam	1-85828-218-7	£8.99	14.95	19.99
Andalucia	1-85828-219-5	9.99	16.95	22.99
Australia	1-85828-220-9	13.99	21.95	29.99
Bali	1-85828-134-2	8.99	14.95	19.99
Barcelona	1-85828-221-7	8.99	14.95	19.99
Berlin	1-85828-129-6	8.99	14.95	19.99
Belgium & Luxembourg	1-85828-222-5	10.99	17.95	23.99
Brazil	1-85828-223-3	13.99	21.95	29.99
Britain	1-85828-208-X	12.99	19.95	25.99
Brittany & Normandy	1-85828-224-1	9.99	16.95	22.99
Bulgaria	1-85828-183-0	9.99	16.95	22.99
California	1-85828-181-4	10.99	16.95	22.99
Canada	1-85828-311-6	12.99	19.95	25.99
China	1-85828-225-X	15.99	24.95	32.99
Corfu	1-85828-226-8	8.99	14.95	19.99
Corsica	1-85828-227-6	9.99	16.95	22.99
Costa Rica	1-85828-136-9	9.99	15.95	21.99
Crete	1-85828-316-7	9.99	16.95	22.99
Cyprus	1-85828-182-2	9.99	16.95	22.99
Czech & Slovak Republics	1-85828-121-0	9.99	16.95	22.99
Dublin Mini Guide	1-85828-294-2	5.99	9.95	12.99
Edinburgh Mini Guide	1-85828-295-0	5.99	9.95	12.99
Egypt	1-85828-188-1	10.99	17.95	23.99
Europe	1-85828-289-6	14.99	19.95	25.99
England	1-85828-301-9	12.99	19.95	25.99
First Time Europe	1-85828-270-5	7.99	9.95	12.99
Florida	1-85828-184-4	10.99	16.95	22.99
France	1-85828-228-4	12.99	19.95	25.99
Germany	1-85828-309-4	14.99	23.95	31.99
Goa	1-85828-275-6	8.99	14.95	19.99
Greece	1-85828-300-0	12.99	19.95	25.99
Greek Islands	1-85828-310-8	10.99	17.95	23.99
Guatemala	1-85828-189-X	10.99	16.95	22.99
Hawaii: Big Island	1-85828-158-X	8.99	12.95	16.99
Hawaii	1-85828-206-3	10.99	16.95	22.99
Holland	1-85828-229-2	10.99	17.95	23.99
Hong Kong	1-85828-187-3	8.99	14.95	19.99
Hotels & Restos	1-85828-306-X	12.99	19.95	25.99
Hungary	1-85828-123-7	8.99	14.95	19.99
India	1-85828-200-4	14.99	23.95	31.99
Ireland	1-85828-179-2	10.99	17.95	23.99
Italy	1-85828-167-9	12.99	19.95	25.99
Jamaica	1-85828-230-6	9.99	16.95	22.99
Kenya	1-85828-192-X	11.99	18.95	24.99
Lisbon Mini Guide	1-85828-297-7	5.99	9.95	12.99
London	1-85828-231-4	9.99	15.95	21.99
Madrid Mini Guide	1-85828-353-1	5.99	9.95	12.99
Mallorca & Menorca	1-85828-165-2	8.99	14.95	19.99
Malaysia, Singapore & Brunei	1-85828-232-2	11.99	18.95	24.99
Mexico	1-85828-044-3	10.99	16.95	22.99
Morocco	1-85828-040-0	9.99	16.95	21.99
Moscow	1-85828-118-0	8.99	14.95	19.99
Nepal	1-85828-190-3	10.99	17.95	23.99
New York	1-85828-296-9	9.99	15.95	21.99
New Zealand	1-85828-233-0	12.99	19.95	25.99
Norway	1-85828-234-9	10.99	17.95	23.99
Pacific Northwest	1-85828-092-3	9.99	14.95	19.99

In the UK, Rough Guides are available from all good bookstores, but can be obtained from Penguin by contacting: Penguin Direct, Penguin Books Ltd, Bath Road, Harmondsworth, West Drayton, Middlesex UB7 0DA; or telephone the credit line on 0181-899 4036 (9am–5pm) and ask for Penguin Direct. Visa and Access accepted. Delivery will normally be within 14 working days. Penguin Direct ordering facilities are only available in the UK and the USA. The availability and published prices quoted are correct at the time of going to press but are subject to alteration without prior notice.

around the world

Paris	1-85828-235-7	8.99	14.95	19.99
Poland	1-85828-168-7	10.99	17.95	23.99
Portugal	1-85828-313-2	10.99	17.95	23.99
Prague	1-85828-318-3	8.99	14.95	19.99
Provence	1-85828-127-X	9.99	16.95	22.99
Pyrenees	1-85828-308-6	10.99	17.95	23.99
Rhodes & the Dodecanese	1-85828-120-2	8.99	14.95	19.99
Romania	1-85828-305-1	10.99	17.95	23.99
San Francisco	1-85828-299-3	8.99	14.95	19.99
Scandinavia	1-85828-236-5	12.99	20.95	27.99
Scotland	1-85828-302-7	9.99	16.95	22.99
Sicily	1-85828-178-4	9.99	16.95	22.99
Singapore	1-85828-237-3	8.99	14.95	19.99
South Africa	1-85828-238-1	12.99	19.95	25.99
Soutwest USA	1-85828-239-X	10.99	16.95	22.99
Spain	1-85828-240-3	11.99	18.95	24.99
St Petersburg	1-85828-298-5	9.99	16.95	22.99
Sweden	1-85828-241-1	10.99	17.95	23.99
Thailand	1-85828-140-7	10.99	17.95	24.99
Tunisia	1-85828-139-3	10.99	17.95	24.99
Turkey	1-85828-242-X	12.99	19.95	25.99
Tuscany & Umbria	1-85828-243-8	10.99	17.95	23.99
USA	1-85828-307-8	14.99	19.95	25.99
Venice	1-85828-170-9	8.99	14.95	19.99
Vietnam	1-85828-191-1	9.99	15.95	21.99
Wales	1-85828-245-4	10.99	17.95	23.99
Washington DC	1-85828-246-2	8.99	14.95	19.99
West Africa	1-85828-101-6	15.99	24.95	34.99
More Women Travel	1-85828-098-2	10.99	16.95	22.99
Zimbabwe & Botswana	1-85828-186-5	11.99	18.95	24.99

Phrasebooks

Czech	1-85828-148-2	3.50	5.00	7.00
Egyptian Arabic	1-85828-319-1	4.00	6.00	8.00
French	1-85828-144-X	3.50	5.00	7.00
German	1-85828-146-6	3.50	5.00	7.00
Greek	1-85828-145-8	3.50	5.00	7.00
Hungarian	1-85828-304-3	4.00	6.00	8.00
Italian	1-85828-143-1	3.50	5.00	7.00
Japanese	1-85828-303-5	4.00	6.00	8.00
Mexican	1-85828-176-8	3.50	5.00	7.00
Portuguese	1-85828-175-X	3.50	5.00	7.00
Polish	1-85828-174-1	3.50	5.00	7.00
Spanish	1-85828-147-4	3.50	5.00	7.00
Swahili	1-85828-320-5	4.00	6.00	8.00
Thai	1-85828-177-6	3.50	5.00	7.00
Turkish	1-85828-173-3	3.50	5.00	7.00
Vietnamese	1-85828-172-5	3.50	5.00	7.00

Reference

Classical Music	1-85828-113-X	12.99	19.95	25.99
European Football	1-85828-256-X	14.99	23.95	31.99
Internet	1-85828-288-8	5.00	8.00	10.00
Jazz	1-85828-137-7	16.99	24.95	34.99
Millennium	1-85828-314-0	5.00	8.95	11.99
Opera	1-85828-138-5	16.99	24.95	34.99
Reggae	1-85828-247-0	12.99	19.95	25.99
Rock	1-85828-201-2	17.99	26.95	35.00
World Music	1-85828-017-6	16.99	22.95	29.99

around the world

Paris	1-85828-235-7	8.99	14.95	19.99
Poland	1-85828-168-7	10.99	17.95	23.99
Portugal	1-85828-313-2	10.99	17.95	23.99
Prague	1-85828-318-3	8.99	14.95	19.99
Provence	1-85828-127-X	9.99	16.95	22.99
Pyrenees	1-85828-308-6	10.99	17.95	23.99
Rhodes & the Dodecanese	1-85828-120-2	8.99	14.95	19.99
Romania	1-85828-305-1	10.99	17.95	23.99
San Francisco	1-85828-299-3	8.99	14.95	19.99
Scandinavia	1-85828-236-5	12.99	20.95	27.99
Scotland	1-85828-302-7	9.99	16.95	22.99
Sicily	1-85828-178-4	9.99	16.95	22.99
Singapore	1-85828-237-3	8.99	14.95	19.99
South Africa	1-85828-238-1	12.99	19.95	25.99
Soutwest USA	1-85828-239-X	10.99	16.95	22.99
Spain	1-85828-240-3	11.99	18.95	24.99
St Petersburg	1-85828-298-5	9.99	16.95	22.99
Sweden	1-85828-241-1	10.99	17.95	23.99
Thailand	1-85828-140-7	10.99	17.95	24.99
Tunisia	1-85828-139-3	10.99	17.95	24.99
Turkey	1-85828-242-X	12.99	19.95	25.99
Tuscany & Umbria	1-85828-243-8	10.99	17.95	23.99
USA	1-85828-307-8	14.99	19.95	25.99
Venice	1-85828-170-9	8.99	14.95	19.99
Vietnam	1-85828-191-1	9.99	15.95	21.99
Wales	1-85828-245-4	10.99	17.95	23.99
Washington DC	1-85828-246-2	8.99	14.95	19.99
West Africa	1-85828-101-6	15.99	24.95	34.99
More Women Travel	1-85828-098-2	10.99	16.95	22.99
Zimbabwe & Botswana	1-85828-186-5	11.99	18.95	24.99
Phrasebooks				
Czech	1-85828-148-2	3.50	5.00	7.00
Egyptian Arabic	1-85828-319-1	4.00	6.00	8.00
French	1-85828-144-X	3.50	5.00	7.00
German	1-85828-146-6	3.50	5.00	7.00
Greek	1-85828-145-8	3.50	5.00	7.00
Hungarian	1-85828-304-3	4.00	6.00	8.00
Italian	1-85828-143-1	3.50	5.00	7.00
Japanese	1-85828-303-5	4.00	6.00	8.00
Mexican	1-85828-176-8	3.50	5.00	7.00
Portuguese	1-85828-175-X	3.50	5.00	7.00
Polish	1-85828-174-1	3.50	5.00	7.00
Spanish	1-85828-147-4	3.50	5.00	7.00
Swahili	1-85828-320-5	4.00	6.00	8.00
Thai	1-85828-177-6	3.50	5.00	7.00
Turkish	1-85828-173-3	3.50	5.00	7.00
Vietnamese	1-85828-172-5	3.50	5.00	7.00
Reference				
Classical Music	1-85828-113-X	12.99	19.95	25.99
European Football	1-85828-256-X	14.99	23.95	31.99
Internet	1-85828-288-8	5.00	8.00	10.00
Jazz	1-85828-137-7	16.99	24.95	34.99
Millennium	1-85828-314-0	5.00	8.95	11.99
Opera	1-85828-138-5	16.99	24.95	34.99
Reggae	1-85828-247-0	12.99	19.95	25.99
Rock	1-85828-201-2	17.99	26.95	35.00
World Music	1-85828-017-6	16.99	22.95	29.99

In the USA, or for international orders, charge your order by Master Card or Visa (US$15.00 minimum order): call 1-800-253-6476; or send orders, with complete name, address and zip code, and list price, plus $2.00 shipping and handling per order to: Consumer Sales, Penguin USA, PO Box 999 – Dept #17109, Bergenfield, NJ 07621. No COD. Prepay foreign orders by international money order, a cheque drawn on a US bank, or US currency. No postage stamps are accepted. All orders are subject to stock availability at the time they are processed. Refunds will be made for books not available at that time. Please allow a minimum of four weeks for delivery.